VOICES OF PROTEST

VOICES OF PROTEST

Documents of Courage and Dissent

EDITED BY FRANK LOWENSTEIN, SHERYL LECHNER, AND ERIK BRUUN

BLACK DOG
& LEVENTHAL
PUBLISHERS
NEW YORK

To our children:
Daniel, Jeffrey, and Max
Elizabeth, Andrew, and Rebecca
who practice dissent often

Published by
Black Dog & Leventhal Publishers, Inc.
151 West 19th Street
New York, NY 10011

Distributed by
Workman Publishing Company
225 Varick Street
New York, NY 10014

Manufactured in the United States of America

Cover and interior design by Elizabeth Driesbach

ISBN 13: 978-1-57912-585-1

h g f e d c b a

Library of Congress Cataloging-in-Publication Data available on file.

TABLE OF CONTENTS

Foreword by Bill McKibben   **7**

Introduction   **9**

Part I: The Roots and Roles of Protest

Chapter 1 Dissent and Liberty   **16**

Chapter 2 Modes of Protest   **45**

Chapter 3 Roots of Dissent   **70**

Part II: Documents of Dissent

Chapter 4 Civil Rights   **100**

Chapter 5 National Self-Determination   **161**

Chapter 6 Economic Justice   **201**

Chapter 7 Environmental Conservation   **256**

Chapter 8 Religious Freedom   **316**

Chapter 9 Peace and War   **380**

Chapter 10 International Political Freedoms   **420**

Part III: The Future of Protest

Chapter 11 Limits of Societal Norms   **464**

Chapter 12 Extreme Protest   **490**

Chapter 13 The Experience of Protest   **514**

Text and Art Credits   **543**

Index of Documents   **549**

Index   **554**

FOREWORD

There is a good deal to be said for the conventional wisdom in any society. It allows community to function, social life to proceed; in its shade we build our lives. Most people will live out those lives without questioning that conventional wisdom; indeed, most will at first resent and fear that small minority who does challenge it, as a threat to the order that provides both their psychological and physical stability.

And yet, looking back at the long course of history as this superb collection does, the voices of protest and dissent against those conventional wisdoms are often precisely what propels human civilization forward and allows it to become unstuck. The history of our own nation is studded with activists, often despised, who in short order became heroes: the Founding Fathers, overthrowing the order represented by the greatest empire of the day; John Brown, converted in a matter of months from terrorist to martyr; Susan B. Anthony, transformed from a figure of ridicule to a face on the dollar coin; Dr. Martin Luther King, Jr., only forty years ago harassed by the FBI, whose birthday we now celebrate as a national holiday. To read these excerpts is to understand what humans are capable of: they demonstrate that we're made for more than a Darwinian drive to survive and procreate and get ahead. They prove we're capable of deep love and anger and outrage, on behalf of ourselves but especially of others, that defies the workaday definition of human nature. And the words are often prelude to the most powerful sacrifices: jail, ostracism, even death.

Not all protests are wise, of course, and not all protesters noble. Having lived through the 20th century, we know that the noble intentions of a Marx can be embodied in ways that crush the human spirit. And having lived through the bloody opening of the 21st, it is hard to read Osama bin Laden's cowardly justifications for murder, especially next to the courageous testimony of Mahatma Gandhi, his opposite in nearly every way. And of course it is worth reflecting that every liberation carries with it the danger of excess—as we read the words of, say, a Wendell Berry, we are reminded that the individual freedoms we have struggled to achieve have too often freed us for a heedless consumerism, one that undermines both planet and community.

Taken as a whole, however, these are the voices of the great human pantheon, greater than the kings and sultans and emperors, greater than the Trumps and Rockefellers. It is our good luck to have their example and their words, for we will need them in the years to come. Humans face perhaps the greatest challenges we've ever known as we confront the environmental devastation and human poverty now staring down at us, and we will need to build a movement like none before to stave off a collective calamity. Last summer, I helped lead a march across the state of Vermont, five days of walking to demand action on global warming. It was, as such things go, a small affair—a thousand people at its height (though that represents, sadly, the biggest rally to date in this country against climate change). But as we walked, despite the long odds against real success when faced with opponents like Exxon Mobil and George W. Bush, we felt more hopeful with every step. The mere act of finally raising our voices, of starting to *move*, seemed somehow to presage victory. Most of the people who drove by down the highway gave us a thumbs-up or a wave, even if they were behind the wheel of some giant SUV; it was as if they too sensed changed needed to come and were glad that someone was saying so (though whether it presages a willingness to pay more for gas remains to be seen).

Perhaps such confidence is what allows dissenters to defy the common order and risk their reputation, their fortune, even their lives. Not the confidence that they will necessarily be there for the triumph, but the certainty that, as with Moses, they will climb to the top of the mountain and glimpse the promised land beyond. It was Dr. King who said so often that the arc of the moral universe is long but that it bends toward justice, and who quoted regularly from the great hymn, 'Once to Every Man and Nation,' based on the poem of James Russell Lowell:

> Truth forever on the scaffold
> Wrong forever on the throne
> But that scaffold sways the future
> And behind the dim unknown
> Standeth God within the shadows
> Keeping watch above his own

This book is proof that Lowell was right—these are the people who have swayed the human future. May there be many, many more.

BILL McKIBBEN

INTRODUCTION

The Essential Protester

Frank Lowenstein

With Sheryl Lechner and Erik Bruun

In 1979, as a freshman in college, I participated in my first protest. With the Massachusetts State Legislature poised to raise the drinking age from eighteen to twenty-one, my roommates and I headed for the statehouse to voice our objections. We and a few hundred other college students stood outside in the chill winter air, chanted, listened to an unintelligible speaker address the crowd through a bullhorn, and clustered around the few reporters present. Our case was simple: how can society assert that eighteen-year-olds are mature enough in their judgment that they can vote, marry, buy a car, buy a house, serve in war, and exercise every other prerogative of adulthood except to purchase certain classes of otherwise legal beverages?

Regardless of the justice of our case (or that of potential counterarguments), our protest had no impact. We did not mobilize many of Boston's 250,000 college students; we threatened the reelection of no politician, the profitability of no major business. We did not articulate our claims in any lasting inspirational document or attract significant press attention. Most importantly, we gave up. Within days the drinking-age bill passed, the issue vanished into the miasma of forgotten causes, and the student population was again quiescent.

Over the years, coeditors Erik Bruun, Sheryl Lechner, and I have participated in many diverse acts of protest. We've dissented from the status quo to try to change draconian criminal penalties, slow the nuclear-arms race, reduce noise in family neighborhoods, stop the oppression of teenagers in our community, and prevent the destruction of biodiversity. As journalists, we've written about protest over school budgets, affordable housing, inappropriate residential development along our nation's coasts, inadequate security for nuclear materials, and the everyday decisions of local governments. We believe that protest is essential to a vital, free society—a belief that is echoed in the first amendment of the United States Constitution, which protects not only freedom of the press, speech, and religion, but also the rights of citizens "peaceably to assemble and to petition the government for a redress of grievances."

Why did our nation's founders place freedom to protest on the same footing as freedom of speech, the press, and religion? Why ensure the right of people to participate in something that is often disruptive, that can in extreme cases threaten to unravel the threads of society, and that many people find uncomfortable even to watch (much less participate in)? There are perhaps two reasons. First, the founders had a collective memory of being part of a society held hostage to the whims of power, in which government was neither of nor for the people; protest thus was seen as a necessary recourse when government becomes unresponsive to the will of the people. Second, in the absence of protest, one is left with conformity, which brings its own dangers to society. As constitutional scholar Cass R. Sunstein put it in his 2003 book *Why Societies Need Dissent*:

> The problem is that widespread conformity deprives the public of information that it needs to have. Conformists follow others and silence themselves, without disclosing knowledge from which others would benefit. . . . Hans Christian Andersen's fable "The Emperor's New Clothes" is an ingenious illustration; because everyone follows everyone else, people do not reveal what their eyes plainly perceive. . . .
>
> Conformists are often thought to be protective of social interests, keeping quiet for the sake of the group. By contrast, dissenters tend to be seen as selfish individualists, embarking on projects of their own. But in an important sense, the opposite is closer to the truth. Much of the time, dissenters benefit others, while conformists benefit themselves. If people threaten to blow the whistle on wrongdoing or to disclose facts that contradict an emerging group consensus, they might well be punished. Perhaps they will lose their jobs, face ostracism, or at least have some difficult months.

We chose to compile this book in hopes of inspiring people around the world to speak up more often and more loudly, and to illustrate the ways in which protest can be helpful to society. The documents we have collected record the actions and thoughts of individuals who spoke against the established consensus of their time and who changed the course of history by their protest. As William Jennings Bryan, three-time candidate for U.S. president, said, with his classic taste for hyperbole, "The humblest citizen in all the land, when clad in the armor of a righteous cause, is stronger than all the hosts of error."

In emphasizing the importance of protest, Bryan joins a host of revered American leaders. Thomas Jefferson, the author of our Declaration of Independence, wrote to Abigail Adams, "The spirit of resistance to government is so valuable on certain occasions, that I wish it to be always kept alive. It will often be exercised when wrong, but better so than not to be exercised at all. I like a little rebellion now and then."

In his famous essay "Self-Reliance," Ralph Waldo Emerson wrote, "Whoso would be a man must be a nonconformist."

Abolitionist leader Frederick Douglass said, "Those who profess to favor freedom and yet depreciate agitation, are men who want crops without plowing up the ground, they want rain without thunder and lightning. They want the ocean without the awful roar of its many waters. This struggle may be a moral one, or it may be a physical one, and it may be both moral and physical, but it must be a struggle. Power concedes nothing without a demand. It never did and it never will."

These spokesmen of American ideals did not value protest for its own sake. Rather they looked to protest to play a crucial role in democratic society—that of enabling a relatively powerless minority to advocate for justice in the face of established dogma or political power. When a minority cannot make its opinions known, it ceases to serve as an effective counterpoint to majority opinion; society proceeds forward in lockstep conformity. As Henry David Thoreau wrote, protesting slavery in his essay "Civil Disobedience": "Cast your whole vote, not a strip of paper merely, but your whole influence. A minority is powerless while it conforms to the majority; it is not even a minority then; but it is irresistible when it clogs by its whole weight."

In American history, citizens of all political persuasions have exercised the right to protest. In recent years, we've seen protest against war and against abortion, against Fidel Castro and against George W. Bush, against gay marriage and against oil drilling in Alaska. In these cases and a thousand more, protesters have contested authority, challenged injustice, or made a public case for changing law or policy.

But protest does not always produce change, as my foray to the Massachusetts statehouse illustrated. As Frances Fox Piven and Richard A. Cloward explained in their seminal work *Poor People's Movements: Why They Succeed, How They Fail:*

> Ordinarily, during periods of stability, governmental leaders have three rather obvious options when an institutional disruption [i.e., a protest] occurs. They may ignore it; they may employ punitive measures against the disruptors; or they may attempt to conciliate them. If the disruptive group has little political leverage in its own right, as is true of lower-class groups, it will either be ignored or repressed. It is more likely to be ignored when the disrupted institution is not central to the society as a whole or to other more important groups. . . . Repression is more likely to be employed when central institutions are affected, as when railroad workers struck and rioted in the late nineteenth century, or when the police struck in Boston after the First World War. Either way, to be ignored or punished is what the poor ordinarily expect from government, because these are the responses they ordinarily evoke. . . .

In many cases, the repression of protest may be brutal and have life-or-death consequences for the protesters. In mining strikes in the western United States during the early 1900s, in the Warsaw ghetto during World War II, in the Kent State antiwar protest of 1970, in East Timor in the early 1980s, and in a host of other individual and mass protests, dissenters have died standing up for what they believed to be right. In other circumstances, the repression of protest may be less deadly, but can still have insidious consequences. The blacklisting of writers and actors for their political views destroyed many promising careers during the days of Senator Joseph McCarthy's influence in the 1950s.

Street protests are particularly likely to face a repressive response. For example, during the 2004 Republican National Convention in New York City, police arrested 1,806 demonstrators to prevent potential disruption of the convention. Peace activist Jeff Paterson, who was himself arrested, described the confusion of the scene:

> While cuffed and sitting in the street awaiting our bus trip to who-knew-where, detainees repeatedly demanded answers to outlandish questions such as "what am I being arrested for?" Initially, the replies were along the lines of "You know what!" or the more honest, "I need to talk to my supervisor first—I'll let you know soon." . . . A woman cop blurted out, "Look, we all know that eventually you guys were going to do something. So why should I follow you around town just waiting for you to do it? It's a lot easier for all of us this way."

A judge's order calling on the city to either immediately release arrested demonstrators or charge them with a crime was ignored until after the convention was over, resulting in contempt charges against New York City. In April 2005 the city settled the contempt charges for $231,200; it still faced $859 million in civil suits over the arrests.

Given the twin tendencies of powerful elites to either ignore protest or repress it, when can it result in positive change? In times of widespread social and economic unrest, change beckons; the aroused populace may join in an increasingly broad range of protest. For example, in the early 1960s in the United States, white liberals joined black activists in demanding improvements in civil rights, and the scope of the civil rights movement gradually expanded to include links to antiwar efforts and even the nascent environmental movement. The civil rights and environmental reforms that followed are examples of successful protest in the wake of societal turmoil.

A catastrophe, such as the death of 146 young, mostly female workers in the Triangle Shirtwaist Factory fire in 1911, can serve as a rallying point for protests and thus create momentum for political action. The importance of timing in facilitating effective protest is also well illustrated by this disaster. The problems underlying that crisis had been recognized for decades. Advocates for workers' right had long complained of unsafe conditions in sweatshops. New York's Joint Board of Sanitary Control had documented fire safety violations at 1,173 of the

1,200 factories it investigated mere months before the fire. As Rabbi Stephen S. Wise said at a protest rally following the disaster, "Some of us did foresee it, and others might have foreseen it, but they chose not to do so." But change occurred rapidly amid the outcry and turmoil that accompanied the disaster.

In selecting documents to include in this book, we have focused on instances in which dissent from authority was publicly expressed and in which the protest had an impact on society. We have included a wide variety of types of documents: essays, news articles, sermons, screenplays, poems, songs, novels, speeches, and letters, as well as images and artwork in the form of photographs, paintings, drawings, and advertisements. We've included works that are themselves protests, as well as documents that record key protests in images or words.

We've also included a broadly international selection of documents. While the United States was born in protest and retains a strong tradition of protest, we believe that dissent and its expression are central to the success of all democratic societies. Moreover, we believe that if globalization is to achieve the broad benefits it promises, protest must be accepted as a fundamental right around the world. Given the increasing speed with which capital and goods flow around the world, there is the potential for wealthier societies to export their problems—such as waste disposal, sweatshop labor, and clear-cutting—to poorer nations. Protest is needed to ensure that these social and environmental ills do not become invisible.

The structure of the book is intended to guide the reader in an exploration of protest. It begins with a selection of documents illustrating the importance of protest to democracy. This selection not only includes records of past protests, but also documents of the legal foundations that protect protest and make it possible. The book then looks at the wide variety of ways to express protest and at documents showing the roots of protest from earliest recorded history to a watershed moment of social upheaval: the Protestant Reformation.

The largest section of the book comprises documents of protest around seven major themes: civil rights, national self-determination, economic justice, environmental conservation, religious freedom, peace and war, and international political freedoms.

The chapter on the limits of societal norms gathers examples of those who have used protest to affect changes in social and cultural mores—or to rebel against such changes. The chapter on extreme forms of protest looks at examples of potentially violent or lethal acts, such as self-immolation, hunger strikes, and sabotage, to explore the boundaries between socially acceptable protest and outlaw action. Where, for instance, does protest end and terrorism or revolution begin?

We hope that you find the book interesting and inspirational, for we believe that American society today is characterized by too much fear and not enough fearlessness, to which we say, "We protest!"

PART I
THE ROOTS AND ROLES
OF PROTEST

DISSENT AND LIBERTY
MODES OF PROTEST
ROOTS OF DISSENT

CHAPTER 1
DISSENT AND LIBERTY

INTRODUCTION

The documents in this chapter outline the principles that allow for—indeed, encourage—dissent in free democratic society.

In exchange for being part of a self-governing society that provides us with security and safety, each of us gives up a measure of our freedom. We assign a portion of our authority to rule over ourselves to a government that we participate in directing. The sovereignty of the government represents the aggregate sovereignty of the citizens who constitute the government.

Each of us carries a set of rights and responsibilities in this arrangement, including the right to have an opinion and to say it out loud. We have the right to think whatever we want without interference from the government, and, within very broad parameters, we can say whatever we please. We trust that no matter how kooky or obscene or offbeat an idea we may have, our fellow citizens have enough wisdom to heed or dismiss it.

Our responsibility lies in both thinking about what it is we say and in respecting the views of our fellow citizens. And in exchange for freedom to dissent, we agree to accept the results of the self-governing process, even if our idea is rejected.

The documents that follow helped define this arrangement; they also explore a few of its many different nuances. They illustrate the vital role that dissent plays in a democratic society. They also demonstrate the challenges of allowing for disagreement in a pluralistic society and of defining the hazy boundary between an individual's personal authority and the government's authority to carry out its responsibilities.

The Magna Carta

In June of 1215, in a meadow known as Runnymede on the banks of the River Thames, King John of England signed the Magna Carta, or Great Charter. Written in Latin, with minor variations in text on each individual hand-printed copy, the Magna Carta represented the first time that the power of the sovereign was limited by a written document. It set the precedent for all future constitutions and thus for all constitutional protections of civil liberties.

The concessions King John made in the Magna Carta were forced by the armed revolt of his own barons. The barons had been driven to this exigency by John's rapacious administration of the country: taxes were high, corruption rampant, justice capricious, and widows and under-age heirs of nobles subject to vicious exploitation. In May the barons captured London, and John sued for peace.

The Magna Carta aimed to limit corruption and exploitation by John and his agents by spec-ifying the rights of "all free men" (a term that encompassed only male nobles). It established pro-cedures for the resolution of future conflicts, including the right for any man to protest mistreatment to a group of barons, and established procedures by which those barons could, by majority rule, decide the justice of such protests.

The language of the Magna Carta presaged both modern protections of civil liberties and regulations ensuring fair trade. It granted protection against unlawful seizure of assets, the right to a speedy trial, judgment by peers, fixed locations of courts, freedom of movement for mer-chants, and standardization of weights and measures.

This excerpt comes from a translation by the British Library, which houses two of the four remaining copies of the document.

JOHN, BY THE GRACE OF GOD King of England, Lord of Ireland, Duke of Normandy and Aquitaine, and Count of Anjou, to his archbishops, bishops, abbots, earls, barons, justices, foresters, sheriffs, stewards, servants, and to all his officials and loyal subjects, Greeting.

Know that before God, for the health of our soul and those of our ancestors and heirs, to the honour of God, the exaltation of the holy Church, and the bet-ter ordering of our kingdom . . . :

To all free men of our kingdom we have also granted, for us and our heirs for ever, all the liberties written out below, to have and to keep for them and their heirs, of us and our heirs:

The guardian of the land of an heir who is under age shall take from it only reasonable revenues, customary dues, and feudal services. He shall do this with-out destruction or damage to men or property. . . .

At her husband's death, a widow may have her marriage portion and inher-itance at once and without trouble. . . .

No widow shall be compelled to marry, so long as she wishes to remain without a husband. . . .

Ordinary lawsuits shall not follow the royal court around, but shall be held in a fixed place. . . .

Earls and barons shall be fined only by their equals, and in proportion to the gravity of their offence. . . .

No constable or other royal official shall take corn or other movable goods from any man without immediate payment, unless the seller voluntarily offers postponement of this. . . .

Neither we nor any royal official will take wood for our castle, or for any other purpose, without the consent of the owner. . . .

There shall be standard measures of wine, ale, and corn . . . throughout the kingdom. There shall also be a standard width of dyed cloth, russett, and haberject, namely two ells within the selvedges. Weights are to be standardised similarly. . . .

To no one will we sell, to no one deny or delay right or justice.

All merchants may enter or leave England unharmed and without fear, and may stay or travel within it, by land or water, for purposes of trade, free from all illegal exactions. . . .

To any man whom we have deprived or dispossessed of lands, castles, liberties, or rights, without the lawful judgement of his equals, we will at once restore these. . . .

All these customs and liberties that we have granted shall be observed in our kingdom in so far as concerns our own relations with our subjects. Let all men of our kingdom, whether clergy or laymen, observe them similarly in their relations with their own men.

Since we have granted all these things for God, for the better ordering of our kingdom, and to allay the discord that has arisen between us and our barons, and since we desire that they shall be enjoyed in their entirety, with lasting strength, for ever, we give and grant to the barons the following security:

The barons shall elect twenty-five of their number to keep, and cause to be observed with all their might, the peace and liberties granted and confirmed to them by this charter.

If we, our chief justice, our officials, or any of our servants offend in any respect against any man, or transgress any of the articles of the peace or of this security, and the offence is made known to four of the said twenty-five barons, they shall come to us—or in our absence from the kingdom to the chief justice—to declare it and claim immediate redress. If we, or in our absence abroad the chief justice, make no redress within forty days, reckoning from the day on which the offence was declared to us or to him, the four barons shall refer the matter to the rest of the twenty-five barons, who may distrain upon and assail us in every way possible, with the support of the whole community of the land, by seizing our castles, lands, possessions, or anything else saving only our own person and those of the queen and our children, until they have secured such redress as they have determined upon. Having secured the redress, they may then resume their normal obedience to us. . . .

In the event of disagreement among the twenty-five barons on any matter referred to them for decision, the verdict of the majority present shall have the same validity as a unanimous verdict of the whole twenty-five, whether these were all present or some of those summoned were unwilling or unable to appear. . . .

Both we and the barons have sworn that all this shall be observed in good faith and without deceit. . . .

Given by our hand in the meadow that is called Runnymede, between Windsor and Staines, on the fifteenth day of June in the seventeenth year of our reign.

Second Treatise of Government
John Locke

The Protestant Reformation changed the way Europeans thought about government. Previously, monarchs were believed to have received God's grace to rule over their respective kingdoms. Protestants, however, believed that all Christians were capable of receiving God's grace. A series of Enlightenment writers in the seventeenth and eighteenth centuries developed a political philosophy that changed the definition of government from one in which government is based on the will of God to one derived from the will of the people, each with his own set of God-given rights and responsibilities.

This change of perspective created a fundamental change in how dissent was viewed. To disagree with your monarch stopped meaning that you were questioning God; it now meant you were exercising one of your proper roles as a member of civil society.

John Locke was one of the most influential Enlightenment writers. Born in England, he participated in the Glorious Revolution of 1688 when Protestants overthrew James II. His *Letters of Toleration* argued against any government attempting to impose religious beliefs on its subjects.

Locke's *Second Treatise of Government*, written in 1689, developed his political theory on the relationship between the ruler and the governed. Locke believed that in the "state of nature" rational people gathered together to form societies aimed at protecting each person's life and property. As part of that arrangement, a social contract was formed between the ruler and the ruled in which citizens agreed to follow the ruler's commands in exchange for protection of their life, liberty, and property. This arrangement means that any government requires the consent of the governed. Locke believed that if the ruler breaks the arrangement—for example by taking citizens' property unfairly or imposing religion on them against their will—then citizens can revoke the contract. The ability of citizens to rebel and dissent, Locke believed, was an essential element in the preservation of each person's rights in the social contract.

The excerpt below from the *Second Treatise of Government* explores the issue of how citizens should respond to the unreasonable exercise of governmental power. The essay was part of a defense of the Glorious Revolution; it was extremely influential on the American Revolution and the formation of a new democracy in the United States.

WHERE-EVER LAW ENDS, TYRANNY BEGINS, if the law be transgressed to another's harm; and whosoever in authority exceeds the power given him by the law, and makes use of the force he has under his command, to compass that upon the subject, which the law allows not, ceases in that to be a magistrate; and, acting without authority, may be opposed, as any other man, who by force invades the right of another. . . .

May the commands then of a prince be opposed? May he be resisted as often as any one shall find himself aggrieved, and but imagine he has not right done him? This will unhinge and overturn all polities, and, instead of government and order, leave nothing but anarchy and confusion.

To this I answer, that force is to be opposed to nothing, but to unjust and unlawful force; whoever makes any opposition in any other case, draws on himself a just condemnation both from God and man; and so no such danger or confusion will follow, as is often suggested: for,

First, As, in some countries, the person of the prince by the law is sacred; and so, whatever he commands or does, his person is still free from all question or violence, not liable to force, or any judicial censure or condemnation. But yet opposition may be made to the illegal acts of any inferior officer, or other commissioned by him. . . .

Secondly, But this privilege, belonging only to the king's person, hinders not, but they may be questioned, opposed, and resisted, who use unjust force, though they pretend a commission from him, which the law authorizes not; as is plain in the case of him that has the king's writ to arrest a man, which is a full commission from the king; and yet he that has it cannot break open a man's house to do it, nor execute this command of the king upon certain days, nor in certain places, though this commission have no such exception in it; but they are the limitations of the law, which if any one transgress, the king's commission excuses him not. . . .

But if either these illegal acts have extended to the majority of the people; or if the mischief and oppression has lighted only on some few, but in such cases, as the precedent, and consequences seem to threaten all; and they are persuaded in their consciences, that their laws, and with them their estates, liberties, and lives are in danger, and perhaps their religion too; how they will be hindered from resisting illegal force, used against them, I cannot tell. This is an inconvenience, I confess, that attends all governments whatsoever.

The Social Contract
Jean-Jacques Rousseau

The French philosopher Jean-Jacques Rousseau expanded on John Locke's theory. In his essay *The Social Contract*, written in 1762, he explored the balance between the rights of an individual and need for a government to keep order. "Man is born free, and everywhere he is in chains," he famously wrote. "'The problem is to find a form of association which will defend and protect with the whole common force the person and goods of each associate, and in which each, while uniting himself with all, may still obey himself alone, and remain as free as before.' This is the fundamental problem of which the Social Contract provides the solution."

Rousseau believed people come together to form governments by their own will. They agree to submit themselves to the authority of the general will in this arrangement. This agreement, however, creates the dilemma of what do when individuals don't agree with the general will—a conflict he discusses in the following excerpt. Balancing the rights of individuals and the needs of authority was the goal of a new government in the United States, and the tension between the two is still at the heart of many of today's political issues.

Rousseau's writings were banned in France and he was forced to live in exile in Switzerland. However, his influence on both the American and French revolutions was enormous.

[E]ACH INDIVIDUAL, AS A MAN, may have a particular will contrary or dissimilar to the general will which he has as a citizen. His particular interest may speak to him quite differently from the common interest: his absolute and naturally independent existence may make him look upon what he owes to the common cause as a gratuitous contribution, the loss of which will do less harm to others than the payment of it is burdensome to himself; and, regarding the moral person which constitutes the State as a *persona ficta*, because not a man, he may wish to enjoy the rights of citizenship without being ready to fulfil the duties of a subject. The continuance of such an injustice could not but prove the undoing of the body politic.

In order then that the social compact may not be an empty formula, it tacitly includes the undertaking, which alone can give force to the rest, that whoever refuses to obey the general will shall be compelled to do so by the whole body. This means nothing less than that he will be forced to be free; for this is the condition which, by giving each citizen to his country, secures him against all personal dependence. In this lies the key to the working of the political machine; this alone legitimizes civil undertakings, which, without it, would be absurd, tyrannical, and liable to the most frightful abuses. . . .

The passage from the state of nature to the civil state produces a very remarkable change in man, by substituting justice for instinct in his conduct, and giving his actions the morality they had formerly lacked. Then only, when the voice of duty takes the place of physical impulses and right of appetite, does man, who so far had considered only himself, find that he is forced to act on different principles, and to consult his reason before listening to his inclinations. Although, in this state, he deprives himself of some advantages which he got from nature, he gains in return others so great, his faculties are so stimulated and developed, his ideas so extended, his feelings so ennobled, and his whole soul so uplifted, that, did not the abuses of this new condition often degrade him below that which he left, he would be bound to bless continually the happy moment which took him from it for ever, and, instead of a stupid and unimaginative animal, made him an intelligent being and a man.

Let us draw up the whole account in terms easily commensurable. What man loses by the social contract is his natural liberty and an unlimited right to everything he tries to get and succeeds in getting; what he gains is civil liberty and the proprietorship of all he possesses. If we are to avoid mistake in weighing one against the other, we must clearly distinguish natural liberty, which is bounded only by the strength of the individual, from civil liberty, which is limited by the general will; and possession, which is merely the effect of force or the right of the first occupier, from property, which can be founded only on a positive title.

We might, over and above all this, add, to what man acquires in the civil state, moral liberty, which alone makes him truly master of himself; for the mere impulse of appetite is slavery, while obedience to a law which we prescribe to ourselves is liberty.

"I confess that I do not entirely approve of this Constitution"

Benjamin Franklin

The debate over how a large number of people with very different perspectives can agree to form a government that has the authority to rule effectively and still leave room for dissent was brought to life at the United States Constitutional Convention of 1787 in Philadelphia. As he was known to do many times, Benjamin Franklin articulated the struggle of finding a balance, citing himself as an example of learning how to dissent from the particulars of a decision but abide by the decision in the interests of a greater good.

At age eighty-two, Franklin had been dispensing wisdom as "Poor Richard" for decades. He was one of the first to call for national union. He had convinced France to come to America's aid in the revolution, and he negotiated the Treaty of Paris, forcing England to recognize American sovereignty. Aside from George Washington, nobody commanded the same respect.

The Constitutional Convention delegates gathered at a time of rising discord within the fledgling nation, a loose collection of states tied together in a weak, confederate form of government. Interstate squabbles and sporadic rebellions were starting to tear the country apart. Leaders looked to the convention as an opportunity—perhaps the last one—to bring order to the new country. "Let prejudices, unreasonable jealousies, and local interests yield," Washington said.

Although he was on the losing side of many arguments leading up to it, Franklin supported the final Constitution. Upon conclusion of the convention on September 17, he had his colleague James Wilson read a speech in favor of the document. The speech included his right to vigorously disagree, but also embodied the spirit of compromise and conciliation that he saw as necessary to forge a democratic nation. The speech was widely circulated throughout America and influenced public opinion in favor of the Constitution. In articulating the spirit of compromise—the ability to remain true to his own beliefs and still support the common good—Franklin marked an indispensable feature of an effective democracy.

MR. PRESIDENT: I confess that I do not entirely approve of this Constitution at present, but Sir, I am not sure I shall never approve it. For having lived long, I have experienced many Instances of being obliged, by better Information or fuller Consideration, to change Opinions even on important Subjects, which I once thought right, but found to be otherwise. It is therefore that the older I grow, the more apt I am to doubt my own Judgment, and to pay more Respect to the Judgment of others. Most Men indeed as well as most Sects in Religion, think themselves in Possession of all Truth, and that wherever others differ from them it is so far Error. Steele, a Protestant in a Dedication tells the Pope, that the only difference between our two Churches in their Opinions of the Certainty of their doctrines is, the Romish Church is infallible, and the Church of England is never in the Wrong. But tho' many private Persons think almost as highly of their own Infallibility, as of that of their Sect, few express it so naturally as a certain French Lady, who in a little Dispute with her Sister, said, I don't know how it happens, Sister but I meet with no body but myself, that's always in the right. . . .

In these Sentiments, Sir, I agree to this Constitution, with all its Faults, if they are such; because I think a General Government necessary for us, and there is no Form of Government but what may be a Blessing to the People if well administered; and I believe farther that this is likely to be well administered for a Course of Years, and can only end in Despotism as other Forms have done before it, when the People shall become so corrupted as to need Despotic Government, being incapable of any other. I doubt too whether any other Convention we can obtain, may be able to make a better Constitution: For when you assemble a Number of Men to have the Advantage of their joint Wisdom, you inevitably assemble with those Men all their Prejudices, their Passions, their Errors of Opinion, their local Interests, and their selfish Views. From such an Assembly can a perfect Production be expected? It therefore astonishes me, Sir, to find this System approaching so near to Perfection as it does; and I think it will astonish our Enemies, who are waiting with Confidence to hear that our Councils are confounded like those of the Builders of Babel, and that our States are on the Point of Separation, only to meet hereafter for the Purpose of cutting one another's Throats. Thus I consent, Sir, to this Constitution because I expect no better, and because I am not sure, that it is not the best. The Opinions I have had of its Errors, I sacrifice to the Public Good. I have never whisper'd a Syllable of them abroad. Within these Walls they were born, and here they shall die. If every one of us in returning to our Constituents were to report the Objections he has had to it, and use his Influence to gain Partizans in support of them, we might prevent its being generally received, and thereby lose all the salutary Effects and great Advantages resulting naturally in our favour among foreign Nations, as well as among ourselves, from our real or apparent Unanimity. Much of the Strength and Efficiency of any Government, in procuring and securing

Happiness to the People, depends on Opinion, on the general Opinion of the Goodness of the Government as well as of the Wisdom and Integrity of its Governors. I hope therefore that for our own Sakes, as a Part of the People, and for the sake of our Posterity, we shall act heartily and unanimously in recommending this Constitution wherever our Influence may extend, and turn our future Thoughts and Endeavours to the Means of having it well administered.

On the whole, Sir, I cannot help expressing a Wish, that every Member of the Convention, who may still have Objections to it, would with me, on this Occasion doubt a little of his own Infallibility, and to make *manifest* our *Unanimity*, put his Name to this instrument.

Preamble to the U.S. Constitution

When the founding fathers of the United States wrote the Constitution, they made the radical assertion that the authority of the government lies with its citizens. The first three words of the Constitution's preamble—"We the people"—make this clear. In the context of the eighteenth century, the term "people" was limited to men with property, a definition that over time has been extended to all adult citizens.

Although some people accused delegates at the 1787 Constitutional Convention of speaking for "the people" without their endorsement, most Americans embraced the concept of government that sprung from themselves as citizens, each with his or her own set of rights and responsibilities. As the United States moves forward toward the ever-elusive goal of "a more perfect Union," it has been the people in all of their diversity who have animated the Constitution and the American government with life and vigor. In the face of the operations of the federal government, which can tend towards seizing authority as its own, it has been a difficult dilemma for many people to step into the authority that each American holds as a citizen with his or her own sovereignty.

WE THE PEOPLE OF THE UNITED STATES, in Order to form a more perfect Union, establish Justice, insure domestic Tranquility, provide for the common defence, promote the general Welfare, and secure the Blessings of Liberty to ourselves and our Posterity, do ordain and establish this Constitution for the United States of America.

U.S. Bill of Rights

Responding to widespread objections that the Constitution did not guarantee liberties and rights, James Madison proposed several amendments to the First Congress in 1789. Within two years, ten amendments known as the Bill of Rights were approved.

In approving the Constitution, several states—including Massachusetts, Virginia, and New York—either attached a series of amendments ensuring individual liberties or recommended that such amendments be included. Two states—North Carolina and Rhode Island—did not ratify the Constitution until after the Bill of Rights was added to the government's founding charter.

These additions have provided the foundation for the protection of fundamental liberties in the United States.

THE CONVENTIONS OF A NUMBER OF THE STATES HAVING, at the time of adopting the Constitution, expressed a desire, in order to prevent misconstruction or abuse of its powers, that further declaratory and restrictive clauses should be added: And as extending the ground of public confidence in the Government, will best ensure the beneficent ends of its institution;

Resolved by the Senate and House of Representatives of the United States of America, in Congress assembled, two thirds of both Houses concurring, that the following Articles be proposed to the Legislatures of the several States, as amendments to the Constitution of the United States; all, or any of which articles, when ratified by three fourths of the said Legislatures, to be valid to all intents and purposes as part of the said Constitution; viz. . . .

Amendment I

Congress shall make no law respecting an establishment of religion, or prohibiting the free exercise thereof; or abridging the freedom of speech, or of the press; or the right of the people peaceably to assemble, and to petition the Government for a redress of grievances.

Amendment II

A well regulated Militia, being necessary to the security of a free State, the right of the people to keep and bear Arms, shall not be infringed.

Amendment III

No Soldier shall, in time of peace be quartered in any house, without the consent of the Owner, nor in time of war, but in a manner to be prescribed by law.

Amendment IV

The right of the people to be secure in their persons, houses, papers, and effects, against unreasonable searches and seizures, shall not be violated, and no Warrants shall issue, but upon probable cause, supported by Oath or affirmation, and particularly describing the place to be searched, and the persons or things to be seized.

Amendment V

No person shall be held to answer for a capital, or otherwise infamous crime, unless on a presentment or indictment of a Grand Jury, except in cases arising in the land or naval forces, or in the Militia, when in actual service in time of War or public danger; nor shall any person be subject for the same offence to be twice put in jeopardy of life or limb; nor shall be compelled in any criminal case to be a witness against himself, nor be deprived of life, liberty, or property, without due process of law; nor shall private property be taken for public use, without just compensation.

Amendment VI

In all criminal prosecutions, the accused shall enjoy the right to a speedy and public trial, by an impartial jury of the State and district wherein the crime shall have been committed, which district shall have been previously ascertained by law, and to be informed of the nature and cause of the accusation; to be confronted with the witnesses against him; to have compulsory process for obtaining witnesses in his favor, and to have the assistance of counsel for his defence.

Amendment VII

In Suits at common law, where the value in controversy shall exceed twenty dollars, the right of trial by jury shall be preserved, and no fact tried by a jury, shall be otherwise reexamined in any court of the United States, than according to the rules of the common law.

Amendment VIII

Excessive bail shall not be required, nor excessive fines imposed, nor cruel and unusual punishments inflicted.

Amendment IX

The enumeration in the Constitution, of certain rights, shall not be construed to deny or disparage others retained by the people.

Amendment X

The powers not delegated to the United States by the Constitution, nor prohibited by it to the States, are reserved to the States respectively, or to the people.

Second Inaugural Address
Abraham Lincoln

When Abraham Lincoln delivered his second inaugural address on March 4, 1865, the end of Civil War seemed imminent. And, indeed, it was only one month away.

Lincoln used the speech to address the profound problem of how to reunite the country after dissent had split the nation in a bitter and bloody civil war for four years. More than 600,000 men had been killed. The North had purposefully destroyed the Southern economy as a military strategy. Disagreement over slavery had led to nationwide loss, sorrow, and anger.

In his address, Lincoln portrayed the war as a national punishment for the evil of slavery, a condition that the full nation had accepted previously. Citing the Bible, he declined to determine whose side was right or wrong. He used the term "adversaries" instead of "enemies" to describe the Southern armies against which the North had fought hundreds of battles. Few would say that the United States has lived up to the goals of the final famous sentence in this address. But Lincoln's articulation of the ideal that people with dissenting views can reunite after the political combat is over remains intact.

AT THIS SECOND APPEARING to take the oath of the presidential office, there is less occasion for an extended address than there was at the first. Then a statement, somewhat in detail, of a course to be pursued, seemed fitting and proper. Now, at the expiration of four years, during which public declarations have been constantly called forth on every point and phase of the great contest which still absorbs the attention and engrosses the energies of the nation, little that is new could be presented. The progress of our arms, upon which all else chiefly depends, is as well known to the public as to myself; and it is, I trust, reasonably satisfactory and encouraging to all. With high hope for the future, no prediction in regard to it is ventured.

On the occasion corresponding to this four years ago, all thoughts were anxiously directed to an impending civil-war. All dreaded it—all sought to avert it. While the inaugural address was being delivered from this place, devoted altogether to *saving* the Union without war, insurgent agents were in the city seeking to *destroy* it without war—seeking to dissolve the Union, and divide effects, by negotiation. Both parties deprecated war; but one of them would *make* war rather than let the nation survive; and the other would *accept* war rather than let it perish. And the war came.

One eighth of the whole population were colored slaves, not distributed generally over the Union, but localized in the Southern part of it. These slaves constituted a peculiar and powerful interest. All knew that this interest was, somehow, the cause of the war. To strengthen, perpetuate, and extend this interest was the object for which the insurgents would rend the Union, even by war; while the government claimed no right to do more than to restrict the territorial enlargement of it. Neither party expected for the war, the magnitude, or the duration, which it has already attained. Neither anticipated that the *cause* of the conflict might cease with, or even before, the conflict itself should cease. Each looked for an easier triumph, and a result less fundamental and astounding. Both read the same Bible and pray to the same God; and each invokes His aid against the other. It may seem strange that any men should dare to ask a just God's assistance in wringing their bread from the sweat of other men's faces; but let us judge not that we be not judged. The prayers of both could not be answered; that of neither has been answered fully. The Almighty has His own purposes. "Woe unto the world because of offences! for it must needs be that offences come; but woe to that man by whom the offence cometh!" If we shall suppose that American Slavery is one of those offences which, in the providence of God, must needs come, but which, having continued through His appointed time, He now wills to remove, and that He gives to both North and South, this terrible war, as the woe due to those by whom the offence came, shall we discern therein any departure from those divine attributes which the believers in a Living God always ascribe to Him? Fondly do we hope—fervently do we pray—that this mighty scourge of war may speedily pass away. Yet, if God wills that it continue, until all the wealth piled by the bonds-men's two hundred and fifty years of unrequited toil shall be sunk, and until every drop of blood drawn with the lash shall be paid by another drawn with the sword, as was said three thousand years ago, so still it must be said "the judgments of the Lord are true and righteous altogether."

With malice toward none; with charity for all; with firmness in the right, as God gives us to see the right, let us strive on to finish the work we are in; to bind up the nation's wounds; to care for him who shall have borne the battle, and for his widow, and his orphan—to do all which may achieve and cherish a just, and lasting peace, among ourselves, and with all nations.

"J'accuse"
Émile Zola

The Dreyfus Affair rocked France in the final years of the nineteenth century. The scandal touched on patriotism, anti-Semitism, free speech, and corruption in the government and military. At the heart of the affair was a passionate act of protest by one man, novelist Émile Zola, who braved charges of disloyalty when he publicly questioned the integrity of the military in his famous newspaper article "J'accuse."

Zola, born in 1840, was a popular novelist with an international reputation. He laid that reputation on the line in 1898 with "J'accuse," an open letter to then-President Félix Faure protesting the wrongful conviction and imprisonment of Army Captain Alfred Dreyfus. Zola's letter—published on the front page of the newspaper L'Aurore and called by one observer a hundred years later "the greatest newspaper article of all time"—was part accusatory screed, part investigative reporting. The letter laid out, in painstaking detail, Zola's examination of the facts of the Dreyfus case. He adamantly asserted that Dreyfus was innocent of espionage; that he was framed because he was Jewish; and that the military was covering up for the army officer who was the actual spy out of a horribly misplaced sense of loyalty. The incendiary nature of Zola's charges were reflected in the bold banner headline, complete with ellipses and exclamation point, that ran across the paper's front page: "J'Accuse…!," meaning "I Accuse…!"

"L 'affaire Dreyfus" began in September 1894 when French Army intelligence intercepted a letter that referred to the delivery of documents about French defense to a German attaché. Military officers suspected the spy who wrote the letter was Dreyfus, a career military man who had risen to be one of the highest-ranking Jews in the army. Major Armand Mercier du Paty de Clam arrested and interrogated Dreyfus, who was then convicted in a military court martial. In December he was sentenced to life imprisonment and deported to Devil's Island, a penal colony off the coast of French Guiana. Two years later, however, French intelligence came into possession of a letter that pointed to army Major Ferdinand Esterhazy as the true author of the treasonous letter. A military court acquitted Esterhazy in January 1898; a few days later an incensed Zola published his famous article, based partly on information supplied by Alfred Dreyfus's brother, Mathieu, and a journalist working on the case. The next year Esterhazy conceded he had written the letter. In 1900, a new French president pardoned Dreyfus, though the conviction remained on his record.

In writing "J'accuse" Zola fully expected to be charged with libel, and said he welcomed the charges since a libel lawsuit would have to take place in open court and would bring more details of the case to light (the military trials had taken place behind closed doors). Zola was indeed charged with libel and convicted. He fled to England to avoid jail. After Dreyfus was pardoned, Zola returned to France. He died in 1902 of carbon monoxide poisoning from a house fire; some charged that anti-Dreyfusards purposely clogged his chimney to murder Zola. Dreyfus attended Zola's funeral, and was reinstated in the military in 1906 after the French courts officially exonerated him. Zola's article, excerpted here, was published January 13, 1898, and ominously foreshadowed the rise of Nazism in Germany.

A COURT MARTIAL, acting on orders, has just dared to acquit such a man as Esterhazy. Truth itself and justice itself have been slapped in the face. And now it is too late, France's cheek has been sullied by that supreme insult, and History will record that it was during your Presidency that such a crime against society was committed.

They have dared to do this. Very well, then, I shall dare too. I shall tell the truth, for I pledged that I would tell it, if our judicial system, once the matter was brought before it through the normal channels, did not tell the truth, the whole truth. It is my duty to speak up; I will not be an accessory to the fact. If I were, my nights would be haunted by the spectre of that innocent man so far away, suffering the worst kind of torture as he pays for a crime he did not commit.

And it is to you, M. le Président, that I will shout out the truth with all the revulsion of a decent man. To your credit, I am convinced that you are unaware of the truth. And to whom should I denounce the evil machinations of those who are truly guilty if not to you, the First Magistrate in the land? . . .

Did anyone really hope that one court martial would undo what another court martial had done in the first place?

I am not even talking about the judges, who could have been chosen differently. Since these soldiers have a lofty idea of discipline in their blood, isn't that enough to disqualify them from arriving at an equitable judgement? Discipline means obedience. Once the Minister of War, the supreme commander, has publicly established the authority of the original verdict, and has done so to the acclamations of the nations' representatives, how can you expect a court martial to override his judgement officially? In hierarchical terms, that is impossible. General Billot, in his statement, planted certain ideas in the judges' minds, and they proceeded to judge the case in the same way as they would proceed to go into battle, that is, without stopping to think. The preconceived idea that they brought with them to the judges' bench was of course as follows: 'Dreyfus was sentenced for treason by a court martial, therefore he is guilty; and we, as a court martial, cannot find him innocent. Now, we know that if we recognize Esterhazy's guilt we will be proclaiming Dreyfus's innocence.' And nothing could make them budge from that line.

They reached an iniquitous verdict which will forever weigh heavy on all our future courts martial and forever make their future decisions suspect. There may be room for doubt as to whether the first court martial was intelligent but there is no doubt that the second has been criminal. Its excuse, I repeat, is that the commander in chief had spoken and declared the previous verdict unattackable, holy and superior to mere mortals—and how could his subordinates dare to contradict him? They talk to us about the honour or the army; they want us to love the army, respect the army. Oh yes, indeed, if you mean an army that would rise up at the very first hint of danger, that would defend French soil; that army is the French people themselves, and we have nothing but affection and respect for it. But the army that is involved here is not the dignified army that our need for justice calls out for. What we are effaced with here is the sabre, the master that may be imposed on us tomorrow. Should we kiss the hit of that sabre, that god, with pious devotion? No, we should not! . . .

[W]hat an accumulation of madness, stupidity, unbridled imagination, low police tactics, inquisitorial and tyrannical methods this handful of officers have got away with! They have crushed the nation under their boots, stuffing its calls for truth and justice down its throat on the fallacious and sacrilegious pretext that they are acting for the good of the country!

And they have committed other crimes. They have based their action on the foul press and let themselves be defended by all the rogues in Paris—and now the rogues are triumphant and insolent while law and integrity go down in defeat. . . . It is a crime to lead public opinion astray, to manipulate it for a death-dealing purpose and pervert it to the point of delirium. It is a crime to poison the minds of the humble, ordinary people, to whip reactionary and intolerant passions into a frenzy while sheltering behind the odious bastion of anti-Semitism. France, the great and liberal cradle of the rights of man, will die of anti-Semitism if it is not cured of it. It is a crime to play on patriotism to further the aims of hatred. And it is a crime to worship the sabre as a modern god when all of human science is labouring to hasten the triumph of truth and justice.

Truth and justice—how ardently we have striven for them! And how distressing it is to see them slapped in the face, overlooked, forced to retreat! . . .

[The article closed with a series of direct accusations against high military officials.]
I accuse Lt-Col du Paty de Clam of having been the diabolical agent of a miscarriage of justice (though unwittingly, I am willing to believe) and then of having defended his evil deed for the past three years through the most preposterous and most blameworthy machinations.

I accuse General Mercier of having been an accomplice, at least by weak-mindedness, to one of the most iniquitous acts of this century.

I accuse General Billot of having had in his hands undeniable proof that Dreyfus was innocent and of having suppressed it, of having committed this crime against justice and against humanity for political purposes, so that the General Staff [of the army], which had been compromised, would not lose face.

I accuse Generals de Boisdeffre and Gonse of having been accomplices to this same crime, one out of intense clerical conviction, no doubt, and the other perhaps because of the esprit de corps which makes the War Office the Holy of Holies and hence unattackable . . .

As for the persons I have accused, I do not know them; I have never seen them; I feel no rancour or hatred towards them. To me, they are mere entities, mere embodiments of social malfeasance. And the action I am taking here is merely a revolutionary means to hasten the revelation of truth and justice.

I have but one goal: that light be shed, in the name of mankind which has suffered so much and has the right to happiness. My ardent protest is merely a cry from my very soul. Let them dare to summon me before a court of law! Let the inquiry be held in broad daylight!

I am waiting.

On Liberty
John Stuart Mill

John Stuart Mill was a prominent nineteenth-century English philosopher and among the most vigorous defenders of free speech. He argued that unpopular opinions should be heard, not to benefit the holders of those opinions, but for the benefit of society as a whole. By clearly articulating the idea that wisdom comes through the challenge of generally accepted ideas, he presaged defenses of free speech offered by U.S. Supreme Court justice Oliver Wendell Holmes in the early twentieth century and by modern constitutional scholar Cass Sunstein. The more firmly convinced a society is of the rightness of an idea, the more firmly that society needs to protect the right of whatever minority holds a contrary idea to advance its arguments. His essay On Liberty, excerpted here, addresses these issues. His views helped shape modern concepts of freedom of speech in both England and the United States.

Mill was also an early advocate for equal rights for women, a tribute perhaps to the influence of his wife, Harriet, on his ideas and intellectual development.

IF ALL MANKIND MINUS ONE, were of one opinion, and only one person were of the contrary opinion, mankind would be no more justified in silencing that one person, than he, if he had the power, would be justified in silencing mankind. Were an opinion a personal possession of no value except to the owner; if to be obstructed in the enjoyment of it were simply a private injury, it would make some difference whether the injury was inflicted only on a few persons or on many. But the peculiar evil of silencing the expression of an opinion is, that it is robbing the human race; posterity as well as the existing generation; those who dissent from the opinion, still more than those who hold it. If the opinion is right, they are deprived of the opportunity of exchanging error for truth: if wrong, they lose, what is almost as great a benefit, the clearer perception and livelier impression of truth, produced by its collision with error.

It is necessary to consider separately these two hypotheses, each of which has a distinct branch of the argument corresponding to it. We can never be sure that the opinion we are endeavouring to stifle is a false opinion; and if we were sure, stifling it would be an evil still.

First: the opinion which it is attempted to suppress by authority may possibly be true. Those who desire to suppress it, of course deny its truth; but they are not infallible. They have no authority to decide the question for all mankind, and exclude every other person from the means of judging. To refuse a hearing to an opinion, because they are sure that it is false, is to assume that *their* certainty is the same thing as *absolute* certainty. All silencing of discussion is an assumption of infallibility. Its condemnation may be allowed to rest on this common argument, not the worse for being common.

Unfortunately for the good sense of mankind, the fact of their fallibility is far from carrying the weight in their practical judgment, which is always allowed to it in theory; for while every one well knows himself to be fallible, few think it necessary to take any precautions against their own fallibility, or admit the supposition that any opinion of which they feel very certain, may be one of the examples of the error to which they acknowledge themselves to be liable. Absolute princes, or others who are accustomed to unlimited deference, usually feel this complete confidence in their own opinions on nearly all subjects. People more happily situated, who sometimes hear their opinions disputed, and are not wholly unused to be set right when they are wrong, place the same unbounded reliance only on such of their opinions as are shared by all who surround them, or to whom they habitually defer: for in proportion to a man's want of confidence in his own solitary judgment, does he usually repose, with implicit trust, on the infallibility of "the world" in general. And the world, to each individual, means the part of it with which he comes in contact; his party, his sect, his church, his class of society: the man may be called, by comparison, almost liberal and large-minded to whom it means anything so comprehensive as his own country or his own age. Nor is his faith in this collective authority at all shaken by his being aware that other ages, countries, sects, churches, classes, and parties have thought, and even now think, the exact reverse. He devolves upon his own world the responsibility of being in the right against the dissentient worlds of other people; and it never troubles him that mere accident has decided which of these numerous worlds is the object of his reliance, and that the same causes which make him a Churchman in London, would have made him a Buddhist or a Confucian in Pekin. Yet it is as evident in itself as any amount of argument can make it, that ages are no more infallible than individuals; every age having held many opinions which subsequent ages have deemed not only false but absurd; and it is as certain that many opinions, now general, will be rejected by future ages, as it is that many, once general, are rejected by the present.

The objection likely to be made to this argument, would probably take some such form as the following. There is no greater assumption of infallibility in forbidding the propagation of error, than in any other thing which is done by public authority on its own judgment and responsibility. Judgment is given to men that they may use it. Because it may be used erroneously, are men to be told that they ought not to use it at all? To prohibit what they think pernicious, is not claiming exemption from error, but fulfilling the duty incumbent on them, although fallible, of acting on their conscientious conviction. If we were never to act on our opinions, because those opinions may be wrong, we should leave all our interests uncared for, and all our duties unperformed. . . .

I answer, that it is assuming very much more. There is the greatest difference between presuming an opinion to be true, because, with every opportunity for contesting it, it has not been refuted, and assuming its truth for the purpose of not permitting its refutation. Complete liberty of contradicting and disproving our opinion, is the very condition which justifies us in assuming its truth for purposes of action; and on no other terms can a being with human faculties have any rational assurance of being right.

. . . Wrong opinions and practices gradually yield to fact and argument: but facts and arguments, to produce any effect on the mind, must be brought before it. Very few facts are able to tell their own story, without comments to bring out their meaning. The whole strength and value, then, of human judgment, depending on the one property, that it can be set right when it is wrong, reliance can be placed on it only when the means of setting it right are kept constantly at hand. In the case of any person whose judgment is really deserving of confidence, how has it become so? Because he has kept his mind open to criticism of his opinions and conduct. Because it has been his practice to listen to all that could be said against him; to profit by as much of it as was just, and expound to himself, and upon occasion to others, the fallacy of what was fallacious. Because he has felt, that the only way in which a human being can make some approach to knowing the whole of a subject, is by hearing what can be said about it by persons of every variety of opinion, and studying all modes in which it can be looked at by every character of mind. No wise man ever acquired his wisdom in any mode but this; nor is it in the nature of human intellect to become wise in any other manner. . . .

Strange it is, that men should admit the validity of the arguments for free discussion, but object to their being "pushed to an extreme;" not seeing that unless the reasons are good for an extreme case, they are not good for any case. Strange that they should imagine that they are not assuming infallibility when they acknowledge that there should be free discussion on all subjects which can possibly be *doubtful*, but think that some particular principle or doctrine should be forbidden to be questioned because it is *so certain*, that is, because *they are certain* that it is certain. To call any proposition certain, while there is any one who would deny its certainty if permitted, but who is not permitted, is to assume that we ourselves, and those who agree with us, are the judges of certainty, and judges without hearing the other side. . . .

Opinion on *Abrams v. United States*
Oliver Wendell Holmes

President Theodore Roosevelt appointed Oliver Wendell Holmes to the Supreme Court in 1902, and Holmes served for nearly thirty years. His influential opinions are still widely quoted, though not all of them have stood the test of time. For example, his 1927 decision in *Buck v. Bell* supported forced sterilization by the government.

Holmes greatly influenced the boundaries of free speech. Two cases based on the 1917 Espionage Act, which made it a crime to advocate policies that would impede the government's military success, gave Holmes the chance to frame the limits of the Constitution's First Amendment.

In 1919, in *Schenck v. United States*, Holmes and a unanimous court upheld the conviction of a socialist leader who had advocated resistance to the draft. Holmes articulated the limits of constitutionally protected free speech using what has come to be known as the clear and present danger test: "The question in every case is whether the words used are used in such circumstances and are of such a nature as to create a clear and present danger that they will bring about the substantive evils that Congress has a right to prevent." The case and the decision attracted much unfavorable attention from prominent legal scholars.

By the time the next test of the law, *Abrams v. United States*, came before the court later that same year, Holmes was ready to draw a finer distinction, perhaps benefitting from the legal controversy following *Schenck*. Holmes's dissent in *Abrams*, excerpted here, defended the First Amendment, arguing for a concept known as the marketplace of ideas. Specifically, Holmes argued that we cannot know ahead of time which points of view may turn out to be right, and hence that the Constitution calls for the minimum amount of restriction on free speech, even of ideas we find hateful.

The facts of the case centered on two brochures that called for workers to avoid building armaments for the U.S. war effort, because they would be used against the Bolsheviks in Russia. Holmes argued that there could be many reasons why one could suggest building fewer armaments—many of them firmly patriotic. Restriction of speech, he asserted, could not be enforced against the author of the brochures simply on the basis of his philosophy. Such restriction of opinions might be logical if one had no doubt of the correct course, but our constitution, Holmes argued, called for a different approach—using public discourse and argument as the basis for finding the right course.

A PATRIOT MIGHT THINK that we were wasting money on aeroplanes, or making more cannon of a certain kind than we needed, and might advocate curtailment with success, yet, even if it turned out that the curtailment hindered and was thought by other minds to have been obviously likely to hinder the United States in the prosecution of the war, no one would hold such conduct a crime. I admit that my illustration does not answer all that might be said, but it is enough to show what I think, and to let me pass to a more important aspect of the case. I refer to the First Amendment to the Constitution, that Congress shall make no law abridging the freedom of speech. . . .

. . . It is only the present danger of immediate evil or an intent to bring it about that warrants Congress in setting a limit to the expression of opinion where private rights are not concerned. Congress certainly cannot forbid all effort to change the mind of the country. Now nobody can suppose that the surreptitious publishing of a silly leaflet by an unknown man, without more, would present any immediate danger that its opinions would hinder the success of the government arms or have any appreciable tendency to do so. . . .

Persecution for the expression of opinions seems to me perfectly logical. If you have no doubt of your premises or your power, and want a certain result with all your heart you naturally express your wishes in law and sweep away all opposition. To allow opposition by speech seems to indicate that you think the speech impotent, as when a man says that he has squared the circle, or that you do not care whole-heartedly for the result, or that you doubt either your power or your premises. But when men have realized that time has upset many fighting faiths, they may come to believe even more than they believe the very foundations of their own conduct that the ultimate good desired is better reached by free trade in ideas—that the best test of truth is the power of the thought to get itself accepted in the competition of the market, and that truth is the only ground upon which their wishes safely can be carried out. That at any rate is the theory of our Constitution. It is an experiment, as all life is an experiment. Every year if not every day we have to wager our salvation upon some prophecy based upon imperfect knowledge. While that experiment is part of our system, I think that we should be eternally vigilant against attempts to check the expression of opinions that we loathe and believe to be fraught with death, unless they so imminently threaten immediate interference with the lawful and pressing purposes of the law that an immediate check is required to save the country. . . . Only the emergency that makes it immediately dangerous to leave the correction of evil counsels to time warrants making any exception to the sweeping command, "Congress shall make no law . . . abridging the freedom of speech."

Freedom of Speech

Norman Rockwell

On January 6, 1941, President Franklin D. Roosevelt delivered his "Four Freedoms Speech" outlining the principles for which the United States would be willing to go to war. "We look forward to a world founded upon four essential freedoms," Roosevelt said. "The first is the freedom of speech and expression—everywhere in the world."

After the Japanese launched a surprise attack on the U.S. naval base at Pearl Harbor on December 7, 1941, painter Norman Rockwell produced a series of paintings illustrating all four freedoms—the others were freedom of worship, freedom from want, and freedom from fear—to help raise money for the war effort. The U.S. Treasury Department and *Saturday Evening Post* sponsored a national tour of the paintings in 1943. More than $130 million was raised through the sale of war bonds.

The painting *Freedom of Speech* was drawn from Rockwell's experience of attending town meetings in his hometown of Arlington, Vermont. In New England, the town meeting is an annual event in which residents vote on the town budget and take action on a variety of topics. Residents have the opportunity to speak about every issue that comes before them. As Rockwell's painting illustrates, it is a two-way process. There is the freedom to express the view,

made obvious by the central figure stating his opinion. But there is also a second element, which is that the rest of the voters need to listen to what is being said. It is a time-consuming, sometimes tedious, process in which all dissenting views are given time to be heard. Rockwell highlights this often-overlooked aspect of free expression by having the speaker standing among the seated audience. While some in the audience are looking at the speaker, listening carefully (Rockwell highlights the ears of three of them), others seem to be gazing off into the distance (or perhaps at a clock on the wall).

"Patriotism is not the *fear* of something; it is the *love* of something"
Adlai Stevenson

Illinois governor Adlai Stevenson II ran for president twice in the 1950s, facing—and losing to—war hero Dwight Eisenhower both times. Stevenson was famous for his intellectual prowess, powerful speeches, service to the nation, and principled stands.

Attacked by Senator Joseph McCarthy as being soft on communism, Stevenson offered his own definition of patriotism in the August 1952 speech excerpted here, given to the American Legion during his first campaign for the presidency. He argued that to defend America is not merely to defend the land, but also the ideas of freedom that define the country. Giving such a speech took great courage, coming as it did just three years after the Soviet Union had acquired the atomic bomb, and as the anticommunist frenzy in the United States moved toward its peak. While Stevenson won only eighty-nine electoral votes in that fall's election, his form of patriotism far outlasted that of McCarthy.

During the Cuban Missile Crisis of 1962, Stevenson served as U.S. ambassador to the United Nations. At an emergency meeting of the U.N. Security Council he famously confronted the Soviet ambassador, demanding to know whether the Soviet Union was installing missiles in Cuba, and then presented aerial photos to prove the falsity of the Soviet denial. On Stevenson's death, President Lyndon Johnson said, "Adlai Stevenson holds a permanent place on that tiny roster of those who will be remembered as long as mankind is strong enough to honor greatness."

WE TALK A GREAT DEAL ABOUT PATRIOTISM. What do we mean by "patriotism" in the context of our times? . . .

The anatomy of patriotism is complex. But surely intolerance and public irresponsibility cannot be cloaked in the shining armor of rectitude and righteousness. Nor can the denial of the right to hold ideas that are different—the freedom of man to think as he pleases. To strike freedom of the mind with the fist of patriotism is an old and ugly subtlety.

And the freedom of the mind, my friends, has served America well. The vigor of our political life, our capacity for change, our cultural, scientific, and industrial achievements, all derive from free inquiry, from the free mind—from the imagination, resourcefulness, and daring of men who are not afraid of new ideas. Most all of us favor free enterprise for business. Let us also favor free enterprise for the mind. For, in the last analysis, we would fight to the death to protect it. Why is it, then, that we are sometimes slow to detect, or are indifferent to, the dangers that beset it?

Many of the threats to our cherished freedoms in these anxious, troubled times arise, it seems to me, from a healthy apprehension about the Communist menace within our country. Communism is abhorrent. It is strangulation of the individual; it is death for the soul. Americans who have surrendered to this misbegotten idol have surrendered their right to our trust. And there can be no secure place for them in our public life.

Yet, as I have said before, we must take care not to burn down the barn to kill the rats. All of us, and especially patriotic organizations of enormous influence like the American Legion, must be vigilant in protecting our birthright from its too zealous friends while protecting it from its evil enemies.

The tragedy of our day is the climate of fear in which we live, and fear breeds repression. Too often sinister threats to the Bill of Rights, to freedom of the mind, are concealed under the patriotic cloak of anticommunism. . . .

It was always accounted a virtue in a man to love his country. With us it is now something more than a virtue. It is a necessity, a condition of survival. When an American says that he loves his country, he means not only that he loves the New England hills, the prairies glistening in the sun, the wide and rising plains, the great mountains, and the sea. He means that he loves an inner air, an inner light in which freedom lives and in which a man can draw the breath of self-respect.

Men who have offered their lives for their country know that patriotism is not the *fear* of something; it is the *love* of something. Patriotism with us is not the hatred of Russia; it is the love of this Republic and of the ideal of liberty of man and mind in which it was born, and to which this Republic is dedicated.

"Let us proclaim—loudly and all together— so that our cry pierces the sky"

Gonzalo Aguirre and Enrique Tarigo

As in several South American countries in the 1970s, the military seized power in Uruguay in 1973, overthrowing a previously elected democratic government. During ten years of military rule, 200 Uruguayans were killed by the government and 400,000 were displaced because of political violence.

In 1983 the military government promised to hold an election the following year, but when hard-line military officers tried to prevent the election, all of the political parties in Uruguay— including the banned parties—joined forces to demonstrate against the action. More than 300,000 people demonstrated for democracy in Montevideo, the nation's capital.

A single speech was given at the event. Two of the leading political figures—Gonzalo Aguirre of the Partido National and Enrique Tarigo of Partido Colorado—who were not restricted from political activity, wrote the speech. Alberto Candeau, the nation's leading actor, read the speech to the audience.

The speech and demonstration proved to be a turning point in the democratization of Uruguay, and the elections were held the following year.

CITIZENS, Uruguay's political parties, all its political parties with no exception, have summoned the nation to celebrate this day—the traditional election day—and to proclaim the irrevocable decision to once again exercise the right to vote a year from today, on the last Sunday of November 1984.

They do so at the foot of the Obelisk of the 1830 forefathers, authors of the first Fundamental Code of the Republic, in which we, the *orientales*, affirmed our will to become a free and sovereign Nation and brought to birth the revered 150 year-old law which established the noble practice of renewing the citizens' representatives through free elections, on a day such as today, on the last Sunday of this month that finishes.

Here you make heard your vibrant call for freedom and democracy, long silenced and yet so alive in the conscience of the people, a call which admits no exceptions or distinctions, because the desire for liberty and the vocation for democracy is the common denominator of all men and women born in this land.

And the people have asserted their presence. Testimony of this is the huge, jubilant, pacific, and hopeful multitude here today. They have asserted their presence because this is a nation that knows its rights, its duties and responsibilities. Because it is a mature nation endowed with civic culture. Because it is capable of giving to the world unique and elevated examples which denote pride, courage and Independence, as is the case that has already made history, when on November 30th of 1980 it said "NO" to the imposition of those in power. Prometheus was great because he said no to the gods. And the Uruguayan nation is great because it said no to the gods with feet of clay: those who—established by force—pretended to legitimize the appropriation of our most sacred rights by way of a constitutional draft that ignored our democratic and republican tradition. . . .

Citizens: we have not come here today as militants of a particular political group, authorized or banned; we do not deny them but uphold them with legitimate pride, each with their own honorable convictions. We have come here as Uruguayans and patriots, heirs to a legacy of liberty, peace, justice, respect and tolerance for all ideas, to a legacy of devotion for the rule of law and repudiation of all use of force and violence.

Leaders, affiliates and sympathizers of all political parties, of those that have been reinstated and of those that have yet to be reinstated, since there can be no democracy without unrestricted political plurality: we hereby make public our conviction that from now on our differences will never go beyond the maintenance of liberty and democracy. No difference can be so profound that it should be possible to compromise the free and democratic fate of this Republic. . . .

This is why we are all here to solemnly proclaim our inalienable commitment, after a decade of repression . . . to give back to the nation its dignity, to the country its prestige, to the Constitution its inviolability, to the political parties their irreplaceable role, to the leaders a respectability than can only emanate from the urns, to the populace the right to choose its leaders, to each citizen the possibility to vote and to be voted, to each family its economic security, and to each Uruguayan the right to earn his bread with the sweat of his brow. . . .

It is with this clear conscience that we demand the immediate and definite removal of all existing proscriptions over citizens and parties. We do so with the knowledge that democracy is incompatible with such arbitrary exclusions to civic life and that only the sovereignty of the people, expressed through the urns, can decide the exclusion of those who nominate themselves for government positions. . . .

Compatriots!: Let us proclaim—loudly and all together—so that our cry pierces the sky and echoes throughout our land, so that none of those who turn deaf ears can say they did not hear: Long live our nation! Long live our liberty! Long live the Republic! Long live democracy!

"Daddy, you're so quaint to believe in hope"
Abbie Hoffman

In November 1986, police arrested a dozen protestors occupying a building at the University of Massachusetts to demonstrate against CIA recruiters on campus. Among those charged with trespassing were Amy Carter, the daughter of former president Jimmy Carter, and Abbie Hoffman.

Hoffman was one of the legendary counterculture figures of the 1960s. He helped start the Youth International Party ("Yippies") and was one of the defendants in the Chicago Seven trial in the wake of violent confrontations between police and protesters at the 1968 Democratic National Convention.

Hoffman was known for his theatrical (and frequently funny) tactics. In 1967, he and a group of protestors threw piles of dollar bills (many of them fake) onto the trading floor of the New York Stock Exchange as a statement against capitalism. Traders who weren't booing the action, scrambled to pick up the money. Another time he organized thousands of demonstrators around the Pentagon to try to use their collective psychic power to levitate the Defense Department headquarters; they were unsuccessful. In the 1970s, Hoffman was charged with selling drugs and hid from authorities for several years to avoid prosecution.

Hoffman strongly believed that his aggressive opposition to governmental authority was a vital part of democracy. He considered himself a patriot. He wore clothing with the design of the American flag on them. He named one of his children "america."

To counter the trespassing charges at the University of Massachusetts, the defense called witnesses to testify about the CIA's secretive policies and abusive tactics. Hoffman, who served as his own attorney, delivered the statement here on April 15, 1987, as his final summary in the trial. All the defendants were acquitted. Hoffman committed suicide two years later. His suicide note stated: "It's too late. We can't win. They've gotten too powerful."

GOOD MORNING, women and men of the jury:

At 50, I am the oldest of the student defendants. In a short time you will retire to deliberate your decision. In examining the exhibits before you, we would draw your attention to Exhibit No. 3, page 1, paragraph 1 of the letter from the administration to the University of Massachusetts community, dated November 21, 1986:

> The university has consistently been committed to providing, promoting and protecting an environment which encourages the free exchange of ideas through formal classes, meetings, public addresses, private conversations, and demonstrations.

Also, we would like you to consider page 2, the first paragraph:

> The university respects the rights of its students to express their views in whatever manner they see fit, including demonstrations, rallies and educational forums.

The defendants have not claimed that the CIA has no right to participate in that free exchange of ideas. To the contrary, the defendants encourage that right of free speech. But recruitment by a company, private or public, is not a right; it is a privilege which is regulated to insure that the laws of the University of Massachusetts, the commonwealth and the United States are being obeyed by the recruiter.

You heard Ralph McGehee's description of how he was recruited into the CIA. He was told that he would be gathering intelligence, and we don't object to that. The country needs intelligence. He wasn't told he would be part of an assassination team, that he would have to "arrange and doctor evidence" that would show the North Vietnamese were invading the South, that he would have to write a white paper to Congress that was a total lie so that Congress could authorize the first bombing of Hanoi. We would draw your attention to Mr. McGehee's remark that the big joke about Congress in the CIA was, "Treat them like mushrooms—keep them in the dark and feed them a lot of manure." Does anyone believe this is what recruiters say? . . .

Free speech is not a license to misinform and lie without accepting challenge. The CIA has been invited to send representatives to debate with the defendants and our witnesses on campus and here in court. After all, in the "necessity defense," we have to prove that bigger laws are being broken. But where is the CIA to refute the evidence we have brought before you? If you accept our necessity defense, the prosecutor must offer some proof that justification was absent beyond reasonable doubt, just as we must prove it was present.

When I was growing up in Worcester, Massachusetts, my father was very proud of democracy. He often took me to town hall meetings in Clinton, Athol and Hudson. He would say, See how the people participate, see how they participate in decisions that affect their lives—that's democracy. I grew up with the idea that democracy is not something you believe in, or a place you hang your hat, but it's something you do. You participate. If you stop doing it, democracy crumbles and falls apart. It was very sad to read last month that the New England town hall meetings are dying off, and, in a large sense, the spirit of this trial is that grass-roots participation in democracy must not die. If matters such as we have been discussing here are left only to be discussed behind closed-door hearings in Washington, then we would cease to have a government of the people.

You travel around this country, no matter where you go, people say, Don't waste your time, nothing changes, you can't fight the powers that be—no one can. You hear it from a lot of young people. I hear it from my own kids: Daddy, you're so quaint to believe in hope. Kids today live with awful nightmares: AIDS will wipe us out; the polar ice cap will melt; the nuclear bomb will go off at any minute. Even the best tend to believe we are hopeless to affect matters. It's no wonder teenage suicide is at a record level. Young people are detached from history, the planet and, most important, the future. I maintain to you that this detachment from the future, the lack of hope and the high suicide rate among youth are connected.

Speakers' Corner

Irene Ng

In 1872, after a series of massive demonstrations, the British Parliament established the northeast corner of London's Hyde Park as an area where people were allowed the right to speak on any topic without fear of government interference. "Speakers' Corner" has since become a site for public speeches and protest demonstrations. Suffragettes in the early 1900s congregated there, as did labor activists and other reformers, including Karl Marx, Vladimir Lenin, and George Orwell. In 2003, Hyde Park officials tried unsuccessfully to prevent demonstrators from gathering to oppose the pending invasion of Iraq. Their resistance provoked a massive protest. More than one million people participated in the demonstration, making it the largest protest in British history.

The idea of a speakers' corner has been copied by several countries throughout the world including Canada, Trinidad, and Australia. On September 1, 2000, the city-state of Singapore established a speakers' corner at Hong Lim Park, which also happens to be where a large police station is located. Although Singapore had previously been notorious for its harsh clamp-downs on free-speech initiatives, government officials made an about-face, albeit with several restrictions. Speakers must register with the police, and religion is off-limits as a topic to be discussed.

Newspaper columnist Irene Ng wrote the article below in the April 4, 2000, for the *Singapore Straits Times* outlining the opportunity that a speakers' corner provided citizens, but also placing the responsibility of its success on the citizenry itself.

More than four hundred people initially registered to participate as speakers and the free-speech zone started off with great success. The energy waned, however, and by 2006 there were only twenty-six registered speakers. The area is called by some Sneakers' Corner, as you are more likely to find a soccer game underway than hear a speech.

THE SPEAKERS' CORNER will be set up here soon. Will it strike a blow for free speech or will it end up as a "Koyok" Corner? And whatever happened to the original Speakers' Corner at Hyde Park in London?

Those who call the Speakers' Corner a mere cosmetic exercise might find the mirror useful.

If you listen to the sceptics, you will note that their views reflect their conceptions of Singaporeans as they knew them, and the Government as they knew it.

They doubt if the masses here will stampede to speak their minds publicly or to hear others do it unless, perhaps, Hello Kitty makes an appearance.

These detractors point to the Government's track record of clamping down on dissent. They reel off its penchant for patrolling out-of-bound boundaries and for filing libel suits.

These reactions are largely predictable, arising mainly from old assumptions.

Not all are invalid. But some seem ripe for revision in the light of changes in recent years.

Some changes seem so gradual and incremental that it would be easy to miss the significance of each step.

Until recently, most people thought that the idea of a Speakers' Corner was dead. Its epitaph read: Too risky to even try it.

Just early last year, the Home Affairs Ministry conducted the funeral rites when it replied solemnly to The Roundtable.

The policy-discussion group had called for "free-speech" venues, which individuals and groups can book on a first-come-first-served basis without the need to apply for a police permit.

In response, the Government trotted out its formulaic retort: "In multi-racial and multi-religious Singapore, we cannot put at risk the racial harmony and sense of public order, peace and safety built up painstakingly over the years. For this reason, we cannot support the setting up of 'free-speech' venues."

That the idea for a Speakers' Corner is now resurrected by the powers-that-be suggests that the Government is revising some of its hitherto iron-clad assumptions. Given an increasingly educated and wired society, it recognises that some slack is in order.

The Government may still harbour reservations, but it seems willing to take a risk and live with some uncertainty. In such a set-up, it will be a challenge to ensure its jealously-guarded right of reply in every instance.

The advent of the Speakers' Corner could thus signify that this political system is moving towards shedding its long-time instinct to lash every moving object tightly to the deck.

The sheer experimental nature of the whole enterprise is one reason, I suspect, the Government has been playing down this move.

The Speakers' Corner will be a high-profile test case of both the maturity of the society as well of the Government in dealing with unsettling changes.

Prime Minister Goh Chok Tong's Press Secretary, Mr Ong Keng Yong, had said that economic recovery and a desire for greater public involvement had influenced the timing of Mr Goh's decision.

"The PM's consistent thinking has been, 'If our society is ready to discuss in a mature, non-agitated way, it's a positive development.'"

Arguably, how positive this will turn out to be depends less on the Government's nerve than the people's verve.

As history would tell us, there is little spontaneous about politics. It depends on deliberate and continuous individual activity.

For a Speakers' Corner to work here, there must be social order.

There must also be some shared idea of "common good." After 35 years of independence, there should be some broad consensus about what should be broached more sensitively and wisely.

It is not so clear how much of this already exists.

This is where the greater responsibility which comes with greater freedom of speech kicks in.

People should show their approval or disapproval, especially at the scene: They could hiss, heckle or boo. Or jump on the soapbox later to put the speaker in his place.

Opportunists who respect neither truth nor justice, and unleash primal passions should not expect applause, however entertaining.

This will require a new mindset from a people long used to being consumers, rather than participants.

CHAPTER 2
MODES OF PROTEST

INTRODUCTION

In the late 1800s, a disgruntled group of Irish peasants sought a way to protest the harsh conditions and low pay on the farm where they worked. They collaborated to make life miserable for the man who managed the farm and for the owner, an English lord. Not only did they refuse to work the fields, but the peasants also shunned the manager—named Charles Boycott—so thoroughly that the hapless man fled the country. Boycott's surname soon came to be used to describe the protest technique.

The fundamental nature of protest has changed very little over the centuries, but the spread of democratic societies, coupled with technological advances, has created a much wider window of opportunity for protest. People have developed incredibly diverse modes for expressing their dissent. Early protesters used speech, song, and drama to convey their arguments. The invention of the printing press meant books, poems, and flyers could be mass-produced instead of transcribed by hand, allowing protesters to disseminate messages to broader audiences. Having these new modes of protest readily available helped shape such significant events as the Protestant Reformation. In later centuries, radio and television again added new avenues for expressing dissent. With the proliferation of personal computers and the Internet, more people can express their dissent today in ways that were unthinkable a century ago. Anyone can post opinions on his or her own blog. Political groups such as MoveOn.org use e-mail alerts to create flash mobs and virtual petitions.

Globalization has provided new fodder for protest, and protest itself has also expanded into new global forms: the coordinated worldwide protests against the war in Iraq, for instance, were perhaps the first global, synchronous outcry.

Over time people have become highly inventive in devising new ways to register protest. In 1917, French artist Marcel Duchamp bought a ceramic urinal, named it "Fountain," and entered his found object in an exhibit to protest the conventions he saw as strangling artistic creation. (The exhibitors rejected the work.) In 2004, another modern artist, American Jenny Holzer, transformed the sides of city buildings into protests against government secrecy by projecting declassified documents onto them.

This chapter includes a sampling of the many different modes of protest, from public nudity to talk radio. The ingenuity of protesters ensures that there will always be as many ways to express objection as there are issues to protest.

"She found herself concerned to go to their Assembly in a very unusual Manner"

Lydia Wardell

Nudity has proved memorable on the infrequent occasions when it has been used to express dissent. That was likely the case among the early settlers of the Massachusetts colony in 1665 when Lydia Wardell, a Quaker, strode naked into the church she had formerly attended.

Wardell took the unusual action to protest the church's religious intolerance. Many settlers had fled England to escape religious persecution there, but found the climate no more tolerant in the New World. The Society of Friends began in England in 1650 as a dissident sect, and its members, commonly called Quakers, were outspoken about their right to worship in their own way. Their protests included refusing to attend mandatory church services, to remove their hats (they saw the gesture as paying homage to man over God), or to pay fees for priests. Massachusetts, like nearly all the colonies, passed laws against the Quakers. Some members of the sect persisted in their protest, disrupting church services and the Puritan status quo in a variety of ways and insisting on professing their beliefs.

This account of Wardell's daring act of dissent appeared in Joseph Besse's history, *Collection of the Sufferings of the People Called Quakers (Volume 2)*. The book was published in London in 1753. Italics, punctuation, and capitalization are original in the custom of the day; hyphens denote missing or unclear letters from the original document.

WE PROCEED TO RELATE the Sufferings of divers others in this Colony, either in this or the Year last preceding, of whom *Eliakim Wardell*, of *Hampton*, was none of the least: He was fined for entertaining *Wenlock Christison* at his House, and had taken from him a Saddle-horse worth about 14 *l.* He was also several Times fined for his Absence from the publick Worship, and had not only his Cattle taken away, but his Marsh and Mea-ow-Lands were also seized, so that almost his whole Substance became a Prey to the Devourers. But remarkable was the Case of *Lydia Wardell*, Wife of the said *Eliakim*, who seeing her Husband's grievous Sufferings for his religious Testimony, and the Cruelty and Wickedness of his Oppressors, became convinced of the Truth of the Principle he professed, and separated herself from the publick Worship of their Church at *Newbury*, of which she had been formerly a *Member*. Upon her withdrawing from their Church-Communion, she was several Times sent for to come to the Congregation, and to give a Reason for such her Separation. At length she found herself concerned to go to their Assembly in a very unusual Manner, and such as was exceeding hard and self-denying to her natural Disposition, she being a Woman of exemplary Modesty in all her Behaviour: The Duty and Concern she lay under, was that of going into their Church at *Newbury* naked, as a Token of that miserable Condition which she esteemed them in, and as a Testimony against their wretched Inhumanity of stripping and whipping many innocent Women as they had done: This she performed, but they, instead of religiously reflecting on their own Condition, which she came in that Manner to represent to them, fell into a Rage, and presently laid Hands on her, and hurried her away to the Court at *Ipswich*, which was held at a Tavern in that Town: The Court, as little considerate of the true Cause of her so appearing, proceeded hastily against her, and sentenced her to be severely whipt at the next Tavern-post. This cruel Sentence was publickly executed on a Woman of exemplary Virtue and unspotted Chastity, for her Obedience to what she believed the Spirit of the Lord had enjoined her to do. Here could these persecuting Rulers of an ignorant People, like those of old complained of by the Prophet *Amos*, sit *at Ease, chaunt to the Sound of the Viol, invent to themselves Instruments of Musick*, (while the Priest, *Cobbet* by Name, diverted them with his Singing) *drink Wine in Bowls*, and not be at all *grieved at the Assi-lions* of the Righteous.

Capoeira: "The Dance of War"

Capoeira's origins are obscure, but many people have portrayed it as a martial art that slaves in Brazil ingeniously disguised as a dancelike game to prevent the white slave owners from realizing that they were training and conditioning themselves. As such, the techniques were a form of protest, helping the blacks resist slavery by preparing for possible rebellion. By using rhythms and movements from their native West Africa, the slaves were able, at the same time, to keep alive their cultural traditions.

Once capoeira became removed from its original plantation setting, it devolved into a more violent martial art, and capoeiristas were seen as ruffians and criminals. Government authorities declared capoeira illegal later in the nineteenth century, and the art nearly died out, surviving only in the province of Bahia, where it had been based. The government ended its oppression of capoeira in the 1930s, according to one source, after foreign diplomats were impressed watching a demonstration by one of the capoeira masters (mestres), Mestre Bimba, and his students. Authorities relented and decided to recognize the cultural significance of the uniquely Brazilian art, allowing Bimba to open the first legal capoeira academy. By the late 1960s and early 1970s, the next wave of Brazilian capoeira masters had begun teaching the art in Europe and the United States, spreading the form around the world. In its modern form, capoeira is highly acrobatic, with cartwheels and flips, but the original blend of dance and potentially lethal fighting and self-defense techniques is still readily apparent.

German artist Johann Moritz Rugendas captured the sport in this 1835 lithograph, captioned "The Game of Capoeira (or the Dance of War)."

"We have no intention whatever of paying your rent to Captain Boycott"
The Irish Land League

The Irish Land League, formed in 1880 by populist leaders Michael Davitt and Charles Stewart Parnell, used boycotts to push for land reform and economic justice for workers. The word "boycott" came into use in the 1880s after a landlord's agent in Ireland, Captain Charles Boycott, so infuriated poor tenants in County Mayo that they began a protest campaign to ostracize him both socially and financially. Boycott was an Englishman who managed the estate of English absentee owner Lord Erne. Irish laborers on the estate had suffered through the great potato famine and several rounds of potato blight. Erne nevertheless kept raising the rents he charged laborers to

farm small plots on his land. When workers petitioned Boycott for rent relief, he refused. Eventually the farmers tired of Boycott's ill treatment. They stopped paying any rent at all and organized a campaign to punish Boycott: ceasing to care for the crops and livestock on the estate, sabotaging fences so animals escaped, even convincing post carriers to refrain from bringing his mail. Someone put Boycott's name to use to describe the actions against him, and the word quickly passed into common usage.

Before the word "boycott" came to be, the tactic was used by American colonists, who urged patriotic citizens to refrain from buying British tea; British abolitionists two decades later urged their citizens to stop buying sugar made in the West Indies because manufacturers there used slave labor. One of the most creative uses of boycott in history may also be one of the oldest, albeit a fictional one: the Greek playwright Aristophanes wrote *Lysistrata* in 411 B.C. about Athenian women who call a boycott of sexual relations until their boyfriends and husbands agree to stop waging war (see chapter 3).

This short excerpt from a protest letter in 1880, addressed to "The Right Honourable, The Earl of Erne," documents the start of the action against Boycott. In the image to the left, Captain Boycott and his family are forced to work on their own farm.

MAY IT PLEASE your Lordship:

We, the tenantry on your Loughmark estate most respectfully beg to intimate to you that we have no intention whatever of paying your rent to Captain Boycott or any person acting for him. But at the same time we have not the slightest objection to paying it to any other person whom your Lordship's better judgment may recommend: which we now request you shall do. Captain Boycott in times past hurted our feelings in every possible way, as Your Lordship might already have understood. For instance he never spoke of us in better terms than *Irish swine*, and for this and manifold reasons we hold him in utter detestation.

"But where is she now?"
Aleksandra Chumakova

Dissidents in the Soviet Union coined the term "samizdat" in the late 1950s to describe writings circulated secretly to evade censorship and repression by the communist government. The word translates as "self-publisher" or "self-published," a sly allusion to the Soviet acronyms for official state publishing outfits (*politizdat*, for instance, was shorthand for the publishing house for political works). Samizdat included all manner of writings, not just those that were directly critical of the government.

Writers in Soviet-bloc nations had a long tradition of circulating clandestine manuscripts, dating to the days when revolutionaries passed hidden manifestos to evade the censorship of the czars. After the Russian Revolution, during Joseph Stalin's dictatorship from 1924 through 1953, those opposing government policies had even more incentive to publish secretly. The price of openly questioning or opposing the government (or being suspected of doing so) was typically imprisonment, exile to forced labor camps in Siberia, or death—or all three. By the 1960s samizdat had become the primary conduit for a burgeoning literature of antigovernment writing, including the works of Aleksandr Solzhenitsyn and Andrei Sahkarov. Since some samizdat writings were smuggled to Western nations, translated, and published to critical acclaim, this mode of protest had far-reaching impact, helping publicize Soviet human rights violations and causing other countries and activist groups to put pressure on the communists to reform.

Aleksandra Chumakova wrote a samizdat manuscript consisting of a series of entries that leave off abruptly, as if unfinished. Chumakova was imprisoned because of her husband's involvement with Communist Party opponents of Stalin, and she described early infighting in the party as well as demonstrations by workers, events that would not have been reported in the state-sanctioned press. Her writings surfaced in 1970 along with the better-known samizdat account, *Memoirs of a Bolshevik-Leninist,* by an anonymous author. The lengthy *Memoirs* described events from early in the Stalin era and continued with descriptions of the author's life in a prison camp. Both it and Chumakova's work served as proof that opposition to Stalin had been real and had persisted despite extensive repression, purges, and censorship.

Chumakova's account here, dated 1936, tells one small tale of a teenage girl who dared, through poetry, to challenge Stalin's disregard for the starvation of the working class.

ONE DAY A YOUNG SCHOOLGIRL who had been arrested was brought into our cell. Her face was the small, sweet face of a child and her hair was held back in two short braids. She was fifteen, and her name was Anya Khromova. For a long time she watched and listened to us carefully without entering into the conversation. But when she had gotten to know us, she told us the story of her life.

Anya had no father, and her mother worked as a conductor on long-distance trains and was nearly always away from home. Anya spent her vacation before her last year of school on a collective farm, where she lived with her grandmother and grandfather. Life on the kolkhoz was very hard that year. The kolkhoz members were being paid next to nothing for their work days, and the peasants were starving and dying from hunger. Her grandmother and grandfather were also suffering from lack of food and had fallen seriously ill.

Previously in that village —the old folks told Anya—there had been plenty of everything. Life had been busy and joyful. But now, all of a sudden, everything had gone bad, as though a terrible plague had struck. No songs were to be heard, nor young maids' laughter. It was like a cemetery around there. All the young people had moved to the city. Only children and old people remained in the village.

Upon returning to Moscow after her stay at the collective farm, Anya wrote a letter to Stalin in verses that described the miserable life in the collectivized village of Russia.

Anya hoped that Stalin would aid the starving kolkhoz and save her grandmother and grandfather from death by starvation. But she was mistaken. Her verse letter was not to Stalin's liking, and he ordered the OGPU [the secret police] to call Anya to account severely.

Soon the dread figure of an OGPU investigator arrived at her school and began an investigation. The director of the school, the teachers, the maintenance people, and even some of the students were all questioned. All those who were questioned liked Anya very much and spoke of her with affection. She was a very intelligent and talented young woman. She was an attentive observer of natural phenomena and of human life and she put down what she saw in vivid images, embodied in both prose and poetry.

No one had anything bad to say about her. They all spoke well of her. But the OGPU investigator was a crusty sort. He found it hard to accept favorable testimony about anyone. He did not believe the testimony of the people at the school. He had his own professional opinion, worked out over many years as an investigator and based on suspicion and mistrust of people. He was certain that the verse letter to Stalin about the collective farms had not been written by Anya but by someone else who was hiding behind the skirts of a schoolgirl. He arrested Anya and took her off to jail, straight from school. The entire school wept, bidding Anya Khromova farewell. But even as she sat, huddled in a corner of the car, she was already whispering new verses to herself.

A few days later Anya was called for questioning. The investigator had decided to expose her "alleged literary talent" and to make her tell the name of the real authors of the letter to Stalin. He felt certain that the author of the letter was some hardened enemy of Soviet power, one who was not going to get away.

When Anya was brought into his office, he gave her pen and paper and proposed that she create a literary work in verse about the women with whom she shared her cell.

The investigator left the room, saying he would return in two hours. Left to herself, Anya fell into thought. She began to call to mind the faces of her bunkmates and selected the most striking images to show how their life in prison had become one of unbearable suffering and torment. Among those sharing our cell at that time were the following:

1. Masha Joffe, daughter of the famous Soviet diplomat, A. A. Joffe.

2. Elena Barbina, wife of an official in the Moscow Soviet.

3. A large group of Young Communist women guides at the Gorky Park for Rest and Recreation, who were accused of wishing to emigrate to England. (That summer the British writer George Bernard Shaw had visited Moscow.)

4. Kabakova, wife of the first secretary of the Sverdlovsk Regional Committee of the party.

After two hours the investigator came back and took the filled-in sheets of paper from Anya. With great irritation, but with eager absorption as well, he pored over the rhythmic phrases of her marvelous poetry. He was overcome with anger, irritation, and chagrin. There in his hands he held a literary work of talent, from whose pages the voice of anguished womanhood cried out, calling for help to the innocent arrested women whose lives were being destroyed in prison.

With great poetic power Anya described one of her bunkmates in prison who had been taken away from her own nursing child by the Chekists [secret police] when they arrested her. Her breasts became painfully swollen from the sudden interruption in nursing, and the inflamed nipples cracked and bled. The unfortunate mother tossed and turned on her bunk, groaning and cursing her fate as a woman and mother.

The investigator no longer had any doubts. He had tested Anya Khromova's literary talent. He no longer suspected someone else of having written the letter to Stalin. Her fate was now sealed. She was sentenced to penal exile in Siberia. In parting she asked us, "Is it true that Dostoevsky and Ryleev spent time in prison?" We told her it was true. "Then," she said, "I no longer fear for my future."

After the prison gates had closed behind her, it was a long time before any of us could speak. Subdued by what had happened we held our tongues. But in our thoughts we all marveled at this amazing young woman, marked by the hand of fate, and gifted with the mind and talent of a poet. Anya had the soul of an artist. The spark of inspiration burned in her. "Unless Siberia extinguishes that spark, the Russian people will yet hear from another inspired lyric voice." Such were our thoughts.

But where is she now?

"Strange Fruit"

Lewis Allen (Abel Meeropol)

Songs have been an important mode of protest for centuries, in part because they are accessible to all people regardless of education or wealth. British commoners in the Middle Ages sang ballads that criticized their lords or protested the unjust taxes and policies of their monarchs. Slave spirituals like "Let My People Go" protested bosses' oppression and voiced yearnings for freedom. Social reformers like Woody Guthrie used songs to rally people for workers' rights, and songs in genres from folk to rock to rap have protested war. Whole styles of music have been developed as protest: in 1960s Brazil, musicians including Caetano Veloso and Gilberto Gil pioneered "tropicália"— a blend of traditional bossa nova rhythms, indigenous folk melodies, and international pop influences—as a protest against the repressive military dictatorship that had come to power in 1964.

One of the most powerful protest songs is "Strange Fruit," first recorded by blues singer Billie Holiday. The song condemned lynching, the summary execution, often by hanging, of young black men. Lynching was usually—but not exclusively—perpetrated by white mobs in the American South and became a widespread tool of racial terror. One study documented 4,743 lynchings in the United States from 1882 to 1968, and more than 70 percent of the victims were African-American. Abel Meeropol, a Jewish schoolteacher and union activist in New York City, wrote the lyrics to "Strange Fruit" (under the pseudonym Lewis Allen) as a poem in 1938 after seeing a photograph of a lynched young black man. Meeropol heard Holiday singing the following year and showed her the poem, and they set it to music. With its graphic images the song was highly controversial, and Holiday's label refused to let her record it; she made the record with another label in 1939. The song provided grist to the antilynching movement, and groups lobbying for federal antilynching legislation used the song to help spread their message.

Southern trees bear a strange fruit
Blood on the leaves and blood at the root
Black body swinging in the southern breeze
Strange fruit hanging from the poplar trees

Pastoral scene of the gallant south
The bulging eyes and the twisted mouth
Scent of magnolia, sweet and fresh
And the sudden smell of burning flesh!

Here is fruit for the crows to pluck
For the rain to gather, for the wind to suck
For the sun to rot, for a tree to drop
Here is a strange and bitter crop.

"The not-raising-hog-business"
J. B. Lee, Jr.

Letters were an effective way to communicate protest in the days before books were affordable and before the invention of the printing press allowed for the mass publication of ideas. Writers conveyed their protest in private letters to spouses, parents, or confidants, as well as in letters directly confronting authority figures from lords to politicians. In more recent times, mass letter-writing campaigns have played a key role in pressuring politicians to take a particular stance. Staff members are known to have literally weighed the voluminous piles of letters sent to an elected official's office to tally public opinion, rather than actually reading the letters. The letters had their impact nonetheless.

In this tongue-in-cheek sample of the letter as protest, the writer, J. B. Lee, Jr., pointedly attacked the absurdity of a government program that paid farmers to refrain from raising pigs. The letter, to U.S. Representative Ed Foreman, was dated March 20, 1963.

DEAR SIR:

My friend over in Terebone Parish received a $1,000 check from the government this year for not raising hogs. So I am going into the not-raising hogs business next year.

What I want to know is, in your opinion, what is the best kind of farm not to raise hogs on and the best kind of hogs not to raise? I would prefer not to raise Razorbacks, but if that is not a good breed not to raise, I will just as gladly not raise any Berkshires or Durocs.

The hardest work in this business is going to be in keeping an inventory of how many hogs I haven't raised.

My friend is very joyful about the future of his business. He has been raising hogs for more than 20 years and the best he ever made was $400, until this year, when he got $1,000 for not raising hogs.

If I can get $1,000 for not raising 50 hogs, then will I get $2,000 for not raising 100 hogs? I plan to operate on a small scale at first, holding myself down to 4,000 hogs which means I will have $80,000 coming from the government.

Now, another thing: these hogs I will not raise will not eat 100,000 bushels of corn. I understand that you also pay farmers for not raising corn. So will you pay me anything for not raising 100,000 bushels of corn not to feed the hogs I am not raising?

I want to get started as soon as possible as this seems to be a good time of the year for not raising hogs.

One thing more, can I raise 10 or 12 hogs on the side while I am in the not-raising-hog-business, just enough to get a few sides of bacon to eat?

Very truly yours,

J. B. Lee, Jr.

Potential Hog Raiser

Mothers of Plaza de Mayo

Street demonstrations are a classic mode of protest, but the idea of regular, weekly silent marches was a 1977 innovation by a group in Argentina called the Mothers of Plaza de Mayo. A dozen women were protesting the disappearances of their children and other family members in Argentina's "Dirty War," the period of military rule from a 1976 coup until 1983, during which thousands of leftists and labor leaders were kidnapped, tortured, and killed. The Argentine government has acknowledged there were as many as nine thousand *desaparecidos*, or disappeared ones, but human rights activists have estimated the toll at up to thirty thousand.

The mothers gathered in the Plaza de Mayo, a Buenos Aires square surrounded by government buildings and the presidential palace. The women marched slowly, in silence, carrying photographs of victims. They marched every Thursday afternoon, and their numbers grew. The group became a political force, winning awards from the United Nations and the European Parliament, and the marches have continued for nearly three decades.

Joanne Omang, who covered the first days of the group in 1977 as a correspondent for *The Washington Post*, wrote recently in *The Nation* about the group's enormous influence. "The Mothers of the Plaza de Mayo became world icons of courageous demands for accountability, the assertion of human rights," she wrote. "Their march inspired poetry and dissidents the world over; it won awards from UNESCO and the European Parliament, among others. What dictator would dare mow down a group of grieving women?

Do the Right Thing
Spike Lee

Film emerged as an artistic medium in the late nineteenth century, and as the twentieth century began filmmakers began using it to tell stories as a new form of entertainment. It didn't take long for filmmakers to put celluloid to use in advocating political points of view. In 1915 D. W. Griffith's classic silent film, *The Birth of a Nation*—which reigned for many years as the country's most successful movie—was an unapologetic justification of lynching and terrorism by groups like the Ku Klux Klan. Russian director Sergei Eisenstein's 1925 classic *The Battleship Potemkin* protested the brutality of czarist troops. Both documentary and fictional films have continued to be vehicles of protest against governments and social norms.

New York director Spike Lee's 1989 movie *Do the Right Thing* attacked racial tension in America, and, in particular, violence by white policemen against blacks. Lee set the movie on one block of the largely black Brooklyn neighborhood of Bedford-Stuyvesant, during the hottest day of the year, and temperatures magnify racial tensions to the boiling point. The movie's main character, Mookie—played by Lee—is a delivery man for Sal's Famous Pizzeria, run by white owner Sal and his two sons Pino (explicitly racist) and Vito, who is friendly with Mookie and the blacks who frequent the shop. Another character, Buggin' Out, tries to organize a boycott of Sal's because he objects to the wall with photos of famous Italian-Americans, but no blacks. In the film's climax Sal responds by angrily smashing the gigantic boom box of another character, Radio Raheem, and, as the script puts it, "all hell breaks loose." This excerpt is from the second draft of Lee's script, which he published in a companion book to the movie, with camera instructions omitted and description in italics.

[Inside Sal's Famous Pizzeria]

We hear the dum-dum-dum of Radio Raheem's box. As everyone turns their heads to the door, Buggin' Out and Radio Raheem are inside already. We have never heard the rap music as loud as it is now. You have to scream to be heard and that's what they do.

SAL: What did I tell ya 'bout dat noise?

BUGGIN' OUT: What did I tell ya 'bout dem pictures?

SAL: What da fuck! Are you deaf?

BUGGIN' OUT: No, are you? We want some Black people up on the Wall of Fame.

SAL: Turn that JUNGLE MUSIC off. We ain't in Africa.

Ahmad, Cee, Punchy, and Ella start to dance while Mookie takes a seat, the impartial observer that he is.

BUGGIN' OUT: Why it gotta be about jungle music and Africa?

SAL: It's about turning that shit off and getting the fuck outta my pizzeria. . . .

VITO: We're closed.

BUGGIN' OUT: You're closed alright, till you get some Black people up on that wall.

Sal grabs his Mickey Mantle bat from underneath the counter and brings it down on Radio Raheem's box, again and again and again. The music stops. . . .

There is an eerie quiet as everyone is frozen, surprised by the suddenness of Sal's action, the swings of his Mickey Mantle bat. All look at Radio Raheem and realize what is about to happen.

Radio Raheem screams, he goes crazy.

RADIO RAHEEM: My music!

Radio Raheem picks Sal up from behind the counter and starts to choke his ass. Radio Raheem's prized possession—his box, the only thing he owned of value—his box, the one thing that gave him any sense of worth—has been smashed to bits. . . . He's gonna make Sal pay with his life.

Vito and Pino jump on Radio Raheem, who only tightens his grip around Sal's neck. Buggin' Out tries to help his friend. Mookie just stands and watches as Ahmad, Cee, Punchy, and Ella cheerlead.

The tangled mass of choking, biting, kicking, screaming confusion flies through the door of Sal's out onto the sidewalk. . . .

. . . We hear sirens, somebody has called da cops.

The cop cars come right through the crowd, almost running over some people. The cops get out with nightsticks and guns drawn. We recognize two of the faces, Officers Long and Ponte. Any time there is a skirmish between a Black man and a white man, you can bet the house on who the cops are gonna go for. You know the deal! Buggin' Out is pulled off first, then Vito and Pino, but Radio Raheem is a crazed man. It takes all six cops to pull him off Sal, who is red as a beet from being choked.

Handcuffs are put on Buggin' Out as he watches the other cops put a choke hold on Radio Raheem to restrain him.

Radio Raheem is still struggling, then he just stops, his body goes limp and he falls to the sidewalk like a fifty-pound bag of Idaho potatoes.

Officers Long and Ponte kick him.

OFFICER LONG: Get up! Get up!

Radio Raheem just lies there like a bump on a log.
The crowd stares at Radio Raheem's still body. He's unconscious or dead.

OFFICER LONG: Quit faking.

The officers all look at each other. They know, they know exactly what they've done. The infamous Michael Stewart choke hold.

OFFICER PONTE: Let's get him outta here.

The officers pick up Radio Raheem's limp body and throw him into the back seat. Buggin' Out is pushed into another car. The cop cars speed off; in their haste to beat it, they have left the crowd. It's at this point the crowd becomes an angry mob. . . .

The mob looks at Sal still on the sidewalk, being helped to his feet by Vito and Pino, who are in bad shape themselves.

The mood/tone of the mob is getting ugly. Once again they have seen one of their own killed before their eyes at the hands of the cops. We hear the murmurs of the folks go through the crowd.

VOICES OF MOB:

THEY KILLED HIM

THEY KILLED RADIO RAHEEM

IT'S MURDER

DID IT AGAIN

JUST LIKE THEY DID MICHAEL STEWART

MURDER

ELEANOR BUMPERS

MURDER

IT'S NOT SAFE

NOT EVEN IN OUR OWN NEIGHBORHOOD

IT'S NOT SAFE

NEVER WAS

NEVER WILL BE

The cops, in their haste to get Radio Raheem out of there, have left an angry mob of Black folks with a defenseless Sal, Vito, and Pino.

The mob looks at them.

VOICES OF MOB:

WON'T STAND FOR IT

THE LAST TIME

FUCKIN' COPS

THE LAST TIME

IT'S PLAIN AS DAY

DIDN'T HAVE TO KILL THE BOY

Mookie looks at the crowd and notices he's on the wrong side. He leaves Sal and his two sons.

Da Mayor walks in front of the crowd.

DA MAYOR: Good people, let's all go home. Somebody's gonna get hurt.

CROWD: Yeah, you!

DA MAYOR: If we don't stop this now, we'll all regret it. Sal and his two boys had nothing to do with what the police did.

CROWD: Get out of the way, old man. You a Tom anyway.

DA MAYOR: Let 'em be.

Mookie picks up a garbage can and dumps it out into the street. He walks through the crowd, up to Da Mayor, Sal, Vito, and Pino.

He screams.

MOOKIE: HATE!!!!

Mookie hurls the garbage can through the plate glass window of Sal's Famous Pizzeria. That's it. All hell breaks loose. The dam has been unplugged, broke. The rage of a people has been unleashed, a fury. A lone garbage can thrown through the air has released a tidal wave of frustration.

Da Mayor pushes Sal, Vito, and Pino out of the way as the mob storms into Sal's Famous Pizzeria.

The people rush into Sal's Famous Pizzeria, tearing it up.

Mock Parking Tickets

Earth on Empty

In the spring of 2001 a few avid bicyclists in the Boston area protested against the large sport-utility vehicles that were becoming prevalent on city streets by devising mock parking tickets to leave on drivers' windshields. The tickets were miniature screeds against SUVs, designed to get people to think about the impact of their consumer choices. They contained statements such as, "Why do you need such a HUGE car? This is not a militarized zone!" The bikers packed the tickets with writings about their objections to SUVs, including the fact that the vehicles got terrible gas mileage, driving up fuel costs for all drivers by increasing demand relative to supply; that they contributed disproportionately to air pollution; and that they made the streets more dangerous for bikers and drivers of smaller, more fuel-efficient vehicles.

The protesters began by ticketing thousands of SUVs around Boston. They later created a Web site called Earth on Empty to spread their message and sell packets of tickets to other protesters. As of 2003 the group had filled orders for nearly a million tickets across the country.

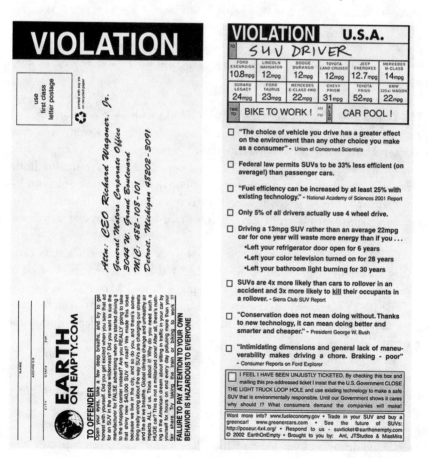

Critical Mass Turns 10: A Decade of Defiance

Joe Garofoli

Critical Mass took the idea of street demonstrations and put it on wheels. The movement began in 1992 as an environmentally-minded call for more bike lanes on the streets of San Francisco and blossomed into a once-a-month event in which cyclists in hundreds of cities worldwide intentionally create traffic jams with their bikes to protest cars' dominance of roads. The rides are intended to be peaceful but sometimes become confrontational; in New York City, for example, police routinely trail riders and typically arrest dozens of them. As a form of protest, the Critical Mass movement is cousin to such public acts as street theater and blockades, a common form of protest in Latin American countries.

"Movement" may be too strong a word to attach to Critical Mass. There is a Web page for "critical-mass.org," but when you arrive you find the following disclaimer: "The '.org' domain notwithstanding, Critical Mass is not an organization, it's an unorganized coincidence. It's a movement . . . of bicycles, in the streets. Accordingly, this isn't the official Critical Mass web page, because there is no official Critical Mass web page." The page offers links to local groups sponsoring rides and lots of articles about the bike jams.

When Critical Mass celebrated its ten-year anniversary in September 2002, riders turned out en masse in San Francisco. This newspaper article in the *San Francisco Chronicle* by staff writer Joe Garofoli looked at the movement's history.

TEN YEARS AGO, Critical Mass started with a dorky name—"Commute Clot"—a couple of dozen riders recruited from flyers passed out on a seedy section of Market Street, and a spin around San Francisco that ended at the Zeitgeist bar.

When several thousand cyclists from around the world roll into Justin Herman Plaza for the 10th anniversary ride Friday, they'll be part of a born-in-San Francisco cultural phenomenon that has spread to 300 cities worldwide. A monthly "spontaneous coincidence" that's rare in these days of corporate-sponsored fun.

Yet despite its influence—San Francisco will celebrate its first "Car-Free Day" Friday afternoon in an unrelated event—the Mass is still feared and loathed in some quarters. The raucous ride in 1997 that followed Mayor Willie Brown's denunciation of cyclists' behavior as "the ultimate arrogance" lingers in the public mind, though police say now they have almost no problems during the monthly Masses.

On the last Friday of every month for the last decade, about 1,000 people have shown up at what they call "Pee-Wee Herman Plaza" to cycle en masse through the begin-the-weekend commute. The Mass stops at red lights, but if the light turns green, the parade doesn't stop until everybody is through.

There's no publicity machine promoting this. No invites. No leadership, no agenda, no definitive map and no Krispy Kremes for sale. It just happens.

"Everybody is there for a different reason," [said] Chris Carlsson, a 45-year-old San Francisco typesetter who passed out flyers on Market Street for the first ride 10 years ago. "Critical Mass: Bicycling's Defiant Celebration," a collection of remembrances that Carlsson edited, just hit stores.

Civil disobedients show up to make a political statement about bike power, and long-suffering cyclists thrill at owning the road for two hours without dodging double-parkers.

"I just go because it's fun, like when about 100 of us all drove through the Moscone Center," said Saboo Takaki, a 24-year-old nightclub doorman.

This monthly guerrilla theater on wheels has inspired a handful of bike-friendly laws and bike lane [sic], and changed the bike-motorist relationship. Sometimes for the better—although there are still a lot of motorists who hate stewing in traffic as the Mass rolls by.

"Back (in 1986), when I first started as a bike messenger, drivers were a lot more aggressive toward pedestrians and bikes," said 34-year-old Craig Traver, who has ridden in several Masses and now works in a rental car agency. "That's mellowed a lot since then."

"Critical Mass has definitely brought attention to bicycle issues, and we wouldn't have been able to do it without them," said Leah Shahun, executive director of the San Francisco Bicycle Coalition.

The coalition isn't affiliated with Critical Mass. Rather, in the words of one bicycle advocate, it operates as Sinn Fein, the Irish political party, does to the more shadowy Irish Republican Army.

Critical Massers grind their gears at that comparison. Carlsson prefers casting the Mass as Earth First to the coalition's Sierra Club. They're the radicals who make the progressives seem more mainstream.

Today, Critical Mass is nearly as politically accepted as the Sierra Club. Almost.

"(Critical Mass) is a mixed bag," said Brown spokesman P. J. Johnston. While it has improved the visibility of bicycle issues, he said, "there are rogue elements that are combative, and they damage the reputation of bicycle advocates. When people are kicking cars and yelling at drivers, that's not good for the bicycle community's cause."

Andrew Lawton, who organized a Friday morning Commonwealth Club seminar on Car-Free Day, praised Critical Mass for effecting change without resorting to violence: "The challenge now is, once the ride is over, where do we go from here? How can we change?"

Despite years of mellow rides, the San Francisco Chamber of Commerce is worrying about this Friday's anniversary celebration.

"We still hear complaints about (Critical Mass) from our members, though not as many as before," said chamber spokeswoman Carol Piasente. "I just hope that this Friday, they take into consideration all the restaurants and retailers who need the roads clear so their customers can get to them."

To hard-core bicyclists, the only thing clogging the roads are cars.

That's what led Carlsson, among others, to approach the Bicycle Coalition 10 years ago with an idea to hold a mass ride around the city as a way to show how unfriendly the roads are for cyclists.

In those days, the coalition had only a few members and met in the back of a Sunset District restaurant. Coalition members agreed with the idea of a ride, Carlsson remembered, but had one request: Just don't attach our name to it.

So he and others passed out flyers, not knowing who would show up. A couple of dozen did. More joined the next month. By the fourth ride, remembered Ted White, a Sebastopol filmmaker who has chronicled Critical Mass, "there were about 100 people, and from then it just grew exponentially. . . . It reminded people how important it is to be a participant in our culture. One of the problems with this country as a whole is that people feel that they don't count. Here, in Critical Mass, everyone riding together does count."

Picasso on the Beach
Greenpeace

On January 19, 2004, more than one thousand people gathered on a Miami beach to create a human facsimile of Pablo Picasso's painting *Amnistia* together with the words "Endangered Freedoms." The living art was a protest of the Bush administration's decision to charge the

environmental group Greenpeace under an obscure 1872 law against sailormongering. The law—which had not been used since 1890—prohibits boarding ships to lure sailors away from their posts with prostitutes. Greenpeace activists had boarded a ship that carried illegal mahogany from the Amazon rain forest and unfurled a banner reading "President Bush: Stop Illegal Logging." Had Greenpeace been convicted, it would have faced fines, potential loss of tax-exempt status, and federal oversight of its activities. The group's members and supporters argued that the law was being selectively applied to discourage Greenpeace's rights to free speech under the First Amendment. The judge in the trial summarily dismissed charges against the organization in May 2004, immediately after the prosecution rested.

Secret Service and White House Charged with Violating Free Speech Rights in ACLU Lawsuit
American Civil Liberties Union

T-shirts, originally used as plain undergarments, have evolved since the 1960s into blank canvasses for declaring viewpoints on any subject. As such, T-shirts and pin-on buttons are easy tools of protest. While many T-shirts do no more than advertise a brand name, and many buttons simply state the wearer's preference of political candidate, others carry strong messages of dissent. Those messages have sometimes tested the limits of free speech. Two teenage girls in Iowa were threatened with punishment by their high school for wearing antiabortion shirts showing pictures of fetuses with the words "Abortion Kills Kids." In February 2006 a university in Poland banned a provocative exhibit of T-shirts with messages such as "I didn't cry when the Pope died" and "I've got AIDS." In 2003 a man was arrested at an Albany, New York, mall for refusing to remove the T-shirt he had put on over his turtleneck with the messages "Give Peace a Chance" and "Peace on Earth" after a security guard ordered him to do so—even though he had just purchased the shirt at the mall. In most states, shoppers in malls are considered exempt from free-speech protection because the malls are private property (though courts in a few states have ruled they are the modern-day equivalent of village squares and thus are considered public for the purposes of free-speech guarantees).

Wearing political T-shirts became an issue in the 2004 presidential campaign after a number of people complained they were asked to leave political events for President George W. Bush, who was seeking election to a second term, because they were wearing anti-Bush shirts or buttons or bearing paraphernalia promoting his opponent, John F. Kerry. In one case a couple went to a Bush campaign rally on Independence Day with anti-Bush T-shirts concealed under other clothes. They were arrested after they revealed their anti-Bush shirts and then refused to take them off or cover them as requested by security staff. The case was detailed in this September 14, 2004, press release from the American Civil Liberties Union announcing it was filing a lawsuit over the couple's arrest, based on a violation of their constitutional rights to free speech.

THE AMERICAN CIVIL LIBERTIES UNION today filed a lawsuit against the United States Secret Service and Greg Jenkins, Deputy Assistant to the President and Director of White House Advance, on behalf of a West Virginia couple who were arrested at a Fourth of July presidential appearance at the state Capitol because they were wearing t-shirts critical of the president.

"This is a simple case," said ACLU Senior Staff Attorney Chris Hansen, who is the lead counsel in the case. "Two Americans went to see their president and to express their disagreement with his policies respectfully and peacefully. They were arrested at the direction of federal officials. That is precisely what the First Amendment was adopted to prevent."

Jeff Rank, 29, who is a registered Republican, and his wife Nicole, 30, had never engaged in political protest in the past, and said that they had no intention to disrupt the president's visit. The Ranks obtained tickets for the event and were admitted to the Capitol grounds without any problems, but drew attention when they removed their outer garments to display t-shirts bearing the international "no" symbol (a circle with a diagonal line across it) superimposed over the word "Bush."

Although the couple stood peacefully on the public grounds with the rest of the audience, two men believed to be working for the Secret Service or White House approached the Ranks and demanded that they remove or cover their t-shirts. When the couple refused, the officials instructed city police to arrest Jeff and Nicole, causing them to be removed from the Capitol grounds in handcuffs, jailed for one to two hours and charged with trespassing. Nicole Rank was also temporarily suspended from her work with the Federal Emergency Management Agency (FEMA).

"We wanted to see the president speak and express our disagreement in what little way we could," said Nicole Rank, who is originally from Corpus Christi, Texas but was assigned to work on a FEMA flood relief project in West Virginia. "We never imagined that we would end up in jail because of a homemade t-shirt."

The charges against the Ranks were ultimately dismissed in court and the mayor and city council publicly apologized for the arrest. City officials also said that local law enforcement was acting at the request of Secret Service.

"It is clear that our Charleston police officers were acting at the request of federal government officials and would otherwise have respected the First Amendment rights of our residents," said ACLU of West Virginia Executive Director Andrew Schneider. "The Ranks were ejected for wearing t-shirts expressing a dissenting opinion while other attendees wearing Bush campaign t-shirts and buttons were allowed to remain."

In September, the ACLU asked a federal court to bar the Secret Service from directing local police to restrict protesters' access to presidential visits. The Secret Service denied engaging in the practice, but agreed with the ACLU that such actions would be inappropriate and unlawful.

"The Secret Service has promised to not curtail the right to dissent at presidential appearances, and yet we are still hearing stories of people being blocked from engaging in lawful protest," said Hansen. "It is time for the Secret Service to stop making empty promises."

The lawsuit, *Rank v. Jenkins*, is seeking unspecified damages as well as a declaration that the actions leading to the removal of the Ranks from the Capitol grounds were unconstitutional.

"The media landscape shifted"
Daily Kos

In the 1990s, improvements in technology, combined with tens of millions of people hooking up to the Internet, created the opportunity and the audience for blogs, shorthand for Web logs. The online diaries mushroomed and seemingly created their own jargon-filled communities overnight. Blogs can be running commentaries on themes such as sports or entertainment, or serve as an online record of one's personal musings and travails. But it is the political blogs that have become the modern-day equivalents of the old street-corner soapboxes. The difference is that the protests mounted from these soapboxes can reach thousands of readers a day, every day, and provide links to commentaries from hundreds of other observers.

A report or accusation made on one popular blog— whether liberal or conservative—can have a rapid ripple effect, since reporters in newspapers and on television and radio now monitor the blogs for leads. Many of these leads end up proving false, but others that have proved true have had significant impact. For example, when former Senate majority leader Trent Lott of Mississippi made remarks in support of Strom Thurmond's one-time presidential run on a segregationist platform, bloggers publicized the comments, which the mainstream media initially failed to report. The ensuing furor forced Lott to resign his leadership post.

One of the most widely read political blogs is Daily Kos, started by Markos Moulitsas Zúniga. Moulitsas (his last name, using the Spanish system of surnames) was born in Chicago but spent some of his childhood in El Salvador, his mother's native country. He later served several years in the U.S. Army, then earned two bachelor's degrees and a law degree before entering the high-tech industry. He started Daily Kos (Kos was his military nickname and rhymes with "prose") in 2002; in traffic statistics on the site he claims twenty million readers a month. The blog places on many lists of the most popular and influential Web logs. In 2006 Moulitsas teamed up with fellow progressive blogger Jerome Armstrong—whose site MyDD.com is another pioneering and widely followed blog—to release a book called *Crashing the Gate: Netroots, Grassroots, and the Rise of People-Powered Politics* about how blogs are helping reform the American political landscape. The Daily Kos entry here, "The GOP and 24/7 News," posted March 9, 2004, talks about the impact of blogs. The jumping-off point is an anecdote about former Bush Administration spokesman Ari Fleischer, and the post also references the Democratic and Republican national committees.

REPUBLICANS AND BUSH, in particular, thrived under the Ari Fleischer school of media management. An old story I read somewhere recounts how Ari, working for a congressman, dealt with a sticky situation. A reporter called to ask why Ari's boss had voted for a certain bill. Fleischer denied the vote. The reporter, flummoxed, said he'd confirm the vote and call back.

Fleischer's boss had voted for the bill. But having confirmed the vote, Fleischer made sure not to take that reporter's call again.

Simple and genius. Lie, force doubt into the reporter's mind, and change the subject as quickly as possible. It worked for Bush in 2000, and a complacent media went along for the ride.

The media stuck with the Bush bandwagon through the first three years of his term, through a disastrous war and one tax-cut-motivated lie after another (tax cuts create jobs! said the Republicans after presiding over the loss of 2.4 million jobs).

But something funny happened in 2003. The media landscape shifted. Suddenly, the Internet became a 24/7 oppo [opposition] research and fact checking tool. The Republicans remain wilfully ignorant of their online would-be allies. The Democratic Party—outgunned, outmanned, outfinanced, and out-of-power—was not so myopic.

Hardly a day goes by when I don't see a blog-inspired email blasted out by some party functionary, be it the DSCC, DCCC, DNC or affiliated organizations. Those institutions—the very core of the "Democratic Party Establishment"—are linking to blogs at increased rates. And the results speak for themselves.

For example, my reader-powered "Bush Flip Flops" post on Saturday hit Andrew Sullivan, WaPo and dozens, if not hundreds, of blogs today. In one fell swoop, we turned a GOP talking point against our candidate against theirs, and people outside of the blogosphere "echo chamber" were receptive to the message.

I didn't write that flip-flop post. Reader TK did. Yet it'll now be picked up by the party and other media outlets when "balancing" out the RNC spin points. We are on our way to neutralizing what might've been the GOP's strongest line of attack against Kerry.

Fact is, this is a brutal time to be in GOoPer politics. The old tricks of the trade don't work anymore. Once upon a time, politicos preyed on the public's short attention span. Say one thing today, pretend you never said that tomorrow knowing no one would call you on it. ("Imminent threat," anyone?)

Bloggers like Bilmon started exposing the administration's blatant lies, and surprise! discovered that they had a hungry audience. It was thus inevitable that such blog-provided "context" started making it into news stories (the Bilmon expose of the WMD quotes was hugely influential in driving down the administration's credibility on the issue). And Google makes political research as easy as typing in a phrase in a text box. No more hours of microfiche headaches at the public library.

The Bush Administration is now in a quandary, never before faced by a political campaign. EVERY WORD IT UTTERS can be instantly fact checked and vetted against previous administration proclamations. And the press, lazy as it is, doesn't even have to do the research. They simply have to read the blogs (and they certainly do). The party can pick the best bits of the day and mold them into spin and talking points. Their overstretched, overworked research departments now have reinforcements of major caliber.

For an administration and a party built on ignorance, short-term memory and outright lies . . . , the harsh glare of this new medium must be excruciating.

The Democratic Party is no longer 75 or 100 employees in Washington, D.C. We are all now adjunct DNCers (whether you like it or not!). When we fact-check Bush, develop new avenues of critique, bring attention to some lonely article in Bismarck, Montpelier, or Dallas . . . and spread the word about the latest GOP lies and/or outrages, we are helping the party do what it can't do on its own—reclaim the nation from the ravages of the GOP wingnuts.

Camp Casey
Cindy Sheehan

Protesters sometimes use encampments to transform street demonstrations into long-term events. In the early 1980s people encamped in front of the White House in Washington, D.C., to protest against nuclear weapons and dubbed their effort "Peace Park." In 1972 in Australia Aboriginal people set up a "tent embassy" on a lawn across from the national parliament, advocating for Aboriginal land rights; the country passed a measure strengthening those rights a few years later.

In August 2005, California resident and antiwar protester Cindy Sheehan traveled to Crawford, Texas, and pitched a tent in a roadside ditch several miles from President George W. Bush's ranch as he began a five-week vacation. Sheehan vowed to stay at Camp Casey—named for her son,

Casey Sheehan, who was killed in action in Iraq—until Bush granted her request for a meeting. While Sheehan never got her meeting with Bush, she captured international publicity, met with two high-level administration officials, and galvanized hundreds of other antiwar protesters who came and joined her in Crawford. Sheehan's effort, carried on by a group she cofounded called Gold Star Families for Peace, helped put a human face on the cost of the war and brought a great deal of attention to the antiwar cause.

Pelosi, Democrats See Only Doom and Gloom
Rush Limbaugh

Long-reigning king of AM talk radio Rush Limbaugh is credited by some observers with personally resuscitating the medium with his nationally syndicated show. Media reports have estimated that the *Rush Limbaugh Show*—with its staunchly right-wing, conservative political bent—draws an estimated thirteen to twenty million listeners each week. The show is a mix of monologue, commentary, listener calls, and occasional guests, but the common denominator is the host's use of the airwaves to attack liberal policies and defend conservatism.

Limbaugh's show runs for three hours each weekday and has been nationally syndicated since 1988. His hallmark is his outspokenness. His unsparing attacks have earned him kudos from fans who like his no-holds-barred approach. Limbaugh has been recognized by industry groups as well. He topped a 2002 list of the greatest talk radio hosts of all time compiled by *Talkers* magazine, and he has won the National Association of Broadcasters award for syndicated radio personality of the year multiple times. Limbaugh has coined a slew of terms to protest liberal causes and politicians; he famously dubbed certain pro-choice feminists "feminazis" and has called some conservation activists "environmentalist wackos." A 1990 *New York Times* article about the then-burgeoning Rush phenomenon described his persona as "comic blowhard" and his style as "a schizoid spritz, bouncing between earnest lecturer and political vaudevillian."

In this transcript from a portion of an April 2006 broadcast, Limbaugh berates the Democratic Party and its leader in the House of Representatives, Nancy Pelosi.

NANCY PELOSI JUST ISSUED A RELEASE, a statement. "House Democratic leader Nancy Pelosi released the following statement today in response to President Bush's remarks this morning on the economy. Quote, 'President Bush should ask American families, millions of whom are struggling to make ends meet and going deeper in debt if they believe there's an economic resurgence that's strong, broad, and benefiting all Americans. With tax cuts for the wealthiest few causing red ink as far as the eye can see, incomes falling and our jobs moving overseas, the economic record of President Bush is dismal for middle-class families. The Bush economy is going in the wrong direction. Gas prices are sky high, health costs are an overwhelming burden for too many Americans.

"'Democrats will not compromise our national security with mountains of debt owned by foreign governments or undercut our domestic strength with an

America that only works for the few. Americans are demanding change and Democrats have a better plan, an America that works for everyone.'" I thought Cynthia McKinney was the stupid one, but now I got second thoughts. This is asinine. This is based solely on, "If Bush says it, we gotta go out and destroy him and disagree with it. Bush is wrong! Bush lies! Bush is crazy!" The economic figures are not "Bush's." He was just announcing them. The economic figures are legitimate.

They come from various departments of the government, jobs, more created, "stunning the experts." Unemployment is down to 4.7 percent. There is no housing bubble. We're not built on a pseudo-stock market that was eventually going to bubble up and bubble out. We're not basing economic strength on accounting schemes and corporate scandals like at Enron and WorldCom and you name 'em. If this economy were happening in the nineties, we would be reading articles about how Bill Clinton's face ought to be the next one on Mount Rushmore and this economy would be the only story that they would be talking about in the drive-by media, and here comes Nancy Pelosi.

This is the stupidest, it's the most asinine—and it falls right into play. They have to make you see doom and gloom. They are obsessed with you looking out over the horizon and seeing smoldering ruins where great jobs once were. They want you to see hopelessness. They want you in utter despair. If a couple of you opened your office window and jumped out and committed suicide, it would make their day. They are trying to foster an attitude of pessimism, hopelessness, defeat, everywhere they go. It's stunning. In the United States of America!

I can understand this if they were down in Mexico. I could understand this if they were in any of a number of other countries in the world, but not here. This is quintessentially not what America is. They are not speaking for quintessential Americans. They have totally lost touch with what it is that makes an American an American. They aren't in touch with it anymore. In fact, they resent it. They privately probably see these numbers and start cursing, getting angry. "This is not supposed to happen. Bush is the worst president! Bush lied! Bush tax cuts for the rich! All this is not supposed to happen." They can't figure it out. They are watching, and what they're seeing is right before their eyes, the very proof that their belief system and their policies fail, and that those they disagree with and oppose succeed, and so they're going to do everything they can to convince you that what's real isn't. They're going to do everything they can—the problem is, they send out airheads like Nancy Pelosi and Harry Reid to do it— and, frankly, who else do they have?

CHAPTER 3
ROOTS OF DISSENT

INTRODUCTION

Sigmund Freud viewed civilization as an uneasy bargain in which individuals subconsciously suppress their natural sexual and aggressive tendencies for the common good of maintaining social order. From this psychosocial viewpoint, peaceful protest is a completely natural expression—perhaps even a stabilizing force—in society since it allows people to vent their discontent in a way that is short of violence. In "rightly finding fault" with our societies and "in doing our utmost to lay bare the roots of its deficiencies by our unsparing criticisms," wrote Freud, "we are undoubtedly exercising our just rights and not showing ourselves enemies of culture."

Whether or not one accepts Freud's theories, it is certainly the case that protest has gone hand in hand with civilization from its inception. This chapter includes examples of protest from early history through the time of the Protestant Reformation, which was a watershed in the time line of protest. Along with the development of the printing press, the Reformation encouraged protest to blossom by promoting the concept that powerful institutions could be challenged and that the views of individuals could actually lead to change.

The roots of modern protest show up in biblical stories and native myths, in which people and characters rebelled against the authority of gods and rulers. Writings from ancient Greece and Rome are filled with fictional and factual accounts of people challenging the societal norms of their day, from the civil disobedience of the fictional Antigone in Sophocles' play, who knowingly defies the law in order to honor her dead brother, to the Roman slaves who led a series of rebellions to protest their oppression.

The documents in this chapter include protests from multiple continents on many issues, from religious freedom to women's rights, from economic justice to war. Though the documents are from various eras and cultures, a common denominator is the assertion that voicing protest is a person's basic underlying right, stemming from a moral authority that supersedes the laws of humankind. As Antigone told her uncle, the king, when he questioned how she could knowingly break the law:

For me it was not Zeus who made that order.
Nor did that Justice who lives with the gods below
mark out such laws to hold among mankind.
Nor did I think your orders were so strong
that you, a mortal man, could over-run
the gods' unwritten and unfailing laws.
Not now, nor yesterday's, they always live,
and no one knows their origin in time.

The Bible (the Tanach)

The books known to Christians as the Old Testament are known to Jews simply as the Bible or by the Hebrew word "Tanach." They were written down and compiled beginning approximately 3,200 years ago; the final writings date from perhaps 2,100 years ago. For millions of religious Jews and Christians around the world, the words of the Tanach are the revealed word of God. Millions more regard them as a source of important moral wisdom, if not actually dictated by God. The books have influenced history, philosophy, law, and literature since they were first committed to parchment or vellum.

And throughout the Bible resound words of protest—many kinds with many meanings. The following three examples of protest found in the Tanach use the lyrical translation of the Artscroll Series Stone Edition from 1996; bracketed phrases are original to the Artscroll text. In the three excerpts, Moses, Micah, and Job all confront authority with their complaints. They do not simply accept the situation as they find it, but rather try to improve the world through their words and actions.

The first selection focuses on a protest against the oppression and mistreatment of Jews by others. Moses and his brother, Aaron, speak to the Egyptian pharaoh, demanding religious rights for the Jews and invoking one of the alternate Hebrew names for God, Hashem. The pharaoh refuses them for economic reasons—the Jews are numerous and their labor too important. God, of course, waits in the background, ready to back up Moses' demands with the awful punishments of the Ten Plagues.

Later in the Tanach the words of the prophets reveal a different kind of protest: protest against immoral actions by the Jews themselves. In general, the books of the prophets forecast that God will cause the downfall of the corrupted Jews, a prophecy that became reality in 587 B.C. when the Jews were forced into exile in Babylonia. In the second excerpt, the prophet Micah forecasts the destruction of Jerusalem. Micah uses the word "Kohanim" to refer to priests.

In the Book of Job, man protests against injustice by God himself. Job, a worthy and god-fearing man, has lost everything he owned and loved for no apparent reason. His friends insist he must have done something evil, but Job protests and demands an explanation from God himself. In the third excerpt, Job calls for horrific divine punishments if ever he had acted immorally. The reader knows that Job's outcry is truthful. He did nothing to deserve the misfortunes that have fallen upon him; they are merely the stakes in a heavenly wager between God and "the

Satan" (which translates from Hebrew as "the Adversary"). Job, in demanding an answer of the highest authority known to the world, serves as the prototype for voices of dissent.

Exodus

Moses and Aaron came and said to Pharaoh, "So said Hashem, the God of Israel, 'Send out My people that they may celebrate for Me in the Wilderness.'"

Pharaoh replied, "Who is Hashem that I should heed His voice to send out Israel? I do not know Hashem, nor will I send out Israel!" So they said, "The God of the Hebrews happened upon us. Let us now go for a three-day journey in the Wilderness and we shall bring offerings to Hashem, our God, lest He strike us dead with the plague or the sword." The king of Egypt said to them, "Moses and Aaron, why do you disturb the people from its work? Go to your own burdens." And Pharaoh said, "Behold! the people of the land are now numerous, and you would have them cease from their burdens."

Micah

Listen, now, to this, O leaders of the House of Jacob and officers of the House of Israel, who detest justice and who twist all that is straight, who build Zion with blood and Jerusalem with iniquity:

Her leaders judge for bribes and her Kohanim teach for a fee and her prophets divine for money—yet they rely on Hashem, saying "Behold Hashem is in our midst; no evil can befall us!" Therefore, because of you, Zion will be plowed over like a field; Jerusalem will become heaps of rubble and the Temple Mount will become like stone heaps in the forest.

Job

If my steps [ever] veered from the [proper] way or if my heart [ever] went after my eyes, or if anything [ever] clung to my hand, then may I sow and let another eat, and may my produce be uprooted! If my heart was [ever] seduced over a woman, or if ever I lay in wait at my neighbor's door, then may my wife grind for another man, and may strangers kneel over her! For that is licentiousness; that is an iniquity for the judges [to punish]! For it is a fire; it consumes unto doom, and it would uproot all my produce.

If ever I spurned justice for my servants and maidservants when they contended with me, then what could I do when God would rise up? When He would attend to me, what could I answer Him? Did not the One Who made me in the belly make him too? Was it not the One Who prepared us in the womb? Never did I withhold the needs of the destitute, nor did I let a widow's eyes long in vain, nor did I eat my bread in solitude, so that an orphan could not eat from it. . . .

Who will grant that someone would hear me; my desire is for the Almighty to answer me!

Lysistrata
Aristophanes

One of the most inventive—albeit fictional—examples of protest in recorded history is also one of the oldest. In ancient Greece the comic playwright Aristophanes penned his ribald antiwar farce, Lysistrata, in which the title character conceives to end the real-life war between Athens and Sparta by staging a sex strike. The women from various city-states bond together and swear an oath not only to refuse sex to their husbands, but also to up the ante by first tantalizing them, until the armies agree to a truce. The play is famous for its bawdy humor, but what is equally arresting about the plot is the way the women leverage their boudoir power to defeat the war. Aristophanes wrote the play for a drama contest, and it was first performed in 411 B.C.E.—the twenty-first year of the Athens-Sparta war.

Poet and author X. J. Kennedy, in a preface to his very contemporary 1999 translation of the play, explained that all translations of Lysistrata are "rough versions," taken from handwritten copies that survive from medieval times and which were themselves the product of much guesswork by earlier translators. Still, it was clear that government officials in Athens had imposed no censorship on the playwright, even during wartime, as the entire play protests war by making fun of warriors. Aristophanes relentlessly skewered the day's leaders and rebuked them for unnecessarily miring the land in an expensive conflict.

In the following excerpt, from a 1964 translation by Douglass Parker (with most stage directions omitted), Lysistrata—whose name means "she who disperses armies"—has called a meeting to lay out her plan to the other women. Among them is Lampito, a woman from Sparta, whose dialogue has been rendered by different translators as some variation on a country drawl.

LAMPITO: The womenfolk's all assemblied. Who-all's notion was this-hyer confabulation?

LYSISTRATA: Mine.

LAMPITO: Git on with the give-out. I'm hankerin' to hear.

MYRRHINE: Me, too! I can't imagine what could be so important. Tell us about it!

LYSISTRATA: Right away. But first, a question. It's not an involved one. Answer yes or no.

MYRRHINE: Well, ASK it!

LYSISTRATA: It concerns the fathers of your children—your husbands, absent on active service. I know you all have men abroad. Wouldn't you like to have them home?

KLEONIKE: My husband's been gone for the last five months! Way up to Thrace, watchdogging military waste. It's horrible!

MYRRHINE: Mine's been posted to Pylos for seven whole months!

LAMPITO: My man's no sooner rotated out of the line than he's plugged back in. Hain't no discharge in this war!

KLEONIKE: And lovers can't be had for love or money, not even synthetics. Why, since those beastly Milesians revolted and cut off the leather trade, that handy do-it-yourself kit's vanished from the open market!

LYSISTRATA: If I can devise a scheme for ending the war, I gather I have your support?

KLEONIKE: You can count on me! If you need money, I'll pawn the shift off my back—[aside] and drink up the cash before the sun goes down.

MYRRHINE: Me, too! I'm ready to split myself right up the middle like a mackerel, and give you half!

LAMPITO: Me, too! I'd climb Taygetos Mountain plumb to the top to git the leastes' peek at Peace!

LYSISTRATA: Very well, I'll tell you. No reason to keep to keep a secret. We can force our husbands to negotiate Peace, Ladies, by exercising steadfast Self-Control—By Total Abstinence . . .

KLEONIKE: From WHAT?

MYRRHINE: Yes, what?

LYSISTRATA: You'll do it?

KLEONIKE: Of course we'll do it! We'd even *die!*

LYSISTRATA: Very well, then here's the program: Total Abstinence from SEX!

The cluster of women dissolves.

Why are you turning away? Where are you going? What's this? Such stricken expressions! Such gloomy gestures! Why so pale? Whence these tears? What IS this? Will you do it or won't you? Cat got your tongue?

KLEONIKE: Afraid I can't make it. Sorry. *On with the war!*

MYRRHINE: Me neither. Sorry. *On with the war!*

LYSISTRATA: *This* from my little mackerel? The girl who was ready, a minute ago, to split herself right up the middle?

KLEONIKE: Try something else. Try anything. If you say so, I'm willing to walk through fire barefoot. But not to give up SEX—there's nothing like it, Lysistrata!

LYSISTRATA: And you?

MYRRHINE: Me, too! I'll walk through fire.

LYSISTRATA: *Women!* Utter sluts, the entire sex! Will-power, nil. We're perfect raw material for Tragedy, the stuff of heroic lays. "Go to bed with a god and then get rid of the baby"—that sums us up! [Turning to Lampito.] Oh, Spartan, be a dear. If *you* stick by me, just you, we still may have a chance to win. Give me your vote.

LAMPITO: Hit's right onsettlin' fer gals to sleep all lonely-like, withouten no humpin'. But I'm on yore side. We shore need Peace, too.

LYSISTRATA: You're a darling—the only woman here worthy of the name!

KLEONIKE: Well, just suppose we *did*, as much as possible, abstain from . . . what you said, you know—not that we *would*—could something like that bring Peace any sooner?

LYSISTRATA: Certainly. Here's how it works: We'll paint, powder, and pluck ourselves to the last detail, and stay inside, wearing those filmy tunics that set off everything we *have*—and then slink up to the men. They'll snap to attention, go absolutely *mad* to love us—but we won't let them. We'll Abstain. I imagine they'll conclude a treaty rather quickly.

LAMPITO: Menelaos he tuck one squint at Helen's bubbies all nekkid, and plumb throwed up. Throwed up his sword.

KLEONIKE: Suppose the men just leave us flat?

LYSISTRATA: In that case, we'll have to take things into our own hands.

KLEONIKE: There simply isn't any reasonable facsimile! Suppose they take us by force and drag us off to the bedroom against our wills?

LYSISTRATA: Hang on to the door.

KLEONIKE: Suppose they beat us?

LYSISTRATA: Give in—but be bad sports. Be nasty about it—they don't enjoy these forced affairs. So make them suffer. Don't worry; they'll stop soon enough.

"I never intentionally wronged anyone"
Socrates

Socrates, at his trial in 399 B.C.E., delivered a speech that protested not his death sentence but the small-mindedness of his fellow Athenians in trying to prevent people from seeking the truth. It is the first great courtroom protest speech in recorded history, notable for Socrates' sarcastic humor and impeccable logic. The speech is, true to form, replete with questions. Socrates' method of using inquiry relied on relentlessly questioning his students to force them to draw their own conclusions using evidence and reasoning. The Socratic method still serves as a foundation of the quest for knowledge. In its very questioning, it is a form of dissent from the status quo, always willing to discard current beliefs in search of deeper truths.

Though Socrates is one of the great pillars of Western civilization, he left no writings, and all our knowledge of him is secondhand. His statement at being condemned to death, excerpted here, is from the account of his trial in the *Apology* (from the Greek word for defense) by his follower Plato. Socrates was born in 469 B.C.E. and spent his life as a teacher—though he insisted he was not one. He was convicted of irreverence toward the official gods of Athens, creating new gods (a reference to his claim of receiving guidance from a mystical inner voice), and corrupting the youth. Socrates ignored pleas from friends to flee, and was put to death.

THERE ARE MANY REASONS why I am not grieved, O men of Athens, at the vote of condemnation. I expected this, and am only surprised that the votes are so nearly equal; for I had thought that the majority against me would have been far larger; but now, had thirty votes gone over to the other side, I should have been acquitted. . . .

. . . What shall be done to the man who has never had the wit to be idle during his whole life; but has been careless of what the many care about—wealth, and family interests, and military offices, and speaking in the assembly, and magistracies, and plots, and parties. Reflecting that I was really too honest a man to follow in this way and live, I did not go where I could do no good to you or to myself; but where I could do the greatest good privately to every one of you, thither I went, and sought to persuade every man among you, that he must look to himself, and seek virtue and wisdom before he looks to his private interests, and look to the state before he looks to the interests of the state; and that this should be the order which he observes in all his actions. What shall be done to such an one? Doubtless some good thing, O men of Athens, if he has his reward; and the good should be of a kind suitable to him. What would be a reward suitable to a poor man who is your benefactor, who desires leisure that he may instruct you? . . .

Perhaps you may think that I am braving you in saying this, as in what I said before about the tears and prayers. But that is not the case. I speak rather because I am convinced that I never intentionally wronged any one, although I can not convince you of that—for we have had a short conversation only; but if there were a law at Athens, such as there is in other cities, that a capital cause should not be decided in one day, then I believe that I should have convinced you; but now the time is too short. I can not in a moment refute great slanders; and, as I am convinced that I never wronged another, I will assuredly not wrong myself. I will not say of myself that I deserve any evil, or propose any penalty. Why should I? Because I am afraid of the penalty of death which Meletus proposes? When I do not know whether death is a good or an evil, why should I propose a penalty which would certainly be an evil? Shall I say imprisonment? And why should I live in prison, and be the slave of the magistrates of the year—of the eleven? Or shall the penalty be a fine, and imprisonment until the fine is paid? There is the same objection. I should have to lie in prison, for money I have none, and can not pay. And if I say exile (and this may possibly be the penalty which you will affix), I must indeed be blinded by the love of life, if I do not consider that when you, who are my own citizens, can not endure my discourses and words, and have found them so grievous and odious that you would fain have done with them, others are likely to endure me. No indeed, men of Athens, that is not very likely. And what a life should I lead, at my age, wandering from city to city, living in ever-changing exile, and always being driven out! For I am quite sure that into whatever place I go, as here so also there, the young men will come to me; and if I drive them away, their elders will drive me out at their desire; and if I let them come, their fathers and friends will drive me out for their sakes.

Some one will say: Yes, Socrates, but can not you hold your tongue, and then you may go into a foreign city, and no one will interfere with you? Now I have great difficulty in making you understand my answer to this. For if I tell you that this would be a disobedience to a divine command, and therefore that I can not hold my tongue, you will not believe that I am serious; and if I say again that the greatest good of man is daily to converse about virtue, and all that concerning which you hear me examining myself and others, and that the life which is unexamined is not worth living—that you are still less likely to believe. And yet what I say is true, although a thing of which it is hard for me to persuade you. Moreover, I am not accustomed to think that I deserve any punishment. Had I money I might have proposed to give you what I had, and have been none the worse. But you see that I have none, and can only ask you to proportion the fine to my means. However, I think that I could afford a mina, and therefore I propose that penalty: Plato, Crito, Critobulus, and Apollodorus, my friends here, bid me say thirty minae, and they will be the sureties. Well, then, say thirty minae, let that be the penalty; for that they will be ample security to you.

Not much time will be gained, O Athenians, in return for the evil name which you will get from the detractors of the city, who will say that you killed Socrates, a wise man; for they will call me wise even although I am not wise when they want to reproach you. If you had waited a little while, your desire would have been fulfilled in the course of nature. For I am far advanced in years, as you may perceive, and not far from death. I am speaking now only to those of you who have condemned me to death. And I have another thing to say to them: You think that I was convicted through deficiency of words—I mean, that if I had thought fit to leave nothing undone, nothing unsaid, I might have gained an acquittal. Not so; the deficiency which led to my conviction was not of words—certainly not. But I had not the boldness or impudence or inclination to address you as you would have liked me to address you, weeping and wailing and lamenting, and saying and doing many things which you have been accustomed to hear from others, and which, as I say, are unworthy of me. But I thought that I ought not to do anything common or mean in the hour of danger: nor do I now repent of the manner of my defence, and I would rather die having spoken after my manner, than speak in your manner and live. For neither in war nor yet at law ought any man to use every way of escaping death. For often in battle there is no doubt that if a man will throw away his arms, and fall on his knees before his pursuers, he may escape death; and in other dangers there are other ways of escaping death, if a man is willing to say and do anything. The difficulty, my friends, is not in avoiding death, but in avoiding unrighteousness; for that runs faster than death. I am old and move slowly, and the slower runner has overtaken me, and my accusers are keen and quick, and the faster runner, who is unrighteousness, has overtaken them. And now I depart hence condemned by you to suffer the penalty of death, and they too go their ways condemned by the truth to suffer the penalty of villainy and wrong; and I must abide by my award—let them abide by theirs. I suppose that these things may be regarded as fated,—and I think that they are well.

"The War of Spartacus," from *Life of Marcus Licinius Crassus*
Plutarch

The civilization of ancient Rome was enlightened in many ways, but its hierarchical social structure also made it fertile ground for dissent. Slaves in Rome staged unrelated rebellions three separate times—none of them ultimately successful—known as the Servile Wars. Armed rebellion can be seen as a form of extreme protest, when people desperate to change their status have no other options. The Roman slave rebellions were the historical precursors of dozens of slave revolts in the western hemisphere more than a thousand years later.

In the First Servile War in 135 B.C.E., slaves on the island of Sicily revolted, banding together and deposing the governor. They occupied part of the island for four years before the Roman army put down the insurrection. Slaves on Sicily rebelled again in 104 B.C.E. after the Roman Senate declared that slaves taken from lands of allies were to be set free, but one governor refused to emancipate the slaves in his territory.

The Third Servile War is well known for its leader, the rebel gladiator Spartacus, whose story is familiar from several modern novels and a popular (but historically inaccurate) movie bearing his name. In the excerpt below, famed Roman historian Plutarch tells the story of the beginning of the third slave rebellion. Spartacus gathered a large rebel force by uniting separate groups of oppressed Romans, including the gladiators (who were often prisoners trained to fight for entertainment) and slaves. His slave army of more than a 100,000 defeated the Roman army in several battles and inflicted heavy losses before it was wiped out—and all surviving rebels crucified—in 71 B.C.E. The story of Spartacus illustrates the snowball effect of protest: in some cases the action of a lone protester or a small group can cause a much larger group to recognize its own dissatisfaction, and thus ignite a large uprising.

THE INSURRECTION of the gladiators and the devastation of Italy, commonly called the war of Spartacus, began upon this occasion. One Lentulus Batiates trained up a great many gladiators in Capua, most of them Gauls and Thracians, who, not for any fault by them committed, but simply through the cruelty of their master, were kept in confinement for this object of fighting one with another. Two hundred of these formed a plan to escape, but being discovered, those of them who became aware of it in time to anticipate their master, being seventy-eight, got out of a cook's shop chopping-knives and spits, and made their way through the city, and lighting by the way on several wagons that were carrying gladiators' arms to another city, they seized upon them and armed themselves. And seizing upon a defensible place, they chose three captains, of whom Spartacus was chief, a Thracian of one of the nomad tribes, and a man not only of high spirit and valiant, but in understanding, also, and in gentleness superior to his condition, and more of a Grecian than the people of his country usually are. When he first came to be sold at Rome, they say a snake coiled itself upon his face as he lay asleep, and his wife, who at this latter time also accompanied him in his flight, his countrywoman, a kind of prophetess, and one of those possessed with the bacchanal frenzy, declared that it was a sign portending great and formidable power to him with no happy event.

First, then, routing those that came out of Capua against them, and thus procuring a quantity of proper soldiers' arms, they gladly threw away their own as barbarous and dishonourable. Afterwards Clodius, the praetor [governor], took the command against them with a body of three thousand men from Rome, and besieged them within a mountain, accessible only by one narrow and difficult passage, which Clodius kept guarded, encompassed on all other sides with steep and slippery precipices. Upon the top, however, grew a great many wild vines, and cutting down as many of their boughs as they had need of, they twisted them into strong ladders long enough to reach from thence to the bottom, by which, without any danger, they got down all but one, who stayed there to throw them down their arms, and after this succeeded in saving himself. The Romans were ignorant of all this, and, therefore, coming upon them in the rear, they assaulted them unawares and took their camp. Several, also, of the shepherds and herdsmen that were there, stout and nimble fellows, revolted over to them, to some of whom they gave complete arms, and made use of others as scouts and light-armed soldiers. Publius Varinus, the praetor, was now sent against them, whose lieutenant, Furius, with two thousand men, they fought and routed. Then Cossinius was sent with considerable forces, to give his assistance and advice, and him Spartacus missed but very little of capturing in person, as he was bathing at Salinae; for he with great difficulty made his escape, while Spartacus possessed himself of his baggage, and following the chase with a great slaughter, stormed his camp and took it, where Cossinius himself was slain. After many successful skirmishes with the praetor himself, in one of which he took his lictors [attendants] and his own horse, he began to be great and terrible; but wisely considering that he was not to expect to match the force of the empire, he marched his army towards the Alps, intending, when he had passed them, that every man should go to his own home, some to Thrace, some to Gaul. But they, grown confident in their numbers, and puffed up with their success, would give no obedience to him, but went about and ravaged Italy; so that now the senate was not only moved at the indignity and baseness, both of the enemy and of the insurrection, but, looking upon it as a matter of alarm and of dangerous consequence, sent out both the consuls to it, as to a great and difficult enterprise.

The Sermon on the Mount
Jesus Christ

Fifteen hundred years after Jesus lived, the father of the Protestant Reformation, Martin Luther, noted the implicit connection of protest and Christianity in his defense against charges of heresy: "I rejoice exceedingly to see the Gospel this day, as of old, a cause of disturbance and disagreement. It is the character and destiny of God's word. 'I came not to send peace unto the earth, but a sword,' said Jesus Christ."

Jesus was a social reformer, continually urging his disciples and followers to question authority. The accounts of his teachings and actions in the Christian Bible include numerous examples of protest. When Jesus visited the temple in Jerusalem, he was incensed by the secular atmosphere in the courtyards outside the sanctuary. He responded with a dramatic, vehement protest, fashioning a whip, scattering the livestock, and overturning the tables of the money changers while quoting Isaiah at them: "It is written, My house shall be called the house of prayer; but ye have made it a den of thieves."

Jesus protested against the religious authorities of the day by preaching different interpretations of scripture; against materialism ("Ye cannot serve God and mammon"); and against meeting violence with violence ("all who draw the sword will die by the sword"). One of his central teachings was the Sermon on the Mount, recorded in the Gospel of Matthew and estimated to have been delivered in the year 30. In his comments on the sermon, Saint Augustine cast Jesus as a dissenter from religious orthodoxies of his time. The teachings of Jesus in the Sermon on the Mount, said Augustine, were God's transmission of "greater precepts of righteousness" compared to those he had previously conveyed in the Ten Commandments.

The Sermon on the Mount opens with the Beatitudes, a series of teachings on how to live righteously that ran counter to expectations by praising the poor and the meek rather than the rich and powerful. The sermon also includes the famous teaching about "turning the other cheek." This passage is the historical touchstone for centuries of nonviolent resistance; among the influential people it inspired are Leo Tolstoy, Mahatma Gandhi, and Martin Luther King, Jr. The following passage of excerpts from the Sermon (Matthew 5 to 7) is from the King James Version of the New Testament.

AND SEEING THE MULTITUDES, he went up into a mountain: and when he was set, his disciples came unto him:
And he opened his mouth, and taught them, saying,

Blessed are the poor in spirit: for theirs is the kingdom of heaven.

Blessed are they that mourn: for they shall be comforted.

Blessed are the meek: for they shall inherit the earth.

Blessed are they which do hunger and thirst after righteousness: for they shall be filled.

Blessed are the merciful: for they shall obtain mercy.

Blessed are the pure in heart: for they shall see God.

Blessed are the peacemakers: for they shall be called the children of God.

Blessed are they which are persecuted for righteousness' sake: for theirs is the kingdom of heaven.

Blessed are ye, when men shall revile you, and persecute you, and shall say all manner of evil against you falsely, for my sake.

Rejoice, and be exceeding glad: for great is your reward in heaven: for so persecuted they the prophets which were before you. . . .

Think not that I am come to destroy the law, or the prophets: I am not come to destroy, but to fulfil.

For verily I say unto you, Till heaven and earth pass, one jot or one tittle shall in no wise pass from the law, till all be fulfilled.

Whosoever therefore shall break one of these least commandments, and shall teach men so, he shall be called the least in the kingdom of heaven: but whosoever shall do and teach them, the same shall be called great in the kingdom of heaven.

For I say unto you, That except your righteousness shall exceed the righteousness of the scribes and Pharisees, ye shall in no case enter into the kingdom of heaven.

Ye have heard that it was said of them of old time, Thou shalt not kill; and whosoever shall kill shall be in danger of the judgment:

But I say unto you, That whosoever is angry with his brother without a cause shall be in danger of the judgment. . . .

Ye have heard that it was said by them of old time, Thou shalt not commit adultery:

But I say unto you, That whosoever looketh on a woman to lust after her hath committed adultery with her already in his heart. . . .

It hath been said, Whosoever shall put away his wife, let him give her a writing of divorcement:

But I say unto you, That whosoever shall put away his wife, saving for the cause of fornication, causeth her to commit adultery: and whosoever shall marry her that is divorced committeth adultery.

Again, ye have heard that it hath been said by them of old time, Thou shalt not forswear thyself, but shalt perform unto the Lord thine oaths:

But I say unto you, Swear not at all; neither by heaven; for it is God's throne:

Nor by the earth; for it is his footstool: neither by Jerusalem; for it is the city of the great King. . . .

Ye have heard that it hath been said, An eye for an eye, and a tooth for a tooth:

But I say unto you, That ye resist not evil: but whosoever shall smite thee on thy right cheek, turn to him the other also.

And if any man will sue thee at the law, and take away thy coat, let him have thy cloak also.

And whosoever shall compel thee to go a mile, go with him twain.

Give to him that asketh thee, and from him that would borrow of thee turn not thou away.

Ye have heard that it hath been said, Thou shalt love thy neighbour, and hate thine enemy.

But I say unto you, Love your enemies, bless them that curse you, do good to them that hate you, and pray for them which despitefully use you, and persecute you;

That ye may be the children of your Father which is in heaven: for he maketh his sun to rise on the evil and on the good, and sendeth rain on the just and on the unjust. . . .

Take heed that ye do not your alms before men, to be seen of them: otherwise ye have no reward of your Father which is in heaven.

Therefore when thou doest thine alms, do not sound a trumpet before thee, as the hypocrites do in the synagogues and in the streets, that they may have glory of men. Verily I say unto you, They have their reward.

But when thou doest alms, let not thy left hand know what thy right hand doeth:

That thine alms may be in secret: and thy Father which seeth in secret himself shall reward thee openly.

And when thou prayest, thou shalt not be as the hypocrites are: for they love to pray standing in the synagogues and in the corners of the streets, that they may be seen of men. Verily I say unto you, They have their reward.

But thou, when thou prayest, enter into thy closet, and when thou hast shut thy door, pray to thy Father which is in secret; and thy Father which seeth in secret shall reward thee openly. . . .

Lay not up for yourselves treasures upon earth, where moth and rust doth corrupt, and where thieves break through and steal:

But lay up for yourselves treasures in heaven, where neither moth nor rust doth corrupt, and where thieves do not break through nor steal:

For where your treasure is, there will your heart be also. . . .

"I advise, I entreat, I exhort, I admonish"
Ambrose, Bishop of Milan

The Roman co-emperors Constantine I and Licinius jointly issued the Edict of Milan in 313 providing for freedom of worship throughout the empire. Later Constantine, who had forced Licinius out and assumed sole power, declared Christianity the state religion. It did not take long for the first signs of friction to appear between the growing religion and the powerful empire. One of Constantine's successors, the emperor Theodosius I, was strongly influenced by Ambrose, the bishop of Milan. The relationship between the two men had plenty of dramatic ups and downs. In 390 Theodosius ordered a horrific massacre of seven thousand men, women, and children from the city of Thessalonica in revenge for the assassination of a city official. Ambrose, appalled, refused to give communion to the emperor and threatened him with excommunication.

Ambrose sent Theodosius a famous letter, excerpted here, in which he firmly protested the actions of the emperor and urged him to follow the lead of King David and other biblical rulers in personally doing penance for his sins. To the amazement of his subjects, Theodosius did indeed become penitent in a very public way for eight months, sometimes dressing like a beggar, and standing outside of the cathedral of Milan to beg forgiveness from Ambrose. In the remaining years of his rule until his death in 395, Theodosius became an ardent promoter of Christianity, passing decrees against pagan rituals and ordering the destruction of non-Christian places of worship.

AN ACT HAS BEEN COMMITTED in the city of Thessalonica, the like of which is not recorded, the perpetration of which I could not prevent, which in my frequent petitions before the court I had declared to be most atrocious, and which by your tardy revocation you have yourself pronounced to be very heinous: such an act as this I could not extenuate. Intelligence of it was first brought to a synod [council] held on the arrival of the Galilean Bishops: all present deplored it, no one viewed it leniently; your friendship with Ambrose, so far from excusing your deed, would have even brought a heavier weight of odium on my head, had there been no one found to declare the necessity of your being reconciled to God.

Is your Majesty ashamed to do that which the Royal Prophet David did, the forefather of Christ according to the flesh? It was told him that a rich man, who had numerous flocks, on the arrival of a guest took a poor man's lamb and killed it, and recognizing in this act his own condemnation, he said, *I have sinned against the Lord.* Let not your Majesty then be impatient at being told, as David was by the prophet, *Thou art the man.* For if you listen thereto obediently and say, *I have sinned against the Lord,* if you will use those words of the royal Prophet, *O come let us worship and fall down, and kneel before the Lord our Maker,* to you also it shall be said, Because thou repentest, *the Lord hath put away thy sin, thou shalt not die . . . .*

And Scripture tells us that when the people were dying, on the very first day and at dinner time, David saw the Angel that smote the people, he said, *Lo, I have sinned and done wickedly; but these sheep, what have they done? let Thine hand, I pray Thee, be against me, and against my father's house.* So the Lord repented, and commanded the Angel to spare the people, and that David should offer sacrifice: for there were then sacrifices for sin, but we have now the sacrifices of penitence. So by that humility he was made more acceptable to God, for it is not wonderful that man should sin, but it is indeed blameable if he do not acknowledge his error, and humble himself before God. . . .

This I have written, not to confound you, but that these royal examples may induce you to put away this sin from your kingdom; for this you will do by humbling your soul before God. You are a man; temptation has fallen upon you; vanquish it. Sin is not washed away but by tears and penitence. Neither Angel nor Archangel can do it. The Lord Himself, *Who alone can say I am with you,* even He grants no remission of sin save to the penitent.

I advise, I entreat, I exhort, I admonish; for I am grieved that you who were an example of singular piety, who stood so high for clemency, who would not suffer even single offenders to be put in jeopardy, should not mourn over the death of so many innocent persons. Successful as you have been in battle, and great in other respects, yet mercy was ever the crown of your actions. The devil has envied you your chief excellence: overcome him, while you still have the means. Add not sin to sin by acting in a manner which has injured so many.

For my part, debtor as I am to your clemency in all other things; grateful as I must ever be for this clemency, which I have found superior to that of many Emperors and equalled only by one, though I have no ground for charging you with contumacy, I have still reason for apprehension: if you purpose being present, I dare not offer the Sacrifice. That which may not be done when the blood of one innocent person has been shed, may it be done where many have been slain? I trow not.

A Song of War Chariots
Du Fu

Du Fu, born in the year 712, is regarded as one of China's great poets. His poems often dealt with war and social criticism. During his lifetime Chinese society was highly militaristic, and many peasants were conscripted to protect the country's boundaries or gain new territory. The later years of his life were shaped by a major rebellion in 755 that killed or displaced millions of Chinese, forced the emperor to abdicate, and disrupted society for years. Du Fu (also called Tu Fu) wrote frequently about the impact of war on the commoners, and sometimes even voiced his dissent by penning poems of advice to the emperor. Du Fu died in 770.

Du Fu traveled extensively and wrote more than four hundred poems. He is believed to have written the following poem, "A Song of War Chariots" (also called "Ballad of the Army Carts"), in 750. Translated by American writer Harold Witter Bynner, it is an early example of protest poetry, still relevant after twelve centuries.

The war-chariots rattle,
The war-horses whinny.
Each man of you has a bow and a quiver at his belt.
Father, mother, son, wife, stare at you going,
Till dust shall have buried the bridge beyond Changan.
They run with you, crying, they tug at your sleeves,
And the sound of their sorrow goes up to the clouds;
And every time a bystander asks you a question,
You can only say to him that you have to go.
. . . We remember others at fifteen sent north to guard the river
And at forty sent west to cultivate the campfarms.
The mayor wound their turbans for them when they started out.
With their turbaned hair white now, they are still at the border,
At the border where the blood of men spills like the sea—
And still the heart of Emperor Wu is beating for war.
. . . Do you know that, east of China's mountains, in two hundred districts
And in thousands of villages, nothing grows but weeds,
And though strong women have bent to the ploughing,
East and west the furrows all are broken down?
. . . Men of China are able to face the stiffest battle,
But their officers drive them like chickens and dogs.
Whatever is asked of them,
Dare they complain?
For example, this winter
Held west of the gate,
Challenged for taxes,
How could they pay?
. . . We have learned that to have a son is bad luck—
It is very much better to have a daughter
Who can marry and live in the house of a neighbour,
While under the sod we bury our boys.
. . . Go to the Blue Sea, look along the shore
At all the old white bones forsaken—
New ghosts are wailing there now with the old,
Loudest in the dark sky of a stormy day.

On the Harmony of Religion and Philosophy
Averroës

Averroës is the name that Westerners use for the twelfth-century Muslim philosopher Ibn Rushd
(his full name was Abu Al-Walid Muhammad Ibn Ahmad Ibn Muhammad Ibn Ahmad Ibn Ahmad

Ibn Rushd). Averroës was born in Córdoba, Spain, in 1126 and was famed for his translations and analyses of Aristotle. He ardently defended the study of classic philosophy as consistent with Islam in a treatise called *The Incoherence of the Incoherence*, countering a charge by an earlier Muslim writer that such study was sacrilegious. Averroës wrote in Arabic, but many of his works were translated into Latin and Hebrew and influenced several non-Muslim philosophers, including Maimonides and Thomas Aquinas. His emphasis on free inquiry presaged later Enlightenment writers. He fell out of favor after the conquest of Moorish Spain by fundamentalist Muslims at the end of the century, and many of his books were burned. Averroës lived his final years in exile, dying in Morocco in 1198.

In his work *On the Harmony of Religion and Philosophy*, written in approximately 1190, Averroës stressed the importance of analytical thinking to proper interpretation of the Koran. In the excerpt below, translated by George F. Hourani, he used a blend of logic and scripture to protest repressive attempts to deter Muslims from studying earlier great thinkers. (Translator's notes have been omitted from the excerpt.)

THAT THE LAW SUMMONS to reflection on beings, and the pursuit of knowledge about them, by the intellect is clear from several verses of the Book of God, Blessed and Exalted, such as the saying of the Exalted, "Reflect, you have vision": this is textual authority for the obligation to use intellectual reasoning, or a combination of intellectual and legal reasoning. Another example is His saying, "Have they not studied the kingdom of the heavens and the earth, and whatever things God has created?": this is a text urging the study of the totality of beings. Again, God the Exalted has taught that one of those whom He singularly honoured by this knowledge was Abraham, peace on him, for the Exalted said, "So we made Abraham see the kingdom of the heavens and the earth, that he might be." The Exalted also said, "Do they not observe the camels, how they have been created, and the sky, how it has been raised up?" and He said, "and they give thought to the creation of the heavens and the earth," and so on in countless other verses.

Since it has now been established that the Law has rendered obligatory the study of beings by the intellect, and reflection on them, and since reflection is nothing more than inference and drawing out of the unknown from the known, and since this is reasoning or at any rate done by reasoning, therefore we are under an obligation to carry on our study of beings by intellectual reasoning. It is further evident that this manner of study, to which the Law summons and urges, is the most perfect kind of study using the most perfect kind of reasoning; and this is the kind called "demonstration."

The Law, then, has urged us to have demonstrative knowledge of God the Exalted and all the beings of His creation. But it is preferable and even necessary for anyone, who wants to understand God the Exalted and the other beings demonstratively, to have first understood the kinds of demonstration and their conditions, and in what respects demonstrative reasoning differs from dialectical, rhetorical and fallacious reasoning. But this is not possible unless he has previously learned what reasoning as such is, and how many kinds it has, and which of them are valid and which invalid. This in turn is not possible unless he has previously learned the parts of reasoning, of which it is composed, i.e., the premises and their kinds. Therefore he who believes in the Law, and obeys its command to study beings, ought prior to his study to gain a knowledge of these things, which have the same place in theoretical studies as instruments have in practical activities.

For just as the lawyer infers from the Divine command to him to acquire knowledge of the legal categories that he is under obligation to know the various kinds of legal syllogisms, and which are valid and which invalid, in the same way he who would know [God] ought to infer from the command to study beings that he is under obligation to acquire a knowledge of intellectual reasoning and its kinds. Indeed it is more fitting for him to do so, for if the lawyer infers from the saying of the Exalted, "Reflect, you who have vision," the obligation to acquire a knowledge of legal reasoning, how much more fitting and proper that he who would know God should infer from it the obligation to acquire a knowledge of intellectual reasoning!

It cannot be objected: "This kind of study of intellectual reasoning is a heretical innovation since it did not exist among the first believers." For the study of legal reasoning and its kinds is also something which has been discovered since the first believers, yet it is not considered to be a heretical innovation. So the objector should believe the same about the study of intellectual reasoning. . . .

Since it has now been established that there is an obligation of the Law to study intellectual reasoning and its kinds, just as there is an obligation to study legal reasoning, it is clear that, if none of our predecessors had formerly examined intellectual reasoning and its kinds, we should be obliged to undertake such an examination from the beginning, and that each succeeding scholar would have to seek help in that task from his predecessor in order that knowledge of the subject might be completed. For it is difficult or impossible for one man to find out by himself and from the beginning all that he needs of that subject, as it is difficult for one man to discover all the knowledge that he needs of the kinds of legal reasoning; indeed this is even truer of knowledge of intellectual reasoning.

But if someone other than ourselves has already examined that subject, it is clear that we ought to seek help towards our goal from what has been said by such a predecessor on the subject, regardless of whether this other one shares our religion or not. . . .

. . . For if we suppose that the art of geometry did not exist in this age of ours, and likewise the art of astronomy, and a single person wanted to ascertain by himself the sizes of the heavenly bodies, their shapes, and their distances from each other, that would not be possible for him, e.g., to know the proportion of the sun to the earth or other facts about the sizes of the stars even though he were the most intelligent of men by nature, unless by a revelation or something resembling revelation. Indeed if he were told that the sun is about 150 or 160 times as great as the earth, he would think this statement madness on the part of the speaker, although this is a fact which has been demonstrated in astronomy so surely that no one who has mastered that science doubts it.

. . . And if someone today wanted to find out by himself all the arguments which have been discovered by the theorists of the legal schools on controversial questions, about which debate has taken place between them in most countries of Islam (except the West), he would deserve to be ridiculed, because such a task is impossible for him, apart from the fact that the work has been done already. Moreover, this is a situation that is self-evident not in the scientific arts alone but also in the practical arts; for there is not one of them which a single man can construct by himself. Then how can he do it with the art of arts, philosophy? If this is so, then whenever we find in the works of our predecessors of former nations a theory about beings and a reflection on them conforming to what the conditions of demonstration require, we ought to study what they said about the matter and what they affirmed in their books. And they should accept from them gladly and gratefully whatever in these books accords with the truth, and draw attention to and warn against what does not accord with the truth, at the same time excusing them.

From this it is evident that the study of the books of the ancients is obligatory by Law, since their aim and purpose in their books is just the purpose to which the Law has urged us, and that whoever forbids the study of them to anyone who is fit to study them, i.e., anyone who unites two qualities, (1) natural intelligence and (2) religious integrity and moral virtue, is blocking people from the door by which the Law summons them to knowledge of God, the door of theoretical study which leads to the truest knowledge of Him; and such an act is the extreme of ignorance and estrangement from God the Exalted.

The Vision of William concerning Piers Plowman

William Langland

In the Middles Ages peasants throughout Europe began to rebel against their economic hardships, especially after the Black Death, a series of pandemics that began in the mid-fourteenth century and killed millions in Europe and elsewhere. Peasants in Flanders rioted against excessive taxes in the 1320s. French peasants rebelled against the nobility in 1358 in a popular uprising called the Jacquerie. Wool carders in Italy staged a revolt against labor conditions in a 1378 event known as the Revolt of the Ciompi.

The masses' growing sense of empowerment became a theme for writers of the era. More than a dozen works in Middle English fell into what is sometimes called the Piers Plowman tradition. Most were written in an allegorical style and featured working-class heroes—often farm laborers—who voiced complaints about the social order and the injustices imposed by rulers, religious leaders, and the upper classes. The seminal work that lent its name to the genre was *The Vision of William concerning Piers Plowman*, attributed to a man named William Langland. Thought to have been written in the 1360s, the long poem is considered one of the great works of medieval literature.

The main character, Piers, goes on a spiritual quest seeking advice from guides called Do Well, Do Better, and Do Best. The poem was hugely popular and very influential; there were more than fifty known copies. Langland's verses protested the practice of the wealthy buying absolution for sins and disregarding the suffering of the lower classes. In its author's questioning of ecclesiastical authority some have seen the seeds of what would grow into the Protestant Reformation.

Many scholars have labored over translations of the various manuscripts, which differ one from another. The following excerpt is from a modernized translation from H. W. Wells, published in 1935. The "four orders" refers to the monastic religious orders active at the time; a "peascod" is a pea pod.

Therefore I warn you rich, who are able in this world
On trust of your treasure to have triennials and pardons,
Be never the bolder to break the ten commandments;
And most of all you masters, mayors and judges,
Who have the wealth of this world, and are held wise by your neighbours,
You who purchase your pardons and papal charters:
At the dread doom, when the dead shall rise
And all come before Christ, and give full accounting,
When the doom will decide what day by day you practiced,
How you led your life and were lawful before him,
Though you have pocketfuls of pardons there or provincial letters,
Though you be found in the fraternity of all the four orders,
Though you have double indulgences—unless Do Well help you
I set your patents and your pardons at the worth of a peascod! . . .

The poor may plead and pray in the doorway;
They may quake for cold and thirst and hunger;
None receives them rightfully and relieves their suffering.
They are hooted at like hounds and ordered off. . . .

Lo, lords, lo, and ladies! witness
That the sweet liquor lasts but a little season,
Like peapods, and early pears, plums and cherries.
What lances up lightly lasts but a moment,
And what is readiest to ripen rots soonest.
A fat land full of dung breeds foul weeds rankly,

And so are surely all such bishops,
Earls and archdeacons and other rich clerics
Who traffic with tradesmen and turn on them if they are beaten,
And have the world at their will to live otherwise.
As weeds run wild on ooze or on the dunghill,
So riches spread upon riches give rise to all vices.
The best wheat is bent before ripening
On land that is overlaid with marle or the dungheap.
And so are surely all such people:
Overplenty feeds the pride which poverty conquers.

"Why should we be kept thus in serfdom?": From a Sermon by John Ball

Jean Froissart

In England, the Peasant Revolt of 1381—also called the Great Rising—was a manifestation of widespread discontent among the lower classes. Workers were particularly angered by a statute that had regulated wages and by the imposition of a burdensome new tax in 1377. One of the instigators of the rebellion was a preacher named John Ball, who was jailed several times for advocating social equality. One clergyman of the era, Henry Knighton, in his writings about the peasant rebellion described Ball as "too pleasing to the laity and extremely dangerous to the liberty of ecclesiastical law and order."

One of the acts that began the 1381 rebellion was a mob's successful effort to spring Ball from a jail in the town of Maidstone. The mob proceeded to London, where it stormed the Tower and killed the archbishop of Canterbury and other high officials. King Richard II agreed to meet the peasants' demands, but actually he was only buying time to regroup his forces and counterattack. The rebel leaders were all captured; Ball was hung and drawn and quartered.

The following account of one of Ball's sermons comes from a well-known French chronicler of medieval times, Jean Froissart.

OF THIS IMAGINATION was a foolish priest in the county of Kent called John Ball, who, for his foolish words, had been three times in the archbishop of Canterbury's prison; for this priest used oftentimes, on the Sundays after mass, when the people were going out of the minster, to go into the cloister and preach, and made the people to assemble about him, and would say thus, "Ah, ye good people, the matter goeth not well to pass in England, nor shall not do so till everything be common, and that there be no villains [serfs] nor gentlemen, but that we may be all united together, and that the lords be no greater masters than we be. What have we deserved, or why should we be kept thus in serfdom? We be all come from one father and one mother, Adam and Eve; whereby can they say or shew that they be greater lords than we be, saving by that they cause us to win and labor for what they dispend? They are clothed in velvet and camlet furred with grise, and we be vestured with poor cloth; they have their wines, spices, and good bread, and we have the drawing out of the chaff and drink water; they dwell in fair houses and we have the pain and travail, rain and wind in the fields; and by what cometh of our labors they keep and maintain their estates: we be called their bondmen, and without we do readily them service, we beaten; and we have no sovereign to whom we may complain, nor that will hear us and do us right. Let us go to the king,—he is young,—and shew him what serfage we be in, and shew him how we will have it otherwise, or else we will provide us with some remedy, either by fairness or otherwise." Thus John Ball said on Sundays, when the people issued out of the churches in the villages; wherefore many of the mean people loved him, and such as intended to no goodness said how he said truth; and so they would murmur one with another in the fields and in the ways as they went together, affirming how John Ball said truth.

The Book of the City of Ladies
Christine de Pizan

The Book of the City of Ladies, written in 1405 by Christine de Pizan, can be considered the pioneering work of feminist thought. De Pizan was born in Italy in 1364 and raised in the court of French king Charles V, whom her father served as a physician and astrologer. She took advantage of the royal archives to read ravenously, learning languages and studying classics, poetry, literature, and science. She married a court secretary at age fifteen and had three children, but her husband died during an epidemic, leaving her a widow at age twenty-four. She had difficulty recovering money from his estate and turned to writing to support her family—making her the first professional woman writer, by some accounts. Her works included poetry, novels, biography, short stories, and feminist polemics.

The misogynistic language in many writings of her time distressed de Pizan. She started a literary debate by challenging the view of women as evil seductresses in one highly popular epic poem of the day, *Romance of the Rose*. In doing so, she demonstrated that women could use rhetorical skills to engage in intellectual debate as well as men. She explored these themes at length in *The Book of the City of Ladies*, structured as a series of dialogues between herself and three wise women who appear to her in a vision: Lady Reason, Lady Rectitude, and Lady Justice. The three ladies answer de Pizan's questions about women's powers of thinking through historical accounts, and as they do so they help her construct the walls of a symbolic utopian city by and for women, from which they can defend themselves against the slanders of male writers.

In the excerpt here, from the opening chapters of the book, de Pizan laments being a woman, because—if male writers are to be believed—women are clearly inferior and serve only as vessels of evil. Her shame is merely a rhetorical device, as quickly becomes clear.

SUNK IN THESE UNHAPPY THOUGHTS, my head bowed as if in shame and my eyes full of tears, I sat slumped against the arm of my chair with my cheek resting on my hand. All of a sudden, I saw a beam of light, like the rays of the sun, shine down into my lap. Since it was too dark at that time of day for the sun to come into my study, I woke with a start as if from a deep sleep. I looked up to see where the light had come from and all at once saw before me three ladies, crowned and of majestic appearance, whose faces shone with a brightness that lit up me and everything else in the place. As you can imagine, I was full of amazement that they had managed to enter a room whose doors and windows were all closed. Terrified at the thought that it might be some kind of apparition come to tempt me, I quickly made the sign of the cross on my forehead.

With a smile on her face, the lady who stood at the front of the three addressed me first: "My dear daughter, don't be afraid, for we have not come to do you any harm, but rather, out of pity on your distress, we are here to comfort you. Our aim is to help you get rid of those misconceptions which have clouded your mind and made you reject what you know and believe in fact to be the truth just because so many other people have come out with the opposite opinion. You're acting like that fool in the joke who falls asleep in the mill and whose friends play a trick on him by dressing him up in women's clothing. When he wakes up, they manage to convince him that he is a woman despite all evidence to the contrary! My dear girl, what has happened to your sense? Have you forgotten that it is in the furnace that gold is refined, increasing in value the more it is beaten and fashioned into different shapes? Don't you know that it's the very finest things which are the subject of the most intense discussion? Now, if you turn your mind to the very highest realm of all, the realm of abstract ideas, think for a moment whether or not those philosophers whose views against women you've been citing have ever been proven wrong. In fact, they are all constantly correcting each other's opinions, as you yourself should know from reading Aristotle's *Metaphysics* where he discusses and refutes both their views and those of Plato and other philosophers. Don't forget the Doctors of the Church either, and Saint Augustine in particular, who all took issue with Aristotle himself on certain matters, even though he is considered to be the greatest of all authorities on both moral and natural philosophy. You seem to have accepted the philosophers' views as articles of faith and thus as irrefutable on every point.

"As for the poets you mention, you must realize that they sometimes wrote in the manner of fables which you have to take as saying the opposite of what they appear to say. You should therefore read such texts according to the grammatical rule of *antiphrasis*, which consists of interpreting something that is negative in a positive light, or vice versa. My advice to you is to read those passages where they criticize women in this way and to turn them to your advantage, no matter what the author's original intention was. . . .

"I neither can nor will retract anything": Speech Before the Diet of Worms

Martin Luther

Few acts of protest in history have been as far-reaching as Martin Luther posting his "Disputation on the Power and Efficacy of Indulgences," better known as the Ninety-Five Theses. Luther posted his declaration, which directly attacked abuses by the Roman Catholic Church, in various public places in the German city of Wittenberg in 1517. A priest and a professor at the University of Wittenberg, Luther was outspoken in his opposition to the church's practice of selling indulgences, which allowed people to buy purported release from punishment of their sins. (The sale of the indulgences was intended to fund work on St. Peter's Basilica.) Luther also mailed a copy of his thesis to the archbishop of Mainz with an accompanying letter in which he explained, "I have no longer been able to keep quiet about this matter, for it is by no gift of a bishop that man becomes sure of salvation."

Pope Leo X excommunicated Luther from the church in January 1521. In April that same year he was summoned by Charles V, the Holy Roman emperor, to a parliamentary council (or diet) in the German city of Worms to defend himself against charges of heresy. At the Diet of Worms, Luther gave this speech, an impassioned defense of his actions and a continued protest against the church. He explicitly rejected the authority of the pope as the highest law and insisted on the scripture as the source of religious law. He bluntly refused to recant the Ninety-Five Theses and other works. In May the emperor issued the Edict of Worms, branding Luther a heretic and banning his writings.

Luther's actions were the culmination of a long line of religious protest against the power of the Catholic Church. Many previous heretics, such as John Wycliffe in England, attracted followers. Others, such as Czech Jan Hus, had paid for their protest by being burned at the stake. In Luther's case, a sufficient groundswell of discontent, among both the masses and the ruling classes, made him so popular that the church didn't dare execute him. Moreover, the development of the printing press in Europe allowed people to rapidly disseminate Luther's ideas, and economic changes bode well for a shift in religious power. Although he was officially silenced, Luther's protest set in motion the radical break with the church that would become the Reformation.

MOST SERENE EMPEROR, and You Illustrious Princes and Gracious Lords:—I this day appear before you in all humility, according to your command, and I implore your majesty and your august highnesses, by the mercies of God, to listen with favour to the defence of a cause which I am well assured is just and right. I ask pardon, if by reason of my ignorance, I am wanting in the manners that befit a court; for I have not been brought up in kings' palaces, but in the seclusion of a cloister.

Two questions were yesterday put to me by his imperial majesty; the first, whether I was the author of the books whose titles were read; the second, whether I wished to revoke or defend the doctrine I have taught. I answered the first, and I adhere to that answer.

As to the second, I have composed writings on very different subjects. In some I have discussed Faith and Good Works, in a spirit at once so pure, clear, and Christian that even my adversaries themselves, far from finding anything to censure, confess that these writings are profitable, and deserve to be perused by devout persons. The pope's bull, violent as it is, acknowledges this. What, then, should I be doing if I were now to retract these writings? Wretched man! I alone, of all men living, should be abandoning truths approved by the unanimous voice of friends and enemies, and opposing doctrines that the whole world glories in confessing!

I have composed, secondly, certain works against popery, wherein I have attacked such as by false doctrines, irregular lives, and scandalous examples afflict the Christian world, and ruin the bodies and souls of men. And is not this confirmed by the grief of all who fear God? Is it not manifest that the laws and human doctrines of the popes entangle, vex, and distress the consciences of the faithful, while the crying and endless extortions of Rome engulf the property and wealth of Christendom, and more particularly of this illustrious nation?

If I were to revoke what I have written on that subject, what should I do . . . but strengthen this tyranny, and open a wider door to so many and flagrant impieties? Bearing down all resistance with fresh fury, we should behold these proud men swell, foam, and rage more than ever! And not merely would the yoke which now weighs down Christians be made more grinding by my retraction—it would thereby become, so to speak, lawful—for, by my retraction, it would receive confirmation from your most serene majesty, and all the States of the Empire. Great God! I should thus be like to an infamous cloak, used to hide and cover over every kind of malice and tyranny.

In the third and last place, I have written some books against private individuals, who had undertaken to defend the tyranny of Rome by destroying faith. I freely confess that I may have attacked such persons with more violence than was consistent with my profession as an ecclesiastic: I do not think of myself as a saint; but neither can I retract these books, because I should, by so doing, sanction the impieties of my opponents, and they would thence take occasion to crush God's people with still more cruelty.

Yet, as I am a mere man, and not God, I will defend myself after the example of Jesus Christ, who said, "If I have spoken evil, bear witness against me" (John xviii, 23). How much more should I, who am but dust and ashes, and so prone to error, desire that every one should bring forward what he can against my doctrine.

Therefore, most serene emperor, and you illustrious princes, and all, whether high or low, who hear me, I implore you by the mercies of God to prove to me by the writings of the prophets and apostles that I am in error. As soon as I shall be convinced, I will instantly retract all my errors, and will myself be the first to seize my writings and commit them to the flames. . . .

Since your most serene majesty and your high mightinesses require of me a simple, clear, and direct answer, I will give one, and it is this: I cannot submit my faith either to the pope or to the council, because it is as clear as noonday that they have fallen into error and even into glaring inconsistency with themselves. If, then, I am not convinced by proof from Holy Scripture, or by cogent reasons, if I am not satisfied by the very text I have cited, and if my judgment is not in this way brought into subjection to God's word, I neither can nor will retract anything; for it cannot be right for a Christian to speak against his conscience. I stand here and can say no more. God help me. Amen.

"To swear it was against my conscience"
Thomas More

Sir Thomas More waged a high-stakes protest against King Henry VIII at the inception of the English Reformation, going to his death rather than betray his religious beliefs and denying the authority of the pope. More was Henry's lord chancellor, one of the highest posts of the realm. For such a public figure to dissent from his king's opinion on such a significant matter was tantamount to signing his own death sentence, as it was intolerable to undermine the monarch, who was seen as ruling by divine right.

In 1527 King Henry began a campaign to dissolve his twenty-year marriage to Catherine of Aragon so he could wed Anne Boleyn and attempt to produce a male heir. When Pope Clement VII refused to annul the marriage, Henry denied his authority, and Parliament passed a series of acts to limit papal jurisdiction in England. More made his dissent public in 1530 by refusing to sign a letter to the pope seeking the annulment. He resigned as chancellor in 1532. The new archbishop of Canterbury supported the annulment, and when Boleyn was crowned in 1533, More refused to attend the coronation. The pope excommunicated Henry, severing the Church of England from the Catholic Church. When Henry and Anne's daughter, Elizabeth, was born, Parliament passed an act of succession declaring her heir to the throne and requiring British subjects, if commanded, to swear an oath supporting the king's supremacy. On April 13, 1534, More refused to swear such an oath. A few days later he was imprisoned in the Tower of London. At his trial in July 1535 More maintained that no man had the right to supersede the pope's authority on religious matters, since that authority had been handed down directly from Jesus through St. Peter.

More wrote this letter to his married daughter, Margaret Roper, a few days after his imprisonment. In the letter he recounts being called before the king's commissioners in the town of Lambeth, and their efforts to pressure him into swearing the loyalty oath. He was convicted of treason and beheaded on July 6, 1535. The Roman Catholic Church considered him a martyr and declared him a saint four centuries later, in 1935. In the 1960s, British playwright Robert Bolt told the story of More's dissent in his play *A Man for All Seasons*, which was later turned into a popular film.

WHEN I WAS BEFORE THE LORDS at Lambeth, I was the first that was called in, albeit Master Doctor the Vicar of Croydon was come before me, and divers others. After the cause of my sending for, declared unto me (whereof I somewhat marveled in my mind, considering that they sent for no more temporal men but me), I desired the sight of the oath, which they showed me under the great seal. Then desired I the sight of the Act of the Succession, which was delivered me in a printed roll. After which read secretly by myself, and the oath considered with the act, I showed unto them that my purpose was not to put any fault either in the act or any man that made it, or in the oath or any man that sware it, nor to condemn the conscience of any other man. But as for myself . . . to swear it was against my conscience.

Unto this my Lord Chancellor said that they all were sorry to hear me say thus, and see me thus refuse the oath. And they said all that on their faith I was the very first that ever refused it; which would cause the King's Highness to conceive great suspicion of me and great indignation toward me. And therewith they showed me the roll, and let me see the names of the lords and the commons which had sworn, and subscribed their names already. Which notwithstanding when they saw that I refused to swear the same myself, not blaming any other man that had sworn, I was in conclusion commanded to go down into the garden, and thereupon I tarried in the old burned chamber, that looketh into the garden and would not go down because of the heat. In that time saw I Master Doctor Latimer come into the garden, and there walked he with divers other doctors and chaplains of my Lord of Canterbury . . . I heard also that Master Vicar of Croydon, and all the remnant of the priests of London that were sent for, were sworn, and that they had such favor at the council's hand that they were not lingered nor made to dance any long attendance to their travail and cost, as suitors were sometimes wont to be, but were sped apace to their great comfort so far forth that Master Vicar of Croydon, either for gladness or for dryness, or else that it might be seen (*quod ille notus erat pontifici*) [because he was known to the pontiff] went to my Lord's buttery bar and called for drink, and drank (*valde familiariter*) [on very familiar terms].

When they had played their pageant and were gone out of the place, then was I called in again. And then was it declared unto me what a number had sworn, even since I went inside, gladly, without any sticking. Wherein I laid no blame in no man, but for my own self answered as before. Now as well before as then, they somewhat laid unto me for obstinacy, that where as before, sith I refused to swear, I would not declare any special part of that oath that grudged my conscience, and open the cause wherefore. For thereunto I had said to them, that I feared lest the King's Highness would as they said take displeasure enough toward me for the only refusal of the oath. And that if I should open and disclose the causes why, I should therewith but further exasperate his Highness, which I would in no wise do, but rather would I abide all the danger and harm that might come toward me, than give his Highness any occasion of further displeasure than the offering of the oath unto me of pure necessity constrained me. . . .

My Lord of Canterbury taking hold upon that that I said, that I condemned not the conscience of them that sware, said unto me that it appeared well that I did not take it for a very sure thing and a certain that I might not lawfully swear it, but rather as a thing uncertain and doubtful. But then (said my Lord) you know for a certainty and a thing without doubt that you be bounden to obey your sovereign lord your King. And therefore are ye bounden to leave off the doubt of your un-sure conscience in refusing the oath, and take the sure way in obeying of your prince, and swear it. Now all was it so that in mine own mind methought myself not concluded, yet this argument seemed to me suddenly so subtle and namely with such authority coming out of so noble a prelate's mouth, that I could again answer nothing thereto but only that I thought myself I might not well do so, because that in my conscience this was one of the cases in which I was bounden that I should not obey my prince, sith that whatsoever other folk thought in the matter (whose conscience and learning I would not condemn nor take upon me to judge), yet in my conscience the truth seemed on the other side.

PART II
DOCUMENTS OF DISSENT
CIVIL RIGHTS
NATIONAL SELF-DETERMINATION
ECONOMIC JUSTICE
ENVIRONMENTAL CONSERVATION
RELIGIOUS FREEDOM
PEACE AND WAR
INTERNATIONAL POLITICAL FREEDOMS

CHAPTER 4
CIVIL RIGHTS

INTRODUCTION

The United States' Declaration of Independence described each citizen's political rights in a democratic society by saying that all men are created equal and that they had certain inalienable rights, including life, liberty, and the pursuit of happiness. These are beautiful words, but many of the men who signed the declaration owned slaves, and none of their wives were allowed to vote.

This chapter explores some of the history of those in the United States—including Native Americans, African Americans, immigrants, women, homosexuals, and other minority groups—who have used protest to obtain and define their portion of the equal rights promised by the country's founders. These groups battled to gain and keep their rights, often incorporating words from the Declaration of Independence into the heart of their protests. They had to fight—and often die—for their rights.

For example, the struggle to emancipate African Americans from slavery required a civil war in which more than 500,000 men were killed. The thirteenth, fourteenth, and fifteenth amendments to the Constitution embedded the rights of black men in official policy, but there is almost nothing equal about the ways blacks in the United States have been treated compared to well-established citizens of European descent.

In 1776, Abigail Adams famously asked her husband John, one of the founding fathers, to consider including women more fully in the new government that emerged from the American Revolution. But it was more than 140 years before the United States allowed women to vote in national elections.

From a governing perspective, the maintenance of individual rights can be a pesky matter. It often seems easier for a governing authority to brush over disagreement and to squelch dissenting views. Political leaders in the United States have often yielded to the temptation to imprison people who disagree with their decisions, especially in times of war. But along with the U.S. civil rights comes the responsibility to exercise those rights, including the right to protest when that very right to dissent may be unjustly restricted.

"We are against this traffic of men"

Resolutions of Germantown Mennonites

The first black Africans brought to a British colony in North America arrived in Jamestown in 1619. Initially, blacks had a status similar to that of white indentured servants and were able to gain emancipation after a period of work.

In most cases, whites preferred white laborers. Gradually, however, the desperate need for workers led white settlers to subjugate native populations and black Africans as permanent slaves. Throughout the second half of the seventeenth century, the bondage of Africans became part of most colonies' civil and criminal law.

Despite the hypocrisy, obvious to us today, of white settlers coming to America for freedom and then enslaving others, few protested. Quakers and Mennonites, however, who were largely outcasts of the more mainstream colonists, did object.

On February 18, 1688, Mennonites in Germantown, Pennsylvania, issued the first formal protest against slavery in British North America at the colony's monthly meeting, held February 18, 1688, at the home of Richard Worrell.

THESE ARE THE REASONS why we are against the traffic of men-body, as followeth: Is there any that would be done or handled at this manner? Viz., to be sold or made a slave for all the time of his life? How fearful and faint-hearted are many at sea, when they see a strange vessel, being afraid it should be a Turk, and they should be taken, and sold for slaves into Turkey. Now, what is this better done, than Turks do? Yea, rather it is worse for them, which say they are Christians; for we hear that the most part of such negers are brought hither against their will and consent, and that many of them are stolen. Now, though they are black, we cannot conceive there is more liberty to have them slaves, as it is to have other white ones. There is a saying, that we should do to all men like as we will be done ourselves; making no difference of what generation, descent, or colour they are. And those who steal or rob men, and those who buy or purchase them, are they not all alike? Here is liberty of conscience, which is right and reasonable; here ought to be likewise liberty of the body, except of evildoers, which is another case. But to bring men hither, or to roll and sell them against their will, we stand against. In Europe there are many oppressed for conscience-sake; and here there are those oppressed which are of a black colour. And we who know that men must not commit adultery—some do commit adultery in others, separating wives from their husbands, and giving them to others: and some sell the children of these poor creatures to other men. Ah! Do consider well this thing, you who do it, if you would be done at this manner—and if it is done according to Christianity! You surpass Holland and Germany in this thing. This makes an ill report in all those countries of Europe, where they hear of [it], that the Quakers do here handel men as they handel there the cattle. And for that reason some have no mind or inclination to come hither. . . .

If once these slaves (which they say are so wicked and stubborn men), should join themselves—fight for their freedom, and handel their masters and mistresses, as they did handel them before; will these masters and mistresses take the sword at hand and war against those poor slaves, like, as we are able to believe, some will not refuse to do? Or, have these poor negers not as much right to fight for their freedom, as you have to keep them slaves?

Now consider well this thing, if it is good or bad. And in case you find it to be good to handel these blacks in that manner, we desire and require you hereby lovingly, that you may inform us herein, which at this time never was done, viz., that Christians have such liberty to do so. To the end we shall be satisfied on this point, and satisfy likewise our good friends and acquaintances in our native country, to whom it is a terror, or fearful thing, that men should be handled so in Pennsylvania.

This is from our meeting at Germantown held the 18th of the 2d month, 1688, delivered to the monthly meeting at Richard Worrell's.

"Opposing arbitrary power"
John Peter Zenger

In the early part of the eighteenth century, John Peter Zenger started a newspaper, the *New-York Weekly Journal*, in opposition to New York governor William Cosby. In 1734, Zenger was arrested and placed in jail for publishing statements criticizing Cosby, such as, "We see men's deeds destroyed, judges arbitrarily displaced, new courts erected, without consent of the legislature, by which it seems to me, trials by jury are taken away when a governor pleases."

Zenger's wife and servants continued to publish the newspaper while he was in jail, often receiving instructions from him through a hole in his prison door.

The first lawyers who tried to defend Zenger were disbarred. Zenger then secretly engaged Andrew Hamilton, the most prominent lawyer in British North America, to defend him against charges of libel, and Hamilton surprised the justices when he walked into the courtroom the first time.

On August 4, 1735, Hamilton asked the jury to ignore the colony's libel law and instead embrace the greater principle of freedom of expression. As Zenger's description of the case, excerpted here, reflects, the jury agreed with Hamilton's appeal, setting the legal foundation for free speech in the United States.

The chief justice, James De Lancey, was appointed by the governor. The attorney general was Richard Bradley.

ATTORNEY GENERAL BRADLEY: . . . The case before the Court is, whether Mr. Zenger is guilty of libeling his Excellency the Governor of New York, and indeed the whole Administration of the Government. Mr. Hamilton has confessed the printing and publishing, and I think nothing is plainer, than that the words in the information are scandalous, and tend to sedition, and to disquiet the minds of the people of this province. And if such papers are not libels, I think it may be said, there can be no such thing as a libel.

MR. HAMILTON: May it please your Honor; I cannot agree with Mr. Attorney. For tho' I freely acknowledge, that there are such things as libels, yet I must insist at the same time, that what my client is charged with, is not a libel; and I observed just now, that Mr. Attorney in defining a libel, made use of the words *scandalous, seditious,* and *tend to disquiet the people;* but (whether with design or not I will not say) he omitted the word "false." . . .

MR. CHIEF JUSTICE: You cannot be admitted, Mr. Hamilton, to give the truth of a libel in evidence. A libel is not to be justified; for it is nevertheless a libel that is true.

MR. HAMILTON: I am sorry the Court has so soon resolved upon that piece of law; I expected first to have been heard to that point. I have not in all my reading met with an authority that says we cannot be admitted to give the truth in evidence, upon an information for a libel.

MR. CHIEF JUSTICE: The law is clear, That you cannot justify a libel. . . .

MR. HAMILTON: I thank your Honor. Then, gentlemen of the jury, it is to you we must now appeal, for witnesses, to the truth of the facts we have offered, and are denied the liberty to prove; and let it not seem strange that I apply my self to you in this manner, I am warranted so to do both by law and reason. The last supposes you to be summoned, out of the neighbourhood where the fact is alleged to be committed; and the reason of your being taken out of the neighbourhood is, because you are supposed to have the best knowledge of the fact that is to be tried. And were you to find a verdict against my client, you must take upon you to say, the papers referred to in the information, and which we acknowledge we printed and published, are false, scandalous and seditious; but of this I can have no apprehension. You are citizens of New-York; you are really what the law supposes you to be, honest and lawful men; and, according to my brief, the facts which we offer to prove were not committed in a corner; they are notoriously known to be true; and therefore in your justice lies our safety. And as we are denied the liberty of giving evidence, to prove the truth of what we have published, I will beg leave to lay it down as a standing rule in such cases, that the suppressing of evidence ought always to be taken for the strongest evidence; and I hope it will have that weight with you. . . .

It is true in times past it was a crime to speak truth, and in that terrible Court of Star-Chamber, many worthy and brave men suffered for so doing; and yet even in that court, and in those bad times, a great and good man dared to say, what I hope will not be taken amiss of me to say in this place, to wit, the practice of informations for libels is a sword in the hands of a wicked King, and an arrant coward to cut down and destroy the innocent; the one cannot, because of his high station, and the other dares not, because of his want of courage, revenge himself in another manner.

ATTORNEY GENERAL BRADLEY: Pray, Mr. Hamilton, have a care what you say, don't go too far neither, I don't like those liberties.

MR. HAMILTON: I hope to be pardon'd, Sir, for my zeal upon this occasion: It is an old and wise caution, that when our neighbor's house is on fire, we ought to take care of our own. For tho', blessed by God, I live in a government where liberty is well understood, and freely enjoy'd; yet experience has shown us all (I'm sure it has to me) that a bad precedent in one government, is soon set up for an authority in another; and therefore I cannot but think it mine, and every honest man's duty, that (while we pay all due obedience to men in authority) we ought at the same time to be upon our guard against power, wherever we apprehend that it may affect ourselves or our fellow-subjects. . . .

I should think it my duty, if required, to go to the utmost part of the land, where my service could be of any use in assisting to quench the flame of prosecutions upon informations, set on foot by the government, to deprive a people of the right of remonstrating (and complaining too) of the arbitrary attempts of men in power. Men who injure and oppress the people under their administration provoke them to cry out and complain; and then make that very complaint the foundation for new oppressions and prosecutions. I wish I could say there were no instances of this kind. But to conclude; the question before the court and you, gentlemen of the jury, is not of small nor private concern, it is not the cause of a poor printer, nor of New-York alone, which you are now trying; No! It may in its consequence, affect every freeman that lives under a British government on the main of America. It is the best cause. It is the cause of liberty; and I make no doubt but your upright conduct, this day, will not only entitle you to the love and esteem of your fellow-citizens; but every man, who prefers freedom to a life of slavery, will bless and honour you, as men who have baffled the attempt of tyranny; and by an impartial and uncorrupt verdict, have laid a noble foundation for securing to ourselves, our posterity, and our neighbours, that to which nature and the laws of our country have given us a right—the liberty—both of exposing and opposing arbitrary power (in these parts of the world, at least) by speaking and writing the truth. . . .

MR. CHIEF JUSTICE: Gentlemen of the jury. The great pains Mr. Hamilton has taken, to show how little regard juries are to pay to the opinion of the judges; and his insisting so much upon the conduct of some judges in trials of this kind; is done, no doubt, with a design that you should take but very little notice of what I may say upon this occasion. I shall therefore only observe to you that, as the facts or words in the information are confessed: the only thing that can come in question before you is, whether the words, as set forth in the information, make a libel. And that is a matter of law, no doubt, and which you may leave to the court. . . .

The Jury withdrew, and in a small time returned, and being asked by the clerk, whether they were agreed of their verdict, and whether John Peter Zenger was guilty of printing and publishing the libels in the information mentioned? They answered by Thomas Bunt, their Foreman, Not Guilty. Upon which there were three Huzzas in the hall which was crowded with people, and the next day I was discharged from my imprisonment.

"I cannot say it without tears"
Fray Carlos José Delgado

By the early eighteenth century, Spanish colonists in Mexico established a significant presence in what is now the southwestern United States. The oppression of native populations by colonists from European countries was commonplace. Rare was the voice of opposition, even from religious authorities. When British colonists massacred hundreds of Native Americans on the Mystic River in 1637, ministers praised the event as a glorification of God.

The Spanish had mercantile and religious concerns in the New World. In addition to seeking gold and promoting commerce, the Catholic nation wanted to convert Native Americans to Christianity.

Conflicts, however, often emerged over these two goals. In this excerpted 1750 letter, Fray Carlos José Delgado protested to his superiors in Spain the cruel treatment of Native Americans by civil and religious authorities in what is now New Mexico.

VERY REVEREND FATHER and our Minister Provincial: I, Fray Carlos José Delgado, preacher general, commissary, notary and censor of the Holy Office, apostolic notary, and missionary in the custodian of the conversion of San Pablo of this province of El Santo Evangelio in the kingdom of New Mexico, appear before your reverence only for the purpose of lamenting before your paternal love the grave extortions that we, the ministers of these missions, are suffering, at the hands of the governors and *alcaldes* of that kingdom. I declare, that of the eleven governors and many *alcaldes mayores* whom I have known in the long period of forty years that I have served at the mission called San Augustin de la Isleta, most of them have hated, and do hate to death, and insult and persecute the missionary religious, causing them all the troubles and annoyances that their passion dictates, without any other reason or fault than the opposition of the religious to the very serious injustices which the said governors and *alcaldes* inflict upon the helpless Indians recently received into the faith, so that the said converts shall not forsake our holy law and flee to the heathen, to take up anew their former idolatries. This is experienced every day, not without grave sorrow and heartfelt tears on the part of those evangelical sowers, who, on seeing that their work is wasted and that the fecund seed of their preaching to those souls is lost and bears no fruit, cry out to heaven and sorrowfully ask a remedy for this great evil. In order that your reverence's exalted understanding may regard as just the reasons which support the said missionaries in their opposition to the aforesaid extortions, even though it should be at the cost of their lives, and also in order that you may come to their aid with the measures best fitted for the total abolition of the said injuries and injustices, I shall specify them in the following manner:

The first annoyance with which the persons mentioned molest the Indians is to send agents every year (contrary to the royal ordinances, and especially to a decree of the most excellent senior, Don Francisco Fernández de la Cueva Henríquez, Duke of Albuquerque, and viceroy of New Spain, issued in this City of Mexico on May 18, 1709, whose content I present, the original being kept in the archive of the *custodia* mentioned) at the time of the harvest, to all the pueblos of the kingdom, under the pretext of buying maize for the support of their households, though most of it is really to be sold in the nearest villages. The said agents take from all the pueblos and missions eight hundred or a thousand *fanegas*, and compel the Indians to transport them to the place where the governor lives. Besides not paying them anything for the said transportation, they do not pay them for the maize at once, and when the date arrives which they have designated for the payment, if the maize is worth two pesos a fanega they give them only one. Even this amount is not in coin or in any article that can be useful to the Indian, but in baubles, such as *chuchumates*, which are glass beads, ill-made knives, relics, awls, and a few handfuls of common tobacco, the value of which does not amount even to a tenth part of what the maize is worth which they extract from them by force, and this even though as has been said, they pay them only half the proper price that is charged throughout the kingdom. From this manifest injustice two very serious evils result: first, the unhappy Indians are left without anything to eat for the greater part of the year; and second, in order not to perish of hunger they are forced to go to the mountains and hunt for game or to serve on the ranches or farms for their food alone, leaving the missions abandoned.

The second oppression that the Indians frequently suffer at the hands of the governors is being compelled arbitrarily and by force, for the small price of an awl or other similar trifle, to work on the buildings that they need, whatever they may be and whether they require little or much time. The Indians also are required to drive cattle as far as the villa of Chihuahua which is more than two hundred leagues distant from the place where the governors live. They receive in payment for this service only a little ground corn, which they call *pinole*, and the Indian cattle drivers are compelled to pay for those [animals] that are lost or die for want of care or by any other accident. A pernicious evil arises from this cattle driving, for the Indians must abandon their families and leave their lands uncultivated, and, as a consequence, be dying of hunger during the greater part of the year.

The third oppression, and the most grievous and pernicious, from which originate innumerable evils and sins against God, and manifest injuries against the missionaries and Indians, is the wicked dissimulation of the governors in regard to the acts of the *alcaldes mayores*, for it is publicly known throughout the realm that when they give them their *varas*, or wands of office, they tell and advise them to make the Indians work without pity.

With such express license, your reverence can imagine how many disturbances will be caused by men who usually take the employment of *alcaldes mayores*, solely for the purpose of advancing their own interests and acquiring property with which to make presents to the governors, so that the latter will countenance their unjust proceedings, even though they be denounced before them, and perhaps will even promote them in office. Every year they make the Indians weave four hundred blankets, or as many woolen sheets; they take from all the pueblos squads of thirty or forty Indians and work them the greater part of the year in planting maize and wheat, which they care for until it is placed in the granaries; they send them among the heathen Indians to trade indigo, knives, tobacco, and *chuchumates*, for cattle and for deer hides. Not even the women are exempt from this tyranny, for if the officials cannot make use of their work in any other way they compel them to spin almost all the wool needed for the said sheets and blankets. And the most lamentable thing about all this is that they recompense them for these tasks with only a handful of tobacco, which is divided among eighteen or twenty.

The most grievous thing for the heathen Indians is that the *alcaldes* and even some of the governors, mix with their wives and daughters, often violating them, and this so openly that with a very little effort the violation of their consorts comes to the knowledge of the husbands, and as a result it often happens that they repudiate their wives and will not receive them until the missionary fathers labor to persuade them. The shameless way in which the officials conduct themselves in this particular is proved by an occasion when a certain governor was in conversation with some missionaries, and an Indian woman came into their presence to charge him with the rape of her daughter, and he, without changing countenance, ordered that she be paid by merely giving her a buffalo skin that he had at hand.

Yet all that I have hitherto related does not drive the Indians to the limits of desperation or cause them to fall away from our holy faith so much as when the said *alcaldes* compel them to deliver to them a quantity of deer skins, lard, sheaves [of grain], chickens, and other things that their desires dictate, saying that they are for the governors, who ask for them. The Indian has to submit to this injustice, for they either take it from him without asking, or, if he does not have what the *alcaldes* ask for or does not give it promptly enough when he has it, he suffers either spoliation or punishment.

These punishments are so cruel and inhuman that sometimes for a slight offense, sometimes because the Indian resists the outrages that they inflict upon him, or sometimes because they are slow in doing what the *alcaldes* order, they are put in jail for many days, are confined in the stocks, or—and I cannot say it without tears—the officials flog them so pitilessly that, their wrath not being appeased by seeing them shed their blood, they inflict such deep scars upon them that they remain for many years. It is a proof of this second point that when I went among the heathens to reduce the apostates there were among them some who, with an aggrieved air, showed me their scars, thus giving me to understand that the reason why they fled and did not return to the pale of the church was their fear of these cruel punishments.

"The late rising of the people"
Daniel Gray

In the wake of the American Revolution, many citizens in the new nation felt their state governments embraced policies similar to those of the oppressive British government they had just rejected. They complained of unfair taxes and the arbitrary enforcement of laws. Compounding these injustices was the fact that for their military service, former soldiers were issued paper currency that many businesses and state governments would not accept.

Residents in western regions, in particular, suffered from policies adopted by governments along the coast, where there was easier access to currency from trade through shipping.

In western Massachusetts, former soldiers and farmers rebelled against the state government when courts started to foreclose on their farms for nonpayment of taxes. Led by a former officer in the American Revolution, Shays's Rebellion highlighted fears throughout the United States that the newborn country was not strong enough to hold together. Leading politicians from the Revolution were alarmed enough to call for a national convention in Philadelphia to write a new Constitution, which would later include a Bill of Rights to protect citizens from some of the arbitrary abuses of power that lead to Shays's Rebellion.

Here, one of the leaders of the rebellion, Daniel Gray, outlined the reasons for the revolt to an audience in Hampshire County. The rebellion was put down by the state militia in a couple of small skirmishes. Two years later all participants had been pardoned and most of the complaints had been resolved.

GENTLEMEN, We have thought proper to inform you of some of the principal causes of the late risings of the people, and also of their present movement, viz.

1st. The present expensive mode of collecting debts, which by reason of the great scarcity of cash, will of necessity fill our gaols with unhappy debtors; and thereby a reputable body of people rendered incapable of being serviceable either to themselves or the community.

2nd. The monies raised by impost and excise being appropriated to discharge the interest of governmental securities, and not the foreign debt, when these securities are not subject to taxation.

3rd. A suspension of the writ of Habeus Corpus, by which those persons who have stepped forth to assert and maintain the rights of the people, are liable to be taken and conveyed even to the most distant part of the Commonwealth, and thereby subjected to an unjust punishment.

4th. The unlimited power granted to Justices of the Peace and Sheriffs, Deputy Sheriffs, and Constables, by the Riot Act, indemnifying them to prosecution thereof; when perhaps, wholly actuated from a principle of revenge, hatred, and envy.

Furthermore, Be assured, that this body, now at arms, despise the idea of being instigated by British emissaries, which is so strenuously propagated by the enemies of our liberties. And also wish the most proper and speedy measures may be taken, to discharge both our foreign and domestic debt.

"The same power which protects the white man, should protect the black"
James Forten

James Forten was a veteran of the American Revolution and one of the wealthiest men in Philadelphia when he wrote this pamphlet in 1813. He was also a free black man who strongly advocated for the rights of African Americans.

At the time, Pennsylvania was one of the most progressive states in the Union, and it had the most active abolitionist group in the country, the Pennsylvania Abolition Society.

It was the first state to pass a gradual abolition law in 1780, freeing the seven thousand black slaves who lived in Pennsylvania, the state where the Declaration of Independence was written. Nevertheless, when the state became a destination for former black slaves, there was a white backlash. In response, the state government attempted to pass a law saying that new black emigrants to Pennsylvania must register with local officials.

Forten wrote a pamphlet, excerpted here, blasting the attempts to restrict the rights of black Americans and pointing out the law's double standard: it applied to blacks but not whites. The law did not pass.

THOSE PATRIOTIC CITIZENS, who, after resting from the toils of an arduous war, which achieved our independence and laid the foundation of the only reasonable Republic upon earth, associated together, and for the protection of those inestimatable rights for the establishments of which they had exhausted their blood and treasure, framed the Constitution of Pennsylvania, have by the ninth article declared, "that all men are born equally free and independent, and have certain inherent and indefeasible rights, among which are those of enjoying life and liberty." Under the restraint of wise and well administered laws, we cordially united in the above glorious sentiment, but by the bill upon which we have been remarking, it appears as if the committee who drew it up mistook the sentiment expressed in this article, and do not consider us as men, or that those enlightened statesmen who formed the constitution upon the basis of experience intended to exclude us from its blessings and protection. If the former, why are we not to be considered as men. Has the God who made the white man and the black, left any record declaring us a different species. Are we not sustained by the same power, supported by the same food, hurt by the same wounds, pleased with the same delights, and propagated by the same means. And should we not enjoy the same liberty, and be protected by the same laws. We would wish not to legislate, for our means of information and the acquisition of knowledge are, in the nature of things, so circumscribed, that we must consider ourselves incompetent to the task: but let us, in legislation be considered men. . . .

It seems almost incredible that the advocates of liberty, should conceive the idea of selling a fellow creature to slavery. It is like the heroes of "Vive la Republic," while the decapitated Nun was precipitate into the general reservoir of death, and the palpitating embryo decorated the point of the bayonet. Ye, who should be our protectors, do not destroy. We will cheerfully submit to the laws, and aid in bringing offenders against them of every colour to justice; but do not let the laws operate so severely, so degradingly, so unjustly against us alone.

Let us put a case, in which the law in question operates peculiarly hard and unjust. I have a brother, perhaps, who, resides in a distant part of the Union, and after a separation of years, actuated by the same fraternal affection which beats in the bosom of a white man, he comes to visit me. Unless that brother be registered in twenty four hours after, and be able to produce a certificate to that effect, he is liable, according to the second and third sections of the bill, to a fine of twenty dollars, to arrest, imprisonment and sale. Let the unprejudiced mind ponder upon this, and then pronounce it to the justifiable act of a free people, if he can. To this we trust our cause, without fear of the issue. The unprejudiced must pronounce any act tending to deprive a free man of his right, freedom and immunities, as not only cruel in the extreme, but decidedly unconstitutional both as regards the letter and spirit of that glorious instrument. The same power which protects the white man, should protect the black.

Memorial of the Cherokee Indians
Cherokee Nation

The Cherokee Indians were one of the tribes most successful at adapting to the European colonization of North America. They embraced many of the laws and practices of the settlers, creating communities that mimicked the white communities around them. As more whites sought opportunities for westward development, however, the state of Georgia, which had signed treaties with the federal government, and treated the tribe as tenants of the state, refused to recognize the sovereign status of the Cherokees. President Andrew Jackson, who was elected in part on his reputation as an Indian fighter, joined Georgia in this view. Jackson strongly favored forcibly relocating Indian tribes westward.

In December 1829, the Cherokee leadership wrote a petition to Congress seeking its assistance. Known as the "Memorial of the Cherokee Nation," this appeal, and several subsequent ones, failed. The Cherokee Indians were removed from their homes and forced to march to arid lands in Oklahoma. About one fourth of the Cherokee population died in the forced march, which would become known as the Trail of Tears.

TO THE HONORABLE SENATE and house of representatives of the United States of America, in congress assembled:

The undersigned memorialists, humbly make known to your honorable bodies, that they are free citizens of the Cherokee nation. Circumstances of late occurrence have troubled our hearts, and induced us at this time to appeal to you, knowing that you are generous and just. As weak and poor children are accustomed to look to their guardians and patrons for protection, so we would come and make our grievances known. Will you listen to us? Will you have pity on us? You are great and renowned—the nation, which you represent, is like a mighty man who stands in his strength. But we are small—our name is not renowned. You are wealthy, and have need of nothing; but we are poor in life, and have not the arm and power of the rich.

By the will of our Father in heaven, the governor of the whole world, the red man of America has become small, and the white man great and renowned. When the ancestors of the people of these United States first came to the shores of America, they found the red man strong—though he was ignorant and savage, yet he received them kindly, and gave them dry land to rest their weary feet. They met in peace, and shook hands in token of friendship. Whatever the white man wanted and asked of the Indian, the latter willingly gave. At that time the Indian was the lord, and the white man the suppliant. But now the scene has changed. The strength of the red man has become weakness. As his neighbors increased in numbers, his power became less, and now, of the many and powerful tribes who once covered these United States, only a few are to be seen—a few whom a sweeping pestilence has left. The northern tribes, who were once so numerous and powerful are now nearly extinct. Thus it has happened to the red man of America. Shall we, who are remnants, share the same fate?

Brothers—we address you according to usage adopted by our forefathers, and the great and good men who have successfully directed the councils of the nation you represent—we now make known to you our grievances. We are troubled by some of your own people. Our neighbor, the state of Georgia, is pressing hard upon us, and urging us to relinquish our possessions for her benefit. We are told, if we do not leave the country, which we dearly love, and betake ourselves to the western wilds, the laws of the state will be extended over us, and the time, 1st of June, 1830, is appointed for the execution of the edict. When we first heard of this we were grieved and appealed to our father, the president, and begged that protection might be extended over us. But we were doubly grieved when we understood, from a letter of the secretary of war to our delegation, dated March of the present year, that our father the president had refused us protection, and that he had decided in favor of the extension of the laws of the state over us.—This decision induces us to appeal to the immediate representatives of the American people. We love, we dearly love our country, and it is due to your honorable bodies, as well as to us, to make known why we think the country is ours, and why we wish to remain in peace where we are. The land on which we stand, we have received as an inheritance from our fathers, who possessed it from time immemorial, as a gift from our common father in heaven. We have already said, that when the white man came to the shores of America, our ancestors were found in peaceable possession of this very land. They bequeathed it to us as their children, and we have sacredly kept it as containing the remains of our beloved men. This right of inheritance we have *never ceded,* nor ever *forfeited.* Permit us to ask, what better right can a people have to a country, than the right of *inheritance* and *immemorial peaceable possession?* We know it is said of late by the state of Georgia, and by the executive of the United States, that we have forfeited this right—but we think this is said gratuitously. At what time have we made the forfeit? What crimes have we committed, whereby we must forever be divested of our country and rights? Was it when we were hostile to the United States, and took part with the king of Great Britain, during the struggle for independence? If so, why was not this forfeiture declared in the first treaty of peace between the United States and our beloved men? Why was not such an article as the following inserted in the treaty: "The United States gives peace to the Cherokees, but, for the part they took in the late war, declare them to be but tenants at our will, to be removed when the convenience of the states within whose chartered limits they live shall require it." This was the proper time to assume such a position. But it was not thought of, nor would our forefathers have agreed to any treaty, whose tendency was to deprive them of their rights and their country. All that they have conceded and relinquished are inserted in the treaties open to the investigation of all people. We would repeat, then, the right of inheritance and peaceable possession which we claim, we have never ceded nor forfeited. . . .

In view of the strong ground upon which their rights are founded, your memorialists solemnly protest against being considered as tenants at will, or as mere occupants of the soil, without possessing the sovereignty. We have already stated to your honorable bodies, that our forefathers were found in possession of this soil in full sovereignty, by the first European settlers; and as we have never ceded nor forfeited the occupancy of the soil and the sovereignty over it, do so solemnly protest against being forced to leave it, either by direct or by indirect measures. To the land of which we are now in possession we are attached—it is our fathers' gift—it contains their ashes—it is the land of our nativity, and the land of our intellectual birth. We cannot consent to abandon it, for another far inferior, and which holds out to us no inducements. We do moreover protest against the arbitrary measures of our neighbor, the state of Georgia, in her attempt to extend her laws over us, in surveying our lands without our consent and in direct opposition to treaties and the intercourse law of the United States, and interfering with our municipal regulations in such a manner as to derange the regular operations of our own laws. To deliver and protect them from all these and every encroachment upon their rights, the undersigned memorialists do most earnestly pray your honorable bodies. Their existence and future happiness are at stake—divest them of their liberty and country, and you sink them in degradation, and put a check, if not a final stop, to their present progress in the arts of civilized life, and in the knowledge of the Christian religion. Your memorialists humbly conceive, that such an act would be in the highest degree oppressive. From the people of these United States, who perhaps, of all men under heaven, are the most religious and free, it cannot be expected.—Your memorialists, therefore, cannot anticipate such a result. You represent a virtuous, intelligent and Christian nation. To you they willingly submit their cause for your righteous decision.

"I will be heard"
William Lloyd Garrison

William Lloyd Garrison was one of the leading abolitionists and social reformers of the mid-nineteenth century. He started writing for his hometown newspaper in Massachusetts as a teenager under the pseudonym Aristides, in reference to the Athenian statesman known as The Just. As a young adult he joined the abolitionist movement and moved to Baltimore to edit a newspaper. Garrison quickly established a reputation for his strong opposition to slavery. He published a regular column entitled the "Black List" describing hardships inflicted on slaves. In one column he revealed the name of a Massachusetts merchant involved in the slave trade; as a result the state of Maryland, which allowed slavery, filed criminal charges against him. Garrison was convicted and received a six-month jail sentence. He was in jail seven weeks, until a wealthy supporter paid a fine to allow for his release.

Garrison returned to Massachusetts in 1821 to start publishing *The Liberator*, a weekly newspaper dedicated to ending slavery. He later supported other reform movements, such as the right of women to vote, Prohibition, and the humane treatment of Native Americans. In 1833, he helped found the American Anti-Slavery Society, incensing Southern opinion. The state of Georgia offered a five-thousand-dollar reward for his arrest and conviction. Garrison, however, remained true to the opening statement in his inaugural issue of *The Liberator*, excerpted here, and never relented in his criticisms of slavery.

DURING MY RECENT TOUR for the purpose of exciting the minds of the people by a series of discourses on the subject of slavery, every place that I visited gave fresh evidence of the fact, that a greater revolution in public sentiment was to be effected in the free states—and particularly in New England—than at the south. I found contempt more bitter, opposition more active, detraction more relentless, prejudice more stubborn, and apathy more frozen, than among slave owners themselves. Of course, there were individual exceptions to the contrary. This state of things afflicted, but did not dishearten me. I determined, at every hazard, to lift up the standard of emancipation in the eyes of the nation, within sight of Bunker Hill and in the birth place of liberty. That standard is now unfurled; and long may it float, unhurt by the spoliations of time or the missiles of a desperate foe—yea, till every chain be broken, and every bondman set free! Let southern oppressors tremble—let their secret abettors tremble—let their northern apologists tremble—let all the enemies of the persecuted blacks tremble.

I deem the publication of my original Prospectus unnecessary, as it has obtained a wide circulation. The principles therein inculcated will be steadily pursued in this paper, excepting that I shall not array myself as the political partisan of any man. In defending the great cause of human rights, I wish to derive the assistance of all religions and of all parties.

Assenting to the "self-evident truth" maintained in the American Declaration of Independence, "that all men are created equal, and endowed by their Creator with certain inalienable rights—among which are life, liberty and the pursuit of happiness," I shall strenuously contend for the immediate enfranchisement of our slave population. In Park-street Church, on the Fourth of July, 1829, in an address on slavery, I unreflectingly assented to the popular but pernicious doctrine of gradual abolition. I seize this opportunity to make a full and unequivocal recantation, and thus publicly to ask pardon of my God, of my country, and of my brethren the poor slaves, for having uttered a sentiment so full of timidity, injustice and absurdity. A similar recantation, from my pen, was published in the Genius of Universal Emancipation at Baltimore, in September, 1829. My conscience is now satisfied.

I am aware, that many object to the severity of my language; but is there not cause for severity? I will be as harsh as truth, and as uncompromising as justice. On this subject, I do not wish to think, or speak, or write, with moderation. No! no! Tell a man whose house is on fire, to give a moderate alarm; tell him to moderately rescue his wife from the hands of the ravisher; tell the mother to gradually extricate her babe from the fire into which it has fallen—but urge me not to use moderation in a cause like the present. I am in earnest—I will not equivocate—I will not excuse—I will not retreat a single inch—AND I WILL BE HEARD. The apathy of the people is enough to make every statue leap from its pedestal, and to hasten the resurrection of the dead.

It is pretended, that I am retarding the cause of emancipation by the coarseness of my invective, and the precipitancy of my measures. The charge is not true. On this question my influence—humble as it is—is felt at this moment to a considerable extent, and shall be felt in coming years—not perniciously, but beneficially—not as a curse, but as a blessing; and posterity will bear testimony that I was right. I desire to thank God, that he enables me to disregard "the fear of man which bringeth a snare," and to speak his truth in its simplicity and power.

And here I close with this fresh dedication:

"Oppression! I have seen thee, face to face,
And met thy cruel eye and cloudy brow;
But thy soul-withering glance I fear not now—
For dread to prouder feelings doth give place
Of deep abhorrence! Scorning the disgrace
Of slavish knees that at thy footstool bow,
I also kneel—but with far other bow
Do hail thee and thy herd of hirelings base:
I swear, while life-blood warms my throbbing veins,
Still to oppose and thwart, with heart and hand,
Thy brutalizing sway—till Africa's chains
Are burst, and Freedom rules the rescued land,
Trampling Oppression and his iron rod:
Such is the vow I take so HELP ME GOD!"

New York Committee of Vigilance for the Year 1837, Together with Important Facts Relative to Their Proceedings
David Ruggles

Before the Amercan Civil War, bands of slave catchers patrolled the streets of Northern cities in search of fugitive slaves to capture and return to the South for bounties. They often seized freed blacks, not bothering to determine the true status of their captives.

Official resistance to these practices was inconsistent. In response, African Americans in some cities joined together to resist this assault on their right to freedom. David Ruggles was the earliest and one of the most aggressive and prolific writers on the topic of Northern blacks organizing themselves in self-defense. Ruggles was unusual in his call for Northern African Americans to help Southern slaves and in his criticisms of Northern white reformers and abolitionists. The document here was from the inaugural organizational meeting of the New York Committee of Vigilance. Because Ruggles served as the committee's secretary, he is therefore the author of the document.

THE ORIGIN AND OBJECT of the New York committee of Vigilance are as follows: At a meeting of The Friends of Human Rights, held in the city of New

York, Nov. 20, 1835, for the purpose of adopting measures to ascertain, if possible, the extent to which the cruel practice of kidnapping men, women and children, is carried on in this city, and to aid such unfortunate persons as may be in danger of being *reduced to Slavery*, in maintaining their rights—ROBERT BROWN, Esq. was called to the Chair, and David Ruggles, appointed Secretary.

The meeting being impressed with the alarming *fact* that any colored person within this State is liable to be arrested as a *fugitive from slavery* and put upon his defence to prove his freedom, and that any such person thus arrested is denied the *right of trial by jury*, and, therefore subject to a hurried trial, often without the aid of a friend or a counselor—We hold ourselves bound by the Golden Rule of our Saviour, to aid them, to *do to others as we would have them do to us*. It is therefore,

Resolved, That William Johnston, David Ruggles, Robert Brown, George R. Barker, J. W. Higgins, be appointed a committee to aid the people of color, legally to obtain their rights.

Resolved, That this Committee be authorized to add to their number and to fill vacancies.

Resolved, That three members shall be a quorum at any meeting regularly called.

Resolved, That this meeting commend the Committee to the confidence of the people of color and to the liberality and support of the friends of Human Rights. . . .

Annual Meeting of the New York Committee of Vigilance

A public meeting will be held, in aid of the people of Color, tomorrow evening, January 16th, at the Third Presbyterian Church, corner of Thompson and Houston streets, to commence at seven o'clock precisely. The attendance of the public is respectfully invited.

W. Johnston, Chairman of Committee of Arrangements.

We, the Committee appointed by the said meeting, being deeply impressed with the important and urgent nature of the duties committed to us, earnestly solicit the aid of the friends of humanity for the accomplishment of the following objects:

1. To protect unoffending, defenceless, and endangered persons of color, by securing their rights as far as practicable.

2. By obtaining for them when arrested, under the pretext of being *fugitive slaves*, such protection as the law will afford.

These objects are so continually pressing themselves on the notice of the friends of our colored brethren especially in the City of New York, that we feel compelled by the dictates of humanity, and by the authority of God to exert ourselves in their behalf, and therefore we appeal to you, to aid in this work of philanthropy and Christian benevolence.

Memorial to the Massachusetts Legislature
Dorothea Dix

In the early 1840s former teacher Dorothea Dix undertook an extensive investigation of the treatment that the insane and mentally disabled suffered in jails in Massachusetts. She wrote the petition, which she called a memorial describing her findings and calling for reforms, including the separation of the mentally ill from criminals. She presented her memorial, excerpted here, to the Massachusetts legislature in 1843.

Despite initial opposition and criticism, the state took up her suggestions and voted to allocate money to expand and improve services for the mentally ill.

Dix conducted similar investigations in New York, Pennsylvania, New Jersey, and other states, leading to similar results over the next decade. She also took her cause to the federal government, and in 1854 Congress passed an act allocating 12.2 million acres of public land among the states to support institutions for the insane and the deaf. President Franklin Pierce, however, vetoed the bill.

I COME TO PRESENT the strong claims of suffering humanity. I come to place before the Legislature of Massachusetts the condition of the miserable, the desolate, the outcast. I come as the advocate of helpless, forgotten, insane, and idiotic men and women; of beings sunk to a condition from which the most unconcerned would start with real horror; of beings wretched in our prisons, and more wretched in our almhouses. And I cannot suppose it needful to enjoy earnest persuasion, or stubborn argument, in order to arrest and fix attention upon a subject only the more strongly pressing in its claims because it is revolting and disgusting in its details.

I must confine myself to a few examples, but am ready to furnish other and more complete details, if required. If my pictures are displeasing, coarse, and severe, my subjects, it must be recollected, offer no tranquil, refined, or composing features. The condition of human beings, reduced to the extremist states of degradation and misery, cannot be exhibited in soft language, or adorn a polished image.

I proceed, gentlemen, briefly to call your attention to the present state of insane persons confined within this Commonwealth, in cages, closets, cellars, stalls, pens! Chained, naked, beaten with rods, and lashed into obedience.

As I state cold, severe facts, I feel obliged to refer to persons, and definitely to indicate localities. But it is upon my subject, not upon localities or individuals, I desire to fix attention; and I would speak as kindly as possible of all wardens, keepers, and other responsible officers, believing that most of these have erred not through hardness of heart and wilful cruelty so much as want of skill and knowledge, and want of consideration. Familiarity with suffering, it is said, blunts the sensibilities, and where neglect once finds a footing other injuries are multiplied. This is not all, for it may justly and strongly be added that, from the deficiency of adequate means to meet the wants of these cases, it has been an absolute impossibility to do justice in this matter. Prisons are not constructed in view of being converted into county hospitals and almshouses are not founded as receptacles for the insane. And yet, in the face of justice and common sense, wardens are by law compelled to receive, and the masters of almshouses not to refuse, insane and idiotic subjects in all stages of mental disease and privation.

It is the Commonwealth, not its integral parts, that is accountable for most of the abuses which have lately and do still exist. I repeat it, it is defective legislation which perpetuates and multiplies these abuses. In illustration of my subject, I offer the following extracts from my Notebook and Journal: . . .

Concord. A woman from the hospital in a cage in the almshouse. In the jail several, decently cared for in general, but not properly placed in prison. Violent, noisy, unmanageable most of the time.

Lincoln. A woman in a cage. *Medford.* One idiotic subject chained, and one in a close stall for seventeen years. *Pepperall.* One often doubly chained, hand and foot; another violent; several peaceable now. *Brookfield.* One man caged, comfortable. *Granville.* One often closely confined; now losing the use of his limbs from want of exercise. *Charlemont.* One man caged. *Savoy.* One man caged. *Lenox.* Two in jail, against whose unfit condition there the jailer protests. . . .

Danvers. November. Visited the almshouse. A large building, much out of repair. Understand a new one is in contemplation. Here are from fifty-six to sixty inmates, one idiotic, three insane; one of the latter in close confinement at all times. . . .

Men of Massachusetts, I beg, I implore, I demand pity and protection for these of my suffering, outraged sex. Fathers, husbands, brothers, I would supplicate you for this boon; but what do I say? I dishonor you, divest you at once of Christianity and humanity, does this appeal imply distrust. If it comes burdened with a doubt of your righteousness in this legislation, then blot it out; while I declare confidence in your honor, not less than your humanity. Here you will put away the cold, calculating spirit of selfishness and self-seeking; lay off the armor of local strife and political opposition; here and now, for once, forgetful of the earthly and perishable, come up to these halls and consecrate them with one heart and one mind to works of righteousness and just judgment. Become the benefactors of your race, the just guardians of the solemn rights you hold in trust. Raise up the fallen, succor the desolate, restore the outcast, defend the helpless, and for your eternal and great reward receive the benediction, "Well done, good and faithful servants, become rulers over many things!" . . .

Gentlemen, I commit to you this sacred cause. Your action upon this subject will affect the present and future conditions of hundreds and of thousands.

Narrative of the Life of William Brown
William Wells Brown

As the abolition movement grew in the northern United States, an increasing number of personal narratives of former slaves were written and published, detailing the cruelty of slavery, the most famous being Frederick Douglass's memoir of his experience as a slave in Maryland.

William Wells Brown was a runaway slave who joined the Northern abolitionist movement. In his 1847 book *Narrative of the Life of William Brown*, excerpted here, he wrote about his experiences as an assistant to a slave trader named Walker. Firsthand accounts such as this one helped further inflame antislavery sentiment in the North. Brown later wrote *Clotel; or, The President's Daughter*, a novel about a slave who was fathered by a president. It is considered to be the first novel written by an African American.

HE SOON COMMENCED purchasing to make up the third gang. We took a steamboat, and went to Jefferson City, a town on the Missouri river. Here we landed, and took stage for the interior of the State. He bought a number of slaves as he passed the different farms and villages. After getting twenty-two or twenty-three men and women, we arrived at St. Charles, a village on the banks of the Missouri. Here he purchased a woman who had a child in her arms, appearing to be four or five weeks old.

We had been traveling by land for some days, and were in hopes to have found a boat at this place for St. Louis, but were disappointed. As no boat was expected for some days, we started for St. Louis by land. Mr. Walker had purchased two horses. He rode one, and I the other. The slaves were chained together, and we took up our line of march, Mr. Walker taking the lead, and I bringing up the rear. Though the distance was not more than twenty miles, we did not reach it the first day. The road was worse than any that I have ever traveled.

Soon after we left St. Charles, the young child grew very cross, and kept up a noise during the greater part of the day. Mr. Walker complained of its crying several times, and told the mother to stop the child's d—d noise, or he would. The woman tried to keep the child from crying, but could not. We put up at night with an acquaintance of Mr. Walker, and in the morning, just as we were about to start, the child again commenced crying. Walker stepped to her, and told her to give the child to him. The mother trembling obeyed. He took the child by one arm, as you would a cat by the leg, walked into the house, and said to the lady.

"Madam, I will make you a present of this little nigger; it keeps such a noise that I can't bear it."

"Thank you, sir," said the lady.

The mother, as soon as she saw her child was to be left, ran up to Mr. Walker, and falling upon her knees begged him to let her have her child; she clung around his legs, and cried, "Oh, my child! O, do, do, do. I will stop its crying, if you will only let me have it again." When I saw this woman crying for her child so piteously, a shudder,—a feeling akin to horror shot through my frame.

Mr. Walker commanded her to return into the ranks with the other slaves. Women who had children were not chained, but those who had none were. As soon as her child was disposed of, she was chained in the gang.

Seneca Falls Declaration of Independence

In 1848 five women in Seneca Falls, New York, called for a declaration of women's rights modeled on the American Declaration of Independence. Led by Elizabeth Cady Stanton and Lucretia Mott, the women wrote a draft declaration of sentiments and resolutions, which included a demand for the right of women to vote. The organizers then advertised a meeting in the *Seneca County Courier*, saying its purpose was "to discuss the social, civil, and religious condition and rights of women." After a two-day convention with extensive discussion and revisions to the document, sixty-eight women and thirty-two men signed the declaration.

The national response to the declaration was largely negative, particularly regarding the call for women's suffrage, which even men who considered themselves progressive reformers often opposed. The declaration, however, helped galvanize localized efforts to promote annual conventions on women's rights throughout much of the country.

The declaration is considered the starting point of the feminist movement in the United States. The right for women to vote became the movement's primary goal during the next several decades. Charlotte Woodward Pierce was the only original signer who lived long enough to vote in the 1920 election, the first time women were allowed to participate in a national election.

1. Declaration of Sentiments

When, in the course of human events, it becomes necessary for one portion of the family of man to assume among the people of the earth a position different from that which they have hitherto occupied, but one to which the laws of nature and of nature's God entitle them, a decent respect to the opinions of mankind requires that they should declare the causes that impel them to such a course.

We hold these truths to be self-evident: that all men and women are created equal; that they are endowed by their Creator with certain inalienable rights; that among these are life, liberty, and the pursuit of happiness; that to secure these rights governments are instituted, deriving their just powers from the consent of the governed. Whenever any form of government becomes destructive of these ends, it is the right of those who suffer from it to refuse allegiance to it, and to insist upon the institution of a new government, laying its foundation on such principles, and organizing its powers in such form, as to them shall seem most likely to effect their safety and happiness. Prudence, indeed, will dictate that governments long established should not be changed for light and transient causes; and accordingly all experience hath shown that mankind are more disposed to suffer while evils are sufferable, than to right themselves by abolishing the forms to which they are accustomed. But when a long train of abuses and usurpations, pursuing invariably the same object, evinces a design to reduce them under absolute despotism, it is their duty to throw off such government, and to provide new guards for their future security. Such has been the patient sufferance of the women under this government, and such is now the necessity which constrains them to demand the equal station to which they are entitled.

The history of mankind is a history of repeated injuries and usurpations on the part of man toward woman, having in direct object the establishment of an absolute tyranny over her. To prove this, let facts be submitted to a candid world.

He has never permitted her to exercise her inalienable right to the elective franchise.

He has compelled her to submit to laws, in the formation of which she had no voice.

He has withheld from her rights which are given to the most ignorant and degraded men—both natives and foreigners.

Having deprived her of this first right of a citizen, the elective franchise, thereby leaving her without representation in the halls of legislation, he has oppressed her on all sides.

He has made her, if married, in the eye of the law, civilly dead.

He has taken from her all right in property, even to the wages she earns.

He has made her, morally, an irresponsible being, as she can commit many crimes with impunity, provided they be done in the presence of her husband. In the covenant of marriage, she is compelled to promise obedience to her husband, he becoming, to all intents and purposes, her master—the law giving him power to deprive her of her liberty, and to administer chastisement.

He has so framed the laws of divorce, as to what shall be the proper causes, and in case of separation, to whom the guardianship of the children shall be given, as to be wholly regardless of the happiness of women—the law, in all cases, going upon a false supposition of the supremacy of man, and giving all power into his hands.

After depriving her of all rights as a married woman, if single, and the owner of property, he has taxed her to support a government which recognizes her only when her property can be made profitable to it.

He has monopolized nearly all the profitable employments, and from those she is permitted to follow, she receives but a scanty remuneration. He closes against her all the avenues to wealth and distinction which he considers most honorable to himself. As a teacher of theology, medicine, or law, she is not known.

He has denied her the facilities for obtaining a thorough education, all colleges being closed against her.

He allows her in Church, as well as State, but a subordinate position, claiming Apostolic authority for her exclusion from the ministry, and, with some exceptions, from any public participation in the affairs of the Church.

He has created a false public sentiment by giving to the world a different code of morals for men and women, by which moral delinquencies which exclude women from society, are not tolerated, but deemed of little account in man.

He has usurped the prerogative of Jehovah himself, claiming it as his right to assign for her a sphere of action, when that belongs to her conscience and to her God.

He has endeavored, every way that he could, to destroy her confidence in her own powers, to lessen her self-respect and to make her willing to lead a dependent and abject life.

Now, in view of this entire disfranchisement of one-half the people of this country, their social and religious degradation—in view of the unjust laws above mentioned, and because women do feel themselves aggrieved, oppressed, and fraudulently deprived of their most sacred rights, we insist that they have immediate admission to all rights and privileges which belong to them as citizens of the United States.

In entering upon the great work before us, we anticipate no small amount of misconception, misrepresentation, and ridicule; but we shall use every instrumentality within our power to effect our object. We shall employ agents, circulate tracts, petition the State and National legislatures, and endeavor to enlist the pulpit and the press in our behalf. We hope this Convention will be followed by a series of Conventions embracing every part of the country.

2. Resolutions

Whereas, The great precept of nature is conceded to be, that "man shall pursue his own true and substantial happiness." Blackstone in his Commentaries remarks, that this law of Nature being coeval with mankind, and dictated by God himself, is of course superior in obligation to any other. It is binding over all the globe, in all countries and at all times; no human laws are of any validity if contrary to this, and such of them as are valid, derive all their force, and all their validity, and all their authority, mediately and immediately, from this original; therefore,

Resolved, That all laws which prevent woman from occupying such a station in society as her conscience shall dictate, or which place her in a position inferior to that of man, are contrary to the great precept of nature, and therefore of no force or authority.

Resolved, That woman is man's equal—was intended to be so by the Creator, and the highest good of the race demands that she should be recognized as such.

Resolved, That the women of this country ought to be enlightened in regard to the laws under which they live, that they may no longer publish their degradation by declaring themselves satisfied with their present position, nor their ignorance, by asserting that they have all the rights they want.

Resolved, That inasmuch as man, while claiming for himself intellectual superiority, does accord to woman moral superiority, it is pre-eminently his duty to encourage her to speak and teach, as she has an opportunity, in all religious assemblies.

Resolved, That the same amount of virtue, delicacy, and refinement of behavior that is required of woman in the social state, should also be required of man, and the same transgressions should be visited with equal severity on both man and woman.

Resolved, That the objection of indelicacy and impropriety, which is so often brought against woman when she addresses a public audience, comes with a very ill-grace from those who encourage, by their attendance, her appearance on the stage, in the concert, or in feats of the circus.

Resolved, That woman has too long rested satisfied in the circumscribed limits which corrupt customs and a perverted application of the Scriptures have marked out for her, and that it is time she should move in the enlarged sphere which her great Creator has assigned her.

Resolved, That it is the duty of the women of this country to secure to themselves the sacred rights to the elective franchise. . . .

Resolved, That the speedy success of our cause depends upon the zealous and untiring efforts of both men and women, for the overthrow of the monopoly of the pulpit, and for the securing to women an equal participation with men in the various trades, professions and commerce.

Resolved, therefore, That, being invested by the creator with the same capabilities, and the same consciousness of responsibility for their exercise, it is demonstrably the right and duty of woman, equally with man, to promote every righteous cause by every righteous means; and especially in regard to the great subjects of morals and religion, it is self-evidently her right to participate with her brother in teaching them, both in private and in public, by writing and by speaking, by any instrumentalities proper to be used, and in any assemblies proper to be held; and this being a self-evident truth growing out of the divinely implanted principles of human nature, any custom or authority adverse to it, whether modern or wearing the hoary sanction of antiquity, is to be regarded as a self-evident falsehood, and at war with mankind.

"And ain't I a woman?"
Sojourner Truth

Sojourner Truth was born as a slave on a Dutch settlement in New York State in 1797. Given the name Isabella Baumfree, she was one of thirteen children and grew up speaking only Dutch until she was eleven years old. Although she learned English, she had a Dutch accent her entire life. Baumfree was sold at least three times to different owners. She escaped from her last owner with her infant son to New York City in 1827, a year before New York emancipated slaves.

Isabella changed her name to Sojourner Truth in 1843 when she became an evangelist. She preached throughout Connecticut and Long Island, New York, before joining a utopian community in Northampton, Massachusetts, where she became involved in the abolitionist movement. Abolitionists published her memoir, *The Narrative of Sojourner Truth: A Northern Slave*, in 1850. When the women's movement started, she became one of the few African-American participants. Her impact was significant. Citing her own personal experiences, she presented a compelling case for women's rights. This speech was given at the 1851 Ohio Women's Rights Convention in Akron.

WELL, CHILDREN, where there is so much racket there must be something out of kilter. I think that 'twixt the Negroes of the South and women of the North, all talking about rights, the white men will be in a fix pretty soon. But what's all this here talking about?

That man over there says that women need to be helped into carriages, and lifted over ditches, and to have the best place everywhere. Nobody ever helps me into carriages, or over mud puddles, or gives me any best place! And ain't I a woman? Look at me! Look at my arm. I have plowed and planted and gathered into barns, and no man could head me! And ain't I a woman? I could work as much and eat as much as a man—when I could get it—and bear the lash as well! And ain't I a woman? I have borne thirteen children, and seen them most all sold off to slavery, and when I cried out with my mother's grief, none but Jesus heard me! And ain't I a woman?

Then they talk about this thing in the head; what's this they call it? [Someone tells her, "intellect."] That's it, honey. What's that got to do with women's rights or Negros' rights? If my cup won't hold but a pint, and yours holds a quart, wouldn't you be mean not let me have my little half-measure full?

Then that little man in black there, he says women can't have as much rights as men, 'cause Christ wasn't a woman! Where did your Christ come from? Where did your Christ come from? From God and a woman! Man had nothing to do with him.

If the first woman God ever made was strong enough to turn the world upside down all alone, these women together ought to be able to turn it back, and get it right side up again! And now they is asking to do it, the men better let them.

Obliged to you for hearing me, and now old Sojourner ain't got nothing more to say.

"Why can't we have a soldier's pay?"
James Henry Gooding

In July 1863, the all-black 54th Massachusetts Regiment of the Union Army suffered casualties of almost 50 percent, including the death of their commander, Colonel Robert Gould Shaw, when it launched a frontal assault against Confederate forces at Fort Wagner outside of Charleston, South Carolina. A published account describing the bravery of the black regiment dispelled widespread doubt about black soldiers' willingness and ability to fight.

The men of the regiment, however, were not paid the same wage as white Union soldiers. Even though in 1862 the United States War Department had promised African Americans the same wages (thirteen dollars per month) as white soldiers, the Union Army had decided to pay black soldiers the salary of black laborers, which Congress had mandated to be ten dollars a month.

James Henry Gooding of New Bedford, Massachusetts, was a corporal with the 54th Regiment. He wrote a column for his hometown newspaper, the *New Bedford Mercury*, while serving as a soldier. After the battle of Fort Wagner, he wrote this letter to Abraham Lincoln asking that he and his fellow black soldiers receive equal pay. Shortly afterward, Congress authorized equal payment for black soldiers. Gooding was killed at the Battle of Olustee Station in Florida in 1864.

YOUR EXCELLENCY will pardon the presumption of a humble individual like myself, in addressing you, but the earnest Solicitation of my comrades in Arms beside the genuine interest felt by myself in the matter is my excuse, for placing before the Executive head of the Nation our Common Grievance.

On the 6th day of the last Month, the Paymaster of the department informed us, that if we would decide to receive the sum of $10 per month, he would come and pay us that sum, but that, on the sitting of Congress, the Regt., would, in his opinion be allowed the other three. He did not give us any guarantee that this would be, as he hoped; certainly he had no authority for making any such guarantee, and we cannot suppose him acting in any way interested.

Now the main question is, Are we Soldiers, or are we Labourers? We are fully armed and equipped, have done all the various Duties pertaining to a Soldier's life, have conducted ourselves to the complete satisfaction of General Officers, who were, if any[thing], prejudiced against us, but who now accord us all the encouragement and honour due us; have shared the perils and Labour of Reducing the first stronghold that flaunted a Traitor Flag; and more, Mr. President. Today the Anglo-Saxon Mother, Wife, or Sister are not alone in tears for departed Sons, Husbands and Brothers. The patient, trusting Descendants of Africa's Clime have dyed the ground with blood, in defense of the Union, and Democracy. Men, too, your Excellency, who know in a measure the cruelties of the Iron heel of oppression, which in years gone by, the very Power their blood is now being spilled to maintain, ever ground them to the dust.

But When the war trumpet sounded o'er the land, when men knew not the Friend from the Traitor, the Black man laid his life at the Altar of the Nation—and he was refused. When the arms of the Union were beaten, in the first year of the War, and the Executive called for more food for its ravaging maw, again the black man begged the privilege of aiding his country in her need, to be again refused.

And now he is in the War, and how has he conducted himself? Let their dusky forms rise up, out the mires of James Island, and give the answer. Let the rich mould around Wagner's parapets be upturned, and there will be found an Eloquent answer. Obedient and patient and Solid as a wall as are they. All we lack is a paler hue and a better acquaintance with the Alphabet.

Now your Excellency, we have done a Soldier's Duty. Why Can't we have a Soldier's pay? You caution the Rebel Chieftan, that the United States knows no distinction in her Soldiers. She insists on having all her Soldiers of whatever creed or Color, to be treated according to the usages of War. Now if the United States exacts uniformity of treatment of her Soldiers from the Insurgents, would it not be well and consistent to set the example herself by paying all her Soldiers alike?

We of this Regt. were not enlisted under any "contraband" act. But we do not wish to be understood as rating our Service of more value to the Government than the service of the ex-slave. Their Service is undoubtedly worth much to the Nation, but Congress made express provision touching their case, as slaves freed by military necessity, and assuming the Government to be their temporary Guardian. Not so with us. Freemen by birth and consequently having the advantage of thinking and acting for ourselves so far as the laws would allow us, we do not consider ourselves fit subject for the Contraband act.

We appeal to you, Sir, as the Executive of the Nation, to have us justly Dealt with. The Regt. do pray that they be assured their service will be fairly appreciated by paying them as American Soldiers, not as menial hirelings. Black men, you may well know, are poor; three dollars per month for a year will supply their needy Wives and little ones with fuel. If you, as Chief magistrate of the Nation, will assure us of our whole pay, we are content. Our Patriotism, our enthusiasm will have a new impetus, to exert our energy more and more to aid our Country. Not that our hearts ever flagged in Devotion, spite the evident apathy displayed in our behalf, but We feel as though our Country spurned us, now that we are sworn to serve her. Please give this a moment's attention.

Dialogue from *United States v. Susan B. Anthony*
Susan B. Anthony and Ward Hunt

Susan B. Anthony and Elizabeth Cady Stanton are credited with leading the women's suffrage movement in the United States. They founded the National Woman Suffrage Association in 1869 to fight for women's right to vote. The daughter of Massachusetts Quakers, Anthony cast a vote in Rochester, New York, on November 5, 1872. She was arrested two weeks later.

Anthony pled "not guilty," stating that the Fourteenth Amendment entitled her to vote as it gives all "persons" born in the United States the rights of citizenship, which she argued included the right to vote. Anthony lost the case. Judge Ward Hunt directed the jury to find Anthony guilty and presented an opinion on the case that he had written before the trial had occurred. Anthony—who had been a hesitant and shy speaker at the start of her career as a reformer—objected strongly to the judge's handling of the case; the text of her objections appears here. Hunt fined Anthony one hundred dollars, which she refused to pay. Hunt did not pursue the payment or order Anthony in jail, thus avoiding an appeal to a higher court.

JUDGE HUNT: The prisoner will stand up. Has the prisoner anything to say why the sentence shall not be pronounced?

ANTHONY: Yes, your honor, I have many things to say; for in your ordered verdict of guilty, you have trampled underfoot, every vital principle of our government. My natural rights, my civil rights, my political rights, are all alike ignored. Robbed of the fundamental privilege of citizenship, I am degraded from the status of a citizen to that of a subject; and not only myself individually, but all of my sex, are, by your honor's verdict, doomed to political subjection under this so-called republican government.

HUNT: The Court can not listen to a rehearsal of arguments the prisoner's counsel has already consumed three hours in presenting.

ANTHONY: May it please your honor, I am not arguing the question, but simply stating the reasons why sentence can not, in justice, be pronounced against me. Your denial of my citizen's rights to vote is the denial of my right of consent as one of the governed, the denial of my right of representation as one of the taxed, the denial of my right to a trial by a jury of my peers as an offender against the law, therefore, the denial of my sacred rights to life, liberty, property, and—

HUNT: The Court can not allow the prisoner to go on.

ANTHONY: Of all my prosecutors, . . . not one is my peer, but each and all are my political sovereigns; and had your honor submitted my case to the jury, as was clearly your duty, even then I should have had cause of protest, for not one of those men was my peer; but, native or foreign, white or black, rich or poor, educated or ignorant, awake or asleep, sober or drunk, each and every man of them was my political superior; hence, in no sense, my peer. . . . [J]ury, judge, counsel, must all be of the superior class.

HUNT: The Court must insist—the prisoner has been tried according to the established forms of law.

ANTHONY: Yes, your honor, but by forms of law all made by men, interpreted by men, administered by men, in favor of men, and against women; and hence, your honor's ordered verdict of guilty, against a United States citizen for the exercise of "that citizen's right to vote," simply because that citizen was a woman and not a man. But, yesterday, the same man-made forms of law declared it a crime punishable with $1,000 fine and six months' imprisonment, for you, or me, or any of us, to give a cup of cold water, a crust of bread, or a night's shelter to a panting fugitive as he was tracking his way to Canada. And every man or woman in whose veins coursed a drop of human sympathy violated that wicked law, reckless of consequences, and was justified in so doing. As then the slaves who got their freedom [had to] take it over, or under, or through the unjust forms of law, precisely so now must women, to get their right to a voice in this Government, take it; and I have taken mine, and mean to take it at every possible opportunity.

HUNT: The Court orders the prisoner to sit down. It will not allow another word.

ANTHONY: When I was brought before your honor for a trial, I hoped for a broad and liberal interpretation of the Constitution and its recent amendments, that should declare all United States citizens under its protecting aegis—that should declare equality of rights the national guarantee to all persons born or naturalized in the United States. But failing to get this justice—failing, even, to get a jury not of my peers—I ask not leniency at your hands—but rather the full rigors of the law.

HUNT: The Court must insist— The prisoner will stand up. The sentence of the Court is that you pay a fine of one hundred dollars and the costs of the prosecution.

ANTHONY: May it please your honor, I shall not pay a dollar of your unjust penalty. All the stock in trade I possess is a $10,000 debt, incurred by publishing my paper—The Revolution—four years ago, the sole object of which was to educate all women to do precisely as I have done, rebel against your man-made, unjust, unconstitutional forms of law, that tax, fine, imprison, and hang women, while they deny them the right of representation in the Government; and I shall work on with might and main to pay every dollar of that honest debt, but not a penny shall go to this unjust claim. And I shall earnestly and persistently continue to urge all women to the practical recognition of the old revolutionary maxim, that "Resistance to tyranny is obedience to God."

What Shall Be Done with the Negro?

Frederick Douglass

A runaway slave who joined the abolitionist movement in Massachusetts, Frederick Douglass was the most powerful black voice for emancipation before and during the Civil War. He remained an articulate spokesman for African-American rights for more than forty years afterward. Douglass was very involved in the Republican party and received several political appointments, including marshal of the District of Columbia and minister to Haiti. Nevertheless, he was the victim of social slights in Republican social circles and often was not invited to ceremonial events.

Douglass advocated equal opportunity for all citizens, saying that African Americans had a right to "voting at the same ballot-box, using the same cartridge-box, going to the same schools, attending the same churches, traveling in the same street cars, in the same railroad cars, on the same steam-boats, proud of the same country, fighting the same war and enjoying the same peace and all its advantages."

Douglass delivered a speech, excerpted here, to the American Missionary Association in 1884. Angry at the lack of progress in achieving his goal of equal opportunity, he advised a young man in 1895 that the best way to advance the cause was to "[a]gitate! Agitate! Agitate!"

IN ANSWER TO THE QUESTION as to what shall be done with the Negro, I have sometimes replied, "Do nothing with him, give him fair play and let him alone." But in reporting me, it has been found convenient and agreeable to place the emphasis of my speech on one part of my sentence. They willingly accepted my idea of letting the Negro alone, but not so my idea of giving the Negro fair play. It has always been easier for some of the American people to imitate the priest and the Levite, rather than the example of the good Samaritan; to let the Negro alone rather than to give him fair play. Even here in New England—the most enlightened and benevolent section of our country—the Negro has been excluded from nearly all profitable employments. I speak from experience. I came here from the South fifty-six years ago, with a good trade in my hands, and might have commanded by my trade three dollars a day, but my white brethren, while praying for their daily bread, were not willing that I should obtain mine by the same means open to them. I was compelled to work for one dollar a day, when others working at my trade were receiving three dollars a day.

But to return. When we consider the long years of slavery, the years of enforced ignorance, the years of injustice, of cruel strifes and degradation to which the Negro was doomed, the duty of the nation is not, and cannot be, performed by simply letting him alone.

If Northern benevolence could send a missionary to a very dark corner of the South, if it could place a church on every hilltop in the south, a schoolhouse in every valley, and support a preacher in the one, and a teacher, in the other, for fifty years to come, they could not then even compensate the poor freedmen for the long years of wrong and suffering he has been compelled to endure. The people of the North should remember that slavery and the degradation of the Negro were inflicted by the power of the nation, that the North was a consenting party to the wrong, and that a common sin can only be atoned and condoned by a common repentance.

Under the whole heavens, there never was a people emancipated under conditions more unfavorable to mental, moral and physical improvement than were the slaves of our Southern States. They were emancipated not by the moral judgment of the nation as a whole; they were emancipated not as a blessing for themselves, but as a punishment to their master; not to strengthen the emancipated but to weaken the rebels, and, naturally enough, taking the emancipation in this sense, the old master class have resented it and have resolved to make his freedom a curse rather than a blessing to the Negro. In many instances they have been quite successful in accomplishing this purpose. Then the manner of emancipation was against the Negro. He was turned loose to the open sky without a foot of earth on which to stand; without a single farming implement; he was turned loose to the elements, to hunger, to destitution; without money, without friends; and to endure the pitiless storm of the old master's wrath. The old master had in his possession the land and the power to crush the Negro, and the Negro in return had no power of defense. The difference between his past condition and his present condition is that in the past the old master class could say to him, "You shall work for me or I will whip you to death"; in the present condition he can say to him, "You shall work for me or I will starve you to death." And today the Negro is in this latter condition. . . .

With all the discouraging circumstances that now surround what is improperly called the Negro problem, I do not despair of a better day. It is sometimes said that the condition of the colored man today is worse than it was in the time of slavery. To me this is simply extravagance. We now have the organic law of the land on our side. We have thousands of teachers, and hundreds and thousands of pupils attending schools; we can now count our friends by the million. In many of the states we have elective franchises; in some of them we have colored office-holders. It is no small advantage that we are citizens of this Republic by special amendment of the Constitution. The very resistance that we now meet on Southern railroads, steamboats and hotels is evidence of our progress. It is not the Negro in his degradation that is objected to, but the Negro educated, cultivated and refined. The Negro who fails to respect himself, who makes no provision for himself or his family, and is content to live the life of a vagabond, meets no resistance. He is just where he is desired by his enemies. Perhaps you will say that this proves that education, wealth and refinement will no nothing for the Negro; but the answer to this is, "that the hair of the dog will cure the bite" eventually. All people suddenly springing from a lowly condition have to pass through a period of probation. At first they are denounced as "upstarts," but the "upstarts" of one generation are the elite of the next.

The history of the great Anglo-Saxon race should encourage the Negro to hope on and hope ever, and work on and work ever. They were once the slaves of Normans; they were despised and insulted. They were looked upon as the coarser clay than the haughty Norman. Their language was despised and repudiated, but where today is the haughty Norman? What people and what language now rock the world by their power?

My hope for the Negro is largely based upon his enduring qualities. No persecutions, no proscriptions, no hardships are able to extinguish him. He neither dies out, nor goes out. He is here to stay, and while here he will partake of the blessings of your education, your progress, your civilization, and your Christian religion. His appeal to you today is for an equal chance in the race of life, and dark and stormy as the present appears, his appeal will not go unanswered.

Letter to the San Francisco Board of Education
Mary Tape

Responding to economic opportunities in California and difficult conditions in China, more than 150,000 Chinese immigrated to California from 1850 to 1880. Possessing a completely different culture and religion, and a willingness to work long hours at low pay, Chinese immigrants posed a threat to white workers in the United States. For example, thousands of Chinese were employed in work gangs to build the transcontinental railroads. In the 1870s a wave of anti-Chinese sentiment swept the West, and violent attacks were committed against the United States' Chinese population.

In 1882 Congress passed the Chinese Exclusion Act, prohibiting Chinese immigration for ten years. This act was followed by the United States–China Treaty of 1894, which barred the exchange of immigrants between the two countries, with some exceptions, for another ten years.

Chinese immigrants who were already in the United States often wanted to assimilate into the American culture but met fierce resistance, including barriers at the governmental level. In San Francisco, Chinese students were not allowed to attend school with white children. One such Chinese student was Mamie Tape, who had been born in the United States and was a U.S. citizen. Although her parents, Mary and Joseph Tape, both Chinese immigrants, appealed to the Board of Education to allow Mamie to attend a white school, the board refused their request several times. Finally Mary Tape wrote the following letter to the board and school superintendent Andrew Moulder expressing her anger at the board's policy.

The case went to the San Francisco Superior Court, which ruled in Tape's favor, saying the board's action was unconstitutional. The California Supreme Court upheld the decision. However, despite her mother's feelings and the court rulings, Mamie attended a special school for Chinese-American children, which the Board of Education set up in Chinatown.

DEAR SIRS: I see that you are going to make all sorts of excuses to keep my child out of the Public schools. Dear sirs, Will you please tell me! Is it a disgrace to be Born a Chinese? Didn't God make us all!!! What right have you to bar my children out of the school because she is a chinese Descend. They is no other worldly reason that you could keep her out, except that. I suppose, you all goes to churches on Sundays! Do you call that a Christian act to compell my little children to go so far to a school that is made in purpose for them. My children don't dress like the other Chinese. They look just as phunny amongst them as the Chinese dress in Chinese look amongst you Caucasians. Besides, if I had any wish to send them to a chinese school I could have sent them two years ago without going to all this trouble. You have expended a lot of Public money foolishly, all because of one poor little Child. Her playmates is all Caucasians ever since she could toddle around. If she is good enough to play with them! Then is she not good enough to be in the same room and studie with them? You had better come and see for yourselves. See if the Tape's is not the same as other Caucasians, except in features. It seems no matter how a Chinese may live and dress so long as you know they Chinese. Then they are hated as one. There is not any right or justice for them.

You have seen my husband and child. You told him it wasn't Mamie Tape you object to. If it were not Mamie Tape you object to, then why didn't you let her attend the school nearest her home! Instead of first making one pretense of some kind to keep her out? It seems to me Mr. Moulder has a grudge against this Eight-year-old Mamie Tape. I know they is no other child I mean Chinese child! Care to go to your public Chinese school. May you, Mr. Moulder, never be persecuted like the way you have persecuted little Mamie Tape. Mamie Tape will nevery attend any of the Chinsese schools of your making! Never!!! I will let the world see sir What justice there is When it is govern by the Race prejudice men! Just because she is of the Chinese decend, not because she don't dress like you because she does. Just because she is decended of Chinese parents I guess she is more a American than a good many of you that is going to prevent her being Educated.

"A Woman's Point of View"
Harriet Stanton Blatch

Harriet Stanton Blatch was one of the foremost suffragists of the early 1900s. The daughter of pioneer women's rights advocate Elizabeth Cady Stanton, she founded the Equality League of Self-Supporting Women in 1907 to bring working women into the women's right movement. The organization later became the National Woman's Party, one of the most militant groups advocating for the right of women to vote.

Here, Blatch, who organized several suffrage marches in New York City, speaks to a crowd of men in Wall Street urging their support for the enfranchisement of women.

After the passage of the Nineteenth Amendment in 1920, Blatch joined the Socialist Party and began to work for the Equal Rights Amendment. She wrote two books about her experiences, *Mobilizing Women Power* (1918) and *A Woman's Point of View* (1920).

Women and the New Race
Margaret Sanger

After working as a public-health nurse, Margaret Sanger started a family-planning and birth-control clinic in Brooklyn, New York, in 1916. It was the first clinic of this sort in the United States. Police raided the clinic, and Sanger was arrested for breaking a post office obscenity law prohibiting birth-control information from being sent through the mail. Sanger moved to Europe to avoid prosecution. When she returned in 1917, she started publishing *The Birth Control Review* and *Birth Control News* and wrote several articles directed to women and teenagers about sexuality. In 1920, she wrote about the subject in her book *Women and the New Race*.

Despite ongoing harassment from authorities for her work, Sanger founded the Birth Control League (now Planned Parenthood) in 1921 to educate women on the use of birth control and advocate its use. She spent the next forty-five years of her life supporting birth-control initiatives in the United States and abroad, helping to fund research for birth-control pills and promoting their distribution once they became available in the United States in the 1960s.

THE PROBLEM OF BIRTH CONTROL has arisen directly from the effort of the feminine spirit to free itself from bondage. Woman herself has wrought that bondage through her reproductive powers and while enslaving herself has enslaved the world. The physical suffering to be relieved is chiefly woman's. Hers, too, is the love of life that dies first under the blight of too-prolific breeding. Within her is wrapped up the future of the race—it is hers to make or mar. All of these considerations point unmistakably to one fact—it is woman's duty as well as her privilege to lay hold of the means of freedom. Whatever men may do, she cannot escape the responsibility. For ages she has been deprived of the opportunity to meet this obligation. She is now emerging from her helplessness. Even as no one can share the suffering of the overburdened mother, so no one can do this work for her. Others may help, but she and she alone can free herself.

The basic freedom of the world is woman's freedom. A free race cannot be born of slave mothers. A woman enchained cannot choose but give a measure of that bondage to her sons and daughters. No woman can call herself free who does not own and control her body. No woman can call herself free until she can chose consciously whether she will or will not be a mother.

It does not greatly alter the case that some women call themselves free because they earn their own livings, while other profess freedom because they defy the conventions of sex relationships. She who earns her own living gains a sort of freedom that is not to be undervalued, but in quantity it is of little account beside the untrammeled choice of mating or not mating, of being a mother or not being a mother. She gains food and clothing and shelter, at least, without submitting to the charity of her companion, but the earning of her own living does not give her the development of her inner sex urge, far deeper and more powerful in its outworkings than any of these externals. In order to have that development, she must still meet and solve the problem of motherhood.

With the so-called "free" woman, who chooses a mate in defiance of convention, freedom is largely a question of character and audacity. If she does attain an unrestricted choice of a mate, she is still in a position to be enslaved through her reproductive powers. Indeed, the pressure of law and custom upon the woman not legally married is likely to make her more of a slave than the woman fortunate enough to marry the man of her choice.

Look at it from any standpoint you will, suggest any solution you will, conventional or unconventional, sanctioned by law or in defiance of law, woman is in the same position, fundamentally, until she is able to determine for herself whether she will be a mother and to fix the number of her offspring. This unavoidable situation is alone enough to make birth control, first of all, a woman's problem. On the very face of the matter, voluntary motherhood is chiefly the concern of the woman.

It is persistently urged, however, that since sex expression is the act of two, the responsibility of controlling the results should not be placed upon woman alone. Is it fair, it is asked, to give her, instead of the man, the task of protecting herself when she is, perhaps, less rugged in physique than her mate, and has, at all events, the normal, periodic inconvenience of her sex?

We must examine this phase of her problem in two lights—that of the ideal, and of the conditions working toward the ideal. In an ideal society, no doubt, birth control would be the concern of the man as well as the woman. The hard, inescapable fact which we encounter today is that man has not only refused any such responsibility, but has individually and collectively sought to prevent woman from obtaining knowledge by which she could assume this responsibility for herself. She is still in the position of a dependent today because her mate has refused to consider her as an individual apart from his needs. She is still bound because she has in the past left the solution of the problem to him. Having left it to him, she finds that instead of rights, she has only such privileges as she has gained by petitioning, coaxing and cozening. Having left it to him, she is exploited, driven and enslaved to his desires.

A Statement Defining the Position of the American Civil Liberties Union on the Issues of the United States Today
American Civil Liberties Union Founders

In the wake of World War I and the "Red Scare" that followed, many people were concerned by some of the heavy-handed tactics of the government to suppress opposition to U.S. involvement in the war, as well as to prevent support of socialist policies afterward. Some states and municipalities banned the teaching of the German language or the display of a red flag, for example. In response, some of the leading progressives in the United States formed the American Civil Liberties Union (ACLU) in 1921 to advocate for the protection of the civil rights defined by the Constitution's Bill of Rights.

Founding members of the ACLU included Roger Baldwin, a conscientious objector during the war; Norman Thomas, who ran for president as a socialist candidate several times; and Jane Addams, a social reformer who would win the Nobel Peace Prize in 1931 for her work. The founders issued the following statement explaining the purpose of the ACLU in 1921.

WE STAND ON THE GENERAL PRINCIPLE that all thought on matters of public concern should be freely expressed without interference. Orderly social progress is promoted by unrestricted freedom of opinion. The punishment of mere opinion, without overt acts, is never in the interests of orderly progress. Suppression of opinion makes for violence and bloodshed.

The principle of freedom of speech, press and assemblage, embodied in our constitutional law, must be reasserted in its application to American conditions today. That application must deal with various methods now used to repress new ideas and democratic movements. The following paragraphs cover the most significant of the tactics of repression in the United States today.

1. Free Speech. There should be no control whatever in advance over what any person may say. The right to meet and to speak freely without permit should be unquestioned.

There should be no prosecutions for the mere expression of opinion on matters of public concern, however radical, however violent. The expression of all opinions, however radical, should be tolerated. The fullest freedom of speech should be encouraged by setting aside special places in streets or parks and in the use of public buildings free of charge, for public meetings of any sort.

2. Free Press. There should be no censorship over the mails by the post-office or any other agency at any time or in any way. Privacy of communication should be inviolate. Printed matter should never be subject to a political censorship. The granting or evoking of second class mailing privileges should have nothing whatever to do with a paper's opinions and policies.

If libelous, fraudulent, or other illegal matter is being circulated, it should be seized by proper warrant through the prosecuting authorities, not by the post-office department. The business of the post-office department is to carry the mails, not to investigate crime or act as censors.

There should be no control over the distribution of literature at meetings or hand to hand in public or private places. No system of license for distribution should be tolerated.

3. Freedom of Assemblage. Meetings in public places, parades and processions should be freely permitted, the only reasonable regulation being the advance notification to the police of the time and place. No discretion should be given the police to prohibit parades or processions, but merely to alter routes in accordance with imperative demands of traffic in crowded cities. There should be no laws or regulations prohibiting the display of red flags or other political emblems.

The right of assemblage is involved in the right to picket in time of strike. Peaceful picketing, therefore, should not be prohibited, regulated by injunction, by order of court or by police edict. It is the business of the police in places where picketing is conducted merely to keep traffic free and to handle specific violations of law against persons upon complaint.

4. The Right to Strike. The right of workers to organize in organizations of their own choosing, and to strike, should never be infringed by law.

Compulsory arbitration is to be condemned not only because it destroys the workers' right to strike, but because it lays emphasis on one set of obligations alone, those of workers to society.

5. Law Enforcement. The practice of deputizing privately paid police as general police officers should be opposed. So should the attempts of private company employees to police the streets or property other than that of the company.

The efforts of private associations to take into their own hands the enforcement of law should be opposed at every point. Public officials, employees of private corporations, and leaders of mobs, who interfere with the exercise of the constitutionally established rights of free speech and free assembly, should be vigorously proceeded against.

The sending of troops into areas of industrial conflict to maintain law and order almost inevitably results in the government taking sides in an industrial conflict in behalf of the employer. The presence of troops, whether or not martial law is declared, very rarely affects the employer adversely, but it usually results in the complete denial of civil rights to the workers.

6. Search and Seizure. It is the custom of certain federal, state and city officials, particularly in cases involving civil liberty, to make arrests without warrant, to enter upon private property, and to seize papers and literature without legal process. Such practices should be contested. Officials so violating constitutional guarantees should be proceeded against.

7. The Right to a Fair Trial. Every person charged with an offense should have the fullest opportunity for a fair trial, for securing counsel and bail in a reasonable sum. In the case of a poor person, special aid should be organized to secure a fair trial, and when necessary, an appeal. The legal profession should be alert to defend cases involving civil liberty. The resolutions of various associations of lawyers against taking cases of radicals are wholly against the traditions of American liberty.

8. Immigration, Deportation, and Passports. No person should be refused admission to the United States on the ground of holding objectionable opinions. The present restrictions against radicals of various beliefs is wholly opposed to our tradition of political asylum.

No alien should be deported merely for the expression of opinion or for membership in a radical or revolutionary organization. This is as un-American a practice as the prosecution of citizens for expression of opinion.

The attempt to revoke naturalization papers in order to declare a citizen an alien subject to deportation is a perversion of a law which was intended to cover only cases of fraud.

Citizenship papers should not be refused to any alien because of the expression of radical views, or activities in the cause of labor.

The granting of passports to or from the United States should not be dependent merely upon the opinions of citizens or membership in radical or labor organizations.

9. Liberty in Education. The attempts to maintain a uniform orthodox opinion among teachers should be opposed. The attempts of educational authorities to inject into public school and college instruction propaganda in the interest of any particular theory of society to the exclusion of others should be opposed.

10. Race Equality. Every attempt to discriminate between races in the application of all principles of civil liberty here set forth should be opposed.

How to get Civil Liberty:

We realize that these standards of civil liberty cannot be attained as abstract principles or as constitutional guarantees. Economic or political power is necessary to assert and maintain all "rights." In the midst of any conflict they are not granted by the side holding the economic and political power, except as they may be forced by the strength of the opposition. However, the mere public assertion of the principle of freedom of opinion in the words or deeds of individuals, or weak minorities, helps win it recognition, and in the long run makes for tolerance and against resort to violence.

Today the organized movements of labor and of the farmers are waging the chief fight for civil liberty throughout the United States as part of their effort for increased control of industry. Publicity, demonstrations, political activities and legal aid are organized nationally and locally. Only by such an aggressive policy of insistence can rights be secured and maintained. The union of organized labor, the farmers, radical and liberal movements is the most effective means to this.

It is these forces which the American Civil Liberties Union serves in their efforts for civil liberty. The practical work of free speech demonstrations, publicity and legal defense is done primarily in the struggles of the organized labor and farmers movements.

"In the interest of true Americanism": Letter to New York governor Alfred Smith
Paul M. Winter

The Ku Klux Klan (KKK) had been founded in the Reconstruction South to resist Northern occupation, including efforts to elevate the status of blacks and give them rights equal to those of whites. In 1922, white Protestant men revived the Klan to maintain, among other things, the supremacy of whites and "pure Americanism." Dressed anonymously in white sheets, the KKK often terrorized blacks, immigrants, and Catholics, sometimes lynching blacks with the tacit approval of the police, especially in the South and Midwest.

Although the rise of the KKK represented one of the virulent strains of intolerance in United States history, some of the group's activities were peaceful and therefore protected by the Bill of Rights. In 1925, forty thousand Klansmen marched in Washington, D.C., and membership was in the millions.

Two years later, the Klan conducted a march in the Jamaica section of Queens (a borough of New York City) that resulted in an altercation with police. Klansmen and a grand jury blamed the incident on the police. In this letter, Klan member Paul M. Winter appealed to New York governor Alfred Smith, a Catholic, to support the group's constitutional right to make a peaceful demonstration.

HONORABLE SIR: Again I am desirous of drawing your attention to the maladministration of justice in Queens County, New York City, relative to the attack precipitated by the police of New York City on a peaceful parade of native-born Americans last Memorial Day, May 30, 1927, in Jamaica, Long Island.

Despite the fact that the Grand Jury of Queens County has placed the blame for the attack on the shoulders of the police and in their decision called upon the Mayor to punish the guilty parties, Mayor James J. Walker has consistently "whitewashed" the affair on the basis that the Klan is illegally operating in the State of New York.

This attitude has not the semblance of an excuse, but merely justifies the clubbing and beating of innocent men and women because they differ religiously with him and have endeavored to exercise their Constitutional rights. The parade of the Klan on Memorial Day was covered by a legal permit. . . .

You are perfectly acquainted, and I believe Mayor Walker is also, with the fact that the Klan incorporated as a Greek letter society and exercising its prerogative changed its name later to the Knights and Women of the Ku Klux Klan. This act made it a legally constituted organization with the same rights enjoyed by any other organization, even the Fascisti.

As the field representative of the Klan in Queens County I am appealing to you in an effort to see that justice is administered and I am making this request for the purpose of determining whether you can separate your religious feelings from things political.

Trusting that the injured feelings of thousands of citizens in Queens County might be healed in the interest of true Americanism, I am

Respectfully yours,
Paul M. Winter

"I have suffered because I was an Italian"
Bartolomeo Vanzetti

In 1921, Italian immigrants Nicola Sacco and Bartolomeo Vanzetti were convicted in Braintree, Massachusetts, of a murder during the robbery of a shoe factory. They were sentenced to death. The prosecution had placed a heavy emphasis on the two men's radical politics, Italian heritage, and opposition to U.S. involvement in World War I. Both men had alibis that were discredited because the witnesses, too, were Italian.

Outraged by the preponderance of evidence presented in the trial about the two men's Italian backgrounds and the lack of evidence about the incident itself, a groundswell of opposition to the sentence emerged. Because of controversy surrounding the trial, the governor appointed a special commission to review the case. The commission sharply criticized the presiding judge's conduct, but sustained the findings. Vanzetti made a statement to the court, reprinted here, upon being sentenced to death (again) after the commission's report.

The executions were carried out on August 23, 1927, despite the widely held belief that Sacco and Vanzetti were innocent. Vanzetti, a fish peddler, told a reporter just prior to his death: "If it had not been for this thing, I might have lived out my life talking at street corners to scorning men. I might have died, unmarked, unknown, a failure. Now we are not a failure. This is our career and our triumph. Never in our full life can we hope to do such work for tolerance, justice, for man's understanding of man, as now we do by accident . . . The taking of our lives, lives of a good shoemaker and a poor fish peddler, all! That last moment belongs to us—that agony is our triumph."

WHAT I SAY IS THAT I AM INNOCENT. . . . Everybody that knows these two arms knows very well that I did not need to go in between the street and kill a man to take the money. I can live with my two arms and live well. But besides that, I can live even without work with my arms for other people. I have had plenty of chance to live independently and to live what the world conceives to be a higher life than not to gain our bread with the sweat of our brow. . . .

Now, I should say that I am not only innocent of all these things, not only have I never committed a real crime in my life—though some sins, but not crimes—not only have I struggled all my life to eliminate crimes that the official law and the official moral condemns, but also the crime that the moral and the official law sanctions and sanctifies, exploitation and the oppression of the man by the man, and if there is a reason why I am here as a guilty man, if there is a reason why you in a few minutes can doom me, it is this reason and none else. . . .

That is what I say: I would not wish to a dog or to a snake, to the most low and misfortunate creature of the earth—I would not wish to any of them what I have had to suffer for things that I am not guilty of. But my conviction is that I have suffered for things that I am guilty of. I am suffering because I am a radical and indeed I am a radical; I have suffered because I was an Italian, and indeed I am an Italian; I have suffered more for my family and for my beloved than for myself; but I am so convinced to be right that you could execute me two times, and I would live again to do what I have done already.

Protests by the Bonus Expeditionary Army

During the depths of the Great Depression, about fifteen thousand World War I veterans marched on Washington, D.C., requesting that they receive early payment of a bonus promised to them for their military service. Congress had earlier pledged to pay $1.25 for each day served overseas and $1 for each day served in the United States; payment was to be made in 1945.

But many soldiers needed the money immediately to feed their families, since at the time there was no unemployment compensation, veterans' benefits, or other forms of financial sup-

port. The soldiers and their families—known as the Bonus Expeditionary Army—camped out peacefully in various places throughout the city in the summer of 1932 and vowed to stay until the government fulfilled its promise.

On July 28, 1932, two of the protesters were killed by police. Fearing violence would break out, President Herbert Hoover ordered the camps cleared. That afternoon, police and troops massed on Pennsylvania Avenue with fixed bayonets and six tanks to disperse the veterans and their families. General Douglas MacArthur ordered the attack. Soldiers and police hurled tear gas into the crowds and set the camps aflame. Scores of people were injured and two babies were killed in the attack.

"The whole scene was pitiful," Dwight Eisenhower, who participated in the attack, later wrote of the assault. "The veterans were ragged, ill-fed, and felt themselves badly abused."

Resignation from the Daughters of the American Revolution
Eleanor Roosevelt

Having completed a very successful concert tour in Europe, African-American contralto Marian Anderson wanted to give a performance at Constitution Hall in Washington, D.C., in 1939. The owner of the hall, the Daughters of the American Revolution (DAR), refused to allow Anderson to perform because she was black.

The organization's most well-known member, First Lady Eleanor Roosevelt, was a forceful advocate for civil rights. Roosevelt was also an admirer of Anderson and had invited her to sing at the White House three years earlier, infuriating some of President Franklin D. Roosevelt's southern supporters. When Mrs. Roosevelt heard that the DAR had refused to let Anderson sing in their hall, she wrote the following letter, resigning from the organization in protest. She then helped organize an Easter concert, in which Anderson sang; the concert was held in front of the Lincoln Memorial and broadcast across the country.

I AM AFRAID that I have never been a very useful member of the Daughters of the American Revolution, so I know it will make very little difference to you whether I resign, or whether I continue to be a member of your organization.

However, I am in complete disagreement with the attitude taken in refusing Constitution Hall to a great artist. You have set an example which seems to me unfortunate, and I feel obliged to send in to you my resignation. You had an opportunity to lead in an enlightened way and it seems to me that your organization has failed.

I realize that many people will not agree with me, but feeling as I do this seems to me the only proper procedure to follow.

"This Land Is Your Land"

Woody Guthrie

Raised in the rural Great Plains, Woody Guthrie wandered the country when the dust storms arrived during the Great Depression. A populist and talented musician, Guthrie played his guitar and wrote songs on behalf of union causes and the impoverished.

In February 1940, Guthrie wrote "This Land Is Your Land" in reaction to Irving Berlin's song "God Bless America." The original lyrics of the song appear here. Guthrie heard Berlin's song repeatedly while traveling across the country. He became increasingly annoyed that it overlooked the lopsided distribution of land and wealth that he had experienced. At the time, 1 percent of the population owned 20 percent of the national wealth.

Guthrie originally entitled his song "God Blessed America for Me," a line repeated at the end of each verse. He changed the lines to "This land was made for you and me" when he first recorded the song in 1944 with Cisco Houston.

This land is your land, this land is my land
From [the] California to the [Staten] New York Island,
From the Redwood Forest, to the Gulf stream waters,
[God blessed America for me.]

As I went walking that ribbon of highway
And saw above me that endless skyway,
And saw below me the golden valley, I said:
[God blessed America for me.]

I roamed and rambled and followed my footsteps
To the sparkling sands of her diamond deserts,
And all around me, a voice was sounding:
[God blessed America for me.]

Was a high wall there that tried to stop me
A sign was painted said: Private Property,
But on the back side it didn't say nothing—
[God blessed America for me.]

When the sun come shining, then I was strolling
In wheat fields waving and dust clouds rolling;
The voice was chanting as the fog was lifting:
[God blessed America for me.]

One bright sunny morning in the shadow of the steeple
By the Relief Office I saw my people—
As they stood hungry, I stood there wondering if
[God blessed America for me.]

Letter to the Minersville, Pennsylvania, School Directors
Billy Gobitas

When the Minersville, Pennsylvania, school system required all of its students to salute the flag, ten-year-old Billy Gobitas and his older sister, Lillian, refused to join their classmates in the morning ritual. The two students had been raised as Jehovah's Witnesses and believed that saluting and pledging allegiance to the flag were acts of idolatry that violated their religious beliefs, specifically the Second Commandment. Billy wrote the following letter to the directors of the school explaining his position. Upon receiving it, the school board expelled him and his sister.

The Watchtower Society of the Jehovah's Witnesses sued on behalf of the Gobitas children. The case went to the Supreme Court in 1940. The court found in favor of the school board. Three years later, however, when the Jehovah's Witness challenged a West Virginia law requiring that students pledge allegiance to the flag, the Supreme Court determined that such a law violates the First Amendment guarantee of free expression.

I DO NOT salute the flag because I have promised to do the will of God. That means that I must not worship anything out of harmony with God's law. In the twentieth chapter of Exodus it is stated, "Thou shalt not make unto thee any graven image, nor bow down to them nor serve them for I the Lord thy God am a jealous God visiting the iniquity of the fathers upon the children unto the third and fourth generation of them that hate me." I am a true follower of Christ. I do not salute the flag not because I do not love my crountry [sic], but I love my crountry and I love God more and I must obey His commandments.

Resolution of the Citizens' Mass Meeting
Montgomery Improvement Association

Like many southern cities, Montgomery, Alabama, required black passengers to sit in the back of city buses and to give up their seats to white passengers if no seats were available in the white section of the bus. On December 1, 1955, Rosa Parks—a seamstress and organizer with the National Association for the Advancement of Colored People (NAACP)—refused to give up her seat for a white man who had gotten on the bus after her. Police were called to arrest Parks, who was fined ten dollars for her crime.

The NAACP and other black organizations in the city used the incident as an opportunity to protest the Jim Crow laws that deprived blacks of equal rights. Black leaders called for a citywide protest that almost the entire black community joined. At the Holt Street Baptist Church, the newly formed Montgomery Improvement Association elected as president a minister new to the Montgomery area: twenty-six-year-old Reverend Martin Luther King, Jr.

"You know, my friends, there comes a time when people get tired of being trampled over by the iron feet of oppression," King told the association's mass meeting on December 5. "There comes a time, my friends, when people get tired of being flung across the abyss of humiliation where they experience the bleakness of nagging despair. There comes a time when people get tired of being pushed out of the glittering sunlight of life's July and left standing amidst the piercing chill of an Alpine November."

Participants at the meeting called for a boycott of Montgomery buses. The text of the resolution calling for the boycott follows. Instead of using buses, protesters carpooled to get to work. Black taxi drivers piled passengers into their cabs, charging the same ten-cent fare required for a bus. Several white employers opted to shuttle their black employees from home to work, sometimes in sympathy for the boycott and other times just because they wanted or needed their work to get done. Many whites fought the boycott. Four churches and the homes of King and fellow civil rights leader Ralph Abernathy were firebombed. Authorities arrested 156 protesters, including King, for "hindering the buses"—a crime that King said he was proud to have committed.

The Supreme Court overturned Montgomery's bus law in November 1956. The decision was one of the first victories of the civil rights movement and made King a national figure.

WHEREAS, there are thousands of Negroes in the city and county of Montgomery who ride busses owned and operated by the Montgomery City Lines, Incorporated, and

Whereas, said citizens have been riding busses owned and operated by said company over a number of years, and

Whereas, said citizens, over a number of years, and on many occasions have been insulted, embarrassed and have been made to suffer great fear of bodily harm by drivers of busses owned and operated by said bus company, and

Whereas, the drivers of said busses have never required a white passenger riding on any of its busses to relinquish his seat and stand so that a Negro may take his seat; however, said drivers have on many occasions too numerous to mention requested Negro passengers on said busses to relinquish their seats and stand so that white passengers may take their seats, and

Whereas, said citizens of Montgomery city and county pay their fares just as all other persons who are passengers on said busses, and are entitled to free and equal treatment, and

Whereas, there has been any number of arrests of Negroes caused by drivers of said busses and they are constantly put in jail for refusing to give white passengers their seats and stand.

Whereas, in March of 1955, a committee of citizens did have a conference with one of the officials of said bus line; at which time said official arranged a meeting between attorneys representing the Negro citizens of this city and attorneys representing Montgomery City Lines, Incorporated and the city of Montgomery, and

Whereas, the official of the bus line promised that as a result of the meeting between said attorneys, he would issue a statement of policy clarifying the law with reference to the seating of Negro passengers on the bus, and

Whereas, said attorneys did have a meeting and did discuss the matter of clarifying the law, however, the official said bus lines did not make public statements as to its policy with reference to the seating of passengers on its busses, and

Whereas, since that time, at least two ladies have been arrested for an alleged violation of the city segregation law with reference to bus travel, and

Whereas, said citizens of Montgomery city and county believe that they have been grossly mistreated as passengers on the busses owned and operated by said bus company in spite of the fact that they are in the majority with reference to the number of passengers riding on said busses.

Be it Resolved As Follows:

That the citizens of Montgomery are requesting that every citizen in Montgomery, regardless of race, color, or creed, to refrain from riding busses owned and operated in the city of Montgomery by the Montgomery City Lines, Incorporated until some arrangement has been worked out between said citizens and the Montgomery City Lines, Incorporated.

That every person owning or who has access to automobiles use their automobiles in assisting other persons to get to work without charge.

That the employers of persons whose employees live a great distance from them, as much as possible afford transportation to your own employees.

That the Negro citizens of Montgomery are ready and willing to send a delegation of citizens to the Montgomery City Lines to discuss their grievances and to work out a solution for the same.

Be it further resolved that we have not, are not, and have no intentions of using an unlawful means or any intimidation to persuade persons not to ride the Montgomery City Lines' busses.

However, we call upon your consciences, both moral and spiritual, to give your whole-hearted support to this undertaking. We believe we have complaint and we are willing to discuss this matter with the proper officials.

"I have a dream"
Martin Luther King, Jr.

Considered one of the greatest speeches of the twentieth century, Martin Luther King, Jr.'s "I Have a Dream" speech capped a massive march on Washington designed to put pressure on Congress and President John F. Kennedy to support civil rights legislation. King delivered his speech on August 23, 1963, from the steps of the Lincoln Memorial before more than one hundred thousand blacks and whites on the Washington Mall. It was also broadcast on national television. King received the Nobel Peace Prize the following year.

Congress responded to many of the demands of the march with the civil rights acts of 1964 and 1965, both of which were supported by President Lyndon Johnson. (Kennedy was assassinated three months after the speech.) King was assassinated in 1968 at the age of thirty-nine.

I AM HAPPY TO JOIN WITH YOU TODAY in what will go down in history as the greatest demonstration for freedom in the history of our nation.

Fivescore years ago, a great American, in whose symbolic shadow we stand today, signed the Emancipation Proclamation. This momentous decree came as a great beacon light of hope to millions of Negro slaves who had been seated in the flames of withering injustice. It came as a joyous daybreak to end the long night of their captivity.

But one hundred years later, the Negro still is not free. One hundred years later, the life of the Negro is still sadly crippled by the manacles of segregation and the chains of discrimination. One hundred years later, the Negro lives on a lonely island of poverty in the midst of a vast ocean of material prosperity. One hundred years later, the Negro is still languished in the corners of American society and finds himself in exile in his own land. And so we've come here today to dramatize a shameful condition.

In a sense we've come to our nation's capital to cash a check. When the architects of our republic wrote the magnificent words of the Constitution and the Declaration of Independence, they were signing a promissory note to which every American was to fall heir. This note was the promise that all men, yes, black men as well as white men, would be guaranteed the "unalienable Rights of Life, Liberty, and the pursuit of Happiness." It is obvious today that America has defaulted on this promissory note insofar as her citizens of color are concerned. Instead of honoring this sacred obligation, America has given the Negro people a bad check, a check which has come back marked "insufficient funds."

But we refuse to believe that the bank of justice is bankrupt. We refuse to believe that there are insufficient funds in the great vaults of opportunity of this nation. And so we've come to cash this check, a check that will give us upon demand the riches of freedom and the security of justice.

We have also come to this hallowed spot to remind America of the fierce urgency of now. This is no time to engage in the luxury of cooling off or to take the tranquilizing drug of gradualism. Now is the time to make real the promises of democracy. Now is the time to rise from the dark and desolate valley of segregation to the sunlit path of racial justice. Now is the time to lift our nation from the quicksands of racial injustice to the solid rock of brotherhood. Now is the time to make justice a reality for God's children.

It would be fatal for the nation to overlook the urgency of the moment. This sweltering summer of the Negro's legitimate discontent will not pass until there is an invigorating autumn of freedom and equality. Nineteen sixty-three is not an end, but a beginning. And those who hope that the Negro needed to blow off steam and will now be content will have a rude awakening if the nation returns to business as usual. There will be neither rest nor tranquility in America until the Negro is granted his citizenship rights. The whirlwinds of revolt will continue to shake the foundations of our nation until the bright days of justice emerges.

But there is something that I must say to my people, who stand on the warm threshold which leads into the palace of justice: In the process of gaining our rightful place, we must not be guilty of wrongful deeds. Let us not seek to satisfy our thirst for freedom by drinking from the cup of bitterness and hatred. We must forever conduct our struggle on the high plane of dignity and discipline. We must not allow our creative protest to degenerate into physical violence. Again and again we must rise to the majestic heights of meeting physical force with soul force. The marvelous new militancy which has engulfed the Negro community must not lead us to a distrust of all white people, for many of our white brothers, as evidenced by their presence here today, have come to realize that their destiny is tied up with our destiny. And they have come to realize that their freedom is inextricably bound to our freedom. We cannot walk alone.

And as we walk, we must make the pledge that we shall always march ahead. We cannot turn back. There are those who are asking the devotees of civil rights, "When will you be satisfied?"

We can never be satisfied as long as the Negro is the victim of the unspeakable horrors of police brutality. We can never be satisfied as long as our bodies, heavy with the fatigue of travel, cannot gain lodging in the motels of the highways and the hotels of the cities. We cannot be satisfied as long as the Negro's basic mobility is from a smaller ghetto to a larger one. We can never be satisfied as long as our children are stripped of their selfhood and robbed of their dignity by signs stating "for whites only." We cannot be satisfied as long as a Negro in Mississippi cannot vote and a Negro in New York believes he has nothing for which to vote. No, no, we are not satisfied and we will not be satisfied until "justice rolls down like waters and righteousness like a mighty stream."

I am not unmindful that some of you have come here out of great trials and tribulations. Some of you have come fresh from narrow jail cells. Some of you have come from areas where your quest for freedom left you battered by the storms of persecution and staggered by the winds of police brutality. You have been the veterans of creative suffering. Continue to work with the faith that unearned suffering is redemptive. Go back to Mississippi, go back to Alabama, go back to South Carolina, go back to Georgia, go back to Louisiana, go back to the slums and ghettos of our northern cities, knowing that somehow this situation can and will be changed. Let us not wallow in the valley of despair.

I say to you today, my friends, that even though we face the difficulties of today and tomorrow, I still have a dream. It is a dream deeply rooted in the American dream.

I have a dream that one day this nation will rise up and live out the true meaning of its creed: "We hold these truths to be self-evident, that all men are created equal."

I have a dream that one day on the red hills of Georgia the sons of former slaves and the sons of former slave owners will be able to sit down together at a table of brotherhood.

I have a dream that one day even the state of Mississippi, a state sweltering with the heat of injustice, sweltering with the heat of oppression, will be transformed into an oasis of freedom and justice.

I have a dream that my four little children will one day live in a nation where they will not be judged by the color of their skin but by the content of their character. I have a dream today.

I have a dream that one day the state of Alabama, with its vicious racists, with its governor having his lips dripping with the words of "interposition" and "nullification," one day right there in Alabama, little black boys and black girls will be able to join hands with little white boys and white girls as sisters and brothers. I have a dream today.

I have a dream that one day "every valley shall be exalted, and every hill and mountain shall be made low; the rough places will be made plain, and the crooked places will be made straight; and the glory of the Lord shall be revealed, and all flesh shall see it together."

This is our hope. This is the faith that I go back to the South with. With this faith we will be able to hew out of the mountain of despair a stone of hope. With this faith we will be able to transform the jangling discords of our nation into a beautiful symphony of brotherhood. With this faith we will be able to work together, to pray together, to struggle together, to go to jail together, to stand up for freedom together, knowing that we will be free one day. This will be the day, this will be the day when all of God's children will be able to sing with a new meaning: "My country, 'tis of thee, sweet land of liberty, of thee I sing. Land where my fathers died, land of the pilgrim's pride, from every mountainside, let freedom ring!"

And if America is to be a great nation, this must become true.

And so let freedom ring from the prodigious hilltops of New Hampshire.

Let freedom ring from the mighty mountains of New York.

Let freedom ring from the heightening Alleghenies of Pennsylvania.

Let freedom ring from the snowcapped Rockies of Colorado.

Let freedom ring from the curvaceous slopes of California.

But not only that: Let freedom ring from Stone Mountain of Georgia.

Let freedom ring from Lookout Mountain of Tennessee.

Let freedom ring from every hill and every molehill of Mississippi.

From every mountainside, let freedom ring.

And when this happens, when we allow freedom [to] ring, when we let it ring from every village and every hamlet, from every state and every city, we will be able to speed up that day when all of God's children, black men and white men, Jews and Gentiles, Protestants and Catholics, will be able to join hands and sing in the words of the old Negro spiritual: "Free at last! Free at last! Thank God Almighty, we are free at last!"

The Autobiography of Malcolm X
Malcolm X

Malcolm X advocated a more aggressive approach to winning civil rights than Martin Luther King, Jr., did, scoffing at nonviolence as being too accommodating to white America. Shortly after the 1963 march on Washington, Malcolm X blasted the march and King's "I Have a Dream" speech as a farce. His view represented the tension within almost all protest movements between moderate and more extreme views.

Ironically, as time passed Malcolm X moderated his firebrand approach, and King became more radical. Both, however, met the same end. Malcolm X was killed by fellow black Muslims in 1965.

NOT LONG AGO, the black man in America was fed a dose of another form of the weakening, lulling, and deluding effects of so-called "integration."

It was that "Farce on Washington," I call it.

The idea of a mass of blacks marching on Washington was originally the brainchild of the Brotherhood of Sleeping Car Porters' A. Phillip Randolph. For twenty or more years the March on Washington idea had floated around among Negroes. And, spontaneously, suddenly now, that idea caught on. . . .

Any student of how "integration" can weaken the black man's movement was about to observe a master lesson.

The White House, with a fanfare of international publicity, "approved," "endorsed," and "welcomed" a March on Washington. . . .

It was like a movie. The next scene was the "big six" civil rights Negro "leaders" meeting in New York City with the white head of a big philanthropic agency. They were told that their money-wrangling in public was damaging their image. And a reported $800,000 was donated to a United Civil Rights Leadership council that was quickly organized by the "big six."

Now, what had instantly achieved black unity? The white man's money. What string was attached to the money? Advice. Not only was there this donation, but another comparable sum was promised, for sometime later on, after the March . . . obviously if it all went well.

The original "angry" March on Washington was now about to be entirely changed. . . .

Invited next to join the march were four famous white public figures: one Catholic, one Jew, one Protestant, and one labor boss. . . .

. . . And suddenly, the previously March-nervous whites began announcing they were going.

It was as if an electrical current shot through the ranks of bourgeois Negroes—the very so-called "middle-class" and "upper-class" who had earlier been deploring the March on Washington talk by grass-roots Negroes.

But white people, now, were going to march.

Why, some downtrodden, jobless, hungry Negro might have gotten trampled. Those "integration"-mad Negroes practically ran over each other trying to find out where to sign up. The "angry blacks" March suddenly had been made chic. Suddenly it had a Kentucky Derby image. For the status-seeker, it was a status symbol. "Were you *there*?" You can hear that right today.

It had become an outing, a picnic.

The morning of the March, any rickety carloads of angry, dusty, sweating small-town Negroes would have gotten lost among the chartered jet planes, railroad cars, and air-conditioned buses. What originally was planned to be an angry riptide, one English newspaper aptly described as "the gentle flood."

Talk about "integrated"! It was like salt and pepper. And, by now, there wasn't a single logistics aspect uncontrolled.

The marchers had been instructed to bring no signs—signs were provided. They had been told to sing one song: "We Shall Overcome." They had been told *how* to arrive, *when, where* to arrive, *where* to assemble, when to *start* marching, the *route* to march. First aid stations were strategically located—even where to *faint*!

Yes, I was there, I observed that circus. Who ever heard of angry revolutionists all harmonizing "We Shall Overcome . . . Suum Day . . ." while tripping and swaying along arm-in-arm with the very people they were supposed to be angrily revolting against? Who ever heard of angry revolutionists swinging their bare feet together with their oppressor in lily-pad park pools, with gospels and guitars and "I Have a Dream" speeches?

Two-Minute Warning: Bloody Sunday

On Sunday, March 7, 1965, six hundred civil rights marchers headed east from Selma, Alabama, to the state capital in Montgomery in a nonviolent march demanding equal voting rights in the state. The march, organized by the Southern Leadership Christian Conference and the Student Nonviolent Coordinating Committee, was held a few days after twenty-six-year-old Jimmy Lee Jackson, a black man, was killed by white state troopers.

The Selma protesters walked six blocks before they were confronted at the Edmund Pettus Bridge by police armed with shotguns and automatic weapons. Governor George Wallace ordered the police to stop the march, if needed with force.

This photograph captures the moment when police gave a two-minute warning to the protestors—led by Hosea Williams and John Lewis—to disperse. The civil rights marchers did not leave. Using tear gas and nightsticks, the troopers pressed forward, beating the protesters. Television cameras captured the attack, which became known worldwide as Bloody Sunday.

After two more attempts, twenty-five thousand protesters reached the state capital on Thursday, March 25. The violence of the police attack and the determination of the civil rights leaders to complete the march helped arouse national opinion in favor of stronger federal legislation for civil rights. Five months later, President Lyndon Johnson signed the Voting Rights Act of 1965.

Statement of Purpose
Founders of the National Organization for Women

Frustrated by inaction by the Equal Employment Opportunity Commission (EEOC) in enforcing sex-discrimination cases, Betty Friedan and twenty-seven other men and women founded the National Organization for Women (NOW) on June 30, 1966. The founders wrote a statement of purpose, reprinted here, focusing on employment opportunities for women. Friedan wrote the first draft on a napkin.

The following year NOW issued a bill of rights for women, broadening the organization's mission to include support for an equal rights amendment to the U.S. Constitution and the legalization of abortion. NOW grew to become the largest feminist group in the United States with more than five hundred thousand members and more than five hundred chapters in all fifty states.

WE, MEN AND WOMEN who hereby constitute ourselves as the National Organization for Women, believe that the time has come for a new movement toward true equality for all women in America, and toward a fully equal partnership of the sexes, as part of the world-wide revolution of human rights now taking place within and beyond our national borders. . . .

We reject the current assumption that a man must carry the sole burden of supporting himself, his wife, and family, and that a woman is automatically entitled to lifelong support by a man upon her marriage, or that marriage, home and family are primarily women's world and responsibility—hers, to dominate—his, to support. We believe that a true partnership between the sexes demands a different concept of marriage, an equitable sharing of the responsibilities of home and children and of the economic burdens of their support. . . .

In the interests of the human dignity of women, we will protest, and endeavor to change, the false image of women now prevalent in the mass media, and in the texts, ceremonies, laws, and practices of the major social institutions. Such images perpetuate contempt for women by society and by women for themselves. . . .

We believe that women will do most to create a new image of women by acting now, and by speaking out in behalf of their own equality, freedom, and human dignity—not in pleas for special privilege, nor in enmity toward men, who are also victims of the current, half-equality between the sexes—but in an active, self-respecting partnership with men. . . .

We Demand:

That the U.S. Congress immediately pass the Equal Rights Amendment to the Constitution to provide that "Equality of rights under the law shall not be denied or abridged by the United States or by any state on account of sex," and such then be immediately ratified by the several states.

That equal employment opportunity be guaranteed to all women, as well as men, by insisting that the Equal Employment Opportunity Commission enforces the prohibitions against racial discrimination.

That women be protected by law to ensure their rights to return to their jobs within a reasonable time after childbirth without loss of seniority or other accrued benefits, and be paid maternity leave as a form of social security and/or employee benefit.

Immediate revision of tax laws to permit the deduction of home and child-care expenses for working parents.

That child-care facilities be established by law on the same basis as parks, libraries, and public schools, adequate to the needs of children from the pre-school years through adolescence, as a community resource to be used by all citizens from all income levels.

That the right of women to be educated to their full potential equally with men be secured by federal and state legislation, eliminating all discrimination and segregation by sex, written and unwritten, at all levels of education, including colleges, graduate and professional schools, loans and fellowships, and federal and state training programs such as the Job Corps.

The right of women in poverty to secure job training, housing, and family allowances on equal terms with men, but without prejudice to a parent's right to remain at home to care for his or her children; revision of welfare legislation and poverty programs which deny women dignity, privacy, and self-respect.

The right of women to control their own reproductive lives by removing from the penal code laws limiting access to contraceptive information and devices, and by repealing penal laws governing abortion.

"I do not feel that I am a piece of property"
Curt Flood

Curt Flood was one of the best outfielders in major league baseball, starring for the St. Louis Cardinals from 1957 to 1969 before being traded to the Philadelphia Phillies, a team he did not want to join. Because Congress had exempted major league baseball from antitrust legislation, baseball players had no choice in selecting their employer.

Flood wrote this letter to baseball commissioner Bowie Kuhn, protesting his lack of rights and requesting that he be allowed to become a free agent. Kuhn refused. Flood brought his appeal to the United States Supreme Court, which ruled against him five to three. Nevertheless, Flood's protest set the stage for free agency in major league baseball in 1974 and in other professional sports thereafter.

AFTER 12 YEARS in the major leagues, I do not feel that I am a piece of property to be bought and sold irrespective of my wishes. I believe that any system that produces that result violates my basic rights as a citizen and is inconsistent with the laws of the United States and the several states.

It is my desire to play baseball in 1970 and I am capable of playing. I have received a contract from the Philadelphia club, but I believe I have the right to consider offers from other clubs before making any decisions. I, therefore, request that you make known to all the major league clubs my feelings in this matter, and advise them of my availability to for the 1970 season.

"The unconstitutional provisions of AFM 39-12 relating to the discharge of homosexuals"
Leonard Matlovich

Leonard Matlovich was a veteran of the Vietnam War, serving as a sergeant in the U.S. Air Force. Shortly after his service in Vietnam, where he had earned a Bronze Star and Purple Heart for combat duty, Matlovich declared his homosexuality in this 1975 letter to the secretary of the Air Force. The military, which banned homosexuals, discharged Matlovich, who then sued the government to stay in the Air Force.

His courtroom battle gained nationwide attention, including a cover photograph of *Time* magazine. The U.S. Court of Appeals ruled that Matlovich's discharge was illegal, but the case was later settled out of court.

With the exception of ancient Greece, homosexuality in the military has largely been discouraged, if not prohibited, as has been the case in the United States for most of its history. The enforcement of the ban has varied. During World War II when the demand for manpower was very high, the military often overlooked same-sex relationships unless they attracted too much attention, in which cases the soldiers received undesirable discharges. After the war, the military became more rigorous in its enforcement of the ban. The Matlovich case brought the issue to the nation's attention. When President Bill Clinton was elected to office in 1993 he implemented a controversial change in the military rules. The new "Don't ask, don't tell" policy distinguished between homosexual behavior and status. Homosexuals can serve in the army provided they keep their sexual orientation to themselves. They are permitted to participate in events advocating for gay rights and read homosexual publications, but they are not allowed to engage in same-gender sexual behavior.

Matolich died of AIDS in 1988. He wrote the following to be engraved on his tombstone: "When I was in the military, they gave me a medal for killing two men, and a discharge for loving one."

1. AFTER SOME YEARS OF UNCERTAINTY, I have arrived at the conclusion that my sexual preferences are homosexual as opposed to heterosexual. I have also concluded that my sexual preference will in no way interfere with my Air Force duties, as my preferences are now open. It is therefore requested that those provisions in AFM 39-12 relating to the discharge of homosexuals be waived in my case.

2. I will decline to answer specific questions concerning the functioning of my sex life, for AFM 39-12 as currently in effect could subject me to a less than fully honorable discharge. However, I will be glad to answer any questions concerning my personal life if reasons are given detailing how the questions relate to specific fitness and security concerns rather than the generally unconstitutional provisions of AFM 39-12 relating to the discharge of homosexuals. If more specific criteria other than the notion of homosexuals are morally unqualified for service in the Air Force can be shown as basis for questioning, I will answer the appropriate questions.

3. Before any specific questions are addressed to me about this matter my attorney, David F. Addlestone, 1346 Connecticut Avenue N.W., Suite 604, Washington, D.C. 20036, requests that he be notified.

4. In sum, I consider myself to be a homosexual and fully qualified for further military service. My almost twelve years of unblemished service supports this position.

Why We Fight

Vito Russo

The onslaught of AIDS (Acquired Immune Deficiency Syndrome) in the late 1970s and early 1980s first hit the gay community and intravenous (IV) drug users. In 1984 doctors identified the Human Immunodeficiency Virus (HIV) as the source of the deadly syndrome. Although thousands of people were dying from the fatal disease, many people believed that the government response to the problem was at best slow, largely because most of the victims were homosexual men, drug users, and people of color. President Ronald Reagan did not publicly mention the disease until 1987, and government-funded educational materials skirted issues of sexuality.

People with HIV and AIDS and public-health advocates fought for public-education and health programs to combat the spread of HIV. In 1987, activists formed the AIDS Coalition to Unleash Power (ACT UP) in New York City to spur government officials into action. They organized civil-disobedience events to raise awareness about the problem.

Vito Russo wrote *The Celluloid Closet* and was a founding member of ACT UP and the Gay and Lesbian Anti-Defamation League. He gave the speech excerpted here at ACT UP events in 1988 in Albany, New York, and Washington, D.C. Russo died of AIDS in 1990 at the age of forty-four.

A FRIEND OF MINE in New York City has a half-fare transit card, which means that you get on buses and subways for half price. And the other day, when he showed his card to the token attendant, the attendant asked what his disability was and he said, I have AIDS. And the attendant said, no you don't, if you had AIDS, you'd be home dying. And so, I wanted to speak out today as a person with AIDS who is not dying.

You know, for the last three years, since I was diagnosed, my family thinks two things about my situation. One, they think I'm going to die, and two, they think that my government is doing absolutely everything in their power to stop that. And they're wrong, on both counts.

So, if I'm dying from anything, I'm dying from homophobia. If I'm dying from anything, I'm dying from racism. If I'm dying from anything, it's from indifference and red tape, because these are the things that are preventing an end to this crisis. If I'm dying from anything, I'm dying from Jesse Helms. If I'm dying from anything, I'm dying from the President of the United States. And, especially, if I'm dying from anything, I'm dying from the sensationalism of newspapers and magazines and television shows, which are interested in me, as a human interest story—only as long as I'm willing to be a helpless victim, but not if I'm fighting for my life.

If I'm dying from anything—I'm dying from the fact that not enough rich, white, heterosexual men have gotten AIDS for anybody to give a shit. You know, living with AIDS in this country is like living in the twilight zone. Living with AIDS is like living though a war which is happening only for those people who happen to be in the trenches. Every time a shell explodes, you look around and you discover that you've lost more of your friends, but nobody else notices. It isn't happening to them. They're walking the streets as though we weren't living through some sort of nightmare. And only you can hear the screams of the people who are dying and their cries for help. No one else seems to be noticing.

And it's worse than a war, because during a war people are united in a shared experience. This war has not united us, it's divided us. It's separated those of us with AIDS and those of us who fight for people with AIDS from the rest of the population.

Two and a half years ago, I picked up *Life* magazine, and I read an editorial which said, "it's time to pay attention, because this disease is now beginning to strike the rest of us." It was as if I wasn't the one holding the magazine in my hand. And since then, nothing has changed to alter the perception that AIDS is not happening to the real people in this country.

It's not happening to us in the United States, it's happening to them—to the disposable populations of fags and junkies who deserve what they get. The media tells them that they don't have to care, because the people who really matter are not in danger. Twice, three times, four times—the *New York Times* has published editorials saying, don't panic yet, over AIDS—it still hasn't entered the general population, and until it does, we don't have to give a shit. . . .

If it is true that gay men and IV drug users are the populations at risk for this disease, then we have a right to demand that education and prevention be targeted specifically to these people. And it is not happening. We are being allowed to die, while low-risk populations are being panicked—not educated, panicked—into believing that we deserve to die. . . .

It is more than a horror story, exploited by the tabloids. AIDS is really a test of us, as a people. When future generations ask what we did in this crisis, we're going to have to tell them that we were out here today. And we have to leave the legacy to those generations of people who will come after us.

Someday, the AIDS crisis will be over. Remember that. And when that day comes—when that day has come and gone, there'll be people alive on this earth—gay people and straight people, men and women, black and white, who will hear the story that once there was a terrible disease in this country and all over the world, and that a brave group of people stood up and fought and, in some cases, gave their lives, so that other people might live and be free. . . .

. . . [A]fter we kick the shit out of this disease, we're all going to be alive to kick the shit out of the system, so that this never happens again.

De Colores Means All of Us
Elizabeth Martínez

In 1968 more than 10,000 Latino students in Los Angeles walked out of their high schools to protest the education system, which they described as racist and insensitive to their heritage. "Chicano Power" was born. Shortly afterward, Latino college students staged similar walkouts in California's higher-education institutions.

Twenty-five years later, a second wave of school blowouts (or student walkouts) occurred, as high school students throughout California and other Western states staged protests demanding more Latino teachers and counselors, ethnic-studies programs, and Latino student-retention programs. Students also often protested other issues, including anticrime laws in California (which they saw as being racially biased) and California's Proposition 187, which denies education and health services to suspected illegal immigrants.

In this excerpt from her 1998 book *De Colores Means All of Us: Latina Views for a Multi-Colored Century*, Elizabeth "Betita" Martínez describes the 1993 student protests. Martínez has been a leading Chicana writer and organizer for many years. She cofounded the Institute of MultiRacial Justice in San Francisco as well as the Chicano Communications Center. She also wrote the bilingual book *500 Years of Chicano History in Pictures*.

CALIFORNIA'S BLOWOUTS focused on public schools in the northern part of the state at first, then spread south. The students, mostly of Mexican or Salvadoran background, came from high school, junior high and sometimes elementary school. Why a walkout during school hours rather than a march or rally on the weekend? Because, as they learned, California's public schools lose $17.20 or more for each unexcused absence per day. This pocketbook damage provided the economic centerpiece of the students' strategy. With it, they made history.

The first wave seemed to burst out of nowhere. On April 1, 1993, more than 1,000 mostly Latino junior high and high school students walked out of a dozen Oakland schools. On September 16, celebrated as Mexican Independence Day, more than 4,000 blew out in Oakland, Berkeley, San Jose, and the town of Gilroy. Arrests and violence were rare, although in Gilroy police did arrest teenager Rebecca Armendariz and harassed her for months with charges of contributing to the delinquency of a minor, apparently because she signed to rent a bus that students used. In right-wing dominated Orange County, 300 students clashed with police while some were beaten and pepper-sprayed.

Another wave of student strikes unrolled in November and December in northern California. In Exeter, a small town in California's generally conservative Central Valley, 500 high school students boycotted classes when a teacher told an embarrassed youth who declined to lead the Pledge of Allegiance in English: "If you don't want to do it, go back to Mexico." It was the kind of remark that had been heard too many times in this school where 40 percent of the 1,200 students—but only six of their teachers—were Latino.

At Mission High School in San Francisco, 200 Latino and other students demonstrated for the same anti-racist reasons as elsewhere, and also for being stereotyped as gangbangers if they wore certain kinds of clothing. The school board agreed to their main demand for Latino Studies, and then offered just one class—to be held before and after the regular school day. The basic message: this concession isn't for real.

On to February 2, 1994, which marked the anniversary of the signing of the 1848 Treaty of Guadalupe Hidalgo confirming the U.S. takeover of half of Mexico—today's Southwest. In Sacramento, the walkout movement spread like wildfire. Some 500 high school students and supporters from various districts shook up the state capital. "The governor wants more prisons, we want schools. He wants more cops, we want more teachers. We want an education that values and includes our culture. We want all cultures to know about themselves," they said, as reported by the local paper *Because People Matter*.

For César Chávez's birthday in March, nearly 150 Latino students from four city schools marched on district offices in Richmond. On April 18, half of the elementary school pupils in the town of Pittsburgh boycotted classes, with parental support, because a Spanish-speaking principal had been demoted. They had their tradition: twenty years before, Pittsburgh elementary school students had boycotted for lack of a Latino principal.

The spring wave climaxed on April 22 with a big, coordinated blowout involving more than 30 schools in northern California. It was unforgettable. Some 800 youth gathered in San Francisco under signs such as "Educate, Don't Incarcerate" and "Our Story Not His-story," with beautiful banners of Zapata and armed women of the Mexican Revolution.

Calls for unity across racial and national lines and against gang warfare rang out all day. "Don't let the lies of the United Snakes divide us!" "Latin American doesn't stop with Mexico," said a Peruvian girl. Another shouted, "It's not just about Latinos or Blacks or Asians, this is about the whole world!" Some of the loudest cheers rang out from a 16-year-old woman who cried "We've got to forget these [gang] colors!" . . .

Cinco de Mayo, May 5, brought more blowouts, followed by a June gathering in Los Angeles of 900 high school students. The youth themselves were startled by their own success. Sergio Arroyo, 16, of Daly City, spoke what others were thinking: "People didn't think it could happen, all that unity, but it did." Lucretia Montez from Hayward High said "We're making history. Yeah, we're making history."

The Growing Surveillance Monster
American Civil Liberties Union

Within weeks after the September 11, 2001, terrorist attacks, Congress and President George W. Bush passed the Patriot Act, loosening federal restrictions on law enforcement agencies so that they could more freely monitor and investigate suspicious behaviors. Although many people objected to the law, the urgent desire to prevent similar terrorist attacks opened the political door for legislation narrowing citizens' rights to privacy.

The American Civil Liberties Union (ACLU) was one of the most forceful opponents of this change. The ACLU wrote several papers detailing the threat to the privacy rights of law-abiding citizens. It noted that the government's capacity to observe citizens' activities coincided with the increase in technological innovations that made this kind of observation possible. The excerpt here is from the introduction of "Bigger Monster, Weaker Chains: The Growth of American Surveillance Society."

PRIVACY AND LIBERTY in the United States are at risk. A combination of lightning–fast technological innovation and the erosion of privacy protection threatens to transform Big Brother from an oft-cited but remote threat into a very real part of American life. We are at risk of turning into a Surveillance Society.

The explosion of computers, cameras, sensors, wireless communication, GPS, biometrics, and other technologies in just the last ten years is feeding a surveillance monster that is growing silently in our midst. Scarcely a month goes by in which we don't read about some new high-tech way to invade people's privacy, from face recognition to implantable microchips, data-mining, DNA chips, and even "brain wave fingerprinting." The fact is, there are no longer any *technical* barriers to the Big Brother regime portrayed by George Orwell.

Even as this surveillance monster grows in power, we are weakening the legal chains that keep it from trampling our lives. We should be responding to intrusive new technologies by building stronger restraints to protect our privacy; instead, we are doing the opposite—loosening regulations on government surveillance, watching passively as private surveillance grows unchecked, and contemplating the introduction of tremendously powerful new surveillance infrastructures that will tie all this information together.

A gradual weakening of our privacy rights has been underway for decades, but many of the most startling developments have come in response to the terrorist attacks of September 11. But few of these hastily enacted measures are likely to increase our protection against terrorism. More often than not, September 11 has been used as a pretext to loosen constraints that law enforcement has been chafing under for years.

It doesn't require some apocalyptic vision of American democracy being replaced by dictatorship to worry about a surveillance society. There is a lot of room for the United States to become a meaner, less open and less just place without any radical change of government. All that's required is the continued construction of new surveillance technologies and the simultaneous erosion of privacy protections.

"Sí se puede." (Yes we can.)

The reaction against the Hispanic immigration into the United States has prompted numerous government crackdowns over the years, especially in California and the southwestern states. In some cases, self-appointed militias have patrolled the Mexican border, seeking to keep out illegal immigrants. But when Congress proposed legislation in 2006 that would penalize employers and people who provide humanitarian aid or other help to undocumented immigrants, as well as build a security wall along the southern U.S. border, immigrants staged some of the largest protests in the nation's history.

On March 25, 2006, more than 500,000 people took to the streets of Los Angeles in a massive protest—the largest in a series of rallies across the country. The protest—in which there were no arrests or injuries—coincided with an initiative spearheaded by the archbishop of Los Angeles urging clergy to defy legislation that would make assisting undocumented immigrants a felony.

Immigrants launched a massive effort to protect their civil rights. Immigrant parents held photographs of adult children in U.S. military uniforms, highlighting the disproportionate number of immigrant recruits in the military who join based on the promise of receiving citizenship. Demonstrators wore white shirts symbolizing peace and waved signs that said "Sí se puede."— Spanish for "Yes we can." Los Angeles mayor Antonio Villaraigosa told the demonstrators, "We cannot criminalize people who are working, people who are contributing to our economy and contributing to the nation."

CHAPTER 5
NATIONAL SELF-DETERMINATION

INTRODUCTION

Most countries as we know them today did not exist a scant three hundred years ago. Their boundaries and identities derive from a concept of national self-determination first articulated in 1689, when John Locke, in his *Two Treatises of Government*, outlined his belief that the power of government should emanate from the consent of the governed. Prior to Locke's work, the power of government derived largely from strength in arms or from a belief in the divine right of monarchs to rule.

During the 1700s and 1800s, the power of central governments increased, in part due to improvements in technology, such as the spread of printing presses and the development of faster ships. These changes not only allowed for more effective centralized government, but also created the possibility of widespread protest movements, such as those that fueled the American Revolution. The American Revolution was the first successful effort to create a nation based on the will of the people. Citizens influenced by the philosophy of Jean-Jacques Rousseau and Locke protested their moral outrage at oppression by England, often while simultaneously declaring their loyalty to King George.

In the twentieth century, the right of the people to choose their form of government gained broader recognition with the emergence of new nations throughout Africa, southeastern Europe, and southern Asia. But the proper boundaries of nations continue to be disputed, particularly when there are differences in how groups identify their geography or when major natural resources are at stake. For example, is it right that tiny Chechnya remains part of Russia, despite the evident desire of its people for self-governance? Should Kurdish peoples living in Iran, Turkey, and Iraq be entitled to their own unified, oil-rich nation. Is it permissible or desirable that Quebec should split from the rest of Canada? These are the questions that protest about national self-determination seeks to address.

The Declaration of Rights of the Stamp Act Congress

It took nearly one hundred and fifty years for British colonists to think of the community they'd created in North America as a nation separate from England. The first serious effort to form a self-governing entity took place in 1754, when representatives from seven colonies met in Albany, New York, to forge a defensive alliance against Indian attacks. Sparked by the idea of colonial unity, Benjamin Franklin drew up a "Plan of Union" to establish a political coalition among the English colonies. Colonial legislatures and the English government rejected the proposal, feeling that it threatened their respective authorities, and the idea faded. One decade later, however, colonists would not be so easily dissuaded.

At the end of the French and Indian War in 1763, British costs for maintaining the American colonies outweighed the financial benefits to the mother country. To cover the difference, the English Parliament passed several acts pertaining to the colonies, including the Sugar Act imposing duties on American imports; the Currency Act prohibiting the colonies from printing their own money; the Quartering Act requiring colonists to provide food and shelter to British troops; and, most notably, the Stamp Act, requiring that printed documents be issued solely on special stamped paper that had a tax associated with it.

Angered that these actions were taken without their input, colonists issued resolutions, called for assemblies of protest, and imposed boycotts. Mobs rioted in the streets. Stamp collectors were forced to resign. Massachusetts called for colonial delegations to meet in New York City in October 1765 to consider taking action against the Stamp Act. Delegates from nine colonies drafted a fourteen-point resolution, reprinted here, protesting the Stamp Act.

"The Declaration of Rights" of the Stamp Act Congress represented the first united act of resistance to British authority by American colonists. The Stamp Act was repealed in 1766.

THE MEMBERS of this congress . . . having considered as maturely as time will permit . . . esteem it our indispensable duty to make the following declarations, of our humble opinions, respecting the most essential rights and liberties of the colonists, and of the grievances under which they labor, by reason of several late acts of Parliament.

1st. That His Majesty's subjects in these colonies owe the same allegiance to the crown of Great Britain that is owing from his subjects born within the realm, and all due subordination to that august body, the Parliament of Great Britain.

2d. That His Majesty's liege subjects in these colonies are entitled to all the inherent rights and liberties of his natural-born subjects within the kingdom of Great Britain.

3d. That it is inseparably essential to the freedom of a people, and the undoubted right of Englishmen, that no taxes be imposed on them, but with their own consent, given personally, or by their representatives.

4th. That the people of these colonies are not, and from their local circumstances, cannot be, represented in the House of Commons in Great Britain.

5th. That the only representatives of the people of these colonies are persons chosen therein, by themselves, and that no taxes ever have been or can be constitutionally imposed on them but by their respective legislature.

6th. That all supplies to the crown, being free gifts of the people, it is unreasonable and inconsistent with the principles and spirit of the British constitution for the people of Great Britain to grant His Majesty the property of the colonists.

7th. That trial by jury is the inherent and invaluable right of every British subject in these colonies.

8th. That the late act of Parliament entitled, "An act for granting and applying certain stamp duties, and other duties in the British colonies and plantations in America, etc.," by imposing taxes on the inhabitants of these colonies, and the said act and several other acts by extending the jurisdiction of the courts of admiralty beyond its ancient limits, have a manifest tendency to subvert the rights and liberties of the colonists.

9th. That the duties imposed by several late acts of Parliament, from the peculiar circumstances of these colonies, will be extremely burdensome and grievous, and, from the scarcity of specie, the payment of them absolutely impracticable.

10th. That as the profits of the trade of these colonies ultimately center in Great Britain, to pay for the manufactures which they are obliged to take from thence, they eventually contribute very largely to all supplies granted there to the crown.

11th. That the restrictions imposed by several late acts of Parliament on the trade of these colonies will render them unable to purchase the manufactures of Great Britain.

12th. That the increase, prosperity, and happiness of these colonies depend on the full and free enjoyment of their rights and liberties, and an intercourse, with Great Britain, mutually affectionate and advantageous.

13th. That it is the right of the British subjects in these colonies to petition the king or either house of Parliament.

Lastly. That it is the indispensable duty of these colonies, to the best of sovereigns, to the mother-country, and to themselves, to endeavor, by a loyal and dutiful address to His Majesty, and humble application to both houses of Parliament, to procure the repeal of the act of granting and applying certain stamp duties, of all clauses of any other acts of Parliament whereby the jurisdiction of the admiralty is extended as aforesaid, and the other late acts for the restriction of American commerce.

"I saw the soldier . . . endeavoring to push me through with his bayonet"

Richard Palmes

The 1766 repeal of the Stamp Act relieved tensions between England and its North American colonies, but conflict soon reignited when the British Parliament passed the Townshend Acts in 1767. This series of acts imposed import duties on all glass, lead, paints, and tea sent from England to the colonies. The Massachusetts House of Representatives called for colonial resistance to the Townshend Acts. In response, the British sent five regiments to Boston.

A crowd of Bostonians attacked a group of these British sentries on March 5, 1770, with snowballs and rocks. As described here in a court statement by Richard Palmes, a Boston resident who witnessed the scene, the British soldiers fired into the crowd, killing three people and fatally wounding two others. Seven of the soldiers, including commanding officer Captain Thomas Preston, were arrested and tried for murder. Future American revolutionary leaders John Adams and Josiah Quincy defended them. Preston and four of the soldiers were acquitted; two soldiers were found guilty of manslaughter.

As often happens, the use of violence in response to protests against a military presence raised the level of interest and intensity in the issues involved. Paul Revere widely published an illustration of the "Boston Massacre" to protest the British shootings. The Boston Massacre led to the repeal of the Townshend Acts, with the exception of the tea tax.

I, RICHARD PALMES, of Boston, of lawful age, testify and say, that between the hours of nine and ten o'clock of the fifth instant, I heard one of the bells ring, which I supposed was occasioned by fire, and enquiring where the fire was, was answered that the soldiers were abusing the inhabitants; I asked where, was first answered at Murray's barracks. I went there and spoke to some officers that were standing at the door, I told them I was surprised they suffered the soldiers go out of the barracks after eight o'clock; I was answered by one of the officers, pray do you mean to teach us our duty; I answered I did not, only to remind them of it. One of them then said, you see that the soldiers are all in their barracks, and why do you not go to your homes. . . . I then saw Mr. Pool Spear going towards the townhouse, he asked me if I was going home, I told him I was; I asked him where he was going that way, he said he was going to his brother David's. But when I got to the town-pump, we were told there was a rumpus at the Customhouse door; Mr. Spear said to me you had better not go, I told him I would go and try to make peace. I immediately went there and saw Capt. Preston at the head of six or eight soldiers in a circular form, with guns breast high and bayonets fixed; the said Captain stood almost to the end of their guns. I went immediately to Capt. Preston (as soon as Mr. Bliss had left him), and asked him if their guns were loaded, his answer was they are loaded with powder and ball; I then said to him, I hope you do not intend they shall fire upon the inhabitants, his reply was, by no means. When I was asking him these questions, my left hand was on his right shoulder; Mr. John Hickling had that instant taken his hand off my shoulder, and stepped to my left, then instantly I saw a piece of snow or ice fall among the soldiers on which the soldier at the officer's right hand stepped back and discharged his gun at the space of some seconds the soldier at his left fired next, and the others one after the other. After the first gun was fired, I heard the word "fire," but who said it I know not. After the first gun was fired, the said officer had full time to forbid the other soldiers not to fire, but I did not hear him speak to them at all; then turning myself to the left I saw one man dead, distant about six feet; I having a stick in my hand made a stroke at the soldier who fired, and struck the gun out of his hand. I then made a stroke at the officer, my right foot slipped, that brought me on my knee, the blow falling short; he says I hit his arm; when I was recovering myself from the fall, I saw the soldier that fired the first gun endeavoring to push me through with his bayonet, on which I threw my stick at his head, the soldier starting back, gave me an opportunity to jump from him into Exchange lane, or I must have been inevitably run through my body. I looked back and saw three persons laying on the ground, and perceiving a soldier stepping around the corner as I thought to shoot me, I ran down Exchange lane, and so up to the next into King Street, and followed Mr. Gridley with several other persons with the body of Capt. Morton's apprentice, up to the prison house, and saw he had a ball shot through his breast; at my return I found that the officers and soldiers were gone to the main guard. To my best observation there were not seventy people in King street at the time of their firing, and them very scattering; but in a few minutes after the firing there were upwards of a thousand.

Proceedings of Farmington, Connecticut, on the Boston Port Act

The Boston Tea Party was a reaction against the British Parliament's 1773 decision to grant the East India Company a virtual monopoly on tea sales in the American colonies. A band of about sixty men, loosely disguised as Mohawk Indians, emptied tea from 342 chests on three British merchant ships in December 1773.

The protest was widely celebrated and imitated in the American colonies. The British reacted with fury. Parliament passed a series of laws known as the Intolerable Acts, closing the port of Boston and sending British troops to occupy the city.

But rather than intimidating Bostonians and other colonists, the acts heightened American anger at the mother country. Many towns and colonies leaped to the city's defense. In Virginia, a delegation called for a general congress of all colonies, noting "that an attack, made on one of our sister colonies, to compel submission to arbitrary taxes, is an attack made on all British America, and threatens ruin to the rights of all." And the town of Farmington, Connecticut, issued a harshly worded proclamation, reprinted here.

May 19, 1774

Early in the morning was found the following handbill, posted up in various parts of town: "To pass through the fire at six o'clock this evening, in honour to the immortal goddess of Liberty, the late infamous Act of the British Parliament for farther distressing the American Colonies; the place of execution will be the public parade, where all Sons of Liberty are desired to attend."

Accordingly, a very numerous and respectable body were assembled of near one thousand people, when a huge pole, just forty-five feet high, was erected and consecrated to the shrine of liberty; after which the Act of Parliament for blocking up the Boston harbour was read aloud, sentenced to the flames and executed by the hands of the common hangman; then the following resolves were passed:

1st. That it is the greatest dignity, interest and happiness of every American to be united with our parent State, while our liberties are duly secured, maintained and supported by our rightful Sovereign, whose person we greatly revere; whose government, while duly administered, we are ready with our lives and properties to support.

2nd. That the present ministry, being instigated by the devil and led on by their wicked and corrupt hearts, have a design to take away our liberties and properties to enslave us forever.

3rd. That the late Act which their malice hath caused to be passed in Parliament, for blocking up the port of Boston, is unjust, illegal and oppressive; and that we and every American are sharers in the insult offered to the town of Boston.

4th. That those pimps and parasites who dared to advise their masters to such detestable measures be held in utter abhorrence by us and every American and their names loaded with the curses of all succeeding generations.

5th. That we scorn the chains of slavery; we despise every attempt to rivet them upon us; we are the sons of freedom and resolved that, till time shall be no more, godlike virtue shall blazon our hemisphere.

"Give me liberty or give me death!"
Patrick Henry

By the spring of 1775, America was ripe for violence. The British army remained encamped in Boston, while Continental militia units openly trained in surrounding towns. The Continental Congress's call for a boycott of British goods had a dramatic impact, cutting trade with British merchants by as much as 99 percent. Both sides became increasingly entrenched in their positions.

In Virginia, colonists strengthened their militias and debated how to respond to British actions in Boston. In March 1775, Virginia legislators of the House of Burgesses met in Richmond to consider the Continental Congress's resolutions. The delegation initially hesitated, but after thirty-nine-year-old Patrick Henry gave a rousing speech, delegates reportedly cheered and shouted, "To arms! To arms!"

Alarmed by Virginia's defiance, the British dissolved the House of Burgesses, seized the colony's gunpowder in Williamsburg, and attempted to incite a slave rebellion. These actions had the combined effect of pushing the relatively moderate colony firmly to the side of the New England radicals. Patrick Henry was later elected governor of Virginia.

The actual words of the speech, as recalled by William Wirt, are subject to some historical doubt; nevertheless, they have become embedded in American legend.

NO MAN THINKS more highly than I do of the patriotism, as well as abilities, of the very worthy gentlemen who have just addressed the House. But different men often see the same subject in different lights; and, therefore, I hope it will not be thought disrespectful to those gentlemen if, entertaining as I do opinions of a character very opposite to theirs, I shall speak forth my sentiments freely and without reserve. This is no time for ceremony. The questing before the House is one of awful moment to this country. For my own part, I consider it as nothing less than a question of freedom or slavery; and in proportion to the magnitude of the subject ought to be the freedom of the debate. It is only in this way that we can hope to arrive at truth, and fulfill the great responsibility which we hold to God and our country. Should I keep back my opinions at such a time, through fear of giving offense, I should consider myself as guilty of treason towards my country, and of an act of disloyalty toward the Majesty of Heaven, which I revere above all earthly kings.

Mr. President, it is natural to man to indulge in the illusions of hope. We are apt to shut our eyes against a painful truth, and listen to the song of that siren till she transforms us into beasts. Is this the part of wise men, engaged in a great and arduous struggle for liberty? Are we disposed to be of the number of those who, having eyes, see not, and, having ears, hear not, the things which so nearly concern their temporal salvation? For my part, whatever anguish of spirit it may cost, I am willing to know the whole truth; to know the worst, and to provide for it.

I have but one lamp by which my feet are guided, and that is the lamp of experience. I know of no way of judging of the future but by the past. And judging by the past, I wish to know what there has been in the conduct of the British ministry for the last ten years to justify those hopes with which gentlemen have been pleased to solace themselves and the House. Is it that insidious smile with which our petition has been lately received? Trust it not, sir; it will prove a snare to your feet. Suffer not yourselves to be betrayed with a kiss. Ask yourselves how this gracious reception of our petition comports with those warlike preparations which cover our waters and darken our land. Are fleets and armies necessary to a work of love and reconciliation? Have we shown ourselves so unwilling to be reconciled that force must be called in to win back our love? Let us not deceive ourselves, sir. These are the implements of war and subjugation; the last arguments to which kings resort. I ask gentlemen, sir, what means this martial array, if its purpose be not to force us to submission? Can gentlemen assign any other possible motive for it? Has Great Britain any enemy, in this quarter of the world, to call for all this accumulation of navies and armies? No, sir, she has none. They are meant for us: they can be meant for no other. They are sent over to bind and rivet upon us those chains which the British ministry have been so long forging. And what have we to oppose to them? Shall we try argument? Sir, we have been trying that for the last ten years. Have we anything new to offer upon the subject? Nothing. We have held the subject up in every light of which it is capable; but it has been all in vain. Shall we resort to entreaty and humble supplication? What terms shall we find which have not been already exhausted? Let us not, I beseech you, sir, deceive ourselves. Sir, we have done everything that could be done to avert the storm which is now coming on. We have petitioned; we have remonstrated; we have supplicated; we have prostrated ourselves before the throne, and have implored its interposition to arrest the tyrannical hands of the ministry and Parliament. Our petitions have been slighted; our remonstrances have produced additional violence and insult; our supplications have been disregarded; and we have been spurned, with contempt, from the foot of the throne! In vain, after these things, may we indulge the fond hope of peace and reconciliation. There is no longer any room for hope. If we wish to be free—if we mean to preserve inviolate those inestimable privileges for which we have been so long contending—if we mean not basely to abandon the noble struggle in which we have been so long engaged, and which we have pledged ourselves never to abandon until the glorious object of our contest shall be obtained—we must fight! I repeat it, sir, we must fight! An appeal to arms and to the God of hosts is all that is left us!

They tell us, sir, that we are weak; unable to cope with so formidable an adversary. But when shall we be stronger? Will it be the next week, or the next year? Will it be when we are totally disarmed, and when a British guard shall be stationed in every house? Shall we gather strength by irresolution and inaction? Shall we acquire the means of effectual resistance by lying supinely on our backs and hugging the delusive phantom of hope, until our enemies shall have bound us hand and foot? Sir, we are not weak if we make a proper use of those means which the God of nature hath placed in our power. The millions of people, armed in the holy cause of liberty, and in such a country as that which we possess, are invincible by any force which our enemy can send against us. Besides, sir, we shall not fight our battles alone. There is a just God who presides over the destinies of nations, and who will raise up friends to fight our battles for us. The battle, sir, is not to the strong alone; it is to the vigilant, the active, the brave. Besides, sir, we have no election. If we were base enough to desire it, it is now too late to retire from the contest. There is no retreat but in submission and slavery! Our chains are forged! Their clanking may be heard on the plains of Boston! The war is inevitable—and let it come! I repeat it, sir, let it come.

It is in vain, sir, to extenuate the matter. Gentlemen may cry, Peace, Peace—but there is no peace. The war is actually begun! The next gale that sweeps from the north will bring to our ears the clash of resounding arms! Our brethren are already in the field! Why stand we here idle? What is it that gentlemen wish? What would they have? Is life so dear, or peace so sweet, as to be purchased at the price of chains and slavery? Forbid it, Almighty God! I know not what course others may take; but as for me, give me liberty or give me death!

The Declaration of Independence

The Declaration of Independence was the culmination of a series of events that made the break from England irreversible. War had broken out in Boston in April 1775, ending with the British abandoning the city. George Washington had been named general of the American forces. In the spring of 1776, he and his army were fighting British forces outside of New York City.

With American colonists in open war against the mother country, the Second Continental Congress began considering a declaration of independence. On June 7, Richard Henry Lee of Virginia introduced a resolution calling for independence. While a majority of delegates favored the motion, the middle states were not ready to break with England. As clumsy and repressive as England's actions had been for the previous twelve years, separation still gave many pause.

A committee consisting of Thomas Jefferson of Virginia, John Adams of Massachusetts, Benjamin Franklin of Pennsylvania, Robert Livingstone of New York, and Roger Sherman of Connecticut was appointed to draft the declaration. Jefferson was charged with the actual writing of the document. In the meantime, several of the moderate colonies swung their votes. In New Jersey, the loyalist governor was ousted from power and a new delegation was sent to Congress, authorized to vote for independence. Maryland, too, changed its position.

On July 1, four states still would not vote for independence. South Carolina and Pennsylvania voted against it, Delaware's delegation was divided, and New York was paralyzed by indecision. But over the next twenty-four hours, Delaware delegate Caesar Rodney traveled to Philadelphia to break his colony's stalemate, the South Carolina and Pennsylvania delegations changed their views, and New York decided to abstain from voting. On July 2, Congress voted unanimously to separate from England. Two days later, after making several changes to Jefferson's original draft, Congress voted unanimously to adopt the Declaration of Independence.

Fifty-five delegates from all thirteen states signed the declaration, a proclamation on the right to self-government and a list of reasons justifying the desire to leave England. Benjamin Franklin famously noted upon signing the document, the delegates would all have to hang together in the cause for independence or "surely we will all hang separately" for treason.

WHEN IN THE COURSE OF HUMAN EVENTS it becomes necessary for one people to dissolve the political bonds which have connected them with another, and to assume among the powers of the earth, the separate and equal station to which the Laws of Nature and of Nature's God entitle them, a decent respect to the opinions of mankind requires that they should declare the causes which impel them to the separation.

We hold these truths to be self-evident, that all men are created equal, that they are endowed by their Creator with certain unalienable Rights, that among these are Life, Liberty and the pursuit of Happiness.—That to secure these rights, Governments are instituted among Men, deriving their just powers from the consent of the governed,—That whenever any Form of Government becomes destructive of these ends, it is the Right of the People to alter or to abolish it, and to institute new Government, laying its foundation on such principles and organizing its powers in such form, as to them shall seem most likely to effect their Safety and Happiness. Prudence, indeed, will dictate that Governments long established should not be changed for light and transient causes; and accordingly all experience hath shewn that mankind are more disposed to suffer, while evils are sufferable, than to right themselves by abolishing the forms to which they are accustomed. But when a long train of abuses and usurpations, pursuing invariably the same Object evinces a design to reduce them under absolute Despotism, it is their right, it is their duty, to throw off such Government, and to provide new Guards for their future security.—Such has been the patient sufferance of these Colonies; and such is now the necessity which constrains them to alter their former Systems of Government. The history of the present King of Great Britain is a history of repeated injuries and usurpations, all having in direct object the establishment of an absolute Tyranny over these States. To prove this, let Facts be submitted to a candid world.

He has refused his Assent to Laws, the most wholesome and necessary for the public good.

He has forbidden his Governors to pass Laws of immediate and pressing importance, unless suspended in their operation till his Assent should be obtained; and when so suspended, he has utterly neglected to attend to them.

He has refused to pass other Laws for the accommodation of large districts of people, unless those people would relinquish the right of Representation in the Legislature, a right inestimable to them and formidable to tyrants only.

He has called together legislative bodies at places unusual, uncomfortable, and distant from the depository of their Public Records, for the sole purpose of fatiguing them into compliance with his measures.

He has dissolved Representative Houses repeatedly, for opposing with manly firmness his invasions on the rights of the people.

He has refused for a long time, after such dissolutions, to cause others to be elected; whereby the Legislative Powers, incapable of Annihilation, have returned to the People at large for their exercise; the State remaining in the mean time exposed to all the dangers of invasion from without, and convulsions within.

He has endeavoured to prevent the population of these States; for that purpose obstructing the Laws for Naturalization of Foreigners; refusing to pass others to encourage their migrations hither, and raising the conditions of new Appropriations of Lands.

He has obstructed the Administration of Justice, by refusing his Assent to Laws for establishing Judiciary Powers.

He has made Judges dependent on his Will alone, for the tenure of their offices, and the amount and payment of their salaries.

He has erected a multitude of New Offices, and sent hither swarms of Officers to harass our people, and eat out their substance.

He has kept among us, in times of peace, Standing Armies without the Consent of our legislatures.

He has affected to render the Military independent of and superior to the Civil Power.

He has combined with others to subject us to a jurisdiction foreign to our constitution, and unacknowledged by our laws; giving his Assent to their Acts of pretended Legislation:

For Quartering large bodies of armed troops among us:

For protecting them, by a mock Trial, from punishment for any Murders which they should commit on the Inhabitants of these States:

For cutting off our Trade with all parts of the world:

For imposing Taxes on us without our Consent:

For depriving us in many cases, of the benefits of Trial by Jury:

For transporting us beyond Seas to be tried for pretended offences:

For abolishing the free System of English Laws in a neighbouring Province, establishing therein an Arbitrary government, and enlarging its Boundaries so as to render it at once an example and fit instrument for introducing the same absolute rule into these Colonies:

For taking away our Charters, abolishing our most valuable Laws, and altering fundamentally the Forms of our Governments:

For suspending our own Legislatures, and declaring themselves invested with power to legislate for us in all cases whatsoever.

He has abdicated Government here, by declaring us out of his Protection and waging War against us.

He has plundered our seas, ravaged our coasts, burnt our towns, and destroyed the lives of our people.

He is at this time transporting large Armies of foreign Mercenaries to compleat the works of death, desolation and tyranny, already begun with circumstances of Cruelty & Perfidy scarcely paralleled in the most barbarous ages, and totally unworthy the Head of a civilized nation.

He has constrained our fellow Citizens taken Captive on the high Seas to bear Arms against their Country, to become the executioners of their friends and Brethren, or to fall themselves by their Hands.

He has excited domestic insurrections amongst us, and has endeavoured to bring on the inhabitants of our frontiers, the merciless Indian Savages, whose known rule of warfare, is an undistinguished destruction of all ages, sexes and conditions.

In every stage of these Oppressions We have Petitioned for Redress in the most humble terms: Our repeated Petitions have been answered only by repeated injury. A Prince whose character is thus marked by every act which may define a Tyrant, is unfit to be the ruler of a free people.

Nor have We been wanting in attentions to our Brittish brethren. We have warned them from time to time of attempts by their legislature to extend an unwarrantable jurisdiction over us. We have reminded them of the circumstances of our emigration and settlement here. We have appealed to their native justice and magnanimity, and we have conjured them by the ties of our common kindred to disavow these usurpations, which, would inevitably interrupt our connections and correspondence. They too have been deaf to the voice of justice and of consanguinity. We must, therefore, acquiesce in the necessity, which denounces our Separation, and hold them, as we hold the rest of mankind, Enemies in War, in Peace Friends.

We, therefore, the Representatives of the United States of America, in General Congress, Assembled, appealing to the Supreme Judge of the world for the rectitude of our intentions, do, in the Name, and by Authority of the good People of these Colonies, solemnly publish and declare, That these United Colonies are, and of Right ought to be Free and Independent States; that they are Absolved from all Allegiance to the British Crown, and that all political connection between them and the State of Great Britain, is and ought to be totally dissolved; and that as Free and Independent States, they have full Power to levy War, conclude Peace, contract Alliances, establish Commerce, and to do all other Acts and Things which Independent States may of right do. —And for the support of this Declaration, with a firm reliance on the protection of Divine Providence, we mutually pledge to each other our Lives, our Fortunes and our sacred Honor.

The American Crisis

Thomas Paine

Thomas Paine was the most influential writer for American independence. More than 100,000 copies of his first pamphlet *Common Sense* were distributed—an unbelievable number considering there were only three million people in the British colonies when it was published in January 1776. In the pamphlet, Paine attacked the ideology of monarchical rule, the belief in American dependence on Britain for economic prosperity, and the notion of British benevolence. Eleven months later, Paine published the first of a series of essays entitled *The American Crisis* (also called *The Crisis*), helping to rally Americans to the struggling cause of independence.

At the time, General George Washington's army had been routed at New York City, chased through northern New Jersey, and had nearly disintegrated by the time it reached the outskirts of Philadelphia. Paine spoke to the military defeats, cited historic low points in other successful ventures, reaffirmed the rightness of the cause, and reminded readers of the poor alternatives to fighting. Inspired by Paine's words, Washington had *The American Crisis* read out loud to his troops.

Although Paine was America's most popular writer, he refused royalties in order to keep the costs of his pamphlets low and thus accessible to as many people as possible. He died in 1809, almost penniless.

THESE ARE THE TIMES that try men's souls. The summer soldier and the sunshine patriot will, in this crisis, shrink from the service of their country; but he that stands by it now, deserves the love and thanks of man and woman. Tyranny, like hell, is not easily conquered; yet we have this consolation with us, that the harder the conflict, the more glorious the triumph. What we obtain too cheap, we esteem too lightly: it is dearness only that gives every thing its value. Heaven knows how to put a proper price upon its goods; and it would be strange indeed if so celestial an article as FREEDOM should not be highly rated. Britain, with an army to enforce her tyranny, has declared that she has a right (not only to TAX) but "to BIND us in ALL CASES WHATSOEVER," and if being bound in that manner, is not slavery, then is there not such a thing as slavery upon earth. Even the expression is impious; for so unlimited a power can belong only to God. . . .

I have as little superstition in me as any man living, but my secret opinion has ever been, and still is, that God Almighty will not give up a people to military destruction, or leave them unsupportedly to perish, who have so earnestly and so repeatedly sought to avoid the calamities of war, by every decent method which wisdom could invent. Neither have I so much of the infidel in me, as to suppose that He has relinquished the government of the world, and given us up to the care of devils; and as I do not, I cannot see on what grounds the king of Britain can look up to heaven for help against us: a common murderer, a highwayman, or a house-breaker, has as good a pretence as he.

'Tis surprising to see how rapidly a panic will sometimes run through a country. All nations and ages have been subject to them. Britain has trembled like an ague at the report of a French fleet of flat-bottomed boats; and in the [fifteenth] century the whole English army, after ravaging the kingdom of France, was driven back like men petrified with fear; and this brave exploit was performed by a few broken forces collected and headed by a woman, Joan of Arc. Would that heaven might inspire some Jersey maid to spirit up her countrymen, and save her fair fellow sufferers from ravage and ravishment! . . .

. . . Not a man lives on the continent but fully believes that a separation must some time or other finally take place, and a generous parent should have said, "If there must be trouble, let it be in my day, that my child may have peace;" and this single reflection, well applied, is sufficient to awaken every man to duty. Not a place upon earth might be so happy as America. Her situation is remote from all the wrangling world, and she has nothing to do but to trade with them. A man can distinguish himself between temper and principle, and I am as confident, as I am that God governs the world, that America will never be happy till she gets clear of foreign dominion. Wars, without ceasing, will break out till that period arrives, and the continent must in the end be conqueror; for though the flame of liberty may sometimes cease to shine, the coal can never expire. . . .

I call not upon a few, but upon all: not on this state or that state, but on every state: up and help us; lay your shoulders to the wheel; better have too much force than too little, when so great an object is at stake. Let it be told to the future world, that in the depth of winter, when nothing but hope and virtue could survive, that the city and the country, alarmed at one common danger, came forth to meet and to repulse it. Say not that thousands are gone, turn out your tens of thousands; throw not the burden of the day upon Providence, but "show your faith by your works," that God may bless you. It matters not where you live, or what rank of life you hold, the evil or the blessing will reach you all. The far and the near, the home counties and the back, the rich and the poor, will suffer or rejoice alike. The heart that feels not now is dead; the blood of his children will curse his cowardice, who shrinks back at a time when a little might have saved the whole, and made them happy. I love the man that can smile in trouble, that can gather strength from distress, and grow brave by reflection. 'Tis the business of little minds to shrink; but he whose heart is firm, and whose conscience approves his conduct, will pursue his principles unto death. My own line of reasoning is to myself as straight and clear as a ray of light. Not all the treasures of the world, so far as I believe, could have induced me to support an offensive war, for I think it murder; but if a thief breaks into my house, burns and destroys my property, and kills or threatens to kill me, or those that are in it, and to "bind me in all cases whatsoever" to his absolute will, am I to suffer it? What signifies it to me, whether he who does it is a king or a common man; my countryman or not my countryman; whether it be done by an individual villain, or an army of them? If we reason to the root of things we shall find no difference; neither can any just cause be assigned why we should punish in the one case and pardon in the other. Let them call me rebel and welcome, I feel no concern from it; but I should suffer the misery of devils, were I to make a whore of my soul by swearing allegiance to one whose character is that of a sottish, stupid, stubborn, worthless, brutish man. I conceive likewise a horrid idea in receiving mercy from a being, who at the last day shall be shrieking to the rocks and mountains to cover him, and fleeing with terror from the orphan, the widow, and the slain of America.

There are cases which cannot be overdone by language, and this is one. There are persons, too, who see not the full extent of the evil which threatens them; they solace themselves with hopes that the enemy, if he succeed, will be merciful. It is the madness of folly, to expect mercy from those who have refused to do justice; and even mercy, where conquest is the object, is only a trick of war; the cunning of the fox is as murderous as the violence of the wolf, and we ought to guard equally against both.

Decree of War to the Death
Simón Bolívar

Simón Bolívar is known in Latin America as El Liberador (The Liberator). During the second decade of the nineteenth century, Spain's government was in turmoil due to the Napoleonic wars. The Spanish colonies in the Americas became restless, and some citizens argued for independence. Bolívar helped foster and eventually led revolts in Ecuador, Bolivia, Columbia, Venezuela, and Panama. His contemporary, José de San Martín, led revolts in Argentina, Chile, and Peru, while Miguel Hidalgo started Mexico's struggle for independence. Of the three, Bolívar was the most prolific writer; his abundant letters and speeches reveal a strong ambivalence about the balance between authority and democracy in government.

For example, in 1819, after the capture of Angostura (today known as Ciudad Bolívar), on the Orinoco River in Venezuela, Bolívar called together the Congress of Angostura to draft a constitution for the area of modern-day Columbia, Venezuela, Panama, and Ecuador. Bolívar's speech to the assembly, known as the Angostura address, focused on the importance of limiting executive power to maintaining freedom: "The continuation of power in the same individual has frequently led to the demise of democratic governments. Periodic elections are essential in popular systems, because nothing is so dangerous as to leave power in the hands of a single citizen over long periods of time." Yet Bolívar at times put forward constitutional proposals that contradicted these words, for example, proposing a president for life in the constitution he wrote for Bolivia.

In 1813, when Bolívar was still proving his skill as a military commander, he issued the "Decree of War to the Death" excerpted below, which threatened Spaniards in the Americas with death unless they actively helped throw off Spanish rule. The decree helped rally support to Bolívar 's military campaign, as did his later emancipation of slaves.

WE ARE SENT TO DESTROY THE SPANIARDS, to protect Americans, and to reestablish the republican governments that formed the Federation of Venezuela. The states protected by our arms are once again ruled by their former constitutions and leaders, in the full enjoyment of their freedom and independence, because our sole mission is to break the chains of servitude that still oppress some of our people, not to make laws or seize power, as the rules of war might authorize us to do. . . .

Despite our just resentment against the foul Spaniards, our generous hearts still see fit one last time to open the way to reconciliation and friendship; we invite them once again to live peacefully among us under the condition that, renouncing their crimes and acting henceforth in good faith, they cooperate with us in the destruction of the Spanish government of occupation and in the reestablishment of the Venezuelan Republic.

Any Spaniard who does not join our fight against tyranny to further our just cause, actively and effectively, will be regarded as an enemy and punished as a traitor to the country and consequently put to death without appeal. On the other hand, a general and absolute pardon is hereby granted to those who come over to our armies, with or without their weapons, and who lend their support to the good citizens who are struggling to shake off the yoke of tyranny. . . . [I]n a word, Spaniards who render distinguished service to the state will be regarded and treated as Americans.

And you Americans who have been led from the path of justice by error or perfidy, be sure that your brothers forgive you and sincerely lament your offenses, convinced in our hearts that you cannot be to blame, and that only blindness and ignorance in which you have been held hitherto by the instigators of your crimes could have led you to commit them. . . . You may count on absolute immunity regarding your honor, your lives, and your property: the mere title of Americans will be your guarantee and your safeguard. . . .

Spaniards and Canarians [citizens of the Spanish Canary Islands], even if you profess neutrality, know that you will die unless you work actively to bring about the freedom of America. Americans, know that you will live, even if you are guilty.

Declaration of the Immediate Causes Which Induce and Justify the Secession of South Carolina from the Federal Union

Almost immediately after the forming of the United States of America, the strength of the bond between the states was tested. Fearing a single powerful government, the country's founders initially created a confederation of states. Deep-seated weaknesses in this structure, however, led to the crafting of the Constitution in 1787 and a much stronger federal government. Regional differences continued, however, and defining the nation and the boundaries of national self-government proved to be very difficult.

The issue of states' rights faced its first severe test in New England in the early 1800s when the national antitrade policies resulted in the War of 1812 and economic hardship for commercial interests in the Northeast. New England states considered seceding from the Union, but abandoned the effort when the war ended.

For the next thirty-five years, the main source of strain came from Southern states, which saw their political power start to diminish as the North's economy grew and new states were created that did not allow slavery. Slaves were a principal source of labor for the South's plantation-based economy, and the Southern states grew increasingly wary of the abolitionist movement in the North. Political compromises were struck in 1820 and 1848 to prevent the South from leaving the Union. But when Abraham Lincoln was elected president in 1860, many Southerners decided they could no longer remain a part of the United States.

South Carolina was the first state to secede, having eight years earlier threatened to do so if the federal government impeded its rights. After Lincoln's election, the South Carolina legislature called for a convention to consider leaving the Union. Delegates voted unanimously on December 20, 1860, to secede and issued a statement, "Declaration of the Immediate Causes Which Induce and Justify the Secession of South Carolina from the Federal Union," justifying the decision. That declaration is excerpted here.

THE PEOPLE of the State of South Carolina, in Convention assembled, on the 26th day of April, A.D. 1852, declared that the frequent violations of the Constitution of the United States, by the Federal Government, and its encroachments upon the reserved rights of the States, fully justified this State in then withdrawing from the Federal Union; but in deference to the opinions and wishes of the other slaveholding States, she forbore at that time to exercise this right. Since that time, these encroachments have continued to increase, and further forbearance ceases to be a virtue.

And now the State of South Carolina having resumed her separate and equal place among nations, deems it due to herself, to the remaining United States of America, and to the nations of the world, that she should declare the immediate causes which have led to this act. . . .

We affirm that these ends for which this Government was instituted have been defeated, and the Government itself has been made destructive of them by the action of the non-slaveholding States. Those States have assumed the right of deciding upon the propriety of our domestic institutions; and have denied the rights of property established in fifteen of the States and recognized by the Constitution; they have denounced as sinful the institution of slavery; they have permitted open establishment among them of societies, whose avowed object is to disturb the peace and to eloign the property of the citizens of other States. They have encouraged and assisted thousands of our slaves to leave their homes; and those who remain, have been incited by emissaries, books and pictures to servile insurrection.

For twenty-five years this agitation has been steadily increasing, until it has now secured to its aid the power of the common Government. Observing the forms of the Constitution, a sectional party has found within that Article establishing the Executive Department, the means of subverting the Constitution itself. A geographical line has been drawn across the Union, and all the States north of that line have united in the election of a man to the high office of President of the United States, whose opinions and purposes are hostile to slavery. He is to be entrusted with the administration of the common Government, because he has declared that that "Government cannot endure permanently half slave, half free," and that the public mind must rest in the belief that slavery is in the course of ultimate extinction.

This sectional combination for the submersion of the Constitution, has been aided in some of the States by elevating to citizenship, persons who, by the supreme law of the land, are incapable of becoming citizens; and their votes have been used to inaugurate a new policy, hostile to the South, and destructive of its beliefs and safety.

On the 4th day of March next, this party will take possession of the Government. It has announced that the South shall be excluded from the common territory, that the judicial tribunals shall be made sectional, and that a war must be waged against slavery until it shall cease throughout the United States.

The guaranties of the Constitution will then no longer exist; the equal rights of the States will be lost. The slaveholding States will no longer have the power of self-government, or self-protection, and the Federal Government will have become their enemy.

Sectional interest and animosity will deepen the irritation, and all hope of remedy is rendered vain, by the fact that public opinion at the North has invested a great political error with the sanction of more erroneous religious belief.

We, therefore, the People of South Carolina, by our delegates in Convention assembled, appealing to the Supreme Judge of the world for the rectitude of our intentions, have solemnly declared that the Union heretofore existing between this State and the other States of North America, is dissolved, and that the State of South Carolina has resumed her position among the nations of the world, as a separate and independent State; with full power to levy war, conclude peace, contract alliances, establish commerce, and to do all other acts and things which independent States may of right do.

"Though I see only gloom before me, I shall follow the Lone Star"

Sam Houston

In February 1861, South Carolina and six other states—Mississippi, Florida, Alabama, Georgia, Louisiana, and Texas—met to form the Confederate States of America, naming Jefferson Davis as president of the new government. Not everyone in these states wanted to leave the Union. One of the strongest voices against secession belonged to Texas governor Sam Houston, who represented a large minority of residents who opposed disunion.

Houston had served as commander of the Texan army in its fight for independence from Mexico in 1836. He was elected as the first president of the Republic of Texas that same year and helped persuade Texas to join the United States ten years later. He served as the first senator from Texas and in 1859 was elected governor.

Houston was an adamant Unionist, declaring "I am for the Union without any 'if' in the case." If Texas were to leave the Union, he preferred that it become an independent republic again instead of joining with the other Southern states. When, despite his objections, Texas voted for secession and joined the Confederacy, Houston issued a proclamation against the decision, a portion of which is excerpted here.

In an act of high-profile public protest, Houston attended the formal ceremony in which state officials were slated to swear their loyalty to the Confederacy, but ignored three requests that he step forward to take the oath. While whittling a stick with his knife, Houston did not even answer to his name. He resigned as governor after the ceremony and returned to his home in Huntsville. He turned down an offer from Abraham Lincoln to send soldiers to help him fight against his own state.

I HAVE DECLARED my determination to stand by Texas in whatever position she assumes. Her people have declared in favor of separation from the Union. I have followed her banners before, when an exile from the land of my fathers. I went back into the Union with the people of Texas. I go out from the Union with them; and though I see only gloom before me, I shall follow the "Lone Star" with the same devotion as of yore. . . .

I love Texas too well to bring civil strife and bloodshed upon her. To avert this calamity, I shall make no endeavor to maintain my authority as Chief Executive of this State, except in the peaceful exercise of my functions. When I can no longer do this, I shall calmly withdraw from the scene, leaving the Government in the hands of those who have usurped its authority; but still claiming that I am its Chief Executive. . . .

I protest in the name of the people of Texas against all the acts and doings of the Convention, and I declare them null and void! I solemnly protest against the acts of its members who are bound by no other than themselves, in declaring my office vacant, because I refuse to appear before it and take the oath prescribed.

The Jewish State
Theodor Herzl

In the early 1890s, Austrian journalist Theodor Herzl covered the flawed and anti-Semitic court-martial of Captain Alfred Dreyfus. Reacting perhaps to that trial (and associated street protests in Paris demanding "Death to the Jews!") and perhaps to the rise of anti-Semitism in his home of Vienna, Herzl published *The Jewish State* in 1896, calling for the creation of Israel. The publication scoffed at the idea that Jews ever would be truly accepted in modern nations, regardless of their assimilation in appearance and customs or of their patriotism. The only solution, Herzl argued, was the creation of a Jewish state, preferably in Palestine, considered by many Jews to be the homeland given to them by God.

In 1897 Herzl founded the World Zionist Organization, and the first Zionist Congress convened in Basel, Switzerland. Herzl was elected president and wrote in his diary after the event: "At Basle, I founded the Jewish State. If I said this out loud today, I would be answered by universal laughter. If not in 5 years, certainly in 50, everyone will know it." Until his death in 1904, Herzl campaigned avidly for this cause, meeting with the German emperor, the sultan of Turkey, and a variety of senior government officials of other European powers. The World Zionist Organization considered locations other than Palestine, including Uganda and Argentina, but ultimately held fast to the dream of a Jewish state in Palestine.

In 1947, after World War II and the horror of the Holocaust, the United Nations General Assembly recommended partitioning Palestine into Jewish and Arab sections. Relying heavily on this recommendation, the state of Israel declared its independence on May 14, 1948, fulfilling Herzl's vision of more than fifty years before.

The following excerpts come from a 1946 translation of *The Jewish State* by Sylvie D'Avigdor.

WE ARE A PEOPLE—*one* people.

We have sincerely endeavored everywhere to merge ourselves in the social life of surrounding communities and to preserve the faith of our fathers. We are not permitted to do so. In vain are we loyal patriots, our loyalty in some places running to extremes; in vain do we make the same sacrifices of life and property as our fellow-citizens; in vain do we strive to increase the fame of our native land in the sciences and in art, or her wealth by trade and commerce. In countries where we have lived for centuries we are still cried down as strangers, and often by those whose ancestors had not yet domiciled in the land where Jews already had the experience of suffering. The majority may decide which are the strangers; for this, as indeed every point which arises in the relations between nations, is a question of might. . . . It is useless, therefore, for us to be loyal patriots, as were the Huguenots, who were forced to emigrate. If only we were left in peace. . . .

But I think we shall not be left in peace.

Oppression and persecution cannot exterminate us. No nation on earth has survived such struggles and sufferings as we have gone through. Jew-baiting has merely stripped off our weaklings; the strong among us were invariably true to their race when persecution broke out against them. This attitude was most clearly apparent in the period immediately following the emancipation of the Jews. Those Jews who were advanced intellectually and materially entirely lost the feeling of belonging to their race. Wherever our political well-being has lasted for any length of time, we assimilated with our surroundings. I think this is not discreditable. Hence, the statesman who would wish to see a Jewish strain added to his nation would have to provide for the duration of our political well-being, and even a Bismarck could not do that.

For old prejudices against us still lie deep in the hearts of the people. He who would have proofs of this need only listen to the people where they speak with frankness and simplicity: proverb and fairy-tale are both anti-Semitic. A nation is everywhere a great child, which can certainly be educated; but its education would, even in the most favorable circumstances, occupy such a vast amount of time that we could, as already mentioned, remove our own difficulties by other means. . . .

No human being is wealthy or powerful enough to transport a nation from one habitation to another. An idea alone can achieve that and this idea of a State probably may have the requisite power to do so. The Jews have dreamt this kingly dream through all the long nights of their history. "Next year in Jerusalem" is our old phrase. It is now a question of showing that the dream can be converted into a living reality.

"My Official Protest to the Treaty", from *Hawaii's Story by Hawaii's Queen*
Queen Liliuokalani

The 1898 absorption of the Hawaiian Islands into the United States represented the first time the United States acquired and held territory that was not part of the North American continent. Foreign business investment in the islands (particularly sugar plantations) had grown throughout the 1800s. In 1887 American planters and businessmen forced King Kalakaua at gunpoint to sign a constitution that stripped him of power, deprived all but the richest Hawaiians of the right to vote for candidates to the upper house of the legislature, and extended the right to vote to European and American residents even if they weren't citizens.

In 1893, Queen Liliuokalani, who had succeeded Kalakaua, began to repeal the Bayonet Constitution, as it was called, and replace it with one that restored more power to native Hawaiians and herself. American expatriates acted swiftly, forming a Committee of Safety, inviting Marines on board the warship USS *Boston* to land in Honolulu harbor, and creating a provisional government. The queen yielded power under protest. The U.S. representative in Hawaii, John Stevens, recognized the new government, and the leaders of the Committee of Safety hastened to Washington with an annexation treaty, which President Benjamin Harrison sent on to the Senate.

But Grover Cleveland soon replaced Harrison and withdrew the annexation treaty, asserting, "By an act of war, committed with the participation of a diplomatic representative of the United States and without authority of Congress, the government of a feeble but friendly and confiding people has been overthrown." Cleveland called for the United States to restore Queen Liliuokalani's government to protect what he called "our national character." Cleveland did not force the issue, however, and Hawaii became an independent "republic," in fact ruled by the wealthy landowners.

On the ascension of President William McKinley in 1897, an annexation treaty was again sent to the Senate. Native Hawaiians submitted a petition protesting "against the annexation of the said Hawaiian Islands to the said United States of America in any form or shape." More than half of the residents of the islands had signed the petitions in just a few weeks' time. (The five hundred fifty-six pages of petitions with more than 21,000 signatures are now in the U.S. National Archives.) Queen Liliuokalani, living in exile in the United States, filed the formal protest excerpted below. Many senators changed their minds, and annexation supporters lacked the two-thirds majority needed for the bill to pass. But in 1898, in the heat of the Spanish American War, Congress passed, by simple majority, a resolution appropriating Hawaii.

In 1993, the U.S. government formally apologized to the native people of Hawaii "for the overthrow of the Kingdom of Hawaii on January 17, 1893, with the participation of agents and citizens of the United States, and the deprivation of the rights of Native Hawaiians to self-determination."

I, LILIUOKALANI OF HAWAII, by the will of God named heir apparent on the tenth day of April, A.D. 1877, and by the grace of God Queen of the Hawaiian Islands on the seventeenth day of January, A.D. 1893, do hereby protest against the ratification of a certain treaty, which, so I am informed, has been signed at Washington by Messrs. Hatch, Thurston, and Kinney, purporting to cede those Islands to the territory and dominion of the United States. I declare such a treaty to be an act of wrong toward the native and part-native people of Hawaii, an invasion of the rights of the ruling chiefs, in violation of international rights both toward my people and toward friendly nations with whom they have made treaties, the perpetuation of the fraud whereby the constitutional government was overthrown, and, finally, an act of gross injustice to me.

Because the official protests made by me on the seventeenth day of January, 1893, to the so-called Provisional Government was signed by me, and received by said government with the assurance that the case was referred to the United States of America for arbitration. . . .

Because that protest and my communications to the United States Government immediately thereafter expressly declare that I yielded my authority to the forces of the United States in order to avoid bloodshed, and because I recognized the futility of a conflict with so formidable a power.

Because the President of the United States, the Secretary of State and an envoy commissioned by them reported in official documents that my government was unlawfully coerced by the forces, diplomatic and naval, of the United States. . . .

Because . . . the [Provisional] government . . . derives its assumed powers from the so-called committee of public safety, organized on or about the seventeenth day of January, 1893, said committee being composed largely of persons claiming American citizenship, and not one single Hawaiian was a member thereof, or in any way participated in the demonstration leading to its existence.

Because my people, about forty thousand in number, have in no way been consulted by those, three thousand in number, who claim the right to destroy the independence of Hawaii. . . .

Because said treaty ignores, not only the civic rights of my people, but, further, the hereditary property of their chiefs. Of the 4,000,000 acres composing the territory said treaty offers to annex . . . 915,000 acres has in no way been heretofore recognized as other than the private property of the constitutional monarch. . . .

Because it is proposed by said treaty to confiscate said property, technically called the crown lands, those legally entitled thereto, either now or in succession, receiving no consideration whatever. . . .

Because said treaty ignores, not only all professions of perpetual amity and good faith made by the United States in former treaties with the sovereigns representing the Hawaiian people, but all treaties made by those sovereigns with other and friendly powers, and it is thereby in violation of international law.

Because, by treating with the parties claiming at this time the right to cede said territory of Hawaii, the Government of the United States receives such territory from the hands of those whom its own magistrates . . . pronounced fraudulently in power and unconstitutionally ruling Hawaii. . . .

Therefore I, Liliuokalani of Hawaii, do hereby call upon the President of that nation, to whom alone I yielded my property and my authority, to withdraw said treaty (ceding said islands) from further consideration. I ask the honorable Senate of the United States to decline to ratify said treaty, and I implore the people of this great and good nation, from whom my ancestors learned the Christian religion, to sustain their representatives in such acts of justice and equity as may be in accord with the principles of their fathers, and to the Almighty Ruler of the universe, to him who judgeth righteously, I commit my cause.

Hind Swaraj
Mohandas K. Gandhi

For more than forty years Mohandas K. Gandhi (known as *Mahatma* or Great Soul) spearheaded the fight for India's independence from the British Empire. Gandhi led his followers in massive campaigns of nonviolent resistance and proved the effectiveness of these techniques. To achieve the necessary fortitude for successful nonviolent protest, Gandhi believed that protesters, and particularly their leaders, had to be capable of controlling their own impatience and desire for power. Such internal *swaraj*, or self-rule, was a prerequisite in his view to achieving external *swaraj*, or independence.

In March of 1930 Gandhi started with seventy-eight followers on a 248-mile march to the sea to make salt, in protest of the British law that granted a monopoly on salt manufacturing and sale to British suppliers. Thousands rushed to join him. On April 9, as the publicity of the march focused the world's attention on him, Gandhi called for more civil disobedience: the manufacture of salt in every village, protests at liquor shops, the burning of British-manufactured cloth, student strikes, and a host of other actions. Sixty thousand nonviolent protesters were arrested as the actions brought the nation to a standstill. Indian troops under British command refused orders to fire on protesters. The British agreed to negotiate, though it would take another seventeen years of periodic protests—during which Gandhi fasted several times as protest and was imprisoned on three occasions—before the dream of an independent India became reality. In the end, Gandhi, who wanted no partition of Hindu from Muslim, was frustrated by the separation of the Indian subcontinent into India and Pakistan.

Gandhi firmly believed that violent resistance corrupted its practitioners, turning them into the same sort of oppressors they sought to remove. As he wrote in his lengthy essay *Hind Swaraj*, considered by many to be his seminal work, "My patriotism does not teach me that I am to allow people to be crushed under the heel of Indian princes, if only the English retire."

Gandhi wrote *Hind Swaraj* in 1909 over just ten days, while traveling by ship from England to South Africa, where he lived at the time. He first published it in December of that year in his own journal, *Indian Opinion*. It is the only one of his works that Gandhi himself translated into English. He crafted the essay, excerpted below, as a dialogue between a doubting reader and an editor, who speaks for Gandhi.

READER: According to what you say, it is plain that instances of this kind of passive resistance are not to be found in history. It is necessary to understand this passive resistance more fully. It will be better, therefore, if you enlarge upon it.

EDITOR: Passive resistance is a method of securing rights by personal suffering; it is the reverse of resistance by arms. When I refuse to do a thing that is repugnant to my conscience, I use soul-force. For instance, the government of the day has passed a law which is applicable to me. I do not like it. If, by using violence, I force the government to repeal the law, I am employing what may be termed body-force. If I do not obey the law, and accept the penalty for its breach, I use soul-force. It involves sacrifice of self.

Everybody admits that sacrifice of self is infinitely superior to sacrifice of others. Moreover, if this kind of force is used in a cause that is unjust, only the person using it suffers. He does not make others suffer for his mistakes. Men have before now done many things which were subsequently found to have been wrong. No man can claim to be absolutely in the right, or that a particular thing is wrong, because he thinks so, but it is wrong for him so long as that is his deliberate judgement. It is, therefore, meet that he should not do that which he knows to be wrong, and suffer the consequence whatever it may be. This is the key to the use of soul-force.

READER: You would then disregard laws—this is rank disloyalty. We have always been considered a law-abiding nation. You seem to be going even beyond the extremists. They say that . . . we must drive out the law-givers even by force.

EDITOR: Whether I go beyond them or whether I do not is a matter of no consequence to either of us. We simply want to find out what is right, and to act accordingly. The real meaning of the statement that we are a law-abiding nation is that we are passive resisters. When we do not like certain laws, we do not break the heads of law-givers, but we suffer and do not submit to the laws. That we should obey laws whether good or bad is a new-fangled notion. There was no such thing in former days. The people disregarded those laws they did not like, and suffered the penalties for their breach. It is contrary to our manhood, if we obey laws repugnant to our conscience. Such teaching is opposed to religion, and means slavery. If the government were to ask us to go about without any clothing, should we do so? If I were a passive resister, I would say to them that I would have nothing to do with their law. But we have so forgotten ourselves and become so compliant, that we do not mind any degrading law.

A man who has realised his manhood, who fears only God, will fear no one else. Man-made laws are not necessarily binding on him. Even the government do not expect any such thing from us. They do not say: 'You must do such and such a thing' but they say: 'If you do not do it, we will punish you.' We are sunk so low, that we fancy that it is our duty and our religion to do what the law lays down. If man will only realise that it is unmanly to obey laws that are unjust, no man's tyranny will enslave him. This is the key to self-rule or home-rule.

It is superstition and an ungodly thing to believe that an act of a majority binds a minority. Many examples can be given in which acts of majorities will be found to have been wrong, and those of minorities to have been right. All reforms owe their origin to the initiation of minorities in opposition to majorities. If among a band of robbers, a knowledge of robbing is obligatory, is a pious man to accept the obligation? So long as the superstition that men should obey unjust laws exists, so long will their slavery exist. And a passive resister alone can remove such a superstition.

To use brute force, to use gunpowder is contrary to passive resistance, for it means that we want our opponent to do by force that which we desire but he does not. And, if such a use of force is justifiable, surely he is entitled to do likewise by us. And so we should never come to an agreement. We may simply fancy, like the blind horse moving in a circle round a mill, that we are making progress. Those who believe that they are not bound to obey laws which are repugnant to their conscience have only the remedy of passive resistance open to them. Any other must lead to disaster.

READER: From what you say, I deduce that passive resistance is a splendid weapon of the weak, but that, when they are strong, they may take up arms.

EDITOR: This is gross ignorance. Passive resistance, that is, soul-force, is matchless. It is superior to the force of arms. How, then, can it be considered only a weapon of the weak? Physical-force men are strangers to the courage that is requisite in a passive resister. Do you believe that a coward can ever disobey a law that he dislikes? Extremists are considered to be advocates of brute force. Why do they, then, talk about obeying laws? I do not blame them. They can say nothing else. When they succeed in driving out the English, and they themselves become governors, they will want you and me to obey their laws. And that is a fitting thing for their constitution. But a passive resister will say he will not obey a law that is against his conscience, even though he may be blown to pieces at the mouth of a cannon.

What do you think? Wherein is courage required—in blowing others to pieces from behind a cannon or with a smiling face to approach a cannon and to be blown to pieces? Who is the true warrior—he who keeps death always as a bosom-friend or he who controls the death of others? Believe me that a man devoid of courage and manhood can never be a passive resister.

This, however, I will admit: that even a man weak in body is capable of offering this resistance. One man can offer it just as well as millions. Both men and women can indulge in it. It does not require the training of an army; it needs no Jiu-jitsu. Control over the mind is alone necessary, and, when that is attained, man is free like the king of the forest, and his very glance withers the enemy.

Passive resistance is an all-sided sword; it can be used anyhow; it blesses him who uses it and him against whom it is used. Without drawing a drop of blood, it produces far-reaching results. It never rusts, and cannot be stolen. Competition between passive resisters does not exhaust. The sword of passive resistance does not require a scabbard. It is strange indeed that you should consider such a weapon to be a weapon merely of the weak.

"Give us our independence": Speech to the U.S. House of Representatives
Luis Muñoz Rivera

Just before the Spanish-American War of 1898, Puerto Rico gained a measure of autonomy from Spain, including both the right to elect its own government and the right to send sixteen members of the Congress of Deputies and three senators to the Spanish parliament, or Cortes. The agreement between Spain and Puerto Rico, known as the Autonomic Charter of 1897, allowed Puerto Rico authority over tariffs, education, and monetary policy, and allowed the island to negotiate commercial treaties.

But in the Treaty of Paris concluding the Spanish-American War in December 1898, Spain turned Puerto Rico, Guam, and the Philippines over to the United States. The Foraker Act of 1900 placed effective rule of the island in Washington. Over the next eighteen years, Puerto Rico's hopes for either independence or statehood were frustrated. In May 1916 the U.S. House of Representatives debated the Jones Act, which would make Puerto Ricans U.S. citizens but without representation in Congress. Puerto Rico's nonvoting resident commissioner, Luis Muñoz Rivera, rose against the bill, giving the passionate speech excerpted here.

Rivera had helped negotiate the Autonomic Charter and had served as chief of the Cabinet (effectively prime minister) during the brief experiment in autonomy from Spain. He decried the unwillingness of the United States to either incorporate Puerto Rico as a state or grant its independence. After Rivera's address, the Jones Act stalled in the Senate, but was passed the following year when the United States entered World War I, thereby allowing Puerto Ricans to serve in the U.S. military.

Perhaps discouraged by the lack of success of Rivera's diplomatic efforts, later activists for Puerto Rican independence advocated violence, including an unsuccessful armed revolt in 1950 and terrorist actions in Washington in 1950 and 1954. Today, a slim majority in the island seems to favor continued commonwealth status; most other residents favor statehood. A small minority continues to advocate for independence.

ON THE 18TH DAY OF OCTOBER 1898, when the flag of this great Republic was unfurled over the fortresses of San Juan, if anyone had said to my countrymen that the United States, the land of liberty, was going to deny their right to form a government of the people, by the people, and for the people of Porto Rico, my countrymen would have refused to believe such a prophecy, considering it sheer madness. The Porto Ricans were living at that time under a regime of ample self-government, discussed and voted by the Spanish Cortes, on the basis of the parliamentary system in use among all the nations of Europe. Spain sent to the islands a Governor, whose power . . . made him the equivalent of those constitutional sovereigns who reign but do not govern. The members of the Cabinet . . . were natives of the island; the representatives in the Senate and in the House were natives of the island; and the administration in its entirety was in the hands of natives of the island. The Spanish Cortes, it is true, retained the power to make statutory laws for Porto Rico, but in the Cortes were 16 Porto Rican representatives and 3 Porto Rican senators having voice and vote. . . .

Two years later, in 1900 . . . the Congress of the United States approved the Foraker Act. Under this act, all of the 11 members of the executive council were appointed by the President of the United States. . . . And this executive council . . . was . . . the supreme arbiter of the island and of its interests. It represents the most absolute contradiction of republican principles.

For 16 years we have endured this system of government, protesting and struggling against it, with energy and without result. We did not lose hope, because if one national party, the Republican, was forcibly enforcing this system upon us, the other national party, the Democratic, was encouraging us by its declarations in the platforms of Kansas City, St. Louis, and Denver. Porto Rico waited, election after election, for the Democratic Party to triumph at the polls and fulfill its promises. At last the Democratic Party did triumph. It is here. It has a controlling majority at this end of the Capitol and at the other end: it is in possession of the White House.

On the Democratic Party rests the sole and undivided responsibility for the progress of events at this juncture. . . .

. . . The legislation you are about to enact will prove whether the platforms of the Democratic Party are more than useless paper, whether the words of its leaders are more than soap bubbles, dissolved by the breath of triumph. . . .

There is no reason which justifies American statesmen in denying self-government to my country and erasing from their programs the principles of popular sovereignty. Is illiteracy the reason? Because if in Porto Rico 60 percent of the electorate cannot read, in the United States in the early days of the Republic, 80 percent of the population were unable to read; and even today there are 20 Republics and 20 monarchies which acknowledge a higher percentage of illiteracy than Porto Rico. . . . There is a reason and only one reason—the same sad reason of war and conquest which let loose over the South after the fall of Richmond thousands and thousands of office seekers, hungry for power and authority, and determined to report to their superiors that the rebels of the South were unprepared for self-government. We are the southerners of the 20th century.

Easter Proclamation
Provisional Government of the Irish Republic

Great Britain had asserted governance over Ireland since the twelfth century, but did not extend control and begin to settle English colonists on the island until the late 1600s. Irish Catholics were oppressed and banned from serving in the Irish Parliament. In 1800, this unrepresentative Irish Parliament passed a bill uniting Ireland with the kingdom of Great Britain.

In the early 1900s, Irish unrest increased, highlighted by the Easter Uprising of 1916, in which armed Irish rebels took over portions of Dublin and declared the creation of an Irish Republic in the proclamation below. The Easter Uprising was put down with a strong military response by Britain, complete with a warship shelling Dublin. Afterward fifteen leaders of the rebellion were executed (all but one without public trial) and martial law was imposed. These acts infuriated many Irish.

In the elections of December 1918, pro-independence Sinn Féin (meaning "We Ourselves") party members won nearly three quarters of Ireland's seats in the British Parliament. The delegates refused to accept their seats, instead meeting together as an independent Assembly of Ireland, the Dáil Éireann. Britain refused to recognize the Dáil Éireann, and guerilla war ensued between the pro-independence Irish Republican Army and Britain's forces.

In 1921 King George V intervened with a speech calling for reconciliation. This led to a truce and ultimately to recognition of Ireland's independence the following year through the Anglo-Irish Treaty. The treaty established the Irish Free State as a member of the British Commonwealth rather than a fully independent republic. In 1949, the Irish Free State amended its constitution, withdrawing from the commonwealth and creating the Irish Republic that we know as Ireland today.

IRISHMEN AND IRISHWOMEN: In the name of God and of the dead generations from which she receives her old tradition of nationhood, Ireland, through us, summons her children to her flag and strikes for her freedom.

Having organised and trained her manhood through her secret revolutionary organisation, the Irish Republican Brotherhood, and through her open military organisations, the Irish Volunteers and the Irish Citizen Army, having patiently perfected her discipline, having resolutely waited for the right moment to reveal itself, she now seizes that moment, and, supported by her exiled children in America and by gallant allies in Europe, but relying in the first on her own strength, she strikes in full confidence of victory.

We declare the right of the people of Ireland to the ownership of Ireland, and to the unfettered control of Irish destinies, to be sovereign and indefeasible. The long usurpation of that right by a foreign people and government has not extinguished the right, nor can it ever be extinguished except by the destruction of the Irish people. In every generation the Irish people have asserted their right to national freedom and sovereignty: six times during the past three hundred years they have asserted it in arms. Standing on that fundamental right and again asserting it in arms in the face of the world, we hereby proclaim the Irish Republic as a Sovereign Independent State, and we pledge our lives and the lives of our comrades-in-arms to the cause of its freedom, of its welfare, and its exaltation among the nations.

The Irish Republic is entitled to, and hereby claims, the allegiance of every Irishman and Irishwoman. The Republic guarantees religious and civil liberty, equal rights and equal opportunities to all its citizens, and declares its resolve to pursue the happiness and prosperity of the whole nation and of all its parts, cherishing all the children of the nation equally, and oblivious of the differences carefully fostered by an alien government, which have divided a minority from the majority in the past.

Until our arms have brought the opportune moment for the establishment of a permanent National Government, representative of the whole people of Ireland and elected by the suffrages of all her men and women, the Provisional Government, hereby constituted, will administer the civil and military affairs of the Republic in trust for the people.

We place the cause of the Irish Republic under the protection of the Most High God, Whose blessing we invoke upon our arms, and we pray that no one who serves that cause will dishonour it by cowardice, inhumanity, or rapine. In this supreme hour the Irish nation must, by its valour and discipline and by the readiness of its children to sacrifice themselves for the common good, prove itself worthy of the august destiny to which it is called.

Declaration of Independence
Ho Chi Minh

During World War II, the Japanese occupied Southeast Asia, ruling what had been the colony of French Indochina (today the nations of Vietnam, Laos, and Cambodia) through a puppet French government. In 1945, the French troops revolted against the Japanese. The rebellion was quickly crushed, and the Japanese took direct control of the country.

In the summer of 1945, fifty American commandos began working behind Japanese lines, fighting alongside the Viet Minh guerillas led by the nationalist leader Ho Chi Minh. The Viet Minh gradually gained control of the countryside and, following the Japanese surrender, took control of the country.

Ho Chi Minh declared Vietnam's independence on September 2, 1945, in this short speech that relied heavily on American ideals and language. The leader of the American commandos—Major Archimedes Patti—stood beside Ho's top military leader, General Vo Nguyen Giap, during the speech. Bands played the "Star Spangled Banner," "God Save the King," and the "Soviet Worker's March"—the national anthems of the Allied countries.

The French were not ready to cede control of their most valuable colony, and despite its earlier show of support for Ho Chi Minh, the West supported France's claims, leading to nearly three decades of conflict, as Ho's troops fought first French, then American troops. In 1975, the last American troops withdrew, leaving Vietnam independent and united under communist control.

"ALL MEN ARE CREATED EQUAL. They are endowed by their Creator with certain inalienable rights, among these are Life, Liberty, and the pursuit of Happiness."

This immortal statement was made in the Declaration of Independence of the United States of America in 1776. In a broader sense, this means: All the peoples on the earth are equal from birth, all the peoples have a right to live, to be happy and free.

The Declaration of the French Revolution made in 1791 on the Rights of Man and the Citizen also states: "All men are born free and with equal rights, and must always remain free and have equal rights." Those are undeniable truths.

Nevertheless, for more than eighty years, the French imperialists, abusing the standard of Liberty, Equality, and Fraternity, have violated our Fatherland and oppressed our fellow citizens. They have acted contrary to the ideals of humanity and justice. In the field of politics, they have deprived our people of every democratic liberty.

They have enforced inhuman laws; they have set up three distinct political regimes in the North, the Center, and the South of Vietnam in order to wreck our national unity and prevent our people from being united.

They have built more prisons than schools. They have mercilessly slain our patriots; they have drowned our uprisings in rivers of blood.

They have fettered public opinion; they have practised obscurantism against our people. To weaken our race they have forced us to use opium and alcohol.

In the fields of economics, they have fleeced us to the backbone, impoverished our people, and devastated our land.

They have robbed us of our rice fields, our mines, our forests, and our raw materials. They have monopolised the issuing of bank-notes and the export trade.

They have invented numerous unjustifiable taxes and reduced our people, especially our peasantry, to a state of extreme poverty.

They have hampered the prospering of our national bourgeoisie; they have mercilessly exploited our workers.

In the autumn of 1940, when the Japanese Fascists violated Indochina's territory to establish new bases in their fight against the Allies, the French imperialists went down on their bended knees and handed over our country to them.

Thus, from that date, our people were subjected to the double yoke of the French and the Japanese. Their sufferings and miseries increased. The result was that from the end of last year to the beginning of this year, from Quang Tri province to the North of Vietnam, more than two million of our fellow-citizens died from starvation. On March 9, the French troops were disarmed by the Japanese. The French colonialists either fled or surrendered, showing that not only were they incapable of "protecting" us, but that, in the span of five years, they had twice sold our country to the Japanese.

On several occasions before March 9, the Vietminh League urged the French to ally themselves with it against the Japanese. Instead of agreeing to this proposal, the French colonialists so intensified their terrorist activities against the Vietminh members that before fleeing they massacred a great number of our political prisoners detained at Yen Bay and Cao Bang. . . .

The French have fled, the Japanese have capitulated, Emperor Bao Dai has abdicated. Our people have broken the chains which for nearly a century have fettered them and have won independence for the Fatherland. Our people at the same time have overthrown the monarchic regime that has reigned supreme for dozens of centuries. In its place has been established the present Democratic Republic.

For these reasons, we, members of the Provisional Government, representing the whole Vietnamese people, declare that from now on we break off all relations of a colonial character with France; we repeal all the international obligation that France has so far subscribed to on behalf of Vietnam and we abolish all the special rights the French have unlawfully acquired in our Fatherland.

I Speak of Freedom
Kwame Nkrumah

In the years following Mohandas Gandhi's successful movement to win independence for India, the British government reluctantly began to allow limited self-government in many of its colonies. These partial concessions did not satisfy demands for full independence, but they did allow for continued dialogue and in many cases for peaceful transition to full independence.

In 1947, African leader Kwame Nkrumah launched a vigorous organizing effort seeking independence for Ghana, culminating with a program of economic noncooperation in 1950, modeled after Gandhi's successful efforts in India. When the country's economic life ground to a standstill, the British government jailed Nkrumah in hopes of stopping the protests. When protests continued, Britain called for elections under a constitution that granted limited autonomy. The still-jailed Nkrumah won a seat in the 1951 elections, while his Convention People's Party took the majority of the parliament. Overnight Nkrumah went from political prisoner to head of the government—but a government of limited power.

The day after his release from prison, Nkrumah gave a speech accepting the conditions offered by Britain, while emphasizing that the focus must remain on full independence. By steering this middle course—accepting compromise while continuing to strive for the ultimate goal of full freedom and national self-determination—he enabled Ghana to earn its independence in 1957 with very little bloodshed. Ghana's success helped start a political tidal wave that swept seventeen African nations to independence in 1960 alone.

In this excerpt from his autobiography, *I Speak of Freedom*, Nkrumah recalled his speech the day after his release from prison in February of 1951.

THE FOLLOWING DAY I gave a Press conference at which I said that the constitution under which I was to act as Leader of Government Business was "bogus and fraudulent" but would serve as a stepping stone to self-government. It was bogus because the ministers were without power. Yet the C.P.P. elected members would accept ministerial posts if they were offered them. While co-operating with the administration, we would not alter our demand for full self-government within the Commonwealth. . . . In a message which I issued a week later to Party members, I referred once more to the Constitution:

> There is a great risk in accepting office under this new Constitution which still makes us half slaves and half free. It is all too easy to identify oneself with such a Constitution and thereby be swayed by considerations of temporary personal advantage, instead of seeking the interest of the people. Hence we call for vigilance and moral courage to withstand the evil manœuvres of imperialism. . . .
>
> The trust which the people have placed in the Convention People's Party is the most precious thing we possess; and as long as that trust and confidence is maintained there is victory for us.

The Battle of Algiers
Franco Solinas

Gillo Pontecorvo's 1966 film *The Battle of Algiers*, scripted by Franco Solinas, constituted a powerful protest against the inevitable violence of colonial occupation and armed revolution. The fictional account looked at the 1954 to 1957 revolt by the Algerian National Liberation Front (NLF) in the city of Algiers. The NLF sought to end French rule of Algeria and relied on terrorist tactics to inspire fear in the country's small European population.

Pontecorvo started the project at the request of a former NLF revolutionary who also plays one of the characters. The film employed a documentary look and feel, and caused a sensation with its realistic scenes of police raids, revolutionary leaders, and terrorized populace. It showed with equal clinical precision the elaborate preparations by the NLF to kill French civilians and the violent torture tactics used by the French to extract information from captured NLF fighters. The movie challenged both repressive occupations and the senseless violence that they breed. It was banned in France, and its torture scenes were edited out of the versions released in the United States and Britain.

In the scene excerpted here, the character of Colonel Mathieu, leader of the French paratroopers called on to restore order, addresses the inevitability of torture if the French were to remain.

PREFECT'S OFFICE. PRESS HALL. INSIDE. DAY. MARCH 4.

Colonel Mathieu is standing. On his face is a brief smile, motionless, his eyes attentive, but half-closed somewhat, due to the camera flashes.

1ST JOURNALIST: Colonel Mathieu . . . the spokesman for the residing minister, Mr. Gorlin, has stated that "Larbi Ben M'Hidi committed suicide in his own cell, hanging himself with pieces of his shirt, that he had used to make a rope, and then attached to the bars of his cell window." In a preceding statement, the same spokesman had specified that: ". . . due to the intention already expressed by the prisoner Ben M'Hidi to escape at the first opportunity, it has been necessary to keep his hands and feet bound continually." In your opinion, colonel, in such conditions, is a man capable of tearing his shirt, making a rope from it, and attaching it to a bar of the window to hang himself?

MATHIEU: You should address that question to the minister's spokesman. I'm not the one who made those statements. . . . On my part, I will say that I had the opportunity to admire the moral strength, intelligence, and unwavering idealism demonstrated by Ben M'Hidi. For these reasons, although remembering the danger he represented, I do not hesitate to pay homage to his memory.

2ND JOURNALIST: Colonel Mathieu . . . Much has been said lately not only of the successes obtained by the paratroopers, but also of the methods that they have employed. . . . Can you tell us something about this?

MATHIEU: The successes obtained are the results of those methods. One presupposes the other and vice versa.

3RD JOURNALIST: Excuse me, colonel. I have the impression that perhaps due to excessive prudence . . . my colleagues continue to ask the same elusive questions, to which you can only respond in an elusive manner. I think it would be better to call things by their right names; if one means torture, then one should call it torture.

MATHIEU: I understand. What's your question?

3RD JOURNALIST: The questions have already been asked. I would only like some precise answers, that's all.

MATHIEU: Let's try to be precise then. The word "torture" does not appear in our orders. We have always spoken of interrogation as the only valid method in a police operation directed against unknown enemies. As for the NLF, they request that their members, in the event of capture, should maintain silence for twenty-four hours, and then, they may talk. Thus, the organization has already had the time necessary to render useless any information furnished. . . . What type of interrogation should we choose? . . . the one the courts use for a crime of homicide which drags on for months?

3RD JOURNALIST: The law is often inconvenient, colonel . . .

MATHIEU: And those who explode bombs in public places, do they perhaps respect the law? When you asked that question to Ben M'Hidi, remember what he said? No, gentlemen, believe me, it is a vicious circle. And we could discuss the problem for hours without reaching any conclusions. Because the problem does not lie here. The problem is: the NLF wants us to leave Algeria and we want to remain. Now, it seems to me that, despite varying shades of opinion, you all agree that we must remain. When the rebellion first began, there were not even shades of opinion. All the newspapers, even the left-wing ones, wanted the rebellion suppressed. And we were sent here for this very reason. And we are neither madmen nor sadists, gentlemen. Those who call us fascists today, forget the contribution that many of us made to the Resistance. Those who call us Nazis, do not know that among us there are survivors of Dachau and Buchenwald. We are soldiers and our only duty is to win. Therefore, to be precise, I would now like to ask you a question: Should France remain in Algeria? If you answer "yes," then you must accept all the necessary consequences.

Prague Spring

Following World War II, the Soviet Union occupied Eastern Europe, including Czechoslovakia, and established communist puppet governments in each nation. In April 1968 the leader of Czechoslovakia's communist party, Alexander Dubcek, launched a series of political and economic reforms, including greater reliance on private enterprise, an emphasis on production of

consumer goods, and the potential for multiparty elections. The reforms were popular, and momentum built for further liberalization. In June, censorship was abolished, and students openly passed out underground newspapers on Prague street corners.

The Soviet Union did not favor the changes, fearing they would inspire widespread democratic reforms or even revolt in the communist nations of Eastern Europe. In August, thousands of Russian tanks and nearly half a million troops rolled into Czechoslovakia and onto the streets of Prague. Western nations objected verbally, but took no concrete action.

But in Prague the reaction was overwhelming. The political and cultural institutions of the country rallied behind the government. Students occupied the streets, blocking the tanks and setting a few on fire. The Soviets were forced to compromise, leaving Dubcek in power temporarily. Eventually an orthodox communist party resumed governance and continued the repression of free speech and close ties to the Soviet Union. Czechoslovakia did not obtain true self-determination until the peaceful Velvet Revolution of 1989. Dubcek lived to see this freedom and served as chairman of Czechoslovakia's Federal Assembly.

Some commentators have assigned broad significance to the Prague Spring reforms and their subsequent suppression. For example, the events showed the people of the communist nations the power of a mobilized populace even in the face of overwhelming force. In this way, Prague Spring may have been the inspiration for events in Moscow nearly twenty years later, when the Soviet regime itself gave way to the winds of change and democratic reform.

"Do not let the olive branch fall from my hand"
Yasser Arafat

On November 13, 1974, the leader of the Palestine Liberation Organization (PLO), Yasser Arafat, addressed the United Nations General Assembly, demanding a unified and democratic Palestine that would be a homeland both for Jews and for Palestinian Muslims. The address represented the first time the head of a revolutionary movement was invited to address the United Nations. The Algerian president of the General Assembly further increased the controversy associated with Arafat's visit by according him the full diplomatic honors due a head of state.

This excerpt from Arafat's speech highlighted a key difference in perception between Israelis and Palestinians. To Arafat, the migration of Jews to Palestine and the 1948 creation of Israel did not represent an acceptable division of land under United Nations supervision, but the colonization and ultimate usurpation of Palestinian lands. He sought a Palestinian state incorporating all of the present area of Israel as well as the West Bank and Gaza. This perception would later drive him to reject a promising peace proposal negotiated under President Bill Clinton's auspices because it did not include a right for Palestinians to return to Israel.

In his 1974 speech, Arafat asserted that the terrorist tactics used by the PLO were morally equivalent to the actions of American revolutionaries, resistance fighters who worked against the Nazis, and participants in African and Asian independence movements.

JUST AS COLONIALISM and its demagogues dignified their conquests, their plunder and limitless attacks upon the natives of Africa with appeals to a "civilizing and modernizing" mission, so too did waves of Zionist immigrants disguise their purposes as they conquered Palestine. Just as colonialism as a system and colonialists as its instrument used religion, color, race and language to justify the African's exploitation and his cruel subjugation by terror and discrimination, so too were these methods employed as Palestine was usurped and its people hounded from their national homeland. . . .

The Jewish invasion of Palestine began in 1881. Before the first large wave of immigrants started arriving, Palestine had a population of half a million; most of the population was either Moslem or Christian, and only 20,000 were Jewish. Every segment of the population enjoyed the religious tolerance characteristic of our civilization. . . .

Between 1882 and 1917 the Zionist Movement settled approximately 50,000 European Jews in our homeland. To do that it resorted to trickery and deceit in order to implant them in our midst. Its success in getting Britain to issue the Balfour Declaration once again demonstrated the alliance between Zionism and imperialism. Furthermore, by promising to the Zionist movement what was not hers to give, Britain showed how oppressive the rule of imperialism was. . . .

By 1947 the number of Jews had reached 600,000; they owned about six percent of Palestinian arable land. The figure should be compared with the population of Palestine which at that time was 1,250,000.

As a result of the collusion between the mandatory Power [Britain] and the Zionist movement and with the support of some countries, this General Assembly early in its history approved a recommendation to partition our Palestinian homeland. . . . When we rejected that decision, our position corresponded to that of the natural mother who refused to permit King Solomon to cut her son in two. . . . The roots of the Palestine question lie here. Its causes do not stem from any conflict between two religions or two nationalisms. Neither is it a border conflict between neighboring states. . . .

If the immigration of Jews to Palestine had had as its objective the goal of enabling them to live side by side with us, enjoying the same rights and assuming the same duties, we would have opened our doors to them, as far as our homeland's capacity for absorption permitted. Such was the case with the thousands of Armenians and Circassians who still live among us in equality as brethren and citizens. But that the goal of this immigration should be to usurp our homeland, disperse our people, and turn us into second-class citizens—this is what no one can conceivably demand that we acquiesce in or submit to. . . .

The difference between the revolutionary and the terrorist lies in the reason for which each fights. For whoever stands by a just cause and fights for the freedom and liberation of his land from the invaders, the settlers and the colonialists, cannot possibly be called terrorist; otherwise the American people in their struggle for liberation from the British colonialists would have been terrorists, the European resistance against the Nazis would be terrorism, the struggle of the Asian, African and Latin American peoples would also be terrorism, and many of you who are in this Assembly Hall were considered terrorists. This is actually a just and proper struggle consecrated by the United Nations Charter and by the Universal Declaration of Human Rights. . . .

I am a rebel and freedom is my cause. I know well that many of you present here today once stood in exactly the same resistance position as I now occupy and from which I must fight. You once had to convert dreams into reality by your struggle. . . .

Why therefore should I not dream and hope? For is not revolution the making real of dreams and hopes? So let us work together that my dream may be fulfilled, that I may return with my people out of exile, there in Palestine to live . . . in one democratic State where Christian, Jew and Moslem live in justice, equality, fraternity and progress. . . .

I appeal to you to enable our people to establish national independent sovereignty over its land.

Today I have come bearing an olive branch and a freedom fighter's gun. Do not let the olive branch fall from my hand.

"I couldn't help noticing the crack in the bell"
The Dalai Lama

The *State of Tibet* has been in flux for the last seven hundred years. It has existed at times as an independent nation, at times under Chinese rule, and at times exercised effective self-rule while nominally part of China. During eras of full or partial self-rule, His Holiness the Dalai Lama—the religious leader of Tibetan Buddhism—has led the nation. Most recently the Dalai Lama ruled from 1912 to 1959.

In 1951, the Chinese army occupied Tibet, taking over the country and imposing severe restrictions on religious freedom and other rights of Tibetans. In 1959, the Dalai Lama fled to India under threat of confinement. He has never acknowledged the legitimacy of the Chinese governance of the country, forming instead a government in exile and maintaining a continuous—and peaceful—campaign to regain independence or, since 1988, at least partial autonomy. In 1989 the Nobel Prize committee awarded him that year's Peace Prize, praising "the fact that the Dalai Lama in his struggle for the liberation of Tibet consistently has opposed the use of violence. He has instead advocated peaceful solutions based upon tolerance and mutual respect in order to preserve the historical and cultural heritage of his people." In recent years some younger Tibetans have been losing patience with this approach, advocating violent resistance to China's occupation.

In 1991, the Dalai Lama spoke to Congress in the rotunda of the U.S. Capitol, articulating his hope to avoid violence and urging the United States and other Western democracies to play a more active role.

WHILE YOUR SOLDIERS WERE FIGHTING Communist Chinese troops in Korea, China invaded Tibet. Almost nine years later, in March, 1959—during the suppression of a nation-wide revolt against Chinese occupation—I was forced to flee to India. Eventually, many thousands of my compatriots followed me. Since then, Tibetan refugees have lived in exile. We were heartened in 1959, 1961 and 1965 by three United Nations Resolutions recognizing the Tibetan people's fundamental rights, including the right to self-determination. Your government supported and voted for these resolutions. China, however, ignored the views of the world community. For almost three decades, Tibet was sealed from the outside world. In that time, as a result of China's efforts to remake our society, 1.2 million Tibetans—one fifth of the population—perished. More than 6,000 of our monasteries and temples were destroyed. Our natural resources were devoured. And in a few short decades the artistic, literary and scientific legacy of our ancient civilization was virtually erased.

In the face of this tragedy, we have tried to save our national identity. We have fought for our country's freedom peacefully. We have refused to adopt terrorism. We have adhered to our Buddhist faith in non-violence. And we have engaged in a vigorous democratic experiment in the exile community as a model for a future free Tibet.

Tibet today continues to suffer harsh oppression. The unending cycle of imprisonment, torture, and executions continues unabated. I am particularly concerned about China's long term policy of population transfer onto the Tibetan plateau.

Tibet is being colonized by waves of Chinese immigrants. We are becoming a minority in our own country. The new Chinese settlers have created an alternate society: a Chinese apartheid which, denying Tibetans equal social and economic status in our own land, threatens to finally overwhelm and absorb us. The immediate result has been a round of unrest and reprisal. In the face of this critical situation, I have made two proposals in recent years.

In September of 1987, here on Capitol Hill, I presented a Five Point Peace Plan. In it, I called for negotiations between Tibet and China, and spoke of my firm resolve that soon Tibet will once again become a Zone of Peace; a neutral, demilitarized sanctuary where humanity and nature live in harmony. In June of 1988, at the European Parliament in Strasbourg, I elaborated on my call for negotiations, and made personal suggestions which would protect the territorial integrity of the whole of Tibet, as well as restore the Tibetan people's right to govern themselves. I also suggested that China could retain overall responsibility for the conduct of Tibet's foreign relations.

It has been almost three years since the Strasbourg Proposal. In that time, many Tibetans have expressed profound misgivings over my stand for being too conciliatory. Beijing did respond: but the response was negative. The Chinese government, it is clear, is unwilling to engage in meaningful dialogue. As recent events in China itself indicate, the Communist leadership refuses even to acknowledge the wishes of its own people. I regret that my sincere efforts to find a mutually beneficial solution have not produced meaningful dialogue. Nevertheless, I continue to believe in a negotiated solution. Many governments and parliaments, as well as the U.S. Congress, support this effort.

For the sake of the people of China as well as Tibet, a stronger stand is needed towards the government of the People's Republic of China. The policy of "constructive engagement," as a means to encourage moderation, can have no concrete effect unless the democracies of the world clearly stand by their principles. Linking bilateral relations to human rights and democracy is not merely a matter of appeasing one's own conscience. It is a proven, peaceful and effective means to encourage genuine change. If the world truly hopes to see a reduction of tyranny in China, it must not appease China's leaders. . . .

Recently, the United States has led the international community in freeing a small country from a cruel occupation. I am happy for the people of Kuwait. Sadly, all small nations can not expect similar support for their rights and freedoms. However, I believe that a "new world order" cannot truly emerge unless it is matched by a "new world freedom." Order without freedom is repression. Freedom without order is anarchy. We need both a new world order that prohibits aggression and a new world freedom that supports the liberty of individuals and nations.

I would like to conclude by recalling a recent and moving experience. On my last trip to the United States, I was taken to Independence Hall in Philadelphia. I was profoundly inspired to stand in the chamber from which your Declaration of Independence and Constitution came. I was then shown to the main floor before the Liberty Bell. My guide explained that two hundred years ago this bell pealed forth to proclaim liberty throughout your land. On examining it, however, I couldn't help noticing the crack in the bell. That crack, I feel, is a reminder to the American people who enjoy so much freedom, while people in other parts of the world, such as Tibet, have no freedom. The Liberty Bell is a reminder that you cannot be truly free until people everywhere are free. I believe that this reminder is alive, and that your great strength continues to come from your deep principles.

CHAPTER 6
ECONOMIC JUSTICE

INTRODUCTION

The documents in this chapter deal with two key economic themes: fair and safe conditions for laborers and the equitable distribution of wealth. In fits and starts over the course of the past four hundred years, society has created more healthful and humane working conditions and laws that protect more vulnerable members of society against the fiercest exploitation. In many cases, protest was part of the impetus for change. Thus protests like that of Richard Oastler (see page 208) over the exploitation of children in England helped bring into place the first child-labor laws in the nineteenth century. Protests over the deaths of more than one hundred young women in the infamous Triangle Shirtwaist Factory fire (see page 231) in 1911 helped to put spine into worker-safety laws first in New York and later throughout the United States.

Economic protests today sometimes take aim at the brand image of major corporations in order to bring these companies to account for their poor treatment of workers. For example, one of the most effective protests of Nike's use of sweatshop labor in Asia occurred in 1997 when inner-city youths—whose hip style had become central to Nike's success—held a "shoe-in" and dumped their old Nike sneakers at the company's store in Manhattan.

Like working conditions, the proper distribution of wealth has long been a subject of protest. In 1649, the True Levelers (see page 202) protested that the wealthy "got your Propriety by murther and theft, and you keep it by the same power from us, that have an equal right to the Land with you, by the righteous Law of Creation." The theme of protest against unequal distribution of wealth is just as pertinent today as it was more than three centuries ago.

Some economic protests that were considered radical when proposed have since come to be so widely accepted as to be taken for granted. For instance, the eight-hour workday, worker safety laws, the minimum wage, and child-labor laws were all at one time or another viewed by powerful elites as having the potential to produce economic catastrophe. The protesters of those times had the vision to see these ideas not as threats to their society's economic stability, but rather as necessary innovations.

A Declaration from the Poor Oppressed People of England
The True Levelers

In the turmoil surrounding the English civil war of 1641 to 1646, citizens began to publicly question the privileges of the nobility. By 1649 food costs had reached excessive levels, driving many citizens to economic desperation. The True Levelers (also known as the Diggers) argued for fair distribution of economic resources, particularly land, as the solution to dramatic impoverishment. In particular, the True Leveler movement attempted to articulate a moral rationale for redistribution of wealth. In the "Declaration from the Poor Oppressed People of England," a group of forty-five leading True Levelers, including the group's founder Gerrard Winstanley, articulated their philosophy, its connection to the scriptures, and its steadfast emphasis on nonviolence. The emphasis on land as the source of wealth reflected the largely agrarian economy of the day.

The True Levelers ultimately set up communal farms in Surrey, attempting to cultivate common land and share the resulting produce among any who came to join them. They were forced from the land by a combination of court action, threats, and physical abuse from local nobility.

WE WHOSE NAMES are subscribed, do in the name of all the poor oppressed people in England, declare unto you, that call your selves Lords of Manors, and Lords of the Land, That in regard the King of Righteousness, our Maker, hath inlightened our hearts so far, as to see, That the earth was not made purposely for you, to be Lords of it, and we to be your Slaves, Servants, and Beggers; but it was made to be a common Livelihood to all, without respect of persons. . . .

And further, in regard the King of Righteousness hath made us sensible of our burthens, and the cryes and groanings of our hearts are come before him: We take it as a testimony of love from him, that our hearts begin to be freed from slavish fear of men, such as you are; and that we find Resolutions in us, grounded upon the inward law of Love, one towards another, To Dig and Plough up the Commons, and waste Lands through England; and that our conversation shall be so unblameable, That your Laws shall not reach to oppress us any longer, unless you by your Laws will shed the innocent blood that runs in our veins.

For though you and your Ancestors got your Propriety by murther and theft, and you keep it by the same power from us, that have an equal right to the Land with you, by the righteous Law of Creation, yet we shall have no occasion of quarrelling (as you do) about that disturbing devil, called Particular propriety: For the Earth, with all her Fruits of Corn, Cattle, and such like, was made to be a common Store-house of Livelihood to all Mankinde, friend, and foe, without exception.

And to prevent your scrupulous Objections, know this, That we Must neither buy nor sell; Money must not any longer (after our work of the Earths community is advanced) be the great god, that hedges in some, and hedges out others; for Money is but part of the Earth: And surely, the Righteous Creator, who is King, did never ordain, That unless some of Mankinde, do bring that Mineral (Silver and Gold) in their hands, to others of their own kinde, that they should neither be fed, nor be clothed; no surely, For this was the project of Tyrant-flesh (which Land-lords are branches of) to set his Image upon Money. And they make this unrighteous Law, That none should buy or sell, eat, or be clothed, or have any comfortable Livelihood among men, unless they did bring his Image stamped upon Gold or Silver in their hands. . . .

For after our work of the Earthly community is advanced, we must make use of Gold and Silver, as we do of other metals, but not to buy and sell withal; for buying and selling is the great cheat, that robs and steals the Earth one from another: It is that which makes some Lords, others Beggers, some Rulers, others to be ruled; and makes great Murderers and Theeves to be imprisoners, and hangers of little ones, or of sincere-hearted men.

And while we are made to labor the Earth together, with one consent and willing minde; and while we are made free, that every one, friend and foe, shall enjoy the benefit of their Creation, that is, to have food and rayment from the Earth, their Mother; and every one subject to give accompt of his thoughts, words, and actions to none, but to the one onely righteous Judg, and Prince of Peace; the Spirit of Righteousness that dwells, and that is now rising up to rule in every Creature, and in the whole Globe. We say, while we are made to hinder no man of his Priviledges given him in his Creation, equal to one, as to another; what Law then can you make, to take hold upon us, but Laws of Oppression and Tyranny, that shall enslave or spill the blood of the Innocent? And so your Selves, your Judges, Lawyers, and Justices, shall be found to be the greatest Transgressors, in, and over Mankinde.

. . . And since the power of the murdering, and theeving Sword, formerly, as well as now of late yeers, hath set up a Govenment, and maintains that Government; for what are prisons, and putting others to death, but the power of the Sword to enforce people to that Government which was got by Conquest and Sword, and cannot stand of it self, but by the same murdering power? That Government that is got over people by the Sword and kept by the Sword, is not set up by the King of Righteousness to be his Law, but by Covetousness, the great god of the world; who hath been permitted to raign for a time, times, and dividing of time, and his government draws to the period of the last term of his allotted time; and then the Nations shall see the glory of that Government that shall rule in Righteousness, without either Sword or Spear. . . .

And thus in love we have declared the purpose of our hearts plainly, without flatterie, expecting love, and the same sincerity from you, without grumbling or quarreling, being Creatures of your own Image and mould, intending no other matter herein, but to observe the Law of righteous action, endeavouring to shut out of the Creation, the cursed thing, called *Particular Propriety*, which is the cause of all wars, bloud-shed, theft, and enslaving Laws, that hold the people under miserie.

Signed for and in behalf of all the poor oppressed people of England, and the whole world. . . .

FINIS.

A Discourse on Political Economy
Jean-Jacques Rousseau

Jean-Jacques Rousseau's impassioned writings on individual rights, social equity, and equality inspired the leaders of both the French and American revolutions. In this excerpt from *A Discourse on Political Economy*, published in 1755, Rousseau addressed the need for progressive taxation to fund public needs, a concept that did not take hold for another 150 years. He also asserted that because a stable society protects the property of the wealthy, the wealthy should contribute more to the maintenance of society.

IT SHOULD BE REMEMBERED that the foundation of the social compact is property; and its first condition, that every one should be maintained in the peaceful possession of what belongs to him. It is true that, by the same treaty, every one binds himself, at least tacitly, to be assessed toward the public wants . . . on the basis of a proportional rating which leaves nothing arbitrary in the imposition of the tax. . . .

These proportions appear at first very easy to note, because, being relative to each man's position in the world, their incidence is always public: but proper regard is seldom paid to all the elements that should enter into such a calculation, even apart from deception arising from avarice, fraud and self-interest. In the first place, we have to consider the relation of quantities, according to which . . . the person who has ten times the property of another man ought to pay ten times as much to the State. Secondly, the relation of the use made, that is to say, the distinction between necessaries and superfluities. He who possesses only the common necessaries of life should pay nothing at all, while the tax on him who is in possession of superfluities may justly be extended to everything he has over and above mere necessaries. To this he will possibly object that, when his rank is taken into account, what may be superfluous to a man of inferior station is necessary for him. But this is false: for a grandee has two legs just like a cow-herd, and, like him again, but one belly. Besides, these pretended necessaries are really so little necessary to his rank, that if he should renounce them on any worthy occasion, he would only be the more honoured. The populace would be ready to adore a Minister who went to Council on foot, because he had sold off his carriages to supply a pressing need of the State. Lastly, to no man does the law prescribe magnificence; and propriety is no argument against right.

A third relation, which is never taken into account, though it ought to be the chief consideration, is the advantage that every person derives from the social confederacy; for this provides a powerful protection for the immense possessions of the rich, and hardly leaves the poor man in quiet possession of the cottage he builds with his own hands. Are not all the advantages of society for the rich and powerful? Are not all lucrative posts in their hands? Are not all privileges and exemptions reserved for them alone? Is not the public authority always on their side? If a man of eminence robs his creditors, or is guilty of other knaveries, is he not always assured of impunity? Are not the assaults, acts of violence, assassinations, and even murders committed by the great, matters that are hushed up in a few months, and of which nothing more is thought? But if a great man himself is robbed or insulted, the whole police force is immediately in motion, and woe even to innocent persons who chance to be suspected. If he has to pass through any dangerous road, the country is up in arms to escort him. If the axle-tree of his chaise breaks, everybody flies to his assistance. If there is a noise at his door, he speaks but a word, and all is silent. If he is incommoded by the crowd, he waves his hand and every one makes way. If his coach is met on the road by a wagon, his servants are ready to beat the driver's brains out, and fifty honest pedestrians going quietly about their business had better be knocked on the head than an idle jackanapes be delayed in his coach. Yet all this respect costs him not a farthing: it is the rich man's right, and not what he buys with his wealth. How different is the case of the poor man! the more humanity owes him, the more society denies him. Every door is shut against him, even when he has a right to its being opened: and if ever he obtains justice, it is with much greater difficulty than others obtain favours. If the militia is to be raised or the highway to be mended, he is always given the preference; he always bears the burden which his richer neighbour has influence enough to get exempted from. On the least accident that happens to him, everybody avoids him: if his cart be overturned in the road, so far is he from receiving any assistance, that he is lucky if he does not get horse-whipped by the impudent lackeys of some young Duke; in a word, all gratuitous assistance is denied to the poor when they need it, just because they cannot pay for it. I look upon any poor man as totally undone, if he has the misfortune to have an honest heart, a fine daughter, and a powerful neighbour.

Another no less important fact is that the losses of the poor are much harder to repair than those of the rich, and that the difficulty of acquisition is always greater in proportion as there is more need for it. "Nothing comes out of nothing," is as true of life as in physics: money is the seed of money, and the first guinea is sometimes more difficult to acquire than the second million. Add to this that what the poor pay is lost to them for ever, and remains in, or returns to, the hands of the rich: and as, to those who share in the government or to their dependents, the whole produce of the taxes must sooner or later pass, although they pay their share, these persons have always a sensible interest in increasing them.

The terms of the social compact between these two estates of men may be summed up in a few words. "You have need of me, because I am rich and you are poor. We will therefore come to an agreement. I will permit you to have the honour of serving me, on condition that you bestow on me the little you have left, in return for the pains I shall take to command you."

Putting all these considerations carefully together, we shall find that, in order to levy taxes in a truly equitable and proportionate manner, the imposition ought not to be in simple ratio to the property of the contributors, but in compound ratio to the difference of their conditions and the superfluity of their possessions.

Manifesto of the Equals
Pierre-Sylvain Maréchal

In 1795, after the Reign of Terror and its wave of beheadings, France adopted a conservative constitution and ended distributions of land. Many of those who participated in the French Revolution felt betrayed, particularly those who believed that the revolution's efforts to achieve equality remained incomplete. Among these was Pierre-Sylvain Maréchal, an anarchist, radical, and author of the innovative calendar adopted by the French Republic so as to avoid endorsing the Christian holidays. In 1796, Maréchal published this impassioned call for renewed commitment to equality, not just in rights but in income and privileges as well. The word *canaille* is a reference to the mobs that took to the streets in the French Revolution.

PEOPLE OF FRANCE! For fifteen centuries you have lived slaves, and therefore unhappy. It is now scarcely six years since you have begun to revive in the hope of independence, happiness and equality.

Equality! First need of nature, first demand of man, and chief bond of all legitimate society! French people! you have not been more favoured than the other nations that vegetate on this wretched globe! Always and everywhere poor humanity, in the hands of more or less adroit cannibals is the tool of every ambition, the pasture of every tyranny. Always and everywhere men were lulled by fine phrases; never and nowhere did they receive the fulfilment with the promise. From time immemorial we have been hypocritically told: *Men are equal:* and from time immemorial the insolent weight of the most degrading and most monstrous inequality has weighed down the human race. Since civilised society began, this finest possession of humanity has been unanimously recognised, yet not once realised; equality was only a fair and sterile fiction of the law. To-day when it is more loudly claimed, we are answered: Silence, wretches! real equality is but a chimera: be content with constitutional equality: you are all equal before the law. *Canaille*, what more do you want?—What more do we want? Legislators, governors, rich proprietors, listen in your turn.

We are all equal, are we not? This principle is uncontested: for with out being mad one cannot say it is night when it is day.

Well, henceforward we are going to live and die equal as we were born; we desire real equality or death: that is what we want.

And we shall have this real equality at all costs. Woe to those who stand between it and us! Woe to those who resist so strong a desire!

The French Revolution is but the precursor of another revolution, far greater, far more solemn, which will be the last.

The people marched over the corpses of the kings and priests who banded against them. They will do the same to the new tyrants and new political Tartuffes who sit in the seats of the others.

What do we want more than equality in law?

We want this equality nor merely written down in the Declaration of the Rights of Man and the Citizen: we want it in our midst, beneath the roofs of our houses. We will consent to everything for it; we will make a clean sweep to hold to it alone. Perish, if need be, all the arts as long as we have real equality!

Legislators and governors who have neither intellect nor honesty, rich and heartless proprietors, you in vain try to neutralize our holy enterprise by saying: They only revive that agrarian law so often demanded before.

Slanderers, hold your peace in your turn, and in silent confusion, hear our demands, dictated by nature and based on justice.

An agrarian law, or the division of lands was the momentary wish of some unprincipled soldiers and some tribes moved by instinct rather than reason. We aim at something more sublime and more just, the COMMON good or the COMMUNITY OF GOODS! No more private property in land: *The earth is nobody's*. We claim, we will the common use of the fruits of the earth: *its fruits are everybody's*. . . .

Let there be no difference now between human beings but in age and sex! Since all have the same needs and the same faculties, let there be for all one education and one standard of life! They are content with one sun and the same air for all, why should not the same portion and quality of food suffice for each?

But already the enemies of a state which is the most natural imaginable, declaim against us.

Disorganisers and factious men, they say to us, all you wish are massacres and booty.

PEOPLE OF FRANCE,

We shall not waste our time in answering them; we shall tell you: The holy enterprise which we are organizing has for its only aim to end civil dissension and the poverty of the people.

Never has more vast a design been conceived and executed. At long intervals some men of genius, some sages have spoken of it in a low and trembling voice. None of them have had the courage to tell the whole truth.

The moment for great measures has come. The evil is at its height, it covers the face of the earth. Chaos has reigned there under the name of politics too many centuries. Everything must be in order and resume its place. Let the elements of justice and happiness crystallize at the voice of Equality. The time has come to found the REPUBLIC OF EQUALS, that great guesthouse of all mankind. The days of restitution have arrived. Weeping families take your seats at the common table, nature spreads for all her children.

PEOPLE OF FRANCE,

For you, then, was reserved the purest of all glories. Yes, it is you that will first offer the world that touching sight!

Ancient habits, archaic prejudices again try to prevent the establishment of the *Republic of Equals*. The organising of real equality, the only state which answers all requirements without making victims or costing sacrifices, perhaps will not at first please everyone. The egoist and ambitious man will scream with rage. Those who possess unjustly will cry out, injustice! Their exclusive delights, their solitary pleasures, their personal ease will leave bitter longings in the hearts of some individuals who have grown effete by their neighbour's toil. Lovers of absolute power, and worthless tools of arbitrary authority, will find it hard to bring their proud chiefs to the level of equality. Their short-sight cannot penetrate into the near future of the common good; but what is the power of a few thousand malcontents against the mass of men, entirely happy and wondering that they sought so long for what was beneath their hand. . . .

PEOPLE OF FRANCE,

Open your eyes and hearts to the fullness of joy. Recognize and proclaim with us THE REPUBLIC OF EQUALS.

On Child Slavery in Yorkshire
Richard Oastler

For Richard Oastler, the transformation from citizen to activist occurred during the course of one 1830 conversation with factory owner John Wood. In early industrial England, the standard workers in the many textile mills were children, and they were worked as virtual slaves. Wood told Oastler that when he read the Bible, he felt condemned for the way that he treated his child workers. He implored Oastler to use his tremendous speaking ability and his influence on behalf of the child textile workers.

The same month Oastler wrote a letter to a Leeds newspaper, signing it "A Briton." Oastler opened by quoting from an abolitionist speech given a week before in Leeds, and then compared the condition of true slaves favorably to the fate of underage factory workers. He emphasized the disposability of the children, anticipating modern concerns about the fate of workers in sweatshops.

Oastler became a leading voice in the nineteenth-century push for the improvement of workers' rights. He testified before Parliament in 1832, participated with thousands of workers in a "pilgrimage of mercy" to the York mills, and became the leading voice of the Ten Hour Movement, which sought to reduce the twelve- to fifteen-hour days required of children and adults in the mills. Parliament passed the Factory Act of 1833, which made it illegal to employ children under the age of nine in mills, except in the silk industry, and limited the hours of all children to no more than twelve hours per day and sixty-nine hours per week. Not until 1861, six years after Oastler's death, were all children limited to ten hours' work per day.

TO THE EDITORS OF THE LEEDS' MERCURY, "It is the pride of Britain that a slave cannot exist on her soil; and if I read the genius of her constitution aright, I find that slavery is most abhorrent to it—that the air which Britons breathe is free—the ground on which they tread is sacred to liberty." Rev. R. W. Hamilton's Speech at the Meeting held in the Cloth-hall Yard, September 22d, 1830.

Gentlemen,—No heart responded with truer accents to the sounds of liberty which were heard in the Leeds Cloth-hall Yard, on the 22d instant, than did mine, and from none could more sincere and earnest prayers arise to the throne of Heaven, that hereafter slavery might only be known to Britain in the pages of her history. One shade alone obscured my pleasure, arising not from any difference in principle, but from the want of application of the general principle to the whole empire. The pious and able champions of negro liberty and colonial rights should, if I mistake not, have gone farther than they did; or perhaps, to speak more correctly, before they had travelled so far as the West Indies, should, at least for a few moments, have sojourned in our own immediate neighbourhood, and have directed the attention of the meeting to scenes of misery, acts of oppression, and victims of slavery, even on the threshold of our homes.

Let truth speak out, appalling as the statement may appear. The fact is true. Thousands of our fellow-creatures and fellow-subjects, both male and female, the miserable inhabitants of a Yorkshire town . . . are this very moment existing in a state of slavery, more horrid than are the victims of that hellish system "colonial slavery." . . . The very streets which receive the droppings of an "Anti-Slavery Society" are every morning wet by the tears of innocent victims at the accursed shrine of avarice, who are compelled (not by the cart-whip of the negro slave-driver) but by the dread of the equally appalling thong or strap of the over-looker, to hasten, half-dressed, but not half-fed, to those magazines of British infantile slavery—the worsted mills in the town and neighbourhood of Bradford! . . .

Thousands of little children, both male and female, but principally female, from seven to fourteen years of age, are daily compelled to labour from six o'clock in the morning to seven in the evening, with only—Britons, blush while you read it! with only thirty minutes allowed for eating and recreation. Poor infants! ye are indeed sacrificed at the shrine of avarice, without even the solace of the negro slave; ye are no more than he is, free agents; ye are compelled to work as long as the necessity of your needy parents may require, or the cold-blooded avarice of your worse than barbarian masters may demand! Ye live in the boasted land of freedom, and feel and mourn that ye are slaves, and slaves without the only comfort which the negro has. He knows it is his sordid, mercenary master's interest that he should live, be strong and healthy. Not so with you. Ye are doomed to labour from morning to night for one who cares not how soon your weak and tender frames are stretched to breaking! You are not mercifully valued at so much per head; this would assure you at least (even with the worst and most cruel masters) of the mercy shown to their own labouring beasts. No, no! your soft and delicate limbs are tired and fagged, and jaded, at only so much per week, and when your joints can act no longer, your emaciated frames are cast aside, the boards on which you lately toiled and wasted life away, are instantly supplied with other victims, who in this boasted land of liberty are HIRED—not sold—as slaves and daily forced to hear that they are free. . . .

The nation is now most resolutely determined that negroes shall be free. Let them, however, not forget that Britons have common rights with Afric's sons.

The blacks may be fairly compared to beasts of burden, kept for their master's use; the whites, to those which others keep and let for hire. If I have succeeded in calling the attention of your readers to the horrid and abominable system on which the worsted mills in and near Bradford is conducted, I have done some good. . . . Christians should feel and act for those whom Christ so eminently loved, and declared that, of such is the Kingdom of Heaven. I remain, yours, etc.,

A Briton.

"The Corn Laws"
Allen Davenport

Sung to the tune of "Auld Lang Syne," this ditty was part of an ultimately successful protest in favor of free trade. During the Napoleonic Wars, grain prices soared due to a reduction in commerce; high grain prices drove the price of farmland in England to high levels. Following the wars, the nobility sought to preserve these profitable conditions by banning grain imports unless grain prices reached a high threshold. The effect of these so-called Corn Laws was to keep food prices excessively high, impoverishing urban workers and enriching rural landowners—primarily members of the nobility. With the majority of workers devoting an excessive portion of their income to food, they had little left over to buy other products. Manufacturing suffered, workers were laid off, and economic stagnation resulted.

In the 1830s, the right to vote was expanded somewhat, and a new protest organization called the Anti-Corn Law League formed. Popular songs and poems were a common tool to spread the message of protest. In 1846, after thirty-one years, the laws were repealed.

Anti-Corn Law League lyricist Allen Davenport published this song sometime between the ascension of Queen Victoria in 1837 and the repeal of the laws. Like many modern protest songs it was set to a well-known tune.

Ye millions that so keenly feel
    The pressure of the times,
To you I earnestly appeal,
    Then listen to my rhymes,
In vain you labour night and day,
    The owners of the soil,
By Corn Laws take the bread away,
    That should reward your toil.

Chorus

Then open every British port,
    And let the poor be fed,
No longer see your children starve,
    And die through want of bread.

The haughty possess the land,
    And wield oppression's rod,
Inspite of that divine command,
    Found in the word of God;
The Corn Laws petrify their hearts,
    And make the nation groan,
For when the people cry for bread,
    They only get a stone.

Chorus

Down, down, with the starvation laws
    And no more be beguiled,
Cheap bread must surely be the cause
    Of woman, man, and child;
All property is insecure,
    And insecure muts [sic] be,
Till they our plundered rights restore
    And make the Corn Trade free.

Chorus

The Corn Laws are the greatest scourge
    That has been since the flood,

Enacted since the time of George,
　　Whose reign was that of blood!
But we have now a Queen beloved,
　　Oh! let it not be said,
That she can see and hear unmoved,
　　Her people cry for bread.

Chorus

The Communist Manifesto
Karl Marx and Friedrich Engels

During the 1840s, political and economic turmoil gripped Europe. Workers' rights movements and democratic revolutions rocked the economic and political foundations of dozens of nations. At the center of the turmoil in Germany were the revolutionary writers and journalists Friedrich Engels and Karl Marx. In late 1847, the workers' organization the League of the Just commissioned Marx and Engels to spell out the goals of the workers movement. By February of 1848, Marx and Engels had produced *The Communist Manifesto*.

The document quickly spread around the world. It was translated from German into Swedish in less than a year, to English in 1871, Russian in 1882, Yiddish in 1889, and Chinese in 1920. The document played a central role in both the Russian and Chinese revolutions of the first half of the twentieth century.

Marx and Engels described a division in the modern world into two classes. In their view, most of society was composed of the proletariat, workers whom Marx and Engels said, "live only so long as they find work, and who find work only so long as their labour increases capital. These labourers, who must sell themselves piece-meal, are a commodity, like every other article of commerce." Set against the proletariat was the bourgeoisie, the social class who make their living via their ownership of property and other capital assets. Marx and Engels argued that as long as the workers were at the service of capital owners, oppression and deprivation would continue.

They advocated a suite of radical solutions: abolition of private property, confiscation of inheritances, and complete replacement of the governing structure and economic framework of society. These radical goals evoked strong negative reaction from existing governments and property owners, and communism for more than 150 years has been, as *The Communist Manifesto* predicted, "a spectre" haunting Europe (and, for that matter, much of the rest of the world).

Within the manifesto, however, were also ideas that have become fairly ordinary in democracies and other governments around the world, including a graduated income tax, free public education, and the abolition of child labor. The excerpt here addresses the concept of free trade and why owners of property might pursue it. Presaging modern free-trade treaties that in some cases may overrule national laws, Marx and Engels prophesied the sacrifice of national industries on the altar of free trade and the creation of a global exchange of goods and ideas. In their analyses, however, such globalization would only lead to oppression of working classes worldwide.

The excerpt is from the 1888 English translation edited by Engels.

THE HISTORY of all hitherto existing societies is the history of class struggles.

Freeman and slave, patrician and plebeian, lord and serf, guild-master and journeyman, in a word, oppressor and oppressed, stood in constant opposition to one another, carried on an uninterrupted, now hidden, now open fight, a fight that each time ended, either in a revolutionary re-constitution of society at large, or in the common ruin of the contending classes. . . .

The modern bourgeois society that has sprouted from the ruins of feudal society has not done away with class antagonisms. It has but established new classes, new conditions of oppression, new forms of struggle in place of the old ones. Our epoch, the epoch of the bourgeoisie, possesses, however, this distinctive feature: it has simplified the class antagonisms. Society as a whole is more and more splitting up into two great hostile camps, into two great classes, directly facing each other: Bourgeoisie and Proletariat. . . .

Modern industry has established the world-market, for which the discovery of America paved the way. This market has given an immense development to commerce, to navigation, to communication by land. This development has, in its time, reacted on the extension of industry; and in proportion as industry, commerce, navigation, railways extended, in the same proportion the bourgeoisie developed, increased its capital, and pushed into the background every class handed down from the Middle Ages.

We see, therefore, how the modern bourgeoisie is itself the product of a long course of development, of a series of revolutions in the modes of production and of exchange.

Each step in the development of the bourgeoisie was accompanied by a corresponding political advance of that class. An oppressed class under the sway of the feudal nobility, an armed and self-governing association in the mediaeval commune; here independent urban republic (as in Italy and Germany), there taxable "third estate" of the monarchy (as in France), afterwards, in the period of manufacture proper, serving either the semi-feudal or the absolute monarchy as a counterpoise against the nobility, and, in fact, corner-stone of the great monarchies in general, the bourgeoisie has at last, since the establishment of Modern Industry and of the world-market, conquered for itself, in the modern representative State, exclusive political sway. The executive of the modern State is but a committee for managing the common affairs of the whole bourgeoisie.

The bourgeoisie, historically, has played a most revolutionary part. . . .

. . . It has resolved personal worth into exchange value, and in place of the numberless and feasible chartered freedoms, has set up that single, unconscionable freedom—Free Trade. In one word, for exploitation, veiled by religious and political illusions, naked, shameless, direct, brutal exploitation.

The bourgeoisie has stripped of its halo every occupation hitherto honoured and looked up to with reverent awe. It has converted the physician, the lawyer, the priest, the poet, the man of science, into its paid wage labourers. . . .

The need of a constantly expanding market for its products chases the bourgeoisie over the whole surface of the globe. It must nestle everywhere, settle everywhere, establish connexions everywhere.

The bourgeoisie has through its exploitation of the world-market given a cosmopolitan character to production and consumption in every country. To the great chagrin of Reactionists, it has drawn from under the feet of industry the national ground on which it stood. All old-established national industries have been destroyed or are daily being destroyed. They are dislodged by new industries, whose introduction becomes a life and death question for all civilised nations, by industries that no longer work up indigenous raw material, but raw material drawn from the remotest zones; industries whose products are consumed, not only at home, but in every quarter of the globe. In place of the old wants, satisfied by the productions of the country, we find new wants, requiring for their satisfaction the products of distant lands and climes. In place of the old local and national seclusion and self-sufficiency, we have intercourse in every direction, universal inter-dependence of nations. And as in material, so also in intellectual production. The intellectual creations of individual nations become common property. National one-sidedness and narrow-mindedness become more and more impossible, and from the numerous national and local literatures, there arises a world literature.

The bourgeoisie, by the rapid improvement of all instruments of production, by the immensely facilitated means of communication, draws all, even the most barbarian, nations into civilisation. The cheap prices of its commodities are the heavy artillery with which it batters down all Chinese walls, with which it forces the barbarians' intensely obstinate hatred of foreigners to capitulate. It compels all nations, on pain of extinction, to adopt the bourgeois mode of production; it compels them to introduce what it calls civilisation into their midst, i.e., to become bourgeois themselves. In one word, it creates a world after its own image.

To the Workmen
The Committee for the Central Labor Union

In the 1880s, momentum built in the United States for a national standard of an eight-hour workday. To support the movement, labor unions called for a nationwide strike on May 1, 1886. In Chicago, a hotbed of labor activism, tens of thousands of workers marched. On May 3, police clashed with workers, killing two. Labor responded with a call for a militant rally on the evening of May 4 at Haymarket Square. As police moved to break up the tail end of the rally, a bomb was thrown, killing one policeman immediately; seven more died from their injuries. The deaths of the policemen provoked a fierce nationwide reaction against labor's demands. The eight-hour-day movement stalled and did not regain momentum until sympathy for labor's plight was aroused by the violent killing of striking miners and their families in Ludlow, Colorado, twenty-eight years later.

In a broadside produced before the May 1 strike, Chicago's Central Labor Union instructed workers on how they could achieve the eight-hour day. The authors felt no need to explain why the eight-hour day was justified, but focused exclusively on the necessary actions to achieve the goal, including a very clear recognition of the role of the media.

. . . THE QUESTION regarding the practicability of the introduction of the eight hour workday has been sufficiently discussed so that we may consider the next necessary question: "What is to be done to secure the eight hour workday and its benefits?"

By virtue of the fact, that a large portion of workingmen are permanently or periodically without employment, and for that reason are compelled to offer their labor at most any price, it is an impossibility for the single working man to demand of his employer a shortening of the hours of labor, increase of wages, etc. as the latter can procure a substitute from those idle workingmen, who are willing to work at smaller wages.

It is therefore a necessity that all workingmen organize themselves in their respective branches of labor, no matter whether they are skilled or unskilled laboringmen. Further, that these organizations maintain connections with each other for the purpose of mutual assistance and united action.

The working population thus organized, will be able to secure the introduction of the eight hour workday. . . .

It is evident, that by the introduction of the eight hour workday and abolition of piece-work, the working class does not secure all the rights, which belong to it, the creator of all wealth. It will not abolish the existing wrongs; the means of production will still be in the hands of the few—the capitalists—who will use the same for their benefit and to the detriment of the people.

The laboring class will not be free from the existing state of misery and want, until the means of life, the land, the means of production, etc., have become the property of the people. Then there will be no ruling, and no ruled class, no possessing and no starving class, but only a class of workers enabled to enjoy life.

. . . And still to-day the working classes rather support this system than battle against it.

For instance you pay moneys and dues to churches and support the preacher, who praises this damnable system of society as an institution created by God.

Therefore, workingmen, away from the church and organize.

Many of you also subscribe for and read capitalistic papers, and thereby nourish the serpent on your own breast. Is it not evident to you, that a press that is dependent on capital, will always praise the existing order of things and endeavor to conceal the evils attending it. . . .

Wealth

Andrew Carnegie

Andrew Carnegie obtained legendary wealth as the founder of the company that eventually became U.S. Steel Corporation. In his 1889 essay "Wealth," published in the *North American Review*, Carnegie responded to critiques of wealth, such as *The Communist Manifesto*, which had been published in America the preceding year. He also was clearly objecting to the behavior of the wealthy.

While he acknowledged that growing inequality in available resources had the potential to set the rich and poor in conflict, he argued that this need not be so. The problem, Carnegie argued, was in what the wealthy chose to do with their resources. He had no patience for hoarding of funds or conspicuous consumption, nor did he feel that leaving wealth to one's descendents was the right course of action. Rather, he felt that the wealthy should spend their resources during their lifetime on works to promote the common good. He agreed with the communists that the government should heavily tax estates, as that would encourage the wealthy toward good works.

By the time of his own death, Carnegie had given away some $350 million toward philanthropic projects, such as establishing over 2,509 public libraries in the United States, Britain, Australia, and New Zealand and funding the construction of the "Palace of Peace" in the Netherlands to house international legal tribunals and a legal library. Today the building serves as headquarters for the International Court of Justice.

THE PROBLEM OF OUR AGE is the administration of wealth, so that the ties of brotherhood may still bind together the rich and poor in harmonious relationship. The conditions of human life have not only been changed, but revolutionized, within the past few hundred years. In former days there was little difference between the dwelling, dress, food, and environment of the chief and those of his retainers. . . . The contrast between the palace of the millionaire and the cottage of the laborer with us today measures the change which has come with civilization.

This change, however, is not to be deplored, but welcomed as highly beneficial. It is well, nay, essential for the progress of the race, that the houses of some should be homes for all that is highest and best in literature and the arts, and for all the refinements of civilization, rather than that none should be so. Much better this great irregularity than universal squalor. . . .

We start, then, with a condition of affairs under which the best interests of the race are promoted, but which inevitably gives wealth to the few. Thus far, accepting conditions as they exist, the situation can be surveyed and pronounced good. The question then arises—and, if the foregoing be correct, it is the only question with which we have to deal—What is the proper mode of administering wealth after the laws upon which civilization is founded have thrown it into the hands of the few? And it is of this great question that I believe I offer the true solution. It will be understood that fortunes are here spoken of, not moderate sums saved by many years of effort, the returns from which are required for the comfortable maintenance and education of families. This is not wealth, but only competence, which it should be the aim of all to acquire.

There are but three modes in which surplus wealth can be disposed of. It can be left to the families of the decedents; or it can be bequeathed for public purposes; or, finally, it can be administered during their lives by its possessors. . . .

. . . Why should men leave great fortunes to their children? If this is done from affection, is it not misguided affection? Observation teaches that, generally speaking, it is not well for the children that they should be so burdened. Neither is it well for the state. Beyond providing for the wife and daughters moderate sources of income, and very moderate allowances indeed, if any, for the sons, men may well hesitate, for it is no longer questionable that great sums bequeathed oftener work more for the injury than for the good of the recipients. Wise men will soon conclude that, for the best interests of the members of their families and of the state, such bequests are an improper use of their means. . . .

As to the second mode, that of leaving wealth at death for public uses, it may be said that this is only a means for the disposal of wealth, provided a man is content to wait until he is dead before it becomes of much good in the world. . . . The cases are not few in which the real object sought by the testator is not attained, nor are they few in which his real wishes are thwarted. . . .

The growing disposition to tax more and more heavily large estates left at death is a cheering indication of the growth of a salutary change in public opinion. . . . Of all forms of taxation, this seems the wisest. Men who continue hoarding great sums all their lives, the proper use of which for public ends would work good to the community, should be made to feel that the community, in the form of the state, cannot thus be deprived of its proper share. By taxing estates heavily at death, the state marks its condemnation of the selfish millionaire's unworthy life. . . .

. . . This policy would work powerfully to induce the rich man to attend to the administration of wealth during his life, which is the end that society should always have in view, as being that by far most fruitful for the people. . . .

There remains, then, only one mode of using great fortunes: but in this way we have the true antidote for the temporary unequal distribution of wealth, the reconciliation of the rich and the poor—a reign of harmony—another ideal, differing, indeed from that of the Communist in requiring only the further evolution of existing conditions, not the total overthrow of our civilization. It is founded upon the present most intense individualism, and the race is prepared to put it in practice by degrees whenever it pleases. Under its sway we shall have an ideal state, in which the surplus wealth of the few will become, in the best sense, the property of the many, because administered for the common good, and this wealth, passing through the hands of the few, can be made a much more potent force for the elevation of our race than if it had been distributed in small sums to the people themselves. Even the poorest can be made to see this, and to agree that great sums gathered by some of their fellow citizens and spent for public purposes, from which the masses reap the principal benefit, are more valuable to them than if scattered among them through the course of many years in trifling amounts.

This, then, is held to be the duty of the man of Wealth: First, to set an example of modest, unostentatious living, shunning display or extravagance; to provide moderately for the legitimate wants of those dependent upon him; and after doing so to consider all surplus revenues which come to him simply as trust funds, which he is called upon to administer, and strictly bound as a matter of duty to administer in the manner which, in his judgment, is best calculated to produce the most beneficial result for the community—the man of wealth thus becoming the sole agent and trustee for his poorer brethren, bringing to their service his superior wisdom, experience, and ability to administer—doing for them better than they would or could do for themselves.

"Labour is the producer of all wealth"
Henry George

Populist American economist Henry George laid out his central thesis in his 1879 work *On Progress and Poverty* and took his ideas on the road, making speeches and distributing pamphlets around the country and overseas. He became one of the most recognized Americans of his day, even running for mayor of New York in 1886 as a labor candidate. He came in second, eclipsing Republican candidate Theodore Roosevelt. In the late 1880s, George traveled around the nation and to Europe and Australia, speaking out against the societal structures that he believed unnecessarily perpetuated poverty. In 1889, he participated in a debate with the well-known British socialist H. M. Hyndman; George's arguments from that debate are excerpted here.

George's views represented a challenge to both classical and Marxist economists. He was a firm defender of free trade, the entrepreneurial spirit, and individual effort. In particular, he argued that people who worked harder should profit from that work, as opposed to commentators who argued for equality of income.

At the same time, George believed that society had stacked the deck against the efforts of labor by allowing private possession of the fundamental resource that labor needs to generate wealth: land. To remedy the situation, he proposed taxing only land and abolishing all other taxes, including those on buildings. This would, in his opinion, have made speculating on land unprofitable—only use of land would yield sufficient profit to pay the tax. The resulting flux of land into the market would lower land prices and bring the value of land into line with the return that labor could produce from it.

Today a strongly held, if small, George-ist movement persists, particularly in Australia. Many analysts believe that George's advocacy of taxing land, rather than labor and its fruits, holds the key to preventing a host of social ills, such as suburban sprawl.

AS TO THE INJUSTICE and wrong of present social conditions, the parties who are here represented tonight both agree. We both agree, moreover, as to the end to be sought—a condition of things in which there shall be opportunities for work for all, leisure for all, a sufficiency of the necessities of life for all, an abundance of the reasonable luxuries of life for all. (Hear, hear.)

We differ as to the means by which that end is to [be] attained. Mr. Hyndman styles himself a Social Democrat: I a Single Tax man. Let me state why we have adopted that name and what we mean by it. Looking over the civilised world today, we see that labour nowhere gets its just dues. (Hear, hear.) We see there is everywhere a fringe of unemployed labour. We see all the phenomena that are called sometimes over-production and industrial depression; we reject as superficial the theory that this is caused by there being too many people; that this is caused by there not being enough work; that this is caused by the multiplication of labour-saving machinery. We say that until human wants are satisfied there can be no such thing as over-production (applause), that until all have enough there is yet plenty of work. (Hear, hear.)

We trace the cause of all these phenomena to one great fundamental wrong. We ask what work is, and we see that what we call productive work is alteration in place or in form of the raw material of the universe that we call land. We see that man is a land animal; that his very body comes from the land; that all his productions consist in but the working up of the land; and that land to him is absolutely necessary; and we behold everywhere the phenomena of which I have spoken. We see everywhere that this element, indispensable to all, has been made the property of some. (Hear, hear.)

To that wrong we trace all the great social evils of which we complain to-day, and we propose to right them by going to the root and removing that wrong. (Loud applause.)

It is perfectly clear that we are all here with equal rights to the use of the universe. We are all here equally entitled to the use of land. How can we secure that equal right? Not by the dividing up of land equally; that in the present stage of civilisation is utterly impossible. Equality could not be secured in that way, nor could it be maintained. The ideal way, the way which wise men, desirous of according to each his equal right, would resort to in a new country, would be to treat the land as the property of the whole, to allow individuals to possess and to use it, paying for the whole a proper rent for any superiority in the piece of land they were using. (Hear.) The ideal plan would allow every man who wished to use land to obtain it, and to possess what he wished to use so long as no one else wished to use it, and if the land be so superior that more than one wanted to use it, a proper payment according to its superiority should be made to the community, and by that community used for the common benefit. (Hear, hear.)

. . . Now if that were done, if the land were let out, those using it paying its premium value to the community, it would amount to precisely the same thing if, instead of calling the payment rent, we called it taxes. "A rose by any other name would smell as sweet." In an old country, however, there is a very great advantage in calling the rent a tax. In an old country there is a very great advantage in moving on that line. People are used to the payment of taxes. They are not used to the formal ownership of land by the community; and to the letting of it out in that way. Therefore, as society is now constituted, and in our communities as they now exist, we propose to move towards our ideal along the line of taxation. (Hear, hear.)

If we were to take the rent of land for the community, one of the first and best uses which would be commended to us would be that of abolishing of taxes that bear in any way upon production, or in any way hamper industry, or in any way increase the price of those things that people wish to use and can use without injury to others. Therefore, as bringing in the idea of abolishing these taxes we call our measure the Single Tax. (Hear, hear.)

We would abolish all taxation that falls on industry, and raise public revenue by this means, and move to our end, the taking of the full rental value of land for the use of the community, in this way. This name, Single Tax, expresses our method; not our ideal. What we are really is liberty men; what we believe in is perfect freedom: What we wish to do is to give each individual in the community the liberty to exert his powers in any way he pleases, bounded only by the equal liberty of others. (Applause.)

We would abolish all taxes, and begin with the most important of all monopolies, the fruitful parent of lesser monopolies, that monopoly which disinherits men of their birthright; that monopoly which puts in the hands of *some*, that element absolutely indispensable to the use of all; and we believe not that labour is a poor weak thing that must be coddled or protected by Government. We believe that labour is the producer of all wealth—(applause)—that all labour wants is a fair field and no favour, and, therefore, as against the doctrines of restriction we raise the banner of liberty and equal right in the gospel of free, fair play. (Loud cheers.). . . .

Capital does not come first. Land and labour are the only two absolutely necessary factors to the production of wealth. (Hear, hear.) Capital is the child of labour exerted upon land. (Cheers.) Give labour access to land and it will produce capital. Give labour access to land and the power of the capitalists to grind the masses must disappear. (Hear, hear.) What does that power came from? Merely from the fact that men are unable to employ themselves upon the land. It is the poverty of the labourers, not the wealth of the capitalist, that is the evil to be removed.

The Oppression of the Worthy Poor
Louis Albert Banks

In the late 1800s, the Industrial Revolution drew poor from rural America and overseas to rapidly growing cities. Many worked long hours at starvation wages. Some of the strongest objections to this exploitation came from clergy, as in this sermon by the Reverend Louis Albert Banks, pastor of St. John's Methodist Episcopal Church in Boston. Banks called for sufficient pay to enable workers not merely to survive, but also to pursue education, worship, and a fulfilling family life.

Expressions of concern from public figures like Banks played a key role in driving voluntary labor improvement efforts such as the Consumers' League, as well as early laws protecting workers. The Consumers' League became a major social force in the early twentieth century; it was an early effort at certifying socially responsible business practices so that consumers could reward those practices with their choices of products. The success of that strategy has inspired diverse efforts visible today in such programs as Energy Star appliances, dolphin-safe tuna, public and private certification programs for organic food, and the Marine Fisheries Stewardship Council.

The Relation of Wages to Morals

There is . . . a great deal said about the dignity of labor which is nothing more than oratorical commonplace—the meaningless froth of the rhetorician. There is no dignity about labor in itself. What is there about piling bricks on top of each other, or mixing mortar, or sewing blue denim into overalls, or trading earthen jars for nickel coin, that has about it any inherent dignity? It is only as there is mixed with the mortar, or builded with the bricks, the holy cement of a moral purpose; only as there is stitched into the cloth the divine thread of hopeful love; only as the deed gathers the aroma of an aspiring human life, is it a dignified transaction. But when you make of the laborer a slave, degrade his work to a mere fight for bread, harass him by continual debt, put him in a vile tenement house that smothers all holy ambition, labor has no longer dignity, it smells rather of the dungeon and the pit.

Honest labor, continued through reasonable hours, paid at a rate which assures a wholesome support, is ennobling; but overwork, that is hopeless of comfortable reward, is degrading in the extreme. . . . Reduce wages to the point where the laborer has to either remain at the shop or take his work home and work into the night, and drive it on through Sunday as well, and you simply brutalize the workman. It is idle, and pharisaical as well, for us to shrug our shoulders and say this is not a question for the pulpit. So intimate is the relation between the body and the soul, that every question which has to do with the feeding or clothing of a human body is, at the last analysis, a moral question. . . .

One of the greatest of physiologists, Moleschott, says: "Courage, readiness, and activity depend in a great measure upon a healthy and abundant nourishment. Hunger makes heart and head empty. No force of will can make up for an impoverished blood, a badly nourished muscle, or an exhausted nerve." All these tend to the one conclusion, that the moral and intellectual life is very largely subject to physiological conditions. A man, of course, may be a scoundrel and well-fed; but, on the other hand, poor food and undue exposure to cold and heat have tremendous influence in breaking down the resistance-power against temptation to evil. Courage is the safeguard both of truth and honesty.

Break down a man's courage by overwork, bad food, and poisonous air, and you have opened the way for lying, theft, and a whole brood of vicious tendencies. . . .

. . . Here are a man and a woman who receive such low wages that they are driven into unhealthy quarters. They ought to have four or five rooms in order to at least approach wholesome living; but poverty herds them in two, or it may be only one, for within the past month I have myself seen many families of father and mother and as many as five children packed into one little room, in one case only seven by nine feet. The air is poisonous; and, after the rent is paid, the food-money is insufficient, and sickness is the result. I do not mean that large numbers of people in Boston are literally starved to death for lack of bread; but I do mean that thousands of men and women and children in this city are compelled to eat such a quality of food that the result is a condition of mind and body which is subject to an insatiable thirst for strong drink, and makes drunkards of those who would otherwise be sober people. . . .

It is a commonplace thing, I know, to say that the American home is the strongest fortress of our civilization. It is one of those things, however, that needs to be said over and over again. Before the church or the state there must be the home. Destroy that, and the whole fabric of our civilization will come crashing to the ground in a common ruin. But the reduction of wages below the comfort point means, inevitably, the deterioration of the home. The father and mother and the children must know each other, if the home is to be welded together with mutual love. Acquaintance of that character, however, requires that they shall be together under such conditions that they may come to enjoy the gifts and talents that each possess. But wages are being reduced to the point where the home is only a sleeping-barrack and a lunch-counter for supper and breakfast. Remember that poor wages mean long hours; and long hours that exhaust all the energy of the laborer mean ignorance; and ignorance, when it is finished, means immorality.

There is only about so much vital force in the average human being. If all this force is put into one's daily toil, there is none left for helpful conversation, for sympathetic communion at home, for uplifting reading, or for worship. Persevere in that course, and you reach barbarism: the road faces that way.

People's Party Platform

In the late 1800s, farmers across the United States found themselves in a difficult financial position. During the second half of the nineteenth century, the population of the United States more than tripled, and there was a corresponding increase in economic activity. But the currency supply was held nearly constant.

The increasing demand for money resulted in deflation—money increased in purchasing power over time. When farmers borrowed money to buy land, to purchase seeds, and for new machinery needed to stay competitive, they had to repay the loan not only with interest, but also with dollars that were worth more than when they were borrowed. Farmers found themselves on a never-ending treadmill of debt; fiscal policy became a populist issue.

Meanwhile corporations and their owners thrived. Railroads were receiving large grants of land as subsidies to encourage their spread. During the Civil War alone, Congress gave 100 million acres of land to various railroad companies. Labor laws also strongly favored corporations and employers. Although the Massachusetts Supreme Judicial Court had legalized unions in 1842, setting a precedent that resonated through the nation, severe limitations on unions and workers' rights persisted in many states. Workplace safety rules and fair-labor laws ranged from nonexistent to unenforced.

In 1877 in Texas, a new Farmer's Alliance began to address these perceived injustices. The organization spread like wildfire through the rural South and Midwest and built links with labor organizations. In 1892, it organized as the People's Party, and fielded a presidential candidate who won twenty-two electoral votes. In 1896, the party put forth the platform excerpted below, featuring many ideas that today are regarded as mainstream, such as direct election of senators and public ownership of highways. The party endorsed William Jennings Bryan, the Democratic Party candidate for president, in the 1896 election and afterward was largely absorbed into the Democratic Party.

THE PEOPLE'S PARTY, assembled in National Convention, reaffirms its allegiance to the principles declared by the founders of the Republic. . . .

We recognize that through the connivance of the present and preceding Administrations the country has reached a crisis in its National life . . . and that prompt and patriotic action is the supreme duty of the hour.

We realize that, while we have political independence, our financial and industrial independence is yet to be attained by restoring to our country the Constitutional control and exercise of the functions necessary to a people's government, which functions have been basely surrendered by our public servants to corporate monopolies. . . . Executive power and patronage have been used to corrupt our legislatures and defeat the will of the people, and plutocracy has thereby been enthroned upon the ruins of democracy. To restore the Government intended by the fathers, and for the welfare and prosperity of this and future generations, we demand the establishment of an economic and financial system which shall make us masters of our own affairs and independent of European control, by the adoption of the following declarations of principles:

The Finances

1. We demand a National money, safe and sound, issued by the General Government only, without the intervention of banks of issue, to be a full legal tender for all debts, public and private. . . .

2. We demand the free and unrestricted coinage of silver and gold at the present legal ratio of 16 to 1, without waiting for the consent of foreign nations.

3. We demand that the volume of circulating medium be speedily increased to an amount sufficient to meet the demand of the business and population, and to restore the just level of prices of labor and production. . . .

7. We demand a graduated income tax, to the end that aggregated wealth shall bear its just proportion of taxation. . . .

8. We demand that postal savings-banks be established by the Government for the safe deposit of the savings of the people and to facilitate exchange.

Railroads and Telegraphs

1. Transportation being a means of exchange and a public necessity, the Government should own and operate the railroads in the interest of the people and on a non-partisan basis, to the end that all may be accorded the same treatment in transportation, and that the tyranny and political power now exercised by the great railroad corporations, which result in the impairment, if not the destruction of the political rights and personal liberties of the citizens, may be destroyed. Such ownership is to be accomplished gradually, in a manner consistent with sound public policy.

2. The interest of the United States in the public highways built with public moneys, and the proceeds of grants of land to the Pacific railroads, should never be alienated, mortgaged, or sold, but guarded and protected for the general welfare. . . .

The Public Lands

1. True policy demands that the National and State legislation shall be such as will ultimately enable every prudent and industrious citizen to secure a home, and therefore the land should not be monopolized for speculative purposes. All lands now held by railroads and other corporations in excess of their actual needs should by lawful means be reclaimed by the Government and held for actual settlers only, and private land monopoly, as well as alien ownership, should be prohibited.

2. We condemn the land grant frauds by which the Pacific railroad companies have through the connivance of the Interior Department, robbed multitudes of bona-fide settlers of their homes and miners of their claims, and we demand legislation by Congress which will enforce the exemption of mineral land from such grants after as well as before the patent.

3. We demand that bona-fide settlers on all public lands be granted free homes, as provided in the National Homestead Law, and that no exception be made in the case of Indian reservations when opened for settlement, and that all lands not now patented come under this demand.

The Referendum

We favor a system of direct legislation through the initiative and referendum, under proper Constitutional safeguards.

Direct Election of President and Senators by the People

We demand the election of President, Vice-President, and United States Senators by a direct vote of the people. . . .

Employment to Be Furnished by Government

In times of great industrial depression, idle labor should be employed on public works as far as practicable.

The Oil War of 1872
Ida Tarbell

Ida Tarbell was born in 1857 in the Oil Regions, that portion of northwestern Pennsylvania that was to the world of that time what Saudi Arabia is today—the area with the largest reserves of oil. Her family first prospered in the oil business and then was driven out by the increasingly centralized power of the trusts, as the large monopolistic corporations of the day were known. As an adult, Tarbell became an immensely popular investigative journalist and took aim at the very interests that had harmed her family during her youth.

From 1902 to 1904, Tarbell wrote a series of nineteen articles detailing the growth and predatory practices of John Rockefeller's Standard Oil Company. The articles were published in book form in 1904. The excerpt shown here is a document of protest in two ways. First, as part of Tarbell's series, it helped spur the antitrust lawsuit that in 1911 resulted in the breakup of Standard Oil. (In recent years, the two largest of the resulting daughter companies—Exxon and Mobil—have rejoined.) Second, it recounts the history of the1872 protest by the Oil Region's producers against attempts by refiners (under Rockefeller's leadership) to take over their trade.

In 1872, the refiners created a new company—the South Improvement Company—that negotiated railroad contracts favorable to its shipments and punitive to the shipments of unaffiliated crude-oil producers and smaller refineries. In Cleveland, South Improvement was able to buy out competing refineries at huge discounts when the punitive freight rates made those businesses suddenly unprofitable. But in the Oil Regions, where the targets were crude-oil producers, the plan failed. The producers banded together to cut off supplies altogether and ultimately secured a temporary revocation of the offending contracts.

IT WAS NOT UNTIL after the middle of February, 1872, that the people of the Oil Regions heard anything of the plan which was being worked out for their "good." Then an uneasy rumour began running up and down the creek. Freight rates were going up. Now an advance in a man's freight bill may ruin his business; more, it may mean the ruin of a region. Rumour said that the new rate meant just this; that is, that it more than covered the margin of profit in any branch of the oil business. The railroads were not going to apply the proposed tariffs to everybody. They had agreed to give to a company unheard of until now—the South Improvement Company—a special rate considerably lower than the new open rate. It was only a rumour and many people discredited it. Why should the railroads ruin the Oil Regions to build up a company of outsiders? . . .

On the morning of February 26, 1872, the oil men read in their morning papers that the rise which had been threatening had come; moreover, that all members of the South Improvement Company were exempt from the advance. At the news all oildom rushed into the streets. Nobody waited to find out his neighbour's opinion. On every lip there was but one word, and that was "conspiracy." . . .

In twenty-four hours after the announcement of the increase in freight rates a mass-meeting of 3,000 excited, gesticulating oil men was gathered in the opera house at Titusville. Producers, brokers, refiners, drillers, pumpers were in the crowd. Their temper was shown by the mottoes on the banners which they carried: "Down with the conspirators"—"No compromise"—"Don't give up the ship!" Three days later as large a meeting was held at Oil City, its temper more warlike if possible; and so it went. They organised a Petroleum Producers' Union, pledged themselves to reduce their production by starting no new wells for sixty days and by shutting down on Sundays, to sell no oil to any person known to be in the South Improvement Company, but to support the creek refiners and those elsewhere who had refused to go into the combination, to boycott the offending railroads, and to build lines which they would own and control themselves. They sent a committee to the Legislature asking that the charter of the South Improvement Company be repealed, and another to Congress demanding an investigation of the whole business on the ground that it was an interference with trade. They ordered that a history of the conspiracy, giving the names of the conspirators and the designs of the company, should be prepared, and 30,000 copies sent to "judges of all courts, senators of the United States, members of Congress and of State Legislatures, and to all railroad men and prominent business men of the country, *to the end that enemies of the freedom of trade may be known and shunned by all honest men.*"

They prepared a petition ninety-three feet long praying for a free pipe-line bill, something which they had long wanted, but which, so far, the Pennsylvania Railroad had prevented their getting, and sent it by a committee to the Legislature; and for days they kept 1,000 men ready to march on Harrisburg at a moment's notice if the Legislature showed signs of refusing their demands. In short, for weeks the whole body of oil men abandoned regular business and surged from town to town intent on destroying the "Monster," the

"Forty Thieves," the "Great Anaconda," as they called the mysterious South Improvement Company. . . .

. . . [T]he oil blockade, to which the Petroleum Producers' Union had pledged itself, was now enforced against the firms listed, and as far as possible against the railroads. All of these refineries had their buyers on the creek, and although several of them were young men generally liked for their personal and business qualities, no mercy was shown them. They were refused oil by everybody, though they offered from seventy-five cents to a dollar more than the market price. They were ordered at one meeting "to desist from their nefarious business or leave the Oil Region," and when they declined they were invited to resign from the oil exchanges of which they were members. So strictly, indeed, was the blockade enforced that in Cleveland the refineries were closed and meetings for the relief of the workmen were held. In spite of the excitement there was little vandalism, the only violence at the opening of the war being at Franklin, where a quantity of the oil belonging to Mr. Watson was run on the ground.

The sudden uprising of the Oil Regions against the South Improvement Company did not alarm its members at first. The excitement would die out, they told one another. All that they needed to do was to keep quiet and stay out of the oil country. But the excitement did not die out. Indeed, with every day it became more intense and more wide-spread.

Summation in the Haywood Trial
Clarence Darrow

On December 30, 1905, a bomb killed Frank Stunenberg, the former governor of Idaho and a notorious opponent of labor unions. Within two days Harry Orchard was arrested and charged with the crime; in his confession Orchard implicated the leaders of the most radical miner's union of the day—the Western Federation of Miners (WFM).

Among the accused leaders of the WFM was the flamboyant Big Bill Haywood—a physically imposing individual who made no secret of his disrespect for the laws that he saw as serving the corporate elite and oppressing the workers. In Haywood's 1907 trial, Orchard testified that since 1903, under orders from the WFM, he had killed nonunion strikebreakers and attempted to kill antiunion politicians and a mining company executive.

Defense lawyer Clarence Darrow's eleven-hour summation, excerpted below, protested Haywood's prosecution as an attack on the labor movement as a whole and as a blow against the rights of the poor. Orchard, he asserted, was a "plant" intended to frame the WFM and Haywood in particular. The jury ultimately acquitted Haywood. In a subsequent trial, George Pettibone, an adviser to the WFM, also was acquitted. Charges were dropped against the last WFM leader, Charles Moyer. Orchard served life in prison for killing Stunenberg.

LET ME TELL YOU, gentlemen, if you destroy the labor unions in this country, you destroy liberty when you strike the blow, and you would leave the poor bound and shackled and helpless to do the bidding of the rich. . . . It would take this country back . . . to the time when there were masters and slaves.

I don't mean to tell this jury that labor organizations do no wrong. I know them too well for that. They do wrong often, and sometimes brutally; they are sometimes cruel; they are often unjust; they are frequently corrupt. . . . But I am here to say that in a great cause these labor organizations, despised and weak and outlawed as they generally are, have stood for the poor, they have stood for the weak, they have stood for every human law that was ever placed upon the statute books. They stood for human life, they stood for the father who was bound down by his task, they stood for the wife, threatened to be taken from the home to work by his side, and they have stood for the little child who was also taken to work in their places—that the rich could grow richer still, and they have fought for the right of the little one, to give him a little of life, a little comfort while he is young. I don't care how many wrongs they committed, I don't care how many crimes these weak, rough, rugged, unlettered men who often know no other power but the brute force of their strong right arm, who find themselves bound and confined and impaired whichever way they turn, who look up and worship the god of might as the only god that they know—I don't care how often they fail, how many brutalities they are guilty of. I know their cause is just.

I hope that the trouble and the strife and the contention has been endured. Through brutality and bloodshed and crime has come the progress of the human race. I know they may be wrong in this battle or that, but in the great, long struggle they are right and they are eternally right, and that they are working for the poor and the weak. They are working to give more liberty to the man, and I want to say to you, gentlemen of the jury, you Idaho farmers removed from the trade unions, removed from the men who work in industrial affairs, I want to say that if it had not been for the trade unions of the world, for the trade unions of England, for the trade unions of Europe, the trade unions of America, you today would be serfs of Europe, instead of free men sitting upon a jury to try one of your peers. The cause of these men is right. . . .

. . . I want to speak to you plainly. Mr. Haywood is not my greatest concern. Other men have died before him, other men have been martyrs to a holy cause since the world began. Wherever men have looked upward and onward, forgotten their selfishness, struggled for humanity, worked for the poor and the weak, they have been sacrificed. They have been sacrificed in the prison, on the scaffold, in the flame. They have met their death, and he can meet his if you twelve men say he must. Gentlemen, you short-sighted men of the prosecution, you men of the Mine Owners' Association, you people who would cure hatred with hate, you who think you can crush out the feelings and the hopes and the aspirations of men by tying a noose around his neck, you who are seeking to kill him not because it is Haywood but because he represents a class, don't be so blind, don't be so foolish as to believe you can strangle the Western Federation of Miners when you tie a rope around his neck. Don't be so blind in your madness as to believe that if you make three fresh new graves you will kill the labor movement of the world. I want to say to you, gentlemen, Bill Haywood can't die unless you kill him. You have got to tie the rope. You twelve men of Idaho, the burden will be on you. If at the behest of this mob you should kill Bill Haywood, he is mortal. He will die. But I want to say that a hundred will grab up the banner of labor at the open grave where Haywood lays it down, and in spite of prisons, or scaffolds, or fire, in spite of prosecution or jury, these men of willing hands will carry it on to victory in the end. . . .

Don't think that you will kill the hopes and the aspirations and the desires of the weak and the poor, you men, unless you people who are anxious for this blood—are you so blind as to believe that liberty will die when he is dead? Do you think there are no brave hearts and no other strong arms, no other devoted souls who will risk their life in that great cause which has demanded martyrs in every age of this world? There are others, and these others will come to take his place, will come to carry the banner where he could not carry it.

Gentlemen, it is not for him alone that I speak. I speak for the poor, for the weak, for the weary, for that long line of men who in darkness and despair have borne the labors of the human race. The eyes of the world are upon you, upon you twelve men of Idaho tonight. Wherever the English language is spoken, or wherever any foreign tongue known to the civilized world is spoken, men are talking and wondering and dreaming about the verdict of these twelve men that I see before me now. If you kill him your act will be applauded by many. If you should decree Bill Haywood's death, in the great railroad offices of our great cities men will applaud your names. If you decree his death, amongst the spiders of Wall Street will go up paeans of praise for those twelve good men and true who killed Bill Haywood. In every bank in the world, where men hate Haywood because he fights for the poor and against the accursed system upon which the favored live and grow rich and fat—from all those you will receive blessings and unstinted praise.

But if your verdict should be "Not Guilty," there are still those who will reverently bow their heads and thank these twelve men for the life and the character they have saved. Out on the broad prairies where men toil with their hands, out on the wide ocean where men are tossed and buffeted on the waves, through our mills and factories, and down deep under the earth, thousands of men and of women and children, men who labor, men who suffer, women and children weary with care and toil, these men and these women and these children will kneel tonight and ask their God to guide your judgment. These men and these women and these little children, the poor, the weak, and the suffering of the world will stretch out their hands to this jury, and implore you to save Haywood's life.

"The Negro is still a slave"
W. E. B. Du Bois

W. E. B. Du Bois had an enormous impact on the efforts of African Americans to obtain justice and economic opportunity. During his long life he was a key black leader in the turbulent civil-rights and economic struggles of the first two-thirds of the twentieth century.

Du Bois became the first African-American to receive a Ph.D. from Harvard. He was a prolific and fiery spokesman for civil rights and one of the founders of the National Association for the Advancement of Colored People. In 1959, he famously declared to an audience in Peking, China, "In my own country for nearly a century I have been nothing but a nigger." He moved to Ghana in 1961 and a year later renounced his U.S. citizenship.

Here, in a column published in the *Cincinnati Times-Star* in 1910, Du Bois railed against the ways in which economic inequality allowed African Americans to be controlled in a way that was almost as strong as the bonds of slavery. He uses the literary device of posing questions to himself, as if he were being interviewed by an objective journalist.

NEGRO SLAVERY EXISTS on a large scale in the United States to-day. . . .

[T]he Negro is still a slave. The law protects him from being branded with the name of a slave. But the law allows him to be enslaved as a matter of grim fact and helps forge the chains.

It's this way: Black Bill comes to white Farmer Jones and asks for work. The farmer hires him as a hand, wages to be paid, not in advance, but when the cotton crop is harvested. That arrangement means that Bill won't get any money for months, sometimes not for a year. He asks Farmer Jones to advance him part of his wages. The farmer seldom does that. But he keeps a store. And he will sell Bill on credit anything that Bill wants, from shoes to tobacco, at an advance of 50 per cent to 100 per cent above the cash price. When Bill's wages become due they aren't enough to pay for his purchases. That keeps Bill constantly in debt to the white man, and just as much at his mercy as in slavery days.

Why doesn't Bill look around for another employer who will treat him more fairly? . . .

The Southern States have passed up-to-date fugitive slave laws, providing for just such emergencies. These laws make it felonious to leave his employer while owing him money. And the wage system is so fixed that the Negro is at almost all times in his employer's debt.

But suppose . . . Bill is an industrious and ambitious fellow, who looks as if he will work harder if he thinks he is his own master. In that case Farmer Jones "rents" Bill a few acres. Bill can keep what he earns, after the rent is paid off, of course. But Farmer Jones always manages to fix the rent so high that after the rent is paid there's very little left. The harder Bill works, the better for Jones. So Bill keeps working his hands off in the vain hope that some day he'll be able to save something. And Jones reaps the benefit of Bill's ambition. . . .

. . . There's no real prejudice, or very little, against the Negro as a man or as a member of a race. There is merely a prejudice against the Negro as the equal of the white man, against allowing him to rise from the position of the servant whose duty it is to do the white man's work for him and demanding nothing in return. Fundamentally, it is the same sort of prejudice as the prejudice against labor unions among a certain class of people up here in the North. Race discrimination is the club with which the white man keeps the Negro in economic subjection to him. It's not a question of sentiment—of the white man's social aversions or aesthetic antipathies. It's a matter chiefly of dollars and cents.

"We have found you wanting"
Rose Schneiderman

In 1911, concerns over exploitation of workers came to a head following the Triangle Shirtwaist Factory disaster. On March 25 a fire in the New York City sweatshop killed 146 workers, mostly women. The victims could not flee the burning building as one exit was locked and the fire escapes were too small. Public outrage and protests eventually led to more than thirty-six new state laws to protect workers.

At a packed public meeting, held April 2 at the Metropolitan Opera House, Rose Schneiderman gave voice to the grief and anger of workers. Schneiderman was an organizer for the International Ladies Garment Workers Union and had led a strike at the Triangle factory two years before. She and other labor advocates had been calling attention to the appalling conditions in the clothing manufacturing shops for nearly two decades. They held the public, government officials, and shop owners all responsible for the deaths of the Triangle workers. The Schneiderman speech was quoted in the April 3, 1911, edition of the *New York Times*, from which this excerpt was taken.

I WOULD BE A TRAITOR to these poor burned bodies . . . if I came here to talk good fellowship. We have tried you good people of the public and we have found you wanting. The old Inquisition had its rack and its thumbscrews and its instruments of torture with iron teeth. We know what these things are to-day; the iron teeth are our necessities, the thumbscrews are the high-powered and swift machinery close to which we must work, and the rack is here in the firetrap structures that will destroy us the minute they catch on fire.

This is not the first time girls have been burned alive in the city. Every week I must learn of the untimely death of one of my sister workers. Every year thousands of us are maimed. The life of men and women is so cheap and property is so sacred. There are so many of us for one job it matters little if 146 of us are burned to death.

We have tried you citizens; we are trying you now, and you have a couple of dollars for the sorrowing mothers, brothers and sisters by way of a charity gift. But every time the workers come out in the only way they know to protest against conditions which are unbearable the strong hand of the law is allowed to press down heavily upon us.

Public officials have only words of warning to us—warning that we must be intensely peaceable, and they have the workhouse just back of all their warnings. The strong hand of the law beats us back, when we rise into the conditions that make life unbearable. . . .

I can't talk fellowship to you who are gathered here. Too much blood has been spilled. I know from my experience it is up to the working people to save themselves. The only way they can save themselves is by a strong working-class movement.

"There Is Power in a Union"
Joe Hill

In the early 1900s, a wave of European immigrants arrived in the United States. A multitude of industries employed these new immigrants in mines, sweatshops, and factories, often under exploitative terms. The new workers lacked both familiarity with American institutions and sufficient resources to effectively fight their exploitation. Their lack of a shared language made it difficult for them to communicate with one another, further increasing their vulnerability. Due to a fear of competition mixed with bigotry, many existing labor unions refused to represent these immigrant workers.

In 1905, radical union activists, anarchists, and socialists formed a new union to represent all workers—the Industrial Workers of the World, known as the IWW or the Wobblies. The Wobblies sought one big union for all workers, including women, blacks, and immigrants of all descriptions, and not just union members.

To overcome their constituents' lack of a common language, the Wobblies pioneered the use of art to convey a universal message, creating hundreds of protest posters and songs. Their willingness to work with all workers transformed the labor movement in America, and their use of art and song became a standard of other movements, such as civil-rights and environmental protests.

The most famous songwriter of the IWW was organizer Joe Hill. His prolific songs were compiled into the *Little Red Song Book*. IWW strikers would sing them on the picket lines and in jail—in one case protecting themselves with mattresses when wardens brought out fire hoses to try to get them to quit singing. Hill's songs remain alive today and are even available online. In his 1913 song "There Is Power in a Union," transcribed here from a recording of U. Utah Phillips, Hill pushed workers to stand up for their rights. Hill was eventually convicted of murder and executed by firing squad. In a final telegram to fellow organizer Big Bill Heywood, he commanded, "Don't waste time mourning. Organize!"

Would you have freedom from wage slavery,
Then come join the Grand Industrial Band.
Would you from mis'ry and hunger be free,
Come on! Do your share, lend a hand.

Chorus

There is pow'r, there is pow'r
In a band of workingfolk,
When we stand hand in hand.
That's a pow'r, that's a pow'r
That must rule in every land—
One Industrial Union Grand.

Would you have mansions of gold in the sky,
And live in a shack, that's away in the back?
Would you have wings up in heaven to fly,
And starve here with rags on your back?

Chorus

If you like sluggers to beat in your head,
Then don't organize, all unions despise.
If you want nothing before you are dead,
Shake hands with your boss and look wise.

Chorus

So come, all ye workers, from every land,
And come join the Grand Industrial Band.
Then we our share of this earth shall demand.
Come on! Do your share, lend a hand.

The Torment of Migrant Workers

John Steinbeck

The Great Depression coincided with an extended drought. Tens of thousands of farmers went bankrupt and lost their land. Rumors of work took many of the newly landless to California, where they joined a vast pool of migrant farm laborers.

John Steinbeck, who later won the Pullitzer Prize for his 1939 novel, *The Grapes of Wrath*, about the plight of these migrants, also wrote about them in popular news magazines, as in this 1936 piece from *The Nation*. Steinbeck called for farmworkers to be allowed to organize and for employers to pay a living wage that would enable them to survive. A living wage would also prevent violence between farmworkers and farm owners, which Steinbeck viewed as the otherwise inevitable outcome of attempts to forcibly suppress the grievances of the farmworkers.

Steinbeck's articles and novel helped raise awareness of the farmworkers' plight, as did the highly successful movie of *The Grapes of Wrath*. But the political power of the farm owners blocked efforts to address farmworkers' grievances within California. Efforts at the federal level stalled with the outbreak of World War II. Not until the 1960s was the farmworkers' right to organize codified.

THERE ARE IN CALIFORNIA . . . two distinct classes of farmers widely separated in standard of living, desires, needs, and sympathies: the very small farmer who more often than not takes the side of workers in disputes, and the speculative farmer, like A. J. Chandler, publisher of the *Los Angeles Times*, or like Herbert Hoover and William Randolph Hearst, absentee owners who possess huge sections of land. Allied with these large individual growers have been the big incorporated farms, owned by their stockholders and farmed by instructed managers, and a large number of bank farms, acquired by foreclosure and operated by superintendents whose labor policy is dictated by the bank. For example, the Bank of America is very nearly the largest farm owner and operator in the state of California.

These two classes have little or no common ground; while the small farmer is likely to belong to the grange, the speculative farmer belongs to some such organization as the Associated Farmers of California, which is closely tied to the state Chamber of Commerce. This group has as its major activity resistance to any attempt of farm labor to organize. Its avowed purpose has been the distribution of new reports and leaflets tending to show that every attempt to organize agricultural workers was the work of red agitators and that every organization was Communist inspired. . . .

. . . The drought in the Middle West has very recently made available an enormous amount of cheap labor. Workers have been coming to California in nondescript cars from Oklahoma, Nebraska, Texas, and other states, parts of which have been rendered uninhabitable by drought. Poverty-stricken after the destruction of their farms, their last reserves used up in making the trip, they have arrived so beaten and destitute that they have been willing at first to work under any conditions and for any wages offered. . . .

During the spring, summer, and part of the fall the man may find some kind of agricultural work. The top pay for a successful year will not be over $400, and if he has any trouble or is not agile, strong, and quick it may well be only $150. It will be seen that rent is out of the question. Clothes cannot be bought. Every available cent must go for food and a reserve to move the car from harvest to harvest. The migrant will stop in one of two federal camps, in a state camp, in houses put up by the large or small farmers, or in the notorious squatters' camps. . . .

. . . The final resource is the squatters' camp, usually located on the bank of some watercourse. The people pack into them. They use the watercourse for drinking, bathing, washing their clothes, and to receive their refuse, with the result that epidemics start easily and are difficult to check. . . . The people in these camps, because of long-continued privation, are in no shape to fight illness. It is often said that no one starves in the United States, yet in Santa Clara County last year five babies were certified by the local coroner to have died of "malnutrition," the modern word for starvation, and the less shocking word, although it its connotation it is perhaps more horrible since it indicates that the suffering has been long drawn out. . . .

These are some of the conditions California offers the refugees from the dust bowl. But the refugees are even less content with the starvation wages and the rural slums than were the Chinese, the Filipinos, and the Mexicans. Having their families with them, they are not so mobile as the earlier immigrants were. If starvation sets in, the whole family starves, instead of just one man. Therefore they have been quick to see that they must organize for their own safety. . . .

The usual repressive measures have been used against these migrants: shooting by deputy sheriffs in "self-defense," jailing without charge, refusal of trial by jury, torture and beating by night riders. But even in the short time that these American migrants have been out here there has been a change. It is understood that they are being attacked not because they want higher wages, not because they are Communists, but simply because they want to organize. And to the men, since this defines the thing not to be allowed, it also defines the thing that is completely necessary to the safety of the workers. . . .

The effect has been far from that desired. There is now in California anger instead of fear. The stupidity of the large grower has changed terror into defensive fury. The granges, working close to the soil and to the men, and knowing the temper of the men of this new race, have tried to put through wages that will allow a living, however small. But the large growers, who have been shown to be the only group making a considerable profit from agriculture, are devoting their money to tear gas and rifle ammunition. The men will organize and the large growers will meet organization with force. It is easy to prophesy this. . . . There is tension in the valley and fear for the future.

It is fervently to be hoped that the great group of migrant workers so necessary to the harvesting of California's crops may be given the right to live decently, that they may not be so badgered, tormented, and hurt that in the end they become the avengers of the hundreds of thousands who have been tortured and starved before them.

"The Oligarchies"
from *Canto general*
Pablo Neruda

Winner of the Nobel Prize for literature in 1971, poet Pablo Neruda of Chile was a fierce radical. In "The Oligarchies," part of his famous epic poem *Canto general*, he dealt with the history of Latin America, and the suppression of the poor first by the Spanish and later by the wealthy class that remained in control following independence across the region. Neruda was considered as an alternative to Salvador Allende as the Communist candidate for Chile's presidency in 1973.

This translation of "The Oligarchies" by Jack Schmitt was included in *The Poetry of Pablo Neruda*, edited by Ilan Stavans.

No, the flags had not yet dried,
the soldiers had not yet slept
when freedom changed clothes,
and was turned into a hacienda:
a caste emerged from
the newly sown lands, a quadrille
of nouveaux riches with coats of arms,
with police and prisons.

They drew a black line:
"Here on our side, Mexico's
Porfiristas, Chile's
"gentlemen," gentry from
the Jockey Club of Buenos Aires,
Uruguay's slicked
freebooters, the Ecuadorian
upper crust, clerical
dandies everywhere."
The poor to the mines, the desert.

Mr. Rodríguez de la Crota
spoke in the Senate with a mellifluous
elegant voice.
            "This law, at long last, establishes
the obligatory hierarchy
and above all the principles
of Christianity.
            It was
necessary as water.
Only the communists, conceived
in hell, as you're well aware,
could object to the Funnel
code sagacious and severe.
But this Asiatic opposition,
proceeding from subman,
is easy to suppress: to jail with
them all, to the concentration camp,
and that way the distinguished

gentlemen and the obliging
Radical Party lackeys
will stand alone."

There was a round of applause
from the aristocratic benches:
what eloquence, how spiritual,
what a philospher, what a luminary!
And everyone ran off to fill
his pockets in his business,
one monopolizing milk,
another racketeering in wire,
another stealing in sugar
and all boisterously proclaiming
themselves patriots, with a monopoly
of patriotism, also accounted for
in the Funnel Law.

Capitalism and Freedom
Milton Friedman

In 1962, in the wake of the New Deal and just before the government interventions that comprised the Great Society, economist Milton Friedman argued what at the time was unorthodox— that government intervention was bad and that greater economic freedom was essential to all forms of freedom. Based on this view, he saw social security, tariffs, the maintenance of national parks, minimum-wage laws, environmental regulation, and welfare programs as impingements on essential freedoms. He outlined his fundamental view of freedom in his 1962 work *Capitalism and Freedom*, excerpted here. Friedman's writings have inspired two generations of conservative economic policies.

FREEDOM IS A RARE and delicate plant. Our minds tell us, and history confirms, that the great threat to freedom is the concentration of power. Government is necessary to preserve our freedom, it is an instrument through which we can exercise our freedom; yet by concentrating power in political hands, it is also a threat to freedom. Even though the men who wield this power initially be of good will and even though they be not corrupted by the power they exercise, the power will both attract and form men of a different stamp.

How can we benefit from the promise of government while avoiding the threat to freedom? Two broad principles embodied in our Constitution give an answer that has preserved our freedom so far, though they have been violated repeatedly in practice while proclaimed as precept.

First, the scope of government must be limited. Its major function must be to protect our freedom both from the enemies outside our gates and from our fellow-citizens: to preserve law and order, to enforce private contracts, to foster competitive markets. Beyond this major function, government may enable us at times to accomplish jointly what we would find it more difficult or expensive to accomplish severally. However, any such use of government is fraught with danger. We should not and cannot avoid using government in this way. But there should be a clear and large balance of advantages before we do. By relying primarily on voluntary co-operation and private enterprise, in both economic and other activities, we can insure that the private sector is a check on the powers of the governmental sector and an effective protection of freedom of speech, of religion, and of thought.

The second broad principle is that government power must be dispersed. If government is to exercise power, better in the county than in the state, better in the state than in Washington. If I do not like what my local community does, be it in sewage disposal, or zoning, or schools, I can move to another local community, and though few may take this step, the mere possibility acts as a check. . . . If I do not like what Washington imposes, I have few alternatives in this world of jealous nations. . . .

The preservation of freedom is the protective reason for limiting and decentralizing governmental power. But there is also a constructive reason. The great advances of civilization, whether in architecture or painting, in science or literature, in industry or agriculture, have never come from centralized government. . . .

Government can never duplicate the variety and diversity of individual action. At any moment in time, by imposing uniform standards in housing, or nutrition, or clothing, government could undoubtedly improve the level of living of many individuals; by imposing uniform standards in schooling, road construction, or sanitation, central government could undoubtedly improve the level of performance in many local areas and perhaps even on the average of all communities. But in the process, government would replace progress by stagnation, it would substitute uniform mediocrity for the variety essential for that experimentation which can bring tomorrow's laggards above today's mean.

Bark Petitions
The Yolngu People

In February 1963, the Australian government granted a bauxite-mining lease on an Aboriginal reserve without consulting or compensating the native Yolngu people at Yirrkala (a community on the north coast of Australia). By August, the Yirrkala residents had protested to Parliament by submitting two petitions, typed in English and their native language, and pasted onto traditional bark artwork (see photo).

The protest action was successful. Over the objections of the interior minister, a Parliamentary inquiry was initiated. At the October 1963 hearings, the Reverend E. A. Wells, who headed the

Methodist mission to Yirrkala, presented the testimony excerpted here. The inquiry recommended compensating the Yolngu and protecting their sacred sites. Lawsuits and legislation following the petition protest eventually produced changes in Australia's constitution, legislation to clarify native rights, and court decisions granting the Aboriginal peoples greater rights over their original lands. The bark petitions are now a featured exhibit in Australia's national archives.

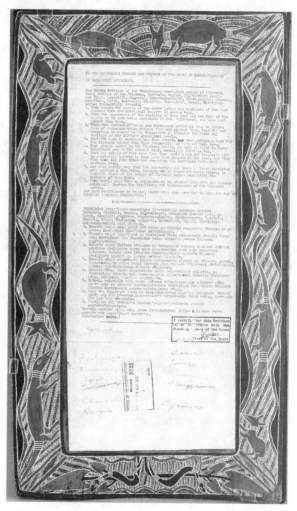

THE ABSOLUTE and final authority generally exercised by white men over dark has suddenly loomed again. I believe a serious error in management was made when a section of the reserve was alienated without previous consultation with anyone residing in the area. . . .

To be suddenly reduced from approximately 200 square miles to an unknown area, under debate as to whether it is 2 square miles or 1 1/2 miles, creates immediate uncertainty, which communicates itself at once in a small community. . . .

It is very cold comfort to tell an aboriginal that he may still walk over land that once was his own, but that by a mysterious process has been acquired by someone else; and that, as the original owner, he can hunt across it until the new owner needs it bit by bit for special sale upon which it is to be removed in very large boats. Insult is added to injury in a final humiliation when he is offered money to shovel away his own sense of spiritual security, as certain places certainly represent to him still.

"We are not beasts of burden"
César Chávez

In the mid-1960s, grape workers in California were poorly paid, exempt from the federal minimum wage, and frequently exposed to pesticides. Filipino grape workers walked out in 1965, but the strike initially had little impact due to the steady flow of new, largely illegal immigrants whom the grape growers could recruit as strikebreakers. Into this difficult setting stepped the soft-spoken young leader of the union that would become the United Farm Workers (UFW)— César Chávez.

Chávez espoused the nonviolent tradition of Martin Luther King, Jr., and Mahatma Gandhi. He reached beyond the relatively powerless workers to organize a consumer boycott of grapes. The boycott was endorsed by diverse groups across the country: insurance workers in Youngstown, Ohio; students in Boston who reenacted the Boston Tea Party with grapes; Mayor John Lindsay in New York City, who ordered city agencies not to buy grapes; and by the national convention of the Jehovah's Witnesses.

The boycott was opposed by the John Birch Society, the American Farm Bureau, Governor Ronald Reagan of California, and of course the grape growers. After Richard Nixon's election as president, the Pentagon increased grape shipments to troops in Vietnam by 800 percent, but still the boycott hurt sales. Growers raised wages but refused to recognize the union. Eventually they sued the union for losses caused by the boycott.

Chávez called attention to the plight of the grape workers with appearances and marches around the country and with a twenty-five-day fast in 1968. By 1969, tensions were rising, and militant elements within the Mexican-American community called for violence to achieve economic justice. Chávez's stubborn resistance to violent protest and devotion to nonviolence are both evident in this 1969 letter to E. L. Barr, leader of the grape growers. By 1975, the UFW had achieved recognition and vastly improved working conditions for the grape workers.

DEAR MR. BARR: I am sad to hear about your accusations in the press that our union movement and table grape boycott have been successful because we have used violence and terror tactics. If what you say is true, I have been a failure and should withdraw from the struggle; but you are left with the awesome moral responsibility, before God and man, to come forward with whatever information you have so that corrective action can begin at once. If for any reason you fail to come forth to substantiate your charges, then you must be held responsible for committing violence against us, albeit violence of the tongue. I am convinced that you as a human being did not mean what you said but rather acted hastily under pressure from the public relations firm that has been hired to try to counteract the tremendous moral force of our movement. How many times we ourselves have felt the need to lash out in anger and bitterness.

You must understand—I must make you understand—that our membership and the hopes and aspirations of the hundreds of thousands of the poor and dispossessed that have been raised on our account are, above all, human beings, no better and no worse than any other cross-section of human society; we are not saints because we are poor, but by the same measure neither are we immoral. We are men and women who have suffered and endured much, and not only because of our abject poverty but because we have been kept poor. The colors of our skins, the languages of our cultural and native origins, the lack of formal education, the exclusion from the democratic process, the numbers of our slain in recent wars—all these burdens generation after generation have sought to demoralize us, to break our human spirit. But God knows that we are not beasts of burden, agricultural implements or rented slaves; we are men. And mark this well, Mr. Barr, we are men locked in a death struggle against man's inhumanity to man in the industry that you represent. And this struggle itself gives meaning to our life and ennobles our dying.

As your industry has experienced, our strikers here in Delano and those who represent us throughout the world are well trained for this struggle. They have been under the gun, they have been kicked and beaten and herded by dogs, they have been cursed and ridiculed, they have been stripped and chained and jailed, they have been sprayed with the poisons used in the vineyards; but they have been taught not to lie down and die nor to flee in shame, but to resist with every ounce of human endurance and spirit. To resist not with retaliation in kind but to overcome with love and compassion, with ingenuity and creativity, with hard work and longer hours, with stamina and patient tenacity, with truth and public appeal, with friends and allies, with mobility and discipline, with politics and law, and with prayer and fasting. They were not trained in a month or even a year; after all, this new harvest season will mark our fourth full year of strike and even now we continue to plan and prepare for the years to come. Time accomplishes for the poor what money does for the rich.

This is not to pretend that we have everywhere been successful enough or that we have not made mistakes. And while we do not belittle or underestimate our adversaries—for they are the rich and the powerful and they possess the land—we are not afraid nor do we cringe from the confrontation. We welcome it! We have planned for it. We know that our cause is just, that history is a story of social revolution, and that the poor shall inherit the land.

Mr. Barr, let me be painfully honest with you. You must understand these things. We advocate militant nonviolence as our means for social revolution and to achieve justice for our people, but we are not blind or deaf to the desperate and moody winds of human frustration, impatience and rage that blow among us. Gandhi himself admitted that if his only choice were cowardice or violence, he would choose violence. Men are not angels, and time and tide wait for no man. Precisely because of these powerful human emotions, we have tried to involve masses of people in their own struggle. Participation and self-determination remain the best experience of freedom, and free men instinctively prefer democratic change and even protect the rights guaranteed to seek it. Only the enslaved in despair have need of violent overthrow.

This letter does not express all that is in my heart, Mr. Barr. But if it says nothing else it says that we do not hate you or rejoice to see your industry destroyed; we hate the agribusiness system that seeks to keep us enslaved, and we shall overcome and change it not by retaliation or bloodshed but by a determined nonviolent struggle carried on by those masses of farm workers who intend to be free and human.

The Modern Little Red Hen
Ronald Reagan

To many, economic justice is found in a fair distribution of wealth in a society, or preventing devastating poverty, or in equal access to resources. Ronald Reagan was a prolific writer and a spokesperson for another view of economic justice. For Reagan, economic justice included the idea that those who worked to achieve something should enjoy the benefits of their effort. Without this incentive, there would be little reason to work to achieve anything and society as a whole would suffer, according to Reagan and his fellow thinkers.

In the mid-1970s, after his term as governor of California, Reagan gave weekly radio addresses that touched on the many themes that would later characterize his presidency. In the address reprinted here, he offers a parable to illustrate his conception of economic justice. As president, Reagan followed through on the concepts outlined in "The Modern Little Red Hen" by cutting taxes.

ABOUT A YEAR AGO I imposed a little poetry on you. It was called "The Incredible Bread Machine" and made a lot of sense with reference to matters economic. You didn't object too much so having gotten away with it once I'm going to try again. This is a little treatise on basic economics called "The Modern Little Red Hen."

The Modern Little Red Hen
Once upon a time there was a little red hen who scratched about the barnyard until she uncovered some grains of wheat. She called her neighbors and said, "If we plant this wheat, we shall have bread to eat. Who will help me plant it?"

"Not I," said the cow.

"Not I," said the duck.

"Not I," said the pig.

"Not I," said the goose.

"Then I will," said the little red hen. And she did. The wheat grew tall and ripened into golden grain. "Who will help me reap my wheat?" asked the little red hen.

"Not I," said the duck.

"Out of my classification," said the pig.

"I'd lose my seniority," said the cow.

"I'd lose my unemployment compensation," said the goose.

"Then I will," said the little red hen, and she did.

At last it came time to bake the bread. "Who will help me bake bread?" asked the little red hen.

"That would be overtime for me," said the cow.

"I'd lose my welfare benefits," said the duck.

"I'm a dropout and never learned how," said the pig.

"If I'm to be the only helper, that's discrimination," said the goose.

"Then I will," said the little red hen.

She baked five loaves and held them up for her neighbors to see.

They all wanted some and, in fact, demanded a share. But the little red hen said, "No, I can eat the five loaves myself."

"Excess profits," cried the cow.

"Capitalist leech," screamed the duck.

"I demand equal rights," yelled the goose.

And the pig just grunted.

And they painted "unfair" picket signs and marched round and round the little red hen, shouting obscenities.

When the government agent came, he said to the little red hen,

"You must not be greedy."

"But I earned the bread," said the little red hen.

"Exactly," said the agent. "That is the wonderful free enterprise system. Anyone in the barnyard can earn as much as he wants. but under our modern government regulations, the productive workers must divide their product with the idle."

And they lived happily ever after, including the little red hen, who smiled and clucked, "I am grateful, I am grateful."

But her neighbors wondered why she never again baked any more bread.

This is Ronald Reagan. Thanks for listening.

"How can you call it a trade union?"

Ela Bhatt and *In Motion* Magazine

The Self-Employed Women's Association (SEWA) in India counts more than 600,000 self-employed women as members; most of them are illiterate or semiliterate, have little capital, and work out of their own homes or in unregulated—and often illegal—street markets. The SEWA membership and goals contrast sharply with those of conventional unions, in which workers sharing a common skill, common employers, or centralized location bond together to extract concessions from corporate owners or managers. SEWA instead works to empower women in highly diverse fields of work and who typically have no employer per se.

The union has relied on Mohandas Gandhi's tradition of nonviolent resistance, or *satyagraha*, to force changes in laws or the enforcement of laws that make the working lives of its members more productive. It has also used more innovative techniques, such as thousands of poor women pooling their meager resources to create a bank that provides low-interest loans, thereby enabling women who could not qualify for standard loans to increase their productivity. This bank has taken the women out of the power of exploitative money lenders, who charged rates of up to 3000 percent interest annually. The union has become one of the world's largest. Here, in a 2003 interview with the online magazine *In Motion*, founder Ela Bhatt recalls some of the union's seminal nonviolent struggles

ELA BHATT: In '72, we started organizing, unionizing the self-employed workers—women. . . .

It was not so easy because the registrar of trade unions said, "How can you call it a trade union? Who is the employer? Against whom are you going to fight?" I argued that the purpose of a union is not only to fight, or to be against somebody, you also have to be for something. And that was for changing so many laws and policies. Women may not be able to pinpoint an employer but we have to fight against certain systems. Like the contract system. Like that whole range of middlemen, of contractors, and subcontractors, and sub-subcontractors. That is something that is an exploitative system.

Or with the public distribution system. Or with the marketplace. Or with the police—the police and the urban development policies who see street vendors as illegal. What we were questioning was, "What is illegal about street vending?" . . .

IN MOTION MAGAZINE: Did you ever use civil disobedience tactics in your struggles?

ELA BHATT: Yes, often we have to resort to that. Also, we have gone on strike as the last weapon, the last tool. We have sit-in strikes. We have satyagraha. . . .

. . . I will tell you of a strike.

Some time back we had a satyagraha of street vendors. We have a downtown market where the women and men sit with baskets of vegetables, fruits, and utility items. The market runs from the beginning of the day until late night and they are all our members, the women.

The municipal corporation wanted to drive them out. We said that we have been here for the last three generations. It is our natural right to be here. Historically, we have been here. And it is true, they are the third or fourth generation that has been sitting there. But in the meantime, many new buildings have come up. And the shops have come up. And these vendors have literally been thrown to the street. They were being removed because they wanted to make a space for a parking lot.

So, where was this taken? The police clamped on a curfew—a five days, six days curfew. The vendors started starving. They had nothing to fall back on.

In the meantime, we had tried everything to explain our situation to the municipal corporation, to the police, everybody. But they didn't listen to us. So, we said, in the most Gandhian way, that, "From tomorrow, 8 o'clock [in the] morning, we are going to sit here. Even if you don't allow that, we are going to sit here."

Already two policemen were standing there, early in the morning when we arrived and, of course, we had certain tactics, we started doing business. The police had a long argument with me and I kept them engaged in argument so when the women were ready they could bring their baskets. And as soon as the baskets were there the customers were ready to buy and the market started. The police didn't know what to do. . . .

For about three days it went on like this. It was such good business because the vendors, they didn't have to pay any fine to any inspector, or to the police— fine or bribe, whatever you say. And in those three days, they didn't have to have any stick beaten to them or their stuff thrown out on the ground. We managed ourselves.

Disposable People
Kevin Bales

Social scientist Kevin Bales pulled the curtain off the largely invisible problem of modern slavery with the publication of *Disposable People* in 1999. Officially slavery is illegal in every country in the world. Bales, who also is director of the advocacy organization Free the Slaves, documented how it persists. Modern slavery is often hidden as a loan secured not by a lien against land or a car, but by the labor of the individual. Or it may take the form of an illegal contract that gives the slaveholder control over where the slave lives, whom he works for, and where and when he is allowed to travel.

Bales also detailed how globalization has increased slavery by disrupting traditional communities, creating a "glut of potential slaves" on the market that drives down the price of slaves. With prices low, slave owners have little inclination to take care of their slaves. Legal systems rarely hold them accountable for the slaves' health. Slavery thrives in countries where the legal system is weak.

Bales showed how slave labor makes its way indirectly into dozens of products consumed in the developing world, such as Brazilian steel manufactured with the help of slave-produced charcoal, and how slave labor drives down wages worldwide by forcing companies in countries where slavery is largely prevented to compete with companies in countries that tolerate the slave labor.

Bales's book produced a storm of media attention and inspired a prize-winning movie, *Slavery: A Global Investigation*. The book provoked both a new U.S. law to toughen penalties on human trafficking and new provisions to fight trafficking in a United Nations convention on organized crime. These actions, according to Bales, helped but will not fully solve the problem. In this excerpt from *Disposable People*, Bales examines the economics and impacts of sexual slavery in Thailand.

WHEN SIRI WAKES it is about noon. In the instant of waking she knows exactly who and what she has become. As she explained to me, the soreness in her genitals reminds her of the fifteen men she had sex with the night before. Siri is fifteen years old. Sold by her parents a year ago, her resistance and her desire to escape the brothel are breaking down and acceptance and resignation are taking their place. . . .

At about five, Siri and the other girls are told to dress, put on their makeup, and prepare for the night's work. By seven the men are coming in, purchasing drinks and choosing girls, and Siri will have been chosen by one or two of the ten to eighteen men who will buy her that night. Many men choose Siri because she looks much younger than her fifteen years. Slight and round faced, dressed to accentuate her youth, she might be eleven or twelve. Because she looks like a child she can be sold as a "new" girl at a higher price, about $15, which is more than twice that charged for the other girls. . . .

Though she is only fifteen Siri is now resigned to being a prostitute. After she was sold and taken to the brothel, she discovered that the work was not what she thought it would be. Like many rural Thais, Siri had a sheltered childhood and she was ignorant of what it meant to work in a brothel. Her first client hurt her and at the first opportunity she ran away. On the street with no money she was quickly caught, dragged back, beaten, and raped. That night she was forced to take on a chain of clients until the early morning. The beatings and the work continued night after night until her will was broken. Now she is sure that she is a bad person, very bad to have deserved what has happened to her. . . . She takes a dark pride in her higher price and in the large number of men who choose her. It is the adjustment of the concentration camp, an effort to make sense of horror. . . .

The boom and bust of Thailand's cyclical economic miracle has had a dramatic impact on northern villages. While the center of the country, around Bangkok, rapidly industrialized, the north was left behind. Prices of food, land, and tools all increased as the economy grew, but the returns for rice growing and other agricultural work were stagnant, held down by government policies guaranteeing cheap food for factory workers in Bangkok. Yet visible everywhere in the north is a flood of consumer goods—refrigerators, televisions, cars and trucks, rice cookers, air conditioners—all of which are extremely tempting. . . .

In the past, daughters were sold in response to a serious family financial crisis. Under the threat of losing their mortgaged rice fields and faced with destitution, a family might sell a daughter to redeem its debt, but for the most part daughters were worth about as much at home as workers as they would realize when sold. Modernization and economic growth have changed all that. Now parents feel a great pressure to buy consumer goods that were unknown even twenty years ago; the sale of a daughter might easily finance a new television set. A recent survey in the northern provinces found that of the families who sold their daughters, two thirds could afford not to do so but "instead preferred to buy color televisions and video equipment." And from the perspective of parents who are willing to sell their children, there has never been a better market.

The brothels' demand for prostitutes is rapidly increasing. The same economic boom that feeds consumer demand in northern villages lines the pockets of laborers and workers of the central plain. . . . Possibly for the first time in their lives, these laborers can do what more well-off Thai men have always done; go to a brothel. The purchasing power of this increasing number of brothel users strengthens the call for northern girls and supports a growing business in procurement and trafficking in girls.

Siri's story was typical. A broker, a woman herself from a northern village, approached the families in Siri's village with assurances of well-paid work for their daughters. Siri's parents probably understood that the work would be as a prostitute—since they knew that other girls from their village had gone south to brothels. After some negotiation they were paid 50,000 baht ($2,000) for Siri, a very significant sum for this family of rice farmers. This exchange began the process of debt bondage that is used to enslave the girls. The contractual arrangement between the broker and parents requires that this money be repaid by the daughter's labor before she is free to leave. . . . In such cases the exorbitant interest charged on the loan means there is little chance that a girl's sexual slavery will ever repay the debt. . . .

Forced prostitution is a great business. The overheads are low, the turnover high, and the profits immense. . . . It is far, far different from the capital-intensive slavery of the past, which required long-term investments and made solid but small profits. The disposability of the women, the special profits to be made from children, all ensure a low-risk, high-return enterprise. For all its dilapidation and filth the brothel is a highly efficient machine that in destroying young girls turns them into gold.

To set up a brothel requires a relatively small outlay. About 80,000 baht ($3,200) will buy all the furniture, equipment, and fixtures that are needed. The building itself will be rented for anywhere from 4,000 to 15,000 baht per month ($160 to $600). . . .

Feeding a prostitute costs 50 to 80 baht per day ($2.00 to $3.20). Slaveholders do not skimp on food, since men want healthy-looking girls with full figures. . . . Bribes are not exorbitant or unpredictable; in most brothels a policeman stops by once a day to pick up 200 to 400 baht ($8 to $16), a monthly expenditure of about 6,000 baht ($240) that is topped off by giving the policeman a girl for an hour if he seems interested. . . .

Income far exceeds expenses. Each of the twenty girls makes about 125 baht ($5) for the brothel with each client she has, and each day she has between ten and eighteen clients for 1,250 to 2,250 baht ($50 to $90). A single day's return is 25,000 to 45,000 baht ($1,000 to $1,800) just on sex.

Resolved to Ruin
Greg Palast

In December 2001, Argentina's middle class rioted in the streets over their inability to purchase food. In the four years preceding the riots, unemployment and foreign debt had soared. Government austerity measures to try to address the debt had provoked peaceful protests in August. Continuing fiscal instability caused a run on the banks in early December. The government responded by limiting withdrawals of bank deposits. Middle-class workers, unable to access their savings, filled the streets and banged pots to call attention to their hunger. The protests attracted international attention, but the sources of the problem remained unclear to most Americans.

In March 2003, journalist Greg Palast, author of *Armed Madhouse*, analyzed the situation for *Harper's* magazine, arguing that International Monetary Fund and World Bank policies exacerbated the crisis to the benefit of financial interests in Europe and United States. Palast presented World Bank documents outlining the policies that were required of Argentina in return for international loans, and then demonstrated the failure of those policies compared to the policies they replaced.

GREEN-HAIRED PROTESTERS in the streets of Seattle were ridiculed for their belief that the World Bank, the International Monetary Fund, and the world's finance ministers enter into secret agreements to impoverish developing nations. Here, in fact, is one such agreement: Argentina's "Country Assistance Strategy Progress Report" from June 2001. This document, nominally produced by the World Bank, represents the interlocking directives of both the Bank and the IMF, as well as, indirectly, the wishes of both institutions' largest patron, the United States Treasury Department. Marked "Confidential" or "Official Use Only," these reports are seldom publicized to the citizenry bound up in their stipulations. Yet for the 100-plus that rely on IMF and World Bank loans—countries such as Argentina, Tanzania, Ecuador, Sierra Leone—such agreements serve as de facto legislation, meticulous in detail and ideological in thrust. Although couched as loan conditions or as helpful development advice, these reports more closely resemble the minutes of a financial coup d'etat.

At the outset, the authors of this Argentina report pause to reflect how their strategy had performed in the past year. Twelve months prior, in June 2000, unemployment stood at 15 percent; the country had already suffered through two years of recession, during which industrial production had declined by more than 10 percent. To cut government spending in such an economy would be akin to turning off the engines of an airplane in stall. And yet in a September 2000 agreement with the IMF, Argentina had been required to cut its budget deficit from $5.3 billion in 2000 to $4.1 billion in 2001. The consequences were predictable: such "austerity" had led, in the first three months of 2001, to a 2.6 percent decline in GDP from the previous year.

To reduce its deficit per IMF decree, Argentina had cut $3 billion from government spending—a cut that was necessary, the authors note here, to "accomodat[e] the increase in interest obligations." These obligations, the report did not need to add, were largely to foreign creditors, including the IMF and World Bank themselves. Since 1994, in fact, Argentina's budget deficits had been entirely attributable to interest payments on foreign loans. Excluding such payments, spending had remained constant at 19 percent of GDP. Despite the visible harm caused by cuts, the new plan ordered more. This, the report promised, would "greatly improve the outlook for the remainder of 2001 and 2002, with growth expected to recover in the later half of 2001." The Bank was slightly off the mark. By December 2001, Buenos Aires' middle class, unaccustomed to hunting the streets for garbage to eat, joined the poor in mass demonstrations.

How had Argentina arrived at such an impasse? In the 1990s the nation was the poster child for globalization, having followed without question the IMF and World Bank program. The "reform" plan for Argentina, as for every nation, has *four steps*. The first of these, *capital-market liberalization*, was achieved by 1991's "Convertibility Plan," which pegged the Argentine peso in a one-to-one relationship with the U.S. dollar. This peg was designed both to keep inflation low and to make deficit spending difficult, in hopes of attracting and comforting foreign investors. Liberalized markets allow free capital to flow in and out across borders. But once Argentina's economy began to wobble, money simply flowed out. . . .

The second step in the IMF/World Bank regimen is *privatization*. Both at the urging of lenders and out of financial necessity, Argentina throughout the nineties sold off what Argentines now ruefully call "las joyas de mi abuela," grandmother's jewels: the state's oil, gas, water, and electric companies and the state banks. It was quite a fire sale. Vivendi of France won rural water systems; Enron of Texas the pipes of Buenos Aires; Fleet of Boston took the provincial banks. By the panic of 2001, there was nothing left to sell: "Almost all the public utilities have already been privatized," this memo laments elsewhere. Once in control, Vivendi raised water prices as much as 200 percent; Enron, too, demanded rate increases, even as its water was inadequately cleaned and its service plagued by interruptions. Former chief World Bank economist Joseph Stiglitz says the wholesale privatizations ordered by the Bank and IMF were so corrupt that he dubbed them "briberizations." . . .

The third prong of the laissez-faire putsch is *market-based pricing*. In Argentina, the main target of this initiative has been labor, that most inflexible of commodities. "A major advance was made to eliminate out dated labor contracts," states this report, noting approvingly that "labor costs" (i.e., wages) had fallen due to "labor market flexibility induced by the de facto liberalization of the market via increased informality." Translation: workers who lost unionized jobs were forced into ad hoc arrangements, with far less protection. Here, the report asks the government to decentralize collective bargaining, a move that would reduce union power. In Tanzania, when the nation's HIV epidemic was beginning in the early nineties, the IMF and World Bank required hospitals to charge "user fees" for visits to government hospitals. After the introduction of such fees in Dar es Salaam in 1994, the number of patients treated in the city's three largest public hospitals dropped by 53 percent. Bowing to pressure, the Bank has in recent years retreated from its demands for user fees. In June 2000 it noted in frustration that, despite its efforts, market reforms had failed to win over the Tanzanians: "One legacy of socialism is that most people continue to believe the State has a fundamental role in promoting development and providing social services."

Far from achieving this goal of "unemployment in single digits," the World Bank and IMF saw the jobless figure in the Buenos Aires area rise from 17 percent to a staggering 22 percent in the year after the report's issuance. The violence and looting that rocked that rocked the city in December 2001 thus represents a stage in the "austerity" process that Stiglitz terms the "IMF riot.". . .

Step four of the IMF/World Bank program is *free trade*. The loan terms of the two institutions had required Argentina to accept "an open trade policy." As recession set in, Argentina's exporters—whose products were effectively priced, via the peg, in U.S. dollars—were forced into a spectacularly unequal competition against Brazilian goods priced in that nation's devalued currency. Argentina grows a special kind of long-grain rice favored by Brazilians, and yet even as Brazil faced a hunger crisis tons of rice went unsold. One of the Bank's first ventures into "liberalizing" African markets was in Ghana, which was directed to end price subsidies for its cotton production; a Bank report from May 2002 admitted that this has left the Ghanaian cotton industry "close to collapse." In a footnote, the same report observed that under the new U.S. farm bill, the share of a typical American farm's cotton revenue that is derived from subsidies will rise to 45 percent. Stiglitz likens the West's hypocritical free-trade policies to the Opium Wars, noting, "That too was about opening markets."

Although they make demands separately, the IMF, the World Bank, and the World Trade Organization have in many ways become interchangeable masks of a single governance system. World Bank borrowers must be members of the IMF, which requires its borrowers to adhere to WTO rules. It is perhaps not a coincidence, then, that the "triggers" of these loans so often are friendly to the interests of Western corporations. In Ecuador's 2000 CAS report, for example, the country's loan was triggered only after it permitted the construction of a controversial gas pipeline over the Andes that had long been sought by British Petroleum. In Sierra Leone, one of the "performance criteria" imposed by the IMF in 2001 was that the nation stop requiring import licenses on foreign-made cigarettes. A study by a Harvard economist found that the IMF alone held borrowing nations to an average of eighty-one "conditionalities" or other requirements.

Although these reports rarely fail to couch their free-market fiats in terms of "reducing poverty," their performance in Argentina on this score is sadly typical. Before 1980, when the World Bank and IMF set out to rearrange the economies of developing nations, nearly all of them adhered to Keynesianism or socialism. Following the "import-substitution model," they built locally owned industry through government investment, behind a protective wall of tariffs and capital controls. In those supposed economic dark ages, spanning roughly from 1960 to 1980, per-capita income grew by 73 percent in Latin America and by 34 percent in Africa. By comparison, since 1980, Latin American income growth has slowed to a virtual halt—to less than 6 percent over twenty years—while African incomes have declined by 23 percent. The IMF itself, in a statement accompanying its April 2000 "World Economic Outlook" report, noted that "in recent decades, too many countries, and nearly one-fifth of the world population, have regressed. . . . This is arguably one of the greatest economic failures of the 20th Century." On this, at least, the IMF had it right.

Wal-Mart: The High Cost of Low Price
Robert Greenwald

Since the early 1970s Wal-Mart has grown from a chain of a few dozen stores in the south-central states to the world's largest corporation, with more than five thousand stores worldwide. Its rampant growth and the impact on Main Streets across the country have evoked strong opposition.

As Don Hunter, the founder of a Middlefield, Ohio, hardware store featured in the 2005 movie *Wal-Mart: The High Cost of Low Price* explained, "I've seen a lot of small communities crucified and forced out—Ma and Pa operations that have been in business for years, they're out on the street. . . . And it appears that that is their intent: To come into a community and force everybody out."

Across the country demonstrations, lawsuits, Congressional investigations, boycott campaigns, and academic studies have alleged that the company drives out individually owned businesses and discriminates against women; that its low pay and poor medical benefits cause its workers to rely excessively on state and federal health-care safety nets; that it flirts with unlawful discrimination in its polices to obstruct unionization of its workforce; and that it relies on sweatshop labor in China and other countries.

Wal-Mart counters that its success is due to the fact that it offers consumers what they want—lower prices. A study commissioned by Wal-Mart and released in late 2005 suggested that Wal-Mart saved an average family $2,329 annually. The company has also undertaken

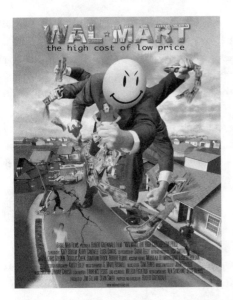

efforts to improve its corporate citizenship, committing in May 2005, for example, to purchase approximately 138,000 acres for wildlife habitat to compensate for lands occupied by its then-existing stores plus its expected growth over the next ten years.

Wal-Mart, by virtue of its success and its global reach, has made issues of economic justice vastly more complex. Is society better off when prices of goods fall, if wages also fall? Are workers overseas better off employed under sweatshop conditions or without those jobs? Do consumers have a responsibility to consider what types of jobs their purchases create and what changes in the community ensue from their purchasing decisions?

In November 2005, director Robert Greenwald tackled these issues in his documentary movie *Wal-Mart: The High Cost of Low Price*. Like *Fahrenheit 9/11* and *Super Size Me*, the movie is intended as a work of protest, not a balanced evaluation; it plays the same role in modern society as Ida Tarbell's early 1900s protest articles against the monopolistic practices of Standard Oil. the *Boston Globe* wrote, "The film convincingly presents the world's largest company as a mendacious, rapacious enemy of the American people. By the final credits you may want to picket Sam Walton's grave."

The Great Corporate Jobs-for-Subsidies Con-Job
Jim Hightower

A crescendo of economic voices bemoans the decline of the middle class in the United States and the associated risks to American society. Harvard law professor Elizabeth Warren has documented how financial security has fallen even as the incomes of two-earner families have risen. James K. Galbraith, professor of government at the University of Texas, has documented the rising disparity in earnings between the top and bottom earners in society. Then there are the populist voices who transform these academic studies into the fire of protest. One of the most persistent of these voices has been Jim Hightower, former secretary of agriculture in Texas.

Hightower writes books with titles like *There's Nothing in the Middle of the Road but Yellow Stripes and Dead Armadillos* and together with colleague Phillip Frazer publishes a monthly news summary and political diatribe called the *Hightower Lowdown* (www.hightowerlowdown.org). In one recent issue they opined that the elite are "so focused on enriching themselves . . . that they have become blind to the looming threat that their avarice poses to the social order. . . Middle-class working families are people who've had a slice of the American pie—and for them to be told now that their slice will be taken from them and their children is not merely to shred the social contract and throw it in their faces, but to dissolve the social glue that holds our big, sprawling, brawling country together."

The July 2005 issue of Hightower and Frazer's monthly newsletter, the *Hightower Lowdown*, analyzed one example of the dissolution of the social contract: tax breaks handed out by states and municipalities to attract new factories and other corporate facilities.

WHAT DO YOU THINK of bums who come into our towns asking for handouts as though they have some right to expect us to underwrite their existence? I don't mean the poor disheveled souls with street names like "Skeeter" and "Gimpy" standing at busy intersections with handwritten cardboard signs saying: "Anything will help. God Bless." No, I'm talking about the real bums, with names like Wal-Mart, Intel, Tyson, Home Depot, Boeing, Dell, Toyota, and Borders. There are two things that these outfits have in common: They are highly profitable, multibillion-dollar corporations . . . and they all go town-to-town, state-to-state, with their hands out, bumming subsidies from us taxpayers. It's not spare change, either—the pinstriped bums suck up a whopping *$50 billion a year* in giveaways doled out by our governors, mayors, and other officials. . . .

. . . When GreatBigGlobalGiantCorp sweeps into town to meet with wide-eyed local politicos, the pitch goes something like this: "We just might build a new facility right here in Greater Bugtussle, creating beaucoup new jobs and scoring big political points for you, Mr. Mayor. All we'd need to seal this sweet deal is for the city and state to give us a few (ahem) 'incentives' to locate here—like, say, a truckload of cash, 40 acres of land, some new buildings and roads, free water and electricity, and an exemption from property taxes. Oh, and by the way, the governor and the mayor up in Recessionville, Ohio, already are promising us all this plus they say they'll personally wash our cars for us once a week if we locate there. But we like the climate and cheap workforce here, so what say y'all come up with a package that makes our hearts go pitty-pat?"

Incredibly, not only does this corporate come-on work, but publicity-seeking politicians all across the country are crawling over each other to be the one who throws the most public money at these hustlers. . . .

Obviously, the public purse (which is already so strained that most states and cities aren't meeting basic needs in education, health care, infrastructure repair, etc.) should not be tapped to play this game, diverting huge sums of taxpayer dollars to some of the richest corporations on the globe. The giants certainly don't need the money, but here's the carefully kept secret that exposes the incentive game as one of the biggest scams ever pulled: *Corporations do not base their expansion decisions on state and local giveaways.* . . .

Paul O'Neill, former CEO of Alcoa and George W's first treasury secretary, put it bluntly: "As a businessman, I never made a decision based on the tax code. . . . If you are giving money away, I will take it. If you want to give me inducements for something I am going to do anyway, I will take it. But good business people do not do things because of inducements." . . .

The corporate executives and political henchmen who pull off these heists should have to wear ski masks at their press conferences, but instead they hide behind one little word that they shout incessantly and at full volume: JOBS!!! The invariable claim is that this shoveling of public money into corporate coffers is all about helping the working stiffs by bringing a mother lode of new jobs to town.

This is where the scam turns sordid. . . .

In Kentucky, state officials bestowed tax credits worth $132 million on Willamette Industries as an incentive to expand its paper mill in Hawesville. Under the terms of the deal, the corporation had to create additional jobs. How many? Fifteen. That's $8.8 million per job! A Willamette exec says that they actually hired 105 new workers. Swell. That brings it down to $1.26 million per job.

In 2003, Boeing set off a bidding frenzy when it announced it would build a $500-million factory somewhere. Forty cities and states came bearing sweet packages to try to "win" the 1,500 jobs Boeing was promising. The top bid came from Seattle, where the city and state offered $3.2 *billion* in subsidies. Hello! That's more than $2 million for each job. Even spread over the 20-year term of the deal, taxpayers were putting up $100,000 a year per job—way more than any worker would ever get.

MLT, a subsidiary of Northwest Airlines, announced in 1999 that it would open a 600-job call center in Minot, North Dakota, after accepting $10.7 million in subsidies. Barely two years later, after having consumed the subsidy (even though it had employed only 400 people), MLT said it was cutting 20 percent of its Minot workforce. A state audit found that officials had no documentation of how many jobs MLT actually created. It was later learned that jobs subsidized by Minot's economic incentive scheme paid 25 percent less than the average wage in the area. When the public was given a chance to extend the subsidy program, 68 percent of Minot voters rejected it. . . .

Study after study has been done on these giveaways, and the overwhelming conclusion is that they create neither jobs nor economic growth, with the clear winner being the corporations that pocket the one tangible benefit that incentive programs deliver: taxpayer cash.

Youth's Future: Protests Against Changes in French Labor Laws

While workers around the world live daily with downsizing and outsourcing, most workers in France are protected from such fates by the country's highly protective labor laws. A proposed revision of these laws sent more than a million young people and union workers into the streets in March and April of 2006. Students took over universities, blocked trains, and marched in the streets.

Outside France, commentators had little sympathy for the demonstrators, who sought to prevent a loosening of the labor laws that would allow employers to fire young workers without cause during the first two years of their employment. Writers in the *New York Times* and the *Economist* argued that the changes would allow France to better compete in a global economy and to drive growth in its lackluster gross domestic product, thereby improving employment prospects for all.

Within France, labor unions and students argued that the new law represented the entry of "savage" capitalism into France, and that the law would undermine employment security for both older workers and younger workers. Older workers might face discrimination from employers who would prefer the flexibility of hiring young workers that they could jettison in the event of a business downturn. Younger workers might face a roller coaster of just-under-two-year-long jobs. The protests also tapped into an undercurrent of youth anger about high unemployment and perceived lack of opportunity. The protests drove French president Jacques Chirac to propose cutting the time of vulnerability back from two years to one, and eventually to withdraw the proposal altogether. Here in a March 16, 2006, protest in Toulouse a young woman raises her fist, echoing the banner showing a policeman raising a bludgeon behind her.

CHAPTER 7
ENVIRONMENTAL CONSERVATION

INTRODUCTION

In its fundamental principles, environmental protest is an extension of civil rights activism. It usually addresses the fundamental right of individuals to a healthy environment or expands individual rights to include protection for animals or even plants.

Environmental protest began as an American phenomenon. Ideas such as national parks, national standards for environmental review, Earth Day, and endangered-species protection laws all originated in the United States and have been widely imitated. The concept of national parks, for example, began with the efforts of a few people to protect Yosemite and Yellowstone parks in California and Wyoming, but have since inspired the conservation of a billion acres of land around the world.

The roots of environmental protest include Henry David Thoreau's 1854 book *Walden* and George Perkins Marsh's 1864 book *Man and Nature*, though neither work was a work of protest itself. Marsh's text was more biology than polemic. It showed how the nation's bountiful forests could, if left unprotected, be degraded to desert. *Man and Nature* sold more than 100,000 copies and was the first bestseller to call attention to environmental issues. Thoreau, in contrast, was unable to sell the three thousand copies of *Walden* he had printed, but the themes of frugality and reliance on nature that he developed have helped inspire protest of overconsumption and isolation from nature for more than 150 years.

Today, environmental protest has grown in subtlety, complexity, and geographic scope. Issues of poverty and economic justice are interwoven with environmental issues, and environmental threats are no longer as visually compelling or as localized as the pollution of the Cuyahoga River in Ohio, which caught fire repeatedly in the mid-twentieth century. (The burning river helped inspire the first Earth Day and the Clean Water Act.)

World leaders now debate appropriate ways to stimulate the global economy and to protect the global climate from carbon-dioxide emissions. Scientists estimate the percentage of solar radiation reaching the earth that is being captured for human use and whether what remains can sustain natural ecosystems. Protesters now seek to influence the actions of multinational corporations, as well as those of governments.

Meanwhile, continued high rates of consumption by industrial nations, growing per capita consumption in developing nations, and worldwide population growth have led to increased demand for clean air, clean water, and open space and to increased protest when these essentials are lost. Harvard biologist E. O. Wilson has noted that for everyone in the world to have the same standard of living as Americans, we would require approximately four earths. But as environmental protesters around the world have pointed out, we only have one.

The American Forests
John Muir

John Muir was perhaps the strongest voice for the American wilderness in the nation's first century and a half of existence. Muir brought Yosemite to the attention of the public and is widely considered responsible for its designation in 1890 as our second national park. In 1892, he founded the Sierra Club to help protect the resources of California's mountains. By 1897 Muir realized that national parks alone would not protect America's forests, and in an article from the *Atlantic*, excerpted here, he argued for wise stewardship of the rest of the 70 million acres of forestland then owned by the federal government.

Muir was an early advocate for setting aside land not only for commercial use but also to protect soil, watersheds, wildlife, and spiritual values. Not until passage of the Wilderness Act in 1964 was Muir's plea answered. Today there are nearly 106 million acres of designated wilderness in the United States. Muir's protest envisioned government as the protector of the weak, presaging themes that would characterize environmental, economic, and civil rights protests throughout much of the twentieth century.

THE AXE AND SAW are insanely busy, chips are flying thick as snowflakes, and every summer thousands of acres of priceless forests, with their underbrush, soil, springs, climate, scenery, and religion, are vanishing away in clouds of smoke, while, except in the national parks, not one forest guard is employed.

All sorts of local laws and regulations have been tried and found wanting, and the costly lessons of our own experience, as well as that of every civilized nation, show conclusively that the fate of the remnant of our forests is in the hands of the federal government, and that if the remnant is to be saved at all, it must be saved quickly.

Any fool can destroy trees. They cannot run away; and if they could, they would still be destroyed,—chased and hunted down as long as fun or a dollar could be got out of their bark hides, branching horns, or magnificent bole backbones. Few that fell trees plant them; nor would planting avail much towards getting back anything like the noble primeval forests. During a man's life only saplings can be grown, in the place of the old trees—tens of centuries old—that have been destroyed. It took more than three thousand years to make some of the trees in these Western woods,—trees that are still standing in perfect strength and beauty, waving and singing in the mighty forests of the Sierra. Through all the wonderful, eventful centuries since Christ's time—and long before that—God has cared for these trees, saved them from drought, disease, avalanches, and a thousand straining, leveling tempests and floods; but he cannot save them from fools,—only Uncle Sam can do that.

Yosemite Against Corporation Greed
I. R. Branson

In the wake of the 1906 San Francisco earthquake and accompanying fire, the city looked for reliable supplies of fresh water. It set its sights on Hetch Hetchy, a remote but spectacularly beautiful valley in Yosemite National Park. When the proposal to dam Hetch Hetchy came to light in 1908, it set off what may well have been the first national debate over land development versus preservation. The debate centered on two issues: should such a beautiful valley be turned into a reservoir, and should development and exclusive franchisement of rights be allowed in a national park? John Muir and the Sierra Club, joined in their outrage by activists across the country, led the unsuccessful fight to preserve Hetch Hetchy. Nebraska firebrand I. R. Branson entered the fray early, publishing this pamphlet in 1909. Excerpts from part I of the pamphlet are included here.

In 1913, a sharply divided Congress authorized the damming of the Hetch Hetchy Valley. Today the valley and its reservoir provide water to 2.4 million residents of the San Francisco Bay area, but in 2005 the State of California began to study the feasibility of replacing the water and electricity supplied by the reservoir, removing the dam, and restoring the valley.

SHALL SAN FRANCISCO be allowed to kidnap Yosemite's great Sister—HETCH-HETCHY—from the American People, together with the "Grand Canyon" of the Tuolumne River, the Tuolumne Meadows, and with them usurp Half of the Yosemite National Park?

Will the great American Press and the People's Patriotism, Congressmen and Senators, the President and his Cabinet come NOW to the Rescue against the dark threat of AVARICE already pending in Congress over that Park?

It is to be deeply regretted that there should be a burning necessity, or any necessity whatever, for such an article as the following; but the necessity is here, for a burning National question is already actually upon us, and one that is more serious than many have dreamed, for it involves the very principle and soul of wrong, as well as most vicious Precedent, directly against the life of Yosemite, and, indirectly, against all our National Parks, and ought to arouse every

American citizen at once to just indignation in a universal campaign of fight and protest against the irretrievable evil and National injury it contemplates.

I refer to the insidious and far reaching design which has at last reached the form of a Bill which San Francisco, after ten years of persistent, (shall we say, covetous audacity?), has succeeded in worming into Congress;—a Bill wherein San Francisco, for the trifling consideration of an ordinary, insignificant "piece of mountain grazing land in the Sierras," called "Hog Ranch," and a trifle other, which she proposes to deed as a dead mule to the Government, seeks, by trampling the already-existing Congressional Statutes under foot, to take from all the people and all posterity, for her own individual use and profit, more than half of the incomparable Yosemite National Park to be usurped by her for her Water Supply and Electric Power System.

The greater half that she is after includes the grand and beautiful Hetch-Hetchy Valley about 12 miles, in a straight line by Government Survey, North and a little West of Yosemite Valley, and through which flows the Tuolumne River, to be fenced up and dammed up, for all time, for a reservoir;—and, just above Hetch-Hetchy and opening into it, the Tuolumne "Grand Canyon" 22 miles long, enclosed in precipitous walls from 1000 to 1200 feet high and wonderfully grand, where the river, not less than 100 feet wide, descends through the gorge 4650 feet in 22 miles in magnificent cascades and water-falls forming, not only some of the most splendid scenery of the world, but also an inexhaustible resource of water and electric power estimated worth "over 40 Millions of Dollars." Nay! instead, to one who knows the situation, there can be no doubt that over a Hundred Millions of Dollars' worth of actual power is there. Yea! so remarkable is the stupendous force of that great 100 foot-wide river descending through the Canyon from a height every mile over 40 feet higher than Niagara for 22 miles, that, reckoning its earning power and value for a century alone, a Hundred Millions of Dollars would still not pay for or measure its remarkable worth. It is the grabbing, seizing, usurping of this enormous water and electric power that San Francisco is so shamelessly after.

And also, to be included in the grant, at the head of this "Grand Canyon," are the great Tuolumne Meadows, about 12 miles in a straight line North East of Yosemite Valley, and through which flows the river, and which are encircled by beautiful groves of mountain forest, and are the best and most available tourist Camping grounds to be had in the whole Park, or, indeed, in the middle Sierras: And this camping room, so handy to Yosemite Valley, is now most urgently needed, because Yosemite is already "crowded to its capacity every summer with campers."

Furthermore, the Tuolumne Meadows afford the best low-altitude, easy-gained point of vantage for one of the most superb mountain views in the United States, embracing the magnificent Mount Dana, Mt. McClure, Mt. Lyell and a world of other peaks with their great snow-caps and flanking glaciers in a towering and far stretching panorama. These great Meadows, with their splendid prospect of mountains, and still more valuable camping grounds, are also designed by San Francisco's scheme to be forever fenced up and dammed up into an immense water hole reservoir. And in addition to the usurpation of all this grand and valuable central group of territory and attractions, would still further be included the vast watersheds of all the mountains surrounding them, where no tourist would be allowed to camp lest the reservoirs, necessarily always guarded by police, should be polluted by the waters from these slopes if campers were allowed, thereby usurping in the scheme the remarkable scope of "more than 500 square miles, or more than half of the whole Yosemite National Park." . . .

. . . And yet, in spite of their sublimity and beauty, in spite of their priceless supplemental value to Yosemite Valley itself, we are confronted with the preposterously astounding demand by San Francisco, through her now pending Bill in Congress, to let her usurp them bodily, destroy their scenery, make the grand and beautiful Hetch-Hetchy and the indispensibly valuable Tuolumne Meadows Camping grounds into reservoir water holes, usurp over 500 square miles, or more than half of the whole Park itself, and seize and exploit the over 100 Millions of Dollars' worth of water and electric power to her self-enrichment, and shut out the whole world and all the unborn millions to come from their use and enjoyment; forever, world without end.

The very thought is outrageous, and an outrageous blot upon the name of the City of the Golden Gate. But it would be a still greater disgrace to the whole Nation and to Congress itself were she authorized legally to carry out her design by being granted the right to thus injure all her sister cities and towns of her own State, the whole American people and all humanity.

Citizens, men and women, this is not only the business of the Public in general, it is your business individually, now;—it is the business of every town and city of the whole country with the cooperation of all their Commercial Clubs and every other working organization;—it is the business of every State and its Governor and leading Officials, and all headed by the great State of California, herself, who has more at stake and hazard financially than all the other States east of the Rocky Mountains;—it is the business of all these and the universal commonwealth of America to rise up now to action with every available means and influence and, without delay, to send petitions, and urging, burning letters by the hundreds of thousands from all parts of the Union to all their Congressmen, Senators, the President and his Cabinet, praying them all as the great representatives, not of San Francisco, but of the great brotherhood of the United States to stand true and overwhelmingly against this dark menace of impending wrong threatening the rights of the whole Nation, and all the world, and all posterity.

Surely the great undivided Press of all America, yea! of all the world, will jointly raise such an unanimous and powerful voice against this Corporation free-booter favoritism that the Bill will have been practically overwhelmingly defeated before it can show its ugly head at the next meeting of Congress.

And not only to defeat this Bill, but to urge the enactment of such legislation as will forestall and prevent any and all future attempts to secure any grant of franchise whatsoever in any of our National Parks.

But, Americans! NOW is the time to defeat the Bill before next Winter's Congress meets, for after the meeting of Congress it would be too late, for then San Francisco, unhindered, would have all her wire-pulling and log-rolling done. Whatever is to be done to defeat the Bill must be done NOW or never.

Sincerely your fellow citizen,

I. R. BRANSON,

Aurora, Nebraska.

Everglades: River of Grass

Marjorie Stoneman Douglas

In 1928, a great hurricane struck south Florida, causing vast Lake Okeechobee to overflow its banks, dealing $100 million dollars of damage to the region's economy and killing thousands of people. In response Congress in 1930 authorized construction of the 143-mile-long Herbert Hoover dike system, which included a 68-mile-long dike across the south end of Lake Okeechobee. But this well-intentioned project, combined with hundreds of miles of drainage canals installed to make the lands around the lake arable, had an unfortunate side effect.

The dike and the drainage canals cut off the flow of water to the widest river in the world, diverting the water instead out to sea. Without the flow of water, the Florida Everglades—the River of Grass, ancestral home of the Seminole Indians—dried and began to burn. The same diversions starved the aquifers that supplied (and still supply today) drinking water for the cities on the east and west coasts of Florida. If water levels in the aquifer dropped enough, salt water would flow in from the sea, making the water less potable.

Public outrage over the fires and damage to the Everglade's unique ecosystem created political will for the formation of the Everglades National Park, as documented in this selection from Marjorie Stoneman Douglas's famous paean to this vast swamp—Everglades: River of Grass, published in 1947.

But the designation did not immediately solve the water problem. During the 1950s the threat of inappropriate water management continued and perhaps even grew worse with the construction of new canals and diversions.

Stoneman went on to found Friends of the Everglades in 1969, and to become one of the most vocal defenders of the park and its environs. In 2000, two years after Douglas's death, President Bill Clinton signed the Everglades Restoration Act to bring the flow of clean water back to this grandest of our nation's wetlands.

THE INDIANS STARED at the smoke, the creeping fires, with the stoic faces of fatalism. This was the end of their world.

But the white man, in all his teeming variety, men of the farms and the

Glades, men of the cities and of the sea, whose inertia and pigheadedness, greed and willfulness had caused all this, as if for the first time seeing what he had done, now, when it was almost too late, the white man was aroused. For the first time in South Florida since the earliest floods, there were mass meetings and protests, editorials, petitions, letters, and excited talk. Thousands, choking in acrid smoke saw for the first time what the drainage of the Glades had brought to pass. . . .

It was a long hot fiery summer, the smoke from the Glades blowing, mosquitoes from the mud and the stagnant last of the pools, and by night the far-off flames. The fires stopped only where there was nothing left to burn, or were checked by the fall rains. Thousands of acres of organic soils were utterly destroyed.

In Dade County people who had really become aroused, thoughtful people, residents and public officials worried at last about the water supply, began to see that it was never just a local problem, to be settled in makeshift bits and pieces. The Everglades were one thing, one vast unified harmonious whole, in which the old subtle balance, which had been destroyed, must somehow be replaced, if the nature of this whole region and the life of the coastal cities were to be saved.

There were two things, and two things only, that gave any hope at all in this eleventh hour of fire and salt. The first was the large number of aroused citizens all over this area, east coast and west, who were now angrily insisting that something constructive must be done, and fast.

An aroused public opinion would have been ineffective if for the first time in the history of the Glades an exact, scientific and complete study had not already been in the making. The University of Florida Experiment Station at Belle Glade, in 1933, had begun its analysis of the varying soils. . . . Even as the fires began, therefore, the engineers worked their way throughout the Glades, in air boats and Glades buggies and tractors and navy "weasels," putting down test wells, studying the rock, the water, the soil, the effects of drainage, and the hope of water control and conservation.

So then at last, with the lands drying and the smoke still drifting from the fires eating at the valuable muck, the problem of the Everglades was seen whole. . . .

It was shown that the productivity of the Everglades soil varied with the distance south from the lake. Its usefulness depended on the depth over the rock of the black saw-grass muck and the dark-brown peaty mucks. . . . If the muck was deeper than five feet they were capable of a high productivity, but only with expensive and continuous operations of drainage and water control and fertilization and pest control. . . .

South of all that, where the muck is less than five feet deep, crops can be grown only under extreme, and therefore dangerous, drainage. . . . But many of these useless lands, it was strongly recommended, should be reconverted into wide natural reservoirs of fresh water, which would help combat salt intrusion and raise the surrounding water tables and no doubt help equalize the temperature. . . .

South still, the scientists recommended that the Glades islands and hammocks and ridges should be left to the tropical hardwoods that clothed them. . . .

The whole lower area of the Everglades, from some distance north of the Tamiami Trail to the warm shallows of Florida Bay and the white beaches of Cape Sable and vast mangrove country is totally unfit for cultivation. It is the last refuge for the roseate spoonbill and the vast flocks of other Everglades birds, of the manatees, the crocodiles and the alligators, of the deer, the raccoon and the otter. . . .

In 1928 Mr. Ernest F. Coe, a landscape architect who was fascinated by the strange beauty of this wilderness, conceived the idea that it should be made a national park. He fought almost single-handed, through years of depression and of disinterest, to gain public backing. His tall, spare figure, his suave voice, the absent gaze of his blue eyes as he talked and wrote and argued and lectured and, as he said, "made a nuisance of himself," was the very figure of a man obsessed. He was laughed at and he laughed at himself. He sacrificed his career to keep the hope of the park going.

The National Park Service approved of the idea. The problem was that the land must be given outright by the state of Florida to the Park Service before it could become a National Park. . . .

It was not until April, 1946, that governor Millard Caldwell set up an Everglades National Park Commission, an official state agency, with the right to acquire land for the park. . . .

The Everglades National Park is at last a reality. It will save the lower Glades and the Cape Sable beaches. It will be the largest national park in the United States. . . . It will be the only national park in which the wild-life, the crocodiles, the trees, the orchids, will be more important than the sheer geology of the country. . . .

Perhaps even in this last hour, in a new relation of usefulness and beauty, the vast, magnificent, subtle and unique region of the Everglades may not be utterly lost.

A Sand County Almanac
Aldo Leopold

In the middle of the twentieth century, writer Aldo Leopold changed the debate about the environment from what constituted the best use of lands to what was right. By framing environmental issues as moral and ethical dilemmas, he encouraged millions of people to have confidence in their own perceptions of right and wrong with respect to the environment. His essays covered the importance of wilderness, the role of wolves in controlling deer and thereby preserving mountains, and the quality of land in shaping history. Perhaps most presciently, Leopold called for extending our concept of rights beyond humans to land, soil, and rivers. His insight opened the door to animal rights movements and to arguments about the legal standing of nonhumans and even inanimate objects. Leopold spelled out these ideas in this excerpt from his 1949 book *A Sand County Almanac*.

WHEN GOD-LIKE ODYSSEUS returned from the wars in Troy, he hanged all on one rope a dozen slave-girls of his household whom he suspected of misbehavior during his absence.

This hanging involved no question of propriety. The girls were property. The disposal of property was then, as now, a matter of expediency, not of right and wrong.

Concepts of right and wrong were not lacking from Odysseus' Greece: witness the fidelity of his wife through the long years before at last his black-prowed galleys clove the wine-dark seas for home. The ethical structure of that day covered wives, but had not yet been extended to human chattels. During the three thousand years which have since elapsed, ethical criteria have been extended to many fields of conduct, with corresponding shrinkages in those judged by expediency only.

The Ethical Sequence

This extension of ethics, so far studied only by philosophers, is actually a process in ecological evolution. Its sequences may be described in ecological as well as in philosophical terms. An ethic, ecologically, is a limitation on freedom of action in the struggle for existence. An ethic, philosophically, is a differentiation of social from anti-social conduct. These are two definitions of one thing. The thing has its origin in the tendency of interdependent individuals or groups to evolve modes of co-operation. The ecologist calls these symbioses. Politics and economics are advanced symbioses in which the original free-for-all competition has been replaced, in part, by co-operative mechanisms with an ethical content.

The complexity of co-operative mechanisms has increased with population density, and with the efficiency of tools. It was simpler, for example, to define the anti-social uses of sticks and stones in the days of the mastodons than of bullets and billboards in the age of motors.

The first ethics dealt with the relation between individuals; the Mosaic Decalogue is an example. Later accretions dealt with the relation between the individual and society. The Golden Rule tries to integrate the individual to society; democracy to integrate social organization to the individual.

There is as yet no ethic dealing with man's relation to land and to the animals and plants which grow upon it. Land, like Odysseus' slave-girls, is still property. The land-relation is still strictly economic, entailing privileges but not obligations.

The extension of ethics to this third element in human environment is, if I read the evidence correctly, an evolutionary possibility and an ecological necessity. It is the third step in a sequence. The first two have already been taken.

Individual thinkers since the days of Ezekiel and Isaiah have asserted that the despoliation of land is not only inexpedient but wrong. Society, however, has not yet affirmed their belief. I regard the present conservation movement as the embryo of such an affirmation. . . .

The Community Concept

All ethics so far evolved rest upon a single premise: that the individual is a member of a community of interdependent parts. His instincts prompt him to compete for his place in the community, but his ethics prompt him also to co-operate (perhaps in order that there may be a place to compete for).

The land ethic simply enlarges the boundaries of the community to include soils, waters, plants, and animals, or collectively: the land.

This sounds simple: do we not already sing our love for and obligation to the land of the free and the home of the brave? Yes, but just what and whom do we love? Certainly not the soil, which we are sending helter-skelter downriver. Certainly not the waters, which we assume have no function except to turn turbines, float barges, and carry off sewage. Certainly not the plants, of which we exterminate whole communities without batting an eye. Certainly not the animals, of which we have already extirpated many of the largest and most beautiful species. A land ethic of course cannot prevent the alteration, management, and use of these "resources," but it does affirm their right to continued existence, and, at least in spots, their continued existence in a natural state.

In short, a land ethic changes the role of *Homo sapiens* from conqueror of the land-community to plain member and citizen of it. It implies respect for his fellow-members, and also respect for the community as such. . . .

The Outlook

It is inconceivable to me that an ethical relation to land can exist without love, respect, and admiration for land, and a high regard for its value. By value, I of course mean something far broader than mere economic value; I mean value in the philosophical sense.

Perhaps the most serious obstacle impeding the evolution of a land ethic is the fact that our educational and economic system is headed away from, rather than toward, an intense consciousness of land. Your true modern is separated from the land by many middlemen, and by innumerable physical gadgets. He has no vital relation to it; to him it is the space between cities on which crops grow. Turn him loose for a day on the land, and if the spot does not happen to be a golf links or a "scenic" area, he is bored stiff. If crops could be raised by hydroponics, instead of farming, it would suit him very well. Synthetic substitutes for wood, leather, wool, and other natural land products suit him better than the originals. In short, land is something he has "outgrown.". . .

"Wilderness Letter" from *The Sound of Mountain Water*

Wallace Stegner

In 1958, President Dwight D. Eisenhower appointed a commission to review the nation's outdoor recreation needs through the year 2000. Among the many comments and suggestions received was the letter excerpted here from Wallace Stegner, already a noted Western novelist and essayist. Most of the letters sent to the commission are collecting dust in file cabinets, but Stegner's letter took on a life of its own. Secretary of Interior Stewart Udall cited it at a conference in San Francisco even before the Outdoor Recreation Resources Review Commission's report was published; the Sierra Club published the letter in the proceedings of that conference; and *The Washington Post* also published it. Stegner himself included it in his book *The Sound of Mountain Water*. It later spread around the world and helped inspire African conservation efforts.

DEAR MR. PESONEN:

I believe that you are working on the wilderness portion of the Outdoor Recreation Resources Review Commission's report. If I may, I should like to urge some arguments for wilderness preservation that involve recreation, as it is ordinarily conceived, hardly at all. Hunting, fishing, hiking, mountain-climbing, camping, photography, and the enjoyment of natural scenery will all, surely, figure in your report. So will the wilderness as a genetic reserve, a scientific yardstick by which we may measure the world in its natural balance against the world in its man-made imbalance. What I want to speak for is not so much the wilderness uses, valuable as those are, but the wilderness *idea*. . . .

I want to speak for the wilderness idea as something that has helped form our character and that has certainly shaped our history as a people. . . .

Something will have gone out of us as a people if we ever let the remaining wilderness be destroyed; if we permit the last virgin forests to be turned into comic books and plastic cigarette cases; if we drive the few remaining members of the wild species into zoos or to extinction; if we pollute the last clear air and dirty the last clean streams and push our paved roads through the last of the silence, so that never again will Americans be free in their own country from the noise, the exhausts, the stinks of human and automotive waste. And so that never again can we have the chance to see ourselves single, separate, vertical and individual in the world, part of the environment of trees and rocks and soil, brother to the other animals, part of the natural world and competent to belong in it. Without any remaining wilderness we are committed wholly, without chance for even momentary reflection and rest, to a headlong drive into our technological termite-life, the Brave New World of a completely man-controlled environment. We need wilderness preserved—as much of it as is still left, and as many kinds—because it was the challenge against which our character as a people was formed. The reminder and the reassurance that it is still there is good for our spiritual health even if we never once in ten years set foot in it. It is good for us when we are young, because of the incomparable sanity it can bring briefly, as vacation and rest, into our insane lives. It is important to us when we are old simply because it is there—important, that is, simply as an idea. . . .

As a novelist, I may perhaps be forgiven for taking literature as a reflection, indirect but profoundly true, of our national consciousness. And our literature, as perhaps you are aware, is sick, embittered, losing its mind, losing its faith. Our novelists are the declared enemies of their society. There has hardly been a serious or important novel in this century that did not repudiate in part or in whole American technological culture for its commercialism, its vulgarity, and the way in which it has dirtied a clean continent and a clean dream. I do not expect that the preservation of our remaining wilderness is going to cure this condition. But the mere example that we can as a nation apply some other criteria than commercial and exploitative considerations would be heartening to many Americans, novelists or otherwise. We need to demonstrate our acceptance of the natural world, including ourselves; we need the spiritual refreshment that being natural can produce. And one of the best places for us to get that is in the wilderness where the fun houses, the bulldozers, and the pavement of our civilization are shut out. . . .

It seems to me significant that the distinct downturn in our literature from hope to bitterness took place almost at the precise time when the frontier officially came to an end, in 1890, and when the American way of life had begun to turn strongly urban and industrial. The more urban it has become, and the more frantic with technological change, the sicker and more embittered our literature, and I believe our people, have become. For myself, I grew up on the empty plains of Saskatchewan and Montana and in the mountains of Utah, and I put a very high valuation on what those places gave me. And if I had not been able to periodically renew myself in the mountains and deserts of western America I would be very nearly bughouse. Even when I can't get to the back country, the thought of the colored deserts of southern Utah, or the reassurance that there are still stretches of prairies where the world can be instantaneously perceived as disk and bowl, and where the little but intensely important human being is exposed to the five directions of the thirty-six winds, is a positive consolation. The idea alone can sustain me. But as the wilderness areas are progressively exploited or "improved," as the jeeps and bulldozers of uranium prospectors scar up the deserts and the roads are cut into the alpine timberlands, and as the remnants of the unspoiled and natural world are progressively eroded, every such loss is a little death in me. In us.

I am not moved by the argument that those wilderness areas which have already been exposed to grazing or mining are already deflowered, and so might as well be "harvested." . . . Better a wounded wilderness than none at all. . . .

. . . Just as a sample, let me suggest the Robbers' Roost country in Wayne County, Utah, near the Capitol Reef National Monument. . . . It is a lovely and terrible wilderness, such a wilderness as Christ and the prophets went out into; harshly and beautifully colored, broken and worn until its bones are exposed, its great sky without a smudge of taint from Technocracy, and in hidden corners and pockets under its cliffs the sudden poetry of springs. Save a piece of country like that intact, and it does not matter in the slightest that only a few people every year will go into it. That is precisely its value. Roads would be a desecration, crowds would ruin it. But those who haven't the strength or youth to go into it and live can simply sit and look. They can look two hundred miles, clear into Colorado; and looking down over the cliffs and canyons of the San Rafael Swell and the Robbers' Roost they can also look as deeply into themselves as anywhere I know. And if they can't even get to the places on the Aquarius Plateau where the present roads will carry them, they can simply contemplate the *idea*, take pleasure in the fact that such a timeless and uncontrolled part of earth is still there.

These are some of the things wilderness can do for us. That is the reason we need to put into effect, for its preservation, some other principle than the principles of exploitation or "usefulness" or even recreation. We simply need that wild country available to us, even if we never do more than drive to its edge and look in. For it can be a means of reassuring ourselves of our sanity as creatures, a part of the geography of hope.

Very sincerely yours,
Wallace Stegner

Silent Spring
Rachel Carson

Rachel Carson's *Silent Spring* is both a detailed work of science and a protest against the poisoning of our atmosphere, water, and land by pesticides. Carson explored the idea of writing an article on the dangers of DDT as early as 1945, and tried to convince E. B. White, a writer for *The New Yorker*, to cover the issue in the late 1950s. Eventually she took it on herself, writing a best-selling book that was excerpted as a three-part series in *The New Yorker*. *Silent Spring* sold 40,000 advance copies before its publication in the fall of 1962 and evoked a storm of public outrage. President John F. Kennedy appointed a commission to study the dangers of pesticides, congressional hearings were held, and CBS ran a documentary based on the book. By the end of 1962, some forty bills to regulate pesticides had been introduced in various states. Largely because of the public outrage that *Silent Spring* evoked, the United States began federal regulation of pesticides for the first time, weighing in on which chemicals would be allowed (it banned DDT in 1972) and how they could be used.

The book owes much of its effectiveness to its opening parable, which calls to mind any small town in the northeastern United States. Carson wove together experiences from many different towns to create a terrifying composite narrative.

Carson's book remains a radical document in at least two ways. First, she called for treating environmental rights much like civil rights. Just as people should be protected from unreasonable search and seizure by the government, so they should be protected from government-endorsed or even government-executed spraying by toxic chemicals. Second, she called not just for moderation in the use of pesticides, but also for a new, more integrative approach to nature and our place within it.

1. A Fable for Tomorrow

There was once a town in the heart of America where all life seemed to live in harmony with its surroundings. The town lay in the midst of a checkerboard of prosperous farms, with fields of grain and hillsides of orchards where, in spring, white clouds of bloom drifted above the green fields. In autumn, oak and maple and birch set up a blaze of color that flamed and flickered across a backdrop of pines. Then foxes barked in the hills and deer silently crossed the fields, half hidden in the mists of the fall mornings.

Along the roads, laurel, viburnum and alder, great ferns and wildflowers delighted the traveler's eye through much of the year. Even in winter the roadsides were places of beauty, where countless birds came to feed on the berries and on the seed heads of the dried weeds rising above the snow. The countryside was, in fact, famous for the abundance and variety of its bird life, and when the flood of migrants was pouring through in spring and fall people traveled from great distances to observe them. Others came to fish the streams, which flowed clear and cold out of the hills and contained shady pools where trout lay. So it had been from the days many years ago when the first settlers raised their houses, sank their wells, and built their barns.

Then a strange blight crept over the area and everything began to change. Some evil spell had settled on the community: mysterious maladies swept the flocks of chickens; the cattle and sheep sickened and died. Everywhere was a shadow of death. The farmers spoke of much illness among their families. In the town the doctors had become more and more puzzled by new kinds of sickness appearing among their patients. There had been several sudden and unexplained deaths, not only among adults but even among children, who would be stricken suddenly while at play and die within a few hours.

There was a strange stillness. The birds, for example—where had they gone? Many people spoke of them, puzzled and disturbed. The feeding stations in the backyards were deserted. The few birds seen anywhere were moribund; they trembled violently and could not fly. It was a spring without voices. On the mornings that had once throbbed with the dawn chorus of robins, catbirds, doves, jays, wrens, and scores of other bird voices there was now no sound; only silence lay over the fields and woods and marsh.

On the farms the hens brooded, but no chicks hatched. The farmers complained that they were unable to raise any pigs—the litters were small and the young survived only a few days. The apple trees were coming into bloom but no bees droned among the blossoms, so there was no pollination and there would be no fruit.

The roadsides, once so attractive, were now lined with browned and withered vegetation as though swept by fire. These, too, were silent, deserted by all living things. Even the streams were now lifeless. Anglers no longer visited them, for all the fish had died.

In the gutters under the eaves and between the shingles of the roofs, a white granular powder still showed a few patches; some weeks before it had fallen like snow upon the roofs and the lawns, the fields and streams.

No witchcraft, no enemy action had silenced the rebirth of new life in this stricken world. The people had done it themselves.

This town does not actually exist, but it might easily have a thousand counterparts in America or elsewhere in the world. I know of no community that has experienced all the misfortunes I describe. Yet every one of these disasters has actually happened somewhere, and many real communities have already suffered a substantial number of them. A grim specter has crept upon us almost unnoticed, and this imagined tragedy may easily become a stark reality we all shall know.

What has already silenced the voices of spring in countless towns in America? This book is an attempt to explain.

2. The Obligation to Endure

. . . It is not my contention that chemical insecticides must never be used. I do contend that we have put poisonous and biologically potent chemicals indiscriminately into the hands of persons largely or wholly ignorant of their potentials for harm. We have subjected enormous numbers of people to contact with these poisons, without their consent and often without their knowledge. If the Bill of Rights contains no guarantee that a citizen shall be secure against lethal poisons distributed either by private individuals or by public officials, it is surely only because our forefathers, despite their considerable wisdom and foresight, could conceive of no such problem.

I contend, furthermore, that we have allowed these chemicals to be used with little or no advance investigation of their effect on soil, water, wildlife, and man himself. Future generations are unlikely to condone our lack of prudent concern for the integrity of the natural world that supports all life.

There is still very limited awareness of the nature of the threat. This is an era of specialists, each of whom sees his own problem and is unaware of or intolerant of the larger frame into which it fits. It is also an era dominated by industry, in which the right to make a dollar at whatever cost is seldom challenged. When the public protests, confronted with some obvious evidence of damaging results of pesticide applications, it is fed little tranquilizing pills of half truth. We urgently need an end to these false assurances, to the sugar coating of unpalatable facts. It is the public that is being asked to assume the risks that the insect controllers calculate. The public must decide whether it wishes to continue on the present road, and it can do so only when in full possession of the facts. In the words of Jean Rostand, "The obligation to endure gives us the right to know."

"What Is Proposed Here Is a Modest Compromise"
Morris K. Udall

From the time Hoover Dam was completed in 1935 until the late 1960s, controversy raged over the damming of the Colorado River and its tributaries. In the 1950s, the Echo Park Dam was proposed for Dinosaur National Monument, and in 1963 dams were proposed for either end of the Grand Canyon. Standing in the way of these dams was David Brower, executive director of the Sierra Club, later dubbed "the Archdruid" by writer John McPhee.

In 1966, Brower and the Sierra Club purchased display ads in the *New York Times* (one of which is shown here) asserting that the proposed dams bracketing the Grand Canyon would flood it, despoiling a national treasure for profit. Running the ads was a bold and innovative stroke for its day, and it clearly illustrated the focus of early environmental protest—create public outrage and use it to influence government action.

The same day the ads appeared, congressman Morris K. Udall (D-AZ), the lead sponsor of the bill to create the two dams, rose before the U.S. House of Representatives to defend the dams and lambaste the Sierra Club. While Udall was generally considered a strong supporter of conservation throughout his career, in this case he spoke in protest against environmentalists and for development.

Udall's stance was unsuccessful. In December 1967, he said, "I must tell you bluntly that no bill providing for a so-called 'Grand Canyon dam' can pass the Congress today." President Lyndon Johnson eventually apologized for ever having supported the proposal. In 1984, the *Washington Post* characterized the dams as "one of the most unpopular development ideas of all time." And the environmental movement, which had lacked organization, structure, and political power going into the fight, came out of it with all three increased.

MR. SPEAKER,

I rise today to express shock and indignation at the dishonest and inflammatory attacks made in Washington and New York newspapers this morning against the Colorado River Basin Project Act, a bill I have introduced along with 36 of my colleagues from Arizona and California. While I have a high regard for many of the people who comprise the Sierra Club, the sponsor of these advertisements, I must say that I have seldom, if ever, seen a more distorted and flagrant hatchet job than this. . . .

These advertisements—there were actually two of them, published in differ-

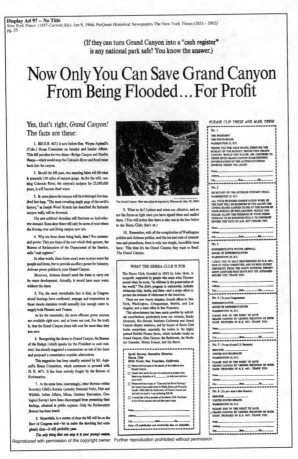

(If they can turn Grand Canyon into a "cash register"
is any national park safe? You know the answer.)

Now Only You Can Save Grand Canyon From Being Flooded... For Profit

ent editions—are so replete with falsehoods and distortions that I should like to deal with them, point by point.

The statement is made that these dams would put an end to the "wild, running Colorado River." Now, I submit that either the river is wild and running now or it isn't. Apparently the Sierra Club is taking the view that it is wild and running. However, I do not believe they can have it both ways. One time they tell you that building a dam upstream of Grand Canyon will regulate the flow and destroy its freeflowing course. Another time they tell you, as they do here, that it is freeflowing now. The trouble with these arguments, of course, is that Glen Canyon Dam already exists upstream of Grand Canyon, and it regulates the flow of the river just as much, or as little, as will Marble Canyon Dam a few miles downstream from it.

Of course, they do not mean just this. They also refer to the "dead water" that will be formed in Grand Canyon. Well, there will be a lake, that is true. It will be the lake behind Hualapai Dam, starting 90 miles downstream of the park and extending for 13 miles along its western boundary. You can call that "dead water," if you like, and the term sounds pretty horrible. However, that lake will enable millions of Americans to see for the first time some of the most remote and inaccessible reaches of the Colorado River and to look up upon thousands of feet of cliffs comprising some of the most awe-inspiring scenery any of us have ever seen. In view of the great interest this area will attain because of the lake, I think a better term for it would be "living water," not "dead water."

A further point. Mr. Brower, with his sweeping language, leaves the impression that the heart of Grand Canyon would lose its "wild, running" nature and become a lake. This is false. The natural river, dropping thousands of feet as it flows through the canyon, will remain untouched for 104 miles, including all of the interior of Grand Canyon National Park, an area larger than the State of Rhode Island. The only effect of any kind on the park would be a backing of the lake for 13 miles along the park's western boundary in an area never seen or visited by the general public, and seldom seen even by hardy outdoorsmen. . . .

I suppose if we had no people in this country, we could leave everything in its pristine purity. We wouldn't turn a spade of earth to build a single highway. We certainly would not build a single dam—on the Colorado, the Columbia, or the Arkansas. But we do have people to serve in this country, and compromises must be made. What is proposed here is a modest compromise that leaves untouched the great heart of the canyon and preserves for all time the geological history revealed in its thousands of feet of depth. . . .

The Energy Crisis: A Radical Solution
Stewart L. Udall

Writing in the first half of 1973—before the Arab-Israeli war in the fall of that year and the subsequent Arab oil embargo, before mile-long gas lines, before hybrid cars or sport utility vehicles—Stewart L. Udall, a former congressman and secretary of the Interior, and brother of Congressman Morris Udall, looked to the future. He argued that expanded imports of Middle Eastern oil would not be a temporary stopgap but a permanent crutch for the U.S. economy. And he suggested that the money sent to the Middle East would have "disastrous" consequences. He called for drastic measures to reduce oil consumption: reduce auto size and horsepower, cut auto travel in half, ration gasoline if necessary, abandon central heating.

The article excerpted here, "The Energy Crisis: A Radical Solution," was published in May 1973 in World Magazine.

THE ENERGY CRISIS in the United States will do more to disrupt and change the American way of life than any other ongoing domestic problem confronting the nation today. Because of it we face, in the near future, severe restrictions in areas of everyday life that Americans now regard as inviolate: automotive travel, including the size and horsepower of our cars; air travel; even home heating. By whatever means necessary, we must end the scandalous waste of our energy resources.

At the root of the energy crisis are our runaway demands for oil, natural gas, and electricity. . . . U.S. energy consumption has doubled every ten to twelve years. . . .

To those of us who are concerned with the energy situation, President Nixon's policies are a severe disappointment. The President is a supporter of the Alaskan pipeline. He acts on the assumption that increases in oil imports from the Middle East will tide us over until we can crank up enough petroleum and coal production to fill the so-called short-term gap. The President and his advisers are technological optimists. They are willing to rely temporarily on Arab oil because they believe a fresh burst of American know-how will provide the fuels we require. Expansion of the GNP is their Holy Grail, and it is almost heretical to suggest to them that consumer demands should be dampened. . . .

If U.S. consumption and production trends are put in a global perspective, the nature of the current crisis is apparent. Annual increases in oil consumption are now so enormous that in the 1970s alone the nations of the world will consume as much oil as was used in the hundred years from 1870 to 1970 (and these projected global demands are scheduled to double again in the 1980s unless consumption patterns are altered). In 1972 the 6 percent of the planet's inhabitants who live in this country used nearly 40 percent of the total energy consumed in the entire world. Two hundred nine million Americans use about as much energy for air conditioning alone as the 800 million mainland Chinese use for all purposes—and Americans waste each year almost as much energy as the Japanese (105 million people) consume annually.

These are alarming statistics, particularly for a nation whose consumption is accelerating so rapidly. They would seem to invite agonizing reappraisals by high-level executives and sharp changes in our energy policies. But our national leaders appear to be inclined to belittle the crisis.

These policies will please the oilmen. They are bullish about further U.S. exploration; they still believe drilling crews will come up with a few "big strikes" that will bail us out. . . .

The electric-power industry is locked into an even more difficult situation. . . . Principally by building larger and larger generating and transmission facilities and by achieving economies of scale, power companies have kept electric costs low and their profits high, and they have managed to stay ahead of the burgeoning demands of their customers.

But the negative side of this scale-up of technology has finally begun to catch up with the industry. Large generating plants mean huge concentrations of pollution, and computerized technical systems have created a mechanical house of cards that can suddenly collapse—as the 1965 Northeast blackout demonstrated. . . .

. . .The trend toward monstrous, "climate controlled" megastructures puts enormous new loads on already strained facilities. . . . To make matters worse, the deterioration of urban environments is causing more and more people to keep the air conditioning on—not just to stay comfortable on the hottest days of summer but to insulate themselves twenty-four hours a day from omnipresent noise and air pollution. . . .

. . .America's cheap energy ride is over. The federal government must call the shots and make the critical decisions. As a start, it must promulgate and enforce a farsighted, all-encompassing national energy policy. Such a policy will not work if it ducks the tough issues or concentrates on increasing the supply of energy without making strenuous efforts to reduce consumer demands.

The high-risk approach of the oilmen—what I call the "dig and drill policy"—is unacceptable. The stakes are too high for us to gamble on emergency programs to fill so-called temporary gaps that are widening daily. The alternative pressed upon us is that we mortgage our energy system to oil imports from a few Middle Eastern countries. This would involve a cost, by 1983, of more than $25 billion a year, which would be disastrous and—given the volatility of some Arab States—politically risky.

Is there no way to avoid these two unpalatable options? Of course there is: by conservation of our energy resources. We cannot come to grips with the real issues until we develop policy guidelines that tie us to an ethic of national thrift, and gear up a huge research effort that will produce environmentally sound solutions to our long-term energy requirements. These policies must embrace: an approach to resources that emphasizes conservation and de-emphasizes consumption; a series of transportation reforms that will save vast quantities of energy; tax and other incentives—rationing if necessary—to reward efficiency and discourage waste; and the development of alternative energy sources that will reduce environmental risks and enable us to achieve energy self-sufficiency.

This search for alternative sources, now in low gear, must receive the kind of support we gave the space program in the 1960s. It should include:

• Exploration of the feasibility of fusion power and the fast breeder nuclear reactor. . . .
• Perfection of technologies that will reduce the enormous waste involved in electric generation and petroleum extraction. . . .
• Development of techniques for storage and use of solar, geothermal, and tidal energy. . . .

- Development of new transportation systems that are efficient and low-polluting. . . .
- Exploration of hydrogen as a versatile gas to replace the fossil fuels. . . .

While these efforts are under way, the paramount task is to mount a wide-ranging energy-conservation program. This program would reduce pressures on all energy industries and make our fuel problems more manageable. Full-scale measures could conceivably reduce fuel demands by as much as 50 percent. We must adopt rational economies now—before millions of Americans experience needless inconvenience and suffering.

In transportation, gasoline consumption should be reduced 50 percent by cutting auto travel in half. It will take time to achieve this objective, but for the present, rationing, car pooling, and/or a doubling of gas prices at the pump would force changes in Americans' extravagant travel habits. Crash efforts to develop cheap, pleasant, convenient mass transit and intercity passenger services would also lead to enormous economies.

The minicar is a must. By imposing stiff taxes on oversized autos (a practice already in effect in some Western European countries) and by forcing reductions in the weight, size, and horsepower, we can double the miles-per-gallon performance of private vehicles. By building fast trains between major urban centers, we can make big reductions in interurban traffic, eliminate short-haul airline service, and thereby achieve major energy savings. . . .

On the residential front. . .[w]e can adopt stiff taxes that will force all energy-wasting appliances off the market. We can provide a safe substitute for gas pilot lights, which use nearly half the gas consumed in homes. And we can even eliminate such extravagances as central heating. Yes, extravagance: I grew up in a house with cold bedrooms and suffered no ill effects, and the same is true for millions of other Americans. . . .

These are only some of the steps that should be taken to depress energy demands that are profligate, or at least unessential. . . . Many of the steps are politically unfeasible at present, but I predict that their implementation will soon become imperative.

In short, the era of "cheap power" is over; a new era of energy thrift must be inaugurated. I am convinced that we can combine conservation and technology to redefine progress—and produce lifestyles that will be leaner and more fulfilling. In the words of Gandhi, our slogan should be: "There can be enough for everybody's need, but not enough for everybody's greed."

The Spirit of the First Earth Day

Jack Lewis

No protest in history has ever exceeded the first Earth Day for sheer number of participants. It is estimated that 20 million Americans turned out to honor the day. Most remarkable of all, this massive protest was largely self-organizing and cut across broad political and cultural spectrums. Senators, congressmen, and mayors from both parties spoke at rallies across the nation. Corporate America rushed to jump on board.

In the wake of Earth Day, Congress passed and President Richard M. Nixon signed a plethora of environmental laws, many of which we take for granted today. These included the Clean Air Act, key pieces of the Clean Water Act, toxic waste cleanup laws, the Federal Environmental Pesticide Control Act, the Endangered Species Act, and the Safe Drinking Water Act. Today, some thirty-five years later, schools and universities across the country still honor April 22 as Earth Day, but the sense of immediate danger that imbued 1970's Earth Day with such power has been lost.

This excerpt is drawn from a 1990 account of the first Earth Day in the *EPA Journal* that commemorated the twentieth anniversary of the event. It was written by *EPA Journal* assistant editor Jack Lewis. The journal has since been discontinued.

IN THE WANING MONTHS of the 1960s, environmental problems were proliferating like a many-headed hydra, a monster no one could understand let alone tame or slay. Rampant air pollution was linked to disease and death in New York, Los Angeles, and elsewhere as noxious fumes, spewed out by cars and factories, made city life less and less bearable. In the wake of Rachel Carson's 1962 best-seller, *Silent Spring*, there was widespread concern over large-scale use of pesticides, often near densely populated communities. In addition, huge fish kills were reported on the Great Lakes, and the media carried the news that Lake Erie, one of America's largest bodies of fresh water, was in its death throes. Ohio had another jolt when Cleveland's Cuyahoga River, an artery inundated with oil and toxic chemicals, burst into flames by spontaneous combustion. . . .

One prominent politician, Gaylord Nelson, then Senator from Wisconsin, had been frustrated throughout the 1960s by the fact that only a "handful" of his Congressional colleagues had any interest in environmental issues. On the other hand, during his travels across the United States, he had been greatly impressed by the dedication and the expertise of the many student and citizen volunteers who were trying to solve pollution problems in their communities.

It was on one such trip, in August 1969, that Nelson came up with a strategy for bridging the gap separating grassroots activists from Congress and the general public. While en route to an environmental speech in Berkeley, California, the Senator was leafing through a copy of *Ramparts* magazine, when an article about anti-war teach-ins caught his eye. It occurred to him that the teach-in concept might work equally well in raising public awareness of environmental issues.

In September, in a ground-breaking speech in Seattle, Senator Nelson announced the concept of the teach-in and received coverage in *Time* and *Newsweek* and on the front page of the *New York Times*. Several weeks later, at his office on Capitol Hill, he incorporated a non-profit, non-partisan organization called Environmental Teach-In, Inc. He announced that it was to be headed by a steering committee consisting of himself, Pete McCloskey, a Congressman from California, and Sidney Howe, then the President of The Conservation Foundation.

The main purpose of the new organization, he declared, was to lay the groundwork for a major nationwide series of teach-ins on the environment early in 1970. The purpose of the teach-ins was, in Nelson's words, to "force the issue [of the environment] into the political dialogue of the country." Very quickly, Environmental Teach-In received pledges from the Senator himself ($15,000), from the United Auto Workers and the AFL-CIO ($2,000 each), as well as from The Conservation Foundation ($25,000) and other organizations.

Early in December, Senator Nelson selected a 25-year-old named Denis Hayes, the dynamic former President of the Stanford student body, as national coordinator. Hayes, postponing plans to enter Harvard Law School, immediately set to work making plans for the inaugural Earth Day.

Hampered from the start by an extremely limited budget (approximately $190,000), he rented an office in Washington and gathered around him an enthusiastic cadre of volunteers, most of them students. The most promising and the most dedicated of these were named coordinators for various regions of the country. Working in an atmosphere Midwest Coordinator Barbara Reid Alexander recalls as "mass confusion," they were inundated each day by torrents of phone calls and overflowing mailbags. . . .

One masterstroke was the purchase of a full-page ad that appeared in the New York Times early in February 1970. The advertisement announced that on April 22, 1970, at locations throughout the United States, citizens would demonstrate for a cleaner environment. Immediately contribution[s] started to roll in, and better yet, the curiosity of network broadcasting giants was piqued.

April 22, 1970, a Wednesday, was a glorious spring day in most parts of the country. Newspapers such as the *New York Times* and the *Washington Post* had given front-page coverage the day before to the roster of scheduled events, and the television networks also had provided enough coverage to give the impending day something of the aura of a national holiday.

Perhaps the most impressive observance was in New York City, whose mayor, John V. Lindsay, had thrown the full weight of his influence behind Earth Day. For two hours, Fifth Avenue was closed to traffic between 14th Street and 59th Street, bringing midtown Manhattan to a virtual standstill. One innovative group of demonstrators grabbed attention by dragging a net filled with dead fish down the thoroughfare, shouting to passersby, "This could be you!" . . .

Public opinion polls indicate that a permanent change in national priorities followed Earth Day 1970. When polled in May 1971, 25 percent of the U.S. public declared protecting the environment to be an important goal—a 2500 percent increase over 1969.

The Crying Indian

Great advertising aims to change behavior. Few protests have changed individual behavior in the realm of environmental conservation as much as Keep America Beautiful's famous 1971–1983 "Crying Indian" campaign. The first of the ads was a television public-service announcement that aired on the second Earth Day in April 1971. A Native American man in a birch bark canoe travels from a beautiful forest into a crowded industrial harbor then disembarks on a litter-strewn shore. The advertisement ends with a bag of food waste bursting over his moccasins at the side of a highway. The actor, Iron Eyes Cody, turns toward the camera as a tear drips from his eye. The advertisement's only words were read in voiceover as the camera zoomed in: "People start pollution. People can stop it."

By the campaign's end, the advertisement was estimated to have reduced littering by 88 percent in some locations. It was selected as one of the top one hundred ads of the twentieth century by *Advertising Age* magazine, and one of the top fifty ads of all time by *Entertainment Weekly* and *TV Guide*. Keep America Beautiful featured the image again in their 1998 campaign, "Back by Popular Neglect."

Here is one of the many print advertisements of the campaign.

Dissenting Opinion from *Sierra Club v. Morton*

William O. Douglas

In his dissent to the Supreme Court's 1972 decision in *Sierra Club v. Morton*, Justice William O. Douglas carried Aldo Leopold's concept of the land ethic (see page 263) from the realm of philosophy to the realm of law.

In order for any legal case to proceed, the party bringing the case must have standing, that is, a legitimate interest at stake under the relevant law. In *Sierra Club v. Morton*, the Sierra Club challenged a proposed resort development in the Mineral King Valley of the Sierra Nevada. A lower court threw the case out on the basis that the Sierra Club lacked standing—a view that was ultimately upheld by a narrow majority of the Supreme Court. Douglas dissented, eloquently.

In addition, Douglas spoke to the importance of "public outrage" as a criteria for legal decision-making. Rarely do the voices of established authority, such as Supreme Court justices, acknowledge the importance and role of protest in decision making. The following is an excerpt from Douglas's dissent (with footnotes and legal citations omitted or simplified).

THE CRITICAL QUESTION of "standing" would be simplified and also put neatly in focus if we fashioned a federal rule that allowed environmental issues to be litigated before federal agencies or federal courts in the name of the inanimate object about to be despoiled, defaced, or invaded by roads and bulldozers and where injury is the subject of public outrage. Contemporary public concern for protecting nature's ecological equilibrium should lead to the conferral of standing upon environmental objects to sue for their own preservation. . . . This suit would therefore be more properly labeled as Mineral King v. Morton.

Inanimate objects are sometimes parties in litigation. A ship has a legal personality, a fiction found useful for maritime purposes. The corporation sole—a creature of ecclesiastical law—is an acceptable adversary and large fortunes ride on its cases. The ordinary corporation is a "person" for purposes of the adjudicatory processes, whether it represents proprietary, spiritual, aesthetic, or charitable causes.

So it should be as respects valleys, alpine meadows, rivers, lakes, estuaries, beaches, ridges, groves of trees, swampland, or even air that feels the destructive pressures of modern technology and modern life. The river, for example, is the living symbol of all the life it sustains or nourishes—fish, aquatic insects, water ouzels, otter, fisher, deer, elk, bear, and all other animals, including man, who are dependent on it or who enjoy it for its sight, its sound, or its life. The river as plaintiff speaks for the ecological unit of life that is part of it. Those people who have a meaningful relation to that body of water—whether it be a fisherman, a canoeist, a zoologist, or a logger—must be able to speak for the values which the river represents and which are threatened with destruction.

. . .The Sierra Club in its complaint alleges that "[o]ne of the principal purposes of the Sierra Club is to protect and conserve the national resources of the

Sierra Nevada Mountains." The District Court held that this uncontested allegation made the Sierra Club "sufficiently aggrieved" to have "standing" to sue on behalf of Mineral King.

Mineral King is doubtless like other wonders of the Sierra Nevada such as Tuolumne Meadows and the John Muir Trail. Those who hike it, fish it, hunt it, camp in it, frequent it, or visit it merely to sit in solitude and wonderment are legitimate spokesmen for it, whether they may be few or many. Those who have that intimate relation with the inanimate object about to be injured, polluted, or otherwise despoiled are its legitimate spokesmen. . . .

The voice of the inanimate object, therefore, should not be stilled. That does not mean that the judiciary takes over the managerial functions from the federal agency. It merely means that before these priceless bits of Americana (such as a valley, an alpine meadow, a river, or a lake) are forever lost or are so transformed as to be reduced to the eventual rubble of our urban environment, the voice of the existing beneficiaries of these environmental wonders should be heard.

Perhaps they will not win. Perhaps the bulldozers of "progress" will plow under all the aesthetic wonders of this beautiful land. That is not the present question. The sole question is, who has standing to be heard?

The Monkey Wrench Gang
Edward Abbey

In 1975 the western writer and one-time National Park Service ranger Edward Abbey wrote a novel about a group of misfits, angry over environmental devastation, who decide to take matters into their own hands. The novel, The Monkey Wrench Gang, became both a best seller and a cult classic. More significantly, the book inspired people worldwide to take direct action to protect the environment.

In this selection three of the four eventual members of the gang conceive the idea of attacking Glen Canyon Dam. Fueled by alcohol, the conspirators gradually expand their thinking to include bulldozers, power plants, and other products of civilization that symbolize the destruction of wilderness. Glen Canyon Dam has long drawn the ire of wilderness lovers, for it flooded a deep and windy canyon of the Colorado River, a reach so inaccessible and wild that few had seen it before it disappeared beneath the rising waters of Lake Powell in 1963. Writer Wallace Stegner said, "Awe was never Glen Canyon's province. That is for the Grand Canyon. Glen Canyon was for delight."

By 1980 the feelings of discontent that Abbey captured in fiction had coalesced in the formation of a radical new organization, Earth First! One of the organization's first acts of public protest was to roll a large plastic banner down the front of the Glen Canyon dam. The banner was designed to look like a crack in the dam.

THE THREE MEN hunched closer to the shrinking fire. The cold night crawled up their backs. They passed Smith's bottle round and around. Then Doc's bottle. Smith, Hayduke, Sarvis. The captain, the bum and the leech. Three wizards on a dead limb. A crafty intimacy crept upon them.

"You know, gentlemen," the doctor said. "You know what I think we ought to do. . . ."

Hayduke had been complaining about the new power lines he'd seen the day before on the desert. Smith had been moaning about the dam again, that dam which had plugged up Glen Canyon, the heart of his river, the river of his heart.

"You know what we ought to do," the doctor said. "We ought to blow that dam to shitaree." (A bit of Hayduke's foul tongue had loosened his own.)

"How?" said Hayduke.

"That ain't legal," Smith said.

"You prayed for an earthquake, you said."

"Yeah, but there ain't no law agin that."

"You were praying with malicious intent."

"That's true. I pray that way all the time."

"Bent on mischief and the destruction of government property."

"That's right, Doc."

"That's a felony."

"It ain't just a misdemeanor?"

"It's a felony."

"How?" said Hayduke.

"How what?"

"How do we blow up the dam?"

"Which dam?"

"Any dam."

"Now you're talking," Smith said. "But Glen Canyon Dam first. I claim that one first."

"I don't know," the doctor said. "You're the demolitions expert."

"I can take out a bridge for you," Hayduke said, "if you get me enough dynamite. But I don't know about Glen Canyon Dam. We'd need an atom bomb for that one."

"I been thinking about that dam for a long time," Smith said. "And I got a plan. We get three jumbo-size houseboats and some dolphins—"

"Hold it!" Doc said, holding up a big paw. A moment of silence. He looked around, into the darkness beyond the firelight. "Who knows what ears those shadows have."

They looked. The flames of their little campfire cast a hesitant illumination upon the bush, the boat half grounded on the sandy beach, the rocks and pebbles, the pulse of the river. The women, all asleep, could not be seen.

"There ain't nobody here but us bombers," Smith said.

"Who can be sure? The State may have its sensors anywhere."

"Naw," Hayduke said. "They're not bugging the canyons. Not yet anyhow.

But who says we have to start with dams? There's plenty of other work to do."

"Good work," the doctor said. "Good, wholesome, constructive work."

"I hate that dam," Smith said. "That dam flooded the most beautiful canyon in the world."

"We know," Hayduke said. "We feel the same way you do, but let's think about easier things first. I'd like to knock down some of them power lines they're stringing across the desert. And those new tin bridges up by Hite. And the god-damned road-building they're doing all over the canyon country. We could put in a good year just taking the fucking goddamned bulldozers apart."

"Hear, hear," the doctor said. "And don't forget the billboards. And the strip mines. And the pipelines. And the new railroad from Black Mesa to Page. And the coal-burning power plants. And the copper smelters. And the uranium mines. And the nuclear power plants. And the computer centers. And the land and cattle companies. And the wildlife poisoners. And the people who throw beer cans along the highways."

"I throw beer cans along the fucking highways," Hayduke said. "Why the fuck shouldn't I throw fucking beer cans along the fucking highways?"

"Now, now. Don't be so defensive."

"Hell," Smith said, "I do it too. Any road I wasn't consulted about that I don't like, I litter. It's my religion."

"Before love canal, I knew nothing about the environment"

Lois Gibbs

In 1978, an obscure working-class neighborhood in Niagara Falls, New York, jumped onto the front pages of local and then national newspapers. Some twenty thousand tons of toxic waste lay shallowly buried under their community in an area known as Love Canal. Some years before, the lands had been conveyed to the local school board for one dollar with a warning about the presence of hazardous chemicals, but this warning was not passed on to future homeowners and renters on the site. An elementary school rested directly over the chemicals.

As testing revealed elevated levels of toxic compounds, citizens in the community organized under the leadership of a determined mother with a high school education—Lois Gibbs. Gibbs hounded her state and federal representatives, the governor, the White House, the Environmental Protection Agency, and the New York Department of Health. She and the other members of the Love Canal Homeowners Association demonstrated, sought celebrity support (from Jane Fonda and Tom Hayden), testified before Congress, and generally insisted that the government protect their children. Within months, the school was closed, and the families closest to the waste were evacuated. Eventually the evacuation was extended to nine hundred families, as evidence of increased birth defects, miscarriages, and developmental problems in children mounted. The school and the closest housing units were demolished.

In 1982, the British magazine *New Internationalist* published the following interview with Gibbs about the Love Canal experience.

BEFORE LOVE CANAL, I knew nothing about the environment and was not particularly concerned. I wanted to live the so-called American Dream—white picket fence, healthy family, well-adjusted children. We moved into Love Canal in 1972. In 1977, I read in a new article that Hooker Chemical Company had used the Canal as a toxic waste dump in the early 1950s and that a variety of health problems could be related to exposure to the chemicals buried beneath the neighbourhood. My son Michael had many of the illnesses that were listed in the article; epilepsy, liver disease, blood disease, asthma and a urinary tract infection which required two surgeries. He had all that before he turned five. Yet, when we first moved to Love Canal, there had been nothing wrong with him. The article got me thinking that there was a connection between the dump site and Michael's health.

Michael attended the 99th Street School, located directly on top of the Canal. And at the start, my primary concern was the school. I went to the Board of Education and said that I wanted Michael to be transferred into a safer school. To be truthful, my initial impulse was selfish. I was concerned for my child's health.

I went to the Board with two doctors' letters, which they had told me I would need. But when I explained that I wanted Michael transferred, they told me that if the school was unsafe for Michael Gibbs, it was unsafe for the other 470 children enrolled there. And they told me they weren't about to close down the school because of one irate hysterical mother with a sickly child. That was the most devastating thing I had ever heard, I came home and could not even talk. How could they say that to me? The child was sick. I had documentation from my physicians. And they refused to help. I was appalled.

So I decided to call my state representatives and my Congressman and even the Governor. I felt very intimidated. I lacked self-confidence. I didn't know whether I had the right to call these people and ask for their help. I felt inadequate talking to them, stuttering and stammering all the way. But after talking to a number of them, my lack of self-confidence and my insecurities quickly turned to anger, because nobody was doing anything. All I could think of was, if something is not done soon and [I] continue to send this child to school[,] I'll lose him. That was the bottom line.

I decided to go out door-to-door and see if other parents were willing to shut down the school and whether they were experiencing similar health problems with their children. That was the most traumatic thing in my life. I put a petition together and practised it at home for about a week. I started with the first ring of homes around the Canal. I do not know what I expected, but when I got to the first door I broke out in a cold sweat. I had to go to the bathroom. So I just picked up and ran all the way home. I just could not do it.

That night, Michael got very sick—a 105F [sic] fever. I had to take him to the emergency room for treatment. That drove home to me the reality that if I continued to be a "scaredy-cat" nothing was going to change. The politicians, the School Board, the neighbours—nobody was doing anything. It was up to me. So after that I went back out[,] took a deep breath as each neighbour opened the door and said what I had to say. I was waiting for people to slam their doors and think I was crazy. But people were very supportive—and they started to ask questions. It was then that I discovered that not just the 99th Street School but the whole damn community was affected. People told me about 12-year-old girls having hysterectomies, men and women with severe cancers. When people realized that their problems were shared by others, we were able to form the Love Canal Committee which later became the Love Canal Home Owners Association.

It was all self-interest that led me to do this. I wanted to protect my children. We had a very low income—my husband made about £10,000 a year. We could not afford to move or even to put Michael in private school. But I felt that something had to be done to protect him. In the end, this is what motivates most people. "You can't do this to my home and my yard. I worked too hard for what little I've got."

There are other Lois Gibbs all across the country, people sitting there knowing that they have a problem and that nobody is doing anything about it. And many of them say to themselves, "I can't do anything. We can't change anything." But with some encouragement and some help, they often can. I received letters and calls from thousands of people asking what they could do in their communities, how they could do a health survey, how they could move government. That led me to set up the Citizen's Clearinghouse on Hazardous Wastes—to help the other Lois Gibbs who have not taken the steps we did in Love Canal.

The one thing I have now that I did not have before is a purpose and a goal in life. I know now that there is something I can do, a contribution I can make. And that gives me a lot of satisfaction. When people call now and say "We won over here" or "We got what we asked for," I feel great.

Ecodefense
Dave Foreman and Bill Haywood, Editors

Five years after the 1980 founding of Earth First!, the group published this how-to manual for radical and destructive protest of economic activities that threaten wilderness and wildlife. *Ecodefense* provided details on how to sink a whaling vessel, take down high-tension power lines, and block off-road vehicles from using wilderness areas.

Early in the book, editor and Earth First! founder Dave Foreman laid down a set of guiding principles for the particular form of ecoterrorism called monkeywrenching (after Edward Abbey's novel, *The Monkey Wrench Gang*). In this excerpt, Foreman asserted that monkeywrenching should be nonviolent toward people but unrelenting toward machines that destroy wilderness. The techniques advocated in the book eschew explosives and firearms in favor of simple tools. For example, metal spikes driven into trees make them useless to sawmills; lightly buried strips of nails laid down in off-road vehicle (ORV) trails produce flat tires.

IT IS TIME FOR WOMEN AND MEN, individually and in small groups, to act heroically in defense of the wild, to put a monkeywrench into the gears of the machine that is destroying natural diversity. Though illegal, this strategic monkeywrenching can be safe, easy, fun, and—most important—effective in stopping timber cutting, road building, overgrazing, oil and gas exploration, mining, dam building, powerline construction, off-road-vehicle use, trapping, ski area development, and other forms of destruction of the wilderness, as well as cancerous suburban sprawl.

But it must be strategic, it must be thoughtful, it must be deliberate in order to succeed. Such a campaign of resistance would adhere to the following principles:

Monkeywrenching is nonviolent

Monkeywrenching is nonviolent resistance to the destruction of natural diversity and wilderness. It is never directed against human beings or other forms of life. It is aimed at inanimate machines and tools that are destroying life. Care is always taken to minimize any possible threat to people, including the monkeywrenchers themselves.

Monkeywrenching is not organized

There should be no central direction or organization to monkeywrenching. Any type of network would invite infiltration, agents provocateurs, and repression. It is truly individual action. Because of this, communication among monkeywrenchers is difficult and dangerous. Anonymous discussion through this book and its future editions seems to be the safest avenue of communication to refine techniques, security procedures, and strategy.

Monkeywrenching is individual

Monkeywrenching is done by individuals or very small groups of people who have known each other for years. Trust and a good working relationship are essential in such groups. The more people involved, the greater the dangers of infiltration or a loose mouth. Monkeywrenchers avoid working with people they haven't known for a long time, those who can't keep their mouths closed, and those with grandiose or violent ideas (they may be police agents or other dangerous crackpots).

Monkeywrenching is targeted

Ecodefenders pick their targets. Mindless, erratic vandalism is counterproductive as well as unethical. Monkeywrenchers know that they do not stop a specific logging sale by destroying any piece of logging equipment they come across. They make sure it belongs to the real culprit. They ask themselves what is the most vulnerable point of a wilderness-destroying project, and strike there. Senseless vandalism leads to loss of popular sympathy.

Monkeywrenching is timely

There are proper times and places for monkeywrenching. There are also times when monkeywrenching may be counterproductive. Monkeywrenchers generally should not act when there is a nonviolent civil disobedience action—e.g., a blockade—taking place against the opposed project. Monkeywrenching may cloud the issue of direct action, and the blockaders could be blamed for the ecotage and be put in danger from the work crew or police. Blockades and monkeywrenching usually do not mix. Monkeywrenching may also not be appropriate when delicate political negotiations are taking place for the protection of a certain area. There are, of course, exceptions to this rule. The Earth warrior always asks, Will monkeywrenching help or hinder the protection of this place?

Monkeywrenching is dispersed

Monkeywrenching is a widespread movement across the United States. Government agencies and wilderness despoilers from Maine to Hawaii know that their destruction of natural diversity may be resisted. Nationwide monkeywrenching will hasten overall industrial retreat from wild areas.

Monkeywrenching is diverse

All kinds of people, in all kinds of situations, can be monkeywrenchers. Some pick a large area of wild country, declare it wilderness in their own minds, and resist any intrusion into it. Others specialize against logging or ORVs in a variety of areas. Certain monkeywrenchers may target a specific project such as a giant powerline, a road under construction, or an oil operation. Some operate in their backyards, while others lie low at home and plan their ecotage a thousand miles away. Some are loners, and others operate in small groups. Even Republicans monkeywrench.

Monkeywrenching is fun

Although it is serious and potentially dangerous, monkeywrenching is also fun. There is a rush of excitement, a sense of accomplishment, and unparalleled camaraderie from creeping about in the night resisting those "alien forces from Houston, Tokyo, Washington, DC, and the Pentagon." As Ed Abbey said, "Enjoy, shipmates, enjoy."

Monkeywrenching is not revolutionary

Monkeywrenchers do not aim to overthrow any social, political, or economic system. Monkeywrenching is merely nonviolent self-defense of the wild. It is aimed at keeping industrial civilization out of natural areas and causing industry's retreat from areas that should be wild. It is not major industrial sabotage. Explosives, firearms, and other dangerous tools are usually avoided; they invite greater scrutiny from law enforcement agencies, repression, and loss of public support.

Monkeywrenching is simple

The simplest possible tool is used. The safest tactic is employed. Elaborate commando operations are generally avoided. The most effective means for stopping the destruction of the wild are often the simplest. There are times when more detailed and complicated operations are necessary. But the monkeywrencher asks, What is the simplest way to do this?

Monkeywrenching is deliberate and ethical

Monkeywrenchers are very conscious of the gravity of what they do. They are deliberate about taking such a serious step. They are thoughtful, not cavalier. Monkeywrenchers—although nonviolent—are warriors. They are exposing themselves to possible arrest or injury. It is not a casual or flippant affair. They keep a pure heart and mind about it. They remember that they are engaged in the most moral of all actions: protecting life, defending Earth.

A movement based on the above principles could protect millions of acres of wilderness more stringently than could any congressional act, could insure the propagation of the Grizzly and other threatened life forms better than could an army of game wardens, and could lead to the retreat of industrial civilization from large areas of forest, mountain, desert, prairie, seashore, swamp, tundra, and woodland that are better suited to the maintenance of native diversity than to the production of raw materials for overconsumptive technological human society.

If logging firms know that a timber sale is spiked, they won't bid on the timber. If a Forest Supervisor knows that a road will be continually destroyed, he won't try to build it. If seismographers know that they will be constantly harassed in an area, they won't go there. If ORVers know that they'll get flat tires miles from nowhere, they won't drive in such areas.

John Muir said that if it ever came to a war between the races, he would side with the bears. That day has arrived.

Voices from Chernobyl
Svetlana Alexievich

Seven years after the Three Mile Island disaster in the United States, a much more serious explosion and meltdown occurred at the Chernobyl nuclear reactor in the Ukraine (then part of the Soviet Union). The Chernobyl explosion and subsequent fire spread deadly radiation over a huge area of Belarus and smaller portions of the Ukraine and Russia. Lower levels of radiation were detected across much of Europe. An area half the size of Italy remains uninhabitable today.

Author Svetlana Alexievich spent three years gathering people's recollections of the disaster's impact on their lives, and published the memoirs in 1997. The entire work is itself a witness to and a protest of the devastation experienced by the people she interviewed. "These people had already seen what for everyone else is still unknown," she wrote. "I felt like I was recording the future."

Here is an excerpt from one of the hundreds of testimonies that Alexievich collected.

Monologue About a Whole Life Written Down on Doors

I want to bear witness. . . .

It happened ten years ago, and it happens to me again every day. . . .

I'm not a writer. I won't be able to describe it. . . . There you are: a normal person. A little person. You're just like everyone else—you go to work, you return from work. You get an average salary. Once a year you go on vacation. You're a normal person! And then one day you're suddenly turned into a Chernobyl person. . . . You want to be like everyone else, and now you can't. . . . The very word "Chernobyl" is like a signal. Everyone turns their head to look at you. He's from there! . . .

. . . We left on the third day. . . .

It was like this: They announced over the radio that you couldn't take your cats. So we put her in the suitcase. But she didn't want to go, she climbed out. Scratched everyone. You can't take your belongings! All right, I won't take all my belongings, I'll take just one belonging. Just one! I need to take my door off the apartment and take it with me. I can't leave the door. I'll cover the entrance with some boards. Our door—it's our talisman, it's a family relic. My father lay on this door. I don't know whose tradition this is, it's not like that everywhere, but my mother told me that the deceased must be placed to lie on the door of his home. He lies there until they bring the coffin. I sat by my father all night, he lay on this door. The house was open. All night. And this door has little etch-marks on it. That's me growing up. It's marked there: first grade, second grade. Seventh. Before the army. And next to that: how my son grew. And my daughter. My whole life is written down on this door. How am I supposed to leave it?

I asked my neighbor, he had a car: "Help me." He gestured toward his head, like, You're not quite right, are you? But I took it with me, that door. At night. On a motorcycle. Through the woods. It was two years later, when our apartment had already been looted and emptied. The police were chasing me. "We'll shoot. We'll shoot." They thought I was a thief. That's how I stole the door from my own home.

I took my daughter and my wife to the hospital. They had black spots all over their bodies. These spots would appear, then disappear. About the size of a five-kopek coin. But nothing hurt. They did some tests on them. I asked for the results. "It's not for you," they said. I said, "Then for who?"

Back then everyone was saying: "We're going to die, we're going to die. By the year 2000, there won't be any Belarussians left." My daughter was six years old. I'm putting her to bed and she whispers in my ear: "Daddy, I want to live, I'm still little." And I had thought she didn't understand anything.

Can you picture seven little girls shaved bald in one room? There were seven of them in the hospital room. . . . But enough! That's it! When I talk about it, I have this feeling, my heart tells me—you're betraying them. Because I need to describe it like I'm a stranger. My wife came home from the hospital. She couldn't take it. "It'd be better for her to die than to suffer like this. Or for me to die, so that I don't have to watch anymore." No, enough! That's it! I'm not in any condition. No.

We put her on the door . . . on the door that my father lay on. Until they brought a little coffin. It was small, like the box for a large doll.

I want to bear witness: my daughter died from Chernobyl. And they want us to forget about it.

Nikolai Fomich Kalugin, father

Cry of the Earth, Cry of the Poor
Leonardo Boff

The clearing of the Amazon rain forest has caused global concern for decades. Scientists argue that the clearing may simultaneously alter the global climate and eliminate the greatest concentration of biodiversity in the world. Most of the area of the Amazon basin is in Brazil, which has made efforts to preserve certain portions of the forest while asserting that development of the remainder is crucial to its economic future. The result has been a rising tide of clearing and the accompanying fragmentation of the remaining rain forest into smaller and smaller patches.

As Brazilian Leonardo Boff explained in his 1997 work *Cry of the Earth, Cry of the Poor*, the Amazon is the "Temple of the Planet's Biodiversity." It is a vastly productive, yet environmentally fragile land, where a few acres may hold more species of plants and insects than all of Europe. Boff describes how modern economic development in the Amazon has wrought a series of ecological disasters—reservoirs that were constructed improperly, causing the death of fish and the proliferation of mosquitoes and disease; clearing and burning of the rain forest resulting in erosion, leaching of nutrients, and the eventual creation of desertlike conditions; death and displacement of indigenous peoples; and the loss of the biological treasure that is the Amazon.

Boff was one of the leading thinkers of liberation theology, a movement within the Catholic Church that asserts that the church has a mission to help the poor. The church forced Boff into silence, which in turn drove him from the priesthood. He has since become one of the leading thinkers on the links between ecology and sustainable livelihoods in the developing world. In 2001, he won the Right Livelihood Award, often called the Alternative Nobel.

In this excerpt, Boff focuses on the alternatives to conventional development proposals in the Amazon. Although Brazil instituted a brief ban on clearing two years after the publication of Boff's work, the rate of clearing has since increased. Approximately a sixth of the great rain forest has now been cleared.

The Dream of Chico Mendes and the Future of the Amazon

The observations we have made about the Amazon—and that we could also make about the Pantanal in Mato Grosso and the Atlantic forest in Brazil—are overwhelming proof of how misguided it is to pursue development along the lines of modernity. Such development ignores nature and is carried out against it, for it sees nature as an obstacle instead of an ally. As we have already indicated, the underlying question lies not in making development sustainable, but rather in starting from the sustainability of nature to create an alternative to the straitjacket of such development. Instead of speaking of development, we must speak of society, defending life, and promoting the quality of human life. Sustainability, as we have seen, is eminently an outgrowth of ecology, just as the category of *development* derives from the economic realm. Sustainability has to do with the dynamic and self-regulating balance (homeostasis) that is inherent in nature as a result of the chain of interdependencies and complementarities among all beings, especially living things that depend on resources that are continually recycled and hence are sustainable without limit. The Amazon is the greatest example of such natural sustainability. We must learn from the technology and sustainability of nature—something that the Amazon megaprojects have denied and continue to deny. This economy of nature must inspire the human economy, which thereby comes to participate in the sustainability of nature.

This was precisely the underlying intuition of Chico Mendes, a genuine representative of the forest peoples and a sharp observer of the logic of nature. Those of us who were close friends with him were aware of how deeply identified he was with the Amazon forest, with its vast biodiversity, with the rubber tappers, with the animals, and with the slightest sign of life in the bush. He was a secular and modern St. Francis. He divided his life between the city and the jungle, but while in the city, he could hear the powerful call of the forest in his body and soul. He experienced himself as part and parcel of the land, and so he used to go back to the rubber area and commune with the wild and the cosmos. It was there that he felt he was in his habitat, his true home. His ecological awareness prompted him to leave the forest temporarily in order to organize rubber tappers, establish labor union cells, and take part in resistance struggles (the famous "standoffs," a strategy by which the rubber tappers, together with their children, old people, and other allies, stood peacefully in the way of those clearing the forest and their machines, preventing them from toppling trees).

In view of the ecological crisis being forced on the Amazon, and speaking for the movement of forest peoples, he suggested that extractive reserves be created. His idea was accepted by the government in 1987. Very realistically he said,

We understand—the rubber tappers understand—that the Amazon cannot be turned into an untouchable sanctuary. However, we also understand that there is an urgent need to avoid the clear cutting that is threatening the Amazon and thereby threatening the life of all the peoples of the planet. Hence we are thinking of an alternative for preserving the forest that can be economically productive at the same time. That is why we are thinking about creating an extractive reserve.

He explained how this mode of production would work:

> In extractive reserves we ourselves are going to sell and manufacture the products that the forest generously grants us. The university must be part of the extractive reserve. It is the only way to keep the Amazon from disappearing. Furthermore, this reserve is not going to have owners. It is going to be the shared property of the community. We will have use but not ownership.

It would thus be possible to devise an alternative to the savage extraction, whose only beneficiaries are speculators. A mahogany tree cut down in Acre costs from one to five dollars; sold on the European market it costs from three to five thousand dollars.

On Christmas Eve 1988, Mendes was murdered with five shots, felled by the enemies of humankind. He departed from life in the Amazon to enter into universal history and into the collective unconscious of those who love our planet and its vast biodiversity. As an archetype Chico Mendes drives the struggle to preserve the Amazon and the forest peoples that has now been assumed by millions of people around the world. A poet of the forest of Pará put it well when he sang, "Ay! Amazon! Amazon! They have buried Chico Mendes, but hope just won't be buried" (João de Jesus Paes Loureiro). . . .

The Wisdom That Builds Community

Greg Watson

A central theme of land-use reform in the United States since World War II has been the decline of inner-city neighborhoods and the flight of higher-income families to the sprawling suburbs. These suburbs eat into the countryside, displacing farms and forests. According to a recent study prepared for The Funders' Network for Smart Growth and Livable Communities, between 1982 and 1997 the population of Massachusetts grew by 6 percent, but the developed area grew by 39 percent. Left in the wake of urban abandonment and suburban sprawl are urban wastelands. Boston's Dudley Street neighborhood, located just two miles south of the city's downtown, was once among them.

Led by the grassroots Dudley Street Neighborhood Initiative (DSNI), the community turned itself around and pioneered a new model of community redevelopment. The DSNI demanded that redevelopment occur with no displacement of existing residents. It sought and eventually received from the city of Boston the power to take land by eminent domain. It then used that power to build a pool of community-owned land with affordable homes that would remain permanently within the financial reach of residents. The DSNI's initiatives relied on a model first put forward by Robert Swann and Susan Witt of the tiny E. F. Schumacher Society.

As Greg Watson, executive director of the DSNI, detailed in his 1997 address as part of the E. F. Schumacher Society's annual lecture series, DSNI demonstrated that solutions to urban blight are possible. The DSNI links environmental progress to social and economic progress.

. . . **THE DUDLEY STREET NEIGHBORHOOD** is one of the poorest communities in all of Massachusetts, with a population of 24,000 Cape Verdean, African-American, Latino, and white residents and with one of the highest rates of unemployment and poverty anywhere in the state. We're not a district, we're not a neat political unit; we are basically an area that was defined by devastation and poverty, an area that has suffered in a number of ways—suffering sometimes even caused by well-intentioned policies and practices. The cumulative effect of this devastation was that by 1984 the Dudley Street area had been reduced to 1300 abandoned lots filled with rubble. You could stand in the middle of the one and a half square mile area that we call the Triangle, and you could literally turn in all directions and not see a building. It was an absolute wasteland, where once there had been a thriving Irish-Catholic and Jewish community.

One of the programs contributing to the changes taking place in Roxbury was the G.I. Bill, which encouraged returning servicemen and their families to go and build homes in the suburbs. And over the years many people did leave the area. Redlining, abandonment, and neglect followed. When immigrants came in from Cape Verde and Puerto Rico, the community changed its character still more, and again people left. The Dudley Street neighborhood became an enclave for the poor and the disenfranchised, and in many cases residents were not citizens of this country.

There were a lot of slumlords in Roxbury who were hoping for urban renewal to make them rich. They were waiting for the same thing that had happened in the West End and the South End of Boston. They were going to hold on to their property until they could make a financial killing. But the community said no. They didn't want urban renewal, and they stopped it. As a result you had a lot of people holding land and buildings they didn't know what to do with. They realized they weren't going to make their "killing," but they were determined they weren't going to suffer, either; they were going to minimize their loss. The way many of them did this was to burn their buildings down. Night after night after night there were fires. Everyone on the outside said, Oh look, they're burning down their own homes, they're destroying their own communities. What's wrong with those people? — It was not the people living there who were destroying their community; it was the slumlords who were burning down their own buildings in order to collect as much insurance money as they could on what they perceived to be a lost cause. They burned until the whole area was virtually flattened. Imagine 1300 abandoned lots in the middle of a community!

As Wendell Berry reminds us, once land is neglected, or looks neglected, it soon becomes even more neglected. Trucks frequently drove through or past Roxbury on their way to the dump, where they were being charged tipping fees to deposit their trash. When the drivers saw all the abandoned lots with no people around, they thought, Why should I pay a fee? So they'd come back after dark, and they'd dump their loads. Then they got so brazen that after a while, because nobody seemed to care, they'd come in the middle of the day and dump. There were sides of beef, there were old refrigerators, there were cars, there were rats and other vermin, there was filth. People were becoming increasingly ill, and finally the community said, No more.

They held a meeting, and they said, We've got to do something about this. We're going to make a stink, and we're going to get these illegal trash transfer stations closed down.—The TV cameras showed up, and right after that, Mayor Ray Flynn showed up. He had no real base of support in communities of color, but now he made a commitment. He said, I'll do whatever you folks need to help you clean up this community. I will do anything: there will be resources, there will be money. You let me know what you want. Ché Madyun and others said, We need rakes and shovels and garbage bags to clean up the lots. And they did clean up. The TV cameras came again, and Ray Flynn looked good; this was a political plus for him.

Then the residents called Mayor Flynn back, and they said, There's something else we need. He thought, Well, that's okay; they probably just want more rakes and shovels. What the community said was, We're going to develop a comprehensive plan to rebuild our neighborhood, and in order to do that we need control over the land, so we'd like the power of eminent domain over the abandoned land in our community. Mayor Flynn gulped and balked at that one; that wasn't what he had expected. But they made a case for eminent domain. Many people rejected the idea. Even in the community there were those who said, No way. That's the very tool that has traditionally been used to force poor people out of their communities. We don't even understand the nature of that power. How do we know we could use it wisely? — The residents held many meetings. They were very deliberate, they thought things through, and they decided that in order to rebuild a wasteland with hundreds of individual owners, they had to have control over the land.

Conventional wisdom says that wealth is having a job. Let's bring in Wal-Mart, let's bring in IBM, and they will give the people jobs. That's not real wealth. Real wealth means you have some assets. It means you build on something that the community owns or that the individuals in the community own. There's no more valuable asset than land. Farmers know that; we know that. The land is the ultimate source of wealth. So through hard work and with the support of Ray Flynn and Stephen Coyle, the director of the Boston Redevelopment Authority, in 1988 the Dudley Street Neighborhood Initiative became the first and to date only community-based organization to be granted the power of eminent domain over a one and a half square mile area right in the heart of Boston.

The Ford Foundation came forward with a two million dollar loan to buy the abandoned parcels of land at fair market value. If there was a building on it, we couldn't buy it; if the land was taken care of, we couldn't buy it. What we were interested in were the parcels that were overgrown, that still had trash on them, that were attracting vermin. And because we weren't acting as individuals but as a community, we formed a community land trust. A community land trust means what it says: land held in trust by the community. It is a democratic, nonprofit vehicle that removes land from the speculative market and holds it for multi-purposes: affordable housing, farming, small businesses, open space. The community land trust uses long-term ground leases to give area residents affordable and secure access to land. Residents own their own homes and pay a small monthly fee to the trust for the use of the land. Resale provisions on the homes ensure that home owners will receive a fair return on the investment in the building, at the same time excluding the value of the land—which has been enhanced by the efforts of the entire community—from the sale price. In this way the homes remain affordable for future residents.

Two hundred and twenty-five affordable homes have been built in and for our community: duplexes, single-family homes, town houses, row houses. The type and location of every single home were determined through a public process. Through sale of the homes and collection of ground-lease fees we were repaid for the cost of land purchase. The development effort was therefore self-supporting. We never had to use one dime of the two million dollars of Ford Foundation money, although it did provide the Initiative with credibility in its initial stages. . . .

. . . Organizing doesn't mean that you always have to be confrontational; it doesn't mean that you have to identify an enemy. It can mean that you identify a shared vision and mobilize residents to make that vision a reality. . . .

Now or Never: What's an Environmentalist to Do?
Bill McKibben

Bill McKibben's 1989 best seller *The End of Nature* first introduced the problem of global warming to a popular audience. The book spelled out in lay terms the global influence of human actions on the environment, extending to the alteration of the very chemistry of the atmosphere and the types of and amount of solar radiation that reach and leave the earth's surface. As a consequence of our power, McKibben argued, humans had an ethical obligation to ensure that the life support functions of the earth remain intact.

In 2001, McKibben wrote the essay excerpted here in the weekly newspaper *In These Times*. McKibben first identified the political problem—despite scientific consensus on the issue, political action has stalled for more than a decade. Since 1995 the Intergovernmental Panel on Climate Change has issued three assessment reports that have—in the restrained language of science—trumpeted the dangers of human influence on climate. Many scientists have suggested that the very foundations of our civilization are at risk.

But as McKibben pointed out, the time frame of climate change makes it more difficult to build a sense of urgency. The dangers of climate change will sneak up on us in seemingly unconnected ways that tempt us to adapt to each new insult—shrinking snowpacks reducing water supplies, progressively more violent weather events, unpredictable harvests, the extinction of organisms whose lifestyle or biology makes them particularly vulnerable. McKibben's solution is to take the issue from the realm of science to the realm of personal moral responsibility. Personal commitment and individual action by a growing minority of Americans, McKibben argued, would change the politics of the issue in similar ways to the growth of the abolitionist movement in the mid-1800s or the civil rights movement in the late 1950s and early 1960s.

WHEN GLOBAL WARMING first emerged as a potential crisis in the late '80s, one academic analyst called it "the public policy problem from hell." The years since have only proven him more astute—15 years into our understanding of climate change, we have yet to figure out how we're going to tackle it. And environmentalists are just as clueless as anyone else: Do we need to work on lifestyles or on lobbying, on politics or on photovoltaics? And is there a difference? How well we handle global warming will determine what kind of century we inhabit—and indeed what kind of planet we leave behind to everyone and everything that follows us down into geologic time. It is *the* environmental question, the one that cuts closest to home and also floats off most easily into the abstract. So far it has been the ultimate "can't get there from here" problem, but the time has come to draw a roadmap—one that may help us deal with the handful of other issues on the list of real, world-shattering problems. . . .

. . . [H]uman beings are changing the planet more fundamentally in the course of a couple of decades than in all the time since we climbed down from the trees and began making clever use of our opposable thumbs. There's never been anything like this.

Yet to judge from the political response, this issue ranks well below, say, the estate tax as a cause for alarm and worry. In 1988, there was enough public outcry that George Bush the Elder promised to combat "the greenhouse effect with the White House effect." In 1992, Bill Clinton promised that Americans would emit no more carbon dioxide by 2000 than they had in 1990—and that his administration would do the work of starting to turn around our ocean liner of an economy, laying the foundation for the transition to a world of renewable energy.

That didn't happen, of course. Fixated on the economy, Clinton and Gore presided over a decade when Americans, who already emitted a quarter of the world's carbon dioxide, actually managed to increase their total output by 12 percent. Now we have a president who seems unsure whether global warming is real, and far more concerned with increasing power production than with worrying about trifles like the collapse of the globe's terrestrial systems. In November [2000], the hope of global controls on carbon dioxide production essentially collapsed at an international conference in the Hague, when the United States refused to make even modest concessions on its use of fossil fuels, and the rest of the world finally walked away from the table in disgust.

In the face of all this, what is an environmentalist to do? The normal answer, when you're mounting a campaign, is to look for self-interest, to scare people by saying what will happen to us if we don't do something: all the birds will die, the canyon will disappear beneath a reservoir, we will choke to death on smog.

But in the case of global warming, those kind of answers don't exactly do the trick, at least in the timeframe we're discussing. At this latitude, climate change will creep up on us. Severe storms have already grown more frequent and more damaging. The seasons are less steady in their progression. Some agriculture is less reliable. But face it: Our economy is so enormous that it handles those kinds of changes in stride. Economists who work on this stuff talk about how it will shave a percentage or two off GNP over the next few decades—not enough to notice in the kind of generalized economic boom they describe. And most of us live lives so divorced from the natural world that we hardly notice the changes anyway. Hotter? Turn up the air conditioning. Stormier? Well, an enormous percentage of Americans commute from remote-controlled garage to office parking garage—they may have gone the last year without getting good and wet in a rainstorm. By the time the magnitude of the change is truly in our faces, it will be too late to do much about it: There's such a lag time with carbon dioxide in the atmosphere that we need to be making the switch to solar and wind and hydrogen right about now. Yesterday, in fact.

So maybe we should think of global warming in a different way—as the great moral crisis of our moment, the equivalent in our time of the civil rights movement of the '60s.

Why a moral question? In the first place, because we've never figured out a more effective way to screw the marginalized and poor of this planet. Having taken their dignity, their resources and their freedom under a variety of other schemes, we now are taking the very physical stability on which they depend for the most bottom-line of existences.

Our economy can absorb these changes for a while, but for a moment consider Bangladesh. A river delta that houses 130 million souls in an area the size of Wisconsin, Bangladesh actually manages food self-sufficiency most years. But in 1998, the sea level in the Bay of Bengal was higher than normal, just the sort of thing we can expect to become more frequent and severe. The waters sweeping down the Ganges and the Brahmaputra from the Himalayas could not drain easily into the ocean—they backed up across the country, forcing most of its inhabitants to spend three months in thigh-deep water. The fall rice crop didn't get planted. We've seen this same kind of disaster in the last few years in Mozambique or Honduras or Venezuela or any of a dozen other wretched spots.

And a moral crisis, too, if you place any value on the rest of creation. Coral reef researchers indicate that these spectacularly intricate ecosystems are also spectacularly vulnerable—rising water temperatures will likely bleach them to extinction by mid-century. In the Arctic, polar bears are 20 percent scrawnier than they were a decade ago: As pack ice melts, so does the opportunity for hunting seals. All in all, this century seems poised to see extinctions at a rate not observed since the last big asteroid slammed into the planet. But this time the asteroid is us.

A moral question, finally, if you think we owe any debt to the future. No one ever has figured out a more thorough-going way to stripmine the present and degrade what comes after. Forget the seventh generation—we're talking 70th generation, and 700th. All the people that will ever be related to you. Ever. No generation yet to come will ever forget us—we are the ones present at the moment when the temperature starts to spike, and so far we have not reacted. If it had been done to us, we would loathe the generation that did it, precisely as we will one day be loathed.

But trying to make a moral campaign is no easy task. In most moral crises, there is a villain—some person or class or institution that must be overcome. Once they're identified, the battle can commence. But you can't really get angry at carbon dioxide, and the people responsible for its production are, well, us. So perhaps we need some symbols to get us started, some places to sharpen the debate and rally ourselves to action. There are plenty to choose from: our taste for ever bigger houses and the heating and cooling bills that come with them; our penchant for jumping on airplanes at the drop of a hat; and so on. But if you wanted one glaring example of our lack of balance, you could do worse than point the finger at sport utility vehicles.

SUVs are more than mere symbol. They are a major part of the problem—one reason we emit so much more carbon dioxide now than we did a decade ago is because our fleet of cars and trucks actually has gotten steadily less fuel efficient for the past 10 years. If you switched today from the average American car to a big SUV, and drove it for just one year, the difference in carbon dioxide that you produced would be the equivalent of opening your refrigerator door and then forgetting to close it for six years. SUVs essentially are machines for burning fossil fuel that just happen to also move you and your stuff around.

But what makes them such a perfect symbol is the brute fact that they are simply unnecessary. Go to the parking lot of the nearest suburban supermarket and look around: the only conclusion you can draw is that to reach the grocery store, people must drive through three or four raging rivers and up the side of a trackless canyon. These are semi-military machines (some, like the Hummer, are not semi at all), Brinks trucks on a slight diet. They don't keep their occupants safer, they do wreck whatever they plow into—they are the perfect metaphor for a heedless, supersized society. And a gullible one, which has been sold on these vast vehicles partly by the promise that they somehow allow us to commune with nature.

That's why we need a much broader politics than the White House–lobbying that's occupied the big enviros for the past decade, or the mass-market mailing that has been their stock in trade for the past quarter century. We need to take all the brilliant and energetic strategies of local grassroots groups fighting dumps and cleaning up rivers, and we need to make those tactics national and international. So that's why some pastors are starting to talk with their congregations about what car they're going to buy, and why some college seniors are passing around petitions pledging to stay away from the Ford Explorers and Excursions and Extraneouses, and why some few auto dealers have begun to notice informational picketers outside on Saturday mornings urging their customers to think about gas mileage when they go inside.

The point is not that by themselves such actions—any individual actions—will make any real dent in the production of carbon dioxide pouring into our atmosphere. Even if you got 10 percent of Americans really committed to changing energy use, their solar homes wouldn't make much of a dent in our national totals. But 10 percent would be enough to change the politics of the issue, to insure the passage of the laws that would cause us all to shift our habits. And so we need to begin to take an issue that is now the province of technicians and turn it into a political issue—just as bus boycotts began to take the issue of race and make it public, forcing the system to respond. That response is likely to be ugly—there are huge companies with a lot to lose, and many people so tied in to their current ways of life that advocating change smacks of subversion. But this has to become a political issue—and fast. The only way that may happen, short of a hideous drought or monster flood, is if it becomes a personal issue first.

Conservationists Sue to Protect Yellowstone from Snowmobiles
Earthjustice

The world's first national park, Yellowstone, was the brainchild of a railroad official who hoped the designation would create a destination resort that would lure a steady stream of tourists to the site, allowing the railroad to build a spur line. Thus from the beginning, U.S. national parks have experienced tension between facilitating use and recreation, and preserving the natural beauty and resources. (see "Yosemite Against Corporation Greed," page 258).

Nowhere has this tension been more evident in recent years than in the bitter battles over snowmobile use in Yellowstone. The conflict has been hard fought not only in court, but in the press too, as both sides seek to galvanize public opinion.

Three National Park Service studies completed as of 2005 have shown that the snowmobiles generate sufficient noise and air pollution that park employees who greet the winter visitors need to wear ear protection and have special ventilation systems in the entrance booths. The air and noise pollution is also alleged to affect wildlife, the ability of park visitors to see distant vistas, and even water quality (when hydrocarbon-laden snow melts in the spring).

The Clinton administration proposed a rule banning the snowmobiles in the park, and ever since lawsuits and counter suits between environmental groups, recreational groups, and local businesses have resounded in federal courts in Wyoming and Washington, D.C. The Bush administration and Congress have intervened to allow several hundred snowmobiles per year on an interim basis while further studies (and, no doubt, lawsuits) progress.

Most of those involved in the dispute agree that snowcoaches (vans with tracks, essentially) should be allowed so that tourists can get to the lodges at Old Faithful in winter. The snowcoaches transport many individuals per trip, and thus produce far less pollution per visitor. But another group, Fund for Animals, contends that all maintenance of over-snow trails harms animals and should be banned. Its lawsuit, temporarily on hold as of this writing, would essentially ban all types of mechanized winter travel in the park.

Protests around the snowmobile issue included Campaign to Protect America's Lands proposal to idle eleven snowmobiles in a Simón Bolívar Park near the Department of Interior in Washington, D.C., to demonstrate the vehicles' noise and fumes. The proposed protest was denied a permit by the National Park Service, as snowmobiles are not allowed in the small park.

Here a 2003 press release from Earthjustice, which provided legal representation to conservation groups, outlines the basic case for removing the snowmobiles from the park.

A COALITION OF CONSERVATION GROUPS today filed suit to challenge the National Park Service's proposal to allow continued snowmobiling in Yellowstone and Grand Teton National Parks. The administration's plan would allow even more snowmobiles in Yellowstone where the noisy machines already disturb wildlife, pollute the air, and spread clouds of exhaust over such famous landmarks as Old Faithful.

"Families visiting Yellowstone in winter shouldn't have to worry about their health, they shouldn't have to wear ear plugs, and park rangers shouldn't have to wear respirators," said Abigail Dillen, an attorney with Earthjustice, who is representing [the] Greater Yellowstone Coalition, National Parks Conservation Association, The Wilderness Society, Natural Resources Defense Council, Winter Wildlands Alliance, and Sierra Club.

"The Park Service's decision flies in the face of overwhelming public sentiment favoring a ban on snowmobiling in Yellowstone. The science says snowmobiles are harmful to Yellowstone, the law requires the National Park Service to protect the park, and polls show that Americans want the service to do its job," said Charles Clusen, director of the Natural Resources Defense Council's National Parks Project. "It's a sad day when we have to file a lawsuit to force this administration to do the right thing."

Federal laws and regulations require the Park Service to preserve Yellowstone's spectacular natural resources "for the enjoyment of future generations." Yet under the Park Service's new snowmobile plan, winter visitors should not expect to enjoy clean air and natural quiet.

Contrary to the administration's public statements, which have touted continued snowmobile use, a recently completed study by the administration identifies ending snowmobile use as best balance between preservation and use of the parks.

That study, completed after two years and $2.4 million, analyzed "cleaner and quieter" snowmobiles and determined that even limited numbers of the newest machines would cause significantly greater impacts than a full transition from snowmobiles to snowcoaches. These greater impacts include haze at Old Faithful, more engine noise, health problems for employees and visitors with sensitive respiratory systems, and chronic disruption of wildlife.

In addition, the Bush administration study concludes that phasing out snowmobiles would not cause great or even moderate economic impact: "Even with the phaseout of snowmobiles, economic impacts to local communities in the five county area have been found to be negligible to minor." These findings are identical to the conclusion that formed the basis for the earlier decision in November 2000 to begin phasing snowmobiles out of both parks.

Air and noise pollution anticipated by the Park Service pose serious health risks, especially to people with respiratory problems and other vulnerable populations such as pregnant women, children, and senior citizens. According to Betsy Buffington of The Wilderness Society, "The Park Service's new decision means that a huge segment of Americans will have to worry about breathing in Yellowstone." The Park Service also reports that employees may experience hearing loss due to constant exposure to the noise of snowmobile engines.

"There's an easy way to solve all the problems caused by snowmobiles. Keep them out of Yellowstone," says Hope Sieck of Greater Yellowstone Coalition. "The Park Service has made it clear that mass-transit snowcoaches are the best way to get visitors into the park, and the public is overwhelmingly behind that approach. So, tell me, why do we still have snowmobiles in the park?"

"On the very first day we planted seven trees"
Wangari Maathai and Amanda Griscom Little

One might not immediately think that planting trees could be an act of protest—or that the person doing the planting could go to prison for subversion. Or, perhaps even more surprisingly, that planting trees would be sufficient to command the Nobel Peace Prize. But all of these are true.

Wangari Maathai founded the Green Belt Movement in Kenya in 1977. The movement established a way for women to improve their lives by planting trees for firewood, building materials, and as protection for wells and water supplies. Today the effort has five thousand local nurseries and has planted twenty million trees in Kenya. And what started as a very small grassroots effort has grown to an international movement; there are Green Belt efforts underway in Tanzania, Uganda, Malawi, Lesotho, Ethiopia, and Zimbabwe.

Maathai was awarded the Nobel Peace Prize in 2004 and spoke with *Grist Magazine's* Amanda Griscom Little in this February 2005 interview.

GRISCOM LITTLE: Tell us about the origins of the Green Belt Movement and why you decided to center your activism around tree planting.

MAATHAI: We started in 1977 to mobilize ordinary women in communities to provide themselves with their basic needs for living, much of which are derived from trees—firewood for energy, building materials and fencing materials, drinking water, rich soil for planting, fodder for their animals. They learned how to separate the soil for crops and protect areas where their waters come from. Much of the drought in Africa is a result of deforestation, which leaches the soil of minerals and moisture.

GRISCOM LITTLE: In only 30 years your organization has grown 30 million trees. Can you talk about the explosive growth of your concept and how it has lifted up communities?

MAATHAI: On the very first day we planted seven trees, and I like to mention this because sometimes people get overwhelmed by 30 million. It is important to understand that this is a process, not something that happens in a bang.

Much more important than the trees themselves is the mobilization of rural populations in large numbers—populations that we normally think are helpless, are dependent, are not able to do things for themselves. They organized themselves and started to address the issues in their own communities to improve their quality of life. At its peak, we've had over 6,000 groups of women planting trees. In the process they educate themselves and address government issues. Eventually we became a pro-democracy movement.

GRISCOM LITTLE: How did you go from a tree-planting activity to a political movement?

MAATHAI: When we started organizing ourselves into many groups, the government started to interfere. We had nearly a dictatorial government that believed in controlling, and they were afraid of why we were organizing. And that's when we contacted the minister of environmental protections, because we realized that in order to protect the environment, we needed to organize and systematically educate ourselves—we needed to create a more democratic state.

GRISCOM LITTLE: I have read that you faced violent opposition from the police.

MAATHAI: We are women [in this organization]. We did not have any guns and we were not going to use force, even when they used force to try to stop us. We realized that all we needed to do to empower ourselves was to understand that we are the ones who can change government, we are the ones who can decide what kind of leaders to put in place. And so we got rid of our fear, we refused to be victims of government intimidation, but instead participated in elections and succeeded in changing leadership. . . .

GRISCOM LITTLE: In your Nobel Prize acceptance speech, you talked about the environment as a path to peace: "A degraded environment leads to a scramble for scarce resources and may culminate in poverty and even conflict."

MAATHAI: Yes, and I think this is a reality in the whole world, not only in Africa, but perhaps more so in Africa. We have not enjoyed peace or enjoyed good government or enjoyed good management of our natural resources, and therefore have had massive poverty and a lot of conflict.

The connection between peace and the environment can be explained using the [analogy of] the traditional African stool, which has three legs that support the base on which we sit. I believe these three legs are symbolic. One represents good management of our natural resources, equitable distribution of the same, and a sense of accountability. Another represents good government—a democratic state that respects humankind so that we can have dignity as human beings. The third represents peace. The base on which we sit is development. If you try to do the development where you have no legs, or where you have two legs or one leg, the base is out of balance. It is unsustainable.

GRISCOM LITTLE: In the United States, it seems our development is based on two of the legs: We have democracy and peace (on our own soil, anyway), but we don't have a broad sense of accountability and equal distribution of resources. The desire to consume in America seems to outpace the sense of responsibility for our resource-intensive lifestyles.

MAATHAI: I know there is a concern about the consumptive pattern in America, but I also know that there are people in America, large numbers, millions of people who really understand this concept and who have been trying to push for this concept and individually live this concept. There are corporations that try to live this concept. Unfortunately, there are also those who don't, and some of those who don't are in power.

But I think you should stop being disempowered. You should focus on the large majority of Americans, for example, who understand, who have power to build a critical mass to shift the politics. That voice is inherently so strong, so practical, so right, and it will be heard.

GRISCOM LITTLE: True, but do you see it as contradictory that the environmental movement in Africa seems to have more resonance with its people than it does in the United States?

MAATHAI: You need to keep perspective. For 30 years I worked putting one foot in front of the other and really didn't think that anybody was listening to me; I felt like I had been talking to myself all my life. And then suddenly, the

Norwegian Nobel Peace Committee tells me that "you're the one that has really been looking at the right balance." I want to encourage those of us who are looking at those issues that way to feel that indeed we are validated. We need to continue that message even more strongly, and even with greater conviction until we win. Because we are the ones who are on the right path.

Petition to the Inter-American Commission on Human Rights Seeking Relief from Violations Resulting from Global Warming Caused by Acts and Omissions of the United States

Sheila Watt-Cloutier, Inuit Circumpolar Conference, et al.

In late December 2005, the Inuit Circumpolar Conference filed a human rights complaint against the United States with the Inter-American Commission on Human Rights, an agency of the Organization of American States. The petition claims that U.S. inaction in preventing global warming constitutes a violation of the Inuit's human rights. A ruling in favor of the Inuit by the commission could open the door for the Inuit to pursue lawsuits that would compel the U.S. government to take action to reduce greenhouse gas emissions or to provide compensation for damages to the Inuit.

The petition is unusual among protests against global warming in that it documents in great detail how changes in climate have affected a people's cultural traditions and economy. For example, weakening of sea ice has reduced the Inuit's safety during over-ice travel to hunting sites, and reduced snowfall has made winter travel by sledge and snowmobile less safe and less reliable.

I. SUMMARY OF THE PETITION

In this petition, Sheila Watt-Cloutier, an Inuk woman and Chair of the Inuit Circumpolar Conference, requests the assistance of the Inter-American Commission on Human Rights in obtaining relief from human rights violations resulting from the impacts of global warming and climate change caused by acts and omissions of the United States. Ms. Watt-Cloutier submits this petition on behalf of herself, 62 other named individuals, and all Inuit of the arctic regions of the United States of America and Canada who have been affected by the impacts of climate change described in this petition. . . .

The Inuit, meaning "the people" in their native Inuktitut, are a linguistic and cultural group descended from the Thule people whose traditional range spans four countries—Chukotka in the Federation of Russia, northern and western Alaska in the United States, northern Canada, and Greenland. . . .

Like many indigenous peoples, the Inuit are the product of the physical environment in which they live. . . . The culture, economy and identity of the Inuit as an indigenous people depend upon the ice and snow.

Nowhere on Earth has global warming had a more severe impact than the Arctic. Building on the 2001 findings of the Intergovernmental Panel on Climate Change, the 2004 Arctic Climate Impact Assessment—a comprehensive international evaluation of arctic climate change and its impacts undertaken by hundreds of scientists over four years—concluded that:

> The Arctic is extremely vulnerable to observed and projected climate change and its impacts. The Arctic is now experiencing some of the most rapid and severe climate change on Earth. Over the next 100 years, climate change is expected to accelerate, contributing to major physical, ecological, social, and economic changes, many of which have already begun.

Because annual average arctic temperatures are increasing more than twice as fast as temperatures in the rest of the world, climate change has already caused severe impacts in the Arctic. . . .

One of the most significant impacts of warming in the Arctic has been on sea ice. Commonly observed changes include thinner ice, less ice, later freezes and earlier, more sudden thaws. Sea ice is a critical resource for the Inuit, who use it to travel to hunting and harvesting locations, and for communication between communities. Because of the loss in the thickness, extent and duration of the sea ice, these traditional practices have become more dangerous, more difficult or, at times, impossible. In many regions, traditional knowledge regarding the safety of the sea ice has become unreliable. As a result, more hunters and other travelers are falling through the sea ice into the frigid water below. The shorter season for safe sea ice travel has also made some hunting and harvest activities impossible, and curtailed others. For the Inuit, the deterioration in sea ice conditions has made travel, harvest, and everyday life more difficult and dangerous.

The quality, quantity and timing of snowfall have also changed. Snow generally falls later in the year, and the average snow cover over the region has decreased ten percent over the last three decades. The spring thaw comes earlier and is more sudden than in the past. As with decreased ice, the shorter snow season has made travel more difficult. In addition, the deep, dense snow required for igloo building has become scarce in some areas, forcing many travelers to rely on tents, which are less safe, much colder and more cumbersome than igloos. The lack of igloo-quality snow can be life threatening for travelers stranded by unforeseen storms or other emergencies. These changes have also contributed to the loss of traditional igloo building knowledge, an important component of Inuit culture.

Permafrost, which holds together unstable underground gravel and inhibits water drainage, is melting at an alarming rate, causing slumping, landslides, severe erosion and loss of ground moisture, wetlands and lakes. The loss of sea ice, which dampens the impact of storms on coastal areas, has resulted in increasingly violent storms hitting the coastline, exacerbating erosion and flooding.

Erosion in turn exposes coastal permafrost to warmer air and water, resulting in faster permafrost melts. These transformations have had a devastating impact on some coastal communities, particularly in Alaska and the Canadian Beaufort Sea region. Erosion, storms, flooding and slumping harm homes, infrastructure, and communities, and have damaged Inuit property, forcing relocation in some cases and requiring many communities to develop relocation contingency plans. In addition, these impacts have contributed to decreased water levels in rivers and lakes, affecting natural sources of drinking water, and habitat for fish, plants, and game on which Inuit depend.

Other factors have also affected water levels. Changes in precipitation and temperature have led to sudden spring thaws that release unusually large amounts of water, flooding rivers and eroding their streambeds. Yet, after spring floods, rivers and lakes are left with unusually low levels of water further diminished by increased evaporation during the longer summer. These changes affect the availability and quality of natural drinking water sources. The fish stocks upon which Inuit rely are profoundly affected by changing water levels. Fish sometimes can not reach their spawning grounds, their eggs are exposed or washed ashore, or northward moving species compete with the native stocks for ecological niches.

The weather has become increasingly unpredictable. In the past, Inuit elders could accurately predict the weather for coming days based on cloud formations and wind patterns, allowing the Inuit to schedule safe travel. The changing climate has made clouds and wind increasingly erratic and less useful for predicting weather. . . . The inability to forecast has resulted in hunters being stranded by sudden storms, trip cancellations, and increased anxiety about formerly commonplace activities. . . .

Increased temperatures and sun intensity have heightened the risk of previously rare health problems such as sunburn, skin cancer, cataracts, immune system disorders and heat-related health problems. Warmer weather has increased the mortality and decreased the health of some harvested species, impacting important sources of protein for the Inuit. Traditional methods of food and hide storage and preservation are less safe because of increased daytime temperatures and melting permafrost.

The current impacts in the Arctic of climate change are severe, but projected impacts are expected to be much worse. . . .

Several principles of international law guide the application of the human rights issues in this case. Most directly, the United States is obligated by its membership in the Organization of American States and its acceptance of the American Declaration of the Rights and Duties of Man to protect the rights of the Inuit described above. Other international human rights instruments give meaning to the United States' obligations under the Declaration. For example, as a party to the International Convention on Civil and Political Rights ("ICCPR"), the United States is bound by the principles therein. As a signatory to the International

Convention on Economic, Social, and Cultural Rights ("ICESCR"), the United States must act consistently with the principles of that agreement. . . .

The impacts of climate change, caused by acts and omissions by the United States, violate the Inuit's fundamental human rights protected by the American Declaration of the Rights and Duties of Man and other international instruments. These include their rights to the benefits of culture, to property, to the preservation of health, life, physical integrity, security, and a means of subsistence, and to residence, movement, and inviolability of the home. . . .

The United States of America, currently the largest contributor to greenhouse emissions in the world, has nevertheless repeatedly declined to take steps to regulate and reduce its emissions of the gases responsible for climate change. . . .

Because this petition raises violations of the American Declaration of the Rights and Duties of Man by the United States of American [sic], the Inter-American Commission on Human Rights has jurisdiction to receive and consider it. The petition is timely because the acts and omissions of the United States that form the basis for the petition are ongoing, and the human rights violations they are causing are increasing. Because there are no domestic remedies suitable to address the violations, the requirement that domestic remedies be exhausted does not apply in this case.

The violations detailed in the petition can be remedied. As such, the Petitioner respectfully requests that the Commission:

1. Make an onsite visit to investigate and confirm the harms suffered by the named individuals whose rights have been violated and other affected Inuit;

2. Hold a hearing to investigate the claims raised in this Petition;

3. Prepare a report setting forth all the facts and applicable law, declaring that the United States of America is internationally responsible for violations of rights affirmed in the American Declaration of the Rights and Duties of Man and in other instruments of international law, and recommending that the United States:

a. Adopt mandatory measures to limit its emissions of greenhouse gases and cooperate in efforts of the community of nations—as expressed, for example, in activities relating to the United Nations Framework Convention on Climate Change—to limit such emissions at the global level;

b. Take into account the impacts of U.S. greenhouse gas emissions on the Arctic and affected Inuit in evaluating and before approving all major government actions;

c. Establish and implement, in coordination with Petitioner and the affected Inuit, a plan to protect Inuit culture and resources, including, *inter alia*, the land, water, snow, ice, and plant and animal species used or occupied by the named individuals whose rights have been violated and other affected Inuit; and mitigate any harm to these resources caused by US greenhouse gas emissions;

d. Establish and implement, in coordination with Petitioner and the affected Inuit communities, a plan to provide assistance necessary for Inuit to adapt to the impacts of climate change that cannot be avoided;

e. Provide any other relief that the Commission considers appropriate and just.

"We should no longer tolerate the low-cost or even free exploitation of public resources"
Call for Public Disclosure of Nujiang Hydropower Development's EIA Report

In 2003, China closed the floodgates of the Three Gorges Dam, the world's largest hydroelectric project, and began filling the reservoir that will eventually flood 350 miles of the Yangtze River and displace more than 1.1 million people. The project's human and environmental impacts were sparingly debated inside China, yet a third of the delegates in China's national assembly abstained or voted no to its final approval—a startling degree of dissent from that usually uniform legislative body.

A clear indication of the growth of free speech in China is the ongoing uproar over a series of dams proposed for the Nujiang River in southeastern China. The Nujiang River tumbles from the Tibetan plateau through some of the world's most rugged and biologically rich terrain. When UNESCO declared the area a World Heritage Site in 2003, it referred to the area as an "epicentre of Chinese biodiversity," as well as an area of outstanding scenic value.

On August 31, 2005, a coalition of sixty-one Chinese organizations and ninety-nine individuals released an open letter demanding that China's environmental laws be enforced in the development of dams along the Nujiang. In particular, the letter seeks the release of the Environmental Impact Assessment [EIA] for the project. (The acronym SEPA refers to China's lead environmental agency, the State Environmental Protection Agency.)

For Americans, most of whom never seek out any of the 50,000 environmental impact statements filed in the United States each year, a protest for the right to review and comment on such documents may seem odd. Yet in China, the fight for citizen access to the review of the Nujiang dams is seen as a critical test of the rule of law and of the rights of citizens to participate in environmental decisions and, more broadly, in the governance of their nation.

SINCE 2003, the plans for damming the Nujiang River have grabbed the attention of people from all walks of life. This river, so very far away, has become linked to the hearts of many people. . . .

We have been informed that the Central Government's planning and environmental departments have reviewed the hydropower development plans for the Nujiang. We think that the EIA for a project such as this that affects the interests of this and future generations, that has attracted worldwide attention, and that carries potentially huge impacts should be publicly disclosed and decided with sufficient prior informed consent and evaluation, following the requirements of the relevant law and the guiding principles of the State Council.

. . . This river is one of only two undammed rivers in China. It is located in an area of high biodiversity, and flows through the Three Parallel Rivers World Heritage Area. This naturally caused concern over its environmental impacts. Meanwhile, dam-building in an area of high mountains, deep valleys and extremely poor farmland threatens the livelihoods and future of tens of thousands of people. . . .

Since the planned dams on the Nujiang became such a focus of public attention, and SEPA expressed concerns, the central government suspended the projects in February 2004. Premier Wen Jiabao called for more careful and prudent studies of the plans, and a "science-based" decision-making process. As a result, the dam developers and relevant government departments were required to conduct a more comprehensive and detailed EIA. . . .

However, since the Nujiang project was suspended, the EIA and related documents concerning the Nujiang project have not been disclosed. There is no way for the public to learn how the developers and local government will avoid environmental damage, how they plan to carry out the resettlement of 50,000 people, and how they will assure the safety and economic feasibility of the dams. . . .

Such a decision-making process does not meet the legal requirements for public participation in China, the internationally recognised requirements for decision-making processes, the requirements of the "Administration Permission Law," and the principles of information disclosure in the "Guidelines of Full Implementation of Law." The EIA law, which became effective on 1 September 2003, clearly states, "The nation encourages relevant units, experts and the public to participate in the EIA process in appropriate ways."

According to the law, "for projects which may cause negative environmental impacts and directly involve public environmental interests, the institutions of project planning should seek opinions from the relevant units, experts and public over the draft EIA report, by holding evaluation meetings, hearings and other forms of meetings, before the draft is submitted.". . .

Recently, we are informed that the Nujiang's hydropower planning has been reviewed by the planning and environmental departments. However, so far the EIA and related documents concerning the Nujiang project still have not been disclosed. There is still no way for the public to learn how the developers and local government plan to avoid environmental damage, or to arrange proper relocation, or to assure the safety and economic feasibility of the dams. We believe that it does not fulfil the legal requirements for such a major plan if it bypasses the public participation requirements in Chinese law. The decision-making under such circumstances lacks the public support and cannot tolerate history's scrutiny.

We sincerely call for the decision-making authorities to disclose the EIA report of the Nujiang dam plans before making a decision, because the right to be informed is a prerequisite for public participation. . . .

Nujiang hydropower development is not an individual case. We hope the process can help develop a set of science-based and democratic decision-making mechanisms, in order to cope with the over-heated and unregulated hydropower development boom in China. In 2004, the installed capacity of China's hydropower reached 100,000 MW, which is the highest in the world. China's hydropower sector plans to increase capacity to 250,000 MW by 2020. On the mainstream of the Jinsha, Min, Dadu, Yalong, Jialing, Wu, Hongshui and Lancang Rivers, hydropower cascades have been planned. Some of them will be amongst the largest dams in the world. Many more dams have been developed on the tributaries of each of these rivers, and in some cases the number of dams top 300 in one watershed. Without a proper procedure, such an abnormally fast pace of development may result in resource exploitation and environmental degradation. Then the beauty of China's natural rivers will be lost, and the affected people in southwest China's mountainous areas may fall into dire poverty.

Today, China has entered the market economy era. Although hydropower development is a major part of our nation's energy development strategy, today's hydropower development is basically a commercial business. We should no longer tolerate the low-cost or even free exploitation of public resources and the earning of huge profits at the expense of our environment. Dam-builders should not externalise the huge costs of dam construction on affected people, the public, the nation's finances and future generations.

We are glad that the State Council, the National Development and Reform Commission and the local governments have taken steps to regulate hydropower development. However, to change the root cause of the current problems, a new decision-making mechanism for hydropower development should be developed, to keep all stakeholders fully informed and allow their participation. When all stakeholders gain the right to know and participate, the social and environmental impacts of hydropower development can then be properly considered, the pros and cons can then be reasonably weighed, the affected people and the environment can then be fully compensated, and alternative solutions can then be seriously considered. Only by doing so, the river resources can then be fairly, openly, scientifically, reasonably and sustainably utilised. This is also the only option to put the science-based development vision and the harmonic development of human beings and nature into practice.

"How to Destroy the Boreal, North America's Largest Ancient Forest, in 3 Easy Steps"

Greenpeace and the Natural Resources Defense Council

Some environmental protest seeks to use consumer pressure to influence corporate behavior. Sometimes these protests take the form of campaigns to change specific corporate behavior, as in the advertisement shown here targeting Kimberly-Clark's logging practices. The ad ran in the national edition of the *New York Times* in early November 2005. In the past, similar campaigns have persuaded Time Inc. to use environmentally sustainable paper in the production of its magazines and encouraged greater environmental responsibility in lending practices.

Advertising has long been used by environmental groups. For example, in the mid-1960s the Sierra Club used advertising to devastating effect in a successful campaign to prevent dams from being built at the foot of the Grand Canyon. But targeting corporations, as opposed to governments, is a significant tactical change, reflecting the growing power of corporations and the globalization of markets.

In the case of this ad, Greenpeace and the Natural Resources Defense Council (NRDC) seek to change the Kimberly-Clark Corporation's behavior in the Canadian wilderness by advertising in the United States. The campaign also has included demonstrations in Seattle, San Francisco, and other American cities, as well as a banner ad on Foxnews.com.

Equator Principles: Compliance Complaint
Center for Human Rights and Environment

Environmental groups increasingly work with industry to endorse common principles. Sometimes this takes the form of third-party certification of environmental responsibility, such as the Equator Principles discussed here, the Marine Fisheries Stewardship Council, or the Forest Stewardship Council. Such collaborative work channels protest into cooperation to fix acknowledged problems and also creates the opportunity for new forms of protest.

The Equator Principles are intended to encourage environmental and economic sustainability in development projects costing more than $50 million. As of the start of 2006, they had been endorsed by more than thirty major financial institutions, including CitiGroup and JPMorgan Chase. Principles, however, are only as powerful as the monitoring and enforcement behind them, just as laws depend on the consent of the majority of the governed to obey them and consistent enforcement against those who don't.

The complaint below, submitted to the Dutch banking group ING, represented the first appeal to one of the signatory banks to enforce the Equator Principles. The bank had committed to two European paper companies (ENCE and Botnia) that it would finance the construction of pulp mills in Uruguay along the Uruguay River, which creates the boundary between Uruguay and Argentina. The mills were to use a chlorine bleaching process to whiten the pulp and thus produce bright white papers. Such processes are being phased out in Europe and the United States due to the extensive pollution produced. In the complaint, the Argentina-based Center for Human Rights and Environment (El Centro de Derechos Humanos y Ambiente, or CEDHA) sought to have ING self-enforce the Equator Principles, especially the requirement for detailed environmental impact review and thorough consultation with those who will be affected by the project. The complaint made reference to a previous complaint filed by CEDHA with the International Financial Corporation or IFC.

In the spring of 2006, ING announced that it was withdrawing from the project.

Complaint Summary

The Center for Human Rights and Environment (CEDHA) denounces the violation of international human rights and international environmental law, . . . violations to the Equator Principles and other procedural violations (especially with respect to stakeholder consultation) regarding the design, preparations and construction of two paper pulp mill industries sponsored by Botnia (Finland) and ENCE (Spain) in Fray Bentos (Uruguay), on the River Uruguay, forming the natural waterway border between Argentina and Uruguay.

CEDHA, in representation of nearly 40,000 affected stakeholders, including local communities and civil society organizations in both Uruguay and Argentina, filed a complaint in September of 2005 to the IFC's independent Compliance Advisory Ombudsman (CAO), and to the Inter-American Commission on Human Rights grounded on these violations. . . . In its Preliminary Assessment Report, released just a short time ago, the CAO expresses its serious concern for the rights and expected impacts on local stakeholders which were not properly consulted. . . .

This Equator Principles Compliance Complaint presents to ING the accusations made in the complaint filed by CEDHA to the CAO, and identifies corresponding violations to the Equator Principles. . . . The complaint denounces and draws attention to severe violations of local, regional and international laws, which are resulting in legal and procedural action not only before the CAO but before international tribunals (such as the Inter-American Commission on Human Rights and/or the International Court of Justice), as well as before local courts (in Uruguay, Argentina, Finland and Spain), and regional courts (such as the European Commission) to hold perpetrators and sponsors of these acts accountable to environmental and human rights obligations.

This complaint is submitted to ING citing ING's moral, ethical and professional obligation to uphold its commitments to the Equator Principles and ensure that as financiers ING is "promoting responsible environmental stewardship and socially responsible development."

The complaint also highlights the enormous risks with ING involvement in these projects in terms of legal process, public opposition, and mounting international advocacy against the types of unsustainable development promoted by the project sponsors.

The complaint requests ING to cease any and all consideration of financing to Botnia and/or ENCE, initiating all and any necessary investigations, considerations and assessments of the violations presented, before any potential financial support to project sponsors is considered.

Background of Projects

The projects involve nearly US$2 billion of foreign direct investment (FDI), the largest single FDI in Uruguayan history, and in the case of Botnia of Finland it is the largest foreign private investment ever of a Finish [sic] company abroad. The combined production of Botnia and ENCE would be the world's largest production of Kraft System paper pulp, utilizing Elemental Chlorine Free technology, technology which has been phased out in European operations by 2007 and is against both European Union and World Bank best practice policy.

The industries will produce 1.5 million tons of pulp, utilizing 4 million tons of wood per year. The plants are sited on the River Uruguay forming the natural waterway border between Argentina and Uruguay, in the town of Fray Bentos

(Uruguay) and across from Gualeguaychú, a tourist driven region of Argentina. The plants are expected to employ 3000 workers during construction and 300 low-paying long-term wage workers in a region that is extremely rich in natural resources and heavily reliant on tourism and fisheries for local livelihoods.

The government of Uruguay has been fomenting eucalyptus tree plantation to feed into the European pulp paper industry for over a decade. Both project sponsors have been operating in Uruguay and in the industry in this context for a number of years, exporting trees for processing in Europe. Both companies had previously acquired land and constructed piers on the Uruguay River for receiving lumbered trees and producing wood chips for subsequent shipping to Europe. The decision to transfer processing technology from Europe to Uruguay coincides with tightening of European legislation and phasing out second-rate technology by 2007. This is a pitiful and unacceptable example of exporting contaminating industries to the global south. . . .

Violations to Equator Principles

ING, as a leader in upholding Equator Principles, has the moral, ethical, and professional obligation to "promote responsible environmental stewardship and socially responsible development" and has promised to finance projects that are "socially responsible and reflect sound environmental management practices." Furthermore, ING recognizes the "significant benefits to ourselves, our customers and other stakeholders" and promises to "review carefully all proposals.". . .

These projects violate the following Equator Principles. . . .

CEDHA Requests to ING

CEDHA and stakeholders requests that ING:

1. Suspend previous, and cease all present and future consideration of financing of these projects until the projects prove to comply with ALL IFC environmental and social safeguard policy, with the Equator Principles as well as with international human rights and environmental law;

2. Initiate any and all internal investigations into the allegations made in this Compliance Complaint and be informed of and consider evidence presented in claims made on these projects to the CAO and to other international and local tribunals based on issues relevant to the Equator Principles;

3. Adhere to CAO recommendations regarding these projects and utilize the CAO Report to inform and guide its own investigation on these projects in terms of compliance with the Equator Principles;

4. Publicly inform clients, customers, stakeholders and the general public on its position with respect to the suspension of financing, or any consideration of financing these projects and the grounds for doing so (or not);

5. Assess and inform itself of project compliance with the Equator Principles and only proceed to provide finance should it be perfectly clear that environmental and social impacts have been properly addressed and mitigated.

CEDHA is available to meet with ING staff and management to provide you with any and all relevant information and evidence that ING may need to bring clarity to any of the issues presented in this and other legal and/or procedural complaints brought against these projects and/or project sponsors.

CHAPTER 8
RELIGIOUS FREEDOM

INTRODUCTION

Globally there are more than a dozen major religions, each with millions of followers and multiple denominations. Along with many additional minor religions, these comprise a myriad of different modes of worship, beliefs about the nature of a divine being, and guidelines for morally correct living. Within each religion, too, there is typically debate about proper belief, worship, and action—debates which probably date to the first organized religions in the world. With so much variation, friction is inevitable between followers of different sects within a religion, between followers of different religions, and between the devout and the secular.

All these religious institutions and their followers exist in a delicate balance with their societies, and religious protest often takes the form of someone seeking to tip that balance in one direction or another. Some protesters—including U.S. founding fathers and presidents James Madison and Thomas Jefferson—have sought a more carefully delineated line between church and state, in order to keep government from intruding into affairs of faith. At the other end of the spectrum are those protesting the exclusion of religion from public life, such as former Alabama Supreme Court judge Roy S. Moore, who in 2001 installed a monument to the Ten Commandments in his courthouse.

Religious protest also includes those who have advocated for freedom to worship as they see fit; examples in this chapter include religious dissidents such as Anne Hutchinson, John Wesley, and Muslims in France who protested a 2004 law that prohibited devout Muslim girls from wearing their traditional head scarves to school. Conversely, atheist Michael Newdow brought a lawsuit to protest his daughter being forced to say the U.S. pledge of allegiance with its phrase "under God."

Other examples of religious protest included here address constraints on people's choice of religion; protest both against inflexible traditions within a particular religion and against straying from those traditions; protest over corruption or immoral behavior by clerics; and, in the case of famous muckraker Upton Sinclair, protest against the basic essence of organized religion itself.

Dialogue from the Examination of Mrs. Hutchinson During Her Trial

Anne Hutchinson and John Winthrop

Anne Marbury Hutchinson was born in England in 1595 and moved to Boston in the Massachusetts Bay Colony with her husband and eleven children in 1634. A midwife who was also deeply religious, she embraced Puritan practice and was moved by the sermons of minister John Cotton. Hutchinson began inviting other women to her home for weekly discussions of Cotton's sermons and the Bible.

The daughter of a minister, she was a highly literate student of the Bible, intellectually sophisticated, and in her element far from the strict confines of the Anglican Church in the homeland. Soon more people, including some men, came to hear her thoughts on scripture as often as to discuss those of clergymen. The meetings set up a classic confrontation between established religious authorities and those individuals pushing the boundaries of religious freedom.

New England's Puritan founders insisted on controlling religious practice. Followers who challenged the authority of religious leaders by holding their own meetings and offering their own interpretations of scripture were considered subversive and were not tolerated—especially a woman. When Hutchinson was ordered to cease her meetings, she defied the order. Even during her trial in 1637, Hutchinson stood her ground. At times in her testimony, she even seems to be toying with Governor John Winthrop, sparring with him intellectually. The court ruled Hutchinson a heretic. She was jailed, then banished to the wilderness of what would later become Rhode Island, where in 1638 she helped found the town of Portsmouth. After her husband died, Hutchinson moved to Pelham, just north of New York City. There, in 1643, she and all but one of her children were killed in an Indian raid.

Some historians believe the Puritans were affronted by Hutchinson's literacy and self-assurance in a time when women were expected to stay in the background, and they consider her America's first feminist. Massachusetts Governor Michael Dukakis officially pardoned Anne Hutchinson in 1987.

GOVERNOR WINTHROP: Mrs. Hutchinson, you are called here as one of those that have troubled the peace of the commonwealth and the churches here; you are known to be a woman that hath had a great share in the promoting and divulging of those opinions that are causes of this trouble, and to be nearly joined not only in affinity and affection with some of those the court had taken notice of and passed censure upon, but you have spoken divers things as we have been informed very prejudicial to the honour of the churches and ministers thereof, and you have maintained a meeting and an assembly in your house that hath been condemned by the general assembly as a thing not tolerable nor comely in the sight of God nor fitting for your sex, and notwithstanding that was cried down you have continued the same, therefore we have thought good to send for you to understand how things are, that if you be in an erroneous way we may reduce you that so you may become a profitable member here among us, otherwise if you be obstinate in your course that then the court may take such course that you may trouble us no further, therefore I would intreat you to express whether you do not assent and hold in practice to those opinions and factions that have been handled in court already, that is to say, whether you do not justify Mr. Wheelwright's sermon and the petition.

MRS. HUTCHINSON: I am called here to answer before you but I hear no things laid to my charge.

WINTHROP: I have told you some already and more I can tell you.

HUTCHINSON: Name one, Sir.

WINTHROP: Have I not named some already?

HUTCHINSON: What have I said or done?

WINTHROP: Why for your doings, this you did harbour and countenance those that are parties in this faction that you have heard of.

HUTCHINSON: That's a matter of conscience, Sir.

WINTHROP: Your conscience you must keep or it must be kept for you.

HUTCHINSON: Must not I then entertain the saints because I must keep my conscience?

WINTHROP: Say that one brother should commit felony or treason and come to his brother's house, if he knows him guilty and conceals him he is guilty of the same. It is his conscience to entertain him, but if his conscience comes into act in giving countenance and entertainment to him that hath broken the law he is guilty too. So if you do countenance those that are transgressors of the law you are in the same fact.

HUTCHINSON: What law do they transgress?

WINTHROP: The law of God and of the state.

HUTCHINSON: In what particular?

WINTHROP: Why in this among the rest, whereas the Lord doth say honour thy father and thy mother.

HUTCHINSON: Ey Sir in the Lord.

WINTHROP: This honour you have broke in giving countenance to them.

HUTCHINSON: In entertaining those did I entertain them against any act (for there is the thing) or what God hath appointed?

WINTHROP: Why the fifth commandment.

HUTCHINSON: I deny that for he saith in the Lord.

WINTHROP: You have joined with them in the faction.

HUTCHINSON: In what faction have I joined with them?

WINTHROP: In presenting the petition.

HUTCHINSON: Suppose I had set my hand to the petition what then?

WINTHROP: You saw that case tried before.

HUTCHINSON: But I had not my hand to the petition.

WINTHROP: You have councelled them.

HUTCHINSON: Wherein?

WINTHROP: Why in entertaining them.

HUTCHINSON: What breach of law is that Sir?

WINTHROP: Why dishonoring of parents.

HUTCHINSON: But put the case Sir that I do fear the Lord and my parents, may not I entertain them that fear the Lord because my parents will not give me leave?

WINTHROP: If they be the fathers of the commonwealth, and they of another religion, if you entertain them then you dishonor your parents and are justly punishable.

HUTCHINSON: If I entertain them, as they have dishonoured their parents I do.

WINTHROP: No but you by countenancing them above others put honor upon them.

HUTCHINSON: I may put honor upon them as the children of God and as they do honor the Lord.

WINTHROP: We do not mean to discourse with those of your sex but only this; you do adhere unto them and do endeavor to set forward this faction and so you do dishonour us.

HUTCHINSON: I do acknowledge no such thing neither do I think that I ever put any dishonour upon you.

WINTHROP: Why do you keep such a meeting at your house as you do every week upon a set day?

HUTCHINSON: It is lawful for me so to do, as it is all your practices and can you find a warrant for yourself and condemn me for the same thing? The ground of my taking it up was, when I first came to this land because I did not go to such meetings as those were, it was presently reported that I did not allow of such meetings but held them unlawful and therefore in that regard they said I was proud and did despise all ordinances, upon that a friend came unto me and told me of it and I to prevent such aspersions took it up, but it was in practice before I came therefore I was not the first.

WINTHROP: For this, that you appeal to our practice you need no confutation. If your meeting had answered to the former it had not been offensive, but I will say that there was no meeting of women alone, but your meeting is of another sort for there are sometimes men among you.

HUTCHINSON: There was never any man with us.

WINTHROP: Well, admit there was no man at your meeting and that you were sorry for it, there is no warrant for your doings, and by what warrant do you continue such a course?

HUTCHINSON: I conceive there lyes a clear rule in Titus, that the elder women should instruct the younger and then I must have a time wherein I must do it.

WINTHROP: All this I grant you, I grant you a time for it, but what is this to the purpose that you Mrs. Hutchinson must call a company together from their callings to come to be taught of you?

HUTCHINSON: Will it please you answer me this and to give me a rule for them, I will willingly submit to any truth. If any come to my house to be instructed in the ways of God what rule have I to put them away?

WINTHROP: But suppose that a hundred men come unto you to be instructed will you forbear to instruct them?

HUTCHINSON: As far as I conceive I cross a rule in it.

WINTHROP: Very well and do you not so here?

HUTCHINSON: No Sir for my ground is they are men.

WINTHROP: Men and women all are one for that, but suppose that a man should come and say Mrs. Hutchinson I hear that you are a woman that God hath given his grace unto and you have knowledge in the word of God. I pray instruct me a little, ought you not to instruct this man?

HUTCHINSON: I think I may. Do you think it not lawful for me to teach women and why do you call me to teach the court?

WINTHROP: We do not call you to teach the court but to lay open yourself.

HUTCHINSON: I desire you that you would then set down a rule by which I may put them away that come unto me and so have peace in so doing.

WINTHROP: You must shew your rule to receive them.

HUTCHINSON: I have done it.

WINTHROP: I deny it because I have brought more arguments than you have.

HUTCHINSON: I say, to me it is a rule.

A Letter Concerning Toleration
John Locke

In his first essay on religion—the 1689 letter excerpted here—English physician and philosopher John Locke protested religious persecution and the involvement of church and state in each other's affairs. Locke argued that religion is an individual matter, in which each person should come to his faith based on his own reason and experience. In Locke's opinion, for government to try to compel people to a particular set of beliefs—such as the Church of England did with its forced loyalty oaths, or the state did with its sanctioned torture during the Spanish Inquisition—was both morally wrong and foolish. Coercion, he argued, would not create true faith. It followed, Locke reasoned, that the state must tolerate people of other faiths and trust that they would come to truth of their own accord.

Locke's plea for toleration had its limits, however. He concluded that the state would have the right to restrict religion when there were compelling political reasons to do so. Roman Catholics, for instance, thought Locke, profess allegiance to the pope, therefore their allegiance to the English king could not be trusted.

Nearly a century later, James Madison and Thomas Jefferson both drew heavily on Locke's concepts as they developed their own practical ideas about the separation of church and state in Virginia.

THAT ANY MAN SHOULD THINK FIT to cause another man, whose salvation he heartily desires, to expire in torments, and that even in an unconverted state, would, I confess, seem very strange to me, and I think, to any other also. But nobody, surely, will ever believe that such a carriage can proceed from charity, love or goodwill. If any one maintain that men ought to be compelled by fire and sword to profess certain doctrines, and conform to this or that exterior worship, without any regard had unto their morals; if any one endeavour to convert those that are erroneous unto the faith, by forcing them to profess things that they do not believe and allowing them to practise things that the gospel does not permit; it cannot be doubted indeed but such a one is desirous to have a numerous assembly joined in the same profession with himself; but that he principally intends by those means to compose a truly christian church, is altogether incredible. It is not, therefore, to be wondered at if those who do not really contend for the advancement of the true religion, and of the church of Christ, make use of arms that do not belong to the christian warfare. If, like the captain of our salvation, they sincerely desired the good of souls, they would tread in the steps and follow the perfect example of that prince of peace, who sent out his soldiers to the subduing of nations, and gathering them into his church, not armed with the sword, or other instruments of force, but prepared with the gospel of peace and with the exemplary holiness of their conversation. This was his method. Though if infidels were to be converted by force, if those that are either blind or obstinate were to be drawn off from their errors by armed soldiers, we know very well that it was much more easy for him to do it with armies of heavenly legions than for any son of the church, how potent soever, with all his dragoons.

The toleration of those that differ from others in matters of religion is so agreeable to the gospel of Jesus Christ, and to the genuine reason of mankind, that it seems monstrous for men to be so blind as not to perceive the necessity and advantage of it, in so clear a light. . . . I esteem it above all things necessary to distinguish exactly the business of civil government from that of religion and to settle the just bounds that lie between the one and the other. If this be not done, there can be no end put to the controversies that will be always arising between those that have, or at least pretend to have, on the one side, a concernment for the interest of men's souls, and, on the other side, a care of the commonwealth. . . .

. . . The care of souls cannot belong to the civil magistrate, because his power consists only in outward force: but true and saving religion consists in the inward persuasion of the mind, without which nothing can be acceptable to God. And such is the nature of the understanding, that it cannot be compelled to the belief of any thing by outward force. Confiscation of estate, imprisonment, torments, nothing of that nature can have any such efficacy as to make men change the inward judgment that they have framed of things. . . .

What I say concerning the mutual toleration of private persons differing from one another in religion, I understand also of particular churches; which stand as it were in the same relation to each other as private persons among themselves; nor has any one of them any manner of jurisdiction over any other; no not even when the civil magistrate, as it sometimes happens, comes to be of this or the other communion. For the civil government can give no new right to the church, nor the church to the civil government. So that whether the magistrate join himself to any church, or separate from it, the church remains always as it was before, a free and voluntary society. It neither acquires the power of the sword by the magistrate's coming to it, nor does it lose the right of instruction and excommunication by his going from it. This is the fundamental and immutable right of a spontaneous society, that it has power to remove any of its members who transgress the rules of its institution: but it cannot, by the accession of any new members, acquire any right of jurisdiction over those that are not joined with it. And therefore peace, equity, and friendship are always mutually to be observed by particular churches, in the same manner as by private persons, without any pretence of superiority or jurisdiction over one another.

That the thing may be made yet clearer by an example, let us suppose two churches, the one of arminians, the other of calvinists, residing in the city of Constantinople. Will any one say, that either of these churches has right to deprive the members of the other of their estates and liberty, as we see practised elsewhere, because of their differing from it in some doctrines and ceremonies; whilst the Turks in the meanwhile silently stand by, and laugh to see with what inhuman cruelty christians thus rage against christians? But if one of these churches hath this power of treating the other ill, I ask which of them it is to whom that power belongs, and by what right? It will be answered, undoubtedly, that it is the orthodox church which has the right of authority over the erroneous or heretical. This is, in great and specious words, to say just nothing at all. For every church is orthodox to itself; to others, erroneous or heretical. Whatsoever any church believes, it believes to be true; and the contrary thereunto it pronounces to be error. So that the controversy between these churches about the truth of their doctrines, and the purity of their worship, is on both sides equal; nor is there any judge, either at Constantinople, or elsewhere upon earth, by whose sentence it can be determined. The decision of that question belongs only to the Supreme Judge of all men, to whom also alone belongs the punishment of the erroneous. In the mean while, let those men consider how heinously they sin, who, adding injustice, if not to their errour, yet certainly to their pride, do rashly and arrogantly take upon them to misuse the servants of another master, who are not at all accountable to them. . . .

. . . Let us now consider what is the magistrate's duty in the business of toleration; which certainly is very considerable.

We have already proved that the care of souls does not belong to the magistrate: not a magisterial care, I mean, if I may so call it, which consists in prescribing by laws, and compelling by punishments. But a charitable care, which consists in teaching, admonishing, and persuading, cannot be denied unto any man. The care therefore of every man's soul belongs unto himself, and is to be left unto himself. But what if he neglect the care of his soul? I answer, what if he neglect the care of his health, or of his estate; which things are nearlier related to the government of the magistrate than the other? Will the magistrate provide by an express law, that such an one shall not become poor or sick? Laws provide, as much as is possible, that the goods and health of subjects be not injured by the fraud and violence of others; they do not guard them from the negligence or ill-husbandry of the possessors themselves. No man can be forced to be rich or healthful, whether he will or no. Nay, God himself will not save men against their wills.

Advice to a People Called Methodist

John Wesley

John Wesley was born in 1703 in Epworth, England. Both he and his younger brother Charles became ministers of the Church of England and missionaries to the colony of Georgia. While attending a prayer meeting in May 1738, Wesley had a transforming religious experience, which he described in his diary: "About a quarter to nine, while he was describing the change which God works in the heart through faith in Christ, I felt my heart strangely warmed. I felt I did trust in Christ, Christ alone for salvation, and an assurance was given me that he had taken away my sins, even mine and saved me from the law of sin and death."

Wesley and his brother began leading a Christian renewal movement that was seen by some as a challenge to church authorities, and by others as heretical and blasphemous. He took the then audacious step of going outside traditional parish bounds to preach to working-class people—who were often excluded from churches—in the open air or under tents in the countryside. Wesley promoted small "faith societies" within the Church of England, emphasizing a serious, methodical observance of religious duties, Bible study, and an ascetic lifestyle. Though he never formally broke with the Anglican Church during his lifetime, Wesley's continued preaching, despite persecution by Church authorities and the public, was an act of protest against the Church's strict control.

In this excerpt from his essay "Advice to a People Called Methodist," Wesley outlined what those who challenged church doctrine—protesters, in essence—could expect as reaction from others, and he urged his followers to stand their ground for their beliefs.

CONSIDERING THESE PECULIAR CIRCUMSTANCES wherein you stand, you will see the propriety of a Second advice I would recommend to you: "Do not imagine you can avoid giving offence." Your very name renders this impossible. Perhaps not one in a hundred of those who use the term *Methodist* have any ideas of what it means. To ninety-nine of them it is still heathen Greek. Only they think it means something very bad,—either a Papist, a heretic, an underminer of the Church, or some unheard-of monster; and, in all probability, the farther it goes, it must gather up more and more evil. It is vain, therefore, for any that is called a Methodist ever to think of not giving offence.

And as much offence as you give by your name, you will give still more by your principles. You will give offence to the bigots for opinions, modes of worship, and ordinances, by laying no more stress upon them; to the bigots against them, by laying so much; to men of form, by insisting so frequently and strongly on the inward power of religion; to moral men, (so called,) by declaring the absolute necessity of faith, in order to gain acceptance with God. To men of reason you will give offence, by talking of inspiration and receiving the Holy Ghost; to drunkards, Sabbath-breakers, common swearers, and other open sinners, by refraining from their company, as well as by that disapprobation of their behaviour which you will often be obliged to express. And indeed your life must give them continual offence: Your sobriety is grievously offensive to a drunkard; your serious conversation is equally intolerable to a gay impertinent: and, in general, that "you are grown so precise and singular, so monstrously strict, beyond all sense and reason, that you scruple so many harmless things, and fancy you are obliged to do so many others which you need not," cannot but be an offence to an abundance of people, your friends and relations in particular. Either, therefore, you must consent to give up your principles, or your fond hope of pleasing men.

What makes even your principles more offensive is, this uniting of yourselves together: Because this union renders you more conspicuous, placing you more in the eye of men; more suspicious,—I mean, liable to be suspected of carrying on some sinister design (especially by those who do not, or will not, know your inviolable attachment to His present Majesty); more dreadful, to those of a fearful temper, who imagine you have any such design; and more odious to men of zeal, if their zeal be any other than fervent love to God and man.

This offence will sink the deeper, because you are gathered out of so many other congregations: For the warm men in each will not easily be convinced, that you do not despise either them or their teachers; nay, will probably imagine, that you utterly condemn them, as though they could not be saved. And this occasion of offence is now at the height, because you are just gathered, or gathering rather, so that they know not where it will end; but the fear of losing (so they account it) more of their members, gives an edge to their zeal, and keeps all their anger and resentment in its strength.

Add to this, that you do not leave them quite, you still rank yourselves among their members; which, to those who know not that you do it for conscience' sake, is also a provoking circumstance. "If you would but get out of their sight!" But you are a continual thorn in their side, as long as you remain with them.

And (which cannot but anger them the more) you have neither power, nor riches, nor learning; yet, with all their power, and money, and wisdom, they can gain no ground against you.

You cannot but expect, that the offence continually arising from such a variety of provocations will gradually ripen into hatred, malice, and all other unkind tempers. And as they who are thus affected will not fail to represent you to others in the same light as you appear to them,—sometimes as madmen and fools, sometimes as wicked men, fellows not fit to live upon the earth; the consequence, humanly speaking, must be, that, together with your reputation, you will lose, first, the love of your friends, relations, and acquaintance, even those who once loved you the most tenderly; then your business, for many will employ you no longer, nor "buy of such an one as you are;" and, in due time, (unless He who governs the world interpose,) your health, liberty, and life.

A Discourse Concerning Unlimited Submission and Non-Resistance to the Higher Powers

Jonathan Mayhew

Jonathan Mayhew was the Congregationalist minister of Boston's West Church from 1747 until his death in 1766. In 1749 he delivered a sermon, "A Discourse Concerning Unlimited Submission and Non-Resistance to the Higher Powers: with Some Reflections on the resistance Made to King Charles I." That sermon was published in 1750 and is excerpted here. In the discourse Mayhew lays out a religious justification for civil disobedience, countering a prevailing doctrine that called for citizens to passively submit to their rulers. Using a blend of scripture and logic, he posited that resistance to a tyrannical ruler is not only permissible, but a Christian duty. Though he makes clear that he is not promoting rebellion, his writings—along with those of other ministers—played a significant role in paving the way for the revolutionary belief that resistance is sanctioned by God.

Mayhew's jumping-off point for his discourse was the hundredth anniversary of the execution of King Charles I, whose contentious reign led to civil war when members of Parliament rebelled against him and eventually had him tried and beheaded. Mayhew drew on the philosophy of John Locke to assert that kings derived their power not from divine right, but from the people; as Mayhew put it, "rulers have no authority from God to do mischief." The minister hoped his observations would prove "that Britons will not be slaves." His sermon, he wrote, should serve as "a warning to all corrupt councillors and ministers, not to go too far in advising to arbitrary, despotic measures."

LET US NOW TRACE the apostle's reasoning in favor of submission to the *higher powers*, a little more particularly and exactly. For by this it will appear, on one hand, how good and conclusive it is, for submission to those rulers who exercise their power in a proper manner: And, on the other, how weak and trifling and inconnected [sic] it is, if it be supposed to be meant by the apostle to show the obligation and duty of obedience to tyrannical, oppressive rulers in common with others of a different character.

The apostle enters upon his subject thus—*Let every soul be subject unto the higher powers; for there is no power but of God: the powers that be, are ordained of God.* Here he urges the duty of obedience from this topic of argument, that civil rulers, as they are supposed to fulfil the pleasure of God, are the ordinance of God. But how is this an argument for obedience to such rulers as do not perform the pleasure of God, by doing good; but the pleasure of the devil, by doing evil; and such as are not, therefore, *God's ministers,* but the devil's! *Whosoever, therefore, resisteth the power, resisteth the ordinance of God; and they that resist, shall receive to themselves damnation.* Here the apostle argues, that those who resist a reasonable and just authority, which is agreeable to the will of God, do really resist the will of God himself; and will, therefore, be punished by him. But how does this prove, that those who resist a lawless, unreasonable power, which is contrary to the will of God, do therein resist the will and ordinance of God? Is resisting those who resist God's will, the same thing with resisting God? . . .

. . . *For, for this cause pay you tribute also; for they are God's ministers, attending continually upon this very thing.* Here the apostle argues the duty of paying taxes from this consideration, that those who perform the duty of rulers, are continually attending upon the public welfare. But how does this argument conclude for paying taxes to such princes as are continually endeavouring to ruin the public? And especially when such payment would facilitate and promote this wicked design! *Render therefore to all their dues; tribute, to whom tribute is due; custom, to whom custom; fear, to whom fear; honor, to whom honor.* Here the apostle sums up what he had been saying concerning the duty of subjects to rulers. And his argument stands thus—"Since magistrates who execute their office well, are common benefactors to society; and may, in that respect, be properly stiled *the ministers and ordinance of God*; and since they are constantly employed in the service of the public; it becomes you to pay them tribute and custom; and to reverence, honor, and submit to, them in the execution of their respective offices." This is apparently good reasoning. But does this argument conclude for the duty of paying tribute, custom, reverence, honor and obedience, to such persons as (although they bear the title of rulers) use all their powers to hurt and injure the public: such as are not *God's ministers,* but *satan's?* such as do not take care of, and attend upon, the public interest, but their own, to the ruin of the public? that is, in short, to such as have no natural and just claim at all to tribute, custom, reverence, honor, and obedience? It is to be hoped that those who have any regard to the apostle's character as an inspired writer, or even as a man of common understanding, will not represent him as reasoning in such a loose incoherent manner; and drawing conclusions which have not the least relation to his premises. For what can be more absurd than an argument thus framed? "Rulers are, by their office, bound to consult the public welfare and the good of society: therefore you are bound to pay them tribute, to honor, and to submit to them, even when they destroy the public welfare, and are a common pest to society, by acting in direct contradiction to the nature and end of their office."

Thus, upon a careful review of the apostle's reasoning in this passage, it appears that his arguments to enforce submission, are of such a nature, as to conclude only in favour of submission *to such rulers as he himself describes*; i.e., such as rule for the good of society, which is the only end of their institution. Common tyrants, and public oppressors, are not intitled [sic] to obedience from their subjects, by virtue of any thing here laid down by the inspired apostle. . . .

If we calmly consider the nature of the thing itself, nothing can well be imagined more directly contrary to common sense, than to suppose that *millions* of people should be subjected to the arbitrary, precarious pleasure of *one single man*; (who has *naturally* no superiority over them in point of authority) so that their estates, and every thing that is valuable in life, and even their lives also, shall be absolutely at his disposal, if he happens to be wanton and capricious enough to demand them. What unprejudiced man can think, that God made ALL to be thus subservient to the lawless pleasure and phrenzy [sic] of ONE, so that it shall always be a sin to resist him! Nothing but the most plain and express revelation from heaven could make a sober impartial man believe such a monstrous, unaccountable doctrine, and, indeed, the thing itself, appears so shocking—so out of all *proportion*, that it may be questioned, whether all the *miracles* that ever were wrought, could make it credible, that this doctrine *really* came from God. At present, there is not the least syllable in scripture which gives any countenance to it. The hereditary, indefeasible, divine right of kings, and the doctrine of non-resistance which is built upon the supposition of such a right, are altogether as fabulous and chimerical, as transubstantiation; or any of the most absurd reveries of ancient or modern visionaries. These notions are fetched neither from divine revelation, nor human reason; and if they are derived from neither of those sources, it is not much matter from *whence they come, or whither they go.* Only it is a pity that such doctrines should be propagated in society, to raise factions and rebellions, as we see they have, in fact, been both in the *last,* and in the *present* REIGN.

Memorial and Remonstrance Against Religious Assessments

James Madison

In 1784, James Madison was a member of the legislative General Assembly in the recently formed Commonwealth of Virginia. He was part of a contingent that believed the state should protect religious freedom and make firm the separation of church and state, beginning with the disestablishment of the Anglican Church. An opposing group, led by Patrick Henry, Virginia's first governor, was concerned that liberalization would spell doom for churches because they would no longer receive tax revenues. Madison had been working closely with Thomas Jefferson to pass the Virginia Statute for Religious Freedom, which Jefferson, also a member of the state assembly, had originally drafted in 1779, three years after he penned the Declaration of Independence.

For years the competing groups remained deadlocked in the assembly, and neither side was able to gain passage of its bill. In 1784, when Jefferson went to France to serve as ambassador, Madison was left to shepherd the religious-freedom bill through to passage. Henry had begun a second term as governor in 1784, and his supporters proposed a compromise that would have ended tax support for churches, but required the commonwealth to pay the wages of all Christian teachers. Madison, not to be swayed from his principles, was spurred to action. He engineered a postponement of the bill. Then, in protest, he wrote the "Memorial and Remonstrance Against Religious Assessments," excerpted here. It was printed and circulated around the state as a petition, and when it was brought to the assembly that fall, it had some eleven thousand signatures. The strategy paid off: the following year the religious-freedom statute was passed.

WE THE SUBSCRIBERS, citizens of the said Commonwealth, having taken into serious consideration, a Bill printed by order of the last Session of General Assembly, entitled "A Bill establishing a provision for Teachers of the Christian Religion," and conceiving that the same if finally armed with the sanctions of a law, will be a dangerous abuse of power, are bound as faithful members of a free State to remonstrate against it, and to declare the reasons by which we are determined. We remonstrate against the said Bill,

Because we hold it for a fundamental and undeniable truth, "that religion or the duty which we owe to our Creator and the manner of discharging it, can be directed only by reason and conviction, not by force or violence." The Religion then of every man must be left to the conviction and conscience of every man; and it is the right of every man to exercise it as these may dictate. This right is in its nature an unalienable right. It is unalienable, because the opinions of men, depending only on the evidence contemplated by their own minds cannot follow the dictates of other men: It is unalienable also, because what is here a right towards men, is a duty towards the Creator. It is the duty of every man to render to the Creator such homage and such only as he believes to be acceptable to him. . . . True it is, that no other rule exists, by which any question which may divide a Society, can be ultimately determined, but the will of the majority; but it is also true that the majority may trespass on the rights of the minority.

Because Religion be exempt from the authority of the Society at large, still less can it be subject to that of the Legislative Body. . . . The preservation of a free Government requires not merely, that the metes and bounds which separate each department of power be invariably maintained; but more especially that neither of them be suffered to overleap the great Barrier which defends the rights of the people. The Rulers who are guilty of such an encroachment, exceed the commission from which they derive their authority, and are Tyrants. The People who submit to it are governed by laws made neither by themselves nor by an authority derived from them, and are slaves.

Because it is proper to take alarm at the first experiment on our liberties. We hold this prudent jealousy to be the first duty of Citizens, and one of the noblest characteristics of the late Revolution. The free men of America did not wait till usurped power had strengthened itself by exercise, and entangled the question in precedents. They saw all the consequences in the principle, and they avoided the consequences by denying the principle. We revere this lesson too much soon to forget it. Who does not see that the same authority which can establish Christianity, in exclusion of all other Religions, may establish with the same ease any particular sect of Christians, in exclusion of all other Sects? that the same authority which can force a citizen to contribute three pence only of his property for the support of any one establishment, may force him to conform to any other establishment in all cases whatsoever?

Because the Bill violates the equality which ought to be the basis of every law. . . . If "all men are by nature equally free and independent," all men are to be considered as entering into Society on equal conditions; as relinquishing no more, and therefore retaining no less, one than another, of their natural rights. Above all are they to be considered as retaining an "equal title to the free exercise of Religion according to the dictates of Conscience." Whilst we assert for ourselves a freedom to embrace, to profess and to observe the Religion which we believe to be of divine origin, we cannot deny an equal freedom to those whose minds have not yet yielded to the evidence which has convinced us. If this freedom be abused, it is an offence against God, not against man: To God, therefore, not to man, must an account of it be rendered. . . .

Because the Bill implies either that the Civil Magistrate is a competent Judge of Religious Truth; or that he may employ Religion as an engine of Civil policy. The first is an arrogant pretension falsified by the contradictory opinions of Rulers in all ages, and throughout the world: the second an unhallowed perversion of the means of salvation.

Because the establishment proposed by the Bill is not requisite for the support of the Christian Religion. To say that it is, is a contradiction to the Christian Religion itself, for every page of it disavows a dependence on the powers of this world: it is a contradiction to fact; for it is known that this Religion both existed and flourished, not only without the support of human laws, but in spite of every opposition from them, and not only during the period of miraculous aid, but long after it had been left to its own evidence and the ordinary care of Providence. . . .

Because experience witnesseth that ecclesiastical establishments, instead of maintaining the purity and efficacy of Religion, have had a contrary operation. During almost fifteen centuries has the legal establishment of Christianity been on trial. What have been its fruits? More or less in all places, pride and indolence in the Clergy, ignorance and servility in the laity, in both, superstition, bigotry and persecution. . . .

Because the proposed establishment is a departure from the generous policy, which, offering an Asylum to the persecuted and oppressed of every Nation and Religion, promised a lustre to our country, and an accession to the number of its citizens. What a melancholy mark is the Bill of sudden degeneracy? Instead of holding forth an Asylum to the persecuted, it is itself a signal of persecution. It degrades from the equal rank of Citizens all those whose opinions in Religion do not bend to those of the Legislative authority. Distant as it may be in its present form from the Inquisition, it differs from it only in degree. The one is the first step, the other the last in the career of intolerance. . . .

Because it will have a like tendency to banish our Citizens. The allurements presented by other situations are every day thinning their number. To superadd a fresh motive to emigration by revoking the liberty which they now enjoy, would be the same species of folly which has dishonoured and depopulated flourishing kingdoms.

Because it will destroy that moderation and harmony which the forbearance of our laws to intermeddle with Religion has produced among its several sects. Torrents of blood have been spilt in the old world, by vain attempts of the secular arm, to extinguish Religious discord, by proscribing all difference in Religious opinion. Time has at length revealed the true remedy. Every relaxation of narrow and rigorous policy, wherever it has been tried, has been found to assuage the disease. The American Theatre has exhibited proofs that equal and compleat liberty, if it does not wholly eradicate it, sufficiently destroys its malignant influence on the health and prosperity of the State. If with the salutary effects of this system under our own eyes, we begin to contract the bounds of Religious freedom, we know no name that will too severely reproach our folly. . . .

Because the policy of the Bill is adverse to the diffusion of the light of Christianity. The first wish of those who enjoy this precious gift ought to be that it may be imparted to the whole race of mankind. Compare the number of those who have as yet received it with the number still remaining under the dominion of false Religions; and how small is the former! Does the policy of the Bill tend to lessen the disproportion? No; it at once discourages those who are strangers to the light of revelation from coming into the Region of it. . . .

Because attempts to enforce by legal sanctions, acts obnoxious to so great a proportion of Citizens, tend to enervate the laws in general, and to slacken the bands of Society. If it be difficult to execute any law which is not generally deemed necessary or salutary, what must be the case, where it is deemed invalid and dangerous? And what may be the effect of so striking an example of impotency in the Government, on its general authority?

Because a measure of such singular magnitude and delicacy ought not to be imposed, without the clearest evidence that it is called for by a majority of citizens, and no satisfactory method is yet proposed by which the voice of the majority in this case may be determined, or its influence secured. . . .

Because finally, "the equal right of every citizen to the free exercise of his Religion according to the dictates of conscience" is held by the same tenure with all our other rights. . . . Either we must say, that the Will of the Legislature is the only measure of their authority; and that in the plenitude of this authority, they may sweep away all our fundamental rights; or, that they are bound to leave this particular right untouched and sacred. Either we must say, that they may controul [sic] the freedom of the press, may abolish the Trial by Jury, may swallow up the Executive and Judiciary Powers of the State; nay that they may despoil us of our very right of suffrage, and erect themselves into an independent and hereditary Assembly or, we must say, that they have no authority to enact into the law the Bill under consideration.

. . . We the Subscribers say, that the General Assembly of this Commonwealth have no such authority. . . .

The Virginia Act for Establishing Religious Freedom
Thomas Jefferson

Thomas Jefferson counted writing the Virginia Act for Establishing Religious Freedom as one of the three great accomplishments of his life. When designing his own tombstone he asked that it state "author of the Declaration of American Independence, of the Statute of Virginia for Religious Freedom, and father of the University of Virginia." First drafted in 1779, the statute was a culmination of the search for religious freedom that had been a driving force of the settling of the nation. It distilled the Enlightenment ideal of the inalienable rights of man into a statement on governance that allowed no wiggle room for intrusion into the citizen's private spiritual belief or practice. The document—with its espousal of the dual principles of religious freedom and the separation of church and state—was Jefferson's protest against what was quickly becoming the young nation's betrayal of the idea of religious tolerance.

Jefferson viewed religious belief as strictly a personal matter, between a man and his God (and if a man chose not to believe, that should also be a protected right, in his view); he saw no justification for the state's intrusion on matters of religion. "The legitimate powers of government extend to such acts only as are injurious to others. But it does me no injury for my neighbor to say there are twenty gods or no god. It neither picks my pocket, nor breaks my leg," Jefferson wrote in his book *Notes on Virginia*.

The Virginia statute was a defining expression of a nation feeling its way to a new relationship between church and state. It became a model for the religious freedom guarantee in the First Amendment of the Bill of Rights, which says, "Congress shall make no law respecting an establishment of religion, or prohibiting the free exercise thereof." In January 1786, a few months after Madison's "Memorial and Remonstrance," the act passed the Virginia Assembly and became law.

WELL AWARE THAT ALMIGHTY GOD hath created the mind free; that all attempts to influence it by temporal punishments or burdens, or by civil incapacitations, tend only to beget habits of hypocrisy and meanness, and are a departure from the plan of the Holy Author of our religion, who being Lord both of body and mind, yet chose not to propagate it by coercions on either, as was in his Almighty power to do; that the impious presumption of legislators and rulers, civil as well as ecclesiastical, who, being themselves but fallible and uninspired men, have assumed dominion over the faith of others, setting up their own opinions and modes of thinking as the only true and infallible, and as such endeavoring to impose them on others, hath established and maintained false religions over the greatest part of the world, and through all time; that to compel a man to furnish contributions of money for the propagation of opinions which he disbelieves, is sinful and tyrannical; that even the forcing him to support this or that teacher of his own religious persuasion, is depriving him of the comfortable liberty of giving his contributions to the particular pastor whose morals he would make his pattern, and whose powers he feels most persuasive to righteousness, and is withdrawing from the ministry those temporal rewards, which proceeding from an approbation of their personal conduct, are an additional incitement to earnest and unremitting labors for the instruction of mankind; that our civil rights have no dependence on our religious opinions, more than our opinions in physics or geometry; that, therefore, the proscribing [of] any citizen as unworthy [of] the public confidence by laying upon him an incapacity of being called to the offices of trust and emolument, unless he profess or renounce this or that religious opinion, is depriving him injuriously of those privileges and advantages to which in common with his fellow citizens he has a natural right; that it tends also to corrupt the principles of that very religion it is meant to encourage, by bribing, with a monopoly of worldly honors and emoluments, those who will externally profess and conform to it; that though indeed these are criminal who do not withstand such temptation, yet neither are those innocent who lay the bait in their way; that to suffer the civil magistrate to intrude his powers into the field of opinion and to restrain the profession or propagation of principles, on the supposition of their ill tendency, is a dangerous fallacy, which at once destroys all religious liberty, because he being of course judge of that tendency, will make his opinions the rule of judgment, and approve or condemn the sentiments of others only as they shall square with or differ from his own; that it is time enough for the rightful purposes of civil government, for its officers to interfere when principles break out into overt acts against peace and good order; and finally, that truth is great and will prevail if left to herself, that she is the proper and sufficient antagonist to error, and has nothing to fear from the conflict, unless by human interposition disarmed of her natural weapons, free argument and debate, errors ceasing to be dangerous when it is permitted freely to contradict them.

Be it therefore enacted by the General Assembly, That no man shall be compelled to frequent or support any religious worship, place, or ministry whatsoever, nor shall be enforced, restrained, molested, or burdened in his body or goods, nor shall otherwise suffer on account of his religious opinions or belief; but that all men shall be free to profess, and by argument to maintain, their opinions in matters of religion, and that the same shall in nowise diminish, enlarge, or affect their civil capacities.

And though we well know this Assembly, elected by the people for the ordinary purposes of legislation only, have no powers equal to our own and that therefore to declare this act irrevocable would be of no effect in law, yet we are free to declare, and do declare, that the rights hereby asserted are of the natural rights of mankind, and that if any act shall be hereafter passed to repeal the present or to narrow its operation, such act will be an infringement of natural right.

"Let My People Go"

African-American Spiritual

Spirituals originated in the late 1700s, when they were sung by African-American slaves. They called the songs "spiritual himes" to distinguish them from the Biblical hymns sung in Protestant churches. While the latter came from the European tradition and were psalms set to music, the spirituals came from a folk-song tradition and often expressed the slaves' yearning for freedom. In this classic spiritual, also known as "Go Down, Moses," the situation of the Southern slaves is mirrored by the enslavement of the Hebrew people in Egypt, who were forced to build pyramids for the pharaoh. The song is an early example of using religious music as vocal protest, a mode that would have enormous impact the following century when the hymn "We Shall Overcome" was employed as a protest song. In the case of the American slaves, singing was a safe way to protest their enslavement without directly confronting their owners.

WHEN ISRAEL was in Egypt's land,
Let my people go;
Oppressed so hard they could not stand,
Let my people go.
    Go down, Moses, way down in Egypt's land,
    Tell old Pharaoh: Let my people go.
The Lord told Moses what to do,
Let my people go;
To lead the children of Israel through,
Let my people go.
    Go down, Moses, way down in Egypt's land,
    Tell old Pharaoh: Let my people go.
The pillar of cloud shall clear the way,
Let my people go;
A fire by night, a shade by day,
Let my people go.
    Go down, Moses, way down in Egypt's land,
    Tell old Pharaoh: Let my people go.
As Israel stood by the water-side,
Let my people go;
At God's command it did divide,
Let my people go.
    Go down, Moses, way down in Egypt's land,
    Tell old Pharaoh: Let my people go.
When they had reached the other shore,
Let my people go;
They sang the song of triumph over,
Let my people go.

Go down, Moses, way down in Egypt's land,
   Tell old Pharaoh: Let my people go.
Oh, let us all from bondage flee,
Let my people go;
And let us all in Christ be free,
Let my people go.
   Go down, Moses, way down in Egypt's land,
   Tell old Pharaoh: Let my people go.

Appeal to the President of the United States
Joseph Smith

Joseph Smith, Jr., founded the Church of Jesus Christ of Latter-day Saints in 1830, and from its inception his followers—commonly known as Mormons—were subject to intense religious persecution. Smith, who was from a poor farming family in upstate New York, was fourteen years old in 1820, when he experienced what he described as a divine revelation. Smith said that as he was in a wooded grove praying to clarify his confusion over which of many competing religious sects to join, Jesus Christ appeared to him and commanded him to join no existing church. During the next ten years he received a series of visions and revelations, culminating in a vision of an angel hovering in his bedroom. The angel, called Moroni, told Smith where to find a series of metal plates, engraved with hieroglyphics, buried in a hill, along with two tablets that provided a translation key. Smith translated the plates, said to be the writings of a prophet named Mormon, who recorded the religious history of people who emigrated from Jerusalem and lived in America between 2200 B.C. and A.D. 421. Smith published the work in 1830 as the Book of Mormon, and it became the fundamental sacred text of the Latter-day Saints.

   The church's central belief is that the original ministry of Jesus went astray after the death of the apostles, and that the true primitive church was resurrected and reestablished by divine revelation to Smith, whom Mormons consider to be a prophet. Though the church proclaimed its Christianity, its adherents were treated with suspicion and disdain. They ventured west, first to Ohio and then in 1831 to Missouri, where their homes and property were vandalized by mobs. In 1838 Smith and his followers were run out of the state by the Missouri militia on orders of the governor. The Mormons moved to Illinois, where they established the community of Nauvoo near the Mississippi River. The community attracted thousands of followers, many of them poor citizens looking to reject the social establishment and start a new life. The community's expansion further inflamed the other settlers' fear and hatred. In 1844, Smith and his brother, Hyrum, were jailed in nearby Carthage, Illinois. On June 27, the jail was attacked by a mob, which murdered Smith and his brother. Afterward, the church's new leader, Brigham Young, led thousands of Mormon pioneers to start a new life far from their persecutors in what would become the state of Utah. Today there are more than twelve million Mormons, more than half of whom live outside the United States.

   Just one week before his death, Joseph Smith wrote this letter to President John Tyler, protesting the religious persecution of his church and asking for the government's protection.

CITY OF NAUVOO, ILL. JUNE 20, 1844

Sir: I have just enclosed to the Governor of the State of Illinois, copies of the enclosed affidavits and extra. I am sorry to say that the State of Missouri, not content with robbery, drinking, and murdering many of the Latter day saints, are now joining the mob of thiz [sic] state for the purpose of "utter extermina-tion" of the Mormons, as they have resolved. And now, Sir, as president of the United States, will you render that protection which the Constitution guaranties [sic] in case of "Insurrection and rebellion," and save the innocent and oppressed from such horrid persecution.

	With great respect
John Tyler	I have the honor
President	to be your obt. Servt.
of the U.S.	Joseph Smith
Washington	Mayor
D.C.	

The Pittsburgh Platform: Declaration of Principles of Reform Judaism 1885 Pittsburgh Conference

The creation of Reform Judaism was a rebellion against ancient rituals and traditions. The Enlightenment had held out the promise of religious tolerance and equality for European Jews, and at times and in places, it seemed the promise might be fulfilled. Governments granted new rights to Jews, but sometimes quickly withdrew them. And the enlightened thinking did not erase deep-seated prejudices. At the same time, advances in science—particularly Charles Darwin's theo-ries—and new ideas about natural law were changing the way people related to their religious history and their sacred texts.

Some Jews—especially in places like Eastern Europe and Russia, where Jews were most threatened by violence—retreated into orthodoxy and insular communities. Others believed the old ways were keeping Jewish Europeans segregated from their societies, and should be adapted to ensure the survival of the religion. In Germany, a group of reform-minded rabbis began meeting in the 1840s. They were losing followers: many Jews desired to assimilate into their secular cultures and were converting to Christianity. To stem the tide, the reform rabbis proposed casting off some of the ancient traditions of Orthodox Judaism, such as kashruth, the kosher dietary laws, and other restrictions that kept Jews alienated from non-Jews. They proposed adopting pragmatic changes that would make Judaism appear less foreign: services with translations from the Hebrew and mixed choral singing, in the manner of Protestant services; men and women being allowed to sit together; confirmation ceremonies for boys and girls entering young adulthood. These modern Jews called their houses of worship "temples" rather than synagogues. Prayers for the coming of the Messiah and the return to Zion were out; prayers recognizing the brotherhood of all humankind were in.

Some of the reform rabbis emigrated to America and continued their meetings. The newfangled services were already catching on in American synagogues when a group of reform rabbis held the Philadelphia Conference of 1869 to begin to formally codify the basic principles of their new movement. At the Pittsburgh Conference, held November 16 through 19, 1885, they adopted the following principles, which formed the basis of the new Jewish denomination. There are now more than nine hundred Reform Jewish congregations, with 1.5 million members, in the United States.

1. WE RECOGNIZE in every religion an attempt to grasp the Infinite, and in every mode, source or book of revelation held sacred in any religious system the consciousness of the indwelling of God in man. We hold that Judaism presents the highest conception of the God-idea as taught in our Holy Scriptures and developed and spiritualized by the Jewish teachers, in accordance with the moral and philosophical progress of their respective ages. We maintain that Judaism preserved and defended midst continual struggles and trials and under enforced isolation, this God-idea as the central religious truth for the human race.

2. We recognize in the Bible the record of the consecration of the Jewish people to its mission as the priest of the one God, and value it as the most potent instrument of religious and moral instruction. We hold that the modern discoveries of scientific researches in the domain of nature and history are not antagonistic to the doctrines of Judaism, the Bible reflecting the primitive ideas of its own age, and at times clothing its conception of divine Providence and Justice dealing with men in miraculous narratives.

3. We recognize in the Mosaic legislation a system of training the Jewish people for its mission during its national life in Palestine, and today we accept as binding only its moral laws, and maintain only such ceremonies as elevate and sanctify our lives, but reject all such as are not adapted to the views and habits of modern civilization.

4. We hold that all such Mosaic and rabbinical laws as regulate diet, priestly purity, and dress originated in ages and under the influence of ideas entirely foreign to our present mental and spiritual state. They fail to impress the modern Jew with a spirit of priestly holiness; their observance in our days is apt rather to obstruct than to further modern spiritual elevation.

5. We recognize, in the modern era of universal culture of heart and intellect, the approaching of the realization of Israel's great Messianic hope for the establishment of the kingdom of truth, justice, and peace among all men. We consider ourselves no longer a nation, but a religious community, and therefore expect neither a return to Palestine, nor a sacrificial worship under the sons of Aaron, nor the restoration of any of the laws concerning the Jewish state.

6. We recognize in Judaism a progressive religion, ever striving to be in accord with the postulates of reason. We are convinced of the utmost necessity of pre-

serving the historical identity with our great past. Christianity and Islam, being daughter religions of Judaism, we appreciate their providential mission, to aid in the spreading of monotheistic and moral truth. We acknowledge that the spirit of broad humanity of our age is our ally in the fulfillment of our mission, and therefore we extend the hand of fellowship to all who cooperate with us in the establishment of the reign of truth and righteousness among men.

7. We reassert the doctrine of Judaism that the soul is immortal, grounding the belief on the divine nature of human spirit, which forever finds bliss in righteousness and misery in wickedness. We reject as ideas not rooted in Judaism, the beliefs both in bodily resurrection and in Gehenna and Eden (Hell and Paradise) as abodes for everlasting punishment and reward.

8. In full accordance with the spirit of the Mosaic legislation, which strives to regulate the relations between rich and poor, we deem it our duty to participate in the great task of modern times, to solve, on the basis of justice and righteousness, the problems presented by the contrasts and evils of the present organization of society.

The Profits of Religion
Upton Sinclair

Upton Sinclair was part of a group of early twentieth-century muckrakers who used literature as a force for social change. He is best known for his groundbreaking work *The Jungle*, first published in 1906. Although it was a novel, *The Jungle* was also an exposé of the horrendous conditions in meatpacking plants. Sinclair shined a spotlight on the sweatshoplike conditions for the mostly immigrant meatpackers, as well as the lack of hygiene in the plants. The latter led the federal government to pass the Pure Food and Drug Act of 1906, which created the Food and Drug Administration and mandated food standards and the hiring of inspectors to enforce them. His Lanny Budd series of novels, published in the 1940s and early 1950s, surveyed many social issues and were highly popular; the third book in the series, *Dragon's Teeth*, about the rise of Nazism, won the Pulitzer Prize in fiction for 1943. Sinclair also dabbled in politics and narrowly lost election to the governorship of California.

In 1918 he self-published *The Profits of Religion: An Essay in Economic Interpretation*. In it, Sinclair savaged the entire institution of organized religion. Using ideas from sociology and economics, he argued that from its inception, religion in all its forms has been a self-serving construct that exploits the underprivileged to the advantage of "the priestly caste." He also railed against what he calls "the supreme crime of the Church": that it encourages in its followers a blind submission to authority and an unquestioning mind. Organized religion, by being "on the side of sloth of mind," argued Sinclair, "banishes brains, it sanctifies stupidity, it canonizes incompetence," and therefore acts as a conservative social force that tries to block important human advancements, such as the abolition of slavery, adoption of just wages and working conditions, teaching of new scientific knowledge, and even inoculations.

While parts of the work are dated (such as his prediction of a Roman Catholic takeover of the United States), others remain vital and especially relevant to a post-9/11 world in which the clash of religions is a driving force of war and terrorism.

WHEN THE FIRST SAVAGE saw his hut destroyed by a bolt of lightning, he fell down upon his face in terror. He had no conception of natural forces, of laws of electricity; he saw this event as the act of an individual intelligence. To-day we read about fairies and demons, dryads and fauns and satyrs, Wotan and Thor and Vulcan, Freie and Flora and Ceres, and we think of all these as pretty fancies, play-products of the mind; losing sight of the fact that they were originally meant with entire seriousness—that not merely did ancient man believe in them, but was forced to believe in them, because the mind must have an explanation of things that happen, and an individual intelligence was the only explanation available. The story of the hero who slays the devouring dragon was not merely a symbol of day and night, of summer and winter; it was a literal explanation of the phenomena, it was the science of early times.

Men imagined supernatural powers such as they could comprehend. If the lightning god destroyed a hut, obviously it must be because the owner of the hut had given offense; so the owner must placate the god, using those means which would be effective in the quarrels of men—presents of roast meats and honey and fresh fruits, of wine and gold and jewels and women, accompanied by friendly words and gestures of submission. And when in spite of all things the natural evil did not cease, when the people continued to die of pestilence, then came the opportunity for hysterical or ambitious persons to discover new ways of penetrating the mind of the god. There would be dreamers of dreams and seers of visions and hearers of voices; readers of the entrails of beasts and interpreters of the flight of birds; there would be burning bushes and stone tablets on mountain-tops, and inspired words dictated to aged disciples on lonely islands. There would arise special castes of men and women, learned in these sacred matters; and these priestly castes would naturally emphasize the importance of their calling, would hold themselves aloof from the common herd, endowed with special powers and entitled to special privileges. They would interpret the oracles in ways favorable to themselves and their order; they would proclaim themselves friends and confidants of the god, walking with him in the night-time, receiving his messengers and angels, acting as his deputies in forgiving offenses, in dealing punishments and in receiving gifts. They would become makers of laws and moral codes. They would wear special costumes to distinguish them, they would go through elaborate ceremonies to impress their followers. . . .

So builds itself up, in a thousand complex and complicated forms, the Priestly Lie. There are a score of great religions in the world, each with scores or hundreds of sects, each with its priestly orders, its complicated creed and ritual, its heavens and hells. Each has its thousands or millions or hundreds of millions of "true believers"; each damns all the others, with more or less heartiness—and each is a mighty fortress of Graft. . . .

In every human society of which we have record there has been one class which has done the hard and exhausting work, the "hewers of wood and drawers of water"; and there has been another, much smaller class which has done the directing. To belong to this latter class is to work also, but with the head instead of the hands; it is also to enjoy the good things of life, to live in the best houses, to eat the best food, to have choice of the most desirable women; it is to have leisure to cultivate the mind and appreciate the arts, to acquire graces and distinctions, to give laws and moral codes, to shape fashions and tastes, to be revered and regarded—in short, to have Power. How to get this Power and to hold it has been the first object of the thoughts of men from the beginning of time.

The most obvious method is by the sword; but this method is uncertain, for any man may take up a sword, and some may succeed with it. It will be found that empires based upon military force alone, however cruel they may be, are not permanent, and therefore not so dangerous to progress; it is only when resistance is paralyzed by the agency of Superstition, that the race can be subjected to systems of exploitation for hundreds and even thousands of years. The ancient empires were all priestly empires; the kings ruled because they obeyed the will of the priests, taught to them from childhood as the word of the gods. . . .

I might fill the balance of this volume with citations from defenses of the "peculiar institution" in the name of Jesus Christ—and not only from the South, but from the North. For it must be understood that leading families of Massachusetts and New York owed their power to Slavery; their fathers had brought molasses from New Orleans and made it into rum, and taken it to the coast of Africa to be exchanged for slaves for the Southern planters. And after this trade was outlawed, the slave-grown cotton had still to be shipped to the North and spun; so the traders of the North must have divine sanction for the Fugitive Slave law. Here is the Bishop of Vermont declaring: "The slavery of the negro race appears to me to be fully authorized both in the Old and New Testaments." Here is the "True Presbyterian," of New York, giving the decision of a clerical man of the world: "There is no debasement in it. It might have existed in Paradise, and it may continue through the Millennium."

And when the slave-holding oligarchy of the South rose in arms against those who presumed to interfere with this divine institution, the men of God of the South called down blessings upon their armies in words which, with the proper change of names, might have been spoken in Berlin in August, 1914. . . .

There came recently to Los Angeles a "world-famous evangelist," known as "Gipsy" Smith. There was a shirt-waist strike at the time, and the girls were starving, and they sent a delegation to this evangelist to ask for help. They told him how they were mistreated, exposed to insults, driven to sell their virtue because their wage would not support life; and to their plea he made answer: "Get Jesus in your hearts, and these questions will take care of themselves!"

So we see the most important of the many services which the churches perform for the merchants—taking the revolutionary hope of Jesus, for a kingdom of heaven upon earth, and perverting it into a dream of a golden harp in an uncertain future. To appreciate the fullness of this betrayal, take the prayer which Jesus dictated—so simple, direct and practical: "Give us this day our daily bread," and put it beside the hymns which the slave-congregations are trained to sing.

"He Calls That Religion"
The Mississippi Sheiks

The Mississippi Sheiks were an early blues band whose music was highly popular in its day. It influenced later blues musicians like Muddy Waters and, years afterward, rock bands like the Grateful Dead. Recordings by the band are included in the archives of the Library of Congress's American Folklife Center.

In his 1993 book *Blues and Evil*, Jon Michael Spencer traced the history of theological polemics in the blues. Where some music historians have dismissed criticisms of the church by blues singers as mere vaudeville, Spencer instead saw a clever use of "the familiar 'sounds' of minstrelsy in order to mask the seriousness of their protest." According to Spencer, one 1920s gospel song intoned that "a lot of preachers are preaching and think they are doing well, when 'all they want is your money and you can go to hell.'"

The Mississippi Sheiks' 1929 song "He Calls That Religion" is part of a long tradition of mocking the hypocrisy of authority figures. The band's take on abuses by Southern preachers is both scathing and humorous. Writers Bo Carter and Walter Vinson questioned preachers' motives toward their female parishioners, using sexual innuendo to attack what parishioners of the time must have been powerless to confront directly.

WELL, THE PREACHER used to preach
To try to save souls
But now he's preachin'
Just to buy jellyroll

> Well, he calls that religion
> Yes, he calls that religion
> Well, he calls that religion
> But I know he's goin' to hell when he dies

It was at a church last night
Happy as I could be
The old preacher

Was tryin' to take my wife from me

> Oh, he calls that religion
> Yes, he calls that religion
> Well, he called that religion
> I know he's goin' to hell when he dies

Preacher always
He was a mighty true man
He gives his commands
And he couldn't understand

> Well, he calls that religion
> Yes, he called that religion
> Well, he called that religion
> I know he goin' to hell when he dies

"Oh yes, he calls that religion"

He will swear he's keepin'
God's command
Have women fussin' 'n fightin'
All over the land

> And then he call that religion
> Well, he calls that religion
> Well, he called that religion
> But I know he's goin' to hell when he dies

The reason the people
Stopped goin' to church
They know that preacher
Was tryin-a do too much

> But still he called that religion
> Still, he called that religion
> Well, he called that religion
> But I know he's goin' to hell when he dies

Old Deacon Jones
He was a preachin' King
They caught him 'round the house
Tryin-a shake that thing

> Oh, he called that religion
> Yes, he called that religion
> Well, he called that religion

But I know he goin' to hell when he dies
"Oh yeah, he calls that religion."

"Christ Climbed Down" from *A Coney Island of the Mind*
Lawrence Ferlinghetti

Poet, artist, publisher, and bookstore owner Lawrence Ferlinghetti was one of the most influential writers of the 1950s Beat movement. His 1955 book *A Coney Island of the Mind* may be the best-selling book of American poetry of all time, with nearly one million copies in print. In this poem, "Christ Climbed Down," Ferlinghetti aimed his barbs at a popular subject for religious protest: the commercialization and secularization of modern American Christianity.

CHRIST CLIMBED DOWN
from His bare Tree
this year
and ran away to where
there were no rootless Christmas trees
hung with candycanes and breakable stars

Christ climbed down
from His bare Tree
this year
and ran away to where
there were no gilded Christmas trees
and no tinsel Christmas trees
and no tinfoil Christmas trees
and no pink plastic Christmas trees
and no gold Christmas trees
and no black Christmas trees
and no powderblue Christmas trees
hung with electric candles
and encircled by tin electric trains
and clever cornball relatives

Christ climbed down
from His bare Tree
this year
and ran away to where
no intrepid Bible salesmen
covered the territory
in two-tone cadillacs

and where no Sears Roebuck creches
complete with plastic babe in manger
arrived by parcel post
the babe by special delivery
and where no televised Wise Men
praised the Lord Calvert Whiskey

Christ climbed down
from His bare Tree
this year
and ran away to where
no fat handshaking stranger
in a red flannel suit
and a fake white beard
went around passing himself off
as some sort of North Pole saint
crossing the desert to Bethlehem
Pennsylvania
in a Volkswagon sled
drawn by rollicking Adirondack reindeer
with German names
and bearing sack of Humble Gifts
from Saks Fifth Avenue
for everybody's imagined Christ child

Christ climbed down
from His bare Tree
this year
and ran away to where
no Bing Crosby carollers
groaned of a tight Christmas
and where no Radio City angels
iceskated wingless
thru a winter wonderland
into a jinglebell heaven
daily at 8:30
with Midnight Mass matinees

Christ climbed down
from His bare Tree
this year
and softly stole away into
some anonymous Mary's womb again
where in the darkest night

of everybody's anonymous soul
He awaits again
an unimaginable
and impossibly
Immaculate Reconception
the very craziest
of Second Comings

Opinion from *Engel v. Vitale*
Hugo Black

In the late 1950s the Board of Regents for public schools in the state of New York drafted a "Statement of Moral and Spiritual Training in the Schools," which included the recitation of a non-denominational prayer by students at the start of each school day. The Board of Education in the town of New Hyde Park directed the school principal to have students recite a prayer each morning, using language that had been composed by the regents: "Almighty God, we acknowledge our dependence upon Thee, and we beg Thy blessings upon us, our parents, our teachers and our Country." After this policy took effect, the parents of ten pupils in the district brought suit in a New York State court challenging the constitutionality of the school prayer based on the First Amendment to the U.S. Constitution, which prohibits the enactment of any law "respecting an establishment of religion." Two levels of state court upheld the prayer, arguing that it did not conflict with the Establishment Clause as long as students were allowed to either remain silent or leave the room.

When the parents appealed to the Supreme Court, however, the justices ruled eight to one that the practice was indeed unconstitutional and overturned the state decisions. The court found that states cannot compose an official prayer and require it to be recited—even if it is non-denominational and individuals may abstain. Many of those who took issue with the ruling—including Justice Potter Stewart, who filed the lone dissent—saw it as divorcing the schools from the spiritual heritage of the nation. The late senator Sam Ervin of North Carolina asked whether the ruling meant that the Supreme Court had found that God was unconstitutional.

Justice Hugo Black's opinion, excerpted here, maintains that his finding is the logical extension of the freedom of religion that was the basis of the nation's founding.

IT IS A MATTER OF HISTORY that this very practice of establishing governmentally composed prayers for religious services was one of the reasons which caused many of our early colonists to leave England and seek religious freedom in America. The Book of Common Prayer, which was created under governmental direction and which was approved by Acts of Parliament in 1548 and 1549, set out in minute detail the accepted form and content of prayer and other religious ceremonies to be used in the established, tax supported Church of England. The controversies over the Book and what should be its content repeatedly threatened to disrupt the peace of that country as the accepted forms of prayer in the established church changed with the views of the particular ruler that happened to be in control at the time. Powerful groups representing some of the varying religious views of the people struggled among themselves to impress their particular views upon the Government and obtain amendments of the Book more suitable to their respective notions of how religious services should be conducted in order that the official religious establishment would advance their particular religious beliefs. Other groups, lacking the necessary political power to influence the Government on the matter, decided to leave England and its established church and seek freedom in America from England's governmentally ordained and supported religion.

It is an unfortunate fact of history that when some of the very groups which had most strenuously opposed the established Church of England found themselves sufficiently in control of colonial governments in this country to write their own prayers into law, they passed laws making their own religion the official religion of their respective colonies. Indeed, as late as the time of the Revolutionary War, there were established churches in at least eight of the thirteen former colonies and established religions in at least four of the other five. But the successful Revolution against English political domination was shortly followed by intense opposition to the practice of establishing religion by law. This opposition crystallized rapidly into an effective political force in Virginia where the minority religious groups such as Presbyterians, Lutherans, Quakers and Baptists had gained such strength that the adherents to the established Episcopal Church were actually a minority themselves. In 1785–1786, those opposed to the established Church, led by James Madison and Thomas Jefferson, who, though themselves not members of any of these dissenting religious groups, opposed all religious establishments by law on grounds of principle, obtained the enactment of the famous "Virginia Bill for Religious Liberty" by which all religious groups were placed on an equal footing so far as the State was concerned. Similar though less far-reaching legislation was being considered and passed in other States.

By the time of the adoption of the Constitution, our history shows that there was a widespread awareness among many Americans of the dangers of a union of Church and State. These people knew, some of them from bitter personal experience, that one of the greatest dangers to the freedom of the individual to worship in his own way lay in the Government's placing its official stamp of approval upon one particular kind of prayer or one particular form of religious services. They knew the anguish, hardship and bitter strife that could come when zealous religious groups struggled with one another to obtain the Government's stamp of approval from each King, Queen, or Protector that came to temporary power. The Constitution was intended to avert a part of this danger by leaving the government of this country in the hands of the people rather than in the hands of any monarch. But this safeguard was not enough. Our Founders were no more willing to let the content of their prayers and their privilege of praying whenever they pleased be influenced by the ballot box than they were to let these vital matters of personal conscience depend upon the succession of monarchs. The First Amendment was added to the Constitution to stand as a guarantee that neither the power nor the prestige of the Federal Government would be used to control, support or influence the kinds of prayer the American people can say—that the people's religions must not be subjected to the pressures of government for change each time a new political administration is elected to office. Under that Amendment's prohibition against governmental establishment of religion, as reinforced by the provisions of the Fourteenth Amendment, government in this country, be it state or federal, is without power to prescribe by law any particular form of prayer which is to be used as an official prayer in carrying on any program of governmentally sponsored religious activity.

There can be no doubt that New York's state prayer program officially establishes the religious beliefs embodied in the Regents' prayer. The respondents' argument to the contrary, which is largely based upon the contention that the Regents' prayer is "non-denominational" and the fact that the program, as modified and approved by state courts, does not require all pupils to recite the prayer but permits those who wish to do so to remain silent or be excused from the room, ignores the essential nature of the program's constitutional defects. . . . When the power, prestige and financial support of government is placed behind a particular religious belief, the indirect coercive pressure upon religious minorities to conform to the prevailing officially approved religion is plain. But the purposes underlying the Establishment Clause go much further than that. Its first and most immediate purpose rested on the belief that a union of government and religion tends to destroy government and to degrade religion. The history of governmentally established religion, both in England and in this country, showed that whenever government had allied itself with one particular form of religion, the inevitable result had been that it had incurred the hatred, disrespect and even contempt of those who held contrary beliefs. That same history showed that many people had lost their respect for any religion that had relied upon the support of government to spread its faith. The Establishment Clause thus stands as an expression of principle on the part of the Founders of our Constitution that religion is too personal, too sacred, too holy, to permit its "unhallowed perversion" by a civil magistrate. Another purpose of the Establishment Clause rested upon an awareness of the historical fact that governmentally established religions and religious persecutions go hand in hand. The Founders knew that only a few years after the Book of Common Prayer became the only accepted form of religious services in the established Church of England, an Act of Uniformity was passed to compel all Englishmen to attend those services and to make it a criminal offense to conduct or attend religious gatherings of any other kind—a law which was consistently flouted by dissenting religious groups in England and which contributed to widespread persecutions of people like John Bunyan who persisted in holding "unlawful [religious] meetings . . . to the great disturbance and distraction of the good subjects of this kingdom . . . ." And they knew that similar persecutions had received the sanction of law in several of the colonies in this country soon after the establishment of official religions in those colonies. It was in large part to get completely away from this sort of systematic religious persecution that the Founders brought into being our Nation, our Constitution, and our Bill of Rights with its prohibition against any governmental establishment of religion. The New York laws officially prescribing the Regents' prayer are inconsistent both with the purposes of the Establishment Clause and with the Establishment Clause itself.

It has been argued that to apply the Constitution in such a way as to prohibit state laws respecting an establishment of religious services in public schools is to indicate a hostility toward religion or toward prayer. Nothing, of course, could be more wrong. The history of man is inseparable from the history of religion. And perhaps it is not too much to say that since the beginning of that history many people have devoutly believed that "More things are wrought by prayer than this world dreams of." It was doubtless largely due to men who believed this that there grew up a sentiment that caused men to leave the cross-currents of officially established state religions and religious persecution in Europe and come to this country filled with the hope that they could find a place in which they could pray when they pleased to the God of their faith in the language they chose. And there were men of this same faith in the power of prayer who led the fight for adoption of our Constitution and also for our Bill of Rights with the very guarantees of religious freedom that forbid the sort of governmental activity which New York has attempted here. These men knew that the First Amendment, which tried to put an end to governmental control of religion and of prayer, was not written to destroy either. They knew rather that it was written to quiet well-justified fears which nearly all of them felt arising out of an awareness that governments of the past had shackled men's tongues to make them speak only the religious thoughts that government wanted them to speak and to pray only to the God that government wanted them to pray to. It is neither sacrilegious nor antireligious to say that each separate government in this country should stay out of the business of writing or sanctioning official prayers and leave that purely religious function to the people themselves and to those the people choose to look to for religious guidance.

Letter from Birmingham Jail
Martin Luther King, Jr.

Martin Luther King, Jr., was a minister and president of the Southern Christian Leadership Conference when he was arrested in Birmingham, Alabama, on April 12, 1963, for breaking a law against demonstrations. An affiliated organization there had asked the Conference to help lead a nonviolent direct-action campaign in protest of humiliating racially discriminatory signs in local shops. While in solitary confinement, King read a letter in the *New York Times*, signed by a group of Alabama clergymen, decrying the protests. He penned his lengthy response in the margins of the newspaper and on other scraps, and then sent the notes out with his aides. King laid out the religious grounds for civil disobedience, citing numerous historical precedents, including Jesus and Socrates. He later published the letter, excerpted here, in his 1964 book *Why We Can't Wait*.

I HAVE HEARD numerous southern religious leaders admonish their worshipers to comply with a desegregation decision because it is the law, but I have longed to hear white ministers declare: "Follow this decree because integration is morally right and because the Negro is your brother." In the midst of blatant injustices inflicted upon the Negro, I have watched white churchmen stand on the sideline and mouth pious irrelevancies and sanctimonious trivialities. In the midst of a mighty struggle to rid our nation of racial and economic injustice, I have heard many ministers say: "Those are social issues, with which the gospel has no real concern." And I have watched many churches commit themselves to a completely other worldly religion which makes a strange, un-Biblical distinction between body and soul, between the sacred and the secular.

I have traveled the length and breadth of Alabama, Mississippi and all the other southern states. On sweltering summer days and crisp autumn mornings I have looked at the South's beautiful churches with their lofty spires pointing heavenward. I have beheld the impressive outlines of her massive religious education buildings. Over and over I have found myself asking: "What kind of people worship here? Who is their God? Where were their voices when the lips of Governor Barnett dripped with words of interposition and nullification? Where were they when Governor Wallace gave a clarion call for defiance and hatred? Where were their voices of support when bruised and weary Negro men and women decided to rise from the dark dungeons of complacency to the bright hills of creative protest?"

Yes, these questions are still in my mind. In deep disappointment I have wept over the laxity of the church. But be assured that my tears have been tears of love. There can be no deep disappointment where there is not deep love. Yes, I love the church. How could I do otherwise? I am in the rather unique position of being the son, the grandson and the great grandson of preachers. Yes, I see the church as the body of Christ. But, oh! How we have blemished and scarred that body through social neglect and through fear of being nonconformists.

There was a time when the church was very powerful—in the time when the early Christians rejoiced at being deemed worthy to suffer for what they believed. In those days the church was not merely a thermometer that recorded the ideas and principles of popular opinion; it was a thermostat that transformed the mores of society. Whenever the early Christians entered a town, the people in power became disturbed and immediately sought to convict the Christians for being "disturbers of the peace" and "outside agitators." But the Christians pressed on, in the conviction that they were "a colony of heaven," called to obey God rather than man. Small in number, they were big in commitment. They were too God-intoxicated to be "astronomically intimidated." By their effort and example they brought an end to such ancient evils as infanticide and gladiatorial contests.

Things are different now. So often the contemporary church is a weak, ineffectual voice with an uncertain sound. So often it is an archdefender of the status quo. Far from being disturbed by the presence of the church, the power structure of the average community is consoled by the church's silent—and often even vocal—sanction of things as they are.

But the judgment of God is upon the church as never before. If today's church does not recapture the sacrificial spirit of the early church, it will lose its authenticity, forfeit the loyalty of millions, and be dismissed as an irrelevant social club with no meaning for the twentieth century.

Responsibility of the Kingdom of God
Oscar Romero

Oscar Romero was born in El Salvador in 1917 and died March 24, 1980, assassinated by a sniper as he celebrated Mass in a hospital chapel. Romero had been named the Roman Catholic archbishop of San Salvador, the capital of El Salvador, in 1977, a time of horrific violence in the country as the military dictatorship cracked down on those pushing for agrarian reform. Prior to his elevation, Romero was rather conservative, particularly compared to some Latin American priests, who were embracing the new Catholic doctrine of liberation theology, which emerged in Latin America in the late 1960s, and held that the church must take an active role in promoting social and economic justice for the poor living under totalitarian regimes. The liberation movement and its adherents, including Jesuit priests, drew a harsh backlash from the ruling elite. The Vatican's enforcer of orthodoxy, Cardinal Joseph Ratzinger—who would become Pope Benedict XVI upon the death of Pope John Paul II in 2005—denounced the movement, saying it bore an uncomfortable resemblance to atheistic Marxism.

Less than a month after he became archbishop, Romero had to identify the body of a close friend, a Jesuit priest who had been brutally murdered with an elderly man and a young boy as they walked to a village to say Mass. The experience was transformative. Romero became an outspoken advocate for the poor and oppressed in El Salvador. The sermon excerpted here was one of many in which Romero used scripture to make his case against the country's inhumane treatment of its citizens. Romero's impact was far-reaching: his sermons were broadcast by radio across the country and to other Latin American nations as well.

WHY DO WE LIVE IN THIS ENVIRONMENT OF VIOLENCE? An environment of violence that makes people fearful to walk the streets? What right does any organization have—it is not important whether they are legitimate or not but their message is important—to threaten with death and expulsion members of the Jesuit community? This is the voice of violence! Violence does not justify Christianity. . . .

My dear sisters and brothers, at this time when the Church is recovering her identity, it is necessary for us to examine ourselves. We must ask ourselves if we have understood what it means to belong to this poor, pilgrim, and detached Church. We must ask ourselves if we understand what it means to depend on Christ who placed his hope in God and not on the powers of the world. We must ask ourselves if we understand that we must build a better world because the Kingdom of God must begin here on earth, but we cannot use violence—the violence that is invented by human persons, institutionalized; the violence that wants to achieve its goals by force. No, we cannot build in this way! Christ calls us to love. Therefore Saint Paul, in the same letter, concludes with a phrase that I would like all of us to remember during these days. My sisters and brothers, Saint Paul writes: *If you go on biting and devouring one another, beware that you are not consumed by one another* (Galatians 5:14). This is the suicide of our country: we are biting one another and destroying one another. So what is the remedy? Saint Paul says: *You shall love your neighbor as yourself* (Galatians 5:14). He then adds: *Live by the Spirit and you will certainly not gratify the desire of the flesh. For the flesh has desires against the Spirit, and the Spirit against the flesh; these are opposed to each other, so that you may not do what you want. But if you are guided by the Spirit, you are not under the law* (Galatians 5:16–18). In other words, love is the power of the Church.

Let us make an effort, my sisters and brother, to forgive and to love. Let us begin by loving God and not offending God and loving our neighbor even though our neighbor may have offended us. This kind of effort will create a better world. The Pope has called us to build a civilization of love. Let us proclaim this civilization of love and make every effort to build it. Is it possible that El Salvador is not civilized! Does civilized mean publishing and communicating by radio brutal threats, like the ones we have recently read and heard! This is a very underdeveloped state of civilization! Is it so impossible to see the light of certain writers! Reason should be combated with reason! Why threaten with arms and death those who with reason communicate the message of the Church? The only way is by conversion. We must confront those who say that the Jesuits do not teach the Church's doctrine and tell them that the Jesuits teach what they have learned from the Church and the Church teaches what she has learned from God.

This then, is the only road that will lead us out of this uncivilized situation in which we now live and in which we are destroying one another. Saint Paul invites us to allow ourselves to be led by the Spirit. He sums this all up in the brief phrase: *You shall love your neighbor as yourself* (Galatians 5:14).

Let us make this effort, my sisters and brothers, for in this way we will make our Church a true torch of freedom—freedom that was proclaimed today in the Word of God and freedom that with one Christian faith we now proclaim.

Controversies at Auschwitz: The Convent and the Cross
Elie Wiesel and Carol Rittner

Postwar Auschwitz was the scene for an intensely emotional debate between Jews and Roman Catholics in the 1980s and 1990s. Two related controversies had their roots in 1979, when Pope John Paul II returned to his native Poland and celebrated Mass for a million Poles at a makeshift altar with a twenty-foot-tall cross near Krakow. The pontiff then visited Auschwitz, where he honored two Catholic martyrs, including a nun known as Sister Teresa Benedicta of the Cross. She was born Edith Stein, a Jew. Stein converted to Catholicism but was killed by the Nazis by virtue of being born a Jew; she was declared a saint by the Vatican in 1998.

The Nazis murdered primarily Jews at Auschwitz, but also killed some quarter of a million non-Jews there. The pope expressed his hope for a place of prayer at the site. In 1984 a group of Polish Carmelite nuns created a convent from a former poison gas storehouse on the Auschwitz compound, in large part to honor Teresa Benedicta, who had been a Carmelite. The international Jewish community protested and was confronted by Catholic counterprotesters. The Catholics said they had every right to honor their dead, while Jews argued that a convent offended their memory of Jewish martyrs by introducing Christian symbols to the site.

The dispute drew lingering anti-Semitism into the open. Protesters outside the gates of Auschwitz got into fights. Some of the Catholics inflamed the situation further when they retrieved the papal cross from Krakow and erected it just outside the death camp. The controversy escalated until the pope himself intervened. He offered to create a new convent for the Carmelites a short distance away and asked the nuns to move; they did so in 1994. Meanwhile, Jews continued to protest the large cross. That dispute continued into 1998 when the Polish government, under pressure from the United States and Israel, agreed to remove the cross. That prompted inflammatory comments by the Polish archbishop Cardinal Jozef Glemp, who argued the cross should remain as a tribute to Catholic martyrs. Supporters began planting hundreds of small crosses outside Auschwitz in protest against the Jewish objectors. Finally, in 1999, the Polish government agreed to a compromise, removing the many small crosses while allowing the large cross to remain.

Carol Rittner, a Roman Catholic nun, interviewed Elie Wiesel about the controversy for a book she coedited, *Memory Offended: The Auschwitz Convent Controversy*. Wiesel, winner of the 1986 Nobel Peace Prize and a Jewish survivor of Auschwitz, placed the controversy in the larger context of the long history of suspicion and strained relations between Christians and Jews.

RITTNER: Frankly, if I were a Polish Catholic who suffered in Auschwitz or lost members of my family there, I don't think I would understand why you object to Carmelite nuns praying in Auschwitz for the victims of the Nazis. After all, you've often said, "Not all victims of the Nazis were Jews, but all Jews were victims." How are we to deal with still unreconciled views about how the victims of Nazism should be memorialized?

WIESEL: First, you must know that I do not differentiate among the victims of the Nazis. All must be remembered. All are *worthy* of being remembered. But as a Jew, I cannot forget that among Hitler's principal goals was the total annihilation of the Jewish people. Six million men, women, and children were isolated, humiliated, hunted down, starved, gassed, reduced to ashes only because they were Jews. And I cannot forget that most of the victims murdered in Auschwitz were Jews.

How do we remember a tragedy of such magnitude? True, there is a problem about how to memorialize the victims of the Nazis, but this is not just a problem in Poland. Human memory is too weak to include so many faces, so many names. God alone can remember everybody and everything. To cheaply universalize the Holocaust would be a distortion of history. The universality of the Holocaust lies in its uniqueness. We must remember the particularity of the Jewish tragedy, without neglecting the suffering of others.

To build a convent on the invisible graves of Jewish people who were murdered in Auschwitz is wrong and offensive. Auschwitz is not the place for a convent. Convents should be among the living, not the dead.

RITTNER: But, Elie, why a Carmelite convent on the site of Dachau and not at Auschwitz?

WIESEL: Dachau was different. It was not primarily a death camp for Jews. Many anti-Nazis from all over Europe—resistance fighters, labor leaders, Jehovah's Witnesses, intellectuals, clergy, including many Catholic priests, and others—were imprisoned there, suffered there. Many died there. There were also Jews in the Dachau concentration camp, but almost always they were sent east, to the death centers.

True: in the beginning, Auschwitz was for Poles, Gypsies, Russian prisoners of war, partisans, others. But when we remember, we must remember the entire past, not only before 1941. Between 1941 and 1945, most victims in Auschwitz—especially Birkenau—were Jews. Nearly two million Jews were murdered in Auschwitz. To establish a convent there, where so many Jewish people were murdered, is simply not acceptable.

Please understand: I respect the Carmelite nuns. I respect their piety, their generosity of spirit, their intent. But since you mention Dachau and the convent there, let me ask you: I heard the Carmelite nuns want to build convents in all the camps, in Belzec, Treblinka, Sobibor, Chelmo. Is this true? If it is, I have only one word, "scandalous"!

I believe in prayer, but not there. It would cause offense and suffering to too many people. This must not be allowed to happen.

Prayer should not offend others, it should help to console them. Surely, these nuns know that the way to God leads through other people, not away from them. Their work of prayer should be a witness to the living, not an insult.

RITTNER: What about the idea of establishing a synagogue *and* a convent at Auschwitz?

WIESEL: I am against it. No religion should build religious institutions at Auschwitz. Not a church, not a synagogue, not a convent. God is God. He listens to all prayers everywhere, from wherever they come. What's the matter with praying to God from five miles away, or ten?

Build the convent outside the area of the camp, as was agreed. Build it in the city of Oswiecim, but not in Auschwitz itself. Nothing should be built there which would further divide people. We have been divided enough.

RITTNER: Is Auschwitz a "holy" place?

WIESEL: I don't like to use the word "holy" when speaking about Auschwitz. It is a special place. A unique place.

If one speaks of Auschwitz as "holy," it is because it has been sanctified by the victims, but there also were killers in that place. How do I combine the holiness of the victims with the unholiness of the murderers? How do I deal with the problem of God in Auschwitz? Where was He? Among the victims? Among the killers? And God's silence? Was He, or was He not silent? And what about man? Where was his humanity? Why didn't their Christian faith serve as a shield to protect the SS men from engaging in such evil acts? Surely these are also questions within the question you ask.

RITTNER: Would you comment on the behavior of the Jewish students who climbed over the wall into the Carmelite convent courtyard?

WIESEL: I do not believe in bad manners, and I surely do not believe in violence. There are other ways. One does not have to offend someone's religious sensitivity to be heard. We must use words: write letters, use arguments, make speeches, talk to people. Surely, at some point, the nuns must listen to what is being said. At least, I hope they will.

RITTNER: What impact does Cardinal Glemp's words about the Auschwitz convent controversy have on Jewish-Catholic relations?

WIESEL: His words are unworthy of a "prince of the church." They are irresponsible. Cardinal Glemp's speeches have helped deepen the crisis. It's not only a matter of theology but of propaganda as well. What he said at Czestochowa is what antisemites used to say: That Jews control the media, that Jews want to dominate everything, that Jews set impossible conditions. And he went further. He said a "squad of seven Jews from New York" wanted to harm the nuns.

Can you imagine if fifty years ago, at the beginning of the war, a cardinal had said such things in Poland, when there were still 3 million Jews? There would have been pogroms.

That other church dignitaries in Europe, in the United States, and also Solidarity, which is, after all, a Polish Catholic movement, have spoken up, disassociating themselves from Cardinal Glemp's statements, is good and encouraging. It satisfies me. Still, I find it troubling that in 1989 a cardinal would make such statements during a religious service.

RITTNER: What about Pope John Paul II's recent comments that God's covenant with the Jewish people was broken by the Jews and is superseded by Christian covenant?

WIESEL: Really, what does the pope want? Does he want us to convert? Then, let him say so, but he will be disappointed. We will remain Jewish.

We Jews have always believed there is more than one way to God, more than one gate open. We have had problems with the God of Israel, but never have we allowed someone else to interfere in our relations with God.

As for the pope's idea that the prophets of Israel came to preach conversion to the new covenant, that is totally wrong, and baffling. Do you think that Jeremiah, Amos, Habakkuk, or others wanted us to convert to Christianity? They wanted us to mend our ways. They wanted us to be *more* Jewish, not less Jewish. This pope wants us to be less Jewish, or to stop being Jewish.

The pope's remarks do not contribute to understanding between Jews and Christians. After Pope John XXIII's spirit, Pope John Paul II seems to be going backward.

RITTNER: What practical steps can Catholics in the United States take to repair Jewish-Catholic relations?

WIESEL: We must deepen our friendships. We must continue to build bridges of understanding among ourselves and strengthen those that exist. We cannot wait for the initiative to come from above. We must create a foundation from below. And we must find ways to work together, to show respect for one another.

Catholics who are offended by the comments of certain church officials should make their views known. Support those cardinals, bishops, and others who have spoken for respect and understanding. And we Jews should let our friends and allies in the Catholic church, and in Poland, know how grateful we are.

Catholics must understand Jews *as Jews*, respecting our tradition and beliefs. Priests, and rabbis too, should preach to encourage understanding and respect. Teachers should teach in the same way. And Christians must respect Jewish sensitivity and memory about the victims of the Holocaust.

RITTNER: Given all the problems facing humankind, where on the list of priorities do you place the controversy over the Auschwitz Carmelite convent?

WIESEL: No people can live alone today, neither Jews nor Christians. The damage done was done to us all. The dangers that face us, face us all. But right now, for Jews, and I think for Catholics, too, the controversy over the convent is a priority, because it is so full of tension and anger. If it continues, it could deepen beyond repair, and we can't allow that to happen.

Of course there are other problems, other priorities which need our attention: Epidemics. Famine. Terrorism. Lebanon, an anguished country committing suicide. Apartheid. In our own country, the ugly face of racism. Refugees. Torture. Drugs. AIDS. Children beaten and killed. Fanaticism. And always the somber threat of nuclear annihilation.

What is so agonizing is that we live in a time when there is more than one number one priority. We cannot ignore any of them. And yet, for Jews, the events of the past weeks and months in Poland remind us of other words, other events, still vivid in our memories. We must find a way to resolve the crisis between Catholics and Jews, without neglecting the needs of our anguished world. It is up to us, after all, to prove that humanity's fate is not sealed, that everything is still possible.

Presentation of the Ten Commandments Monument at the Alabama Supreme Court
Roy S. Moore

When Roy S. Moore, chief justice of the Alabama Supreme Court, delivered this speech, it was the culmination of his nearly decade-long campaign to acknowledge God as the foundation for the legal system. Moore's speech marked the August 2001 installation of a 5,280-pound carved granite monument to the Ten Commandments at the Alabama Supreme Court building in Montgomery. Moore was appointed a circuit judge in 1992. He hung a wooden plaque of the commandments behind his bench and began opening his court sessions with a prayer, later explaining that he wanted to establish the moral foundation of American law. When the American Civil Liberties Union

(ACLU) threatened to sue over issues of separation of church and state, Moore refused to back down, and the resultant publicity seemed to transform him into a populist hero.

The ACLU did sue him in 1995. Moore again stood his ground, and the case was thrown out on a technicality in 1998. When the seat of chief justice on the state's high court, the Alabama Supreme Court, opened the next year, Moore entered the race as a long shot, stressing his belief that the state needed to "return God to our public life." He was elected in November 2000 and took office in January 2001. Set on furthering his cause, Moore commissioned the monument to be carved from a block of Vermont granite; it features tablets with the Ten Commandments on its top surface and inscriptions from such figures as George Washington and Thomas Jefferson on its sides. When federal judges ordered the monument removed, Moore defied the court order, triggering a state judicial ethics case that ended in his being deposed from the bench in November 2003. Since then, Moore has toured the state and beyond—sometimes with "the Rock" along, displayed on a flatbed truck—spreading his message that "separation of church and state does not mean separation of God and government!" In the fall of 2005, Moore announced his intention to run for governor of Alabama.

BY THE AUTHORITY vested by the Constitution of the State of Alabama in the Chief Justice of the Alabama Supreme Court and as the administrative head of the judicial system of the State of Alabama; and

By the authority vested by Alabama Code Section 41-10-275 in the Chief Justice of the Alabama Supreme Court as the Authorized Judicial System Representative of the Unified Judicial System of the State of Alabama; and

By the authority vested in the Chief Justice as such Authorized Representative under the lease of the Alabama Judicial Building in Montgomery, Alabama;

I am pleased to present this monument depicting the moral foundation of law, and hereby authorize it to be placed in the Rotunda of the Alabama Judicial Building.

It is altogether fitting that this monument be placed in the Rotunda of the building housing the Alabama Supreme Court, the Alabama Court of Criminal Appeals, the Alabama Court of Civil Appeals, the Alabama State Law Library, and of Alabama's Administrative Office of Courts. This monument serves to remind the Appellate Courts and the judges of the Circuit and District Courts of this State and members of the bar who appear before them, as well as the people of Alabama who visit the Alabama Judicial Building, of the truth stated in the Preamble to the Alabama Constitution that in order to establish justice we must invoke "the favor and guidance of Almighty God."

"The institutions of our society are founded on the belief that there is an authority higher than the authority of the State; that there is a moral law which the State is powerless to alter; that the individual possesses rights, conferred by the Creator which government must respect."

The Declaration of Independence stated the now familiar theme: "We hold these Truths to be self evident, that all Men are created equal, that they are endowed by their Creator with certain inalienable Rights, that among these are Life, Liberty, and the Pursuit of Happiness."

"And the body of the Constitution as well as the Bill of Rights enshrined these principles."

Some of you might think that the words I just spoke are my words, carefully structured to fit my own ends—or perhaps a quote from a long ago past, but certainly not true or of relevance to our law today. On the contrary; those are neither my words nor an ancient quote irrelevant to law.

Those were the words of Justice William O. Douglas of the United States Supreme Court in the 1961 case of *McGowan vs. Maryland.*

Today, a mere forty years later, many judges and other government officials deny any higher law and forbid the teaching to our children that they are created in the image of an Almighty God while they purport that it is government—and not God—who gave us our rights.

Not only have they turned away from those absolute standards that serve as the moral foundation of law and which form the basis of morality, but also they have divorced our Constitution and Bill of Rights from these principles.

As they have sown the wind, so we have reaped the whirlwind in our schools, in our homes, and in our workplaces.

When I ran for the office of Chief Justice of the Alabama Supreme Court, I made a pledge to restore the moral foundation of law.

It is axiomatic that to restore morality we must first recognize the source from which all morality springs. From our earliest history in 1776 when we were declared to be the United States of America, our forefathers recognized the sovereignty of God. And as late as 1954, the United States Congress placed the phrase "Under God" in our Pledge of Allegiance. Judges, legislators, and executive officers have, since our nation's birth, consistently pledged under oath—"so help me God" —to uphold the Constitution.

Immediately after my election in November of 2000, I contacted Mr. Richard Hahnemann, an accomplished sculptor, to assist me in the construction and design of this monument. Based upon my specifications, he, together with my attorney, Mr. Stephen Melchior, and myself, have worked for the past eight months to complete this monument.

No tax funds were used in its construction or installation, which was accomplished last evening so as not to conflict with the workplace.

I would like to recognize Clark Memorial and Mr. Pierre Tourney, Jr., for their assistance in both the construction and installation of this monument.

What an appropriate date it is to unveil this monument, for it was on August 1, 1776, exactly 225 years ago today, that Samuel Adams stood before a rather large crowd on the steps of the Philadelphia Statehouse, where he delivered a speech before the formal signing of the Declaration of Independence the next day.

Adams began by stating:

"We have explored the temple of Royalty and found that the Idol that we have bowed down to has Eyes which see not, Ears that hear not our Prayers, and a heart like the nether Millstone."

Today a cry has gone out across our land for the acknowledgment of that God upon whom we are dependent as a nation, and for those simple truths that our forefathers found to be "self evident." But once again we find that those cries have fallen upon "eyes which see not and ears that hear not our prayers."

Samuel Adams concluded his remarks by saying:

"We have this day restored the Sovereign to whom alone all men ought to be obedient; He reigns in Heaven, and with a propitious Eye beholds his Subjects assuming that freedom of thought, and dignity of self direction, which He bestowed upon them. From the rising to the setting Sun, may his Kingdom come."

May this day mark the beginning of the restoration of the moral foundation of law to our people and a return to the knowledge of God in our land.

Response of the Faithful: A Declaration to the Pope
Voice of the Faithful

The clergy abuse scandal that rocked the Roman Catholic Church in the first years of the new millennium first came to light in Boston in June 2001. Cardinal Bernard F. Law, archbishop of Boston, revealed in a court document that the archdiocese had transferred a priest, John Geoghan, from parish to parish despite knowing that he had abused young boys. Though the church had defrocked Geoghan in 1998, his case was the spark that ignited a bonfire of protest. Once Law acknowledged Geoghan's abuse—and the church's cover-up of the crimes—other victims came forward to reveal their stories of being abused by priests.

Hundreds of victims, men and women, went public during 2002 with their tales. Journalists' investigations continued to reveal more details of the scandal. An outraged laity, as well as other priests, began calling for Law to resign. Boston-area parishioners formed a new group, Voice of the Faithful, which drew more than four thousand people to its initial conference in June 2002. The group began to organize protests and to work to heal the suffering of clergy abuse victims. It also called for restructuring within the church to prevent further abuses or cover-ups by church authorities.

As the year progressed, the scope of the scandal became ever wider, spreading across the country and across the world. Victims began filing lawsuits seeking millions of dollars in damages, and prosecutors began filing criminal charges against priests. In December 2002 Law met with Pope John Paul II at the Vatican to discuss the scandal, and on December 13 the pope accepted Law's resignation as archbishop of Boston.

The following declaration was overwhelmingly ratified by participants at Voice of the Faithful's July 2002 convention. It is a protest of clergy abuse and church practices, addressed directly to the pope

.

WE THE FAITHFUL, in order to form a more perfect Church, gather in Boston on this 20th day of July 2002, to affirm the role of the laity in the constant renewal of the Catholic Church, as proclaimed in *Lumen Gentium* and other documents of the Second Vatican Council. Sharing actively in Christ's priestly, prophetic, and kingly functions in the fulfillment of our lay apostolate, we meet to express our opinion on those things that concern the good of the Church.

We acknowledge with grief and anger the profound suffering of untold numbers of boys and girls, men and women, who have been sexually abused by our clergy. We honor those heroic survivors who have come forward to tell the terrible truth.

We support the decisions of the American bishops in Dallas and commit to work for the full and immediate implementation of the Charter approved there. We petition the Holy Father to support this Charter and to hold accountable any bishop who reassigned an abusive priest or concealed his crimes, and any member of the Curia who participated in these practices.

We dedicate our apostolate to building up a Church in which these crimes and the abuse of power that made them possible will not happen again.

Therefore we affirm the mission of the Voice of the Faithful:

To provide a prayerful voice, attentive to the Spirit, through which the Faithful can actively participate in the governance and guidance of the Catholic Church.

We unite around three goals: To support those who have been abused; to support priests of integrity; and to shape structural change within the Church.

In accordance with our mission and goals, we commit individually and collectively to realize fully the renewal of the Church and the role of the laity envisioned by the Second Vatican Council. We do so as loving members of the Catholic Church, the People of God, called to fulfill the mission of Christ in the Church and in the world.

Testimony Before the U.S. Congressional Human Rights Caucus
Amal al-Qahtani

Amal al-Qahtani, Ph.D., a Saudi Arabian woman, protested the oppression of Saudi women by religious police in this June 2002 testimony before the U.S. Congressional Human Rights Caucus. Caucus members were holding hearings as part of their investigation into religious freedom.

Wahhabism, the branch of Islam practiced in Saudi Arabia, has been criticized—mostly outside that country—for strictly enforcing religious edicts based on extremist interpretations of Islamic code. For Saudi women and girls, the religious control can be a matter of life and death. Women are denied medical care at hospitals if they lack permission from a male family member, and they are prohibited from driving. In March 2002, fourteen girls were burned to death in a Saudi school fire. Witnesses reported that local officials thwarted rescue efforts, and some of the girls who tried to escape were pushed back into the burning building because they were not wearing the head-to-toe cloaks required for older females.

IN THIS TWENTY-FIRST CENTURY where civilization has made a great deal of progress and change worldwide, one may think that most people would have gained their basic human rights that enable them to live as full functioning and respected citizens. The sad thing about this assumption is that it is not always true, at least not where I come from, Saudi Arabia.

As a Saudi woman, I am still struggling to obtain my basic human rights. Saudi women undergo sexual discrimination that restricts their presence in the society as productive citizens. Unlike men, who are privileged with opportunities in education, jobs, governmental institutions, and all aspects of life, women have come second and are only allowed to use the limited resources offered to them.

The government has given the Wahhabi religious extremists control over the whole country. Those religious people, or as we call them "The Matawa," focus most of their efforts on policing women and punishing them if they don't listen to their orders. The Matawa follow women in markets, streets, outside schools, public libraries, parks, restaurants, hospitals, and in any place they can gain access.

They stop and interrogate couples walking hand in hand and question whether they are a husband and wife. They force women to dress in dark Abyas that cover them from head to toe as the Wahhabi doctrine teaches. Moreover, the Wahhabi Matawa harass and sometimes beat any woman who is not dressed as they see appropriate. Thus, they force their understanding of religion on all people even though the Saudi people come from different religious backgrounds and creeds.

As women, we cannot travel without a male guardian or the written approval of a male guardian. We also cannot have ID cards or apply to university without the same approval. The law prohibits us from driving, free market trade, pursuing job opportunities (other than the acceptable medical, educational, and banking areas). We are not allowed to apply to colleges that are restricted to only men. We are even forbidden from getting married without the approval of a male guardian.

This treatment, which is directed by the Wahhabi Matawa with the approval of the government, restricts us and makes us feel like minors, since we cannot do anything without the approval of a male in the family. It is restricting our lives in ways that make us dependent on men and we are consequently forced to accept our lives even if they are abusive and unfair.

There are no laws that protect women from sexual harassment or abuse. Hence, when a woman files a complaint of a sexual harassment in the job or in a public place, or a charge of spousal abuse, she has nowhere to turn but to the Wahhabi Matawa, who have adopted an extreme view of Islam toward women and always blame the female for such issues.

Most women have accepted their fate and are sadly conducting their lives inside their homes while others object silently for fear of being caught and punished. We have tried to speak up and voice our demands, but every time we are silenced and sometimes punished. For example, some Saudi women protested against the ban on driving by driving their own cars, but unfortunately, they were stopped and expelled from their jobs to satisfy the rage of the religious extremists who view women's activity as a sinful act that signals the deep corruption in society.

I can tell you that the suffering of the Afghani women is nearly matched by the experiences of Saudi women. Just as the world united to end the Taliban's oppression of Afghani women, we need to end this sad and painful control over us in Saudi Arabia by the Wahhabi religious authority.

We need the world community to help us have better and decent lives that enable us to live in a healthy society and therefore produce healthy generations of women that are neither angry nor bitter at life.

Statement Protesting the Ordination of Bishop V. Gene Robinson
American Anglican Council

The debate over whether to consecrate V. Gene Robinson—a divorced and openly gay priest in New Hampshire—as that state's bishop tore apart the Episcopal (Anglican) Church in 2003. The crisis, which some leaders in the church have labeled "a pastoral emergency," has strained relations between American Episcopals and the church's worldwide governing body, under the archbishop of Canterbury, and will likely have lasting reverberations.

The House of Bishops was deeply divided over the question. The August 5 vote in Minneapolis on whether to elevate Robinson was sixty-two bishops in favor and forty-three against. Robinson called the vote "a huge step for gay and lesbian folk in the church." Some of the opposing bishops formally rejected the vote, paving the way for a possible schism in the American Anglican church, which is the U.S. presence of the Church of England.

The Reverend Canon David C. Anderson, an Episcopal priest and president of the American Anglican Council, said in an interview with *Time* magazine that opponents "consider Gene Robinson's election invalid, null and void. It is illegal, in that it violates the moral standards the church has established and uses for the evaluation of who can be a bishop or even a priest." The council, a conservative alliance of Episcopal clergy and laity formed in 1996, issued this statement protesting Robinson's elevation on November 2, 2003—the day of his consecration ceremony in New Hampshire.

TODAY IS A GRIEVOUS DAY in the history of our Church. Heresy has been held up as Holy. Blasphemy has been redefined as blessing. The hope of the transforming love of Jesus Christ has been denied. Holy Scripture has been abandoned and sin celebrated over sanctification. The arrogance of the leaders of the Diocese of New Hampshire and the Episcopal Church is nothing less than stunning.

The world has now seen the foul fruits of "anything goes" spirituality and the leaders that have pushed it in the Episcopal Church. The Apostle Paul says: "For the time will come when men will not put up with sound doctrine. Instead, to suit their own desires, they will gather around them a great number of teachers to say what their itching ears want to hear." (2 Tim. 4:3,5)

The time has come. Our family is now split and the whole cloth of the Anglican Communion is torn. Realignment has begun.

But it is out of brokenness that God brings restoration; out of death God brings new life. Jesus died on the cross as a substitution for the very sin that the Episcopal Church now celebrates. Jesus rose again to offer us a second chance—all of us. Therefore, we continue to earnestly pray that the Episcopal Church will repent and return to God. So many are broken in our Church and desperately in need of the healing and transforming love, and new life, that Jesus has to offer.

We stand at an incredible moment in history—a moment of profound new hope. Mainstream Anglicans in America are moving forward, secure in purpose, standing for the truth and proclaiming the Good News. So even as we grieve, we rejoice. God still reigns, just as he did yesterday and will tomorrow. God does not change. His truth is still truth. His love is still deep, and He has promised to care for His faithful children.

In the footsteps of those great Church reformers of the past, it is now our time to boldly and unashamedly take a stand for righteousness. The cost may be high, but we must not be afraid. We must hold firm, confident in our salvation and not forgetting that the vast majority of Anglicans in the world stand with us. We are the mainstream, and the Episcopal Church has left us.

The AAC will work tirelessly to insure that Mainstream Anglicans in America have a safe place to call home. We seek a home free from harassment and persecution where the Gospel can again be proclaimed unhindered. The AAC has already developed guidelines and an application form for congregations wishing to request Adequate Episcopal Oversight. . . .

So to all mainstream Anglicans in America we say, "Take heart! You are not alone. The AAC stands with you. The Anglican Primates stand with you. Most Christians in America share your beliefs. Two thousand years of church tradition support you. Holy Scripture supports you. You are not alone."

Please pray for the Episcopal Church, the leaders of the worldwide Anglican Communion, the AAC, and for each other. Redirect your financial giving to ministries or organizations that call Jesus Lord. "Keep your head in all situations, endure hardship, do the work of an evangelist, discharge all the duties of your ministry." (2 Tim. 4:35)

Ours is a future of hope. God is our strength and He will prevail. Jesus Christ is Lord!

Protest of French Muslim Head Scarf Ban

In early 2004 France's national assembly passed a controversial bill that forbids conspicuous religious symbols in the country's secular public schools. While the law cut across religions, banning students from wearing large Christian crosses, Jewish yarmulkes, or Muslim head scarves, many saw it as targeting Muslims. A devout Muslim girl, required by her faith to cover her head with a scarf, or *hajib*, would be forced to choose between uncovering her head or dropping out of school.

The law prompted widespread protest in the French Muslim community—the largest Muslim community of any country in Western Europe—and across Europe. It also prompted a more radical response: in August 2004, just as the law was set to take effect for the start of the school year, a radical Islamic group in Iraq kidnapped two French journalists and demanded that France rescind the head scarf ban. (The journalists were released after several months in captivity.)

Some French supporters of the ban said the law was necessary to keep the schools strictly secular and to prevent Muslim extremists from treating French schools as recruiting centers for terrorists. Opponents, though, said the law was an unfair constraint on religious freedom. Although many people of other religions—including Pope John Paul II—joined Muslims in opposition to the law, supporters were not dissuaded, and it remained in place.

Oral Argument from *Elk Grove Unified School Dist. v. Newdow*

Michael A. Newdow and the Supreme Court of the United States

The right to religious freedom can sometimes take the form of the right to practice no religion at all. Many organizations, including the American Civil Liberties Union, are adamant in enforcing what they see as strict separation of government and the establishment of religion. Atheist Michael A. Newdow, a doctor in California, objected to the inclusion of the words "under God" in the Pledge of Allegiance. He decided to press the issue by bringing a lawsuit against the school district where his daughter attended school and where students were asked to recite the pledge daily in the classroom.

Newdow maintains that the inclusion of "under God" in the pledge—an amendment to the original wording that was inserted by an act of Congress in the 1950s, explicitly as a repudiation of Communism—is "a gross violation of one of our foremost Constitutional mandates." The First Amendment to the Constitution states that "Congress shall make no law respecting an establishment of religion," but Newdow—representing himself before the highest court of the land—argued that having a religious reference in the pledge violates that right. Using the courts as a bully pulpit for his protest and appealing to legal reason, Newdow prevailed in his initial suit before the Ninth Circuit Court of Appeals in California. When the three-judge panel there ruled in Newdow's favor, the decision caused a public uproar. Newdow was vilified and received death threats, but when the decision was appealed to the Supreme Court he persevered in defending his views. Newdow presented arguments before the court in March 2004, but lost that case when the justices ruled he did not have the proper legal standing to bring suit. A subsequent California court decision in the fall of 2005 again ruled the pledge unconstitutional.

MR. NEWDOW: MR. CHIEF JUSTICE, AND MAY IT PLEASE THE COURT:

Every school morning in the Elk Grove Unified School District's public schools, government agents, teachers, funded with tax dollars, have their students stand up, including my daughter, face the flag of the United States of America, place their hands over their hearts, and affirm that ours is a nation under some particular religious entity, the appreciation of which is not accepted by numerous people, such as myself. We cannot in good conscience accept the idea that there exists a deity.

I am an atheist. I don't believe in God. And every school morning my child is asked to stand up, face that flag, put her hand over her heart, and say that her father is wrong. . . .

. . . I am saying I as her father have a right to know that when she goes into the public schools she's not going to be told every morning to be asked to stand up, put her hand over her heart, and say your father is wrong, which is what she's told every morning. That is an actual, concrete, discrete, particularized, individualized harm to me, which gives me standing, and not only gives me standing, demonstrates to this Court how the—

QUESTION: Well, she does have a right not to participate.

MR. NEWDOW: She has a—yes, except under Lee v. Weisman she's clearly coerced to participate. If there was coercion in Lee v. Weisman—

QUESTION: That was a prayer.

MR. NEWDOW: Well, I'm not sure this isn't a prayer, and I'm—I am sure that the Establishment Clause does not require prayer. President Bush, and this is in the Americans United brief, stated himself that when we ask our citizens to pledge allegiance to one nation under God, they are asked to participate in an important American tradition of humbly seeking the wisdom and blessing—

QUESTION: Yeah, but I suppose reasonable people could look at the pledge as not constituting a prayer.

MR. NEWDOW: Well, President Bush said it does constitute a prayer.

QUESTION: Well, but he—we certainly don't take him as the final authority on this.

(Laughter.) . . .

MR. NEWDOW: . . . I'm—I'm saying that she—that my right to inculcate my religious beliefs includes the right to know that government will not in the public schools influence her one way in—or the other. And government is coming in here every morning to start off the morning, say put your hand on your heart, pledge to that flag and incorporate in that Pledge of Allegiance that there exists this purely religious dogma that your father has told you doesn't exist, and government may not do that.

QUESTION: What—what do you make of—of this argument? I will assume, and I—I do assume, that—that if you read the pledge carefully, the—the reference to under God means something more than a mere description of how somebody else once thought. We're pledging allegiance to the flag and to the republic. The republic is then described as being under God, and I think a fair reading of that would—would be I think that's the way the republic ought to be conceived, as under God. So I think—I think there's some affirmation there. I will grant you that.

What do you make of the argument that in actual practice the—the—the affirmation in the midst of this civic exercise as a religious affirmation is—is so tepid, so diluted then so far, let's say, from a compulsory prayer that in fact it— it should be, in effect, beneath the constitutional radar. It's—it's sometimes, you know the phrase, the Rostow phrase, the ceremonial deism.

What—what do you make of—of that argument, even—even assuming that, as I do, that there is some affirmation involved when the child says this as a technical matter?

MR. NEWDOW: I think that that whole concept goes completely against the ideals underlying the Establishment Clause. We saw in Minersville v. Gobitis and West Virginia v. Barnette something that most people don't consider to be religious at all to be of essential religious value to those Jehovah's Witnesses who objected. And for the Government to come in and say, we've decided for you this is inconsequential or unimportant is—is an arrogant pretension, said James Madison. He said in his memorial—

QUESTION: Well, I think the argument is not that the Government is—is saying, we are defining this as inconsequential for you. I think the argument is that simply the way we live and think and work in schools and in civic society in which the pledge is made, that the—that whatever is distinctively religious as an affirmation is simply lost. It—it's not that the—that the Government is saying, you've got to pretend that it's lost. The argument is that it is lost, that the religious, as distinct from a civic content, is close to disappearing here.

MR. NEWDOW: And again, I—I don't mean to go back, but it seems to me that is a view that you may choose to take and the majority of Americans may choose to take, but it doesn't—it's not the view I take, and when I see the flag and I think of pledging allegiance, I—it's like I'm getting slapped in the face every time, bam, you—you know, this is a nation under God, your religious belief system is wrong.

And here, I want to be able to tell my child that I have a very valid religious belief system. . . .

. . . But here we're not—it's not a question of being hostile to religion. It's—it's indoctrinating children and Congress said that was the purpose. This Court is supposed to give credence and . . .

QUESTION: Well, we're—I don't know. I mean, that's the point where—I have no doubt that it offends you and I respect the fact that you're—your right to be offended. I understand that. But the question is whether Congress, whether—whether the—whether the Government has the power to work that kind of offense. And on that, because you say, well, it doesn't have the right. Well, why doesn't it have the right? It isn't that divisive if, in fact, you have a very broad understanding of God. It's not a prayer, it's in a ceremonial context, and it has a long history of being evoked for civic purposes. Of course, some people will be offended, but those people who are offended can in fact ask the child, where they have custody, to be excused or not to say the words, under God.

So it's not perfect, it's not perfect, but it serves a purpose of unification at the price of offending a small number of people like you. So tell me from ground one why—why the country cannot do that?

MR. NEWDOW: Well, first of all, for 62 years this pledge did serve the purpose of unification and it did do it perfectly. It didn't include some religious dogma that separated out some—and I don't think there's anything in the Constitution that says what percentage of people get separated out. Additionally, again, we can use that example that I raised before with one nation under Jesus. That would also separate out just a few people relatively in our country. There's not that many more. It's about 86 percent to 93 percent, somewhere in that vicinity, so we're separating out another amount of people, but again, the principle is the same. We are separating out people. We don't need to.

Again, the Pledge of Allegiance did absolutely fine and with—got us through two world wars, got us through the Depression, got us through everything without God, and Congress stuck God in there for that particular reason, and the idea that it's not divisive I think is somewhat, you know, shown to be questionable at least by what happened in the result of the Ninth Circuit's opinion. The country went berserk because people were so upset that God was going to be taken out of the Pledge of Allegiance.

"Our religious identities have . . . become an increasingly potent source of human conflict"
Sam Harris

In his controversial 2004 book *The End of Faith: Religion, Terror, and the Future of Reason*, Sam Harris protested not aspects of a religion but the entire institution of organized religion itself. He attacked what he views as a misplaced sense of religious tolerance that makes people unwilling to criticize the faith of others. This tolerance allows fundamentalism to flourish, provides false hope that all religions can coexist peacefully, and threatens to allow faith to triumph over reason, wrote Harris.

As *New York Times* science writer Natalie Angier put it in her review of the book, "Sam Harris presents major religious systems like Judaism, Christianity and Islam as forms of socially sanctioned lunacy, their fundamental tenets and rituals irrational, archaic and, important when it comes to matters of humanity's long-term survival, mutually incompatible." *The End of Faith* won the 2005 PEN Award for nonfiction and made the *New York Times* bestseller list. Harris, who has a philosophy degree from Stanford University, explained many of his basic contentions in this Question & Answer feature on his Web site.

1. IN YOUR BOOK YOU SEEM TO ARGUE for a kind of religious intolerance. Do you mean to suggest that we need not respect a person's religious beliefs?

Yes. Our history of religious conflict had led us to be very cautious about criticizing the religious beliefs of others. We are right to be wary of religious intolerance, but it is time we recognized that our religious identities have themselves become an increasingly potent source of human conflict. The notion that God wrote one or another book has always been a source of dangerous and unnecessary divisions in our world. Given the spread of modern weapons and other disruptive technology, these divisions are fast becoming antithetical to civilization itself.

Notice that no one is ever faulted in our culture for not "respecting" another person's beliefs about mathematics or history. When people have reasons for what they believe, we consider those reasons, and when they are good, we find ourselves believing likewise. When they have no reasons, or bad ones, we dismiss their beliefs as a symptom of ignorance, delusion, or stupidity. Except on matters of religion.

2. Yes, but isn't religion different?

Only in so far as we treat it differently. We have been lulled into ignoring just how strange and insupportable many of our religious beliefs are. How comforting would it be to hear the President of the United States assure us that almighty Zeus is on our side in our war on terrorism? The mere change of a single word in his speech—from God to Zeus—would precipitate a national emergency. If I believe that Christ was born of a virgin, resurrected bodily after death, and is now literally transformed into a wafer at the Mass, I can still function as a respected member of society. I can believe these propositions because millions of others believe them, and we have all been taught to overlook how irrational this picture of reality is. If, on the other hand, I wake up tomorrow morning believing that God is communicating with me through my hairdryer, I'll be considered a nut, even in church. The beliefs themselves are more or less on a par—in so far as they are in flagrant violation of the most basic principles of reason. The perversity of religion is that it allows sane people to believe the unbelievable *en masse*.

3. And what is the link, as you see it, between religion and violence?

It's quite simple and direct. And inevitable. If you truly believe that your neighbor is going to hell for his unbelief, and you believe that his ideas about the world are putting the souls of your children in peril, it is quite sensible to drive him from your community, or kill him. Religion, by promising an eternity of supernatural rewards and punishments, raises the stakes enormously. Which is worse, a child molester or a heretic? If you really believe that the heretic can endanger your child for all time, there's simply no contest.

4. Doesn't the fact that no one is being killed for his religious beliefs in our country suggest that religion, in a democracy, can become a benign and even ennobling social force?

It only suggests that we have come to our senses on so many fronts that killing people for heresy—when you need these people to collaborate with, to sell your goods to, to employ, etc.—is no longer an option. This does not mean, however, that no one is dying on account of American-style religion.

Consider the fact that we have allocated a third of our budget for AIDS prevention in the developing world to the teaching of abstinence. Rather than provide as many condoms as possible, we have elected to spend millions of dollars on a program of bogus and ineffectual moral instruction. This is catastrophically stupid. Given that millions of people could be infected with AIDS unnecessarily, this is an example of Christian morality literally herding people into mass graves. Inadvertently, perhaps—but innocent people will die all the same.

5. Why is it that you think religious moderates bear some responsibility for the religious conflict in our world? It would seem that religious moderates are precisely the people who abhor violence in the name of faith.

Yes, but their indulgence of religious faith perpetuates an attachment to religious texts and to religious identities that, in turn, perpetuate human conflict. Religious moderates may ignore or overlook the more barbaric passages in their religious books, but by venerating the books in general, they leave us powerless to really oppose the belief systems of fundamentalists. And because moderates tend to ignore the most lunatic parts of scripture, they lose touch with how dangerous these books are when taken literally. In fact, they have trouble believing that anyone *does* still take these books literally, and so they tend not to recognize the role that faith plays in inspiring human violence. Religious moderates are blinded by their own moderation. When college-educated jihadists stare into a video camera and declare that "we love death more than the infidels love life," and then blow themselves up along with dozens of innocent bystanders, religious moderates rack their brains wondering what motivated these killers to do what they did. The respect that moderates accord to religious faith has blinded them to the fact that the atrocities of September 11th were a religious exercise. Religious moderates seem incapable of realizing that our problem is not terrorism, but Islam.

6. But isn't our conflict just with Muslim fundamentalists?

The distinction between "fundamentalists" and "moderates" has not really emerged in the Muslim world. Most Muslims are "fundamentalist" in the sense that they really appear to believe that the Koran is the literal and inerrant word of God. In any case, Islamic fundamentalism is only a problem for us because the *fundamentals of Islam* are a problem for us. There is a pervasive piece of wishful thinking circulating among religious moderates, and it could get a lot of us killed. The idea is that all religions, at their core, teach the same thing. This is myth. The principal tenet of Jainism is non-harming. Observant Jains will literally not harm a fly. Fundamentalist Jainism and fundamentalist Islam do not have the same consequences, neither logically nor behaviorally. Read the Koran. Osama bin Laden is playing it more or less by the book. Anyone who says that there is no basis for his worldview in the doctrine of Islam is either dangerously ignorant or just dangerous.

We must hope that the Muslim world is full of moderates who abhor the worldview of Osama bin Laden. But where are they? We cannot just assume that they exist. And the horrible truth is that if they do exist, they will be easily marginalized by their coreligionists.

7. But we've all seen moderate Muslims in the news, disavowing the actions of Islamic militants.

Have we? We've seen the occasional Muslim disavow the actions of Osama bin Laden, saying things like "Islam is a religion of peace," but this is not a sign of Muslim moderation. We'll know there are Muslim moderates in this world when they get on television and say things like: "There is much in the doctrine of Islam that should not be taken literally. It is, for instance, unacceptable to believe that people can get into Paradise by killing infidels and dying in the process. In fact, we're not even sure Paradise exists. Nor are we sure that the Koran was written by the Creator of the universe. The Koran is an ancient book of religious wisdom, some of it applies to our modern circumstance and some of it does not." Find a Muslim who can talk this way, and you will have found a Muslim moderate. You will also have found someone who is guilty of blasphemy and liable to be killed in almost any Muslim community on this earth. This is the problem with Islam.

8. This is all pretty inflammatory.

Yes. There really is a deal-breaker lurking here, and there is no use denying it. We should all be genuinely shaken by the knowledge that an entire civilization appears to think that the Koran is the wisest book ever written. How we have a conversation with 1.3 billion people about the dangerousness and illegitimacy of their core beliefs is a problem for which there may be no easy answer. But we must come to terms with the fact that the spread of technology has moved us to a crisis point. There is no possibility at all of our having a cold war with an Islamist regime that has acquired long-range nuclear weapons. More importantly, moderate Muslims, wherever they are, must come to terms with this. And they must find some way of marginalizing and containing the cult of death and martyrdom that has emerged in the Muslim world.

9. But some would say that it is not religion, but history, that explains Muslim—and specifically Arab—intolerance. Doesn't the Israeli occupation play a role here?

You cannot deny that the Israeli occupation is at least part of the problem. The Israelis settlers are themselves religious extremists who are putting us all in danger. Their notion of God as some omniscient real-estate broker is one of the principal sources of conflict between the West and Islam. But anyone who thinks western or Israeli imperialism solves the riddle of Muslim violence must explain why we don't see Tibetan suicide bombers killing Chinese children. The Tibetans have suffered every bit as much as the Palestinians. Over a million of them died as a direct result of the Chinese occupation of their country. Where are the Tibetan suicide bombers? Where is their cult of martyrdom? Where are the throngs of Tibetans seething with hatred, calling for the deaths of the Chinese? They are not likely to exist. What is the difference that makes the difference? Religion.

10. This brings us to one of the other implications of your book: you argue that not all cultures are morally equal, and that those that are morally superior have the right to impose their cultural values on others.

Yes. I think the civilized world has the duty, ultimately, to rescue the poor people in the developing world who are living under tyranny. It does not much matter if this tyranny is imposed from the top, by a dictator, or from all sides, by the tyranny of ignorance. This should really be viewed as a problem of education. People who don't understand how diseases like AIDS spread must be educated. People who don't understand that women should be accorded all the civic and moral privileges of men must be educated. People who think you can get to heaven by flying planes into buildings must be educated. Whether they must be conquered first and then educated is for them to decide.

11. What would you say to someone who has had a profound religious experience and simply knows that there is a God?

I would have to know the details of the religious experience. Such experiences rarely suggest anything at all about the structure of the universe. What they do prove, beyond any possibility of doubt, is that it is possible to have extraordinary experiences. We have to realize that there is no conflict between spiritual experience and reason. The conflict is between reason and those who make unreasonable claims to knowledge on the basis of such experiences—or worse, on the basis of books that recount the experiences of men who have been dead for centuries. Spiritual experience is arguably the most important human pursuit. But nothing needs to be taken on faith for us to pursue it.

12. You seem to have focused on all that is wrong with religion and overlooked all that is right with it. Religion has inspired some of the greatest art, architecture, moral teachings, and humanitarian acts.

The fact that people do wonderful things in the name of faith does not suggest that these things are *best* done in the name of faith. There is nothing to suggest that similar acts of beauty would not occur in the absence of religious dogmatism. There are very good reasons—which is to say justifiable, rational reasons—to create art, to build beautiful spaces for people to inhabit, and to treat other human beings well.

13. Do you really think that we can apply rational standards to religion? Isn't the whole point of faith that it is not bound by reason?

I happen to think that the so-called "leap of faith" is a myth. Beliefs have a certain logical relationship to one another, to language, and to sensory experience. We are not free merely to believe whatever we want about the world. In any case, the leap of faith is doubly a myth because people of faith rely upon reason whenever they can. The moment something in their experience appears to corroborate their faith, they seize it with both hands. The moment prayer actually seems to *work*—the tumor shrinks, the child is pulled from the wreckage unscathed—people of faith are elated to find their faith confirmed. The problem is that they are not inclined to view the totality of the evidence with an open mind. Any honest appraisal of the state of our world, or of human history, will lead you to conclude that the evidence for an omniscient, omnipotent, and benevolent Creator who takes an interest in the affairs of men and women is impossible to find.

Take Back the Faith
Jim Wallis

Sojourners is one of a number of contemporary Christian social-action organizations in the United States. Founded in 1971 by religious activists who opposed the Vietnam War, Sojourners identifies itself as "a Christian ministry whose mission is to proclaim and practice the biblical call to integrate spiritual renewal and social justice." Jim Wallis is the group's executive director and editor in chief of *Sojourners Magazine*. This essay came out during the heated political climate of the 2004 presidential election, when candidates' religious convictions became a campaign issue.

MANY OF US FEEL that our faith has been stolen, and it's time to take it back. An enormous public misrepresentation of Christianity has taken place. Many people around the world now think Christian faith stands for political commitments that are almost the opposite of its true meaning. How did the faith of Jesus come to be known as pro-rich, pro-war, and pro-American? And how do we get back to a historic, biblical, and *genuinely* evangelical faith rescued from its contemporary distortions?

That rescue operation is even more crucial today, in the face of a social crisis that cries out for prophetic religion. The problem is clear in the political arena, where strident voices claim to represent Christians, when they clearly don't speak for *most* of us. We hear politicians who love to say how religious they are but utterly fail to apply the values of faith to their public leadership and political policies. It's time to take back our faith in the public square, especially in a time when a more authentic social witness is desperately needed.

When we do, we discover that faith challenges the powers that be to do justice for the poor, instead of preaching a "prosperity gospel" and supporting politicians that further enrich the wealthy. We remember that faith hates violence and tries to reduce it, and exerts a fundamental presumption against war, instead of justifying it in God's name. We see that faith creates community from racial, class, and gender divisions and prefers international community over nationalist religion, and we see that "God bless America" is found nowhere in the Bible. And we are reminded that faith regards matters such as the sacredness of life and family bonds as so important that they should never be used as ideological symbols or mere political pawns in partisan warfare.

The media likes to say, "Oh, then you must be the Religious Left." No, and the very question is the problem. Just because a Religious Right has fashioned itself in one predictable ideological guise does not mean that those who question this political seduction must be their opposite political counterpart. The best public contribution of religion is precisely *not* to be ideologically predictable nor a loyal partisan. To raise the moral issues of human rights, for example, will challenge both left- and right-wing governments who put power above principles. And religious action is rooted in a much deeper place than "rights"—that being the image of God in every human being.

Similarly, when the poor are defended on moral or religious grounds, it is not "class warfare" but rather a direct response to the overwhelming focus in the scriptures that claims the poor are regularly neglected, exploited, and oppressed by wealthy elites, political rulers, and indifferent affluent populations. Those scriptures don't simply endorse the social programs of liberals or conservatives, but make clear that poverty is indeed a religious issue and that the failure of political leaders to help uplift those in poverty will be judged a moral failing.

It is precisely because religion takes the problem of evil so seriously that it must always be suspicious of concentrated power—politically and economically—either in totalitarian regimes or in huge multinational corporations, which now have more wealth and power than many governments. It is indeed our theology of evil that makes us strong proponents of both political and economic democracy—not because people are so good, but because they often are not and need clear safeguards and strong systems of checks and balances to avoid the dangerous accumulations of power and wealth.

It's why we doubt the goodness of *all* superpowers and the righteousness of empires in any era, *especially* when their claims of inspiration and success invoke theology and the name of God. Given human tendencies for self-delusion and deception, is it any wonder that hardly a religious body in the world regards unilateral and pre-emptive war as "just"? Religious wisdom suggests that the more overwhelming the military might, the more dangerous its capacity for self and public deception.

The loss of religion's prophetic vocation is terribly dangerous for any society. Who will uphold the dignity of economic and political outcasts? Who will question the self-righteousness of nations and their leaders? Who will question the recourse to violence and the rush to wars long before any last resort has been unequivocally proven? Who will not allow God's name to be used to simply justify ourselves, instead of calling us to accountability?

In an election year, the particular religiosity of a candidate, or even how devout they might be, is less important than how their religious and/or moral commitments and values shape their political vision and their policy commitments. Understanding the moral compass they bring to their public lives and how their convictions shape their political priorities is the true litmus test.

"We have to snap out of our denial"
Irshad Manji

Irshad Manji, a Canadian writer, journalist, and feminist, is also a Muslim activist. She has been outspoken in calling for a spirit of debate and reform within Islam, and is uniting moderate, reform-minded Muslims globally through her Web site muslim-refusenik.com. Her 2003 book *The Trouble with Islam Today: A Muslim's Call for Reform in Her Faith* has been translated into multiple languages, including Arabic, and has drawn both strong praise and harsh condemnation.

In her book, lectures, and interviews, Manji has advocated forcefully for equal rights for Muslim women. She has also pushed to resuscitate the dormant Islamic tradition of *ijtihad*, or independent critical thinking—a tradition that ended in the eleventh century when clerics declared the "gates of *ijtihad*" closed and said that Muslims must refrain from questioning the Koran or forging new interpretations of its verses. Ultraconservative imams, according to Manji, have hijacked the original message and intent of the teachings of the prophet Mohammad, who intended women to be honored as equal partners with men, as evidenced by his own marriage with an older, entrepreneurial woman. Instead, Manji has protested, in many countries Muslim women are treated as commodities whose lives can be sacrificed to assert men's honor.

Manji wrote the following open letter to Australian Prime Minister John Howard as he prepared to host a summit with Muslim clerics in Canberra in August 2005. It appeared in the newspaper *The Australian*.

DEAR PRIME MINISTER JOHN HOWARD,

Today you meet 14 of Australia's top Muslim clerics at the Islamic summit. As my own Prime Minister in Canada recently did, you'll be asking for their support in the effort to stop Islamist terror.

But sir, as a reform-minded Muslim, I urge you to keep this in mind: Dialogue will not be enough. You'll need to extract honesty about the practice of Islam today. And for that you'll have to move beyond platitudes to ask pointed questions.

Why are Westerners, both Muslim and non-Muslim, being held hostage by what's happening between the Palestinians and the Israelis?

What's with the stubborn streak of anti-Semitism in Islam?

Who's the real coloniser of Muslims, the US or Saudi Arabia?

Above all, why did the frenzy of fatwas against terror begin only recently? After New York. After Kabul. After Bali. After Beslan. After Baghdad. After Beirut. After Madrid. After Moscow. After Istanbul. After London. Why has clerical condemnation taken so bloody long?

While the London bombings have roused many Muslims from our slumber, we still have trouble. The trouble with Islam today is that literalism is mainstream.

Even moderate Muslims take the Koran as the final word of God: unfiltered, unchanged and unchangeable. This supremacy complex inhibits us from asking hard questions about what happens when faith becomes dogma. Such a path can lead only to a dead end of more violence.

Please ask the imams: Is this the justice they seek for the world that God has leased to us all? If it's not, then why don't more of them say so publicly?

What they're bound to say is that Muslims are the targets of a backlash. It's true that from time to time we're subject to hate. Our community leaders are adroit at showing us how to assert our rights, something most of us wouldn't have in Islamic countries. In the spirit of reciprocity, it's worth asking: What about the Koran's incitement of hate against Jews? Shouldn't Muslims who invoke the Koran to justify anti-Semitism be open to a lawsuit? Or would this amount to more backlash? What makes Muslims righteous and everybody else racist?

Which brings me to the R-word: racist. I beg you not to back off if you hear it. Remind your accusers that in the past 100 years alone, more Muslims have been tortured and murdered at the hands of other Muslims than at the hands of any foreign imperial power. That's not to deny Western colonialism. It's to point out that colonialism comes in many shades and colours. When you stand up for human rights in Islam, the people you're helping are ordinary Muslims. What's so racist about that? Ask the imams.

They'll want to assure you that a faith that violates human rights isn't true Islam. Excellent. That's why you're meeting them: because you believe that Muslims are capable of being more thoughtful and humane than the terrorists suggest.

But for the sake of an honest discussion, please challenge the clerics to come clean about the Islam they reflexively defend.

Is this Islam in its real form or Islam as an ideal? Let's face it; everything is wonderful as an ideal. Communism is egalitarian as an ideal. Capitalism is fair as an ideal. The US constitution guarantees liberty and justice for all as an ideal. Muslims know the reality is different. As people of conscience, Muslims have to address Islam's realities, too.

The prophet Mohammad would have embraced this distinction between the real and the ideal. When he was asked to define religion, he reportedly replied that religion is the way we conduct ourselves towards others. A fine definition, simple without being simplistic. Yet, by that definition, how we Muslims behave, not in theory but in actuality, is Islam, which means our complacency is Islam. It also means the power is ours to restore Islam's better angels, those who care about the human rights of women and minorities.

To do that, though, we have to snap out of our denial. By insisting that there's nothing the matter with Islam today, we're sweeping the reality of our religion under the rug of Islam as an ideal, thereby absolving ourselves of responsibility for our fellow human beings, including Muslims, in Australia and beyond.

Prime Minister, you have a sterling opportunity to tell the imams that you won't be hoodwinked by silky-smooth chatter. Diplomacy is not accountability. Winning this war will require one more than the other.

Our Endangered Values: America's Moral Crisis
Jimmy Carter

Since he left the White House in 1980, former U.S. president Jimmy Carter has been a prolific writer and an activist for human rights and political freedoms. Through his nonprofit, nonpartisan organization, the Carter Center, he has traveled to many nations to monitor elections, mediate conflicts, and promote public health and economic development initiatives. His work earned him the Nobel Peace Prize in 2002. But he has also been outspoken on domestic political issues. In his 2005 book *Our Endangered Values: America's Moral Crisis*, Carter harshly criticized the administration of George W. Bush and the Republican conservative agenda, particularly on the issue of separation of church and state.

In the book Carter describes himself as deeply religious and an evangelical Christian. Nevertheless, he decries what he views as a hijacking of political leadership by some right-wing conservative Christians. These religious conservatives, he asserts, have used access to the highest levels of U.S. government to inject a radical religious agenda into government policy. He also protests how religious fundamentalists have derailed their own institutions: Carter was heavily involved for many years in the Southern Baptist Convention, but it became so politicized and restrictive that he severed his ties with the group.

In the first of two excerpts from his book, Carter protests what he sees as the effort by fundamentalist Christians to break down the "wall of separation" between church and state, arguing that to do so will be to the detriment of both. In a later chapter on "the distortion of American foreign policy," Carter registers his strong protest against the influence of the end-of-days fundamentalists.

THE GOVERNMENT AND THE CHURCH are two different realms of service, and those in political office have to face a subtle but important difference between the implementation of the high ideals of religious faith and public duty. In a speech to my fellow Baptists in 1978, I tried to explain the duality of my personal responsibilities as a president and as a Christian:

> Thomas Jefferson, in the original days of our country, said he was fearful that the church might influence the state to take away human liberty. Roger Williams, who created the first Baptist church in our country, was afraid that the church might be corrupted by the state. These concerns led

to the First Amendment, which prohibits the establishment of any official state church and, in the same sentence, prohibits the passing of any laws that might interfere with religious freedom. . . .

During the twenty-seven years since I made that speech, there has been a much more public effort to break down what Thomas Jefferson espoused as "a wall of separation between church and state."

Referring to this premise, *700 Club* host Pat Robertson said, "There is no such thing in the Constitution. It's a lie of the left, and we're not going to take it anymore." He repeatedly attacks public schools and calls for their replacement with religious academies.

Chief Justice William Rehnquist, in a U.S. Supreme Court minority opinion, has written, "The 'wall of separation between church and state' is a metaphor based on bad history, a metaphor which has proved useless as a guide to judging. It should be frankly and explicitly abandoned."

In 2000, Southern Baptist Convention leaders dropped from their new creed "The state has no right to impose taxes for the support of any form of religion." They have subsequently espoused vouchers for private schools and a constitutional amendment to authorize mandatory prayer in public schools, and they are openly challenging "the strict separation of church and state."

Government funding of social programs through "faith-based initiatives" appeals to religious groups who have no qualms about breaking down the historic wall between religion and government. They substitute certain charitable services in a religious environment for more broad and equitable government programs that address the wider needs of the poor for economic justice, with access to training for jobs, affordable housing, health care, sound education, and a livable wage. These initiatives bypass the historic implementation of the First Amendment by channeling taxpayers' dollars to churches and other religion-based providers of social services under contrived rules that allow for proselytizing and putting religious tests on hiring employees. The initiative even provides taxpayers' money to build and renovate houses of worship. There is no doubt that the goal is to finance programs that are clearly religious, and the annual level of somewhat surreptitious government funding through religious institutions has now reached about $2 billion.

ONE OF THE MOST BIZARRE ADMIXTURES of religion and government is the strong influence of some Christian fundamentalists on U.S. policy in the Middle East. Almost everyone in America has heard of the Left Behind series, by Tim LaHaye and Jerry B. Jenkins, twelve books that have set all-time records in sales. Their religious premise is based on a careful selection of Bible verses, mostly from the book of Revelation, and describes the scenario for the end of the world. When the Messiah returns, true believers will be lifted into heaven, where, with

God, they will observe the torture of most other humans who are left behind. This transcendent event will be instantaneous, and the timing unpredictable. There are literally millions of my fellow Baptists and others who believe every word of this vision, based on self-exaltation of the chosen few along with the condemnation and abandonment, during a period of "tribulation," of family members, friends, and neighbors who have not been chosen for salvation.

It is the injection of these beliefs into America's governmental policies that is a cause for concern. These believers are convinced that they have a personal responsibility to hasten this coming of the "rapture" in order to fulfill biblical prophecy. Their agenda calls for a war in the Middle East against Islam (Iraq?) and the taking of the entire Holy Land by Jews (occupation of the West Bank?), with the total expulsion of all Christians and other gentiles. This is to be followed by infidels (Antichrists) conquering the area, and a final triumph of the Messiah. At this time of rapture, all Jews will either be converted to Christianity or be burned.

Based on these premises, some top Christian leaders have been in the forefront of promoting the Iraqi war, and make frequent trips to Israel, to support it with funding, and lobby in Washington for the colonization of Palestinian territory. Strong pressure from the religious right has been a major factor in America's quiescent acceptance of the massive building of Israeli settlements and connecting highways on Palestinian territory in the West Bank. Some Israeli leaders have utilized this assistance while conveniently ignoring the predicted final plight of all Jews.

CHAPTER 9
PEACE AND WAR

INTRODUCTION

Few public issues generate as much turmoil as a government's decision to go to war. In the service of national interest, countries ask (or force) their citizens—usually young men—to put their lives at risk and kill other people whom they do not know. Even when a war seems fully justified, many people struggle to reconcile their civic obligation to support their government and their personal commitment to living in peace. In matters of protest, when the issue is about killing and being killed in war, you are no longer talking about abstract or distant principles. Passions rise as stakes get higher.

The entries in this chapter reflect responses to this conflict during different episodes in history, particularly in the United States. Protests against military service took place in the American colonies soon after the first European colonists arrived. Basing their pacifism on religious beliefs, many Quakers and Mennonites refused to fight in colonial wars and the American Revolution and often suffered grave retaliation from colonial authorities.

Over time, the United States government found less punitive ways to address the beliefs of conscientious objectors. However, people who protest a government's decision to go to war often feel ostracized. Questioning the merits of a war can be seen as failing to support the soldiers in the field. It raises the discomforting possibility that the deaths and injuries suffered in war served no purpose or were in the service of an unworthy cause.

The intensity of this issue has produced some classic examples of protest literature. Henry David Thoreau's *Civil Disobedience* voiced his strong objections to the United States invasion of Mexico. Writers distressed by the suffering of men who fought in World War I, living in the squalid trenches and killing each other, prompted a generation of antiwar literature and poetry. Protests against the Vietnam War divided the country into bitter factions: young resisters against older veterans of World War II; privileged families who could avoid the draft versus the poor and minorities who could not; those who insisted upon the right to dissent from authority versus those who believed you obey your country, right or wrong.

A Collection of the Sufferings of the People called Quakers

Joseph Besse

Quakerism started in England in the 1650s and quickly took hold in the American colonies. The British Quakers issued a declaration in January 1661 to the restored monarchy of Charles II, stating "that the Spirit of God . . . will never move us to fight and war . . . with outward weapons, neither for the Kingdom of Christ nor the Kingdoms of the world." The Quaker peace testimony included the obligation to refuse to personally participate in any form of military service.

Many Quakers refused to serve in the military even before the declaration. Pennsylvania, founded by the Quaker William Penn, was the only colony to allow Quakers to take this stance without punishment. Quakers also believed that they should not pay fines, saying that a person should not be punished for what he or she considered to be right. This belief often resulted in authorities imposing harsh penalties and confiscating properties.

The first recorded case of Quakers being punished in America for their conscientious objection stance took place in Maryland in 1658. As the report from Joseph Besse's 1753 book *A Collection of the Sufferings of the People called Quakers, for the Testimony of a Good Conscience*, excerpted here, shows, they were treated very severely. (The currency is in British sterling. A laborer would earn about ten pounds (£10) a year.)

THE BEGINNING OF OUR ACCOUNT of sufferings in this province may appear somewhat abrupt, because we find not, among our papers collected, any exact account of the first settlement of the people called Quakers here, and the earliest sufferings we meet with are without any particular dates. Only in general the reader may observe, that such of them are so, appear to us to have been transacted in or before the year 1658, *viz.*

William Fuller and Thomas Homewood, for their conscientious refusal to obey the orders of court made by the officers of Cecilius Lord Baltimore, respecting the militia, had taken from them goods to the value of £8.15s.6d.

Richard Keene, for refusing to be trained as a soldier, had taken from him the sum of £6.15s. and was abused by the sheriff, who drew his cutlass, and therewith made a pass at the breast of the said Richard, and struck him on the shoulders, saying *You Dog, I could find in my heart to split your brains.* This sheriff's name was Coarsey. At another time one John Odber a captain, and a justice of the peace, named Ashcomb, with many rude associates attending them, having heated themselves by drinking out several casks of wine, came to the houses of Richard Keene and others to take away their goods, under pretence of defaults in appearing at arms, but indeed to raise money to pay for the wine they had drank; and when Richard Keene's wife reproved the said justice for his drunkenness, his answer was as sottish as his practice, *viz. A man is never drunk if he can get out of a cart's way when it is coming towards him.* Thus even the magistrates did glory in the commission of those vices, which it was the duty of their office to have punished.

William Muffit, for refusing to be trained, was fined £6.15s. and an officer gave the orders to the sheriff, *if he could not get his goods, to take his chest, and if not his chest, his shirts.*

John Knap, for refusing to be trained, had goods taken from him to the value of £7.10s. with a chest. He was also fined £3.10s. for not swearing. These distresses were a great suffering to a poor labouring man, above sixty years of age, being a considerable part of the small remains of many years' pain and industry. . . .

Michael Brooks was fined £7.10s. because he could not swear, and £4.10s. for refusing to bear arms under the command of John Odber Captain, a man so profane as to affirm in the hearing of many persons, that *They were not fit to be soldiers who could not swear, be drunk, and whore.* To such men as these the properties of sober and conscientious men stood exposed, and were often sacrificed to their unruly passions and domineering tempers. Edmund Hinchman was also fined £4.10s. for not bearing arms under the said Capt. Odber. . . .

Thomas Mears had also taken from him by John Norwood sheriff goods worth £5 because his son had refused to bear arms. . . .

Susanna Elliot, for default of her servant's appearing in arms, had goods taken away worth 16s. . . .

Hugh Drew being fined £4.10s for refusing to bear arms, but being very poor and in debt, he sold his cow with intent to pay his debt, but the officers understanding it, seized the money the cow was sold for, being £5.5s. for the said fine.

Journal of the Life, Travels, and gospel Labours of That Faithful Servant and Minister of Christ, Job Scott

Job Scott

The American Revolution placed greater pressure on religious peace groups such as Quakers and Mennonites. Mennonites and members of the German Baptist Brethren and Moravian Church refused to serve in the military, but they did often support the military with construction work, transportation, and other activities that did not involve actual fighting.

Quakers, however, took the most extreme positions, refusing to do any activity that could be construed as supporting militancy. "We have enlisted ourselves as soldiers under the Prince of Peace, [and] must [therefore] wear his uniform and march according to his step," New England Quakers declared in July 1776. This stance included declining to pay taxes to the government or accepting currency used by the new American government to support the war effort, as described in this journal entry by Job Scott, a Quaker member. (The Continental Congress had established the dollar currency during the American Revolution to finance the war.)

Although colonial officials often punished conscientious objectors for their positions, Quakers and other religious pacifists were often left alone during the American Revolution, as they represented a neutral position in the very sharp and violent division between those who supported and opposed independence. Prior to the Revolution, George Washington had taken a lenient attitude toward Quaker conscripts who refused to fire weapons under his command. After letting seven Quakers go free, he requested "that if ever he should fall as much into their power as they had been in his—they would treat him with equal kindness."

THE RULERS OF AMERICA having made a paper currency professedly for the special purpose of promoting or maintaining said war; and it being expected that Friends would be tried by requisitions for taxes, principally for the support of war, I was greatly exercised in spirit, both on the account of taking and passing said money, and in regard to the payment of [war] taxes, neither of which felt easy to my mind. I believed a time would come when christians would not so far contribute to the encouragement and support of war and fightings as voluntarily to pay the taxes that were mainly, or even in considerable proportion, for defraying the expences thereof; and it was also impressed upon my mind, that if I took and passed money that I knew was made on purpose to uphold war, I should not bear a testimony against war that for me, as an individual, would be a faithful one. I knew the people's minds were in a rage against such as, from any motive whatever, said or acted any thing tending to discountenance the war. I was sensible that refusing to pay the taxes, or to take the currency, would immediately be construed as a pointed opposition to the present war in particular, as even our refusing to bear arms was, notwithstanding our long and wellknown testimony against it. I had abundant reason to expect great censure and some suffering in consequence of my faithfulness, if I should stand faithful in these things, though I knew that my scruples were unconnected with any party considerations, and uninfluenced by any motives but such as respect the propriety of a truly christian conduct in regard to war at large. I had no desire to promote the opposition to Great-Britain; neither had I any desire on the other hand to promote the measure or success of Great-Britain. I believed it my business not to meddle with any thing from such views; but to let the potsherds of the earth alone in their smiting one against another: but I wished to be clear in the sight of God, and to do all that he might require of me towards the more full introduction and coming of his peaceable kingdom and government on earth. I found many well concerned brethren, who seemed to have little or nothing of these scruples and some others who were like-minded with me herein. . . .

About the latter end of the 6th month this year [1776], an old acquaintance of mine, being now collector of rates, came and demanded one of me. I asked him what it was for? He said, to sink the paper money. I told him, as that money was made expressly for the purpose of carrying on war, I had refused to take it; and for the same reason could not pay a tax to sink it, believing it my duty to bear testimony against war and fighting. I informed him that for divers years past, even divers years before the war began, and when I had no expectation of ever being tried in this way, it had been a settled belief with me that it was not right to pay such taxes; at least not right for me, nor, in my apprehension, right in itself; though many sincere brethren may not at present see its repugnancy to the pure and peaceable spirit of the gospel. I let him know I did not wish to put him to any trouble, but would be glad to pay it if I could consistently with my persuasion. He appeared moderate, thoughtful and rather tender; and after a time of free and pretty full conversation upon the subject, went away in a pleasant disposition of mind, I being truly glad to him so. Divers such demands were made of me in those troublesome times for divers years: I ever found it best to be very calm and candid; and to open, as I was from time to time enabled, the genuine grounds of my refusal; and that if possible, so far as to reach the understanding of those who made the demand.

The Third of May, 1808, or *The Execution on Principe Pio Hill*

Francisco José de Goya y Lucientes

Francisco José de Goya y Lucientes's painting *The Third of May, 1808,* or *The Execution on Principe Pio Hill*, celebrates the Spanish people who rose up against Napoleon's French army, which defeated and occupied Spain during the early 1800s.

Goya had been the official painter of the Spanish court before Napoleon's invasion and was commissioned to do two paintings: one marking the Spanish uprising on May 2, 1808, and another of the massacre of the captured insurrectionists the following day. Goya defied the orthodoxy of the day by choosing anonymous participants as the subjects of the painting instead of well-known heroic aristocratic or royal leaders.

The central hero in this painting represents the thousands of unknown, uncelebrated men killed as a result of the war. Standing as though he were being crucified, he appears to be sacrificed to the dark, monolithic, and impersonal French soldiers about to execute him. Goya has

even given his right hand a scar that makes it look similar to Jesus' hand as it was nailed to the cross. The dark and silent church stands ominously in the background, symbolizing the church's indifference to the sacrifices of the people, while individual monks who have joined the people in their plight are splayed dead on the ground or praying as they are about to be killed.

Goya touches upon the theme of individuals being sacrificed for indifferent economic, religious, and national interests—the same sacrifice that many future antiwar leaders would speak out against.

Despite the power of the paintings, the Spanish Court that commissioned the works did not display them. Goya went on to do hundreds of etchings and prints illustrating the horrors of war in French-occupied Spain.

The dramatic imagery of the *Third of May, 1808,* inspired many future artists and illustrators, including Spanish artist Pablo Picasso, who painted *Guernica* nearly 125 years later.

On the Duty of Civil Disobedience
Henry David Thoreau

Like many abolitionists who opposed the Mexican-American War in the 1840s, Henry David Thoreau believed the conflict was designed to expand slavery westward. The United States attacked Mexico to seize land that now includes California and most of the U.S. Southwest. As an act of protest to the war, Thoreau refused to pay his poll tax in 1846 and spent a night in jail before a relative paid the tax on Thoreau's behalf—much to his annoyance. He explained his action in a speech to his fellow townsmen in Concord, Massachusetts, shortly afterward. Three years later, Thoreau's lecture was published as "On the Duty of Civil Disobedience," which is excerpted here.

Widely ignored or scorned in its day, Thoreau's essay on the duties of an individual to act upon his conscience has had a worldwide influence, affecting the writings of Leo Tolstoy, Mohandas Gandhi's revolutionary movement, and the American civil rights movement of the 1950s and 1960s. Although Thoreau's decision and explanation represented the capacity of an individual act, his words helped inspire mass movements.

I HEARTILY ACCEPT THE MOTTO, "That government is best which governs least"; and I should like to see it acted up to more rapidly and systematically. Carried out, it finally amounts to this, which also I believe—"That government is best which governs not at all"; and when men are prepared for it, that will be the kind of government which they will have. Government is at best but an expedient; but most governments are usually, and all governments are sometimes, inexpedient. The objections which have been brought against a standing army, and they are many and weighty, and deserve to prevail, may also at last be brought against a standing government. The standing army is only an arm of the standing government. The government itself, which is only the mode which the people have chosen to execute their will, is equally liable to be abused and perverted before the people can act through it. Witness the present Mexican war, the work of comparatively a few individuals using the standing government as their tool; for in the outset, the people would not have consented to this measure.

This American government—what is it but a tradition, though a recent one, endeavoring to transmit itself unimpaired to posterity, but each instant losing some of its integrity? It has not the vitality and force of a single living man; for a single man can bend it to his will. It is a sort of wooden gun to the people themselves. But it is not the less necessary for this; for the people must have some complicated machinery or other, and hear its din, to satisfy that idea of government which they have. Governments show thus how successfully men can be imposed on, even impose on themselves, for their own advantage. It is excellent, we must all allow. Yet this government never of itself furthered any enterprise, but by the alacrity with which it got out of its way. It does not keep the country free. It does not settle the West. It does not educate. The character inherent in the American people has done all that has been accomplished; and it would have done somewhat more, if the government had not sometimes got in its way. For government is an expedient by which men would fain succeed in letting one another alone; and, as has been said, when it is most expedient, the governed are most let alone by it. Trade and commerce, if they were not made of india-rubber, would never manage to bounce over the obstacles which legislators are continually putting in their way; and if one were to judge these men wholly by the effects of their actions and not partly by their intentions, they would deserve to be classed and punished with those mischievous persons who put obstructions on the railroads.

But, to speak practically and as a citizen, unlike those who call themselves no-government men, I ask for, not at once no government, but at once a better government. Let every man make known what kind of government would command his respect, and that will be one step toward obtaining it.

After all, the practical reason why, when the power is once in the hands of the people, a majority are permitted, and for a long period continue, to rule, is not because they are most likely to be in the right, nor because this seems fairest to the minority, but because they are physically the strongest. But a government in which the majority rule in all cases cannot be based on justice, even as far as men understand it. Can there not be a government in which majorities do not virtually decide right and wrong, but conscience?—in which majorities decide only those questions to which the rule of expediency is applicable? Must the citizen ever for a moment, or in the least degree, resign his conscience to the legislator? Why has every man a conscience, then? I think that we should be men first, and subjects afterward. It is not desirable to cultivate a respect for the law, so much as for the right. The only obligation which I have a right to assume is to do at any time what I think right. It is truly enough said that a corporation has no conscience; but a corporation of conscientious men is a corporation with a conscience. Law never made men a whit more just; and, by means of their respect for it, even the well-disposed are daily made the agents of injustice. A common and natural result of an undue respect for law is, that you may see a file of soldiers, colonel, captain, corporal, privates, powder-monkeys, and all, marching in admirable order over hill and dale to the wars, against their wills, ay, against their common sense and consciences, which makes it very steep marching indeed, and produces a palpitation of the heart. They have no doubt that it is a damnable business in which they are concerned; they are all peaceably inclined. Now, what are they? Men at all? or small movable forts and magazines, at the service of some unscrupulous man in power? Visit the Navy Yard, and behold a marine, such a man as an American government can make, or such as it can make a man with its black arts—a mere shadow and reminiscence of humanity, a man laid out alive and standing, and already, as one may say, buried under arms with funeral accompaniments, though it may be,

> "Not a drum was heard, not a funeral note,
> As his corse to the rampart we hurried;
> Not a soldier discharged his farewell shot
> O'er the grave where our hero we buried."

The mass of men serve the state thus, not as men mainly, but as machines, with their bodies. They are the standing army, and the militia, jailers, constables, posse comitatus, etc. In most cases there is no free exercise whatever of the judgment or of the moral sense; but they put themselves on a level with wood and earth and stones; and wooden men can perhaps be manufactured that will serve the purpose as well. Such command no more respect than men of straw or a lump of dirt. They have the same sort of worth only as horses and dogs. Yet such as these even are commonly esteemed good citizens. Others—as most legislators, politicians, lawyers, ministers, and office-holders—serve the state chiefly with their heads; and, as they rarely make any moral distinctions, they are as likely to serve the devil, without intending it, as God. A very few—as heroes, patriots, martyrs, reformers in the great sense, and men—serve the state with their consciences also, and so necessarily resist it for the most part; and they are commonly treated as enemies by it.

Report of New York City Draft Riot

Congress passed an act on March 3, 1863, during the height of the Civil War, authorizing conscription and punishing speech and actions resistant to the law. No provisions were made for conscientious objectors, but men could avoid military service by finding a substitute or paying the government three hundred dollars, roughly the equivalent of a year's wages for many working men.

The law was very unpopular, particularly in parts of the country such as New York City, where people opposed waging war to hold the Union together. Before the war, New York City was known as a center for slave-catchers, who snatched fugitive slaves from the city's streets.

Ten days after the Battle of Gettysburg, on July 13, 1863, the deadliest riots in United States history erupted when a mob sacked a draft office on East Forty-sixth Street and Second Avenue in Manhattan. Tens of thousands attacked police stations, rampaged through businesses, and burned buildings, including an orphanage for black children. Mobs chased down and killed dozens of black men, and 40 percent of the black population was made homeless. Many rioters targeted African Americans because they resented having to go to war to end slavery.

The riots were finally put down when seasoned troops, just off the Gettysburg battlefield, arrived and confronted the mobs, even firing guns point-blank into the gangs of protesters. The following report was part of the official army record written by an officer who helped put down the riots.

ABOUT SIX O'CLOCK P.M., General Dodge and Colonel Mott informed General Brown, that the troops at Gramercy Park had marched down Twenty-second Street, and been attacked by an armed mob; that they had been driven back, leaving their dead in the street. The general ordered me to take my company, and a portion of the Twentieth and Twenty-eighth New York volunteer batteries, about eighty men, armed as infantry, commanded by Lieutenant B. F. Ryer. Lieutenant Ryer had with him Lieutenant Robert F. Joyce and Lieutenant F. M. Chase, Twenty-eighth New York battery. My whole command amounted to one hundred and sixty men.

With this force I marched to the Gramercy Hotel. At a short distance from the hotel, I saw some of the rioters fire from a house on some of Colonel Mott's command. I immediately sent Lieutenant Joyce with a few men to search the house. The search was fruitless, the men having escaped to the rear. I then told the women in the house that the artillery would open on the house, if any more shots were fired from it. We then marched down Twenty-second Street, between Second and Third Avenues, found the body of a sergeant of Davis' Cavalry, who had been killed two hours before. I ordered a livery-stable keeper to put his horses to a carriage, and accompany me, for the purpose of carrying the dead and wounded. He replied that the mob would kill him if he did, and that he dare not do it. He was informed that he would be protected if he went, but if he refused he would be instantly shot. The horses were speedily harnessed, and the body put into the carriage. The mob at this time commenced firing on us from the houses. We at once commenced searching the houses, while my skirmishers drove the rioters back from every window and from the roofs. The houses were searched from cellar to the roof. The mob made a desperate fight, and evidently seemed to think they could whip us. Every house that was used to conceal these rioters was cleared. A large number was killed, and several prisoners were taken. We then marched to Second Avenue, where we found the mob in great force and concealed in houses. They fired on us from house-tops, and from windows, and also from cross streets. We soon cleared the streets, and then commenced searching the houses. We searched thirteen houses, killed those within that resisted, and took the remainder prisoners. Some of them fought like incarnate fiends, and would not surrender. All such were shot on the spot. The soldiers captured a large number of revolvers of large size, which I allowed them to keep. The mob at this place were well armed; nearly every one had some kind of fire-arms, and had one blunderbuss which they fired on us.

If they had been cool and steady, they might have done us great harm. As it was, they fired wildly, running to a window and firing, and then retreating back out of danger.

When my soldiers once got into a house they made short work of it. The fight lasted about forty minutes and was more severe than all the rest in which my company was engaged. There were none of my men killed. Sergeant Cadro, of company F, Twelfth Infantry (my own), was slightly wounded in the hand; private Krouse was also slightly wounded.

The mob being entirely dispersed, we returned to head-quarters.

"I am for peace on almost any terms"
Jonathan Worth

Minorities in both the North and the South opposed the American Civil War. Northern opponents, known as "Copperheads," were more vocal in their criticisms of President Abraham Lincoln and his handling of the war. Many Copperheads sympathized with the Southern cause and supported the continuation of slavery. As the number of killed and wounded grew, Northern wariness of the death toll nearly undermined the war.

In the South, the calls for peace were much more muted. Supporting the cause of independence was a paramount position of almost all public officials. However, underneath the loud proclamations was a growing belief that the war was a mistake, as shown by the following letter by Jonathan Worth, written to Jesse G. Henshaw in August, 1863, shortly after the South had suffered major losses at the battles of Vicksburg and Gettysburg. Worth had fought secession in 1861, but went with his state when North Carolina joined the Confederacy. He served as North Carolina state treasurer and became governor in 1865.

I HARDLY KNOW whether I am in favor of the peace meetings or not. On the one hand, it is very certain that the President and his advisors will not make peace, if not forced into it by the masses and the privates in the army. Their cry echoed by almost every press is: "Independence, or the last man and the last dollar." The North will not make peace on the basis of Independence. The real question which nobody—not even Holden—will squarely present is, shall we fight on with certain desolation and impoverishment and probably ultimate defeat; or make peace on the basis of reconstruction? Nearly every public man—every journal, political and religious, and every politician, in the fervor of their patriotism, has vociferously declared in favor of "the last man and the last dollar" cry. These classes cannot be consistent unless they still cry war. Many believe the masses in their saner hours never approved war and would rather compromise on the basis of the Constitution of the U.S. with such additional securities against any future rupture as could be agreed on. If there be any sense in peace meetings they mean reconstruction. They may rather do mischief if they are not so imposing as to force the administration to reconstruction. They will be impotent and mischievous if the army is still for to the last man and the last dollar. I do not know the sentiments of the rank and file of the army.

I am for peace on almost any terms and fear we shall never have it until the Yankees dictate it. Upon the whole I would not go into a peace meeting now or advise others to go into one, particularly Randolph—but I have no repugnance to them in other places and see no other chance to get to an early end of this wicked war, but by the action of the masses who have the fighting to do. If an open rupture occurs between Gov. V[ance] and Mr. Holden, it will be ruinous to us. There ought to be none and I trust there will be none. There is no difference between them that justifies a breach. The Governor concedes the right of the people to hold meetings and express their wishes, but he deems such meetings inexpedient and tending to dissatisfaction and disorganization in the army and that no honorable peace can be made, after we cease to present a strong military front. The Gov. acts consistently and in the eminent difficult position he occupied. I doubt whether any pilot could manage the crippled ship in such a storm with more skill. Repress all expressions of dissatisfaction against him. He values the extravagant eulogiums of the fire-eaters at their worth. They are playing an adroit game. They would get up dissention between the Gov. and Holden and then break up the Conservative party and seize the helm of Government.

"I am opposed to having the eagle putting its talons on any other land"

Mark Twain

At the beginning of the twentieth century, the United States victory in the Spanish-American War and President Theodore Roosevelt's "big stick" expansionary policy marked the high point of American imperial ambitions of that era. The United States occupied former Spanish colonies in Cuba and the Philippines.

Not everyone in the United States favored this militaristic expansion. Observing that the United States had once been a colony itself, many questioned the need, morality, and wisdom of the country becoming a colonial power, particularly in the distant Philippines.

Satirist Mark Twain reversed his views on the country's imperial ambitions after visiting the Philippines to get a firsthand look at U.S. colonialism. Upon returning he wrote the following commentary about his journey in the October 15, 1900, edition of the *New York Herald* newspaper. He subsequently wrote several more articles and essays criticizing the country's imperialistic policies. Twain saved his sharpest satire for the role patriotism plays in the service of self-serving expansionary policies. "There is nothing that training cannot do," he wrote of patriotism. "Nothing is above its reach or below it. It can turn bad morals to good, good morals to bad; it can destroy principles, it can recreate them; it can debase angels to men and lift men to angelships. And it can do any one of these miracles in a year—even in six months."

I LEFT THESE SHORES,

at Vancouver, a red-hot imperialist. I wanted the American eagle to go screaming into the Pacific. It seemed tiresome and tame for it to content itself with the Rockies. Why not spread its wings over the Philippines, I asked myself? And I thought it would be a real good thing to do.

I said to myself, here are a people who have suffered for three centuries. We can make them as free as ourselves, give them a government and country of their own, put a miniature of the American constitution afloat in the Pacific, start a brand new republic to take its place among the free nations of the world. It seemed to me a great task to which we had addressed ourselves.

But I have thought some more, since then, and I have read carefully the treaty of Paris, and I have seen that we do not intend to free, but to subjugate the people of the Philippines. We have gone there to conquer, not to redeem.

It should, it seems to me, be our pleasure to make those people free, and let them deal with their own domestic questions in their own way. And so I am an anti-imperialist. I am opposed to having the eagle put its talons on any other land.

Notes for Officers
Leo Tolstoy

Leo Tolstoy served as an officer in the Russian army when he was a young man. The experience helped inform his great novels *War and Peace* and *Anna Karenina*, as well as many of his famous short stories on military life. He later renounced his past military life, however, and became a passionate advocate of civil disobedience.

This essay, "Notes for Officers," was accompanied by a second essay, "Notes for Soldiers," urging men in the military to find the courage to resist the increasingly repugnant tasks that Russian soldiers were being ordered to do. It was the decision by Russian soldiers and sailors to turn against their generals and the czar in 1917 that ultimately tipped the country toward revolution.

IN ALL RUSSIAN BARRACKS there hang, nailed to the wall, the so-called "Notes for Soldiers" composed by General Dragomiroff. These notes are a collection of stupidly braggart sentences intermixed with blasphemous citations from the Gospels, and written in an artificial barrack slang, which is, in reality, quite strange to every soldier. The Gospel citations are quoted in order to corroborate the statements that soldiers should kill and tear with their teeth the enemy: "If your bayonet breaks, strike with your fists; if your fists give way, bite with your teeth." The notes conclude with the statement that God is the soldiers' General: "God is your General."

Nothing illustrates more convincingly than these notes that terrible degree of unenlightenment, servile submissiveness, and brutality which Russian men have attained to at present. Since this most horrible blasphemy appeared and was first hung up in all the barracks (a considerable time ago), not one commander, nor priest—whom this distortion of the meaning of the Gospel texts would seem to concern directly—has expressed any condemnation of this obnoxious work and it continues to be published in millions of copies and to be read by millions of soldiers who accept this dreadful production as a guide to their conduct.

These notes revolted me long ago, and now, being afraid I may otherwise miss the opportunity of doing so before my death, I have now written an appeal to soldiers, in which I have endeavored to remind them that as men and Christians they have quite other duties toward God than those put forward in the notes. And a similar reminder is required, I think, not only of the soldiers, but still more so by the officers . . . who enter the military service or continue in it, not by compulsion as privates do, but their own free will. . . .

In past times, in the days say of Nicholas I (1825–1855), it entered into no one's head that troops are necessary chiefly to shoot at unarmed populaces. But at present troops are permanently stationed in every large town and manufacturing centre for the purpose of being ready to disperse gatherings of workmen; and seldom a month passes without soldiers being called out of their barracks with ball cartridges and hidden in secret places in readiness to shoot the populace down at any moment.

The use of troops against the people has become indeed not only customary—they are mobilized in advance to be in readiness for this very purpose; and the Governments do not conceal the fact that the distribution of recruits in the various regiments is intentionally conducted in such a way that the men are never drafted into a regiment stationed in the place from which they are drawn. This is done for the purpose of avoiding the possibility of soldiers having to shoot at their own relations. . . .

I know that there are many officers, especially of the higher grades, who by various arguments on the themes of orthodoxy, autocracy, integrity of the State, eternal inevitableness of war, necessity of order, inconsistency of socialistic ravings, and so on, try to prove to themselves that their activity is rational and useful, and contains nothing immoral. But in the depths of their soul they themselves do not believe in what they say, and the more intelligent and the older they become the less they believe.

I remember how joyously I was struck by a friend and old comrade of mine, a very ambitious man, who had dedicated his whole life to military service, and had attained the highest honors and grades (General Aide-de-Camp and Major-General), when he told me that he had burnt his "Memoirs" of the wars in which he had participated because he had changed his view of the military activity, and now regarded every war as an evil deed, which should not be encouraged by participation, but, on the contrary, should be discredited in every way. Many officers think the same, although they do not say so while they serve. And indeed no thoughtful officer can think otherwise. Why, one has only to recall to mind what forms the occupation of all officers, from the lowest to the highest—to the Commandant of an Army Corps. From the beginning to the end of their service—I am alluding to officers in the active service—their activity, with the exception of the few and short periods when they go to war and are occupied with actual murder, consists in the attainment of two aims: in teaching soldiers the best methods of killing men, and in accustoming them to an obedience which enables them to do mechanically, without argument, everything their commander orders. In olden times it used to be said, "Flog two to death, and train one," and so they did.. . . .

When we see trained animals accomplishing things contrary to nature: dogs walking on their forelegs, elephants rolling barrels, tigers playing with lions, and so on, we know that all this has been attained by the torments of hunger, whip, and red-hot iron. And when we see men in uniforms with rifles standing motionless, or performing all together at the same movement—running, jumping, shooting, shouting, and so on—in general, producing those fine reviews and maneuvers which emperors and kings so admire and show off one before the other, we know the same. One cannot cauterize out of a man all that is human and reduce him to the state of a machine without torturing him, and torturing not in a simple way but in the most refined cruel way—at one and the same time torturing and deceiving him.

And all this is done by you officers. In this all your service consists, from the highest grade to the lowest, with the exception of those rare occasions when you participate in real war. . . .

It is therefore not astonishing that amongst you more than amongst any other class everything which will stifle conscience flourishes: smoking, cards, drunkenness, depravity; and that suicides occur amongst you more frequently than anywhere else.

"It is impossible but that offenses will come, but woe unto him through whom they come."

You often say that you serve because if you did not the existing order would be destroyed and disturbances and every kind of calamities would occur.

But firstly, it is not true that you are concerned with the maintenance of the existing order: you are concerned only with your own advantages.

Secondly, even if your abstinence from military service did destroy the existing order, this would in no way prove that you should continue to do what is wrong, but only that the order which is being destroyed by your abstinence should be destroyed. Were establishments of the most useful kind—hospitals, schools, homes, to depend for their support on the profits from houses of ill-fame, no consideration of the good produced by these philanthropic establishments would retain in her position the woman who desired to free herself from her shameful trade.

"It is not my fault," the woman would say, "that you have founded your philanthropic institutions on vice. I no longer wish to live in vice. As to your institutions, they do not concern me." And so should every soldier say if the necessity of maintaining the existing order founded on his readiness to murder were put before him. "Organize the general order in a way that will not require murder," the soldier should say. "And then I shall not destroy it. I only do not wish to and cannot be a murderer."

Many of you say also: "I was educated thus. I am tied to my position, and cannot escape." But this also is not true.

You can always escape from your position. If, however, you do not, it is only because you prefer to live and act against your conscience rather than lose certain worldly advantages which your dishonest service affords. Only forget that you are an officer and recall to mind that you are a man, and the way of escape from your position will immediately disclose itself to you. This way of escape in its best and most honest form would consist in your calling together the men of whom you are in command, stepping in front, and asking their pardon for all the evil you have done them by deception—and then cease to serve in the army. Such an action seems very bold, demanding great courage, whereas in reality much less courage is required for such an action than to storm a fortification or to challenge a man to a duel for an insult to the uniform—which you as a soldier are always ready to do, and do.

But even without being capable of acting thus you can always, if you have understood the criminality of military service, leave it and give preference to any other activity though less advantageous.

But if you cannot do even this, then the solution for you of the question whether you will continue to serve or not will be postponed to that time—and this will soon appear for each one of you—when you will stand face to face with an unarmed crowd of peasants or factory workers, and be ordered to shoot at them. And then, if anything human remains in you, you will have to refuse to obey, and, as a result, to leave the service. . . .

So that in our time, when the fratricidal function of the army has become evident, officers not only can no longer continue in the ancient traditions of military self-complacent bravado—they cannot continue the criminal work of teaching murder to simple men confiding in them, and themselves to prepare for participation in murdering unarmed populaces, without the consciousness of their human degradation and shame.

It is this which should be understood and remembered by every thinking and conscientious officer of our time.

"We drifted back to our trenches and the fraternization ended"
Johannes Niemann

In the weeks leading up to World War I, socialist leaders throughout Europe called for the people of different countries to rise above their national loyalties and not participate in a war fought against their fellow workers. Their arguments collapsed with the onset of hostilities. The most prominent socialist leader in Europe, the Frenchman Jean Juarès, was assassinated the day France entered the war in 1914, ending the possibility of an international boycott. Working-class men from Germany, France, and Great Britain suddenly found their fellow workers were now enemy soldiers.

But on Christmas morning in 1914, soldiers on both the German and French/British sides of the western front in France defied their commanders' orders and stepped out of their trenches to celebrate the holiday with each other, finding unity through a common sense of humanity. All across the front, men who had shot and killed each other for months sang songs, drank beer together, swapped stories, exchanged addresses, and even played soccer. When the generals learned of the fraternization on the front lines, many ordered that the cross-national celebrations of Christmas cease.

When Christmas Day, 1914, ended, the war began anew and lasted for almost four more years. But for that one day in modern history, soldiers on both sides of a brutal war protested their roles in the conflict by refusing to treat their opponents as enemies. This account of the famous Christmas truce of 1914 was written by a German officer, Lieutenant Johannes Niemann of the 133rd Royal Saxon Regiment.

WE CAME UP TO TAKE OVER THE TRENCHES on the front between Frelinghien and Houplines, where our Regiment and the Scottish Seaforth Highlanders were face to face. It was a cold, starry night and the Scots were a hundred or so meters in front of us in their trenches where, we discovered, like us they were up to their knees in mud. My Company Commander and I, savouring the unaccustomed calm, sat with our orderlies round a Christmas tree we had put up in our dugout.

Suddenly, for no apparent reason, our enemies began to fire on our lines. Our soldiers had hung little Christmas trees covered with candles above the trenches and our enemies, seeing the lights, thought we were about to launch a surprise attack. But, by midnight it was calm once more.

Next morning the mist was slow to clear and suddenly my orderly threw himself into my dugout to say that both the German and Scottish soldiers had come out of their trenches and were fraternizing along the front. I grabbed my binoculars and looking cautiously over the parapet saw the incredible sight of our soldiers exchanging cigarettes, schnapps and chocolate with the enemy. Later a Scottish soldier appeared with a football which seemed to come from nowhere and a few minutes later a real football match got underway. The Scots marked their goal mouth with their strange caps and we did the same with ours. It was far from easy to play on the frozen ground, but we continued, keeping rigorously to the rules, despite the fact that it only lasted an hour and that we had no referee. A great many of the passes went wide, but all the amateur footballers, although they must have been very tired, played with huge enthusiasm.

Us Germans really roared when a gust of wind revealed that the Scots wore no drawers under the kilts—and hooted and whistled every time they caught an impudent glimpse of one posterior belonging to one of "yesterday's enemies." But after an hour's play, when our Commanding Officer heard about it, he sent an order that we must put a stop to it. A little later we drifted back to our trenches and the fraternization ended.

The game finished with a score of three goals to two in favor of Fritz against Tommy.

Strike Against War

Helen Keller

After World War I broke out in Europe in 1914, the United States began to move toward entering the conflict. One of the first voices of opposition to U.S. involvement was Helen Keller, who gave this speech on January 5, 1916, at Carnegie Hall. Although widely known today as having overcome being blind and deaf, Keller was also a leading social activist. She was a member of the Socialist Party and the Industrial Workers of the World (IWW). She linked industrial and financial interests to the start of the war.

Keller wrote that her activism was driven by her desire to prevent blindness and other disabilities: "I was appointed on a commission to investigate the conditions for the blind. For the first time I, who had thought blindness a misfortune beyond human control, found, that too much of it was traceable to wrong industrial conditions, often caused by the selfishness and greed of employers. . . . I found that poverty drove women to a life of shame that ended in blindness."

Many newspapers that had previously praised Keller for her courage in overcoming her own blindness criticized her when she started to speak out for political causes, including the right for women to vote. Keller responded that her critics were "socially blind and deaf." Keller continued to advocate for women, workers, minorities, and the disabled until her death in 1968.

THE FUTURE OF THE WORLD rests in the hands of America. The future of America rests on the backs of 80,000,000 working men and women and their children. We are facing a grave crisis in our national life. The few who profit from the labor of the masses want to organize the workers into an army which will protect the interests of the capitalists. You are urged to add to the heavy burdens you already bear, the burden of a larger army and many additional warships. It is in your power to refuse to carry the artillery and the dread-noughts and to shake off some of the burdens, too, such as limousines, steam yachts and country estates. You do not need to make a great noise about it. With the silence and dignity of creators you can end wars and the system of selfishness and exploitation that causes wars. All you need to do to bring about this stupendous revolution is to straighten up and fold your arms.

We are not preparing to defend our country. Even if we were as helpless as Congressman [Augustus] Gardner says we are, we have no enemies foolhardy enough to attempt to invade the United States. The talk about attack from Germany and Japan is absurd. Germany has its hands full and will be busy with its own affairs for some generations after the European war is over.

With full control of the Atlantic Ocean and the Mediterranean Sea, the allies failed to land enough men to defeat the Turks at Gallipoli; and then they failed again to land an army at Salonica in time to check the Bulgarian invasion of Serbia. The conquest of America by water is a nightmare confined exclusively to ignorant persons and members of the Navy League.

Yet, everywhere, we hear fear advanced as argument for armament. It reminds me of a fable I read. A certain man found a horseshoe. His neighbor began to weep and wail because, as he justly pointed out, the man who found the horseshoe might someday find a horse. Having found the shoe, he might shoe him. The neighbor's child might some day go so near the horse's heels as to be kicked, and die. Undoubtedly the two families would quarrel and fight, and several valuable lives would be lost through the finding of the horseshoe. You know the last war we had we quite accidentally picked up some islands in the Pacific Ocean which may some day be the cause of a quarrel between ourselves and Japan. I'd rather drop those islands right now and forget about them than go to war to keep them. Wouldn't you?

Congress is not preparing to defend the people of the United States. It is planning to protect the capital of American speculators and investors in Mexico, South America, China, and the Philippine Islands. Incidentally this preparation will benefit the manufacturers of munitions and war machines. . . .

Every modern war has had its roots in exploitation. The Civil War was fought to decide whether the slaveholders of the South or the capitalists of the North should exploit the West. The Spanish-American War decided that the United States should exploit Cuba and the Philippines. The South African War decided that the British should exploit the diamond mines. The Russo-Japanese War decided that Japan should exploit Korea. The present war is to decide who shall exploit the Balkans, Turkey, Persia, Egypt, India, China, Africa. And we are whetting our sword to scare the victors into sharing their spoils with us. Now, the workers are not interested in the spoils; they will not get any of them anyway.

The preparedness propagandists have still another object, and a very important one. They want to give the people something to think about besides their own unhappy condition. They know the cost of living is high, wages are low, employment is uncertain and will be much more so when the European call for munitions stops. No matter how hard and incessantly the people work, they often cannot afford the comforts of life; many cannot obtain the necessities.

Every few days we are given a new war scare to lend realism to their propaganda. They have had us on the verge of war over the Lusitania, the Gulflight, the Ancona, and now they want the workingmen to become excited over the sinking of the Persia. The workingman has no interest in any of these ships. The Germans might sink every vessel on the Atlantic Ocean and the Mediterranean Sea, and kill Americans with every one—the American workingman would still have no reason to go to war.

All the machinery of the system has been set in motion. Above the complaint and din of the protest from the workers is heard the voice of authority.

"Friends," it says, "fellow workmen, patriots; your country is in danger! There are foes on all sides of us. There is nothing between us and our enemies except the Pacific Ocean and the Atlantic Ocean. Look at what has happened to Belgium. Consider the fate of Serbia. Will you murmur about low wages when your country, your very liberties, are in jeopardy? What are the miseries you endure compared to the humiliation of having a victorious German army sail up the East River? Quit your whining, get busy and prepare to defend your firesides and your flag. Get an army, get a navy; be ready to meet the invaders like the loyal-hearted freemen you are."

Will the workers walk into this trap? Will they be fooled again? I am afraid so. The people have always been amenable to oratory of this sort. The workers know they have no enemies except their masters. They know that their citizenship papers are no warrant for the safety of themselves or their wives and children. They know that honest sweat, persistent toil and years of struggle bring them nothing worth holding on to, worth fighting for. Yet, deep down in their foolish hearts they believe they have a country. Oh blind vanity of slaves!

The clever ones, up in the high places, know how childish and silly the workers are. They know that if the government dresses them up in khaki and gives them a rifle and starts them off with a brass band and waving banners, they will go forth to fight valiantly for their own enemies. They are taught that brave men die for their country's honor. What a price to pay for an abstraction—the lives of millions of young men; other millions crippled and blinded for life; existence made hideous for still more millions of human beings; the achievement and inheritance of generations swept away in a moment—and nobody better off for all the misery! . . .

Strike against all ordinances and laws and institutions that continue the slaughter of peace and the butcheries of war. Strike against war, for without you no battles can be fought. Strike against manufacturing shrapnel and gas bombs and all other tools of murder. Strike against preparedness that means death and misery to millions of human beings. Be not dumb, obedient slaves in an army of destruction. Be heroes in an army of construction.

"I am opposed to this and all other wars"
Roger N. Baldwin

After the United States entered World War I in 1917, more than twenty thousand men filed claims to be classified as objectors. The Conscription Act of 1917 gave objectors the option to fulfill non-military roles. Several hundred men, however, refused all forms of service.

One of them was Roger N. Baldwin, who objected to the use of violence for moral reasons, as his statement to the draft board, reprinted here, reflects. A member of the upper class in Boston, Baldwin had opposed the war and attempted to use his family connections to convince government officials to treat conscientious objectors with respect. His efforts were constantly stymied, however, and he was sentenced to jail for one year for resisting the draft.

After being released in 1919, Baldwin renewed his campaign. He founded the American Civil Liberties Union to advocate for citizens' rights as defined by the U.S. Constitution Bill of Rights.

THE COMPELLING MOTIVE for refusing to comply with the draft act is my uncompromising opposition to the principle of conscription of life by the state for any purpose whatever, in time of war or peace. I not only refuse to obey the present conscription law, but I would in future refuse to obey any similar statute which attempts to direct my choice of service and ideals. I regard the principle of conscription of life as a flat contradiction of all our cherished ideals of individual freedom, democratic liberty, and Christian teaching.

I am the more opposed to the present act, because it is for the purpose of conducting war. I am opposed to this and all other wars. I do not believe in the use of physical force as a method of achieving any end, however good. . . .

But, I believe most of us are prepared even to die for our faith, just as our brothers in France are dying for theirs. To them we are comrades in spirit—we understand one another's motive, though our methods are wide apart. We both share deeply the common experience of living up to the truth as we see it, whatever the price.

Though at the moment I am of a tiny minority, I feel myself just one protest in a great revolt surging up from among the people—the struggle of the masses against the rule of the world by the few—profoundly intensified by the war. It is a struggle against the political state itself, against exploitation, militarism, imperialism, authority in all forms. . . .

Having arrived at the state of mind in which those views mean the dearest things in life to me, I cannot consistently, with self-respect, do other than I have, namely, to deliberately violate an act which seems to me to be a denial of everything which ideally and in practice I hold sacred.

"We frankly admit that we are disloyalists"
Eugene Debs

Eugene Debs ran for president of the United States four times as the Socialist Party candidate at the turn of the twentieth century. He strongly opposed U.S. involvement in World War I.

In 1917, Congress passed the Espionage Act, making it illegal to for citizens to use "disloyal" language against the government or its wartime policies. On June 18, 1918, Debs purposefully defied the law in a speech at a workers' rally in Ohio. He was arrested and put in jail for this speech, reprinted here. He told the jury that found him guilty, "I have been accused of obstructing the war. I admit it. Gentlemen, I abhor war. I would oppose the war if I stood alone."

SAM JOHNSON DECLARED that "patriotism is the last refuge of the scoundrel." He must have had . . . [the] Wall Street gentry in mind, or at least their prototypes, for in every age it has been the tyrant, the oppressor and the exploiter who has wrapped himself in the cloak of patriotism, or religion, or both to decree and overawe the people.

They would have you believe that the Socialist Party consists in the main of disloyalists and traitors. It is true in a sense not at all to their discredit. We frankly admit that we are disloyalists and traitors to the real traitors of this nation; to the gang that on the Pacific coast are trying to hang Tom Mooney and Warren Billings in spite of their well-known innocence and the protest of practically the whole civilized world. . . .

Every solitary one of these aristocratic conspirators and would-be murderers claims to be an arch-patriot; every one of them insists that the war is being waged to make the world safe for democracy. What humbug! What rot! What false pretense! These autocrats, these tyrants, these red-handed robbers and murderers, the "patriots," while the men who have the courage to stand face to face with them, speak the truth, and fight for their exploited victims—they are the disloyalists and traitors. If this be true, I want to take my place side by side with the traitors in this fight. . . .

Max Eastman has been indicted and his paper [*The Masses*] suppressed, just as the papers with which I have been connected have all been suppressed. What a wonderful compliment they pay us! They are afraid that we may mislead and contaminate you. You are their wards; they are your guardians and they know what is best for you to read and hear and know. They are bound to see to it that our vicious doctrines do not reach your ears. And so in our great democracy, under our free institutions, they flatter our press by suppression; and they ignorantly imagine that they have silenced revolutionary propaganda in the United States. What an awful mistake they make for our benefit! As a matter of justice to them we should respond with resolutions of thanks and gratitude. Thousands of people who had never before heard of our papers are now inquiring for and insisting upon seeing them. They have succeeded only in arousing curiosity in our literature and propaganda. And woe to him who reads Socialist literature from curiosity! He is surely a goner. I have known of a thousand experiments but never one that failed. . . .

Wars throughout history have been waged for conquest and plunder. In the Middle Ages when the feudal lords who inhabited the castles whose towers may still be seen along the Rhine concluded to enlarge their domains, to increase their power, their prestige and their wealth they declared war upon one another. But they themselves did not go to war any more than the modern feudal lords, the barons of Wall Street go to war. The feudal barons of the Middle Ages, the economic predecessors of the capitalists of our day, declared all wars. And their miserable serfs fought all the battles. The poor, ignorant serfs have been taught to revere their masters; to believe that when their masters declared war upon one another, it was their patriotic duty to fall upon one another and cut one another's throats for the profit and glory of the lords and barons who held them in contempt. And that is war in a nutshell. The master class has always declared the wars; the subject class has always fought the battles. The master class has had all to gain and nothing to lose, while the subject class has had nothing to gain and all to lose—especially their lives.

They have always taught and trained you to believe it to be your patriotic duty to go to war and to have yourselves slaughtered at their command. But in all the history of the world you, the people, have never had a voice in declaring war, and strange as it certainly appears, no war by any nation in any age has ever been declared by the people.

And here let me emphasize the fact—and it cannot be repeated too often—that the working class who fight all the battles, the working class who make the supreme sacrifices, the working class who freely shed their blood and furnish the corpses, have never yet had a voice in either declaring war or making peace. It is the ruling class that invariably does both. They alone declare war and they alone make peace.

> Yours not to reason why;
> Yours but to do and die.

That is their motto and we object on the part of the awakening workers of this nation.

If war is right let it be declared by the people. You who have your lives to lose, you certainly above all others have the right to decide the momentous issue of war or peace.

Guernica
Pablo Picasso

On April 27, 1937, Nazi warplanes bombed the Basque town of Guernica to support Francisco Franco's fascist forces in the Spanish Civil War. Guernica was the capital of the state of Basque, which the Spanish government had granted autonomy. It was the world's first sustained aerial bombardment of a civilian population, and more than sixteen hundred people were killed.

When Spanish artist Pablo Picasso saw photographs of Guernica in ruins, he began working on this mural, which was exhibited at the 1937 International World's Fair, as a powerful statement against the violence of war.

The painting is filled with symbolism. The gored and speared horse in agony is the Spanish Republic, while the powerful bull standing over the anguished shrieking woman holding a dead child represents Franco. The falling figure on the right with outstretched arms harkens back to Goya's imagery from *The Third of May*.

Picasso's use of abstract cubist art brings out the anguish, arrogance, tragedy, and pain of the bombing that photographs could not do. "Art is a lie that tells the truth," Picasso said.

Catch-22
Joseph Heller

Joseph Heller's 1961 novel *Catch-22* blends satire and a keen understanding of military bureaucracy to portray the insanity of war. Eccentric characters are trapped in a maze of impersonal and nonsensical rules with comic and tragic consequences. The book centers on Yossarian, an American bomber pilot in World War II trying to avoid thousands of people who he does not know, but who appear to want to kill him every time he flies a mission.

Yossarian's goal is to fly the number of missions required to complete his military service. The problem is that every time he approaches the number, Colonel Cathcart raises the requirement. Yossarian's attempts to excuse himself from his obligations are thwarted by the sinister bureaucratic regulation that inspires the title of the book.

In this excerpt, Doc Daneeka introduces Yossarian to the dilemma of Catch-22—a man is considered insane if he willingly continues to fly dangerous combat missions, but if he makes the required formal request to be relieved of the missions, the act of making the request proves that he is sane and thereby ineligible to be relieved.

IT WAS A HORRIBLE JOKE, but Doc Daneeka didn't laugh until Yossarian came to him one mission later and pleaded again, without any real expectation of success, to be grounded. Doc Daneeka snickered once and was soon immersed in problems of his own, which included Chief White Halfoat, who had been challenging him all that morning to Indian wrestle, and Yossarian, who decided right then and there to go crazy.

"You're wasting your time," Doc Daneeka was forced to tell him.

"Can't you ground someone who is crazy?"

"Oh sure. I have to. There's a rule saying I have to ground anyone who's crazy."

"Then why don't you ground me? I'm crazy. Ask Clevinger."

"Clevinger? Where is Clevinger? You find Clevinger and I'll ask him."

"Then ask any of the others. They'll tell you how crazy I am."

"They're crazy."

"Then why don't you ground them?"

"Why don't they ask me to ground them?"

"Because they're crazy, that's why."

"Of course they're crazy," Doc Daneeka replied. "I just told you they're crazy, didn't I? And you can't let crazy people decide whether you're crazy or not, can you?"

Yossarian looked at him soberly and tried another approach. "Is Orr crazy?"

"He sure is," Doc Daneeka said.

"Can you ground him?"

"I sure can. But first he has to ask me to. That's part of the rule."

"Then why doesn't he ask you to?"

"Because he's crazy," Doc Daneeka said. "He has to be crazy to keep flying combat missions after all the close calls he's had. Sure, I can ground Orr. But first he has to ask me to."

"That's all he has to do to be grounded?"

"That's all. Let him ask me."

"And then you can ground him?" Yossarian asked.

"No. Then I can't ground him."

"You mean there's a catch?"

"Sure there's a catch," Doc Daneeka replied. "Catch-22. Anyone who wants to get out of combat duty isn't really crazy."

There was only one catch and that was Catch-22, which specified that a concern for one's own safety in the face of dangers that were real and immediate was the process of a rational mind. Orr was crazy and could be grounded. All he had to do was ask; and as soon as he did, he would no longer be crazy and would have to fly more missions. Orr would be crazy to fly more missions and sane if he didn't, but if he was sane he had to fly them. If he flew them he was crazy and didn't have to; but if he didn't want to he was sane and had to. Yossarian was moved very deeply by the absolute simplicity of this clause of Catch-22 and let out a respectful whistle.

"That's some catch, that Catch-22," he observed.

"It's the best there is," Doc Daneeka agreed.

"I have nothing to lose by standing up for my beliefs"
Muhammad Ali

In 1966, the world heavyweight boxing champion Muhammad Ali announced that he would petition for a religious exemption to military service in the U.S. army. Ali had changed his name from Cassius Clay two years earlier, at the same time that he had converted to Islam. He said that his former name had been his slave name. He made his announcement, reprinted here, in his hometown of Louisville, Kentucky, at a time when U.S. involvement in the Vietnam War was escalating.

The military denied his petition. He was stripped of his boxing title and sentenced to serve five years in prison. Ali fought the sentence in the courts, and the decision was reversed in 1971. He also reclaimed his boxing title through a series of matches.

WHY SHOULD THEY ASK ME to put on a uniform and go ten thousand miles from home and drop bombs and bullets on brown people in Vietnam while so-called Negro people in Louisville are treated like dogs and denied simple human rights? No, I am not going ten thousand miles from home to help murder and burn another poor nation simply to continue the domination of white slave masters of the darker people the world over. This is the day when such evils must come to an end. I have been warned that to take such a stand would put my prestige in jeopardy and could cause me to lose millions of dollars which should accrue to me as the champion. But I have said it once and I will say it again. The real enemy of my people is right here. I will not disgrace my religion, my people or myself by becoming a tool to enslave those who are fighting for their own justice, freedom and equality. . . .

If I thought the war was going to bring freedom and equality to twenty-two million of my people, they wouldn't have to draft me, I'd join tomorrow. But I either have to obey the laws of the land or the laws of Allah. I have nothing to lose by standing up for my beliefs. So I'll go to jail. We've been in jail for four hundred years.

"It is no longer clear what is service and what is disservice"

Bill Clinton

Like many young men in the 1960s, President Bill Clinton was confronted with the difficult dilemma of whether or not to join the military and fight in the Vietnam War. Clinton had marched against the war and supported others in their demonstrations against it. But before becoming a Rhodes Scholar at Oxford University in England, Clinton avoided the draft by signing up for the Reserve Officers' Training Corps (ROTC) program at the University of Arkansas Law School. He wrote the following letter to ROTC director Colonel Eugene J. Holmes, explaining his deeply conflicted feelings about opposing the war but not wanting to act too strongly on those convictions for fear of jeopardizing his own future. Holmes was persuaded to defer Clinton's military-service start date.

Clinton subsequently drew a very high number in the draft, which meant he would not have to serve in the army. He instead went to Yale Law School.

December 3, 1969

Dear Col. Holmes,

I am sorry to be so long writing. I know I promised to let you hear from me at least once a month, and from now on you will, but I have had to have some time to think about this first letter. Almost daily since my return to England I have thought about writing, about what I want to and ought to say.

First, I want to thank you, not just for saving me from the draft, but for being so kind and decent to me last summer, when I was as low as I have ever been. One thing which made the bond we struck in good faith somewhat palatable to me was my high regard for you personally. In retrospect, it seems that the admiration might not have been mutual had you known a little more about me, about my political beliefs and activities. At least you might have thought me more fit for the draft than for R.O.T.C.

Let me try to explain. As you know, I worked for two years in a very minor position in the Senate Foreign Relations Committee. I did it for the experience and the salary but also for the opportunity, however, small, of working every day against a war I opposed and despised with a depth of feeling I had reserved solely for racism in America before Vietnam. I did not take the matter lightly but studied it carefully, and there was a time when not many people had more information about Vietnam at hand that I did.

I have written and spoken and marched against the war. One of the national organizers of the Vietnam Moratorium is a close friend of mine. After I left Arkansas last summer, I went to Washington to work in the national headquarters of the Moratorium, then to England to organize the Americans here for demonstrations Oct. 15 and Nov. 16.

Interlocked with the war is the draft issue, which I did not begin to consider separately until early 1968. For a law seminar at Georgetown I wrote a paper on the legal arguments for and against allowing, within the Selective Service System, the classification of selective conscientious objection, for those opposed to participation in a particular war, not simply to "participation in war in any form."

From my work, I came to believe that the draft system is illegitimate. No government really rooted in limited, parliamentary democracy should have the power to make its citizens fight and kill and die in a war they may oppose, a war which even possibly may be wrong, a war which, in any case, does not involve immediately the peace and freedom of the nation.

The draft was justified in World War II because the life of the people collectively was at stake. Individuals had to fight, if the nation was to survive, for the lives of their countryman and their way of life. Vietnam is no such case. Nor was Korea an example where, in my opinion, certain military action was justified but the draft was not, for the reasons stated above.

Because of my opposition to the draft and the war, I am in great sympathy with those who are not willing to fight, kill, and maybe die for their country (i.e., the particular policy of a particular government) right or wrong. Two of my friends at Oxford are conscientious objectors. I wrote a letter of recommendation for one of them to his Mississippi draft board, a letter which I am more proud of than anything else I wrote at Oxford last year. One of my roommates is a draft resister who is possibly under indictment and may never be able to go home again. He is one of the bravest, best men I know. His country needs men like him more than they know. That he is considered a criminal is an obscenity.

The decision not to be a resister and the related subsequent decisions were the most difficult of my life. I decided to accept the draft in spite of my beliefs for one reason: to maintain my political viability within the system. For years I have worked to prepare myself for a political life characterized by both practical political ability and concern for rapid social progress. It is a life I still feel compelled to try to lead. I do not think our system of government is by definition corrupt, however dangerous and inadequate it has been in recent years. (The society may be corrupt, but that is not the same thing, and if that is true we are all finished anyway.)

When the draft came, despite political convictions, I was having a hard time facing the prospect of fighting a war I had been fighting against, and that is why I contacted you. R.O.T.C. was the one way left in which I could possibly, but not positively, avoid both Vietnam and resistance. Going on with my education, even coming back to England, played no part in my decision to join R.O.T.C. I am back here, and would have been at Arkansas Law School because there is nothing else I can do. In fact, I would like to have been able to take a year out perhaps to teach in a small college or work on some community action project and in the process to decide whether to attend law school or graduate school and how to begin putting what I have learned to use.

But the particulars of my personal life are not nearly as important to me as the principles involved. After I signed the R.O.T.C. letter of intent I began to wonder whether the compromise I had made with myself was not more objectionable than the draft would have been, because I had no interest in the R.O.T.C program in itself and all I seemed to have done was to protect myself from physical harm. Also, I began to think I had deceived you, not by lies—there were none—but by failing to tell you all the things I'm writing now. I doubt that I had the mental coherence to articulate them then.

At that time, after we had made our agreement and you had sent my 1-D deferment to my draft board, the anguish and loss of my self-regard and self-confidence really set in. I hardly slept for weeks and kept going by eating compulsively and reading until exhaustion brought sleep. Finally, on Sept. 12 I stayed up all night writing a letter to the chairman of my draft board, saying basically what is in the preceding paragraph, thanking him for trying to help in a case where he really couldn't, and stating that I couldn't do the R.O.T.C. after all and would he please draft me as soon as possible.

I never mailed the letter, but I did carry it on me every day until I got on the plane to return to England. I didn't mail the letter because I didn't see, in the end, how my going in the army and maybe going to Vietnam would achieve anything except a feeling that I had punished myself and gotten what I deserved. So I came back to England to try to make something of this second year of my Rhodes scholarship.

And that is where I am now, writing to you because you have been good to me and have a right to know what I think and feel. I am writing too in the hope that my telling this one story will help you to understand more clearly how so many fine people have come to find themselves still loving their country but loathing the military, to which you and other good men have devoted years, lifetimes, of the best service you could give. To many of us, it is no longer clear what is service and what is disservice, or if it is clear, the conclusion is likely to be illegal.

Forgive the length of the letter. There was much to say. There is still a lot to be said, but it can wait. Please say hello to Col. Jones for me.

4 Kent State Students Killed by Troops
John Kifner

By the spring of 1970, student opposition to the Vietnam War was at a boiling point. Demonstrations against the war, the secret invasion of Cambodia, and the draft sprang up at universities and college campuses across the country, including at Kent State University in Ohio.

Tension between Kent State students and police and military officials reached a violent climax on May 4, 1970, as described in the article below by *New York Times* reporter John Kifner. Four students were killed and nine wounded when National Guardsmen opened fire on the protesters. The deaths sparked a renewed wave of concern and protests throughout the United States, raising the stakes of continuing the war and stirring greater resentment on both sides.

STUDENTS HERE, ANGERED BY the expansion of the war into Cambodia, have held demonstrations for the last three nights. On Saturday night [May 2], the Army Reserve Officers Training Corps building was burned to the ground and the [National] Guard was called in and martial law was declared.

Today's rally, called after a night in which the police and guardsmen drove students into their dormitories and made 69 arrests, began as students rang the iron Victory Bell on the Commons, normally used to herald football victories.

A National Guard jeep drove onto the Commons and an officer ordered the crowd to disperse. Then several canisters of tear gas were fired and the students straggled up a hill that borders the area and retreated into buildings.

A platoon of guardsmen, armed—as they have been since they arrived here with loaded M-1 rifles and gas equipment—moved across the green and over the crest of the hill, chasing the main body of protesters.

The youths split into two groups, one heading farther downhill toward a dormitory complex, the other eddying around a parking lot and girls' dormitory just below Taylor Hall, the architecture building.

The guardsmen moved into a grassy area just below the parking lot and fired several canisters of tear gas from their short, stubby launchers.

Three or four youths ran to the smoking canisters and hurled them back. Most fell far short, but one landed near the troops and a cheer went up from the crowd, which was chanting "Pigs off campus" and cursing the war.

A few youths in the front of the crowd ran into the parking lot and hurled stones or small chunks of pavement in the direction of the guardsmen. Then the troops began moving back up the hill in the direction of the college.

The students in the parking lot area, numbering about 500, began to move towards the rear of the troops, cheering. Again, a few in front picked up stones from the edge of the parking lot and threw them at the guardsmen. Another group of several hundred students had gathered around the sides of Taylor Hall, watching.

As the guardsmen, moving up the hill in a single file, reached the crest, they suddenly turned, forming a skirmish line and opening fire.

The crackle of the rifle volley cut the suddenly still air. It appeared to go on, as a solid volley, for perhaps a full minute or a little longer.

Some of the students dived to the ground, crawling on the grass in terror. Others stood shocked or half-crouched, apparently believing the troops were firing into the air. Some of the rifle barrels were pointed upward.

Near the top of the hill at the corner of Taylor Hall, a student crumpled over, spun sideways and fell to the ground, shot in the head.

When the firing stopped, a slim girl, wearing a cowboy shirt and faded jeans, was lying face down on the road at the edge of the parking lot, blood pouring out onto the macadam, about 10 feet from this reporter.

The youths stood stunned, many of them clustered in small groups staring at the bodies. A young man cradled one of the bleeding forms in his arms. Several girls began to cry. But many of the students who rushed to the scene seemed almost too shocked to react. Several gathered around an abstract steel sculpture in front of the building and looked at a .30-caliber bullet hole drilled through one of the plates.

"Witness for Peace needs to reflect on the true meaning of peace"

Sharon Hostetler

The nonprofit organization Witness for Peace maintained the longest nonviolent presence in an active war zone in United States history when it worked in Nicaragua in the 1980s. The organization started after a 1983 incident. U.S.-backed contra rebels, who were trying to overthrow the Sandinista government in Nicaragua, balked when they saw thirty Americans from the Carolina Interfaith Task Force standing in the tobacco farm they planned to attack.

During the next ten years Witness for Peace sent more than 4,500 delegates to experience the war in Nicaragua. The trips were designed to both discourage attacks through the simple act of having U.S. citizens bear witness and to give them firsthand knowledge of the war to help influence U.S. policy. Sharon Hostetler served as the coordinator of the agency's work in Nicaragua. In this excerpt from *Witness for Peace* newsletter, she reflects on her experience and the role that being a witness can play in advancing peace, both during times of war and peace.

Witness for Peace's mission is "to support peace, justice and sustainable economies in the Americas by changing U.S. policies and corporate practices which contribute to poverty and oppression in Latin America and the Caribbean." It has sent groups throughout the region, including Colombia, Bolivia, Venezuela, Cuba, Haiti, and the Chiapas region of Mexico. Hostetler, a Mennonite, served as the organization's international program coordinator after her work in Nicaragua.

OUR COMMITMENTS ARE DEEP; they are rooted in our hearts where we ponder the pain and injustices we see reflected in the eyes of a people who have suffered for centuries the results of U.S. policies which have waged war on the poor. Thousands of us have come to Nicaragua since the beginning of Witness for Peace in 1983. We came to bear witness and to respond by going into a war zone to say "no" to an immoral policy.

We heard a grandmother from Teotecacinte tell how her four year old granddaughter, Suyapa, was killed by a mortar when she ran from the bomb shelter to rescue her pet chicken. We stood in silence at the cross which marks the place where Suyapa took her last step. In Jinotega we saw the remains of a civilian transport truck blasted into a ravine after it passed over a land mine. Thirty-five people were killed—14 women, nine men, and 12 children, including three infants. Petrona Torres wept as she told us that her 22-year-old daughter, Maria, was running for shelter with her young niece when they were both gunned down. The WFP Long Term Team and Short-Term Delegates documented 500 civilians killed by contras supported by our government.

We accompanied mourners at all-night wakes, and we still can remember the smells—the stench of death mixed with the odor of wilted flowers that covered the coffins and the smell of fresh dirt at the cemeteries. The cries of "Presente!" ring in our ears as we remember the sound of dirt hitting the crude wooden boxes of all sizes holding the victims of the U.S. government-sponsored aggression. Our arms still feel the weight of the crosses and markers we carried along the road to San Juan de Limay. We planted them at the sites where innocent road workers and others were murdered with weapons bought with our tax dollars. Our mouths still open and close as we try to utter words of comfort.

Our commitments found expression in non-violent actions directed at stopping the war and changing our government's foreign policy toward Nicaragua. We accompanied people in cooperatives and communities when they predicted imminent attacks. We traveled roads that often held the threat of ambushes and land mines. We accompanied priests and nuns who knew that to continue their mission could mean death. We drove an ambulance in an area where it was not safe for a Nicaraguan to drive. We chartered a small fishing boat and headed out to the Pacific Ocean to confront a U.S. warship, protesting that Nicaragua was not a threat to the security of the United States. We set out on a mission of peace on the beautiful San Juan River knowing that contra soldiers had orders to fire on any boat that passed beyond a certain point. We vowed that we were willing to risk our lives for peace as many had risked their lives for war.

Our deep commitments were not a guarantee of success. We were not able to stop the suffering, death and destruction that the U.S. policy of low-intensity warfare imposed on the Nicaraguan people. The U.S. Congress continued funding the contras until the Arias Central American Peace Plan was signed by the five Central American presidents. We were not successful in stopping the economic embargo or the blocking of loans from international lending agencies. Those policies changed only after the U.S. massively intervened in the 1990 elections and ensured the election of "our" candidate.

After the elections, one of our partners declared, "Witness for Peace needs to reflect on the true meaning of peace. The military war is over, but there is still violence—unemployment, poverty, and instability. Is this peace? Witness for Peace needs to reflect on the actual U.S. policy toward this poor country and educate the people in the U.S. about its effects on the people of Nicaragua."

Our commitments call us to engage in a process of deep reflection and analysis. The military manifestations of the U.S. policy and its consequences on the civilian population which motivated our initial response are gone. However, U.S.

Latin American policy in the 1990s—neo-liberal economics, the North American Free Trade Agreement, GATT, etc.—taken together kill the poor just as surely as did the military policy of the 1980s. We no longer go to all-night wakes; or document ambushes, kidnappings, and murders; or plant crosses and markers in the cemeteries. Yet every day we see the pain of a different kind of violence. We know that 60 percent of the work force, many of whom are single mothers, are unemployed; we see the disastrous effects of U.S. AID policies that provide no credit for small and medium-sized producers; we see the suffering that results when 69 percent of the population, of which more than half are children, suffer severe nutritional deficiency. We see the disintegration of a society where children no longer can afford to go to school or to the neighborhood health clinic. We realize that our struggle has only begun. . . .

"Washington Bullets"
The Clash

The British punk rock band The Clash made a name for itself in the late 1970s and early 1980s with its fast-based beat and antiauthoritarian message. Although many of their songs directed anger at British institutions and social conditions, The Clash also targeted the United States. The song "Washington Bullets" was recorded on their album *Sandinista*. The lyrics refer to U.S. military intervention in the domestic affairs of Chile, Cuba, and Nicaragua, as well as similar intrusions by the Soviet Union, China, and Great Britain during the same decades.

Oh! Mama, Mama look there!
Your children are playing in that street again
Don't you know what happened down there?
A youth of fourteen got shot down there
The Cocaine guns of Jamdown Town
The killing clowns, the blood money men
Are shooting those Washington bullets again

As every cell in Chile will tell
The cries of the tortured men
Remember Allende, and the days before,
Before the army came
Please remember Victor Jara,
In the Santiago Stadium,
Es verdad—those Washington Bullets again

And in the Bay of Pigs in 1961,
Havana fought the playboy in the Cuban sun,
For Castro is a colour,

Is a redder than red,
Those Washington bullets want Castro dead
For Castro is the colour . . .
. . . That will earn you a spray of lead

Sandinista!

For the very first time ever,
When they had a revolution in Nicaragua,
There was no interference from America
Human rights in America

Well the people fought the leader,
And up he flew . . .
With no Washington bullets what else could he do?
Sandinista!

'N' if you can find a Afghan rebel
That the Moscow bullets missed
Ask him what he thinks of voting Communist . . .
. . . Ask the Dalai Lama in the hills of Tibet,
How many monks did the Chinese get?
In a war-torn swamp stop any mercenary,
'N' check the British bullets in his armoury
Que?
Sandinista!

Statement of Refusal to Participate in Interventionist Wars
Erik Larsen

In the summer of 1990, Iraq invaded Kuwait. President George H. W. Bush led a coalition of countries from around the world in an effort to force Iraq out of the oil-producing nation. The debate about whether to launch a military attack against Iraq was extremely contentious and continued right up to the invasion, which took place in early 1991. Three California cities—San Francisco, Berkeley, and Oakland—declared themselves sanctuaries for Gulf War objectors, as did many churches across the country. During the buildup and subsequent Persian Gulf war, about two thousand men and women in the U.S. military applied for conscientious objector status. Marine Corps lance corporal Erik Larsen made this statement at a press conference announcing his intention to file on August 28, 1990.

The war proved to be very brief, ending after a few weeks, and there were far fewer U.S. casualties than feared, making Bush extremely popular. For a brief time after the war, he had a 90 percent favorability rating.

HELLO AND GOOD MORNING: My name is Erik Larsen. I am a Lance Corporal in the United States Marine Corps Reserve and a radar mechanic for the HAWK missile system. I am stationed in Hayward, California, with the Fourth Light Anti-Aircraft Missile Battalion, Fourth Marine Aircraft Wing.

On April 21, 1986, I joined the Marine Corps to defend the American dream, which first attracted my parents to this country in 1958. I emerged from boot camp three months later, a fully indoctrinated fighting machine willing to go anywhere in the world to defend the ideals and freedoms stated in the Constitution of the United States of America.

I first became aware of the realities of U.S. policies through student activists at Chabot Community College. They introduced me to alternative newspapers and books, and exposed me to the writings and speeches of Archbishop Oscar Romero of El Salvador.

I learned about a Central American history of U.S.-sponsored exploitive polices motivated by corporate and personal greed. 70,000 Salvadorans have been killed over the last ten years as a result of U.S. policies. I realized that I could no longer blindly follow orders from my Commander-in-Chief but that my actions were ultimately accountable to a higher authority—namely God.

My deeply rooted moral convictions have led me to declare my objection to the escalation of tensions and seemingly inevitable war in the Middle East.

It sickens me to hear Mr. Bush announce that 40,000 of my fellow reservists and 80,000 of my active duty brothers and sisters are going to wage war in the Middle East to protect "our American lifestyle." Oil imports could be cut in half if a sound energy policy focusing on renewable resources and conservation was in effect.

Our oil consuming western lifestyle is destroying the earth and it is our wasteful society that has brought the world to the brink of a preventable war.

Our presence in the Middle East has destroyed any hope of any of us ever receiving a peace dividend. We are wasting more than 24 million dollars a day in Saudi Arabia while the Oakland school system is still in shambles, with homeless people still walking the streets, and while the [Savings & Loan] criminals are still on the loose.

I've been listening to a lot of experts on public radio and they share my concern that the use of chemical and nuclear weapons is a possibility in the event a war does occur.

I have experienced firsthand the frightening power of chemical weapons and I never want to go through that again. I had two buddies who were involved in a chemical incident when I was on an exercise this summer at Dugway Proving Grounds in Utah. They were rushed to an aid station while a decontamination team swept the area.

While standing upwind from the contamination area which had been the site of chemical testing for the last fifty years I made a vow to my buddies. Never again will I allow myself or others to be put into a chemical environment.

The suggestion that nuclear weapons could be used in addition to chemical weapons scares the hell out of me. The use of chemical-biological agents and nuclear arms is completely unjustified.

Eight years ago the Reagan-Bush administration encouraged the sale of chemical weapons to Saddam Hussein. Bush said nothing at the time about human rights when Hussein used the weapons on his own people. Bush wants us to forget that he turned his eyes when innocent men, women, and children were being gassed.

Now he wants the American public to turn our eyes and forget about humanity, as he prepares to use me and others in the service as fodder for his cannon. I spent three long months in boot camp to learn to view human beings as targets. It has taken me almost three years to begin to see people as individuals once again. And I'll be damned if I'm going to be part of this militaristic feeding frenzy.

I will refuse orders to activate me into the regular Marines.

I will refuse orders to ship me to Saudi Arabia to defend our polluting, exploitive lifestyle.

I will refuse to face another human being with a gas mask covering my face and my M-16 drawn.

I declare myself as a conscientious objector.

Here is my sea bag full of personal gear. Here is my gas mask. I will return them to the government. I no longer need them; I am no longer a Marine.

Thoughts in the Presence of Fear

Wendell Berry

On September 11, 2001, Islamic terrorists slammed hijacked airplanes into the World Trade Center in New York City and the Pentagon in Washington, D.C. President George W. Bush responded with a statement saying that the United States had entered a new "War on Terror." Although there was near-universal condemnation of the attacks and support for a vigorous response, some people expressed concern about what the United States reaction would be.

Wendell Berry is a Kentucky farmer-poet-writer who for many years had linked the decline of local farming communities with decreasing national economic security. He expressed strong concerns about the conditions that led to the attack and the anticipated response to September 11. His essay, labeled "Thoughts in the Presence of Fear," was published as an ad in the *New York Times* and was subsequently translated into seventy languages.

I. THE TIME WILL SOON COME when we will not be able to remember the horrors of September 11 without remembering also the unquestioning technological and economic optimism that ended on that day.

II. This optimism rested on the proposition that we were living in a "new world order" and a "new economy" that would "grow" on and on, bringing a prosperity of which every new increment would be "unprecedented."

III. The dominant politicians, corporate officers, and investors who believed this proposition did not acknowledge that the prosperity was limited to a tiny percent of the world's people, and to an ever smaller number of people even in the United States; that it was founded upon the oppressive labor of poor people all over the world; and that its ecological costs increasingly threatened all life, including the lives of the supposedly prosperous.

IV. The "developed" nations had given to the "free market" the status of a god, and were sacrificing to it their farmers, farmlands, and communities, their forests, wetlands, and prairies, their ecosystems and watersheds. They had accepted universal pollution and global warming as normal costs of doing business.

V. There was, as a consequence, a growing worldwide effort on behalf of economic decentralization, economic justice, and ecological responsibility. We must recognize that the events of September 11 make this effort more necessary than ever. We citizens of the industrial countries must continue the labor of self-criticism and self-correction. We must recognize our mistakes. . . .

VII. We did not anticipate anything like what has now happened. We did not foresee that all our sequence of innovations might be at once overridden by a greater one: the invention of a new kind of war that would turn our previous innovations against us, discovering and exploiting the debits and the dangers that we had ignored. We never considered the possibility that we might be trapped in the webwork of communication and transport that was supposed to make us free.

VIII. Nor did we foresee that the weaponry and the war science that we marketed and taught to the world would become available, not just to recognized national governments, which possess so uncannily the power to legitimate large-scale violence, but also to "rogue nations," dissident or fanatical groups and individuals—whose violence, though never worse than that of nations, is judged by the nations to be illegitimate.

IX. We had accepted uncritically the belief that technology is only good; that it cannot serve evil as well as good; that it cannot serve our enemies as well as ourselves; that it cannot be used to destroy what is good, including our homelands and our lives.

X. We had accepted too the corollary belief that an economy (either as a money economy or as a life-support system) that is global in extent, technologically complex, and centralized is invulnerable to terrorism, sabotage, or war, and that it is protectable by "national defense." . . .

XIII. One of the gravest dangers to us now, second only to further terrorist attacks against our people, is that we will attempt to go on as before with the corporate program of global "free trade," whatever the cost in freedom and civil rights, without self-questioning or self-criticism or public debate.

XIV. This is why the substitution of rhetoric for thought, always a temptation in a national crisis, must be resisted by officials and citizens alike. It is hard for ordinary citizens to know what is actually happening in Washington in a time of such great trouble; for all we know, serious and difficult thought may be taking place there. But the talk that we are hearing from politicians, bureaucrats, and commentators has so far tended to reduce the complex problems now facing us to issues of unity, security, normality, and retaliation.

XV. National self-righteousness, like personal self-righteousness, is a mistake. It is misleading. It is a sign of weakness. Any war that we may make now against terrorism will come as a new installment in a history of war in which we have fully participated. We are not innocent of making war against civilian populations. The modern doctrine of such warfare was set forth and enacted by General William Tecumseh Sherman, who held that a civilian population could be declared guilty and rightly subjected to military punishment. We have never repudiated that doctrine.

XVI. It is a mistake also—as events since September 11 have shown—to suppose that a government can promote and participate in a global economy and at the same time act exclusively in its own interest by abrogating its international treaties and standing apart from international cooperation on moral issues. . . .

XVIII. In a time such as this, when we have been seriously and most cruelly hurt by those who hate us, and when we must consider ourselves to be gravely threatened by those same people, it is hard to speak of the ways of peace and to remember that Christ enjoined us to love our enemies, but this is no less necessary for being difficult.

XIX. Even now we dare not forget that since the attack of Pearl Harbor—to which the present attack has been often and not usefully compared—we humans have suffered an almost uninterrupted sequence of wars, none of which has brought peace or made us more peaceable.

XX. The aim and result of war necessarily is not peace but victory, and any victory won by violence necessarily justifies the violence that won it and leads to further violence. If we are serious about innovation, must we not conclude that we need something new to replace our perpetual "war to end war"?

XXI. What leads to peace is not violence but peaceableness, which is not passivity, but an alert, informed, practiced, and active state of being. We should recognize that while we have extravagantly subsidized the means of war, we have almost totally neglected the ways of peaceableness. We have, for example, several national military academies, but not one peace academy. We have ignored the teachings and the examples of Christ, Gandhi, Martin Luther King, [Jr.,] and other peaceable leaders. And here we have an inescapable duty to notice also that war is profitable, whereas the means of peaceableness, being cheap or free, make no money.

XXII. The key to peaceableness is continuous practice. It is wrong to suppose that we can exploit and impoverish the poorer countries, while arming them and instructing them in the newest means of war, and then reasonably expect them to be peaceable.

XXIII. We must not again allow public emotion or the public media to caricature our enemies. If our enemies are now to be some nations of Islam, then we should undertake to know those enemies. Our schools should begin to teach the histories, cultures, arts, and language of the Islamic nations. And our leaders should have the humility and the wisdom to ask the reasons some of those people have for hating us.

XXIV. Starting with the economies of food and farming, we should promote at home, and encourage abroad, the ideal of local self-sufficiency. We should recognize that this is the surest, the safest, and the cheapest way for the world to live. We should not countenance the loss or destruction of any local capacity to produce necessary goods.

XXV. We should reconsider and renew and extend our efforts to protect the natural foundations of the human economy: soil, water, and air. We should protect every intact ecosystem and watershed that we have left, and begin restoration of those that have been damaged.

XXVI. The complexity of our present trouble suggests as never before that we need to change our present concept of education. Education is not properly an industry, and its proper use is not to serve industries, either by job-training or by industry-subsidized research. Its proper use is to enable citizens to live lives that are economically, politically, socially, and culturally responsible. This cannot be done by gathering or "accessing" what we now call "information"—which is to say facts without context and therefore without priority. A proper education enables young people to put their lives in order, which means knowing what things are more important than other things; it means putting first things first.

XXVII. The first thing we must begin to teach our children (and learn ourselves) is that we cannot spend and consume endlessly. We have got to learn to save and conserve. We do need a "new economy," but one that is founded on thrift and care, on saving and conserving, not on excess and waste. An economy based on waste is inherently and hopelessly violent, and war is its inevitable by-product. We need a peaceable economy.

So You Want to Be a CO?
Peace-Out

The United States occupation of Iraq, which started with the 2003 invasion of the Persian Gulf nation, prompted a renewed interest in conscientious objectors. Employing the latest communication technology, supporters of conscientious objectors started a Web page called peace-out.com, offering direct advice to soldiers on how to apply for conscientious objector (CO) status. The page includes a lengthy list of agencies that support soldiers, as well as connections to other former soldiers who have been designated as COs.

The U.S. military allows members of all five branches—Army, Marines, Navy, Air Force, and Coast Guard—to obtain a discharge as a conscientious objector. Each service has a standard policy with strict criteria, including interviews with a psychiatrist, chaplain, and military investigator. Several nonprofit organizations, including former veterans groups, have established programs to support and advise conscientious objectors.

MAKING THE DECISION to be a conscientious objectors is hardly an easy one. There are a number of different factors that may influence you, but let's start with the most important:

Your beliefs

Do you feel that war is wrong? Do you feel uncomfortable carrying a weapon or training for combat? Was there one particular experience that changed the way you look at war? Do these beliefs come from religious conviction or a more personal, philosophical position?

Here are the important things to remember about your beliefs in regards to CO application:

1. The military does not allow for a nuanced position on war and violence. To be granted CO status, you MUST be opposed to ALL wars. If your application to be a CO is based on the wrongness of a particular war, your packet will be rejected. Additionally, you must be personally committed to peace over violence in almost every situation.

2. Your beliefs on war cannot be political in nature to be considered a CO.

3. Assuming that you volunteered to join the military, you must have come to the conclusion that war is wrong AFTER your enlistment. You may have been asked if you were a CO when you joined, and you probably answered "no." To be considered a CO following enlistment, you must prove that your beliefs against war crystallized AFTER enlisting. This is far from uncommon, as many soldiers simply do not realize how they feel about war until they are actually deployed or start to understand the implications of a deployment.

Friends and Family

Everyone around you will have an opinion on the subject of conscientious objection, and it is likely that not all of them will be supportive towards your feelings about war. Though the people around you are clearly important, you have to remember that this is a deeply personal decision, and no one can make it for you. If you truly feel that war is fundamentally an unethical way to solve problems, then you may need to seek CO status regardless of what those around you think. Once you make the decision to say "no" to war, you can hope that friends and family have the maturity to recognize your conviction.

Other Soldiers

Some soldiers in your unit may not be supportive of your decision to seek CO status, but others may understand what you are doing and feel similar. It is unlikely that someone will give you a hard time, accusing you of being a coward or saying that you are just trying to get out. Remember, the most courageous thing a person can do is stand up for what they believe in. Other soldiers may believe that war is good, so they are acting on their ethics by remaining in the military. Why should you be denied the same right? You will be following a perfectly legal process recognized by the Uniform Code of Military Justice, and if they don't agree with the process, they should take it up with the Pentagon.

As for your NCO's and Chain of Command, they may give you a hard time because many of them are lifers and believe in the ethical application of war. However, if you are firm in your convictions and make sure to be clear that you are not judging or putting down your fellow soldiers for supporting war, they may respect your decision. Ultimately, most leaders would prefer not to have CO's in their units. Who wants to risk deploying someone who might think twice in the face of the enemy?

Your Benefits

You may be concerned about your benefits if your CO application is accepted. In terms of benefits, you may or may not receive full benefits following discharge as a CO, depending on the characterization of your discharge. Some people mistakenly believe that all CO's lose their VA [Veterans Administration] benefits. They are probably referring to this passage: "the discharge of persons on the grounds that they are conscientious objectors who refuse to perform military duty, wear the uniform, or otherwise comply with lawful orders of competent military authority, will bar all their rights under the laws administered by the Veterans Administration (VA)."

All this is saying is that if you refuse orders while still in the service, you may get a dishonorable discharge and thus lose all VA benefits. It is possible for you to get an honorable discharge, but that is at the discretion of your commander. Your commander may characterize your discharge as "other than honorable," and in this case you will not be eligible for most VA benefits.

Another potential loss to be aware of is your enlistment bonus. If you received a cash bonus upon enlistment, you may be forced to repay a portion of it for not completing your entire commitment.

By applying for CO status, you do risk the loss of money and benefits. This possibility for personal loss is a test of your convictions as someone opposed to war, and should be taken into account before making the decision to submit your application.

CHAPTER 10
INTERNATIONAL POLITICAL FREEDOMS

INTRODUCTION

When the United Nations approved the Universal Declaration of Human Rights in 1948, that document became a manifesto of global expectations for how societies and governments should treat their citizens and those of fellow nations. This chapter looks at examples of protest pertaining to many basic human rights issues in nations other than the United States. These examples date from centuries before the U.N. declaration and the decades since.

The documents center on the rights of citizens to fair elections, to freedom of speech and creative expression, and to freedom from the random violence and restrictions of authoritarian regimes. Several documents from political activists and artists of the seventeenth, eighteenth, and nineteenth centuries register protests over slavery and the abuse of power. The documents from the twentieth century and recent years include protests over well-known issues, such as the Nazi genocide and the ongoing genocide in Darfur, and protests by famous dissidents such as Daw Aung San Suu Kyi of Burma (also called Myanmar).

The universal yearning to live peacefully, free from fear, has also inspired countless lesser known, but no less eloquent, voices of protest. These voices include Chanrithy Him, who grew up during the genocidal regime of Cambodia's Khmer Rouge, and Angel Cuadra, an imprisoned and exiled Cuban poet who envisions a free land where he and his American translator could walk together, "speaking the word of Love that has existed since before the age of man."

An Agreement of the Free People of England
John Lilburn, William Walwyn, Thomas Prince, and Richard Overton

John Lilburn was a prominent leader in the group of British reformers known as the Agitators just before, and continuing after, the English Civil Wars of 1642 to 1651. As a young man, Lilburn was arrested for importing unlicensed religious material. His experience of the criminal justice system turned Lilburn into a passionate advocate for basic human rights—which he called his "freeborn rights," earning him the nickname Freeborn John. Lilburn demanded such things as the right to have the charges against him read in English (as opposed to Latin, which was customary for legal writing at the time). The authorities' response to Lilburn's demands was to torture, gag, and repeatedly imprison him. In the wake of the harsh treatment accorded Lilburn, the British Parliament reformed the criminal justice system, abolishing the Star Chamber, a special, secretive court infamous for abuses of power. Lilburn is cited in the opinion by U.S. Supreme Court Chief Justice Earl Warren in the famous 1966 case *Miranda v. Arizona*, which enshrined protections for the accused in constitutional law.

Lilburn later fought with the Parliamentary Army in the first English civil war, which pitted Oliver Cromwell's forces against the Royalists loyal to the Stuart monarchs. After resigning from the army, he resumed his agitation for natural rights. His work inspired followers in 1647 to draft the first version of "An Agreement of the Free People," a document that codified various political rights for commoners. A revised version was presented to Parliament in 1649 in the form of a petition, signed by hundreds of London citizens. Later that year Lilburn himself, with three fellow reformers, all imprisoned in the Tower of London, wrote a third version, excerpted below, which they smuggled out of prison. As protests of the usurpation of natural rights by the ruling elite (particularly, as referred to in the document, by representatives in the House of Commons), these works were an important influence on the American colonists who crafted the U.S. Constitution more than a century later, and have come to be seen as some of the formative documents of modern democracy.

WE AGREE AND DECLARE, . . .

XVI. That it shall not be in the power of any Representative, to punish, or cause to be punished, any person or persons for refusing to answer questions against themselves in Criminall cases.

XVII. That it shall not be in their power, after the end of the next Representative, to continue or constitute any proceedings in Law that shall be longer then Six months in the final determination of any cause past all Appeal, nor to continue the Laws or proceedings therein in any other Langueage then English, nor to hinder any person or persons from pleading their own Causes, or of making use of whom they please to plead for them. . . .

XVIII. That it shall not be in their power to continue to make any Laws to abridge or hinder any person or persons, from trading or merchandising into any place beyond the Seas, where any of this Nation are free to trade.

XIX. That it shall not be in their power to excise Customes upon any sort of Food, or any other Goods, Wares or Commodities, longer than four months after the beginning of the next Representative, being both of them extreme burthensome and oppressive to Trade, and so expensive in the Receipt, as the moneys expended therein (if collected as Subsidies have been) would extend very far towards defraying the publick Charges; and forasmuch as all Moneys to be raised are drawn from the People; such burthensome and chargeable wayes, shall never more be revived, nor shall they raise Moneys by any other ways (after the aforesaid time) but only by an equal rate in the pound upon every reall and person-all estate in the Nation.

XX. That it shall not be in their power to make or continue any Law, whereby mens reall or personall estates, or any part thereof, shall be exempted from payment of their debts; or to imprison any person for debt of any nature, it being both unchristian in itself, and no advantage to the Creditors, and both a reproach and prejudice to the Common-wealth.

XXI. That it shall not be in their power to continue any Law, for taking away any mans life except for murther, or other the like hainous offences destructive to humane Society, or for endevouring by force to destroy this our Agreement, but shall use their uttermost endeavour to appoint punishments equall to offences: that so mens Lives, Limbs, Liberties, and estates, may not be liable to be taken away upon trivial or slight occasions as they have been; and shall have speciall care to preserve, al sorts of people from wickedness misery and beggery: nor shall the estate of any capitall offendor be confiscate but in cases of treason only; and in all other capitall offences recompense shall be made to the parties damnified, as well out of the estate of the Malifactor, as by loss of life, according to the conscience of his jury.

XXII. That it shall not be in their power to continue or make any Law, to deprive any person, in case of Tryals for Life, Limb, Liberty, or Estate, from the benefit of witnesses, on his, or their behalf; nor deprive any person of those priviledges, and liberties, contained in the *Petition of Right*, made in the third yeer of the late King Charls.

"On the Late Massacre in Piedmont"
John Milton

British poet John Milton, celebrated for his epic poem *Paradise Lost*, wrote this sonnet in 1655 in protest of the massacre of some 1,700 members of the Protestant Waldensian sect in the Piedmont region of northwest Italy. The Waldensians (also called the Waldenses) were a dissident sect of Christianity founded in the twelfth century by Peter Waldo (also known as Peter Valdes). Waldo was a prosperous medieval merchant in Lyon, France, who renounced worldly possessions to live a life of poverty and religious preaching modeled after the apostles. He advocated a personal and direct relationship with Jesus through the Bible—a direct contradiction of the authority of the pope. The Waldensians criticized the materialism of the Roman Catholic Church and questioned some of its dogma. Not surprisingly, the sect was branded heretical; Waldo was excommunicated and his followers were heavily persecuted for centuries.

Waldensian communities sprouted in many areas of Europe, but steady persecution reduced them to small enclaves, including a group in the Piedmont. Eventually the sect formally rejected the pope's authority and, in the sixteenth century, connected with the burgeoning Protestant movement, bringing further violence against its followers. French kings ordered crusades against them, and in the mid-seventeenth century the Duke of Savoy began a campaign to suppress the Piedmont Waldensians. During Easter week of 1655, he allowed five thousand French soldiers to cross the border to invade Waldensian settlements and murder the inhabitants. "The triple tyrant" of Milton's sonnet refers to the pope, with his three-crowned tiara. Protestants often linked the city of Babylon, a symbol of vice, with the Holy See.

Avenge, O Lord, thy slaughtered saints, whose bones
    Lie scattered on the Alpine mountains cold,
    Even them who kept thy truth so pure of old
    When all our fathers worshiped stocks and stones,
Forget not: in thy book record their groans
    Who were thy sheep and in their ancient fold
    Slain by the bloody Piedmontese that rolled
    Mother with infant down the rocks. Their moans
The vales redoubled to the hills, and they
    To Heaven. Their martyred blood and ashes sow
    O'er all th' Italian fields where still doth sway
The triple tyrant: that from these may grow
    A hundredfold, who having learnt thy way
    Early may fly the Babylonian woe.

"Am I Not a Man and a Brother?": Anti-slavery Medal from the Shop of Josiah Wedgwood

The British Empire of the eighteenth century was dependent on cheap goods produced by slave labor in distant colonies, such as sugar from the Caribbean. Slavery, in fact, was so widespread and accepted that it was a radical notion to even consider the world functioning without it. Adam Hochschild, in his 2005 book *Bury the Chains*, an account of the British abolitionist movement, wrote, "At the end of the eighteenth century, well over three quarters of all people alive were in bondage of

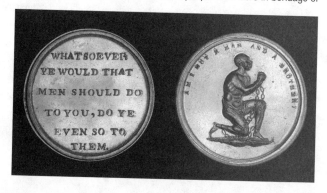

one kind or another, not the captivity of striped prison uniforms, but of various systems of slavery or serfdom. The age was a high point in the trade in which close to eighty thousand chained and shackled Africans were loaded onto slave ships and transported to the New World each year."

In 1787 two Britons, Thomas Clarkson and Granville Sharp, created the Society for the Abolition of the Slave Trade, and advocated fiercely for an end to British slavery with the help of their powerful ally in Parliament, William Wilberforce. Many of their techniques—including petitions to politicians and the use of logos, pamphlets, mass mailings, and fund-raising letters—prefigure modern grassroots organizing campaigns and protest movements.

One prominent citizen who joined the new group was the famous pottery designer and manufacturer Josiah Wedgwood (the grandfather of another reformer, Charles Darwin). Wedgwood had one of his craftsmen create a design of a kneeling, chained slave with the words, "Am I Not a Man and a Brother?" The 1787 design became a logo of sorts for the abolitionist movement. It was made into a seal for the society, and Wedgwood also struck a brass medal version, pictured here, with a moral imperative on the reverse: "Whatsoever ye would that men would do to you, do ye even so to them." The medals, and the British anti-slavery movement, became an inspiration to leaders in the nascent American nation. In 1788 Wedgwood sent medals to Benjamin Franklin in Pennsylvania, and they proved a huge success. Women had the medals made into jewelry and hairpins, and the design proliferated on everything from snuffboxes to tea caddies to cuff links. Hochschild likens the image to that of a modern political campaign button.

The British abolitionist campaign lasted fifty years. Slaves in British lands were freed by an act of Parliament in 1833. The success of the campaign inspired both the American antislavery movement and British activism for other political, human rights, and economic justice causes.

Liberty Leading the People
Eugène Delacroix

A leader of the Romanticism movement, Eugène Delacroix broke from the tradition of painting scenes from ancient history and mythology to tackle unconventional subjects, such as current political events. In his early years his subjects were more traditional, though his treatment of them created a stir. His first major painting was accepted at the prestigious Salon in 1822 when he was twenty-four; entitled *The Barque of Dante*, it featured a dramatic scene from Dante's *Inferno*. Delacroix began keeping a journal and sought inspiration in his own views and experience—a completely radical notion for an artist of the time. For his next subjects he turned to the Greek War of Independence with Turkey. *The Massacre of Chios*, shown at the 1824 Salon, commemorated one of the most horrifying episodes of the war, when Turks killed twenty thousand Greeks on the island of Chios in April and May 1822.

Liberty Leading the People (La Liberté Guidant le Peuple), painted in 1830, is seen as Delacroix's masterpiece and depicts the current political events of his country. The July Revolution that year had forced the abdication of King Charles X when the people rose up to protest his rollback of reforms. Charles was replaced by King Louis-Philippe, the "citizen king," who assumed the monarchy with conditions limiting his power, marking the beginning of the country's constitutional monarchy. Delacroix's Liberty is a bare-breasted woman warrior, rallying the people with the tricolor flag of the French Revolution in one hand and a bayonet in the other. The French government bought the painting, which now hangs in the Louvre in Paris. Foreshadowing modern political posters, the painting is a potent reminder of the power of the citizenry to rise up to assert its political rights.

"An inconceivable miscarriage of justice"
Sir Arthur Conan Doyle

Sir Arthur Conan Doyle was famed mostly for his books about detective Sherlock Holmes. But he also penned many other stories, novels, and works of nonfiction. In 1906, not long after the death of his first wife, Doyle immersed himself in investigating a true crime story: the case of George Edalji. His protests of the handling of the case and the violation of Edalji's rights helped bring about the establishment of a criminal appeals court.

Edalji was the son of an Indian man who had married a British woman, converted to Christianity, and become vicar of a church in the small country town of Great Wyrley. The family was treated by some with suspicion, and by others with outright racial hatred. Edalji was well educated and eventually became a lawyer. In 1903, he was accused of a bizarre series of crimes, in which a number of farm animals were mutilated. He was convicted and sent to prison. He was released three years later after a judge championed his cause and collected more than ten thousand signatures on petitions demanding his release. The conviction remained on Edalji's record, however. Working to clear his name so he could resume his career, he contacted Doyle, who made his own investigation and quickly surmised that Edalji had been framed. Doyle advocated for a full pardon, with an apology and restitution. In a series of articles published in the London newspaper the *Daily Telegraph*, Sir Arthur vehemently protested the abuse of authority by the local police, who seemed more intent on jailing Edalji than on objectively investigating the vicious crimes that terrorized the community.

The Edalji family had for many years prior to the maimings been harassed and threatened through anonymous letters and phony newspaper advertisements. While the animal attacks were occurring, more anonymous letters circulated around the village claiming that a gang headed by George Edalji was behind the attacks. Prosecutors accused Edalji himself of writing the letters— even those threatening his family. The "Mr. Gurrin" referred to was later discredited after his false handwriting testimony in a different case caused an innocent man to be wrongly convicted.

THE FIRST SIGHT WHICH I EVER HAD of Mr. George Edalji was enough in itself to convince me both of the extreme improbability of his being guilty of the crime for which he was condemned, and to suggest some at least of the reasons which had led for his being suspected. He had come to my hotel by appointment, but I had been delayed, and he was passing the time by reading the paper. I recognised my man by his dark face, so I stood and observed him. He held the paper close to his eyes and rather sideways, proving not only a high degree of myopia, but marked astigmatism. The idea of such a man scouring fields at night and assaulting cattle while avoiding the watching police was ludicrous to anyone who can imagine what the world looks like to eyes with myopia of eight diopters—the exact value of Mr. Edalji's myopia according to Mr. Kenneth Scott of Manchester-square. But such a condition, so hopelessly bad that no glasses availed in the open air, gave the sufferer a vacant, bulge-eyed staring appearance, which, when taken with his dark skin, must assuredly have made him seem a very queer man to the eyes of an English village, and therefore to be naturally associated with any queer event. There, in a single physical defect, lay the moral certainty of his innocence, and the reason why he should become the scapegoat.

Before seeing him I had read the considerable literature which had been sent to me about his case. After seeing him I read still more, saw or wrote to everyone who could in any way throw light upon the matter, and finally visited Wyrley and had a useful day's work upon the spot. The upshot of my whole research has been to introduce me to a chain of circumstances which seem so extraordinary that they are far beyond the invention of the writer of fiction. At all times in my inquiries I have kept before my mind the supreme necessity of following truth rather than any preconceived theory, and I was always prepared to examine any point against the accused with as much care as if it made for his innocence, but I have felt at last that it was an insult to my intelligence to hold out any longer against the certainty that there had been an inconceivable miscarriage of justice. . . .

The ground over which the prosecution advanced is already familiar to the reader. We have the clothes which have now become "wet." They were merely "damp" in the previous inquiry, and we have the word of the vicar that this dampness was imperceptible to him, coupled with the fact that any bloodstains would then have been liquid. We have the down-at-heel boot, which was fitted into impressions which must have been made after rain, whereas the whole police theory was that the crime was committed before the rain. We have the bloodstains which sank from smears into two threepenny-bit patches, and we have the hairs which made their appearance thirteen hours after the coat had been in the hands of the police, and after it had been associated with the strip of horse's hide.

Then came the letters. There was a strong probability that whoever wrote the letters knew something of the crimes. What matter that the letters actually accused Edalji himself and vilified him in all sorts of ways? What matter that one villainous postcard in the same writing as the others was posted at Wolverhampton when he was at Aberystwith? What matter that in the original series of anonymous letters the writer had said, "Do you think we cannot imitate your kid's writing?" None of these things weighed as compared with the expression of opinion by an expert that the letters were in George Edalji's own writing. As the unfortunate prisoner listened to such an opinion he must have felt that he was in some nightmare dream. And who was the expert who expressed these views which weighed so heavily with the jury? It was Mr. Thomas Gurrin. . . . And what is the record of Mr. Thomas Gurrin? His nemesis was soon to come. Within a year he had to present himself before the Beck Committee, and admit the terrible fact that through his evidence an innocent man had suffered prolonged incarceration. Does this fact alone not convince my readers that an entire reconsideration of the Edalji case is a most pressing public duty?

There is absolutely the whole evidence—the coat-boot-razor business, the letter business, the so-called incriminating expressions which I have already analyzed, and the one fact, which I admit did really deserve consider consideration, that a group of schoolboys with whom once a month young Edalji may have traveled were known also to the writer of the letters. That is all. I have shown what each link is worth. And on that evidence a young gentleman, distinguished already in an honourable profession, was torn from his family, suffered all the indignities of a convict, was immured for three of the best years of his life, was struck from the roll on which with such industry and self-denial he had written his name, and had every torture made ten-fold more bitter by the thought of the vicar at home, of his mother and of his sister, so peculiarly sensitive, from their position in the church, to the scoff and the derision of those around them. It is a tale which makes a man hot with indignation as he reads it.

"The Stalin Epigram"

Osip Mandelstam

Considered among the great poets of revolutionary-era Russia, Osip Mandelstam (or Mandelshtam) was one in a long pantheon of Russian writers—from Dostoyevsky and Tolstoy to Pasternak and Solzhenitsyn—who used their poetry and fiction to protest social conditions and government policies. Born in Warsaw in 1891, he was raised in St. Petersburg and educated in

Paris, Germany, and Russia. Mandelstam was also an essayist, journalist, translator, and author of children's books. He became one of the leaders of the Acmeist school of poets, which also included Anna Akhmatova. The group came together in 1910, rejecting symbolism and instead emphasizing gritty realism.

Mandelstam may have written his own death sentence when he penned his poem "The Stalin Epigram," in 1933. It's hard to imagine a more pointed—and personal—literary attack on a dictator than Mandelstam's criticism of Stalin in this poem. He was arrested in 1934 after reading it aloud to a group of friends, one of whom is presumed to have been an informer. Mandelstam was sentenced only to exile, but was rearrested in 1938 and sentenced to five years in a labor camp. He died in December 1938 in a transit camp near Vladivostok. Much of his later work remained unpublished until after Stalin's death; it survived to publication by the efforts of his widow, Nadezhda Mandelstam, who was persecuted for many years and, distrusting paper, committed his poems to memory (she later wrote two memoirs). This translation of the poem is by W. S. Merwin and Clarence Brown.

Our lives no longer feel ground under them.
At ten paces you can't hear our words.

But whenever there's a snatch of talk
it turns to the Kremlin mountaineer,

the ten thick worms his fingers,
his words like measure of weight,

the huge laughing cockroaches on his top lip,
the glitter of his boot-rims.

Ringed with a scum of chicken-necked bosses
he toys with the tributes of half-men.

One whistles, another meows, a third snivels.
He pokes out his finger and he alone goes boom.

He forges decrees in a line like horseshoes,
One for the groin, one the forehead, temple, eye.

He rolls the executions on his tongue like berries.
He wishes he could hug them like big friends from home.

A Year in Treblinka Horror Camp
Yankel Wiernik

On August 2, 1943, during a prisoner's revolt at the Treblinka concentration camp, several dozen prisoners escaped. They told their story to the Polish resistance, and a London-based paper, *Polish Labor Fights*, quickly published accounts of the atrocities. The *New York Times* picked up the story and reported on the death camp on August 8, 1943. Despite pleas from Jewish groups, American armed forces chose not to divert bombers from other targets in order to destroy the railroad tracks to Treblinka and other concentration camps. At Treblinka alone, up to twenty thousand Jews were exterminated every day at the height of the camp's operations.

Yankel Wiernik, born in 1889 in Poland, was one of the prisoners who escaped. In 1944 Wiernik published a memoir of the terrors at Treblinka as a desperate attempt to raise the alarm over the killings. His account was translated from Yiddish and first published in English in 1945 by the General Jewish Workers' Union of Poland, based in New York. The excerpt presented here comes from the 1968 *Anthology of Holocaust Literature* published by the Jewish Publication Society of America.

WHEN I ARRIVED AT THE CAMP, three gas chambers were functioning. The remaining ten were added during my stay. Each chamber measured about twenty-five square meters and was two meters high. The roof opening was hermetically sealed, and the terra-cotta floor sloped toward the debarkation platform.

The brick building was separated from Camp One by a wooden wall. Both walls, of wood and of masonry, formed a corridor rising eighty centimeters above the roof. The gas chambers were connected with the corridor. Hermetically closed steel doors provided entry into each chamber. A platform, raised above the ground, connected the three chambers. The doors of every room on the side of Camp Two opened only from the outside, swinging upward and out with the help of iron supports, and were shut by bolts fixed in sash frames. The victims were ushered through the doors from the corridor, and their bodies were dragged through the doors facing Camp Two. Along the gas chambers stood an electric station, about as large as the chambers but somewhat higher. This station provided light for both camps. A motor from a Soviet tank pumped in the gas, which reached the chambers through influx valves. The speediness of the execution depended upon the quantity of the gas intake.

Two Ukrainians operated the death machines. One was called Ivan, a tall man with pleasant eyes, nevertheless a sadist. He found much enjoyment in the tortures and agonies of the victims. More than once he ran to us and nailed our ears to the walls, or ordered us to lie down and beat us savagely. In his sadistic frenzy he joked and laughed uproariously. He murdered his victims in various ways, according to his whims. The other, Nicholai, was shorter, pale and looked as if spiritually possessed.

The day I first saw men, women and children being led to their doom I nearly went mad. I tore my hair and wept unrestrainedly. I suffered most when I looked at the little ones walking beside their mothers, or at the others walking alone, who had no thought of the quick and cruel death impending. Their eyes were wide with fear and wonder. "What is all this? What is it for?" seemed to be congealed on their lips. When they saw the stony faces of their parents, however, they kept silent and prepared for whatever might come. They remained stock still or nestled against one another or cuddled up to their parents, awaiting the ghastly end. Suddenly the entrance doors would swing open. Ivan would appear with a thick gas pipe, a meter long. Nicholai was with him, swinging a sword. At a signal the victims would be driven in, clubbed and lashed without mercy. To this day the fearful screams of the women and the crying of the children ring in my ears. There was despair and agony in the screams, a plea for mercy, a cry to God for vengeance. I shall never forget the horrible sights there.

Into the chamber of twenty-five square meters 450 to 500 people were jammed. The congestion was unbelievable. The victims carried in the children, somehow hoping thus to save them from death. On their way to die they were beaten and driven by truncheons and gas pipes. Dogs were set upon them; barking, they threw themselves upon the victims. Everyone, eager to escape the blows and the dogs, rushed screaming into the lethal chamber. The stronger pushed the weaker. But the tumult did not long endure. The doors closed with a clang on the packed chamber. The motor was connected with the inflow apparatus and switched on. In twenty-five minutes, at the most, all lay dead. But they did not really lie, for they had no room to fall. They died standing, their legs and arms entangled. There were no more screams. Mothers and children were clasped in death's embrace. There was no friend or foe, no envy. No one was more beautiful or ugly—all were suffocated, yellowed by gas. No rich, no poor—all were alike before the Lord.

Why all this? I found it most difficult to stay alive, but I had to live, to give the world the story of this depravity, this bestial depravity.

Nineteen Eighty-Four
George Orwell

British journalist, essayist, critic, and novelist George Orwell—the pen name of Eric Blair—was born in 1903 to British parents living in India. He was raised and educated in England. Orwell's early experience working in Burma made him an ardent anti-imperialist, and his socialist politics were cemented by years of poverty and menial jobs in London and Paris as he worked to support himself while launching his writing career. His experience fighting on the side of the Loyalists in the Spanish Civil War (captured in his book *Homage to Catalonia*) turned Orwell against Stalinist communism, which he blasted in the allegorical *Animal Farm*. He wrote *Nineteen Eighty-Four* in his final years, as his health declined from the tuberculosis he had contracted years earlier. The novel presents Orwell's bleak cautionary vision of a totalitarian system in which the government of the future gains control of every aspect of the individual's life. It was published in June 1949, and Orwell died in January 1950 at age forty-six. *Animal Farm* and *Nineteen Eighty-Four* are widely considered to be among the most influential books of the twentieth century.

The main character in *Nineteen Eighty-Four*, Winston Smith, works for the Ministry of Truth, the role of which is to provide propaganda and misinformation to keep the citizens of Oceania subservient and loyal to the ruling party. (Orwell drew on his own experience working for the British Broadcasting Corporation during World War II.) All aspects of their lives are controlled, from the telescreens that observe their every move and the ubiquitous posters that proclaim that the party leader, known as Big Brother, "is watching you." The government is so totalitarian that it controls all public information. All truth is subsidiary to the ends of the ruling party. Any noncon-forming facts are altered retroactively—and all traces of the original destroyed—to make the party appear utterly infallible. Thus the authorities are completely in control of reality, leaving Smith and all workers completely divorced from the truth of both their present and their history.

WITH THE DEEP, UNCONSCIOUS SIGH which not even the nearness of the tele-screen could prevent him from uttering when his day's work started, Winston pulled the speakwrite toward him, blew the dust from its mouthpiece, and put on his spectacles. Then he unrolled and clipped together four small cylinders of paper which had already flopped out of the pneumatic tube on the right-hand side of his desk.

In the walls of the cubicle there were three orifices. To the right of the speak-write, a small pneumatic tube for written messages; to the left, a larger one for newspapers; and in the side wall, within easy reach of Winston's arm, a large oblong slit protected by a wire grating. This last was for the disposal of waste paper. Similar slits existed in thousands or tens of thousands throughout the building, not only in every room but at short intervals in every corridor. For some reason they were nicknamed memory holes. When one knew that any doc-ument was due for destruction, or even when one saw a scrap of waste paper lying about, it was an automatic action to lift the flap of the nearest memory hole and drop it in, whereupon it would be whirled away on a current of warm air to the enormous furnaces which were hidden somewhere in the recesses of the building.

Winston examined the four slips of paper which he had unrolled. Each con-tained a message of only one or two lines, in the abbreviated jargon—not actu-ally Newspeak, but consisting largely of Newspeak words—which was used in the Ministry for internal purposes. They ran:

times 17.3.84 bb speech malreported africa rectify
times 19.12.83 forecasts 3 yp 4th quarter 83 misprints verify current issue
times 14.2.84 miniplenty malquoted chocolate rectify
times 3.12.83 reporting bb dayorder doubleplusun-good refs unpersons rewrite fullwise upsub antefiling.

With a faint feeling of satisfaction Winston laid the fourth message aside. It was an intricate and responsible job and had better be dealt with last. The other three were routine matters, though the second one would probably mean some tedious wading through lists of figures.

Winston dialed "back numbers" on the telescreen and called for the appropri-ate issues of the *Times*, which slid out of the pneumatic tube after only a few minutes' delay. The messages he had received referred to articles or news items which for one reason or another it was thought necessary to alter, or, as the official phrase had it, to rectify. For example, it appeared from the *Times* of the seventeenth of March that Big Brother, in his speech of the previous day, had predicted that the South Indian front would remain quiet but that a Eurasian offensive would shortly be launched in North Africa. As it happened, the Eurasian Higher Command had launched its offensive in South India and left North Africa alone. It was therefore necessary to rewrite a paragraph of Big Brother's speech in such a way as to make him predict the thing that had actually happened. Or again, the *Times* of the nineteenth of December had published the official forecasts of the output of various classes of consumption goods in the fourth quarter of 1983, which was also the sixth quarter of the Ninth Three-Year Plan. Today's issue contained a statement of the actual output, from which it appeared that the forecasts were in every instance grossly wrong. Winston's job was to rectify the original figures by making them agree with the later ones. As for the third message, it referred to a very simple error which could be set right in a couple of minutes. As short a time ago as February, the Ministry of Plenty had issued a promise (a "categorical pledge" were the official words) that there would be no reduction of the chocolate ration during 1984. Actually, as Winston was aware, the chocolate ration was to be reduced from thirty grams to twenty at the end of the present week. All that was needed was to substitute for the original promise a warning that it would probably be necessary to reduce the ratio at some time in April.

As soon as Winston had dealt with each of the messages, he clipped his speak-written corrections to the appropriate copy of the *Times* and pushed them into the pneumatic tube. Then, with a movement which was as nearly as possible unconscious, he crumpled up the original message and any notes that he himself had made, and dropped them into the memory hole to be devoured by the flames.

What happened in the unseen labyrinth to which the pneumatic tubes led, he did not know in detail, but he did know in general terms. As soon as all the corrections which happened to be necessary in any particular number of the *Times* had been assembled and collated, that number would be reprinted, the original copy destroyed, and the corrected copy placed on the files in its stead. This process of continuous alteration was applied not only to newspapers, but to books, periodicals, pamphlets, posters, leaflets, films, sound tracks, cartoons, photographs—to every kind of literature or documentation which might conceivably hold any political or ideological significance. Day by day and almost minute by minute the past was brought up to date. In this way every prediction made by the Party could be shown by documentary evidence to have been correct; nor was any item of news, or any expression of opinion, which conflicted with the needs of the moment, ever allowed to remain on record. All history was a palimpsest, scraped clean and reinscribed exactly as often as was necessary. In no case would it have been possible, once the deed was done, to prove that any falsification had taken place. The largest section of the Records Department, far larger than the one in which Winston worked, consisted simply of persons whose duty it was to track down and collect all copies of books, newspapers, and other documents which had been superseded and were due for destruction. A number of the *Times* which might, because of changes in political alignment, or mistaken prophecies uttered by Big Brother, have been rewritten a dozen times still stood on the files bearing its original date, and no other copy existed to contradict it. Books, also, were recalled and rewritten again and again, and were invariably re-issued without any admission that any alteration had been made. Even the written instructions which Winston received, and which he invariably got rid of as soon as he had dealt with them, never stated or implied that an act of forgery was to be committed; always the reference was to slips, errors, misprints, or misquotations which it was necessary to put right in the interests of accuracy.

But actually, he thought as he readjusted the Ministry of Plenty's figures, it was not even forgery. It was merely the substitution of one piece of nonsense for another. Most of the material that you were dealing with had no connection with anything in the real world, not even the kind of connection that is contained in a direct lie. Statistics were just as much a fantasy in their original version as in their rectified version. A great deal of the time you were expected to make them up out of your head. For example, the Ministry of Plenty's forecast had estimated the output of boots for the quarter at a hundred and forty-five million pairs. The actual output was given as sixty-two millions. Winston, however, in rewriting the forecast, marked the figure down to fifty-seven millions, so as to allow for the usual claim that the quota had been overfulfilled. In any case, sixty-two millions was no nearer the truth than fifty-seven millions, or than a hundred and forty-five millions. Very likely no boots had been produced at all. Likelier still, nobody knew how many had been produced, much less cared. All one knew was that every quarter astronomical numbers of boots were produced on paper, while perhaps half the population of Oceania went barefoot. And so it was with every class of recorded fact, great or small. Everything faded away into a shadow-world in which, finally, even the date of the year had become uncertain.

Ten Years of Madness
Feng Jicai

The ten years from 1966 to 1976, known as the Cultural Revolution in the People's Republic of China, were marked by social chaos, arbitrary arrests and murders, political persecution, and massive suppression of freedom. Students were enlisted into units of the Red Guard and, along with local authorities, were charged with rooting out remnants of bourgeois thought and set to spy on their fellow citizens. The period ended with the death of party leader Mao Zedong and the arrest of four high-level party officials known as the Gang of Four, which included Mao's widow. In an effort to collect people's stories from those years, Chinese novelist Feng Jicai ran a newspaper advertisement. Feng collected hundreds of stories from among the thousands who answered his ad and in 1996 published a selection of the pieces in *Ten Years of Madness: Oral Histories of China's Cultural Revolution.* The book included recollections of those who were part of the machinery of state repression, as well as those who were its victims. In the introduction to his book, reprinted here, Feng related his own experience of living in the city of Tianjin and of the Communist regime's stranglehold on free expression—which bore an uncanny resemblance to the fictional society of George Orwell's *Nineteen Eighty-Four.* The repression led Feng to an obsession with preserving personal stories on hidden scraps of paper as a way of resisting state control.

ON A WINDY WINTER NIGHT of 1967, there was a knock on my door. For a family like mine whose house had been frequently ransacked, a knock on the door was usually a bad omen. But this time, it was gentle and soft. It turned out to be a good friend of mine. He was a Chinese teacher at a suburban middle school. Ever since the Cultural Revolution started, we had completely lost touch with each other. I figured he must also have been a target of persecutions. And I was right. He had just been released from the "cow shed." During the time he was locked up there, several of his former students who knew he had the habit of sleep talking took turns waiting by his side at night in order to record anything he said. The next day he would be forced to confess the "reactionary meaning" of his slurring "black words." Therefore he was always afraid to sleep. In the end, he miraculously lost his ability to sleep. As a result, his health was damaged, and his spirit collapsed. Seeing him in front of me, I had the eerie feeling that he had been reduced to a dehydrated kernel.

At that time, both my family and my fiancée's family had been ransacked with very little left. At the mercy of the neighborhood security office, we were given a small room of several square meters so that we could get married and start a family. Because of our problematic class background, we lived nervously every day in the terror of the Cultural Revolution.

Both of us knew that the reality was even worse than we could imagine. Even though we hadn't seen each other for over half a year, we had nothing to say at this moment. All we did was smoke, one cigarette after another. They were low quality cigarettes, named "Fighting." The stinky smoke filled the small room, so dense that we could hardly see each other's faces. The only sound came from the twigs and leaves of an old tree outside the house that was gnawing in the wind, as if a beast was grinding its teeth. But suddenly he broke the silence and said in a loud voice, "Tell me, will people of future generations know what kind of life we are living now? Will they understand our situation and our miseries? If it goes on like this for a few decades, we will all have died. Then who will live to tell the real stories of our generation? Will we suffer for nothing? Do you think there are people who are writing down our sufferings today? Of course, that's impossible. Who would risk his life for that?"

In the dense smoke he struggled to open his eyes, the very eyes that had fought against sleep for six months and were now swamped with blood vessels. He looked desperately depressed.

From then on, I began to quietly write down the stories of people around me. Knowing that this could be a crime punishable by death, I changed the names and places to foreign names, and the time to the last century. Then I signed the stories with names of foreign authors, writers such as Thomas Mann, Gide, and Steinbeck. If they were ever discovered, I could claim that they were excerpts from foreign novels that I had copied many years before. I also chose to write on small pieces of papers that were easy to conceal. As soon as I finished a story, I'd hide it underneath a brick, inside a wall crack, in a flower pot, or in between quilts. Sometimes I glued a number of pieces together, covered them with Chairman Mao's quotations or Cultural Revolution posters, and hung them on the wall. I exhausted my brain trying to hide these "reactionary" writings. But for a person who has something to hide, the more skillful and secretive you think you are, the more you believe they might be discovered. So I dug them out and hid them again in other places. For a long time, it became my habit to write, hide, dig out, and hide again.

Once during the movement, we were assembled in a stadium for a public sentencing. The audience was assigned spaces according to their work units. We stood in rows, facing an ad hoc stage that was set up with wooden planks. On the stage were some loudspeakers and microphones. When the criminals—altogether twenty-two of them—were led onto the stage, the noises from the handcuffs and shackles were magnified by the loudspeakers and heard throughout the stadium, sending shivers of fear to everyone in the audience. Then the crimes of those criminals were read. One of them was charged with writing "counterrevolutionary" articles and journals. The most lenient sentence that day was twenty years imprisonment. Most of the accused were sentenced to death. The one who wrote "counterrevolutionary" articles was sentenced to life imprisonment.

When I went home and saw my wife, I was suddenly overwhelmed by a depressed feeling. What if I was also sentenced to life imprisonment, like the one who wrote "counterrevolutionary" articles? She would then have to live like a widow for the rest of her life. This was not just a psychotic fantasy. That disastrous era was full of disastrous possibilities. I hurried to dig out my writings and copied the most important ones onto some thinner paper. Then I disposed of the original pieces and rolled up the new ones. I wrapped them in oil paper and inserted them into my bicycle tube. But as soon as I felt a little safer, I began to worry that my bike might be stolen. At that time, people were mobilized to search for "clues of hidden enemies." I often fantasized that someone would spring at my bike and fish out my writings. Those were enough to sentence me to death. Eventually I could not stand the fears in my heart and quietly took out the papers in the bicycle tube. I tried to memorize the stories before I burnt some of the papers and flushed others in the toilet. I subsequently changed my way of writing. Whenever I had the urge to write, I would put my material on paper, memorize it, and then burn the paper. I couldn't afford to leave any trace of it. I carried on with this writing habit until the end of the Cultural Revolution.

The Great Tangshan Earthquake took place on July 28, 1976. And Tianjin was also affected. For me it was a double disaster. Our house collapsed. When I crawled out of the wreckage with my family, the first thing that came to my mind was to clean up the ruins. I knew that there were still pieces of my writings that I had left in cracks of the wall and underneath the bricks. The Cultural Revolution was not over yet, and I couldn't afford to let other people discover them. However, I couldn't just work on my own house. That would make others suspicious. So I offered to help my neighbors clean up their houses first. When it was finally time to clean up my own place, I turned down my neighbors' offer for help and carefully rummaged through the ruins to look for my writings. In the end, I collected a whole bagful of small pieces of paper.

In the 1980s, a Swedish TV station learned of my story and requested an interview with me. Talking about this peculiarity of my writing habits, which could only be imaginable for that era, they asked me, "What did you feel about those pieces of paper."

"Responsibility," I replied.

The Declaration of Barbados
World Council of Churches and the Programme to Combat Racism

In January 1971 delegates from South American nations gathered on the Caribbean island of Barbados for a symposium on the rights of aboriginal peoples. The symposium was sponsored by the World Council of Churches and the Programme to Combat Racism. The statement the participants composed, known as the Declaration of Barbados, was a groundbreaking assertion of aboriginal rights as well as a blueprint for what governments, anthropologists, and religious missionaries should do to protect those rights. The document called for far-reaching changes: "Irrelevant are those Indian policy proposals that do not seek a radical break with the existing social situation; namely, the termination of colonial relationships, internal and external; breaking down of the class system of human exploitation and ethnic domination; a displacement of economic and political power from a limited group or an oligarchic minority to the popular majority; the creations of a truly multi-ethnic state in which each ethnic group possesses the right to self-determination and the free selection of available social and cultural alternatives."

The group argued that several Latin American countries failed to provide basic rights to native peoples, motivated in part by a desire to appropriate their lands and resources. Governments were, in some cases, responsible for "crimes of genocide and ethnocide." Further, the delegates had harsh words for evangelical missionaries, accusing some of using a "religious pretext" to justify exploitation of aboriginal groups—both for economic gain and in a competition between religious groups for souls to convert. The declaration also charged that some anthropologists studying native cultures, perhaps unwittingly, reinforced inequality for Indians. The opening statement of the declaration, printed here, is titled "For the Liberation of the Indians."

THE INDIANS OF AMERICA remain dominated by a colonial situation which originated with the conquest and which persists today within many Latin American nations. The result of this colonial structure is that lands inhabited by Indians are judged to be free and unoccupied territory open to conquest and colonization. Colonial domination of the aboriginal groups, however, is only a reflection of the more generalised system of the Latin American states' external dependence upon the imperialist metropolitan powers. The internal order of our dependent countries leads them to act as colonising powers in their relations with the indigenous peoples. This places the several nations in the dual role of the exploited and the exploiters, and this in turn projects not only a false image of Indian society and its historical development, but also a distorted vision of what constitutes the present national society.

We have seen that this situation manifests itself in repeated acts of aggression directed against the aboriginal groups and cultures. There occur both active interventions to "protect" Indian society as well as massacres and forced migrations from the homelands. These acts and policies are not unknown to the armed forces and other governmental agencies in several countries. Even the official "Indian policies" of the Latin-American states are explicitly directed towards the destruction of aboriginal culture. These policies are employed to manipulate and control Indian populations in order to consolidate the status of existing social groups and classes, and only diminish the possibility that Indian society may free itself from colonial domination and settle its own future.

As a consequence, we feel the several States, the religious missions and social scientists, primarily anthropologists, must assume the unavoidable responsibilities for immediate action to halt this aggression and contribute significantly to the process of Indian liberation.

"Get Up, Stand Up"
Bob Marley and Peter Tosh

In the 1970s, Jamaican reggae superstar Bob Marley helped introduce socially conscious themes about the struggles of Third World people into mainstream music. While some of his songs were rhythmically driven romantic ballads, others, such as "Get Up Stand Up," were elegant distillations of the strivings of the underprivileged for political rights and economic justice. With his band the Wailers (which at first included Peter Tosh, cowriter of "Get Up Stand Up"), Marley helped ignite the world music movement, and he was a strong influence on the political lyrics of punk bands like the Clash. Marley died of cancer in 1981 at the age of thirty-six.

CHORUS

Get up, stand up
Stand up for your rights
Get up, stand up
Stand up for your rights
Get up, stand up
Stand up for your rights
Get up, stand up
Don't give up the fight

Preacher man don't tell me
Heaven is under the earth
I know you don't know
what life is really worth
it's not all that glitters is gold
half the story has never been told
so now you see the light
stand up for your rights

Repeat chorus

Most people think
great good will come from the skies
take away everything
and make everybody feel high
but if you know what life is worth
you would look for yours on earth
and now you've seen the light
You stand up for your rights

Chorus

Get up, stand up (Yeah Yeah)
Stand up for your rights (Oh)
Get up, stand up (Get up, stand up)
Don't give up the fight (Life is your right)
Get up, stand up (So we can't give up the fight)
Stand up for your right (Lord Lord)
Get up, stand up (People struggling on)
Don't give up the fight (Yeah)

We're sick and tired of your ism and skism game
to die and go to heaven in Jesus' name
we know and understand
almighty God is a living man

you can fool some people sometimes
but you can't fool all the people all the time
And now we've seen the light (What you gonna do)
we gonna stand up for our rights

Repeat chorus and fade

"Brief Letter to Donald Walsh (in memoriam)"
Angel Cuadra

Angel Cuadra (also known as Angel Cuadra Landrove) was born in Havana in 1931. He was trained as a lawyer and was a supporter of the Cuban revolution. He published his first book of poetry in 1959. After the Castro regime slipped into dictatorship, the government began to brand his work as counterrevolutionary. He was prohibited from traveling to Spain for a cultural conference in 1964, and in 1967 he was arrested and charged with conspiracy and spreading antigovernment propaganda. He was sentenced to fifteen years in prison. He was released in 1976 but forbidden to write poetry. Defying that order, he smuggled a book of his poems out of the country and was arrested again in 1977. Amnesty International campaigned for his release, and family and friends appealed to the Commission on Human Rights of the Organization of American States, asserting that Cuadra was a political prisoner whose only crime was his poetry. Cuadra was released in 1982 and allowed to go into exile in Miami, Florida. There, he has served for many years as president of the PEN Cuban Writers in Exile, a branch of the international literary group PEN, which advocates for freedom of expression and human rights.

Cuadra wrote this poem on March 22, 1980, in Boniato Prison. Walsh had been the translator of Cuadra's poems. The poem expressed his gratitude to the man who helped free his words from bondage. It was also an indictment of a regime so repressive that it stifled poetry and outlawed something as mundane as a poet meeting to discuss his work with his translator. This translation is by Katherine Rodriguez Nieto.

My friend:
In what language shall we begin our conversation?
How can I begin to celebrate
the support your voice gives me
in sending out my songs, drenched in your accents,
to live in this world?
And not know what the warmth of your hand is like in friendship;
only this music shining from the soul,
stretching like a bridge between us:
you in your country open to the stars,
I behind bars of rancor,

dying since the dawn.
Yet even so we meet.
The hands of friends
brought your name to me with the morning dew.
And you are here, and I am talking to you.

Because I've learned that not everything is hatred.
I want to declare another word,
sow it as it were in furrows
of goodness and of hope.

There are some men who crush my words,
tear me to pieces for producing beauty,
bring my poem to trial
and sentence it to run the gauntlet:
the drops of blood my poem sheds
form a constellation among the stars.

But there are other men who rescue me
and save my poem like unransomed light,
who gather up its pieces of suffering clay
and, like Prometheus, lend me fire for it.
The fire of love, I proclaim now,
that is the word I will defend
in martyrdom, among the thorns.
My poem, the grape of pain
for which I bleed and grow.

And you exist, Donald Walsh.
I knew nothing of your musical being,
of that gemstone clear and high, transparent.
Don't leave now
that I have found days dawning in my heart
that were sent me by your hand.
Don't leave now
that we begin to speak in a language
that unites the souls of Whitman and Martí.
And on the streets of all the world
—without bars, without bitterness or fear
—you and I will walk together, speaking
the word of Love that has existed since before the age of man.

Man Against Tanks

This photograph of a lone protester trying to halt the crackdown on pro-democracy demonstrators by standing in front of tanks became the iconic image of the Tiananmen Square protests in

spring 1989 in Beijing. According to the original caption from Associated Press photographer Jeff Widener, bystanders pulled the unidentified man away, and the tanks continued. Widener took the picture June 5, 1989, a day after Chinese troops opened fire on student-led demonstrators, who had been protesting and staging hunger strikes in front of Communist Party headquarters to demand democratic reforms.

Although the protester's actions at the moment had little impact, the fact that a photographer captured the scene allowed the man's intentions to create a huge effect beyond the particular time and place. The exquisite symbolism of one person, alone, standing up to a row of powerful government machines trying to crush his opposition needed no translation as it reverberated around the world. While the Chinese government tried to squelch internal protest and keep a lid on the flow of information into and out of the country, this single universal image conveyed the true situation.

Freedom from Fear
Daw Aung San Suu Kyi

Since 1989, Daw Aung San Suu Kyi has spent the majority of her time under house arrest or in jail for her leadership of nonviolent pro-democracy efforts against the military leadership of Burma, also called Myanmar. She is the daughter of General U Aung San, leader of the country's liberation from colonialism, who was assassinated in 1947 when she was two years old. As a child Aung San Suu Kyi (her four-part surname) lived in India, while her mother served as Burma's ambassador there. She later studied philosophy, economics, and politics at Oxford in England and worked for several years at the United Nations. She married Michael Aris, a British citizen who was a professor of Asian studies at Oxford. The couple had two children before Aung San Suu Kyi returned to Burma in 1988 to care for her ailing mother.

Her return to the country coincided with a series of student protests against the military regime, culminating in a nationwide uprising in August 1988. The government crackdown that followed, in which thousands of citizens were killed, inflamed the pro-democracy protests even more. Aung San Suu Kyi called for democratic reforms, speaking to a huge rally in Rangoon, and in September she was named general secretary of the newly formed National League for Democracy. In July 1989 the government placed her under house arrest, citing a martial-law provision allowing detention without charge or trial for three years. She has been released several times, but on each occasion the military junta found reason to arrest her anew after a short period of freedom. In 1999, during her house arrest, Aris, then in London, was dying of prostate cancer. He had been refused a visa by the Burmese authorities, and Aung San Suu Kyi was unwilling to leave the country for fear she would be prevented from returning. She did not see her husband before his death.

Aung San Suu Kyi's essay "Freedom from Fear," excerpted below, was published widely in 1991, in newspapers from the *New York Times* to the *Far East Economic Review* and the *Bangkok Post*. Her supporters arranged the publication to coincide with her being awarded the Sakharov Prize for Freedom of Thought, the human rights prize of the European Parliament. The award ceremony was held in her absence in Strasbourg, France, on July 10, 1991. That fall, when she was awarded the 1991 Nobel Peace Prize, she was again unable to attend the ceremony. Amnesty International has declared Aung San Suu Kyi a prisoner of conscience—one of more than 1,300 political prisoners the organization said were being held by the Myanmar government as of 2005.

IT IS NOT POWER that corrupts but fear. Fear of losing power corrupts those who wield it and fear of the scourge of power corrupts those who are subject to it. Most Burmese are familiar with the four a-gati, the four kinds of corruption. Chanda-gati, corruption induced by desire, is deviation from the right path in pursuit of bribes or for the sake of those one loves. Dosa-gati is taking the wrong path to spite those against whom one bears ill will, and moga-gati is aberration due to ignorance. But perhaps the worst of the four is bhaya-gati, for not only does bhaya, fear, stifle and slowly destroy all sense of right and wrong, it so often lies at the root of the other three kinds of corruption. Just as chanda-gati, when not the result of sheer avarice, can be caused by fear of want or fear of losing the goodwill of those one loves, so fear of being surpassed, humiliated or injured in some way can provide the impetus for ill will. And it would be difficult to dispel ignorance unless there is freedom to pursue the truth unfettered by fear. With so close a relationship between fear and corruption it is little wonder that in any society where fear is rife corruption in all forms becomes deeply entrenched.

Public dissatisfaction with economic hardships has been seen as the chief cause of the movement for democracy in Burma, sparked off by the student demonstrations of 1988. It is true that years of incoherent policies, inept official measures, burgeoning inflation and falling real income had turned the country into an economic shambles. But it was more than the difficulties of eking out a barely acceptable standard of living that had eroded the patience of a traditionally good-natured, quiescent people—it was also the humiliation of a way of life disfigured by corruption and fear.

The students were protesting not just against the death of their comrades but against the denial of their right to life by a totalitarian regime which deprived the present of meaningfulness and held out no hope for the future. And because the students' protests articulated the frustrations of the people at large, the demonstrations quickly grew into a nationwide movement. Some of its keenest supporters were businessmen who had developed the skills and the contacts necessary not only to survive but to prosper within the system. But their affluence offered them no genuine sense of security or fulfilment, and they could not but see that if they and their fellow citizens, regardless of economic status, were to achieve a worthwhile existence, an accountable administration was at least a necessary if not a sufficient condition. The people of Burma had wearied of a precarious state of passive apprehension where they were "as water in the cupped hands" of the powers that be.

Emerald cool we may be
As water in cupped hands
But oh that we might be
As splinters of glass
In cupped hands.

Glass splinters, the smallest with its sharp, glinting power to defend itself against hands that try to crush, could be seen as a vivid symbol of the spark of courage that is an essential attribute of those who would free themselves from the grip of oppression. Bogyoke Aung San regarded himself as a revolutionary and searched tirelessly for answers to the problems that beset Burma during her times of trial. He exhorted the people to develop courage: "Don't just depend on the courage and intrepidity of others. Each and every one of you must make sacrifices to become a hero possessed of courage and intrepidity. Then only shall we all be able to enjoy true freedom."

The effort necessary to remain uncorrupted in an environment where fear is an integral part of everyday existence is not immediately apparent to those fortunate enough to live in states governed by the rule of law. Just laws do not merely prevent corruption by meting out impartial punishment to offenders. They also help to create a society in which people can fulfil the basic requirements necessary for the preservation of human dignity without recourse to corrupt practices. Where there are no such laws, the burden of upholding the principles of justice and common decency falls on the ordinary people. It is the cumulative effect of their sustained effort and steady endurance which will change a nation where reason and conscience are warped by fear into one where legal rules exist to promote man's desire for harmony and justice while restraining the less desirable destructive traits in his nature.

In an age when immense technological advances have created lethal weapons which could be, and are, used by the powerful and the unprincipled to dominate the weak and the helpless, there is a compelling need for a closer relationship between politics and ethics at both the national and international levels. The Universal Declaration of Human Rights of the United Nations proclaims that "every individual and every organ of society" should strive to promote the basic rights and freedoms to which all human beings regardless of race, nationality or religion are entitled. But as long as there are governments whose authority is founded on coercion rather than on the mandate of the people, and interest groups which place short-term profits above long-term peace and prosperity, concerted international action to protect and promote human rights will remain at best a partially realized struggle. There will continue to be arenas of struggle where victims of oppression have to draw on their own inner resources to defend their inalienable rights as members of the human family. . . .

Within a system which denies the existence of basic human rights, fear tends to be the order of the day. Fear of imprisonment, fear of torture, fear of death, fear of losing friends, family, property or means of livelihood, fear of poverty, fear of isolation, fear of failure. A most insidious form of fear is that which masquerades as common sense or even wisdom, condemning as foolish, reckless, insignificant or futile the small, daily acts of courage which help to preserve man's self-respect and inherent human dignity. It is not easy for a people conditioned by fear under the iron rule of the principle that might is right to free themselves from the enervating miasma of fear. Yet even under the most crushing state machinery courage rises up again and again, for fear is not the natural state of civilized man.

The wellspring of courage and endurance in the face of unbridled power is generally a firm belief in the sanctity of ethical principles combined with a historical sense that despite all setbacks the condition of man is set on an ultimate course for both spiritual and material advancement. It is his capacity for self-improvement and self-redemption which most distinguishes man from the mere brute. At the root of human responsibility is the concept of perfection, the urge to achieve it, the intelligence to find a path towards it, and the will to follow that path if not to the end at least the distance needed to rise above individual limitations and environmental impediments. It is man's vision of a world fit for rational, civilized humanity which leads him to dare and to suffer to build societies free from want and fear. Concepts such as truth, justice and compassion cannot be dismissed as trite when these are often the only bulwarks which stand against ruthless power.

"The novel is not the crime"
Salman Rushdie

Indian-born author Salman Rushdie was forced to go into hiding for nearly ten years when the fundamentalist Islamic leader of the Iranian revolution, Ayatollah Ruhollah Khomeini, issued a fatwa (an Islamic legal pronouncement) in 1989 calling for devout Muslims to assassinate the writer in response to his novel *The Satanic Verses*, published in September 1988. The novel featured passages critical of Islam which many Muslims deemed blasphemous. Many Islamic countries banned the book, and it was the subject of protests and book burnings around the globe. Rushdie went into hiding under the protection of security forces in Great Britain, where he was then living. The fatwa also incited Muslims to kill others associated with the book's publication; the book's Japanese translator was murdered in 1991, and both its Italian translator and Norwegian publisher were violently attacked and severely injured. Many western nations put political pressure on the government of Iran to retract the fatwa, which it apparently did in 1998. Rushdie resumed his public life and later moved to New York City, although an article in the official Iranian news agency in 2003 reported that the fatwa was in fact irrevocable and remained in place, with an Iranian foundation offering a multimillion-dollar bounty for Rushdie's murder.

At times since the book's publication, Rushdie has attempted to mitigate the situation by expressing respect for Islam, while still defending his right to freedom of creative expression and to be critical of his religion. He has addressed the fatwa issue repeatedly both in his fiction and in numerous essays and articles, ardently protesting the violation of basic human rights when religious extremists use their views as a reason to suppress—or to threaten or kill—others. The following is a speech he made in April 1992 to the International Conference on Freedom of Expression in Washington, D.C.

I'D LIKE TO THANK ALL THOSE who helped make this trip possible. It wasn't a simple matter, and how odd that is! For a writer interested in freedom of expression to attend a conference on the subject should be a simple matter. It should not be necessary for his travel plans to be shrouded in secrecy. The security forces should not need to pay me any special attention. It feels a little like being inside one of those science-fiction yarns in which the present has been altered, so that the Inquisition appears in Piccadilly Circus, and there are witch-burnings on the Potomac.

The fatwa of Imam Khomeini bent the world out of shape. Ancient bloodlusts were unleashed, armed with state-of-the-art modern technology. Battles that we thought no longer needed to be fought—battles against such concepts as "blasphemy" and "heresy," which throughout human history have been the stormtroopers of bigotry—were re-enacted in our streets. Many people who should have known better defended the real and threatened violence and blamed its victims. Even now, in Britain, there is a powerful lobby which regularly denigrates my character. It is hard for me to be my own advocate in this matter, hard for me to insist on my own value. When I do, I am accused of arrogance and ingratitude. But when I don't fight my corner, my case is swiftly forgotten. Quite a double-bind.

As we used to say in the Sixties, there is a fault in reality. Do not adjust your minds. What has been done to *The Satanic Verses*, its author, publishers, translators and booksellers, is a crime against freedom. The novel is not the crime; the author is not the criminal.

Of course I know I'm not the only writer under attack. I have tried hard during the past three years to point out that those words, "blasphemy" and "heresy," have been launched against writer after writer, especially in the Muslim world. I have tried repeatedly to remind people that we are witnessing a war against independence of mind, a war for power.

The peculiar evil of silencing the expression of an opinion is that it is robbing the human race, posterity as well as the existing generation—[robbing] those who dissent from the opinion, still more than those who hold it. [For] if the opinion is right, they are deprived of the opportunity of exchanging error for truth; if wrong, they lose what is almost as great a benefit, the clearer perception and livelier impression of truth produced by its collision with error.

Those words are from John Stuart Mill's great essay, *On Liberty*. It is extraordinary how much of Mill's essay applies directly to the case of *The Satanic Verses*. The demand for the banning of this novel and indeed the eradication of its author is precisely what Mill called the "assumption of infallibility". Those who make such demands do so, just as Mill anticipated, because they find the book and its author "immoral and impious."

"But," he writes, "this is the case in which [the assumption of infallibility] is most fatal. These are exactly the occasions on which the men of one generation commit those dreadful mistakes which excite the astonishment and horror of posterity." Mill gives two examples of such occasions: the cases of Socrates and of Jesus Christ. To these can be added a third case, that of Galileo. All three men were accused of blasphemy and heresy. All three were attacked by the stormtroopers of bigotry. And yet they are, as is plain to anyone, the founders of the philosophical, moral and scientific traditions of the West. We can say, therefore, that blasphemy and heresy, far from being the greatest evils, are the methods by which human thought has made its most vital advances. The writers of the European Enlightenment, who all came up against the stormtroopers at one time or another, knew this. It was because of his nervousness of the power of the Church, not of the State, that Voltaire suggested that it was advisable for writers to live in close proximity to a frontier, so that, if necessary, they could hop across it into safety. Frontiers will not defend a writer now; not if this new form of terrorism, terrorism by edict and bounty, is allowed to have its day.

Many people say the Rushdie case is a one-off, that it will never be repeated. This complacency, too, is an enemy to be defeated. I return to John Stuart Mill.

The dictum that truth always triumphs over persecution is one of those pleasant falsehoods which all experience refutes. History teems with instances of truth put down by persecution. If not suppressed for ever, it may be thrown back for centuries. . . Persecution has always succeeded, save where the heretics were too strong a party to be effectually persecuted.

There it is in a nutshell. Religious persecution is never a matter of morality, always a question of power. To defeat the modern-day witch-burners, it is necessary to show them that our power, too, is great—that our numbers are greater than theirs, and our resolve, too. This is a battle of wills.

Free societies are societies in motion, and with motion comes friction. Free people strike sparks, and those sparks are the best evidence of freedom's existence. Totalitarian societies seek to replace the many truths of freedom by the one truth of power, be it secular or religious; to halt the motion of society, to snuff out its spark. Unfreedom's primary purpose is invariably to shackle the mind. . . .

Land Mines and Measures to Eliminate Them
Jody Williams

In the early 1990s a handful of humanitarian groups came together in a coordinated effort to ban antipersonnel land mines and seek assistance for civilian land-mine victims. These weapons— small explosive devices that can be planted in the ground to detonate upon contact, sometimes decades later—had been in use since the U.S. Civil War and the Crimean War, but their use had proliferated to the point where they constituted a humanitarian crisis. Hundreds of millions of land mines have been sown since the beginning of World War II, and millions of these persist in places where conflict has ended, particularly in developing nations. The coalition of nongovernmental organizations in 1992 formed an umbrella group, the International Campaign to Ban Land Mines, which grew within five years to include more than one thousand organizations in sixty countries. The campaign's coordinator, Jody Williams, and the group itself were jointly awarded the Nobel Peace Prize in 1997 for their work. That year they helped draft an international treaty, signed by 121 countries, banning land mines.

The International Committee of the Red Cross is one of the campaign's member groups. In this excerpt from an article in the August 1995 issue of the Red Cross publication *International Review of the Red Cross*, Williams laid out the basic arguments of the protest against the continued use of land mines. For countries to continue manufacturing, stockpiling, or using such indiscriminate weapons, she asserted, amounted to a massive violation of basic human rights.

[M]INES AS THEY ARE KNOWN TODAY were originally developed during the First World War to defend against tanks. Given the size of anti-tank mines, it was relatively easy for enemy troops to enter minefields and remove the weapons for their own use. This led to the development of the anti-personnel mine, a much smaller delayed-action explosive device which was sown throughout anti-tank minefields to deter enemy soldiers from entering. First used to protect the more valuable anti-tank mine, the anti-personnel mine has taken on a life of its own. . . .

What sets the weapon apart is its time-delay function. Not designed for immediate effect, landmines lie dormant until triggered by a victim. While mines can be directed against a legitimate military target, what might have been one at the time of sowing will in most cases, because of their delayed action, not remain so over the entire life span of the weapons. In many cases, particularly during the wars and internal conflicts of the past couple of decades, landmines have been used as offensive weapons to cut off access by opposition forces and their civilian supporters to large tracts of land.

Often designed to maim, their psychological impact on the enemy is undeniable. In addition to demoralizing combatants, landmine casualties can also overload military logistical support systems since most mine victims require more extensive medical and rehabilitative attention than other types of war-related casualties. Moreover, landmines do not discriminate between the logistical support systems of the military and those of society as a whole. They terrorize and demoralize civilians, and their impact on the fragile health systems of the countries where they are used in great numbers can be overwhelming. Post-conflict landmine casualties are almost exclusively civilian.

The impact of landmines extends beyond just health-care systems. When much of a country has become the theatre of battle—as in Afghanistan, Angola, Cambodia, Mozambique, Somalia, the former Yugoslavia, and the list goes on—little is spared. Used offensively, landmines are deployed to depopulate areas, to disrupt agriculture and to interrupt the flow of goods and services. Transportation systems are affected, as are power systems, agricultural and grazing lands, religious sites, national parks and forests, and villages and the people living in them or fleeing from them. In short, all that makes up the fabric of a country can be contaminated by landmines. Unlike other weapons of war, landmines and explosive devices which act like landmines are not silenced by any peace agreement. They continue to kill and maim for generations. . . .

Humanitarian law, or the law of war, seeks to limit as much as possible destruction and injury to the civilian population during armed conflicts. The basic tenets, which apply also to landmines, say essentially that soldiers may not use any means to achieve their ends, that there are limits. There must be a balance between military need and consequences to the civilian population—and that balance must be proportional. Combatants must distinguish between civilians, who must not be targeted in war, and other combatants. As part of customary law, these tenets apply to all States regardless of other treaty obligations. . . .

A few questions about landmines were recently posed by Russell W. Ramsey from the United States Army School of the Americas at Fort Benning, Georgia, in his assessment of the book *Landmines: A Deadly Legacy*, by Human Rights Watch and Physicians for Human Rights. In commenting on the book for *Military Review*, Ramsey asked:

"What crop costs a hundred times more to reap than to plant and has no market value when harvested? What weapon is still lethal to unsuspecting human targets when the soldiers who brought it to the battlefield have become old men? What Cold War legacy has the greatest mathematical probability of claiming victims now and for the next couple of generations? What weapon employed by US forces in scrupulous adherence to the laws of land warfare may have inflicted more friendly than enemy casualties in several campaigns?"

The answer is, of course, anti-personnel landmines. These weapons have a huge impact on societies. Their effects, as briefly outlined above, are all the more pervasive because they are not conflict-limited. They continue for decades. Thus societies are affected not only in the immediate term but for generations. Landmines are not simply the cause of an immediate crisis in a country in conflict, they are also a long-term obstacle to total peace and post-conflict development of a society and its people. Thus, children now living with landmines are affected. But so will their children be, and their children's children. The only way to end this scourge is to move quickly to fulfill the goal stated by the international community in last year's United Nations resolution on landmines and to eliminate landmines from the world's arsenals once and for all.

Republic of Fear
Kanan Makiya

Iraqi dissident Kanan Makiya was born in Baghdad and trained as an architect at Massachusetts Institute of Technology before turning to a career in writing and academia. Now a professor of Islamic and Middle Eastern Studies at Brandeis University in Massachusetts, Makiya spent five years writing his first book, *Republic of Fear: The Politics of Modern Iraq*. The book is a blistering attack on totalitarianism, and on the massive human rights violations of the country—including a genocidal campaign against ethnic Kurds—under Saddam Hussein (Makiya uses the alternate spelling Husain for the former Iraqi leader). First published in 1989 under the pseudonym Samir al-Khalil, the book gained wide readership after Hussein's 1990 invasion of Kuwait.

Makiya published an updated edition of *Republic of Fear* in 1998. As an articulate dissident and vocal opponent of Saddam's regime, Makiya became a highly influential figure advising the second Bush administration as it planned the 2003 invasion of Iraq. The excerpt below is from the new introduction written for the 1998 edition of *Republic of Fear*.

ON AUGUST 18, 1994, six weeks before President Saddam Husain began redeploying his troops to make the world think that he was about to do the unthinkable—invade Kuwait a second time—he promulgated Law 109. It read: "According to Section 1, Article 42, of the Iraqi Constitution, the Revolutionary Command Council has decreed that . . . the foreheads of those individuals who repeat the crime for which their hand was cut off will be branded with a mark in the shape on an X. Each intersecting line will be one centimeter in length and one millimeter in width." The crimes "for which their hand was cut off" were theft and desertion. Branding with a red-hot iron was being introduced in Saddam Husain's post–Gulf War Iraq as a new form of punishment for these crimes.

Soldiers and car thieves were singled out for prosecution on the basis of the new laws. Iraqi newspapers reported that thirty-six thousand cars had been stolen in 1993, many of them in broad daylight on the main streets of Baghdad. This, in a police state that took pride in the fact that the crime rate under its regime, especially since the middle 1970s, had plummeted.

The new law was formulated in general terms: stealing anything worth more than 5,000 dinars—worth roughly 12 dollars in 1994—by anyone who was not a minor had become punishable in Iraq by amputation in the first instance and in the second by branding. Something must have gone wrong in the case of thirty-seven-year-old 'Ali 'Abed 'Ali, because he had his hand amputated and his forehead branded with an X at the same time. His crime: stealing a television set and 250 Iraqi dinars (worth roughly 50 cents at the time). . . .

The number of ways in which the state was publicly disfiguring the bodies of its citizens was mushrooming. Depending on the crime, the foreheads of offenders got branded with a horizontal line three to five centimeters long, or with a circle, along with the X spelled out in Law 109. Some army deserters and draft dodgers, and those who sheltered them, got special treatment: the outer part of one ear was to be cut off for the first offense; a repeat offense resulted in the amputation of the other ear and a circle being branded on the forehead. (Unconfirmed rumor from inside Iraq claimed that the word *jaban*, "coward," was also being branded on some people's foreheads, and two parallel horizontal lines three to five centimeters in length.) Only after being caught for desertion a third time would a soldier be executed. This was an improvement on the situation before the passage of these new laws, when the instant and unquestioned penalty for desertion was a firing squad. The nature of crime and punishment was changing in Saddam Husain's Iraq.

The reaction of ordinary Iraqis to the new laws was also unprecedented. Two men whose ears had been cut off immolated themselves in central Baghdad in October 1994. Following the murder of a doctor in the southern city of Nassirriyya by an amputee, and the storming of the headquarters of the Ba'th party in the city of 'Amara by a crowd that cut off the ears of the Ba'thi officials it got its hands on, several hundred doctors went on strike to protest having to carry out the new punishments. Upon being threatened with having their own ears cut off, the doctors called off their strike. Law 117 was then promptly issued, directed at the whole medical profession. It threatened immediate amputation of the ear for anyone who assisted in the cosmetic improvement of an officially disfigured body part. . . .

Since I finished writing *Republic of Fear* in 1986, the chamber of horrors that is Saddam Husain's Iraq has grown into something that not even the most morbid imagination could have dreamed up. *Republic of Fear* is about how such horror stories became the norm inside a hitherto ordinary developing country. It describes how a new, Kafkaesque world came into being, one ruled and held together by fear. In this world, the ideal citizen became an informer. Lies and "analysis" filled public discourse to the exclusion of everything else. Fear, the book argued, was not incidental or episodic, as in more "normal" states; it had become constitutive of the Iraqi body politic. The Ba'th developed the politics of fear into an art form, one that ultimately served the purpose of legitimizing their rule by making large numbers of people complicit in the violence of the regime.

When Broken Glass Floats
Chanrithy Him

Chanrithy Him's memoir, *When Broken Glass Floats: Growing Up under the Khmer Rouge*, published in 2000, recounted her harrowing experience as a child from the late 1960s through the 1970s, during the guerrilla war that culminated with the takeover of her native Cambodia by the Khmer Rouge rebels. The Khmer Rouge tried to implement an extremist vision of a utopian Communist society on the nation. All citizens would be equal "comrades" working together to support the country. In reality, the Khmer Rouge perpetrated a horrifying genocide on its own people. Between 1975 and 1979, an estimated 1.7 million Cambodians died—21 percent of the population. The Khmer Rouge were able to recruit members in part because of bitterness about the U.S. bombing of the country during the Vietnam War—an effort to destroy Vietcong bases there—which killed an estimated 100,000 Cambodians before the Khmer Rouge came to power in 1975. Because the country continued to be a political pawn of other nations, the genocide was not officially recognized for many years; the United Nations began preparations for a war-crimes tribunal in Cambodia in 2004.

Him's account grimly recorded many of the regime's casualties: the Cambodians who died during long marches that followed forced evacuations of millions from cities; those who died of starvation under meager food rationing; those who perished under the primitive conditions of makeshift villages with no sanitation and potable water; and others who died of treatable diseases because there was no medical care. Many were simply executed. Chanrithy Him lost both parents, her grandmother, and several siblings. She and her remaining siblings survived the forced labor camps that came to be called the killing fields, and emigrated to the United States in 1981. Him attended high school and college in Oregon, and worked on a research study of post-traumatic stress disorder among Cambodian survivors. Her intent in writing the memoir, she said, was to educate people about the atrocities of the Khmer Rouge and to speak for those who had died because of its actions. Her book also aimed "to give Cambodian survivors in the Khmer diaspora a sense of justice," said Him.

In this excerpt, Him is a ten-year-old, forced with her large family to leave their two-story home in the city to live in a squalid hut they must construct in a labor camp. The Khmer Rouge has rounded up a group of men, including her father—a well-educated man who had worked as an import-export official for the government, but who also had medical training. The family has had no word of his whereabouts. In Cambodian, the word *Pa* is father, *Mak* is mother, *Kong* is grandpa. *Athy* is Him's childhood nickname (from the last syllable of her first name). *Chea* is her elder sister. *Angka Leu* translates as "the high organization," the Khmer Rouge governing authority. Takeo and Year Piar are cities.

DAYS HAVE GONE BY since the Khmer Rouge took *Pa* and my uncles away. I've counted the days until *Pa* is due back, noting them carefully with pen and paper. I draw my own calendar, recording each day without him. A month, *Mak* told me, which was what the Khmer Rouge had told her. During the day I return to the orchard. I cry alone, calling out to *Pa*. Like the earth without the sun, I'm drifting in the dark, thinking of him, wondering where he is, what he's doing. Whether he misses us, misses me.

After the sun surrenders to the might, I'm still thinking of *Pa*. I'm no longer scared of the informant hiding below us. I sit on *Pa's* scooter, parked under the house where the informant used to eavesdrop on us. Holding on to the black rubber handles, *Pa's* last handprints. I'm connected to the world as it was when *Pa* was with us. As painful as it is, I journey back in time, revisiting the past as my wet eyes gaze at the tachometer, the red needle aligned at the zero mark.

Zero. Our lives are at zero. Year zero.

I reminisce about better times, when *Pa* took us out to restaurants and to the palace where the royal family lived. I remember nights in Takeo. *Pa* would wake everyone up for pâté sandwiches. He'd carry me from my bed to the dining table. He'd feed me until my mind woke up, then my eyes would open to find a platter of meats, cucumbers, and French bread. My memory speaks until it hurts. Until I break down.

"Athy, why are you crying? Are you okay?" Chea comes to rescue me.

"Chea, I miss *Pa*. I miss *Pa* very much."

"Stop crying, *p'yoon srey* [younger sister]. I miss *Pa*, too."

Chea reaches out and pulls me close to her. In her arms, I cry harder, letting out pain that I've hidden from my family. Chea hugs me tight. Her hand massages my head, a soothing touch that softens my sorrow. It allows me to sleep, lying in the room beside my sisters, hugging *Pa's* shirt. I hug him in my mind as I inhale his odor from his shirt. I inhale it deeply and hungrily. I love *Pa*—words I've never actually uttered. I miss him; the way I would miss a piece of my own body. I am adrift.

One month has gone by. Still *Pa* hasn't returned. Now the Khmer Rouge order *Mak* to a meeting with the other women whose husbands were taken away. At the meeting the Khmer Rouge ask everyone if they want to go to their husbands and work with them in an "office." All of them say yes. *Who wouldn't want to be with their husbands? Mak* wouldn't. She tells the Khmer Rouge that she would rather stay in the village and work for *Angka Leu. Mak* would have told them otherwise if it weren't for Som, whose husband had worked for *Kong Houng* before the Khmer Rouge "liberated" Year Piar. Som secretly came to *Mak* the day before the meeting and told her what to say. Even though there was no reason given, *Mak* obeyed, repeating her lines to Khmer Rouge leaders. *Mak's* intuition to trust Som's words saves my family. In time, those women who volunteered to be with their husbands are taken away.

Walking in the village days later, *Mak* see a man wearing *Pa's* shirt—a cream-colored short-sleeved dress shirt with one pocket. In this village of poverty, a simple office shirt stands out. Without fear, she follows the man and demands to know where he got it. Baffled by *Mak's* abrupt confrontation, he mutters that it has been distributed to him. *Mak* rages at the idea of someone giving away her husband's belongings. Biting back her anger, she turns and heads to Som's hut in search of the truth. *Mak* figures Som will know since her husband is one of the local people who now works for the Khmer Rouge who took *Pa* and my uncles to "orientation."

Som whispers urgently to *Mak*, asking her to tone down her voice. In her hut, lit only by the rays of sun that sneak in, she confides to *Mak*, revealing what happened to *Pa*—a truth that shakes the core of *Mak's* already wilted soul.

Pa, Uncle Surg, Uncle Sorn, and the other men were not taken to an orientation. They were taken to a remote field outside Year Piar to be executed. Upon their arrival, they were unloaded off the oxcarts and forced to dig their own graves. After they finished, the Khmer Rouge cadres tied them up, then killed each one with a hoe. The bodies tumbled into the very pits they had readied to catch them.

"Your husband fought back while being tied up," Som whispers. "He called them liars and traitors. They killed him right away."

Mak's face gorges with blood, burning with sorrow and anger. The women who wanted to be with their husbands, along with their children and elderly parents, were also executed. Their bodies were buried in the empty field, but their personal belongings were brought back to Year Piar to be distributed among the villagers—*Pa's* belongings as well as my uncles'. Possessions of the dead passed out as a gruesome prize to the living.

Mak returns, telling us all at once. She is composed, unraveling the bad news carefully. There is no outward grieving, even as a family. Like other emotions, it must be tucked away. She delivers the news in a tone of resignation—relieved that Som has told her. There is no more wondering. And in a dull way, I am not surprised.

But inside, questions bubble up. More confusion than rage. *What has Pa done to be killed this way?* He has never been anything but a caring father, a responsible husband, and a devoted son. Contemplating it all, I'm first baffled by this senseless killing, rather than sad. In this era, the rules are twisted: having education is a crime and honesty doesn't pay. *What will?* I wonder. I answer this question myself. I recall a Cambodian proverb that I heard grown-ups quote among themselves: *Don't give up on the winding road, but don't tread the straight one.*

Mak had treaded the winding road and lied to the Khmer Rouge. Her false act of patriotism prompted by Som's secret warning saved our lives.

Fascism's Firm Footprint in India

Arundhati Roy

Indian writer Arundhati Roy won the prestigious Booker Prize in 1997 for her novel *The God of Small Things*. She is also internationally known as a political essayist and India's progressive conscience. Roy was awarded the 2002 Lannan Foundation Prize for Cultural Freedom. The article excerpted below appeared in the September 30, 2002, issue of *The Nation*, and a longer version was published in Roy's book *War Talk*, a collection of nonfiction published in 2003. The essay is a powerful indictment of religious-inspired nationalism and how it breeds not only cycles of violence, but also despair.

GUJARAT, THE ONLY MAJOR STATE IN INDIA with a government headed by the Bharatiya Janata Party (BJP), has for some years been the petri dish in which Hindu fascism has been fomenting an elaborate political experiment. In spring 2002, the initial results were put on public display.

It began within hours of the Godhra outrage—in which fifty-eight Hindus were killed when a train returning from the disputed site of Ayodhya on February 27 was set alight as it pulled out of a station in Godhra, in Gujarat. Even now, months later, nobody knows who was responsible for the crime. The Forensic Department report clearly says that the fire was started inside the coach. This raises a huge question mark over the theory that the train was set alight by a Muslim mob that had gathered outside the train. However, the then-Home Minister (now elevated to the post of Deputy Prime Minister), L. K. Advani, immediately announced—with no evidence to back his statement—that the attack was a Pakistani plot.

On the evening of February 27, Hindu nationalists in the Vishva Hindu Parishad (VHP, the World Hindu Council) and the Bajrang Dal movement put into motion a meticulously planned pogrom against the Muslim community. Press reports put the number of dead at just over 800. Human rights organizations have said it is closer to 2,000. As many as 100,000 people, driven from their homes, now live in refugee camps. Women were stripped and gang-raped, and parents were bludgeoned to death in front of their children. In Ahmedabad, the former capital of Gujarat and the second-largest industrial city in the state, the tomb of Wali Gujarati, the founder of the modern Urdu poem, was demolished and paved over in the course of a night. The tomb of the musician Ustad Faiyaz Khan was desecrated. Arsonists burned and looted shops, homes, hotels, textile mills, buses and cars. Hundreds of thousands have lost their jobs.

Across Gujarat, thousands of people made up the mobs. They were armed with petrol bombs, guns, knives and swords. Apart from the VHP and Bajrang Dal's usual lumpen constituency, there were Dalits (untouchables) and Adivasis (indigenous peoples), who were brought in on buses and trucks. Middle-class people participated in the looting. (On one memorable occasion, a family arrived in a Mitsubishi Lancer.) The leaders of the mob had computer-generated lists marking out Muslim homes, shops and businesses. They used mobile phones to coordinate the action. They had not just police protection and police connivance, but also covering fire. The cooking-gas cylinders they used to burn Muslim homes and establishments had been hoarded weeks in advance, causing a severe gas shortage in Ahmedabad.

While Gujarat burned, our prime minister, Atal Bihari Vajpayee, was on MTV promoting his new poems. (Reports say cassettes have sold 100,000 copies.) It took him more than a month—and two vacations in the hills—to make it to Gujarat. When he did, he gave a speech at the Shah Alam refugee camp. His mouth moved, he tried to express concern, but no real sound emerged except the mocking of the wind whistling through a burned, bloodied, broken world. Next we knew, he was bobbing around in a golf cart, striking business deals in Singapore.

One hundred and thirty million Muslims live in India. Hindu fascists regard them as legitimate prey. The lynch mob continues to be the arbiter of the routine affairs of daily life: who can live where, who can say what, who can meet whom and where and when. Its mandate is expanding quickly. From religious affairs, it now extends to property disputes, family altercations, the planning and allocation of water resources. Muslim businesses have been shut down. Muslim people are not served in restaurants. Muslim children are not welcome in schools. Muslim parents live in dread that their infants might forget what they've been told and give themselves away by saying "Ammi!" or "Abba!" in public and invite sudden and violent death.

Notice has been given: This is just the beginning. . . .

While the parallels between contemporary India and prewar Germany are chilling, they're not surprising. (The founders of the Rashtriya Swayamsevak Sangh [RSS], the National Volunteer Force that is the moral and cultural guild of the BJP, have in their writings been frank in their admiration for Hitler and his methods.) One difference is that here in India we don't have a Hitler. We have instead the hydra-headed, many-armed Sangh Parivar—the "joint family" of Hindu political and cultural organizations, with the BJP, the RSS, the VHP and the Bajrang Dal each playing a different instrument. Its utter genius lies in its apparent ability to be all things to all people at all times. . . .

Whipping up communal hatred is part of the mandate of the Sangh Parivar. It has been planned for years. Hundreds of RSS *shakhas* across the country (*shakha* literally means "branch," and RSS *shakhas* are "educational" cells) have been indoctrinating thousands of children and young people, stunting their minds with religious hatred and falsified history, including unfactual or wildly exaggerated accounts of the rape and pillaging of Hindu women and Hindu temples by Muslim rulers in the precolonial period. In states like Gujarat, the police, the administration and the political cadres at every level have been systematically penetrated. It has huge popular appeal, which it would be foolish to underestimate or misunderstand. The whole enterprise has a formidable religious, ideological, political and administrative underpinning. This kind of power, this kind of reach, can only be achieved with state backing.

Under this relentless pressure, what will most likely happen is that the majority of the Muslim community will resign itself to living in ghettos as second-class citizens, in constant fear, with no civil rights and no recourse to justice. What will daily life be like for them? Any little thing, an altercation at a cinema or a fracas at a traffic light, could turn lethal. So they will learn to keep very quiet, to accept their lot, to creep around the edges of the society in which they live. Their fear will transmit itself to other minorities. Many, particularly the young, will probably turn to militancy. They will do terrible things. Civil society will be called upon to condemn them. Then President Bush's canon will come back to us: "You're either with us or with the terrorists."

Those words hang frozen in time like icicles. For years to come, butchers and genocidists will fit their grisly mouths around them ("lip-sync," filmmakers call it) to justify their butchery. . . .

Fascism is about the slow, steady infiltration of all the instruments of state power. It's about the slow erosion of civil liberties, about unspectacular, day-to-day injustices. Fighting it does not mean asking for RSS *shakhas* and *madrassahs* that are overtly communal to be banned. It means working toward the day when they're voluntarily abandoned as bad ideas. It means keeping an eagle eye on public institutions and demanding accountability. It means putting your ear to the ground and listening to the whispering of the truly powerless. It means giving a forum to the myriad voices from the hundreds of resistance movements across the country that are speaking about real issues—about mining, about bonded labor, marital rape, sexual preferences, women's wages, uranium dumping, weavers' woes, farmers' worries. It means fighting displacement and dispossession and the relentless, everyday violence of abject poverty.

"You know the people's choice"
Viktor Yushchenko

In the fall of 2004 Viktor Yushchenko ran for president of Ukraine against the prime minister, Viktor Yanukovich. The contest was marred by charges that Yushchenko's opponents had poisoned him with dioxin. Yushchenko had to leave the country for treatment of the poisoning, which doctors said was nearly fatal and which permanently disfigured his face. When Yanukovich was declared the winner of the November 21 runoff election, Yushchenko and his supporters brought charges of widespread election fraud. Ukraine's Supreme Court blocked Yanukovich's victory, and the country remained in a political impasse for several weeks. The streets of the capital city, Kiev, filled day after day with thousands of protesters waving banners of bright orange—Yushchenko's campaign color—leading people to dub the phenomenon the Orange Revolution.

On November 24 Yushchenko delivered this speech addressed to "soldiers, law-enforcers, commanders and heads of Armed Forces and the forces of order of Ukraine." Government authorities had urged soldiers and police to crack down on demonstrators. While security forces often serve as agents of repression, here Yushchenko instead called on them to reject corruption and side with the people. In January 2005 Yushchenko was declared to have won the election and became president of Ukraine.

I, VICTOR YUSHCHENKO, appeal to you on the behalf of the people of Ukraine who elected me President. Our nation has come out to squares in hundreds of towns and cities. The people demand that their will is acknowledged.

The voting took place right before your eyes. You were closer than anybody else to ballot boxes and saw how the vote count proceeded and protocols signed. You know the people's choice. You also know how their choice was disregarded.

Crimes are committed right before your eyes. They are carried out by the government that wants to preserve the regime of lawlessness, corruption, and disrespect for human dignity in Ukraine. Having stolen the votes of your brothers and sisters, having stolen many of your votes, state authorities want to force the people into submission. They want to do it with your hands and your weapons.

Today, however, as always, you are bound by your oath and not by criminal orders. Thousands of people in epaulettes, tens of army regiments and departments of internal affairs have already validated their oath. They are with the people of Ukraine. The place of every honest person is on the side of the people.

You should know that criminals want to send you to the barricades. The sons of the people that will have dragged you into shedding blood will not be there. They will run away and you and we will have to build the new Ukraine. It needs your honesty, experience, and professionalism.

I am calling on the heads of the forces of order—you are the ones responsible for preserving order, and preventing disaster. You must forbid all the forces under your command to use weapons against the people.

You see that there are only peaceful protests. Public peace can be disturbed only by provocations. It is your duty to prevent them.

It is also your duty to prevent foreign armed forces on Ukrainian soil under any conditions.

Issue the corresponding orders and make the necessary arrangements. Make sure that they can be transmitted through mass media. Silence is unacceptable. Being silent means aiding crimes or becoming their accessories.

I am calling on all to whom the people have entrusted weapons—come to the aid of the country. We are a part of it. The time has come to defend our parents, our brothers and sisters, and our children.

Ukraine needs your courage. There is only one more step till truth triumphs. Make it together with the people.

Glory to Ukraine!

"Will We Say 'Never Again' Yet Again?"

Nicholas D. Kristof

The United Nations in early 2004 called the plight of people in the Darfur region of Sudan a "dire humanitarian situation." Since the tribal and racial cleansing began in 2003, an estimated 180,000 people have died from illness or starvation, many others have been murdered, and two million people have been displaced to refugee camps. Sudanese authorities have tacitly allowed armed militias, known as the Janjaweed, to kill, rape, and torture black Darfur villagers and destroy their property in a blatant effort to terrorize them into leaving their lands. A U.N. fact-finding mission charged in a January 2005 report that the Sudan government was abetting the violence, including providing air cover for the pillaging militias. The mission's report concluded "that the Government of the Sudan and the Janjaweed are responsible for serious violations of international human rights and humanitarian law amounting to crimes under international law," although it stopped short of calling the violence genocide, which would have required action by U.N. member nations. Many governments, individuals, and humanitarian groups—including the United States government—have not shied from calling the atrocities a case of genocide by the Sudanese government against its own people.

Nicholas D. Kristof, a columnist for the *New York Times*, has been one of the most persistent voices urging action to stop the violence and help the victims of Darfur. This column, one of the first he wrote about Darfur, was filed from a location along the Chad-Sudan border and published March 27, 2004.

FOR DECADES, whenever the topic of genocide has come up, the refrain has been, "Never again."

Yet right now, the government of Sudan is engaging in genocide against three large African tribes in its Darfur region here. Some 1,000 people are being killed a week, tribeswomen are being systematically raped, 700,000 people have been driven from their homes, and Sudan's Army is even bombing the survivors.

And the world yawns.

So what do we tell refugees like Muhammad Yakob Hussein, who lives in the open desert here because his home was burned and his family members killed in Sudan? He now risks being shot whenever he goes to a well to fetch water. Do we advise such refugees that "never again" meant nothing more than that a Führer named Hitler will never again construct death camps in Germany?

Interviews with refugees like Mr. Hussein—as well as with aid workers and U.N. officials—leave no doubt that attacks in Darfur are not simply random atrocities. Rather, as a senior U.N. official, Mukesh Kapila, put it, "It is an organized attempt to do away with a group of people."

"All I have left is this jalabiya," or cloak, said Mr. Hussein, who claimed to be 70 but looked younger (ages here tend to be vague aspirations, and they usually emerge in multiples of 10). Mr. Hussein said he'd fled three days earlier after an attack in which his three brothers were killed and all his livestock stolen:

"Everything is lost. They burned everything."

Another man, Khamis Muhammad Issa, a strapping 21-year-old, was left with something more than his clothes—a bullet in the back. He showed me the bulge of the bullet under the skin. The bullet wiggled under my touch.

"They came in the night and burned my village," he said. "I was running away and they fired. I fell, and they thought I was dead."

In my last column, I called these actions "ethnic cleansing." But let's be blunt: Sudan's behavior also easily meets the definition of genocide in Article 2 of the 1948 convention against genocide. That convention not only authorizes but also obligates the nations ratifying it—including the U.S.—to stand up to genocide.

The killings are being orchestrated by the Arab-dominated Sudanese government, partly through the Janjaweed militia, made up of Arab raiders armed by the government. The victims are non-Arabs: blacks in the Zaghawa, Massaliet and Fur tribes. "The Arabs want to get rid of anyone with black skin," Youssef Yakob Abdullah said. In the area of Darfur that he fled, "there are no blacks left," he said.

In Darfur, the fighting is not over religion, for the victims as well as the killers are Muslims. It is more ethnic and racial, reflecting some of the ancient tension between herdsmen (the Arabs in Darfur) and farmers (the black Africans, although they herd as well). The Arabs and non-Arabs compete for water and forage, made scarce by environmental degradation and the spread of the desert.

In her superb book on the history of genocide, "A Problem from Hell," Samantha Power focuses on the astonishing fact that U.S. leaders always denounce massacres in the abstract or after they are over—but, until Kosovo, never intervened in the 20th century to stop genocide and "rarely even made a point of condemning it as it occurred." The U.S. excuses now are the same ones we used when Armenians were killed in 1915 and Bosnians and Rwandans died in the 1990's: the bloodshed is in a remote area; we have other priorities; standing up for the victims may compromise other foreign policy interests.

I'm not arguing that we should invade Sudan. But one of the lessons of history is that very modest efforts can save large numbers of lives. Nothing is so effective in curbing ethnic cleansing as calling attention to it.

President Bush could mention Darfur or meet a refugee. The deputy secretary of state could visit the border areas here in Chad. We could raise the issue before the U.N. And the onus is not just on the U.S.: it's shameful that African and Muslim countries don't offer at least a whisper of protest at the slaughter of fellow Africans and Muslims.

Are the world's pledges of "never again" really going to ring hollow one more time?

North Korea: Denial of Right to Food

Amnesty International

The human rights group Amnesty International issued this press release in January 2004 to publicize a report protesting ongoing violations of basic rights in North Korea (formally the Democratic People's Republic of Korea). Under its extremely repressive totalitarian government, the country has drawn broad condemnation for infringements of human rights. A 2005 U.S. State Department annual report on human rights charged that the North Korean government "continued to control almost all aspects of citizens' lives, denying freedoms of speech, religion, the press, assembly, association, and movement, as well as workers' rights." Amnesty's press release, which opens with quotations from an aid worker and a refugee, decried in particular the country's use of food as a political tool.

"PUBLIC EXECUTIONS were highest between 1996 and 1998 when the famine was at its peak. People were stealing the infrastructure of society such as electric lines and copper wires and selling it."
(Interview by Amnesty International with Lee Sung-yong of the Seoul-based NGO, Good Friends—Centre for Peace, Human Rights & Refugees on 4 December 2002)
"I saw a 15 or 16 year old boy die; the boy was there [in detention] as he had sold glass from his school. After 15 days' detention, the boy died, because of malnutrition. There was so little food."
(Lee, North Korean man in his early forties, who gave testimony to Amnesty International on 3 December 2002)

North Korea is one of the world's most closed and isolated nations. For more than a decade, the people of North Korea have suffered from famine or food crisis. In a new report, Amnesty International argues that the North Korean government should ensure that food shortages are not used as a tool to persecute perceived political opponents and that humanitarian organizations, in particular UN agencies, have free and unimpeded access to all parts of North Korea.

"Hundreds of thousands of people have died as a result of acute food shortages caused by a series of natural disasters, the loss of support from the former Soviet Union and economic mismanagement. Several million children suffer from chronic malnutrition, impairing their physical and mental development," Amnesty International emphasized.

Government policies are at least partly to blame. The government appears to have distributed food unevenly, favouring those who are economically active and politically loyal. Government restrictions on freedom of movement prevent North Koreans searching for food or moving to an area where food supplies are better, as they face punishment including detention if they leave their towns or villages without permission. They also hamper the movement, access and monitoring of international humanitarian agencies who have been involved in distributing food aid. This has contributed to donor fatigue and a fall in food aid commitments.

"The right to food is a basic human right, and the government of North Korea appears to be failing in its duties to respect, protect and fulfil this right," Amnesty said.

Widespread malnutrition has led to the movement of tens of thousands of people into China. Thousands have been forcibly repatriated by the Chinese authorities, and have then been detained by North Korean authorities in appalling conditions. Detainees are reported to have died of hunger. Many have reportedly been tortured during interrogations by the North Korean authorities.

Some North Koreans have been publicly executed because they have stolen food or goods to survive—school children have reportedly been taken to see the executions.

Children, women and the elderly are reported to be among the principle victims of North Korea's famine. Many women forced to go to China in search of food have been preyed on by trafficking gangs, which operate on both sides of the China-North Korea border.

Efforts by the international community to assist in the provision of food to North Korea have been undermined by the government's refusal to allow swift and equitable distribution of this food, and by the restrictions on freedom of information.

"Notwithstanding the obstacles to providing assistance, foreign states able to help must also provide the necessary food aid, to enable the North Korean government to fulfil its obligations to respect, protect and fulfil the right to food," Amnesty said.

"Provison of humanitarian aid should be guided at all times by human rights considerations and should never be used by any government as a bargaining tool to further political or economic interests."

PART III
THE FUTURE OF PROTEST
LIMITS OF SOCIETAL NORMS
EXTREME PROTEST
THE EXPERIENCE OF PROTEST

CHAPTER 11
LIMITS OF SOCIETAL NORMS

INTRODUCTION

Going against the tide of societal opinion is one of the most difficult things a person can do. "For nonconformity the world whips you with its displeasure," Ralph Waldo Emerson wrote in his 1841 essay "Self-Reliance." Emerson urged his readers to become nonconformists despite the potential backlash, writing: "It is easy in the world to live after the world's opinion; it is easy in solitude to live after our own; but the great man is he who in the midst of the crowd keeps with perfect sweetness the independence of solitude."

Tolerant societies resist the urge to enforce a rigid conformity and thus clamp down on dissent. The collective willingness to enter forbidden realms by allowing citizens to press for change can, when successful, move societies to a higher plane of civilization. This has been the case in past and present efforts to abolish slavery, for instance.

Societies that allow dissenters to challenge societal norms also run a very real risk. Such norms often support society's political infrastructure; to allow them to be openly challenged through protest can lead to the unraveling of the social fabric and political foundations. When Copernicus declared that the earth was not the center of the universe, for example, he defied the Catholic Church, which in turn had sanctioned God's grace upon the royal monarchies. Using observation and science to explain the world instead of taking the church's word on how things worked threatened to undermine the religious authorities and, by extension, the kings.

This chapter looks at a sampling of cases in which ordinary people protested oppressive aspects of everyday life. The documents here include examples by those who objected to societal norms that constrained their rights, whether those norms were as subtle as opposing the accumulation of written knowledge in an encyclopedia or as blatant as using the term "negro" to reinforce racial prejudice. Conversely, protesters can also argue against changing norms they deem overly liberal, such as Jesse Helms's protest against an edgy piece of modern art or the protest by Muslim women in Kashmir, India, against the celebration of Valentine's Day.

Encyclopedia
Denis Diderot

The Age of Enlightenment in seventeenth- and eighteenth-century Europe overthrew the religious basis upon which society functioned. Instead of relying on a church's explanation of God's laws, Enlightenment thinkers turned to the knowledge they drew from nature and experience to explain the world. Reason was a more reliable source of information than faith, they claimed. Rapid advances in science fueled the later industrial revolution, but Enlightenment thinkers faced fierce resistance from church leaders, who saw their influence being eclipsed.

Denis Diderot was named editor of *Encyclopedia* in 1747 in Paris, France, the center of Enlightenment thinking. Diderot applied Enlightenment philosophy in the encyclopedia as a way to store important information. Although hardly considered an act of heresy today, the writing of an encyclopedia represented a threat to the power of the church and the underlying basis of its authority. Jesuits criticized the publication of the first two volumes of the *Encyclopedia*. In 1752, the French government tried to stop their publication, saying the volumes were subversive. King Louis XIII's mistress, Madame de Pompadour, a friend of Diderot, intervened however, and a third volume soon appeared.

The entry here is an excerpt from Diderot's article "Encyclopedia," written in 1755 for the fifth volume. The translation is by Stephen Gendzier.

ENCYCLOPEDIA, f. n. (PHILOSOPHY). This word means the *interrelation of all knowledge*; it is made up of the Greek prefix *en*, in, and the nouns, *kyklos*, circle, and *paideia*, instruction, science, knowledge. In truth, the aim of an *encyclopedia* is to collect all the knowledge scattered over the face of the earth, to present its general outlines and structure to the men with whom we live, and to transmit this to those who will come after us, so that the work of past centuries may be useful to the following centuries, that our children, by becoming more educated, may at the same time become more virtuous and happier, and that we may not die without having deserved well of the human race. . . .

We have seen that our *Encyclopedia* could only have been the endeavor of a philosophical century; that this age has dawned, and that fame, while raising to immortality the names of those who will perfect man's knowledge in the future, will perhaps not disdain to remember our own names. We have been heartened by the ever so consoling and agreeable idea that people may speak to one another about us, too, when we shall no longer be alive; we have been encouraged by hearing from the mouths of our contemporaries a certain voluptuous murmur that suggests what may be said of us by those happy and educated men in whose interests we have sacrificed ourselves, whom we esteem and whom we love, even though they have not yet been born. . . .

I have said that it could only belong to a philosophical age to attempt an *encyclopedia*; and I have said this because such a work constantly demands more intellectual daring than is commonly found in ages of pusillanimous taste. All things must be examined, debated, investigated without exception and without regard for anyone's feeling. . . . We must ride roughshod over all these ancient puerilities, overturn the barriers that reason never erected, give back to the arts and sciences the liberty that is so precious to them. . . . We have for quite some time needed a reasoning age when men would no longer seek the rules in classical authors but in nature, when men would be conscious of what is false and true about so many arbitrary treatises on aesthetics.

Self-Reliance
Ralph Waldo Emerson

Ralph Waldo Emerson served as an inspiration to reformers and was the leader of the Transcendentalism movement of the 1830s and 1840s in New England. A mediocre student at Harvard and unsuccessful in his first ministry, Emerson soared to prominence in 1837 with a famous address on "The American Scholar," which dared scholars to chart their own intellectual course.

Emerson's essay "Self-Reliance," excerpted below, describes the importance and challenge of listening to your own voice in the face of society's judgment. His emphasis on the individual as a source of change helped build his reputation as one of the towering figures in American literature and leading influences of his time. "Self-Reliance" was published in Emerson's first book, *Essays*, in 1841.

WHOSO WOULD BE A MAN, must be a nonconformist. He who would gather immortal palms must not be hindered by the name of goodness, but must explore if it be goodness. Nothing is at last sacred but the integrity of your own mind. Absolve you to yourself, and you shall have the suffrage of the world. I remember an answer which when quite young I was prompted to make to a valued adviser who was wont to importune me with the dear old doctrines of the church. On my saying, What have I to do with the sacredness of traditions, if I live wholly from within? My friend suggested,—"But these impulses may be from below, not from above." I replied, "They do not seem to me to be such; but if I am the Devil's child, I will live then from the Devil." No law can be sacred to me but that of my nature. Good and bad are but names very readily transferable to that or this; the only right is what is after my constitution, the only wrong what is against it. A man is to carry himself in the presence of all opposition, as if every thing were titular and ephemeral but he. I am ashamed to think how easily we capitulate to badges and names, to large societies and dead institutions. Every decent and well-spoken individual affects and sways me more than is right. I ought to go upright and vital, and speak the rude truth in all ways. . . . [D]o not tell me, as a good man did to-day, of my obligation to put all poor men in good situations. Are they *my* poor? I tell thee, thou foolish philanthropist, that I grudge the dollar, the dime, the cent, I give to such men as do not belong to me and to whom I do not belong. There is a class of persons to whom by all spiritual affinity I am bought and sold; for them I will go to prison if need be; but your miscellaneous popular charities; the education at college of fools; the building of meeting-houses to the vain end to which many now stand; alms to sots, and the thousandfold Relief Societies;—though I confess with shame I sometimes succumb and give the dollar, it is a wicked dollar which by and by I shall have the manhood to withhold.

Virtues are, in the popular estimate, rather the exception than the rule. There is the man *and* his virtues. Men do what is called good action, as some piece of courage or charity, much as they would pay a fine in expiation of daily non-appearance on parade. Their works are done as an apology or extenuation of their living in the world,—as invalids and the insane pay a high board. Their virtues are penances. I do not wish to expiate, but to live. My life is for itself and not for a spectacle. I much prefer that it should be of a lower strain, so it be genuine and equal, than that it should be glittering and unsteady. I wish it to be sound and sweet, and not to need diet and bleeding. I ask primary evidence that you are a man, and refuse this appeal from the man to his actions. I know that for myself it makes no difference whether I do or forbear those actions which are reckoned excellent. I cannot consent to pay for a privilege where I have intrinsic right. Few and mean as my gifts may be, I actually am, and do not need for my own assurance or the assurance of my fellows any secondary testimony.

What I must do is all that concerns me, not what the people think. This rule, equally arduous in actual and intellectual life, may serve for the whole distinction between greatness and meanness. It is the harder, because you will always find those who think they know what is your duty better than you know it. It is easy in the world to live after the world's opinion; it is easy in solitude to live after our own; but the great man is he who in the midst of the crowd keeps with perfect sweetness the independence of solitude. . . .

For nonconformity the world whips you with its displeasure. And therefore a man must know how to estimate a sour face. The by-standers look askance on him in the public street or in the friend's parlour. If this aversion had its origin in contempt and resistance like his own, he might well go home with a sad countenance; but the sour faces of the multitude, like their sweet faces, have no deep cause, but are put on and off as the wind blows and a newspaper directs. Yet is the discontent of the multitude more formidable than that of the senate and the college. It is easy enough for a firm man who knows the world to brook the rage of the cultivated classes. Their rage is decorous and prudent, for they are timid, as being very vulnerable themselves. But when to their feminine rage the indignation of the people is added, when the ignorant and the poor are aroused, when the unintelligent brute force that lies at the bottom of society is made to growl and mow, it needs the habit of magnanimity and religion to treat it godlike as a trifle of no concernment.

The other terror that scares us from self-trust is our consistency; a reverence for our past act or word because the eyes of others have no other data for computing our orbit than our past acts, and we are loath to disappoint them.

But why should you keep your head over your shoulder? Why drag about this corpse of your memory, lest you contradict somewhat you have stated in this or that public place? Suppose you should contradict yourself; what then? It seems to be a rule of wisdom never to rely on your memory alone, scarcely even in acts of pure memory, but to bring the past for judgment into the thousand-eye present, and live ever in a new day. . . .

A foolish consistency is the hobgoblin of little minds, adored by little statesmen and philosophers and divines. With consistency a great soul has simply nothing to do. He may as well concern himself with his shadow on the wall. Speak what you think now in hard words, and to-morrow speak what to-morrow thinks in hard words again, though it contradict everything you said to-day.—"Ah, so you shall be sure to be misunderstood."—Is it so bad, then, to be misunderstood? Pythagoras was misunderstood, and Socrates, and Jesus, and Luther, and Copernicus, and Galileo, and Newton, and every pure and wise spirit that ever took flesh. To be great is to be misunderstood.

"Sexual love is not naturally restricted to pairs"
John Noyes

Long before "free love" and the "sexual revolution" of the 1960s, there was the Oneida Community, the most successful and notorious of the utopian communities established during the Age of Reform in the United States in the 1840s. John Noyes founded Oneida in 1848 in upstate New York with the goal of changing the societal notion of marriage.

Noyes sought to reshape the relationship between men and women. He developed a complex communal marriage system in which every man and woman in the community was married to each other. Each man had sexual access to every woman, and each woman had the same for every man. To avoid "special love" couplings, each community member had his or her own bedroom. Similar communities were formed in Putney and Cambridge, Vermont; Newark, New Jersey; and Wallingford, Connecticut, but they all disbanded after a few years.

Under Noyes's direct leadership Oneida flourished, growing to as many as three hundred people. The community prospered as an agricultural and commercial enterprise. External pressures and Noyes's declining ability to lead with age led to the dissolution of the community in 1881. Several members continued the commercial businesses, which eventually became the publicly owned silverware company Oneida Limited.

Noyes wrote this description of the community's marriage system in 1870.

CHAPTER II. Showing that Marriage is not an institution of the Kingdom of Heaven, and must give place to Communism.

PROPOSITION 5. In the Kingdom of Heaven, the institution of marriage, which assigns the exclusive possession of one woman to one man, does not exist. Matt. 22: 23–30.

6. In the Kingdom of Heaven the intimate union of life and interest, which in the world is limited to pairs, extends through the whole body of believers; i.e., complex marriage takes the place of simple. John 17:21. . . .

8. Admitting that the Community principle of the day of Pentecost, in its actual operation at that time, extended only to material goods, yet we affirm that there is no intrinsic difference between property in persons and property in things; and that the same spirit which abolished exclusiveness in regard to money, would abolish, if circumstances allowed full scope to it, exclusiveness in regard to women and children. Paul expressly places property in women and property in goods in the same category, and speaks of them together, as ready to be abolished by the advent of the Kingdom of Heaven. "The time, says he, "is short; it remaineth that they that have wives be as though they had none; and they that buy as though they possessed not; for the fashion of this world passeth away." I Cor. 7:29–31.

9. The abolishment of appropriation is involved in the very nature of a true relation to Christ in the gospel. This we prove thus: The possessive feeling which expresses itself by the possessive pronoun mine, is the same in essence when it relates to persons, as when it relates to money or any other property. Amativeness and acquisitiveness are only different channels of one stream. They converge as we trace them to their source. . . .

10. The abolishment of exclusiveness is involved in the love-relation required between all believers by the express injunction of Christ and the apostles, and by the whole tenor of the New Testament. "The new commandment is, that we love one another," and that, not by pairs, as in the world, but en masse. We are required to love one another fervently. The fashion of the world forbids a man and a woman who are otherwise appropriated, to love one another fervently. But if they obey Christ they must do this; and whoever would allow them to do this, and yet would forbid them (on any other ground than that of present expediency), to express their unity, would "strain at a gnat and swallow a camel"; for unity of hearts is as much more important than any external expression of it, as a camel is larger than a gnat. . . .

13. The law of marriage is the same in kind with the Jewish law concerning meats and drinks and holy days, of which Paul said that they were "contrary to us, and were taken out of the way, being nailed to the cross." Col. 2:14. The plea in favor of the worldly, social system, that it is not arbitrary, but founded in nature, will not bear investigation. All experience testifies (the theory of the novels to the contrary notwithstanding), that sexual love is not naturally restricted

to pairs. Second marriages are contrary to the one-love theory, and yet are often the happiest marriages. Men and women find universally (however the fact may be conceded), that their susceptibility to love is not burnt out by one honeymoon, or satisfied by one lover. On the contrary, the secret history of the human heart will bear out the assertion that it is capable of loving any number of times and any number of persons, and that the more it loves the more it can love. This is the law of nature, thrust out of sight and condemned by common consent, and yet secretly known to all.

14. The law of marriage "worketh wrath." 1. It provokes to secret adultery, actual or of the heart. 2. It ties together unmatched natures. 3. It sunders matched natures. 4. It gives sexual appetite only a scanty and monotonous allowance, and so produces the natural vices of poverty, contraction of taste and stinginess or jealousy. It makes no provision for the sexual appetite at the very time when that appetite is the strongest. By the custom of the world, marriage, in the average of cases, takes place at about the age of twenty-four; whereas puberty commences at the age of fourteen. For ten years, therefore, and that in the very flush of life, the sexual appetite is starved. This law of society bears hardest on females, because they have less opportunity of choosing their time of marriage than men. This discrepancy between the marriage system and nature, is one of the principal sources of the peculiar diseases of women, of prostitution, masturbation, and licentiousness in general.

De Profundis
Oscar Wilde

Oscar Wilde was one of the leading artistic and intellectual voices of late nineteenth-century England. His plays, poems, and essays delighted audiences with their wit and daring assaults on convention. Wilde's life became notorious, however, when it was revealed he had a sexual affair with Sir Alfred Douglas, a much younger man in his early twenties. Wilde was convicted of sodomy and sentenced to jail in the Reading Prison for two years.

Wilde wrote an eighty-page letter from his jail cell to Douglas in 1896–97. When he was released from jail he gave the letter to a friend and asked him to publish it after his death. "I do not defend my conduct. I explain it," he wrote in his cover letter of the manuscript. The essay, *De Profundis*, was published in 1949.

Wilde's life and writings represent a witty and fiercely intelligent attack on orthodoxy. He wrote: "Agitators are a set of interfering, meddling people, who come down to some perfectly contented class of the community and sow the seeds of discontent amongst them. That is the reason why agitators are so absolutely necessary."

In *De Profundis* he explains his own personal history and, in the passage here, describes how the life of Jesus Christ represented a model for living a life as an individual in the face of a resistant society.

CHRIST HAD NO PATIENCE with the dull lifeless mechanical systems that treat people as if they were things, and so treat everybody alike: as if anybody, or anything for that matter, was like aught else in the world. For him there were no laws: there were exceptions merely.

That which is the very keynote of romantic art was to him the proper basis of actual life. He saw no other basis. And when they brought him one taken in the very act of sin and showed him her sentence written in the law and asked him what was to be done, he wrote with his finger on the ground as though he did not hear them, and finally, when they pressed him again, looked up and said, "Let him of you who has never sinned be the first to throw the stone at her." It was worth while living to have said that.

Like all poetical natures, he loved ignorant people. He knew that in the soul of one who is ignorant there is always room for a great idea. But he could not stand stupid people, especially those who are made stupid by education—people who are full of opinions not one of which they even understand, a peculiarly modern type, summed up by Christ when he describes it as the type of one who has the key of knowledge, can't use it himself, and won't allow other people to use it, though it may be made to open the gate of God's Kingdom. His chief war was against the Philistines. That is the war every child of light has to wage. Philistinism was the note of the age and community in which he lived. In their heavy inaccessibility to ideas, their dull respectability, their tedious orthodoxy, their worship of vulgar success, their entire preoccupation with the gross materialistic side of life, their ridiculous estimate of themselves and their importance, the Jew of Jerusalem in Christ's day was the exact counterpart of the British Philistine of our own. Christ mocked at the "whited sepulchers" of respectability, and fixed the phrase for ever. He treated worldly success as a thing absolutely to be despised. He saw nothing in it at all. He looked on wealth as an encumbrance to a man. He would not hear of life being sacrificed to any system of thought or morals. He pointed out that forms and ceremonies were made for man, not man for forms and ceremonies. He took Sabbatarianism as a type of the things that should be set at nought. The cold philanthropies, the ostentatious public charities, the tedious formalisms so dear to the middle-class mind, he exposed with utter and relentless scorn. To us, what is termed Orthodoxy is merely a facile unintelligent acquiescence, but to them, and in their hands, it was a terrible and paralyzing tyranny. Christ swept it aside. He showed that the spirit alone was of value. He took a keen pleasure in pointing out to them that though they were always reading the Law and the Prophets they had not really the smallest idea of what either of them meant. In opposition to their tithing of each separate day into the fixed routine of prescribed duties, as they tithed mint and rue, he preached the enormous importance of living completely for the moment.

Those whom he saved from their sins are saved simply for beautiful moments in their lives. Mary Magdalen, when she sees Christ, breaks the rich vase of alabaster that one of her seven lovers had given her, and spills the odorous spices over his tired, dusty feet, and for that one moment's sake sits for ever with Ruth and Beatrice in the tresses of the snow-white Rose of Paradise. All that Christ says to us by way of a little warning is that *every* moment should be beautiful, that the soul should *always* be ready for the coming of the Bridegroom, *always* waiting for the voice of the Lover, Philistinism being simply that side of man's nature that is not illumined by the imagination, he sees all the lovely influences of life as modes of Light: the imagination itself is the world-light . . . : the world is made by it, and yet the world cannot understand it: that is because the imagination is simply a manifestation of Love, and it is love and the capacity for it, that distinguishes one human being from another.

But it is when he deals with a Sinner that he is most romantic, in the sense of most real. The world had always loved the Saint as being the nearest possible approach to the perfection of God. Christ, through some divine instinct in him, seems to have always loved the sinner as being the nearest possible approach to the perfection of man. His primary desire was not to reform people, any more than his primary desire was to relieve suffering. To turn an interesting thief into a tedious honest man was not his aim. He would have thought little of the Prisoners' Aid Society and other modern movements of the kind. The conversion of a Publican into a Pharisee would not have seemed to him a great achievement by any means. But in a manner not yet understood of the world he regarded sin and suffering as being in themselves beautiful, holy things, and modes of perfection. It *sounds* a very dangerous idea. It is so. All great ideas *are* dangerous. That it was Christ's creed admits of no doubt. That it is the true creed I don't doubt myself.

"I came to Wichita expecting to get in trouble and here I am": A Report of the Arrest of Carrie Nation
Topeka Daily Capital

The temperance movement of the late 1800s and early 1900s in the United States led to the Eighteenth Amendment to the Constitution in 1919, banning the manufacture, sale, or transportation of alcohol. The most infamous combatant in this struggle was Mrs. Carrie A. Nation. A formidable woman who stood nearly six feet tall, she wielded a hatchet to smash the interiors of approximately thirty taverns.

Nation's hatred of intoxicating liquors stemmed from the experience of her marriage to Dr. Charles Glayd, a severe alcoholic who died less than two years after they were married. She became a teacher after his death and married David Nation several years later. In 1889 the couple moved to Medicine Lodge, Kansas, where she ran a hotel and became involved in the local temperance movement.

As described in this December 27, 1900, article from the *Topeka Daily Capital* newspaper, Nation believed she was sanctioned to destroy liquor-serving bars, taverns, and saloons. She was arrested approximately thirty times for smashing saloons, sometimes accompanied by hymn-singing women. Nation died in 1911, eight years before Prohibition went into effect.

Although today Prohibition is largely viewed as a failure, it did have some positive effects, particularly in rural America. The cirrhosis death rates and admissions to state mental hospitals for alcoholism both dropped by 50 percent during Prohibition.

MRS. CARRIE NATION, president of Barber County Women's Christian Temperance Union, began today a raid on the saloons in Wichita. As a result of her work she is now under arrest and placed behind the bars at the county jail.

At 9:45 this morning she entered the saloon in the basement of the Carey hotel and without a word of warning pulled from a bundle of papers which she carried in her hands two large stones. Before the clerks and bartenders could realize what was going on, Mrs. Nation sent one of the stones whizzing through a large oil painting of Cleopatra nude at the Roman bath. The painting was valued at $100. As a result of the stone hitting the painting the picture is completely spoiled.

After damaging this picture, the woman suddenly turned herself about and with much force sent another stone through a valuable $1,500 mirror which is situated directly back of the bar. She then left the saloon.

While in the saloon she also broke about $25 worth of bottled goods and also a window. As soon as she left the saloon she was arrested. . . .

Last night Mrs. Nation visited all the saloons in Wichita and demanded that they close their doors. She called at the Carey barroom last night where she saw this costly picture hanging on the wall. She told the bartender to remove it. The bartender refused to do so. Today, while the stones were being hurled, the bartender, Edward Parker, hid himself behind the bar.

Mrs. Nation, when seen by a reporter for the *Capital*, said:

"I am a law abiding citizen and I have not gone out of the bounds of the law. I have a husband who is a lawyer and he says they cannot prosecute me. . . ."

She dared the officers to place her in a cell. She said if they did, she would sue the city for false imprisonment. . . .

Members of the Women's Christian Temperance Union of Wichita who heard of the actions of Mrs. Nation say they do not approve of them, and believe there are other ways to shut up the saloons in Wichita.

Mrs. Nation was removed to the county jail tonight. . . .

"I came to the Governor's town," she said, "to destroy the finest saloon in it, hoping thus to attract public attention to the flagrant violation of a Kansas law, under the very eye of the chief executive of the state."

The damage done to the saloon is hard to estimate. It was finished with stucco secured from the World's Fair building and many blocks of it are shattered. The painting of Cleopatra cost Mr. Noble, its author, nine months' time painting it and was still his property, being rented by the saloon. It has been seen at nearly all the street fairs from Canada to the Gulf.

"I came to Wichita expecting to get into trouble and here I am. I have brought my clothes and some eating along so as to be as comfortable as possible. . . . I studied the law and asked competent lawyers if I can be prosecuted for destroying the property of the jointists and they say I cannot for the reason that the saloon men here have no rights under the state laws. I telegraphed my husband this morning not to come here and interfere with my work, but to leave me alone."

The course of Mrs. Nation's fight for temperance started from the cause of the death of her first husband twenty-five years ago, who died from the result of delirium tremens. His name was Dr. Charles Glayd and she was married to him against the wishes of her parents. . . . Word is received in Wichita that Mrs. Nation is well respected in Medicine Lodge. She is considered eccentric at some times.

Manifesto of Futurism
Filippo T. Marinetti

The turn of the twentieth century was a time of massive change. The automobile, telephone, and airplane had just been invented. Industrial cities were becoming gigantic metropolises. Thinkers such as Karl Marx and Friedrich Nietzsche challenged people's views of morality, truth, and other traditional issues. Several artistic movements grew out of this environment, radically changing the way people thought about art, literature, and philosophy. Literature by writers such as Henry Miller and James Joyce explored the depths of Sigmund Freud's theories of the unconscious and sexuality. Cubism abandoned any pretense of realism in painting.

In Italy a group of artists started Futurism. Unlike most avant-garde movements, which called for utopian visions of the future, Futurism believed in machinery, modern technology, and militarism. In 1909, Futurist poet and editor Filippo Tommaso Marinetti issued a statement of the goals and ambitions of the movement. Comparing the hood of automobiles to breasts and art museums to cemeteries, he called for the overhaul of traditional ways and the embracing of modernity. Marinetti's statement also unveiled his group's eleven-point "Manifesto of Futurism."

The movement was short-lived in part because the onset of World War I dashed any notion of militarism as a romantic ideal. Nevertheless, many people consider its ideas as a precursor to fascist movements that took power in Italy in the 1920s and Germany in the 1930s.

1. WE WANT TO SING THE LOVE OF DANGER, the habit of energy and rashness.

2. The essential elements of our poetry will be courage, audacity and revolt. . . .

3. Literature has up to now magnified pensive immobility, ecstasy and slumber. We want to exalt movements of aggression, feverish sleeplessness, the double march, the perilous leap, the slap and the blow with the fist.

4. We declare that the splendor of the world has been enriched by a new beauty: the beauty of speed. A racing automobile with its bonnet adorned with great tubes like serpents with explosive breath . . . a roaring motor car which seems to run on machine-gun fire, is more beautiful than the Victory of Samothrace [a classical sculpture of the Greek goddess Nike].

5. We want to sing the man at the wheel, the ideal axis of which crosses the earth, itself hurled along its orbit.

6. The poet must spend himself with warmth, glamour and prodigality to increase the enthusiastic fervor of the primordial elements.

7. Beauty exists only in struggle. There is no masterpiece that has not an aggressive character. Poetry must be a violent assault on the forces of the unknown, to force them to bow before man.

8. We are on the extreme promontory of the centuries! What is the use of looking behind at the moment when we must open the mysterious shutters of the impossible? Time and Space died yesterday. We are already living in the absolute, since we have already created eternal, omnipresent speed.

9. We want to glorify war—the only cure for the world—militarism, patriotism, the destructive gesture of the anarchists, the beautiful ideas which kill, and contempt for woman.

10. We want to demolish museums and libraries, fight morality, feminism and all opportunist and utilitarian cowardice.

11. We will sing of the great crowds agitated by work, pleasure and revolt; the multi-colored and polyphonic surf of revolutions in modern capitals: the nocturnal vibration of the arsenals and the workshops beneath their violent electric moons: the gluttonous railway stations devouring smoking serpents; factories suspended from the clouds by the thread of their smoke; bridges with the leap of gymnasts flung across the diabolic cutlery of sunny rivers: adventurous steamers sniffing the horizon; great-breasted locomotives, puffing on the rails like enormous steel horses with long tubes for bridle, and the gliding flight of aeroplanes whose propeller sounds like the flapping of a flag and the applause of enthusiastic crowds.

"This word as used in the picture is not an oath or a curse"

David O. Selznick

In the wake of a series of Hollywood scandals involving murders, sex, and drugs, the film industry adopted the Production Code, which set moral standards for Hollywood movies. Among other things, the 1930 code prohibited nudity, suggestive dancing, rude language, the depiction of illegal drugs, and the ridicule of religion. The sanctity of marriage and home were to be upheld and the American flag "was to be treated respectfully."

The code was largely ignored until 1934 when all films were required by the Hollywood association to get a certificate of approval from the Production Code Administration, which had no governmental authority. Joseph Breen was named as the chief enforcer of the code. He quickly earned a reputation for his rigid interpretations of the code and determination to enforce it.

Several controversies erupted, and accusations of censorship were made against the administration. The first involved the 1934 film *Tarzan and His Mate*, from which Breen successfully forced the sponsoring studio to remove nude scenes. Breen also refused to grant a certificate for the 1943 film *The Outlaw* directed by Howard Hughes because of the film's emphasis on starring actress Jane Russell's breasts.

In 1939, Breen refused to give a certificate for the eagerly anticipated movie *Gone With the Wind* because of Rhett Butler's final line ending his relationship with Scarlet O'Hara: "Frankly, my dear, I don't give a damn." Breen deemed the word "damn" to be too vulgar. In this letter, producer David O. Selznick appealed Breen's decision to William Hays, the head of the office in charge of ensuring that Hollywood films did not lower the nation's moral standards. The line stayed in the movie. The Production Code remained in place until 1964.

AS YOU PROBABLY KNOW, the punch line of *Gone With the Wind*, the one bit of dialogue which forever establishes the future relationship between Scarlett and Rhett, is, "Frankly, my dear, I don't give a damn."

Naturally I am most desirous of keeping this line and, to judge from the reactions of two preview audiences, this line is remembered, loved, and looked forward to by the millions who have read this new American classic.

Under the code, Joe Breen is unable to give me permission to use this sentence because it contains the word "damn," a word specifically forbidden by the code.

As you know from my previous work with such pictures as *David Copperfield, Little Lord Fauntleroy, A Tale of Two Cities*, etc., I have always attempted to live up to the spirit as well as the exact letter of the producers' code. Therefore, my asking you to review the case, to look at the strip of film in which this forbidden word is contained, is not motivated by a whim. A great deal of the force and drama of *Gone With the Wind*, a project to which we have given three years of hard work and hard thought, is dependent on that word.

It is my contention that this word as used in the picture is not an oath or a curse. The worst that could be said against it is that it is a vulgarism, and it is so described in the *Oxford English Dictionary*. Nor do I feel that in asking you to make an exception in this case, I am asking for the use of a word which is considered reprehensible by the great majority of American people and institutions. A canvass of the popular magazines shows that even such moral publications as *Woman's Home Companion, Saturday Evening Post, Collier's* and *The Atlantic Monthly*, use this word freely. I understand the difference, as outlined in the code, between the written word and the word spoken from the screen, but at the same time I think the attitude of these magazines toward "damn" gives an indication that the word itself is not considered abhorrent or shocking to audiences.

I do not feel that your giving me permission to use "damn" in this one sentence will open up the floodgates and allow every gangster picture to be peppered with "damns" from end to end. I do believe, however, that if you were to permit our using this dramatic word in its rightfully dramatic place, in a line that is known and remembered by millions of readers, it would establish a helpful precedent, a precedent which would give to Joe Breen discretionary powers to allow the use of certain harmless oaths and ejaculations whenever, in his opinion, they are not prejudicial to public morals.

"Please stop using the word 'Negro'"
Mary Church Terrell

Because of their particular use throughout history, certain words develop strong connotations not easily lost in the context of conversation or debate. A longtime civil rights leader, Mary Church Terrell was one of the first to start to change the way Americans described African Americans, forcefully arguing against the term "Negro." Terrell wrote the following letter to the *Washington Post* in 1949, expressing her concerns about how language could be used to sustain or change racial stereotypes.

When Terrell wrote the letter she had been an activist for sixty years. She was born in 1863 to former slaves. In 1884, she received a bachelor's degree from Oberlin College, making her one of the first African-American women to graduate from college. She helped found and was the first president of the National Association of Colored Women (NACW) in the 1890s. The NACW established many parenting and children's programs. It also resisted segregation laws and advocated for the right of women to vote.

Terrell was a founding member of the National Association for the Advancement of Colored People (NAACP) executive committee and the first black woman to serve on a municipal school board, in this case in Washington, D.C. After writing the letter below, at age eighty-seven, she launched a campaign of boycotts and sit-ins against segregated restaurants in Washington, D.C. She was part of a lawsuit against Thompson Restaurant for refusing her and other African Americans service. On June 8, 1953, the Supreme Court ruled that it was unconstitutional for restaurants to be segregated. Terrell died one year later.

Although it took several decades to accomplish, the use of the term "negro" decreased and was gradually replaced first with the term "black" and later "African American."

PLEASE STOP using the word "Negro." Several days ago "BAN ON WORD ASKED" was the Post's title of an appeal made by a leper who stood before a congressional committee urging that the Federal Government ban the use of the word "leper." He said the word "leper" should be removed from the dictionary because of its unjust and shameful stigma which hurts its victims and efforts to control and wipe the disease out. He wants the affliction to be called "Hansen's Disease," because lepers are treated unfairly owing to "public misunderstanding."

For a reason similar to the one given by the leper I am urging the Post and others willing to advance our interest and deal justly with our group to stop using the word "Negro." The word is a misnomer from every point of view. It does not represent a country or anything else except one single, solitary color. And no one color can describe the various and varied complexions in our group. In complexion we range from deep black to the fairest white with all the colors of the rainbow thrown in for good measure. When twenty or thirty of us are meeting together it would be as hard to find three or four of us with the same complexion as it would be to catch greased lightning in a bottle. We are the only human beings in the world with fifty-seven varieties of complexions who are classed together as a single racial unit. Therefore, we are really, truly colored people, and that is the name in the English language which accurately describes us.

To be sure the complexion of the Chinese and Japanese is yellow. But nobody refers to an individual in either group as a colored man. . . . They say he is Chinese. . . . When I studied abroad and was introduced as an "American," (generally speaking, everybody from the United States used to be called an "American" in Europe) occasionally somebody would say "you are rather dark to be an American, aren't you?" "Yes," I would reply, "I am dark, because some of my ancestors were Africans." I was proud of having the continent of Africa part of my ancestral background. "I am an African-American," I would explain. I am not ashamed of my African descent. Africa had great universities before there were any in England and the African was the first man industrious and skillful enough to work in iron. If our group must have a special name setting it apart, the sensible way to settle it would be to refer to our ancestors, the Africans, from whom our swarthy complexions come.

There are at least two strong reasons why I object to designating our group as Negroes. If a man is a Negro, it follows as the night the day that a woman is a Negress. "Negress" is an ugly, repulsive word—virtually a term of degradation and reproach which colored women of this country can not live down in a thousand years. I have questioned scores of men who call themselves "Negroes," and each and every one of them strenuously objected to having his wife, or daughter or mother or any woman in his family called a "Negress."

In the second place, I object to . . . Negro because our meanest detractors and most cruel prosecutors insist that we shall be called by that name, so that they can humiliate us by referring contemptuously to us as "niggers," or "Negras" as [Theodore] Bilbo [a Mississippi senator] used to do. Some of our group say they will continue to classify us as Negroes, until an individual referred to as such will be proud of that name. But that is a case of wishful thinking and nothing else. For the moment one hears the word Negro in this country, instantly, automatically, in his mind's eye he sees a human being who is ignorant, segregated, discriminated against, considered inferior and objectionable on general principles from every point of view. God alone knows how long it will take our minority group under prevailing conditions in this country to reach such heights that a representative of it will be proud to be called a Negro. That would be a double, back action, super-duper miracle indeed! . . .

It is a great pity the word "Negro" was not outlawed in the Emancipation Proclamation as it certainly should have been. After the people have been freed, it is a cruel injustice to call them by the same name they bore as slaves. It is painful and shocking indeed that those in our group who have enjoyed educational opportunities; that officials in the National Association for the Advancement of Colored People, founded forty years ago which repudiated the word "Negro" should continue to use the slave term and thereby increase the difficulties of their group in their effort to reach the worthy goal toward which they strive.

The founders of the N.A.A.C.P. which has been and still is waging such a holy warfare against disfranchisement, segregation and discrimination of all kinds certainly deserves our gratitude for not naming that wonderful, powerful instrument for good "The National Association for the Advancement of Negroes."

"Hair"
James Rado and Gerome Ragni

The play *Hair*, which celebrated the hippie counterculture of the 1960s, was first performed in a New York City club called the Cheetah in 1967. Subtitled *The American Tribal Love/Rock Musical*, it soon found its way to the Biltmore Theater on Broadway. Nearly two thousand performances were given in both the Broadway and London productions.

Hair was created by two out-of-work actors, James Rado and Gerome Ragni. They said they wanted to bring the excitement of the long-haired, free-spirited hippies onto the stage. With songs celebrating drugs, sexual acts that some consider deviant, and peace, *Hair*, despite its popularity, provoked a heavy dose of controversy. It was shut down after one night in Mexico, and all the performers ordered to leave the country or go to jail. Clive Barnes, theater critic of the *New York Times,* wrote: "Since I have had a number of letters from people who have seen previews asking me to warn readers, and, in the urbanely quaint words of one correspondent, 'Spell out what is happening on stage' this I had better do. Well, almost, for spell it out I cannot, for this remains a family newspaper."

The play's name and title song celebrated the desire of young people, including boys and young men, to grow their hair very long. This was seen as an act of rebellion against the short or restrained hairstyles of their parents' generation.

She asks me why . . . I'm just a hairy guy?
I'm hairy noon and night; Hair that's a fright.
I'm hairy high and low,
Don't ask me why; don't know!
It's not for lack of bread
Like the Grateful Dead; darling

Gimme a head with hair, long beautiful hair
Shining, gleaming, steaming, flaxen, waxen
Give me down to there, hair!
Shoulder length, longer (hair!)
Here baby, there mama, Everywhere daddy daddy

Chorus

Hair! (hair, hair, hair, hair, hair, hair)
Flow it, Show it;
Long as God can grow it, My Hair!

Let it fly in the breeze and get caught in the trees
Give a home to the fleas in my hair
A home for fleas, a hive for bees
A nest for birds, there ain't no words
For the beauty, the splendor, the wonder of my

Chorus

I want it long, straight, curly, fuzzy
Snaggy, shaggy, ratty, matty
Oily, greasy, fleecy, shining
Gleaming, steaming, flaxen, waxen
Knotted, polka-dotted; Twisted, beaded, braided
Powdered, flowered, and confettied
Bangled, tangled, spangled and spaghettied!

O-oh, Say can you see; my eyes if you can,
Then my hair's too short!
Down to here, down to there,
Down to where, down to there;
It stops by itself!
doo doo doo doo doot-doot doo doo doot

They'll be ga-ga at the go-go
when they see me in my toga
My toga made of blond, brilliantined, Biblical hair
My hair like Jesus wore it

Hallelujah I adore it
Hallelujah Mary loved her son
Why don't my Mother love me?

Black Power
Tommie Smith and John Carlos

In 1968, after the assassination of Martin Luther King, Jr., many black athletes in the United States formed the Olympic Project for Human Rights (OPHR) and contemplated boycotting the Summer Olympics in Mexico City. Although the Olympics had often been used by governments to advance their political agendas, it was highly unusual for individual athletes to use the sporting event as a platform to assert their political beliefs.

The boycott never happened, but the 1968 Olympics provided the forum for one of the most powerful images of the civil rights movement. In the 200-meter dash, Tommie Smith (center) won the gold medal and John Carlos (right) won the bronze. Both had taken part in the boycott discussion, and as they prepared to accept their medals, they spontaneously worked out the details of a silent protest in which they would raise their fists, the symbol of black power.

Both men stepped onto the podium in black socks with no shoes. "We wanted the world to know that in Mississippi, Alabama, Tennessee, South Central Los Angeles, Chicago, that people were still walking back and forth in poverty without even the necessary clothes to live," Carlos later said. Carlos wore beads around his neck, symbolizing blacks who had been lynched. A black scarf around Smith's neck represented black pride.

At the suggestion of silver medalist Peter Norman (left) of Australia, Smith and Carlos divided a pair of black leather gloves. As the American flags rose as part of the medal ceremony, Smith and Carlos raised their fists above their head. Norman stood motionless, but wore an OPHR badge in support of the American athletes.

Smith and Carlos were immediately kicked off the United States Olympic team and banished from the Olympic Village. Many people were furious at the two men for using an international sports event to make a political statement. Despite the uproar and death threats against them and their families, Carlos and Smith were unrepentant.

"We didn't come up there with any bombs," said Carlos, who had spoken with King shortly before he was assassinated. "We were trying to wake the country up and wake the world up too."

"We . . . demand to be busted by policewomen only"
New York Radical Women

The feminist movement of the 1960s gave voice to the unspoken resentments many women felt for years of being given second-class status in American society. Central to their argument were the effects of gender stereotyping. Society's response to women based on their appearance and "feminine" qualities was sharply condemned as being patronizing and as a way to subjugate women.

The annual Miss America Pageant in Atlantic City epitomized everything the feminist movement objected to in chauvinistic American society. In 1968, the feminist group New York Radical Women launched a militant protest against the event. Bearing "freedom trash cans" in which to dump symbols of the oppression of women, the New York Radical Women were barred from the convention hall, but staged a protest outside. The demonstration attracted national media attention. Protestors distributed the following handout, stating their position to the media and spectators on the Atlantic City boardwalk.

ON SEPTEMBER 7 IN ATLANTIC CITY, the Annual Miss America Pageant will again crown "your ideal." But this year, reality will liberate the contest auction-block in the guise of "genyoine" de-plasticized, breathing women. Women's Liberation Groups, black women, high-school and college women, women's peace groups, women's welfare and social-work groups, women's job-equality groups, pro-birth control and pro-abortion groups—women of every political persuasion—all are invited to join us in a day-long boardwalk-theater event, starting at 1:00 p.m. on the Boardwalk in front of Atlantic City Convention Hall. We will protest the image of Miss America, an image that oppresses women in every area in which it purports to represent us. There will be: Picket Lines; Guerrilla Theater; Leafleting; Lobbying Visits to the contestants urging our sisters to reject the Pageant Farce and join us; a huge Freedom Trash Can (into which we will throw bras, girdles, curlers, false eye-lashes, wigs, and representative issues of *Cosmopolitan, Ladies' Home Journal, Family Circle,* etc.—bring any such women-garbage you have around the house); we will also announce a Boycott of all those commercial products related to the pageant, and the day will end with a Women's Liberation rally at midnight when Miss America is crowned on live television. Lots of other surprises are being planned (come and add your own!) but we do not plan heavy disruptive tactics and so do not expect a bad police scene. It should be a groovy day on the Boardwalk in the sun with our sisters. In case of arrests, however, we plan to reject all male authority and demand to be busted by policewomen only. (In Atlantic City, women cops are not permitted to make arrests—dig that!)

Male chauvinist-reactionaries on this issue had best stay away, nor are male liberals welcome in the demonstrations. But sympathetic men can donate money as well as cars and drivers.

Male reporters will be refused interviews. We reject patronizing reportage. Only newswomen will be recognized.

We Protest:

The Degrading Mindless-Boob-Girlie Symbol. The Pageant contestants epito-mize the roles we are all forced to play as women. The parade down the runway blares at the metaphor of the 4-H Club county fair, where the nervous animals are judged for teeth, fleece, etc. and where the best "specimen" gets the blue ribbon. So are women in our society forced daily to compete for male approval, enslaved by ludicrous "beauty" standards we ourselves are conditioned to take seriously.

Racism with Roses. Since its inception in 1921, the pageant has not had one Black finalist, and this has not been for a lack of test-case contestants. There has never been a Puerto Rican, Alaskan, Hawaiian, or Mexican-American winner. Nor has there ever been a true Miss America—an American Indian.

Miss America as a Military Death Mascot. The highlight of her reign each year is a cheerleader-tour of American troops abroad—last year she went to Vietnam to pep-talk our husbands, fathers, sons and boyfriends into dying and killing with a better spirit. She personifies the "unstained patriotic womanhood our boys are fighting for." The Living Bra and the Dead Soldier. We refused to be used as Mascots for Murder.

The Consumer Con-Game. Miss America is a walking commercial for the Pageant's sponsors. Wind her up and she plugs your product on promotion tours and TV—all in an "honest, objective" endorsement. What a shill.

Competition Rigged and Unrigged. We deplore the encouragement of the American myth that oppresses men as well as women: the win-or-you're-worthless competitive disease. The "beauty contest" creates only one winner to be "used" and forty-nine losers who are "useless."

The Woman as Pop Culture Obsolescent Theme. Spindle, mutilate, and then discard tomorrow. What is so ignored as last year's Miss America? This only reflects the gospel of our society, according to Saint Male: women must be young, juicy, malleable—hence age discrimination and the cult of youth. And we women are brainwashed into believing this ourselves!

The Unbeatable Madonna-Whore Combination. Miss America and *Playboy's* centerfold are sisters over the skin. To win approval, we must be both sexy and wholesome, delicate but able to cope, demure yet titillatingly bitchy. Deviation of any sort brings, we are told, disaster. "You won't get a man!!"

The Irrelevant Crown on the Throne of Mediocrity. Miss America represents what women are supposed to be: unoffensive, bland, apolitical. If you are tall, short, over or under what weight The Man prescribes you should be, forget it. Personality, articulateness, intelligence, commitment—unwise. Conformity is the key to the crown—and, by extension, to success in our society.

Miss America as Dream Equivalent To—? In this reputedly democratic society, where every little boy supposedly can grow up to be president, what can every little girl hope to grow up to be? Miss America. That's where it is at. Real power to control our own lives is restricted to men, while women get patronizing pseudo-power, an ermine cloak, and a bunch of flowers; men are judged by their actions, women by their appearance.

Miss America as Big Sister Watching You. The Pageant exercises Thought Control, attempts to sear the Image onto our minds, to further make women oppressed and men oppressors; to enslave us all the more in high-heeled, low-status roles; to inculcate false values in young girls; to use women as beasts of buying; to seduce us to prostitute ourselves before our own oppression.

NO MORE MISS AMERICA

Criticism and Response to *Piss Christ*
Jesse Helms and Andres Serrano

Often artists push the envelope of free expression with their work, breaking social, religious, or sexual taboos and putting forth extreme forms of social or political commentary. Because of its extreme nature, such commentary can be seen by critics not as having value but as self-serving or highly offensive.

In 1989, the schism between contemporary artists and the general public burst into the public debate when North Carolina senator Jesse Helms's condemned of Andres Serrano's artwork "Piss Christ," which had received a National Endowment for the Arts subsidy. Helms helped insert a restriction on future NEA expenditures prohibiting contributions for art that may be considered obscene.

The following are Helms's remarks on the floor of the Senate and the artist's response via a letter to the NEA.

MR. PRESIDENT, . . . I do not know Mr. Andres Serrano, and I hope I never meet him because he is not an artist, he is a jerk.

Let us examine exactly what this bird did to get the American taxpayer to subsidize his $15,000 award through the so-called National Endowment for the Arts. Let me first say that if the Endowment has no better judgment than this, it ought to be abolished and all funds returned to the taxpayer.

What this Serrano fellow did to create this blasphemy was to fill a bottle with his own urine and then he stuck a crucifix—the Lord Jesus Christ on a cross—down in the urine, set the bottle on the table and took a picture of it.

For that, the National Endowment for the Arts contributed to a $15,000 award to honor him as an artist.

I say again, Mr. President, he is not an artist. He is a jerk. He is taunting a large segment of the American people, just as others are, about their Christian faith. I resent it, and I do not hesitate to say so.

I am not going to call the name that he applied this work of art. In naming it he sought to create indignation, and let there be no question that he succeeded in that regard.

It is all right for him to be a jerk but let him be a jerk on his own time and with his own resources. Do not dishonor the Lord. Again, I resent it and I think the vast majority of our American people resent the National Endowment for the Arts spending the taxpayers' money to honor this individual.

The Federal program which honored Mr. Serrano, called the Awards in Visual Arts, is supported by the National Endowment for the Arts and administered by the Southeastern Center for Contemporary Arts. They call it SECCA and I am sorry to say it is in my home state.

After Mr. Serrano's selection, this deplorable photograph and some of his other works were exhibited in several cities around the country with the approval and the support of the National Endowment.

Horsefeathers. If we have sunk so low in this country as to tolerate and condone this sort of thing, then we have become a part of it.

The question is obvious. On what conceivable basis does anybody who would engage in such blasphemy and insensitivity toward the religious community deserve to be honored? The answer to that is that he does not. He deserves to be rebuked and ignored because he is not an artist. Anybody who would do such a despicable thing—and get a tax-subsidized award of $15,000 for it—well, it tells you something about the state of this government and the way it spends our hard-earned tax dollars.

So no wonder all of the people calling my office are indignant. The Constitution may prevent the government from prohibiting Mr. Serrano's—laughably, I will describe it—"artistic expression." But the Constitution certainly does not require the American taxpayers or the federal government to fund, promote, honor, approve, or condone it.

Mr. President, the National Endowment's procedures for selecting artists and works of art deserving of taxpayer support are badly, badly flawed if this is an example of the kind of programs they fund with taxpayers' money.

I have sent word to the Endowment that I want them to review their funding criteria to ensure abuses such as this never happen again. The preliminary report we got from one person with whom we talked was sort of "Down, boy, we know what we are doing."

Well, they do not know what they are doing. By promoting, approving, and funding Mr. Serrano's sacrilege, the National Endowment for the Arts has insulted the very precepts on which this country was founded. I say again, that as an American and as a taxpayer, I resent it.

[Serrano's response]

I am concerned over recent events regarding the misrepresentation of my work in Congress and consequent treatment in the media. The cavalier and blasphemous intentions ascribed to me on the Congressional floor bear little resemblance to reality. I am disturbed that the rush to judgment by certain members of Congress has been particularly swift and vindictive.

I am appalled by the claim of "anti-Christian bigotry" that has been attributed to my picture, "Piss Christ." The photograph, and the title itself, are ambiguously provocative but certainly not blasphemous. Over the years, I have addressed religion regularly in my art. My Catholic upbringing informs this work which helps me to redefine and personalize my relationship with God. My use of such bodily fluids as blood and urine in this context is parallel to Catholicism's obsession with "the body and blood of Christ." It is precisely in the exploration and juxtaposition of these symbols from which Christianity draws its strength. The photograph in question, like all my work, has multiple meanings and can be interpreted in various ways. So let us suppose that the picture is meant as a criticism of the billion dollar Christ-for-profit industry and the commercialization of spiritual values that permeates our society. That it is a condemnation of those who abuse the teachings of Christ for their own ignoble ends. Is the subject of religion so inviolate that it is not open to discussion? I think not.

In writing the majority opinion in the flag burning case, Justice William J. Brennan concluded, "We never before have held that the government may insure that a symbol be used to express one view of that symbol or its referents . . . to conclude that the government may permit designated symbols to be used to communicate only a limited set of messages would be to enter into having no discernible or defensible boundaries."

Artists often depend on the manipulation of symbols to present ideas and associations not always apparent in the symbols. If all such ideas and associations were evident there would be little need for artists to give expression to them. In short, there would be no need to make art.

Do we condemn the use of a swastika in a work of art that does not unequivocally denounce Nazism as anti-Semitic? Not when the artist is Jewish. Do we denounce as racist a painting or photograph that is demeaning African Americans? Not if the artist is black. When art is decontextualised, however, it can pose a problem and create misunderstanding.

Debate and discussion are at the heart of our democracy. In a free society, ideas, even difficult ones, are not dangerous. The only danger lies in repressing them.

"This action was illegal, but . . . it was legitimate"
José Bové

The French sheep farmer José Bové emerged in the late 1990s as one of the most controversial and well-known opponents of globalization. Alarmed by the impact of multinational agricultural and capitalist practices on farming and national cultures, Bové resorted to numerous civil disobedience tactics to raise public resistance.

His most notorious action took place in 1999 in Mileau, France, when he led a small group of activists in the dismantling of a McDonald's restaurant that was under construction. He alerted the police in advance, and the activists did the work in the middle of the day. The action was done in retaliation against a United States tariff against French cheese.

"This is a fight against free trade global capitalism," Bové said. "It's about the logic of a certain economic system, not an American system. It can be a struggle against any country, this one or that one. It's not against those who have an American passport."

Bové has also directed his actions against the agricultural industry many times. For example, in Brazil, he and more than one thousand Brazilian farmers raided a plantation owned by the United States company Monsanto and uprooted thousands of corn and soy bean plants, burned seeds, and destroyed numerous documents.

The transcript excerpted here comes from a court statement he made in 1998 after he and some colleagues destroyed stocks of genetically modified maize in France. When a French court sentenced him to jail for ten months, tens of thousands of people protested the sentence. French president Jacques Chirac reduced the sentence to six months. Two years later, Bové was sent to jail again for destroying genetically engineered corn.

TODAY, I AM PRESENT IN THIS COURT together with René Riesel and Francis Roux, accused of committing a serious crime according to the law. The alleged crime is: the destruction of sacks of genetically modified maize.

Yes, this is serious, and that's why I assume full responsibility. I am not going to hide behind collective, anonymous responsibility. . . . The strength of our union movement rests on this determination to mobilize free individuals who accept all the consequences of their acts knowing fully the motive for them.

Yes, on January 8, I participated in the destruction of genetically modified maize, which was stored in Novartis' grain silos in Nerac. And the only regret I have now is that I wasn't able to destroy more of it.

I knew that by acting in this way I was doing something illegal. But it was necessary, and we had no other choice. The way in which genetically modified agricultural products have been imposed on European countries didn't leave us with any alternative.

When was there a public debate on genetically modified organisms? When were farmers and consumers asked what they think about this? Never.

The decisions have been taken at the level of the World Trade Organization (WTO), and state machinery complies with the law of market forces. The WTO dictates its own law on the opening of trade barriers. The obligation to import bovine somatotropin meat from the USA is a good example of this. The Panel of the WTO, the true policeman of world trade, decides what's "good" for both countries and their people, without consultation or a right of appeal.

The countries or groups of countries which refuse the importation of bovine somatotropin meat or genetically modified products have to prove that these are dangerous, and not the inverse! The Codex Alimentarius, the norm dictated by the multinationals, is there to fix the rules of the game!

Why refuse something which is presented as "progress"? It's not because of old fashionedness, or regret for the "good old days." It's because of concern for the future, and because of a will to have a say in future development. I am not opposed to fundamental research. I think that it would be illusory and detrimental to want to curb it. On the other hand, I don't think that every application of research is necessarily desirable, at the human, social or environmental level. . . .

By destroying the genetically modified maize seeds on January 8 at the Novartis factory in Nerac, we wanted to put this short-sighted logic into the spotlight.

Yes, this action was illegal, but I lay claim to it because it was legitimate.

A democratic debate simply doesn't exist. The conspiracy of silence organized by the companies and the sovereign states is the sole logic which prevails. As with blood contaminated with the HIV virus, or mad cow disease, the public mustn't be alarmed. Everything has to be allowed to continue in silence.

By appearing before you today, I'm aware of being in breach of the law which wants every citizen to be content with expressing her or his views by simply putting their vote in the urn every six years.

But it's not in this way that social and economic problems are resolved—on the contrary. Through the action which we undertook and for which we are being judged, we kicked off a vast citizen's movement which refuses the use of GMOs in foodstuffs for animals and for humans. These actions will stop when this mad logic comes to a halt.

Yes, this action was illegal, but I lay claim to it because it was legitimate. I don't demand clemency, but justice. Either we have acted in everyone's interest and you will acquit us, or we have shaken the establishment and in that case you will punish us.

There is no other issue.

Protests Against Western Valentine's Day
Dukhtaran-e-Millat

Many groups in foreign cultures around the world have resisted the imposition of Western values. While some resistance focuses on the globalization, advances in technology, communication, and transportation that have allowed multinational corporations to push their products in non-Western nations with greater and greater ease, other protests focus on the prevalence of Western culture in movies, magazines, and music.

One perceived cultural threat is Valentine's Day. The Kashmiri Islamic group Dukhtaran-e-Millat (meaning "Daughters of the Community") took to the streets February 14, 2006, in central Srinagar in India to burn Valentine's Day cards, symbols of the Western idea of love being imposed on young Muslims. The Dukhtaran-e-Millat has been operating in Srinagar, which is part of the Kashmir section of India, since the early 1990s, when it initiated a campaign for Muslim women to wear burqas (or veils), which most Muslim women in Kashmir do not use. Activists applied spray paint to women who did not wear a veil.

CHAPTER 12
EXTREME PROTEST

INTRODUCTION

Extreme protest often blurs the line between protest and terrorism, between dissent and crime. Many protests today considered righteous were crimes when they occurred. The protesters were labeled criminals both by repressive dictatorships and sometimes by democratic governments. For example, Martin Luther King, Jr., and Mohandas K. Gandhi both spent time in jail for their protest actions, although today their actions are widely admired as examples of nonviolent protest.

Violent protesters, when they justify their actions at all, usually invoke the acts of such respected protesters. For example, the leaders of the American Revolution are repeatedly cited to justify taking up weapons in many different causes. What separates extreme protest from criminal activity seems to depend on one's perspective. Even within protest movements there is sometimes disagreement on the boundary; Benjamin Franklin strenuously objected to the Boston Tea Party because of its wanton destruction of property—that is, tea.

This chapter examines examples of protest deemed extreme based on one of two criteria. The first thread comprises protesters who aim to accomplish their goals by putting their own lives at risk. Self-immolation by Buddhist monks protesting religious oppression, volunteers who place themselves in the path of tanks or bulldozers to protect the innocent, and tree-sitters who spend weeks or even years living high above the ground to protect old-growth forests all fit this model of extreme protest.

The second thread comprises those who place the lives (or in slightly less extreme cases, the property) of others at risk, often targeting individuals with little or no direct responsibility for the acts being protested. The plotters of the 1605 attack on the British Parliament; John Brown, who attempted to foster slave revolts in the 1850s; and legions of modern-day suicide bombers, including the perpetrators of the September 11, 2001, attacks on the United States, all expected to kill the innocent along with the guilty.

Each of the documents presented in this chapter will be acceptable to some readers and objectionable to others. As editors, we, too, would define some of the events recorded as unacceptable forms of protest. However, collectively, these events and documents help to define the line between protest that benefits society and protest that harms it.

"Out of the love that I bear to some of your friends"

In 1605, a small group of British Catholics, distressed by continuing persecution from the Protestant leadership of England, decided to murder the king, queen, and most of the Protestant nobility by exploding a massive quantity of gunpowder in the cellars of the Parliament building. Their grievances included a law instituted by King James that imposed fines on those who did not attend Protestant church services. The plotters also planned to capture other members of the royal family and instigate a widespread Catholic rebellion. The conspirators, led by Robert Catesby, stored thirty-six barrels of gunpowder under Parliament—enough to have destroyed that building and a considerable surrounding area.

Less than two weeks before the appointed day, the rebels sent a letter to Lord Monteagle, a Catholic noble, in hopes of preventing the bomb from killing several Catholic members of Parliament. Lord Monteagle, however, proved less of an ally than the conspirators had hoped. He showed the letter to a member of King James's inner circle. A search of the cellars of Parliament ensued, and one of the conspirators, Guy Fawkes, was discovered guarding the gunpowder.

Fawkes was arrested, and King James authorized his torture to extract the names of the co-conspirators, who were also soon arrested. In 1606, the members of the conspiracy were hung, then drawn and quartered. *The Weekely Newes* reproduced the letter to Monteagle, as shown below, in its January 31, 1606, edition as part of its coverage of the executions.

MY LORD,—OUT OF THE LOVE that I bear to some of your friends I have a care of your preservation, therefore I would advise you, as you tender your life, to devise some excuse to shift of your attendance at this Parliament: for God and man have concurred to punish the wickedness of this time. And think not slightly of this advertisement, but retire yourself into your own country, where you may expect the event in safety. For though there be no appearance of any stir, yet I say they shall receive a terrible blow this Parliament, and yet they shall not see who hurt them. This counsel is not to be contemned, because it may do you good, and can do you no harm, for the danger is passed as soon as you have burnt this letter, and I hope God will give you the grace to make good use of it—to whose holy protection I commend you.

"Rally, Mohawks! Bring out your axes"

In 1767, in order to alleviate financial strain brought on by war, the British government passed the Townshend Acts, imposing stiff duties on certain products shipped from England to the American colonies, including tea.

In 1773, Parliament passed the Tea Act, allowing the East India Company to ship tea directly to the American colonies on its own ships, thereby avoiding the tax. This was a direct threat to colonial merchants and shippers, as it would allow the East India Company to sell tea at prices below those of American smugglers, and it cost colonial ships business. Colonists saw this as an attempt by the British government to enslave them economically and to violate their civil rights as British citizens. In protest, ships carrying the East India Company tea were turned away from Philadelphia and New York. In Boston, the governor—appointed by the crown—made plans to unload the tea under the protection of the British military.

On November 29 a handbill was distributed throughout Boston and surrounding towns. "Friends! Brethren! Countrymen! That worst of plagues, the detested tea, shipped for this port by the East India Company, is now arrived in the harbor; the hour of destruction, or manly opposition to the machinations of tyranny stares you in the face. Every friend to his country, to himself and posterity, is now called upon to meet at Faneuil Hall, at nine o'clock THIS DAY . . . to make united and successful resistance to this last, worst, and most destructive measure of administration."

The rebels' organizational meetings attracted up to five thousand people. On the night of December 16, 1773, some sixty colonists, partially disguised as Mohawk Indians, boarded the ships, and threw ninety thousand pounds of tea into the harbor—an event known in history as the Boston Tea Party. Two thousand people stood on Griffin's wharf to watch. As the "Mohawks" worked, they supposedly sang the song reproduced here. The "Warren and Revere" referred to were Joseph Warren, a physician and grand master of the Boston Lodge of Freemasons, and Paul Revere, patriot, silversmith, and senior grand deacon of the Boston Freemasons. The "Green Dragon" was a tavern in Boston's North End used by colonists as a meeting place to plan their acts of rebellion.

The event triggered a massive reaction. Mobs in other American port towns held similar "tea parties." Many, however, saw this not as justified protest, but simply as vandalism. Benjamin Franklin called it "an act of violent injustice" and offered to pay for the lost tea himself. The British government revoked Massachusetts's limited self-governance, closed the port of Boston (at the time one of the busiest in the colonies), and required colonists to provide room and board for British soldiers. These acts—part of the set of laws known in the colonies as the Intolerable Acts—inflamed colonial passions and led directly to the Revolutionary War.

Rally, Mohawks! Bring out your axes,
And tell King George we'll pay no taxes
On his foreign tea;
His threats are vain, and vain to think
To force our girls and wives to drink
His vile Bohea!
Then rally, boys, and hasten on
To meet our chiefs at the Green Dragon.

Our Warren's there and bold Revere,
With hands to do, and words to cheer,
For liberty and laws;

Our country's "braves" and firm defenders
Shall ne'er be left by true North-Enders
Fighting Freedom's cause!
Then rally, boys, and hasten on
To meet our chiefs at the Green Dragon.

"I must like them publish a card of denial"
Charles H. Langston

John Brown was among the most violently radical abolitionists. In 1856, in the midst of the feud over whether Kansas would be a free or slave territory, Brown and his followers brutally killed several pro-slavery whites by splitting open their heads and cutting off their arms.

By 1859, Brown decided to raid the federal arsenal at Harpers Ferry and use the 100,000 rifles and muskets stored there to arm slaves for a mass revolt. Brown succeeded in taking the arsenal on October 16, 1859, but the Virginia militia and a squad of Marines arrived more swiftly than any slaves who might have been bold enough to join him. Most of Brown's nineteen raiders were killed or captured, and Brown himself was hung for murder, treason, and inciting insurrection.

Brown's attack captivated the country and divided the public. Throughout the South he was condemned, reviled, and believed a madman. But many in the North saw his actions not as terrorism, but as a justified attack upon the unacceptable institution of slavery. Henry David Thoreau responded to Brown's execution by saying, "Some 1800 years ago, Christ was crucified. This morning, Captain Brown was hung." On the day of his execution, Brown said, "I, John Brown, am now quite certain that the crimes of this guilty land will never be purged away but with blood." Within two years his prophecy had come true, and soldiers in the Union army were marching to the morbid song "John Brown's Body":

John Brown was a hero, undaunted, true and brave;
Kansas knew his valor when he fought her rights to save;
And now though the grass grows green above his grave,
His truth is marching on.

He captured Harpers Ferry with his nineteen men so few,
And he frightened "Old Virginny" till she trembled through and through,
They hung him for a traitor, themselves a traitor crew,
But his truth is marching on.

Many African Americans saw Brown as a hero. Here, in an excerpt of a letter printed in the *Cleveland Plain Dealer* the month after the raid, Charles H. Langston (the grandfather of twentieth-century poet Langston Hughes) offers his "card," or denial, of involvement in the plot. Such cards were common in the weeks following the raid, as authorities searched for individuals who had perhaps conspired with Brown but not been present at the raid. But Hughes's card is unusual in its frank admiration for Brown.

MR. EDITOR—Card writing seems to be the order of the day, particularly with reference to Capt. John Brown and his insurrectionary movements at Harper's Ferry. We have heard through the public journals from many of the great men and some of the great women too who are said to be connected with the "bloody attempt to dissolve the Union," "to subvert and overturn the Government," "to push forward the irrepressible conflict," "and to incite the slaves of Virginia and Maryland to cut their masters' throats." Giddings, Hale, Smith, the Plumbs, and others have denied any knowledge of, or connection with the "mad scheme or its crazy perpetrators." Why the hasty denial? Why all this hot haste to throw off the imaginary disgrace or danger, which may grow out of complicity with this daring friend of Liberty and lover of mercy? Were the noble old hero and his brave and faithful followers, engaged in a mean, selfish, and dastardly work? Were they "plotting crime" against the rights or liberties of any human being? Were they in Virginia to take the property or lives of men who respect the rights of life, liberty or property in others? Capt. Brown was engaged in no vile, base, sordid, malicious or selfish enterprise. His aims and ends were lofty, noble, generous, benevolent, humane and Godlike. His actions were in perfect harmony with, and resulted from the teaching of the Bible, of our Revolutionary fathers and of every true and faithful anti-slavery man in this country and the world.

Does not the holy Bible teach that it is the duty of the strong and powerful to assist the weak and helpless, that the rich should succor the poor and needy? Does it not command us to remember those in bonds as being bound with them? Does it not tell us to loose the bonds of wickedness, undo the heavy burdens and let the oppressed go free? Does not the Bible plainly say, "whatsoever ye would that man shall do to you, do ye even so to them?" and further: "he that stealeth a man and selleth him or if he be found in his hand, he shall surely be put to death."

Did not Capt. Brown act in consonance with these Biblical principles and injunctions? . . . His actions then are only the results of his faithfulness to the plain teaching of the word of God.

The renowned fathers of our celebrated revolution taught the world that "resistance to tyrants is obedience to God," that all men are created equal, and have the inalienable right to life and liberty. . . . They also ordained and established a constitution to secure the blessings of liberty to themselves and their *posterity*. (It is to be remembered that they have a large colored posterity in the Southern States). And they further declared that when any government becomes destructive of these ends, namely, life, liberty, justice and happiness, it is the right of the people to abolish it and to institute a new government.—On these pure and holy principles they fearlessly entered into a seven years war against the most powerful nation of the earth. . . .

Did not Capt. Brown act in accordance with the foregoing revolutionary principles? Did not he obey God by resisting tyrants? Did he not in all things show his implicit faith in the equality of all men? and their unalienable right to life and liberty? When he saw that the governments of the South were destructive of these ends, did he not aim to abolish them and to institute a new government laying its foundation on such principles as to him seemed most likely to secure the happiness and safety of the people? . . .

If then, Brown acted on these pure and righteous principles, why are the friends of justice, liberty and right so hasty in denying all connections with him or sympathy with his ends and aims? Perhaps they see the bloody gallows of the "affrighted chivalry" rising before them in awful horror. Or more probably they see a political grave yearning to receive them.

But to speak of myself I have no political prospects and therefore no political fears! for my black face and curly hair doom me in the land of equality to political damnation and that beyond the possibility of redemption. But I have a neck as dear to me as Smith's, Hale's or Giddings', and therefore I must like them publish a card of denial. So here it is. But what shall I deny? I cannot deny that I feel the very deepest sympathy with the Immortal John Brown in his heroic and daring efforts to free the slaves.

"An oppressed class which does not strive to . . . use arms . . . deserves to be treated like slaves"
Vladimir I. Lenin

Vladimir Ilyich Lenin was the most famous of the revolutionaries who overthrew the tsarist government of Russia in 1917, and he eventually became the first communist dictator of the Soviet Union. While many socialists during World War I advocated pacifism, Lenin saw armed struggle as necessary if the powerless were to achieve their goals.

The essay excerpted here was published by the magazine *Jugend-Internationale* in October 1917, just as Lenin led the Bolsheviks against the provisional government that had replaced the czar. In it, Lenin argued for armed struggle and even said that women of the proletariat—or working class—should encourage their sons to enroll in the military so they could learn military tactics to use against the bourgeoisie, or moneyed class. An unwillingness to use violence to pursue the rights of the proletariat, Lenin asserted, was as much as agreeing to remain oppressed.

Lenin's reliance on force continued after the revolution. He established a secret police, killed political opponents, and limited freedom of the press. In the national assembly election of November 1917, Lenin's Bolshevik party won only a quarter of the more than 40 million votes cast; Lenin dissolved the elected national assembly after its first meeting.

AN OPPRESSED CLASS which does not strive to learn to use arms, to acquire arms, only deserves to be treated like slaves. We cannot, unless we have become bourgeois pacifists or opportunists, forget that we are living in a class society from which there is no way out, nor can there be, save through the class struggle. In every class society, whether based on slavery, serfdom, or, as at present, wage-labor, the oppressor class is always armed. Not only the modern standing army, but even the modern militia—and even in the most democratic bourgeois republics, Switzerland, for instance—represent the bourgeoisie armed *against* the proletariat. That is such an elementary truth that it is hardly necessary to dwell upon it. Suffice it to point to the use of troops *against* strikers in all capitalist countries.

A bourgeoisie armed against the proletariat is one of the biggest fundamental and cardinal facts of modern capitalist society. . . . Our slogan must be: arming of the proletariat to defeat, expropriate and disarm the bourgeoisie. These are the only tactics possible for a revolutionary class, tactics that follow logically from, and are dictated by, the whole *objective development* of capitalist militarism. Only *after* the proletariat has disarmed the bourgeoisie will it be able, without betraying its world-historic mission, to consign all armaments to the scrap-heap. And the proletariat will undoubtedly do this, but *only when this condition has been fulfilled, certainly not before.* . . .

. . . Today the imperialist bourgeoisie militarizes the youth as well as the adults; tomorrow, it may begin militarizing the women. Our attitude should be: All the better! Full speed ahead! For the faster we move, the nearer shall we be to the armed uprising against capitalism. . . .

. . . Women and teenage children fought in the Paris Commune side by side with the men. It will be no different in the coming battles for the overthrow of the bourgeoisie. Proletarian women will not look on passively as poorly armed or unarmed workers are shot down by the well-armed forces of the bourgeoisie. They will take to arms, as they did in 1871, and from the cowed nations of today—or more correctly, from the present-day labor movement, disorganized more by the opportunists than by the governments—there will undoubtedly arise, sooner or later, but with absolute certainty, an international league of the "terrible nations" of the revolutionary proletariat.

The whole of social life is now being militarized. Imperialism is a fierce struggle of the Great Powers for the division and redivision of the world. It is therefore bound to lead to further militarization in all countries, even in neutral and small ones. How will proletarian women oppose this? Only by cursing all war and everything military, only by demanding disarmament? The women of an oppressed and really revolutionary class will never accept that shameful role. They will say to their sons: "You will soon be grown up. You will be given a gun. Take it and learn the military art properly. The proletarians need this knowledge not to shoot your brothers, the workers of other countries, as is being done in the present war, and as the traitors to socialism are telling you to do. They need it to fight the bourgeoisie of their own country, to put an end to exploitation, poverty and war, and not by pious wishes, but by defeating and disarming the bourgeoisie."

"What happened exceeded our boldest dreams"
Mordecai Anielewicz

At the beginning of 1943, some fifty thousand Jews remained in the Warsaw ghetto, where they had been herded by the German army for transport to death camps. More than three hundred thousand Jews had already been shipped out of Warsaw for extermination in gas chambers. The remaining Jews made the decision to band together and fight for their lives. They took control of the ghetto in January. On April 19, the Germans attempted to recapture it by force.

Under the leadership of twenty-four-year-old Mordecai Anielewicz, the Jews resisted, driving out the *Schutzstaffel* (better known as the SS) and the German army. The Germans brought in tanks, artillery, and more than two thousand soldiers to deal with the ragtag, poorly armed Jewish resistance. They eventually burned most of the ghetto, taking the command center on May 8 and retaking the ghetto as a whole by May 16.

Anielewicz killed himself to avoid capture. He wrote the letter excerpted here on April 23, 1943, to Yitzhak Cukierman, a Jewish resistance fighter who found himself outside the ghetto as the uprising began and was unable to subsequently return. Cukierman led a Jewish force in the general uprising of Warsaw in 1944 and survived the war.

IT IS IMPOSSIBLE to put into words what we have been through. One thing is clear, what happened exceeded our boldest dreams. The Germans ran twice from the ghetto. One of our companies held out for 40 minutes and another for more than 6 hours. The mine set in the "brushmakers" area exploded. Several of our companies attacked the dispersing Germans. Our losses in manpower are minimal. That is also an achievement. Y. [Yechiel] fell. He fell a hero, at the machine-gun. I feel that great things are happening and what we dared do is of great, enormous importance. . . .

Beginning from today we shall shift over to the partisan tactic. Three battle companies will move out tonight, with two tasks: reconnaissance and obtaining arms. Do you remember, short-range weapons are of no use to us. We use such weapons only rarely. What we need urgently: grenades, rifles, machine-guns and explosives.

It is impossible to describe the conditions under which the Jews of the ghetto are now living. Only a few will be able to hold out. The remainder will die sooner or later. Their fate is decided. In almost all the hiding places in which thousands are concealing themselves it is not possible to light a candle for lack of air.

With the aid of our transmitter we heard the marvelous report on our fighting by the "Shavit" radio station. The fact that we are remembered beyond the ghetto walls encourages us in our struggle. Peace go with you, my friend! Perhaps we may still meet again! The dream of my life has risen to become fact. Self-defense in the ghetto will have been a reality. Jewish armed resistance and revenge are facts. I have been a witness to the magnificent, heroic fighting of Jewish men in battle.

Self-immolations of Vietnamese Buddhist Monks: "His body was slowly withering and shriveling up, his head blackening and charring"

On May 8, 1963, in the city of Hue, South Vietnamese soldiers opened fire on marchers peacefully celebrating the Buddha's 2,527th birthday, killing nine of them. The killings were part of ongoing oppression of Buddhists by the government of Vietnamese president Ngo Dinh Diem.

Soon daily protests began in Saigon. These protests escalated on June 11, 1963, when Buddhists organized the voluntary immolation of the monk Thich Quang Duc; other monks helped to set him on fire, and a small demonstration was held to prevent fire trucks from reaching the scene. The self-immolations continued through October and included the one pictured here, photographed on October 5, 1963. A total of seven Vietnamese monks and nuns sacrificed themselves in protest of oppression of Buddhists.

The self-immolations brought public attention in the United States, South Vietnam's main international supporter. In the week following the first immolation, the *New York Times* covered the protests on the front page. *New York Times* reporter David Halberstam described the event in

his 1965 book *The Making of a Quagmire*: "Flames were coming from a human being; his body was slowly withering and shriveling up, his head blackening and charring. In the air was the smell of burning human flesh; human beings burn surprisingly quickly. Behind me I could hear the sobbing of the Vietnamese who were now gathering. I was too shocked to cry, too confused to take notes or ask questions, too bewildered to even think. . . . As he burned he never moved a muscle, never uttered a sound, his outward composure in sharp contrast to the wailing people around him."

President Diem declared martial law in August and sent troops into the Buddhist temples to round up leaders of the demonstrating sects. Army officers, who had long been dissatisfied with Diem and did not like being blamed for the actions against the Buddhists, began planning a coup, with at least tacit acquiescence from the United States government. President Diem was deposed on November 1, 1963, and assassinated the next day, leading to a period of turmoil. Several different governments took office and resigned throughout 1964. Ineffective governance in South Vietnam opened the door for North Vietnamese military success, which in turn drew the United States into the conflict.

"It is an idea for which I am prepared to die": Statement at the Opening of the Rivonia Trial
Nelson Mandela

Nelson Mandela became the first president of a racially integrated South Africa in 1994. His presidency capped a remarkable transformation of South African society and came after he had served twenty-six years of a life sentence for terrorism. His conviction sprang from his violent actions against the apartheid laws, which created strict separation of the races and denied basic civil rights (including the right to vote) to black South Africans, who made up three-fourths of the nation's population.

Mandela was one of the founders and the first commander of the military wing of the African National Congress—*Umkhonto we Sizwe*—usually translated as "Spear of the Nation." At his 1964 trial for sabotage, Mandela made the opening statement excerpted below, carefully laying out both the reasons for resorting to violence and the types of violence planned. Mandela laid out the history of black African leaders' peaceful quest for equal rights, beginning with reasoned arguments, and progressing to nonviolent resistance. The apartheid regime's response to these actions—not compromise or reform, but increasing repression—made peaceful protest less and less possible. Mandela argued that the controlled violence aimed at economic targets was the only option available to prevent a bloody civil war.

I AM THE FIRST ACCUSED. I hold a Bachelor's Degree in Arts and practised as an attorney in Johannesburg for a number of years in partnership with Oliver Tambo. I am a convicted prisoner serving five years for leaving the country without a permit and for inciting people to go on strike at the end of May 1961.

At the outset, I want to say that the suggestion made by the State in its opening that the struggle in South Africa is under the influence of foreigners or communists is wholly incorrect. I have done whatever I did, both as an individual and as a leader of my people, because of my experience in South Africa and my own proudly felt African background, and not because of what any outsider might have said. . . .

Having said this, I must deal immediately and at some length with the question of violence. Some of the things so far told to the Court are true and some are untrue. I do not, however, deny that I planned sabotage. I did not plan it in a spirit of recklessness, nor because I have any love of violence. I planned it as a result of a calm and sober assessment of the political situation that had arisen after many years of tyranny, exploitation, and oppression of my people by the Whites.

I admit immediately that I was one of the persons who helped to form Umkhonto we Sizwe, and that I played a prominent role in its affairs until I was arrested in August 1962. . . .

I deny that Umkhonto was responsible for a number of acts which clearly fell outside the policy of the organisation, and which have been charged in the indictment against us. I do not know what justification there was for these acts, but to demonstrate that they could not have been authorized by Umkhonto, I want to refer briefly to the roots and policy of the organization.

I have already mentioned that I was one of the persons who helped to form Umkhonto. I, and the others who started the organization, did so for two reasons. Firstly, we believed that as a result of Government policy, violence by the African people had become inevitable, and that unless responsible leadership was given to canalize and control the feelings of our people, there would be outbreaks of terrorism which would produce an intensity of bitterness and hostility between the various races of this country which is not produced even by war. Secondly, we felt that without violence there would be no way open to the African people to succeed in their struggle against the principle of white supremacy. All lawful modes of expressing opposition to this principle had been closed by legislation, and we were placed in a position in which we had either to accept a permanent state of inferiority, or to defy the Government. We chose to defy the law. We first broke the law in a way which avoided any recourse to violence; when this form was legislated against, and then the Government resorted to a show of force to crush opposition to its policies, only then did we decide to answer violence with violence.

But the violence which we chose to adopt was not terrorism. We who formed Umkhonto were all members of the African National Congress, and had behind us the ANC tradition of non-violence and negotiation as a means of solving political disputes. We believe that South Africa belongs to all the people who live in it, and not to one group, be it black or white. We did not want an interracial war, and tried to avoid it to the last minute. . . .

The African National Congress was formed in 1912 to defend the rights of the African people which had been seriously curtailed by the South Africa Act, and which were then being threatened by the Native Land Act. For thirty-seven years—that is until 1949—it adhered strictly to a constitutional struggle. It put forward demands and resolutions; it sent delegations to the Government in the belief that African grievances could be settled through peaceful discussion and that Africans could advance gradually to full political rights. But White Governments remained unmoved, and the rights of Africans became less instead of becoming greater. In the words of my leader, Chief Lutuli, who became President of the ANC in 1952, and who was later awarded the Nobel Peace Prize:

> who will deny that thirty years of my life have been spent knocking in vain, patiently, moderately, and modestly at a closed and barred door? What have been the fruits of moderation? The past thirty years have seen the greatest number of laws restricting our rights and progress, until today we have reached a stage where we have almost no rights at all.

Even after 1949, the ANC remained determined to avoid violence. At this time, however, there was a change from the strictly constitutional means of protest which had been employed in the past. The change was embodied in a decision which was taken to protest against apartheid legislation by peaceful, but unlawful, demonstrations against certain laws. Pursuant to this policy the ANC launched the Defiance Campaign, in which I was placed in charge of volunteers. This campaign was based on the principles of passive resistance. More than 8,500 people defied apartheid laws and went to jail. Yet there was not a single instance of violence in the course of this campaign on the part of any defier. . . .

During the Defiance Campaign, the Public Safety Act and the Criminal Law Amendment Act were passed. These Statutes provided harsher penalties for offences committed by way of protests against laws. Despite this, the protests continued and the ANC adhered to its policy of non-violence. In 1956, 156 leading members of the Congress Alliance, including myself, were arrested on a charge of high treason and charges under the Suppression of Communism Act. . . . We were acquitted on all counts. . . .

In 1960 there was the shooting at Sharpeville, which resulted in the proclamation of a state of emergency and the declaration of the ANC as an unlawful organization. My colleagues and I, after careful consideration, decided that we would not obey this decree. The African people were not part of the Government and did not make the laws by which they were governed. We believed in the words of the Universal Declaration of Human Rights, that "the will of the people shall be the basis of authority of the Government," and for us to accept the banning was equivalent to accepting the silencing of the Africans for all time. The ANC refused to dissolve, but instead went underground. We believed it was our duty to preserve this organization which had been built up with almost fifty years of unremitting toil. I have no doubt that no self-respecting White political organization would disband itself if declared illegal by a government in which it had no say. . . .

It must not be forgotten that by this time violence had, in fact, become a feature of the South African political scene. There had been violence in 1957 when the women of Zeerust were ordered to carry passes; there was violence in 1958 with the enforcement of cattle culling in Sekhukhuniland; there was violence in 1959 when the people of Cato Manor protested against pass raids; there was violence in 1960 when the Government attempted to impose Bantu Authorities in Pondoland. Thirty-nine Africans died in these disturbances. In 1961 there had been riots in Warmbaths, and all this time the Transkei had been a seething mass of unrest. Each disturbance pointed clearly to the inevitable growth among Africans of the belief that violence was the only way out—it showed that a Government which uses force to maintain its rule teaches the oppressed to use force to oppose it. . . .

At the beginning of June 1961, after a long and anxious assessment of the South African situation, I, and some colleagues, came to the conclusion that as violence in this country was inevitable, it would be unrealistic and wrong for African leaders to continue preaching peace and non-violence at a time when the Government met our peaceful demands with force.

This conclusion was not easily arrived at. It was only when all else had failed, when all channels of peaceful protest had been barred to us, that the decision was made to embark on violent forms of political struggle, and to form Umkhonto we Sizwe. We did so not because we desired such a course, but solely because the Government had left us with no other choice. In the Manifesto of Umkhonto published on 16 December 1961, which is Exhibit AD, we said:

> The time comes in the life of any nation when there remain only two choices—submit or fight. That time has now come to South Africa. We shall not submit and we have no choice but to hit back by all means in our power in defence of our people, our future, and our freedom.

This was our feeling in June of 1961 when we decided to press for a change in the policy of the National Liberation Movement. I can only say that I felt morally obliged to do what I did. . . .

Four forms of violence were possible. There is sabotage, there is guerrilla warfare, there is terrorism, and there is open revolution. We chose to adopt the first method and to exhaust it before taking any other decision.

In the light of our political background the choice was a logical one. Sabotage did not involve loss of life, and it offered the best hope for future race relations. Bitterness would be kept to a minimum and, if the policy bore fruit, democratic government could become a reality. . . .

This then was the plan. Umkhonto was to perform sabotage, and strict instructions were given to its members right from the start, that on no account were they to injure or kill people in planning or carrying out operations. . . .

During my lifetime I have dedicated myself to this struggle of the African people. I have fought against white domination, and I have fought against black domination. I have cherished the ideal of a democratic and free society in which all persons live together in harmony and with equal opportunities. It is an ideal which I hope to live for and to achieve. But if needs be, it is an ideal for which I am prepared to die.

The Legacy of Luna
Julia Butterfly Hill

Extreme protest is not always violent. In November of 1997, a young woman named Julia Butterfly Hill sought out activists working to save ancient redwoods in California and volunteered for a tree-sit—a direct action in which protesters live 24/7 in trees scheduled for harvest. The assumption—usually correct—is that logging companies won't cut down trees with people in them.

For Hill, it was the start of two years living on a tiny platform 180 feet off the ground in a one thousand-year-old tree known as Luna. With the help of a support team that brought provisions and carried away her trash, Hill survived hurricane-force winds, ice storms, frostbite, a prolonged effort by the logging company to halt her food deliveries, and two years without hot showers or other everyday comforts. She came down when the Pacific Lumber Company agreed to preserve the tree and a two-hundred-foot buffer area around it.

In this selection from her memoir *The Legacy of Luna*, Hill had been living in the tree for six months.

BY MANY GAUGES, the tree-sit had been a tremendous success. It had become known across the country, even around the world, informing and inspiring many. Incredible press coverage, both domestic and international, had helped to legitimize direct action in mainstream society, which represented a huge shift away from earlier negative stereotyping of *environmentalists*. Already, these factors alone had taken the tree-sit far beyond my wildest imaginings and expectations.

But many people continued to ask, "What has it really accomplished?" A thousand-year-old tree, condemned to death, had been granted a reprieve for six months, while the devastating clear-cuts and the destruction of old-growth forests continued all around me.

The largest local paper, the *Times-Standard,* published in Eureka, California, ran an editorial entitled, "Time's Right to Put an End to Protest." They said:

Six months in a tree is an astonishing physical accomplishment, which hardly needs to be prolonged. There is a curve of diminishing effect in attention-seeking—the most arresting novelty eventually becomes stale news. A year in a tree is not necessarily a bigger story than six months in a tree, and two or three years ceases to be news at all.

That's what the local press thought of this tree-sit—it was a story, a novelty, an attention-getting device. It was narrow-minded and myopic. They called it "an open-ended endurance test," and they said that Luna was not "an especially notable tree" because it did not set any "size records."

How could they have so totally missed the point? I did not go up to live in Luna because she sets any size records. I did not stay to set any endurance records. To me, the tree-sit was not about records of any kind. It was not just a "novelty." It wasn't even about me. If it had been about any of those things, I would have gone down long before this point. I had put my life in a critical position to try to show people what was really at stake. These old-growth forests, once destroyed, would never return. This was not to gain a spotlight for me but to shine a beacon on something that was about to vanish forever. It was about the forests.

Letter to America

Osama bin Laden

Osama bin Laden is the founder and leader of the al-Qaeda terrorist network. In 1996 he issued a fatwa, or religious legal declaration, calling on believers to attack the United States. On September 11, 2001, al-Qaeda conducted a coordinated attack on New York City and Washington, D.C., using four hijacked airliners as suicide bombs. Two of the airliners crashed into the World Trade Center, destroying it, while a third hit the Pentagon. The fourth crashed in a field in Pennsylvania after passengers rebelled against the hijackers. To Americans and other Westerners, the attacks were horrific acts of terrorism, but to bin Laden and his sympathizers they represented justified acts of protest.

While hiding from the ensuing worldwide manhunt, bin Laden released videotapes and letters putting forward his views, as in the November 2002 open letter to America excerpted below. The letter first appeared on Islamic Web sites sympathetic to al-Qaeda and was translated and printed in full by the *Observer* in the United Kingdom. (The following excerpt is taken from that translation.) U.S. papers did not print the letter, perhaps in part because it was impossible to authenticate. The *New York Times*, for example, referred to the letter only in a four-sentence aside in an article on the capture of an al-Qaeda member in Kuwait.

In the letter, as in many of his other writings, bin Laden portrayed attacks against the United States as righteous protest in response to U.S. actions. In sections of the letter not included here, bin Laden cited the following U.S. activities as offensive to Muslims: pollution of the atmosphere and the refusal to sign the Kyoto protocol, refusal to convert to Islam, charging interest on loans, tolerance of homosexuality, use of women in advertising and marketing, obsession with sex, use of alcohol and drugs, alleged tolerance of incest, and unwillingness to follow Islamic laws based on the Koran.

SOME AMERICAN WRITERS have published articles under the title "On what basis are we fighting?" These articles have generated a number of responses, some of which adhered to the truth and were based on Islamic Law, and others which have not. Here we wanted to outline the truth—as an explanation and warning—hoping for Allah's reward, seeking success and support from Him.

While seeking Allah's help, we form our reply based on two questions directed at the Americans:

(Q1) Why are we fighting and opposing you?

(Q2) What are we calling you to, and what do we want from you?

As for the first question: Why are we fighting and opposing you? The answer is very simple:

(1) Because you attacked us and continue to attack us.

a) You attacked us in Palestine:

(i) Palestine, which has sunk under military occupation for more than 80 years. The British handed over Palestine, with your help and your support, to the Jews, who have occupied it for more than 50 years; years overflowing with oppression, tyranny, crimes, killing, expulsion, destruction and devastation. The creation and continuation of Israel is one of the greatest crimes, and you are the leaders of its criminals. . . .

(ii) It brings us both laughter and tears to see that you have not yet tired of repeating your fabricated lies that the Jews have a historical right to Palestine, as it was promised to them in the Torah. Anyone who disputes with them on this alleged fact is accused of anti-Semitism. This is one of the most fallacious, widely-circulated fabrications in history. The people of Palestine are pure Arabs and original Semites. It is the Muslims who are the inheritors of Moses (peace be upon him) and the inheritors of the real Torah that has not been changed. . . .

(b) You attacked us in Somalia; you supported the Russian atrocities against us in Chechnya, the Indian oppression against us in Kashmir, and the Jewish aggression against us in Lebanon.

(c) Under your supervision, consent and orders, the governments of our countries which act as your agents, attack us on a daily basis;

(i) These governments prevent our people from establishing the Islamic Shariah [a code of laws based on the Koran], using violence and lies to do so.

(ii) These governments give us a taste of humiliation, and places us in a large prison of fear and subdual.

(iii) These governments steal our Ummah's wealth and sell them to you at a paltry price [Ummah refers to all Muslims collectively].

(iv) These governments have surrendered to the Jews, and handed them most of Palestine, acknowledging the existence of their state over the dismembered limbs of their own people.

(v) The removal of these governments is an obligation upon us, and a necessary step to free the Ummah, to make the Shariah the supreme law and to regain Palestine. And our fight against these governments is not separate from our fight against you.

(d) You steal our wealth and oil at paltry prices because of your international influence and military threats. This theft is indeed the biggest theft ever witnessed by mankind in the history of the world.

(e) Your forces occupy our countries; you spread your military bases throughout them; you corrupt our lands, and you besiege our sanctities, to protect the security of the Jews and to ensure the continuity of your pillage of our treasures.

(f) You have starved the Muslims of Iraq, where children die every day. It is a wonder that more than 1.5 million Iraqi children have died as a result of your sanctions, and you did not show concern. Yet when 3000 of your people died, the entire world rises and has not yet sat down.

(g) You have supported the Jews in their idea that Jerusalem is their eternal capital, and agreed to move your embassy there. With your help and under your protection, the Israelis are planning to destroy the Al-Aqsa mosque. Under the protection of your weapons, Sharon entered the Al-Aqsa mosque, to pollute it as a preparation to capture and destroy it.

(2) These tragedies and calamities are only a few examples of your oppression and aggression against us. It is commanded by our religion and intellect that the oppressed have a right to return the aggression. Do not await anything from us but Jihad, resistance and revenge. Is it in any way rational to expect that after America has attacked us for more than half a century, that we will then leave her to live in security and peace?!! . . .

. . . America does not understand the language of manners and principles, so we are addressing it using the language it understands.

(Q2) As for the second question that we want to answer: What are we calling you to, and what do we want from you?

(1) The first thing that we are calling you to is Islam.

(a) The religion of the Unification of God; of freedom from associating partners with Him, and rejection of this; of complete love of Him, the Exalted; of complete submission to His Laws; and of the discarding of all the opinions, orders, theories and religions which contradict with the religion He sent down to His Prophet Muhammad (peace be upon him). Islam is the religion of all the prophets, and makes no distinction between them—peace be upon them all.

It is to this religion that we call you; the seal of all the previous religions. It is the religion of Unification of God, sincerity, the best of manners, righteousness, mercy, honour, purity, and piety. It is the religion of showing kindness to others, establishing justice between them, granting them their rights, and defending the oppressed and the persecuted. It is the religion of enjoining the good and forbidding the evil with the hand, tongue and heart. It is the religion of Jihad in the way of Allah so that Allah's Word and religion reign Supreme. And it is the religion of unity and agreement on the obedience to Allah, and total equality between all people, without regarding their colour, sex, or language. . . .

(2) The second thing we call you to, is to stop your oppression, lies, immorality and debauchery that has spread among you.

(a) We call you to be a people of manners, principles, honour, and purity; to reject the immoral acts of fornication, homosexuality, intoxicants, gambling's [sic], and trading with interest.

We call you to all of this that you may be freed from that which you have become caught up in; that you may be freed from the deceptive lies that you are a great nation, that your leaders spread amongst you to conceal from you the despicable state to which you have reached.

(b) It is saddening to tell you that you are the worst civilization witnessed by the history of mankind. . . .

My Name Is Rachel Corrie

Rachel Corrie

Alan Rickman and Katharine Viner, editors

On March 16, 2003, a twenty-three-year-old American was run over and killed by an Israeli army bulldozer. Rachel Corrie was in the Gaza Strip, then occupied by Israel, as part of the International Solidarity Movement (ISM), an organization founded in 2001 by Palestinian, Israeli, and American activists to promote nonviolent resistance to Israeli occupation of Gaza and the West Bank. Like many other extreme protesters, ISM volunteers knowingly put their lives at risk, in this case by serving as human shields for Palestinian civilians and by standing or sitting in the path of tanks and bulldozers that were attempting to demolish Palestinian homes.

Corrie's death evoked tremendous controversy, much of it around the still-disputed question as to whether the bulldozer driver had seen Corrie or not, and thus whether her death was an accident or a murder.

In 2005, a one-woman play based on Corrie's journals and e-mails opened in London. Journalist Katharine Viner and actor Alan Rickman edited Corrie's writings into a compelling narrative. The play, directed by Rickman, was first presented at the Royal Court Theater, London on April 7, 2005, and revived at the Royal Court Theater in October 2005; gaining both critical and audience acclaim. It was scheduled for production in spring 2006 in New York when the theater hosting the production suddenly withdrew—creating still more controversy. The play subsequently transferred to the Playhouse Theater in London's West End in March 2006 and was first produced in the U.S. at the Minetta Lane Theater in New York City in October 2006.

In the final moments of the play, excerpted below, Corrie muses in an e-mail to her mother on the situation in Gaza and her role there. The play concludes with an eyewitness account of Corrie's death from another ISM volunteer.

MOM.

. . . I thought a lot about what you said about Palestinian violence not helping the situation. 60,000 people from Rafah worked in Israel two years ago. Now only 600 can go there for jobs. . . .

Sources of economic growth are all completely destroyed—the airport (runways demolished, totally closed); the border for trade with Egypt (now with a sniper tower in the middle of the crossing); access to the ocean (completely cut off the last two years). . . .

If any of us had our lives and welfare completely strangled and lived with children in a shrinking place where we knew that soldiers and tanks and bull-dozers could come for us at any moment, with no means of economic survival and our houses demolished; if they came and destroyed all the greenhouses that we'd been cultivating for the last however long do you not think, in a similar situation, most people would defend themselves as best they could?

. . . The vast majority of Palestinians right now, as far as I can tell are engaging in Gandhian non-violent resistance. Who do you think I'm staying with, in houses that are going to be demolished amid gunfire? Who do you think are staffing the human-rights centers? What do you think this Palestinian-led movement is that I joined that engages in non-violent direct action? Who do you think these families are that I tell you about, who won't take any money from us even though they are very, very poor, and who say to us: "We are not a hotel. We help you because we think maybe you will go and tell people in your country that you lived with Muslims. We think they will know that we are good people. We are quiet people. We just want peace"? Do you think I'm hanging out with Hamas fighters? These people are being shot at every day and they continue to go about their business as best they can in the sights of machine guns and rocket launchers. Isn't that basically the epitome of non-violent resistance? . . .

I'm having a hard time right now. Just feel sick to my stomach from being doted on very sweetly, by people who are facing doom. I know that from the United States it all sounds like hyperbole. A lot of the time the kindness of the people here, coupled with the willful destruction of their lives, makes it seem unreal to me. I can't believe that something like this can happen in the world without a bigger outcry. . . .

For a long time I've been operating from a certain core assumption that we are all essentially the same inside, and that our differences are by and large situational. That goes for everybody—Bush, Bin Laden, Tony Blair, me, you, Sarah, Chris, Dad, Gram, Palestinians, everybody of any particular religion. I know there is a good chance that this assumption actually is false. But it's convenient, because it always leads to questions about the way privilege shelters people from the consequences of their actions. It's also convenient because it leads to some level of forgiveness, whether justified or not. . . .

. . . Anyway, I'm rambling. Just want to tell my mom that I'm really scared, and questioning my fundamental belief in the goodness of human nature. This has to stop. I think it is a good idea for us all to drop everything and devote our lives to making this stop. I don't think it's an extremist thing to do any more. I still really want to dance around to Pat Benatar and have boyfriends and make comics for my co-workers. But I also want this to stop. . . .

When I come back from Palestine I probably will have nightmares and constantly feel guilty for not being here, but I can channel that into more work. Coming here is one of the better things I've ever done.

I love you and Dad. Sorry for the diatribe.

A door opens.

Okay, some strange men are offering me some peas, so I need to eat and thank them.

She leaves.

From the TV set, a recording of the transcript of an eyewitness account by Tom Dale.

Rachel walked to place herself in between the home and the bulldozer. As the bulldozer turned towards them, it had about 20 metres or 10 seconds clear time directly with her in its view to see where she was. It continued toward her at some pace with a mound of earth building up in front of it. And as the mound of earth reached Rachel she obviously felt that in order to keep her balance, to keep her footing she had to climb on to this mound of earth to prevent being overwhelmed by it. When she did this it put her head and shoulders clearly above the top of the bulldozer blade and therefore clearly in the view of the bulldozer driver, so he knew absolutely that she was there.

She falls down the mound of earth and out of sight of the driver; so he has essentially pushed her forward down the mound of earth. And then she starts to slide and then you see one then both of her feet disappear and he simply continued until she was, or the place where she had been, was directly beneath the cockpit of the bulldozer. They waited a few seconds then withdrew leaving his scoop on the ground. Only later when it was much clear of her body did it raise its scoop.

I ran for an ambulance, she was gasping and her face was covered in blood from a gash cutting her face from lip to cheek. She was showing signs of brain haemorrhaging. She died in the ambulance a few minutes later.

"Is there any point at which all of the legal remedies will not suffice?"

Confession of Eric Rudolph

During the 1996 Summer Olympics in Atlanta, Georgia, a bomb killed one spectator and injured 111 others. During the next two years, abortion clinics in an Atlanta suburb and in Birmingham, Alabama, and a gay and lesbian bar in Atlanta were bombed. Two people were killed in the Birmingham bombing.

Eventually all of the bombings were attributed to Eric Rudolph, and the FBI began a five-year effort to capture him. He lived in the wilds of the southern Appalachians until his arrest in 2003.

In April 2005 he pleaded guilty to the Birmingham bombing to avoid the death penalty and issued a lengthy and unapologetic confession, excerpted below.

Like many other violent protesters, Rudolph justified his actions by saying the government was ignoring a moral imperative—in this case, stopping the destruction of unborn children. He acknowledged the potential of abortion being stopped through the political system, but he alleged that during the time it would take for nonviolent means to accomplish that goal, too many fetuses would die.

THE FACT THAT I HAVE ENTERED AN AGREEMENT with the government is purely a tactical choice on my part and in no way legitimates the moral authority of the government to judge this matter.

Abortion is murder. And when the regime in Washington legalized, sanctioned and legitimized this practice, they forfeited their legitimacy and moral authority to govern. At various times in history men and women of good conscience have had to decide when the lawfully constituted authorities have overstepped their moral bounds and forfeited their right to rule. This took place in July of 1776 when our Forefathers decided that the British Crown had violated the essential rights of Englishmen, and therefore lost its authority to govern. . . .

I am not an anarchist. I have nothing against government or law enforcement in general. It is solely for the reason that this govt [sic] has legalized the murder of children that I have no allegiance to nor do I recognize the legitimacy of this particular government in Washington.

Because I believe that abortion is murder, I also believe that force is justified in an attempt to stop it. Because this government is committed to the policy of maintaining the policy of abortion and protecting it, the agents of this government are the agents of mass murder, whether knowingly or unknowingly. And whether these agents of the government are armed or otherwise they are legitimate targets in the war to end this holocaust, especially those agents who carry arms in defense of this regime and the enforcement of its laws. This is the reason and the only reason for the targeting of so-called law enforcement personnel. . . .

. . . There is no more fundamental duty for a moral citizen than to protect the innocent from assault. . . . Would you protect your children from the clutches of a murderer? Would you protect your neighbors' children when they were under assault? If you answered yes to both of these, then you must support the use of force as justified in attempting to prevent the murder that is abortion. . . .

There are those who would say to me that the system in Washington works. They say that pro-life forces are making progress, that eventually Roe v. Wade will be overturned, that the culture of life will ultimately win over the majority of Americans and that the horror of abortion will be outlawed. Yet, in the meantime thousands die everyday [sic]. They say that the mechanism through which this will be achieved is the Republican party, and under the benevolent leadership of men like George W. Bush the wholesale slaughter of children will be a thing of the past. But with every day that passes another pile of corpses is added to the pyre. George W. will appoint the necessary justices to the Supreme Court and Roe will be finished, they say. All of this will be achieved through the lawful, legitimate democratic process. And every year a million and a half more die. I ask these peaceful Christian law-abiding Pro-Life citizens, is there any point at which all of the legal remedies will not suffice and you would fight to end the massacre of children? How many decades have to pass, how many millions have to die? Is there any point when the cries of children will not go unanswered? I think that your inaction after three decades of slaughter is a sufficient answer to all of these questions. . . .

Tell me plastic people, are you not the ones waving the flag in support of the coward Bush's operation in Iraq? Do you not say that Washington's cause justifies the bombing and shooting of thousands of people? Answer me, is the causus belli of promoting democracy in the Middle East more weighty for waging war than the systematic murder of millions of your own citizens? . . .

. . . For many years I thought long and hard on these issues and then in 1996 I decided to act. In the summer of 1996, the world converged upon Atlanta for the Olympic Games. Under the protection and auspices of the regime in Washington millions of people came out to celebrate the ideals of global socialism. Multinational corporations spent billions of dollars, and Washington organized an army of security to protect these best of all games. Even though the conception and purpose of the so-called Olympic movement is to promote the values of global socialism, as perfectly expressed in the song "Imagine" by John Lennon, which was the theme of the 1996 games—even though the purpose of the Olympics is to promote these despicable ideals, the purpose of the attack on July 27th was to confound, anger and embarrass the Washington government in the eyes of the [world] for its abominable sanctioning of abortion on demand.

The plan was to force the cancellation of the Games, or at least create a state of insecurity to empty the streets around the venues and thereby eat into the vast amounts of money invested. The plan was conceived in haste and carried out with limited resources, planning and preparation — it was a monster that kept getting out of control the more I got into it. Because I could not acquire the necessary high explosives, I had to dismiss the unrealistic notion of knocking down the power grid surrounding Atlanta and consequently pulling the plug on the Olympics for their duration.

The plan that I finally settled upon was to use five low-tech timed explosives to be placed one at a time on successive days throughout the Olympic schedule, each preceded by a forty to fifty minute warning given to 911. The location and the time of detonation was to be given, and the intent was to thereby clear each of the areas, leaving only uniformed arms-carrying government personnel exposed to potential injury.

. . . However, I knew that the weapons used (highly uncontrollable timed explosives) and the choice of tactics (placing them in areas frequented by large numbers of civilians) could potentially lead to a disaster wherein many civilians could be killed or wounded. There is no excuse for this, and I accept full responsibility for the consequences of using this dangerous tactic.

Protests Against Cartoons Depicting the Prophet Mohammad: "They featured evil, shameless images"

In September 2005, the Danish newspaper *Jyllands Posten* published a dozen cartoons showing the Prophet Mohammad. In much of the Islamic world any visual depiction of Mohammad is considered heresy. Although the cartoons were immediately castigated by Muslim clerics in Denmark as disrespectful of Islam, neither the cartoons nor the objections to them attracted much attention at the time.

But in February 2006, following a visit by Danish clerics to the Middle East, worldwide riots erupted in protest to the cartoons. Muslim protesters in Syria, Iran, and Lebanon burned the embassies of Denmark, Sweden, and France. A Danish mission in Beirut was also burned; the fire is shown in the photo here. Protesters in London called for beheading the cartoonists, as did a religious leader in the Gaza Strip. Riots and street demonstrations took place in Egypt, Indonesia, India, Nigeria, Afghanistan, Pakistan, Malaysia, and Belgium, among other countries. Most Europeans and Americans watched the riots with disbelief.

Commentators from Western nations around the world spoke of the cartoons as legitimate free speech (even if in poor taste) that must be defended. As Harvard law professor Alan Dershowitz wrote in *Time* magazine, "A separate standard is being applied here out of fear of physical retaliation. Whatever is fair to say about one group must be fair to say about another . . . When you see them [the cartoons], you see the extent of the overreaction. They are not nearly as bad as cartoons that routinely run in the Muslim media against Jews, Christians, the U.S. and Israel."

For Muslims, however, the extreme event was not the protests, but the publication of satiric depictions of the prophet Mohammad. As an unnamed commentator on the Web site www.islam-select.com explained, "Whom was this newspaper mocking? It was mocking the greatest man ever created . . . the leader of all the Prophets. . . . They featured evil, shameless images of him . . . as shameless as any disbeliever's imagination can be."

In the aftermath of the riots, many European media reprinted the cartoons in protest of the intimidation of free speech. This caused still further outrage on the streets of Muslim countries, since the offence the cartoons provided was already known.

CHAPTER 13
THE EXPERIENCE OF PROTEST

INTRODUCTION

Mohandas Gandhi's first experience with protest was a far cry from the iconic image of him leading hundreds of followers on long marches. In his memoir, Gandhi described how, when he was a young man newly arrived to South Africa, a bigoted coachman usurped the seat he had paid for and made him sit outside on the coachbox. When Gandhi got up the nerve to protest, he did so alone and trembling with fear. To read his vivid description of the incident—the punches that rained down on him from the angry coachman, the shouts of the other passengers—is to gaze through a window of time and be a witness to the experience of protest.

The documents in this chapter reveal the gritty reality of protest. These accounts transcend lofty arguments over the moral or political basis of protest to focus instead on what it feels like to be a protester on the ground. Here are the sights, sounds, and emotions of protest, along with the tension and violence that can attend it. A nineteenth-century Kentucky man who protested the injustice of slavery by providing sanctuary to a young escaped slave wrote about her capture, "This morning our family was aroused by the screams of a young colored girl, who has been living with us nearly a year past; but we were awakened only in time to see her borne off by three white men, ruffians indeed, to a carriage at our door, and in an instant she was on her way to the South." Rose Winslow, an American suffragist in the early twentieth century, was among a group of women protesters who went to jail, where they staged a hunger strike and were force-fed by their jailers. Describing the experience, she wrote: "I had a nervous time of it, gasping a long time afterward, and my stomach rejecting during the process. I spent a bad, restless night, but otherwise I am all right. The poor soul who fed me got liberally besprinkled during the process."

Many of the protesters featured in this book have, from the distance afforded by time, come to be seen as heroes. But some of these people, like Gandhi, were, at the time, just simple people standing up for their rights. This is a potent reminder that the right to protest belongs to all. We hope the documents in this chapter, and in the book as a whole, will inspire you to read more fully about protest and to experience it firsthand, exercising both your rights and responsibilities as a citizen of the earth.

Declaring America's Independence
Benjamin Rush

This excerpt of a letter from Dr. Benjamin Rush to John Adams recalls the tension at Independence Hall in Philadelphia (then the Pennsylvania State House) at the moment in August 1776 that most of the signers of the Declaration of Independence put pen to paper and publicly declared their split from Britain. Only two men actually signed the document when it was formally adopted on July 4, 1776: John Hancock, president of the Continental Congress, and Congress secretary Charles Thomson. The identities of the other fifty-six men who voted to approve the declaration were kept secret for several months as a precaution against reprisals from British forces and loyalists.

Most of those who signed the declaration—including Rush and Adams, the future president—did so on August 2 after an official parchment copy had been prepared. In his letter Rush captured the solemn mood of the men who understood the dangers of their public protest, should the colonies' move to break ties with England fail.

Rush, who addressed the letter "Dear Old Friend," shared a long correspondence with Adams; this letter was written in July 1811. The founder of Dickinson College in Pennsylvania, Rush also served as a surgeon-general in the Continental Army but left after becoming disillusioned with the state of military hospitals.

THE 4TH OF JULY HAS BEEN CELEBRATED in Philadelphia in the manner I expected. The military men, and particularly one of them, ran away with all the glory of the day. Scarcely a word was said of the solitude and labors and fears and sorrows and sleepless nights of the men who projected, proposed, defended, and subscribed the Declaration of Independence. Do you recollect your memorable speech upon the day on which the vote was taken? Do you recollect the pensive and awful silence which pervaded the house when we were called up, one after another, to the table of the President of Congress to subscribe what was believed by many at that time to be our own death warrants? The silence and the gloom of the morning were interrupted, I well recollect, only for a moment by Colonel Harrison of Virginia [Benjamin Harrison, father of future president William Henry Harrison], who said to Mr. [Elbridge] Gerry at the table: "I shall have a great advantage over you, Mr. Gerry, when we are all hung for what we are now doing. From the size and weight of my body I shall die in a few minutes, but from the lightness of your body you will dance in the air an hour or two before you are dead." This speech procured a transient smile, but it was soon succeeded by the solemnity with which the whole business was conducted.

"This sight froze the blood in my veins"

Ernesto Teodoro Moneta

The year 1848 was one of widespread political unrest. Rebellions rocked countries across Europe in what are collectively known as the Revolutions of 1848. Citizens rose up against autocratic governments, economic injustice, and foreign rulers, and the revolts inspired others as far away as Brazil.

At that time Italy was a collection of states. Milan was part of a state ruled by the Hapsburg empire of Austria. In January 1848 Milanese citizens began a boycott of tobacco and the lottery in order to cut into Austria's revenues from those items. Austrian soldiers responded by shooting and killing dozens of residents. Italians in Milan then took up arms in a violent rebellion, later dubbed the Five Days of Milan, aimed at expelling the Austrians. One fifteen-year-old who took part was Ernesto Teodoro Moneta. In this brief account he highlighted the impact of violent protest on those who participated. Moneta became a journalist and an international peace activist, though he also served in the military and pressed ardently for Italian unification (the Italian states were united as a kingdom in 1861). He wrote a four-volume work, *Le guerre, le insurrezioni e la pace nel secolo XIX (Wars, Insurrections and Peace in the Nineteenth Century)* between 1903 and 1910. In 1907 he was awarded the Nobel Peace Prize. This excerpt is from the Nobel lecture he gave in August 1909, after a delay due to ill health. Moneta died in 1918.

I WAS A YOUNG MAN WHEN, in March, 1848, Milan along with the other cities of Lombardy rose in revolt against the ruling [Austrian government]. . . . While the tocsin [alarm bell] sounded, we were putting up the barricades; we fought, mingling cries of joy with the shots and the crash of tiles and bricks thrown from windows. If this magnificent and epic struggle, which passed into history under the name of the "Five Days," demonstrated the courage of our people in the face of danger, it also demonstrated their generosity in the face of victory, which was free of reprisals even against the most notorious police agents. They fought heroically but without hatred for the poor foreign soldiers who were obliged by discipline to fight in spite of themselves. For our fighters it was practically a cause for celebration whenever, by catching the enemy unawares, they were able to capture them without bloodshed. The enemy prisoners and wounded were all well treated.

One day when my father and brothers were absent, I watched, from the windows of my home, three Austrian soldiers fall amid a hail of bullets. Apparently dead, they were carried away to a neighboring square. I saw them again two hours later: one of them was still in the throes of dying. This sight froze the blood in my veins and I was overcome by a great compassion. In these three soldiers I no longer saw enemies but men like myself, and with remorse as keenly suffered as if I had killed them with my own hands, I thought of their families who were perhaps at that very moment preparing for their return.

In that instant I felt all the cruelty and inhumanity of war which sets peoples against one another to their mutual detriment, peoples who should have every interest in understanding and being friends with each other. I was to feel this way many times as I looked at the dead and the wounded in all the wars for our independence in which I took part.

The Underground Rail Road
William Still

Abolitionist, writer, and businessman William Still of Philadelphia was called the Father of the Underground Railroad for his unflagging involvement in aiding blacks escaping from slavery. He was born a freeman in New Jersey in 1821, one of eighteen children of two former slaves. One of the hundreds of slaves he helped turned out to be his own brother, Peter, whom their mother had left behind in the South as a slave when she escaped decades earlier with two other children.

In 1872 Still published *The Underground Rail Road*, a remarkable collection of documents by and about both the blacks who sought freedom and those who aided them. As an epigraph to the book, he used a quotation from the Bible: "Thou shalt not deliver unto his master the servant that has escaped from his master unto thee" (Deuteronomy 23:15).

The verse is especially pertinent to the first of two excerpts here, an April 1848 letter to Still from a woman named Mary B. Thomas of Downingtown, Pennsylvania, whose home was a safe house on the railroad. Thomas's letter describes how bounty hunters entered her home and kidnapped the slave the family was harboring. The letter and a subsequent one quoted by Still relate both the first-person experience of those who actively resisted slavery, as well as the emotional devastation when their efforts to help slaves failed. Still's introduction to the letters reads, "Daring outrage! Burglary and kidnapping! The following letter tells its own startling and most painful story. Every manly and generous heart must burn with indignation at the villainy it describes, and bleed with sympathy for the almost broken-hearted sufferers."

The second excerpt from *The Underground Rail Road* is a letter from William S. Bailey to Anna H. Richardson in Newcastle, England, written in November 1859. Richardson was a supporter of American antislavery efforts and had sent money to Bailey, who lived in Newport, Kentucky. Bailey ran a press on which he printed abolitionist literature. The asterisks appear in the original document.

THIS MORNING OUR FAMILY WAS AROUSED by the screams of a young colored girl, who has been living with us nearly a year past; but we were awakened only in time to see her borne off by three white men, ruffians indeed, to a carriage at our door, and in an instant she was on her way to the South. I feel so much excited by the attendant circumstances of this daring and atrocious deed, as scarcely to be able to give you a coherent account of it, but I know that it is a duty to make it known, and, I therefore write this immediately.

As soon as the house was opened in the morning, these men who were lurking without, having a carriage in waiting in the street, entered on their horrid errand. They encountered no one in their entrance, except a colored boy, who was making the fire; and who, being frightened at their approach, ran and hid himself; taking a lighted candle from the kitchen, and carrying it up stairs, they went directly to the chamber in which the poor girl lay in a sound sleep. They lifted her from her bed and carried her down stairs. In the entry of the second floor they met one of my sisters, who, hearing an unusual noise, had sprung from her bed. Her screams, and those of the poor girl, who was now thoroughly awakened to the dreadful truth, aroused my father, who hurried undressed from his chamber, on the ground floor. My father's efforts were powerless against the three; they threw him off, and with frightful imprecations hurried the girl to the carriage. Quickly as possible my father started in pursuit, and reached West Chester only to learn that the carriage had driven through the borough at full speed, about half an hour before. They had two horses to their vehicle, and there were three men besides those in the house. These particulars we gather from the colored boy Ned, who, from his hiding-place, was watching them in the road.

Can anything be done for the rescue of this girl from the kidnappers? We are surprised and alarmed! This deliberate invasion of our house, is a thing unimagined. There must be some informer, who is acquainted with our house and its arrangements, or they never would have come so boldly through. Truly, there is no need to preach about Slavery in the abstract, this individual case combines every wickedness by which human nature can be degraded. . . .

From my letter of the 7th inst. you will have learned the sad intelligence that my printing-office has been destroyed by a brutal mob of Pro-Slavery men. Through the money I received from you and other friends in this country I was moving the cause of freedom in all parts of Kentucky. The people seemed to grasp our platform with eagerness, and the slave-holders became alarmed to see their wish to read and discuss its simple truths. Hence they plotted together to devise a stratagem by which they could destroy *The Free South*, and in the meantime the Harper's Ferry difficulty, by Mr. Brown, was seized upon to excite the people against me, and the most extravagant lies were told about me, as trying to excite slaves to rebellion; intending to seize the United States barracks at this place, arm the negroes, and commence war upon slave-holders. All these lies were told as profound secrets to the people by the tools of the slave-power. But these lies have already exploded, and the people are resuming their common sense again.

I tried your plan of non-resistance with all my power. I pleaded with all the earnestness of my soul, and so did my wife and daughters, but though I am certain many were moved in conscience against the savage outrage, and did their work with a stinging heart, yet they felt that they must stick to their party, and complete the destruction. Slavery, indeed, makes the most hardened savages the world ever knew. The savage war-whoop of the Indian never equalled their dastardly cry of "shoot him," "cut his throat," "stab him," and such like words most maliciously spoken. * * * Slavery is the cause of this devilish spirit in men; but this outrage has gained me many friends, and will do much towards putting down Slavery in the state. It will also add many thousand votes to the republican presidential candidate in 1860. God grant it may work out a great good! * * * I want to get started again as soon as I possibly can. As soon as I can raise 1,000 dollars, I can make a beginning, and soon after you will see *The Free South* again, and I trust a much handsomer sheet than it was before.

"I sat speechless and prayed to god to help me"
Mohandas K. Gandhi

Mohandas K. Gandhi—later given the name Mahatma, meaning "great soul"—is regarded as one of history's greatest leaders of protest. He spent his life teaching his belief in nonviolent resistance and worked for economic justice, racial equality, and independence for India. Gandhi rejected the idea of passive resistance and instead developed the concept of *satyagraha*, a new term he coined from the words for "truth" and "firmness." Satyagraha emphasized a forceful adherence to truth in resistance to injustice; protesters should be nonviolent, he taught, but in an assertive, active, and loving manner.

Gandhi was born in 1869 in India and studied law in England. He later described himself as an ineffectual lawyer and teacher who was nearly crippled by shyness. He took a one-year position as a lawyer in South Africa to defend Indians living there, and his experiences with racial discrimination transformed him from mild-mannered businessman to committed activist. He studied theological writings, Tolstoy, and Thoreau, and renounced materialism, dedicating himself to a simple lifestyle based on vegetarianism, celibacy, and fighting for freedom. Gandhi stayed in South Africa for twenty-one years, advocating relentlessly for racial equality through speeches, letters, marches, and boycotts.

In *An Autobiography: The Story of My Experiments with Truth*, Gandhi described his first days in South Africa. The society was strictly segregated. Whites referred to Indians as "samis" or "coolies," derogatory terms for unskilled Asian laborers who came to the country as indentured servants. Gandhi was treated like an unskilled laborer despite dressing, in those days, in European-style suits (though he also wore a turban). In this excerpt he writes about traveling to Johannesburg and spending a night in a railway station after getting kicked off the train; he had refused to give up his first-class seat when train authorities demanded he do so despite having a ticket. The next day he sent a telegram to the railroad company protesting his treatment and took another train to the town of Charlestown before getting on a coach, where he encountered further prejudice. His description captures the fear and anxiety that often come with the decision to challenge authority.

THE TRAIN REACHED CHARLESTOWN in the morning. There was no railway, in those days, between Charlestown and Johannesburg, but only a stage-coach, which halted at Standerton for the night *en route*. I possessed a ticket for the coach, which was not cancelled by the break of the journey at Maritzburg for a day; besides, Abdulla Sheth had sent a wire to the coach agent at Charlestown.

But the agent only needed a pretext for putting me off, and so, when he discovered me to be a stranger, he said, "Your ticket is cancelled." I gave him the proper reply. The reason at the back of his mind was not want of accommodation, but quite another. Passengers had to be accommodated inside the coach, but as I was regarded as a "coolie" and looked a stranger, it would be proper, thought the "leader," as the white man in charge of the coach was called, not to seat me with the white passengers. There were seats on either side of the coachbox. The leader sat on one of these as a rule. Today he sat inside and gave me his seat. I knew it was sheer injustice and an insult, but I thought it better to pocket it. I could not have forced myself inside, and if I had raised a protest, the coach would have gone off without me. This would have meant the loss of another day, and Heaven only knows what would have happened the next day. So, much as I fretted within myself, I prudently sat next the coachman.

At about three o'clock the coach reached Pardekoph. Now the leader desired to sit where I was seated, as he wanted to smoke and possibly to have some fresh air. So he took a piece of dirty sack-cloth from the driver, spread it on the footboard and, addressing me said, "*Sami*, you sit on this, I want to sit near the driver." The insult was more than I could bear. In fear and trembling I said to him, "It was you who seated me here, though I should have been accommodated inside. I put up with the insult. Now that you want to sit outside and smoke, you would have me sit at your feet. I will not do so, but I am prepared to sit inside."

As I was struggling through these sentences, the man came down upon me and began heavily to box my ears. He seized me by the arm and tried to drag me down. I clung to the brass rails of the coachbox and was determined to keep my hold even at the risk of breaking my wristbones. The passengers were witnessing the scene— the man swearing at me, dragging and belabouring me, and I remaining still. He was strong and I was weak. Some of the passengers were moved to pity and exclaimed: "Man, let him alone. Don't beat him. He is not to blame. He is right. If he can't stay there, let him come and sit with us." "No fear," cried the man, but he seemed somewhat crestfallen and stopped beating me. He let go my arm, swore at me a little more, and asking the Hottentot servant who was sitting on the other side of the coachbox to sit on the footboard, took the seat so vacated.

The passengers took their seats and, the whistle given, the coach rattled away. My heart was beating fast within my breast, and I was wondering whether I should ever reach my destination alive. The man cast an angry look at me now and then and, pointing his finger at me, growled: "Take care, let me once get to Standerton and I shall show you what I do." I sat speechless and prayed to God to help me.

"I did not mince matters, yet there was no arrest"
Emma Goldman

American radical Emma Goldman (1869–1940) was born in Russia, moved to the United States as a child, and worked in sweatshops as a young woman before moving to New York City and devoting the rest of her life to various progressive causes. Goldman became notorious for her anarchist political beliefs—for which she was permanently deported from the country in 1917—but she lectured and wrote on many subjects including peace, free love, literature, birth control, and reform of labor laws. She was jailed many times—often preferring to be jailed on principle rather than paying a fine she deemed unjust. She founded an anarchist magazine, *Mother Earth*, which was shut down by the federal government in 1917 under the Espionage Act, which made it illegal to obstruct conscription or voice disloyalty to the military. She was a fiery orator who purposely tested the limits of free speech by addressing proscribed topics and passing out illegal pamphlets.

In this excerpt from her 1931 autobiography *Living My Life*, she describes a period in 1915 when she was actively defying national obscenity laws by talking openly about contraception. The "Comstock" referred to was Anthony Comstock, a crusader against lewdness, gambling, and drinking who saw himself as a protector of public morality. Comstock founded the New York Society for the Suppression of Vice. A federal anti-obscenity law named after him was passed in 1873 and was used for many years to arrest people who dared to disseminate information about sex education and birth control. William Sanger, the husband of birth-control activist Margaret Sanger, was arrested under this law for passing out one of his wife's pamphlets.

E. C. WALKER, president of the Sunrise Club, had invited me to speak at one of its fortnightly dinners. His organization was among the few libertarian forums in New York open to free expression. I had often lectured there on various social topics. On this occasion I chose birth-control as my theme, intending openly to discuss methods of contraception. I faced one of the largest audiences in the history of the club, numbering about six hundred persons, among them physicians, lawyers, artists, and men and women of liberal views. Most of them were earnest people who had come together to lend moral support to the test case that this first public discussion represented. Everyone felt certain that my arrest would follow, and some friends had come prepared to go bail for me. I carried a book with me in case I should have to spend the night in the station-house. That possibility did not disturb me, but I did feel uneasy because I knew that some of the diners had come out of curiosity, for the sex thrills they expected to experience on this evening.

I introduced my subject by reviewing the historical and social aspects of birth-control and then continued with a discussion of a number of contraceptives, their application and effects. I spoke in the direct and frank manner that I should use in dealing with ordinary disinfection and prophylaxis. The questions and the discussion that followed showed that I had taken the right approach. Several physicians complimented me on having presented so difficult and delicate a subject in a "clean and natural manner."

No arrest followed. Some friends feared I might be picked up on my way home, and insisted on seeing me to my door. Days passed and the authorities had taken no steps in the matter. It was the more surprising in view of the arrest of William Sanger for something he had not said nor written himself. People wondered why I, who had been so frequently arrested when I had not broken the law, should be allowed to go unpunished when I had done so deliberately. Perhaps Comstock's failure to act was due to the fact that he knew that those who were in the habit of attending the Sunrise Club gatherings were probably already in possession of contraceptives. I must therefore deliver the lecture at my own Sunday meetings, I decided.

Our hall was packed, mostly with young people, among them students from Columbia University. The interest evinced by my audience was even greater than at the Sunrise dinner, the questions put by the young folks of a more direct and personal nature. I did not mince matters, yet there was no arrest.

"We don't want other women ever to have to do this over again"
Rose Winslow

In the second decade of the twentieth century women stepped up their demands for the right to vote. Dozens of women started to picket the White House. Starting in the summer of 1917, several of the women were arrested for obstructing traffic. Although the first groups were pardoned, several were sentenced to seven months in prison.

In jail the women demanded that they be treated as political prisoners and not criminals. They staged a hunger strike. In response, jailers force-fed the women. One of the suffragists, Rose Winslow, described the experience in letters to her husband and friends, which were smuggled from the prison. Less than three years later, in 1920, the Nineteenth Amendment to the U.S. Constitution was ratified, giving women the right to vote.

IF THIS THING IS NECESSARY we will naturally go through with it. Force is so stupid a weapon. I feel so happy doing my bit for decency—for *our* war, which is after all, real and fundamental.

The women are all so magnificent, so beautiful. Alice Paul is as thin as ever, pale and large-eyed. We have been in solitary for five weeks. There is nothing to tell but that the days go by somehow. I have felt quite feeble the last few days—faint, so that I could hardly get my hair brushed, my arms ached so. But to-day I am well again. Alice Paul and I talk back and forth though we are at opposite ends of the building and a hall door also shuts us apart. But occasionally—thrills— we escape from behind our iron-barred doors and visit. Great laughter and rejoicing!

My fainting probably means nothing except that I am not strong after these weeks. I know you won't be alarmed.

Alice Paul is in the psychopathic ward. She dreaded forcible feeding frightfully, and I hate to think how she must be feeling. I had a nervous time of it, gasping a long time afterward, and my stomach rejecting during the process. I spent a bad, restless night, but otherwise I am all right. The poor soul who fed me got liberally besprinkled during the process. I heard myself making the most hideous sounds. . . . One feels so forsaken when one lies prone and people shove a pipe down one's stomach.

This morning but for an astounding tiredness, I am all right. I am waiting to see what happens when the President realizes that brutal bullying isn't quite a states-manlike method for settling a demand for justice at home. At least, if men are supine enough to endure, women—to their eternal glory—are not.

They took down the boarding from Alice Paul's window yesterday, I heard. It is so delicious about Alice and me. Over in the jail a rumor began that I was considered insane and would be examined. Then came Doctor White, and said he had come to see "the thyroid case." When they left we argued about the mat-ter, neither of us knowing which was considered "suspicious." She insisted it was she, and, as it happened, she was right. Imagine any one thinking Alice Paul needed to be "under observation!" The thick-headed idiots!

Yesterday was a bad day for me in feeding. I was vomiting continually during the process. The tube has developed an irritation somewhere that is painful.

Never was there a sentence like ours for such an offense as ours, even in England. No woman ever got it over there even for tearing down buildings. And during all that agitation *we* were busy saying that never would such things happen in the United States. The men told us they would not endure such frightfulness.

Mary Beard and Helen Todd were allowed to stay only a minute, and I cried like a fool. I am getting over that habit, I think.

I fainted again last night. I just flopped over in the bathroom where I was wash-ing my hands and was led to bed when I recovered, by a nurse. I lost consciousness just as I got there again. I felt horribly faint until 12 o'clock, then fell asleep for awhile.

I was getting frantic because you seemed to think Alice was with me in the hos-pital. She was in the psychopathic ward. The same doctor feeds us both, and told me. Don't let them tell you we take this well. Miss Paul vomits much. I do, too, except when I'm not nervous, as I have been every time against my will. I try to be less feeble-minded. It's the nervous reaction, and I can't control it much. I don't imagine bathing one's food in tears very good for one.

We think of the coming feeding all day. It is horrible. The doctor thinks I take it well. I hate the thought of Alice Paul and the others if I take it well.

We still get no mail; we are "insubordinate." It's strange, isn't it; if you ask for food fit to eat, as we did, you are "insubordinate"; and if you refuse food you are "insubordinate." Amusing. I am really all right. If this continues very long I perhaps won't be. I am interested to see how our so-called "splendid American men" will stand for this form of discipline.

All news cheers one marvelously because it is hard to feel anything but a bit desolate and forgotten here in this place.

All the officers here know we are making this hunger strike [so] that women fighting for liberty may be considered political prisoners; we have told them. God knows we don't want other women ever to have to do this over again.

"Those who dare to stand in a strong sun and cast a sharp shadow"

Robert Moses

Robert Moses left a teaching job in New York City to become field secretary for the Student Nonviolent Coordinating Committee (SNCC) in the civil rights movement in Mississippi in 1961. The Harvard graduate became a member of the Freedom Riders, helping to lead voter registration drives for blacks.

When two students were expelled from Burgland High School in McComb, Mississippi, for trying to integrate a Greyhound bus station, many fellow students boycotted the school. Moses and other SNCC members started teaching classes to the students above a local grocery store. The school was dubbed "Nonviolent High." In October 1961 local police arrested all of the teachers, who were imprisoned when they could not make bail. In this letter about their jail experience, Moses took note of both the casualness of their response to being jailed and their determination to prevail. The letter conveys a common experience of protest: down time in jail.

Moses later organized the Mississippi Freedom Democratic Party, which challenged the legitimacy of the Mississippi Democratic Party at the 1964 Democratic Party Convention. Ultimately disillusioned by his civil rights experiences, Moses moved to Tanzania to teach. He later returned to the United States and founded the Algebra Project, a nationally recognized math-literacy program.

WE ARE SMUGGLING THIS NOTE from the drunk tank of the county jail in Magnolia, Mississippi. Twelve of us are here, sprawled out along the concrete bunker; Curtis Hayes, Hollis Watkins, Ike Lewis and Robert Talbert, four veterans of the bunker, are sitting up talking—mostly about girls; Charles McDew ("Tell the story") is curled into the concrete and the wall; Harold Robinson, Stephen Ashley, James Wells, Lee Chester Vick, Leotus Eubanks, and Ivory Diggs lay cramped on the cold bunker; I'm sitting with smuggled pen and paper, thinking a little, writing a little; Myrtis Bennett and Janie Campbell are across the way wedded to a different icy cubicle.

Later on, Hollis will lead out with a clear tenor into a freedom song, Talbert and Lewis will supply jokes, and McDew will discourse on the history of the black man and the Jew. McDew—a black by birth, a Jew by choice, and a revolutionary by necessity—has taken on the deep hates and deep loves which America and the world reserve for those who dare to stand in a strong sun and cast a sharp shadow. . . .

This is Mississippi, the middle of the iceberg. Hollis leading off with his tenor, "Michael row the boat ashore, Alleluia; Christian brothers don't be slow, Alleluia; Mississippi's next to go, Alleluia." This is a tremor in the middle of the iceberg—from a stone that the builders rejected.

"Saturday night, the pink panthers are back in full force"
Edmund White

The Stonewall Riots marked the beginning of the gay-rights movement, as gays publicly rebelled against government-sanctioned persecution. The conflict—also called the Stonewall rebellion—took place over several nights in New York City in 1969. On Friday, June 27, police raided the Stonewall Inn, a popular gay bar in Greenwich Village. Police raids on gay bars were common around the country, but this time the bar's clientele "acted up," actively resisting the police action and fighting back. The police found themselves confronting an angry mob of several hundred gay, lesbian, bisexual, and transgender persons. Several gay-liberation groups were formed in the wake of the riots, and a large gay-liberation rally was held in New York's Central Park on the one-year anniversary of the rebellion.

Edmund White, author of *A Boy's Own Story* and *The Farewell Symphony*, witnessed the riot. The prominent gay writer described the experience in a letter to his friends Alfred and Ann Corn. The letter was later published in *The Violet Quill Reader: The Emergence of Gay Writing After Stonewall*, edited by David Bergman.

WELL, THE BIG NEWS HERE is Gay Power. It's the most extraordinary thing. It all began two weeks ago on a Friday night. The cops raided the Stonewall, that mighty Bastille which you know has remained impregnable for three years, so brazen and so conspicuous that one could only surmise that the Mafia was paying off the pigs handsomely. Apparently, however, a new public official, Sergeant Smith, has taken over the Village, and he's a peculiarly diligent lawman. In any event, a mammoth paddy wagon, as big as a school bus, pulled up to the Wall and about ten cops raided the joint. The kids were all shooed into the street;

soon other gay kids and straight spectators swelled the ranks to, I'd say, about a thousand people. Christopher Street was completely blocked off and the crowds swarmed from the *Voice* office down to the Civil War hospital.

As the Mafia owners were dragged out one by one and shoved into the wagon, the crowd would let out Bronx cheers and jeers and clapping. Someone shouted "Gay Power," others took up the cry—and then it dissolved into giggles. A few more prisoners—bartenders, hatcheck boys—a few more cheers, someone starts singing "We Shall Overcome"—and then they started camping on it. A drag queen is shoved into the wagon; she hits the cop over the head with her purse. The cop clubs her. Angry stirring in the crowd. The cops, used to the cringing and disorganization of the gay crowds, snort off. But the crowd doesn't disperse. Everyone is restless, angry, and high-spirited. No one has a slogan, no one even has an attitude, but something's brewing.

Some adorable butch hustler boy pulls up a *parking meter*, mind you, out of the pavement, and uses it as a battering ram (a few cops are still inside the Wall, locked in). The boys begin to pound at the heavy wooden double doors and windows; glass shatters all over the street. Cries of "Liberate the Bar." Bottles (from hostile straights?) rain down from the apartment windows. Cries of "We're the Pink Panthers." A mad Negro queen whirls like a dervish with a twisted piece of metal in her hand and breaks the remaining windows. The door begins to give. The cops turn a hose on the crowd (they're still within the Wall). But they can't aim it properly, and the crowd sticks. Finally the door is broken down and the kids, as though working to a prior plan, systematically dump refuse from waste cans into the Wall, squirting it with lighter fluid, and ignite it. Huge flashes of flame and billows of smoke.

Now the cops in the paddy wagon return, and two fire engines pull up. Clubs fly. The crowd retreats.

Saturday night, the pink panthers are back in full force. The cops form a flying wedge at the Greenwich Avenue end of Christopher and drive the kids down towards Sheridan Square. The panthers, however, run down Waverly, up Gay Street, and come out *behind* the cops, kicking in a chorus line, taunting, screaming. Dreary middle-class East Side queens stand around disapproving but fascinated, unable to go home, as though torn between their class loyalties, their desire to be respectable, and their longing for freedom. Sheridan Square is cordoned off by the cops. The United Cigar store closes, Riker's closes, the deli closes. No one can pass through the square; to walk up Seventh Avenue, you must detour all the way to Bleecker.

A mad left-wing group of straight kids called the Crazies is trying to organize the gay kids, pointing out that Lindsay is to blame (the Crazies want us to vote for Procaccino, or "Prosciutto," as we call him). A Crazy girl launches into a tirade against Governor Rockefeller, "Whose Empire," she cries, "Must Be Destroyed." Straight Negro boys put their arms around me and say we're comrades (it's okay with me—in fact, great, the first camaraderie I've felt with blacks in years). Mattachine (our NAACP) hands out leaflets about "what to do if arrested." Some man from the Oscar Wilde bookstore hands out a leaflet describing to newcomers what's going on. I give a stump speech about the need to radicalize, how we must recognize we're part of a vast rebellion of all the repressed. Some jeers, some cheers. Charles Burch plans to make a plastique [an explosive device] to hurl at cops.

Sunday night, the Stonewall, now reopened—though one room is charred and blasted, all lights are smashed, and only a few dim bulbs are burning, no hard liquor being sold—the management posts an announcement: "We appreciate all of you and your efforts to help, but the Stonewall believes in peace. Please end the riots. We believe in peace." Some kids, nonetheless, try to turn over a cop car. Twelve are arrested. Some straight toughs rough up some queens. The queens beat them up. Sheridan Square is again blocked off by the pigs. That same night a group of about seventy-five vigilantes in Queens chops down a wooded part of a park as vengeance against the perverts who are cruising in the bushes. "They're endangering our women and children." The *Times*, which has scarcely mentioned the Sheridan Square riots (a half column, very tame) is now so aroused by the *conservation* issue that it blasts the "vigs" for their malice toward *nature*.

Wednesday. The *Voice* runs two front-page stories on the riots, both snide, both devoted primarily to assuring readers that the authors are straight.

Praying Crowd Halts Marcos Tank Column
John Burgess

This article, published in the *Washington Post* by John Burgess, on February 24, 1986, gave an on-the-ground view of a street protest in Manila, the capital of the Philippines, the previous day. While Burgess's account of the protest revealed the ebullient mood of the crowd it is clear that, with a slight shift in circumstance, the scene could have become the story of a violent massacre.

Philippines President Ferdinand Marcos, first elected in 1965 and reelected in 1969, had declared martial law in 1972, allowing him to stay in power. Marcos became increasingly dictatorial, and opposition against him grew as charges of corruption piled up. In 1981 Marcos lifted martial law and won reelection in balloting that was widely boycotted. Two years later former Filipino senator Benigno Aquino, Jr.—the opposition leader and reformer whom Marcos had jailed for many years—was murdered at the Manila airport as he returned from exile in the United States, despite having a heavy military escort. Years of frustration over continuing poverty, government corruption, and authoritarian rule exploded into widespread protest throughout the archipelago.

In November 1985 Marcos called a "snap" election. Aquino's widow, Corazon, known as Cory, who had taken up the mantle of leader of the opposition "People Power" movement, declared herself a candidate. In the election on February 7, 1986, both Aquino and Marcos claimed victory. On February 15 the country's Catholic bishops denounced the elections as fraudulent and called for civil disobedience. Since the Philippines is a strongly Catholic country, it was the death knell for the Marcos regime. One week later, Marcos's defense minister and another high-ranking administration official defected to the Aquino camp. Some Aquino supporters in the military seized bases. When Marcos ordered loyalist troops to retake the bases, protesters formed a human blockade to insulate the rebel leaders' camp—a protest that was to prove pivotal. The troops refused to fire on civilians. Two days later, after more than two decades in power, Marcos fled to Hawaii, and Corazon Aquino became president.

THE CHOICE GIVEN to the Philippine marines manning two tanks stopped on Ortigas Avenue Sunday afternoon, as tensions first began to build, was simple. If they wanted to reach their objective, they would have to roll over the crowd that was enveloping them.

In its ranks were Catholic nuns reciting the words, "Hail Mary, full of grace. . . ." There were priests with heads bowed in prayer and young women offering orchids to any soldier who would take them.

So the marines bluffed. Over and over, they fired up their tanks' mammoth diesel engines and edged forward. Shouts of "Sit down! Sit down!" would ring out. People would drop to the pavement and the tanks would stop. Applause and cries of rapture would go up at this new victory.

In the end, after four hours, the tanks and the armored column of about 1,000 marines they were leading went back to their barracks, having unexpectedly met with a remarkable display of citizen activism by supporters of opposition leader Corazon Aquino.

In the early hours of Monday morning, troops came back elsewhere, according to widespread reports, using tear gas and truncheons against crowds. But those troops also failed in their mission.

The withdrawal of the military in the confrontation on Sunday brought jubilation.

"Liberation day!" declared a young man surveying the scene with others from atop a bus.

The danger to the crowd was probably not as high as it might have seemed. From the start it was clear that the marines, many of whom had been flown to Manila only days ago from duty fighting Communist insurgents on Mindanao Island, did not have their hearts in the task. Many flashed the *laban* ("fight!") hand signal of the opposition.

The crowd treated them not with contempt but as errant brothers they hoped would return to the fold.

"We are all Filipinos—there is no fight here," shouted one man as a column of marines weighted down with M60 machine guns and a bazooka passed by.

The marines left Ft. Bonifacio, a major military base in Manila, in early afternoon. Their mission, officers said, was to proceed to Camp Aguinaldo, the Defense Ministry headquarters where military rebels who support Aquino's claim to the presidency were in control.

Their tracked vehicles chewed up soft pavement as they rumbled across the city through light Sunday traffic on Epifanio de los Santos Avenue. Crowds of people watched from overpasses and sidewalks.

At the intersection with Ortigas Avenue, about one mile from the camp, Aquino supporters had blocked passage with about two dozen commandeered buses. As the crowd of about 20,000 looked on, the marines turned off the avenue and crashed through a wooden fence, entering a vacant lot of about 10 acres in an apparent effort to skirt the barrier. Two tanks broke through a wall at the field's far side and entered Ortigas Avenue. The crowd closed in and that was as far as the soldiers got.

The marine commandant, Brig. Gen. Artemio Tadiar, dressed in a camouflage jump suit, waded into the crowd around the tanks and tried to work out passage with a businessman who had emerged as a spokesman. "If we can't clear this and it gets dark, there will be trouble," he told reporters later.

The crowd's spirits were high and the general drew applause when he climbed atop a tank to address them with a loudspeaker.

"Let us just move," he pleaded.

"No! No!" the crowd responded.

He tried again: "We want to go on quietly and I want to assure you there'll be no trouble." That appeal also was rejected.

Women moved among the soldiers, giving out purple orchids. A marine packing an M16 rifle stuck one in his shoulder harness. Sandwiches were passed forward by the crowd and given to the marines.

"Look at the faces of the soldiers. They are not the faces of people who want to fight," said Freddie Aldeguer, a salesman for a pharmaceutical company.

The first sign of victory for the crowd came when the tanks lurched back through the hole in the wall about 4:45 p.m. and rejoined the rest of the force in the field. "It seems we cannot go forward without hurting someone," a colonel said.

People began feeling bolder. Ignoring gestures of admonition, women strode into the field to deliver marigolds to sheepish soldiers.

When a helicopter set down in the center, they rushed toward it and chanted, "Cory! Cory!" at the men who got out.

A colonel said there would be no violence from the soldiers. "We told them not to follow unlawful orders," he said. "Killing people is unauthorized. That's why we didn't push through. Some of us have relatives in the opposition. Some of us have relatives in the mountains," a reference to the Communist insurgency.

The gathering acquired even more of a fiesta atmosphere as dusk approached. A family posed for a photo against an armored car. Two men volunteered to a reporter that the Filipino people would welcome U.S. intervention.

The marines began leaving as darkness fell. The buses were removed and the crowd parted. The tanks, armored cars, personnel carriers, jeeps and trucks picked their way through amid applause.

People grabbed the hands of soldiers walking out, often drawing warm smiles in return, and joined the convoy in a victory march as it rolled back toward Ft. Bonifacio.

It is unclear why the order to withdraw was given. President Ferdinand Marcos said tonight he gave it after the rebels pleaded with him not to use force. But to the crowd, the victory was all theirs.

Li Peng Meets Fasting Student Protesters
Beijing Television Service

The pro-democracy protests of April through June 1989 in the People's Republic of China saw an estimated one million demonstrators in the streets of Beijing and thousands of students and workers occupying Tiananmen Square. When Communist Party leaders refused to meet with students to discuss their demands for reform, protesters began a hunger strike outside the Great Hall of the People. Several thousand people joined in. As the strike moved toward the end of a full week, Premier Li Peng and other party officials agreed to meet with student leaders. The May 18 meeting was videotaped, and a transcript was later published in the official Communist Party newspaper *Renmin Ribao (People's Daily)*. The transcript was posted on a Web site that accompanied a documentary about the uprising, "The Gate of Heavenly Peace," shown on public television in the United States.

The lengthy meeting transcript, excerpted here, gave an unvarnished look at the tense behind-the-scenes maneuvering as demonstrators and government officials worked to avert mass deaths from the hunger strike, but also wrangled over their conflicting goals. Li Peng and other high-ranking officials sought to portray the protests as disruption incited by a small antigovernment contingent, while the student leaders portrayed themselves as patriotic reformers pressing the government toward increased responsiveness to the needs of the people. The talks failed to breach the impasse, and on May 20 the government declared martial law. Students converted the hunger strike to a sit-in and continued the occupation for several weeks. On June 4 the Chinese Army moved on the demonstrators, killing or injuring many and clearing people out of Tiananmen Square at gunpoint. The Chinese government acknowledged that more than two hundred people were killed, including scores of soldiers and police; human rights groups have put the number substantially higher, to as many as five thousand.

In this excerpt the speakers are student leaders Wu'er Kaixi, Wang Dan, Xiong Yan, Wang Zhixin, and Shao Jiang, and party officials Lie Tieying and Premier Li Peng.

LI PENG: DELIGHTED TO MEET YOU. This meeting came a little late. I apologize for this. Some of your fellow students are now waiting for you at the east side of the Great Hall, making me feel as if under siege [laughing]. I hope that we will have a frank conversation instead of [indistinct]. I would like to discuss only one topic today and shelve other topics until some time in the future. The topic I would like to discuss is how to relieve the fasting comrades of their predicament as soon as possible. The party and the government are very much concerned about the students. Therefore, I would like to exchange views with you mainly on this question, and on how a solution can be found so that we can discuss other questions. . . .

WU'ER KAIXI: The time is pressing. We can sit down and have a drink here, but the students are sitting on the cold ground and starving on the square. I'm sorry I had to butt in. We hope we can enter into a substantial dialogue as soon as possible. Sorry I have to interrupt. . . . You have just said that this meeting is a little late. The fact is that we asked for a meeting with you as early as April 22 at Tiananmen Square. Therefore, this meeting is not only a little late, but too late. . . . Let me tell you, Teacher Li. First of all, the problem now lies not in dissuading us—a handful of student representatives. We have already stated clearly that you need not dissuade us because we too wish very much for the students to leave the square. Second, even if you succeed in utterly rebuking us here, it is still useless. The situation at the square now is dictated by 99.9 percent of the students who rule over the remaining 0.1 percent. If a student refuses to leave, then thousands of others will also stay.

WANG DAN: . . . I would like to take this opportunity to clearly state once again our demands. First, the current student movement should be evaluated as a democratic, patriotic movement and not unrest. Second, [indistinct].

WU'ER KAIXI: I would like to add my explanation to the above two demands. We hope that the verdict will be reversed and that the editorial [in the official party newspaper claiming a small group of students were creating unrest to overthrow the Community Party] will be negated immediately. . . .

XIONG YAN, BEIJING UNIVERSITY: I want to say a few words. We hold that whether it is recognized by the government or other sectors of society as a great patriotic democratic movement or not, history will recognize the current student movement as a great patriotic democratic movement. But why do students still want the government to particularly recognize it as a patriotic democratic movement? I think that their desire is the same—all want to see whether our own government is still our own government. In fact, herein lies the problem. This is the first point. Second, comrades, we all are fighting for communism. To save one life is already a job of prime importance, let alone saving thousands of lives. Many of our students have fainted. We are all people of good conscience. We are human beings. To solve this problem, we should forget face and other things of secondary importance. Even if the people's government admits its own mistakes, the people will still support it. I think that the masses of people will do so. This is the second point. Third, our criticism of Premier Li Peng is not directed at you personally. We criticize you because you are the premier of the Republic. In fact, you have just said that your coming out is too late. I have nothing more to say.

LI PENG: Any other student who wants to . . .

WANG ZHIXIN, UNIVERSITY OF POLITICAL SCIENCE AND LAW, Interrupting: If this is put off any longer, not only the students but also citizens in general will not be able to control themselves. [Video shows Li Peng nodding his head.] I think that these questions should be clarified. First, the current movement is no longer simply a student movement; it has become a democratic movement. . . .

WU'ER KAIXI: Fellow students, fellow students. I feel that we are almost finished with things of a practical nature. With a sense of responsibility toward the students in the square, we must try to make it as brief as possible.

LI PENG: Any other student? Since you are here, speak as much as possible. . . . If there is no one else, I will make this demand. Please do not interrupt as we speak. We have already fully . . . If you interrupt when we speak, then it will be difficult for us to continue. . . .

YAN MINGFU, Interrupting: If you do not have any more questions . . .

LI PENG, Interrupting: If you still have questions, then I hope that you will continue to speak. Since you have this many representatives here, fully air your views.

WU'ER KAIXI: Does this mean that when you finish talking, we can no longer talk? Is that what you mean?

LI PENG: What I mean is that when we are talking, do not interrupt us.

SHAO JIANG, BEIJING UNIVERSITY: Yes, yes. We hope that the current state of affairs will not become more serious, for China really should maintain a stable social order to develop itself and to become prosperous. At this stage, however, the student movement has already begun to change directly. Perhaps it has become a movement of the whole people. The student movement itself, as the central authorities have admitted, is relatively reasonable. However, we cannot guarantee that this movement of the whole people is a reasonable one. Thus, I would like to ask you gentlemen to calm this situation down as soon as possible by meeting our two demands. . . .

LI PENG: I would like to express my views on several points. Everyone is interested in discussing essential issues. First I want to discuss one essential issue. I propose that the China Red Cross Society and its chapter in Beijing responsibly and safely send those on hunger strike to various hospitals. I hope that all other students at the square would help and support this operation. . . .

Another point is that neither the government nor the party Central Committee, has ever said that the broad masses of students are creating disorder.

We have never said such a thing. We have unanimously affirmed the patriotic fervor of the students. Their patriotic aspirations are good. Many of the things they have done are correct. A considerably large number of their complaints are also problems that our government seeks to solve. I will tell you in all honesty that you have played an excellent role in helping us solve these problems. We plan to solve these problems, but there will probably be many obstacles. Some of the problems are difficult to solve. The students have actually helped the government overcome the difficulties on our road of advance by pointedly bringing up these problems. Therefore, your efforts are positive. Nevertheless, things often develop independently of your good will, fine ideas, and patriotic fervor. No one is able to control this objective law.

There is complete chaos in Beijing. Moreover, chaos has spread throughout the country. I can tell you students that yesterday our lifeline, our railway lifeline, was blocked for three hours in Wuhan, suspending our important means of transportation. At present, many urban students have come to Beijing. Others who are not students but who are people without fixed duties in society have also come to Beijing under the banner of students. I can state that during the past few days, Beijing has been in a state of anarchy. I hope you students will think for a moment what consequences might have been brought about by this situation. . . .

. . . If we insist on endless quibbling over this issue today, in my view, this is inappropriate. This is unreasonable. I want to appeal to you for the last time: if you think that you comrades present at this meeting cannot, well, either command or—however you may describe it—your partners, if you cannot have complete control over their actions, then I would like to appeal, through you, directly to our fellow students on the hunger strike in the square. I hope that they will stop their hunger strike and go to the hospital for treatment as soon as possible. Once again, on behalf of the party and the government, I extend cordial greetings to them. I hope that they will be able to accept this very simple, but also very pressing, request made to them by the government. I have finished what I wanted to say.

Standoff at Oka
Peter Blue Cloud

Tensions between Canadian First Nations and government officials over land rights hit a boiling point in 1990, when the small town of Oka, near Montreal, proposed to expand its municipal golf course into an area claimed by the Canadian Mohawk nation in the Kanesatake Indian reserve. In March 1990, after tribal members exhausted all conventional appeals to block the development, they created a road barricade to obstruct the bulldozers. The blockade continued for months, and authorities from Oka asked the provincial police to intervene. Natives from the nearby Kahnawake reserve, to show their support, set up another blockade on a bridge used by commuters, jamming traffic routes into the city. The scene captivated the nation, and tensions continued to mount. After one of the protesters shot dead a provincial soldier, the Quebec premier asked the Canadian army to come maintain order. The standoff ended when Mohawks dismantled their barriers in late September. The golf course expansion was never built, and the protest eventually helped fuel changes in Canadian laws addressing rights of native peoples.

Peter Blue Cloud, a member of the Mohawk tribe, was present during the protest. Blue Cloud, who won an American Book Award in 1981 for his poetry, recorded his experience of the standoff. An excerpt was published in the book *Native American Testimony*, edited by Peter Nabokov.

THE ST. LAWRENCE RIVER VALLEY AREA around Montreal, Quebec, is but a fraction of what is still rightfully the territories of the Mohawk Nation. Larger still are the territories of the Iroquois Six Nations Confederacy of which the Mohawk Nation is a part. These territories are mostly in what is now called the United States of America, but were ours long before the coming of the Europeans.

Kanesatake, on the north shore of Lake St. Louis, some fifteen miles from Montreal, was permanently settled in the early 1700s by natives, including many Mohawks from Kahnawake, on the south shore. The Sulpicians, a Catholic order, were given Kanesatake lands to hold in trusteeship for the natives, to remain their property until natives left them or died out. But the Sulpicians sold and leased out large tracts of these lands, including the town of Oka, which borders Kanesatake. That started the trouble, since the Mohawks never left Kanesatake, and so those sales and leases were illegal.

Recently, the town of Oka wanted to expand its nine-hole golf course to eighteen holes. The expansion was to take place in the Pines, a forest planted by natives almost two hundred years before. The area includes a cemetery of the Mohawk people and holds the remains of their parents and grandparents.

The Mohawks tried to fight the expansion by legal means, but they lost and the lands were declared no longer theirs. There was no other recourse but to declare it Indian Land.

On March 11, 1990, the Mohawks set up a barricade to prevent any development of the Pines. They were armed and ready to defend their land.

On June 30, 1990, the Oka town council won a court order to have the roadblock removed. The Mohawks began reinforcing their barricades.

On July 11, 1990, Quebec's Provincial Police, the Sûreté du Québec, began arriving in great numbers just before dawn. The first assault against the Mohawk people began. As this news reached Kahnawake, our traditional clan mothers ordered our Warriors to blockade the highways going through our lands, to support our relatives at Kanesatake.

During the long standoff we witnessed our Warriors burned in effigy at our borders, saw rioting non-natives attacking their own police with rocks and Molotov cocktails, watched as a caravan of our children, elders, and women, fearing invasion and trying to leave, were stoned by a mob while police stood by.

We were subjected to rationing as police hindered the delivery of food, fuel, and other necessities. When we used boats to get food and supplies from nearby towns, we faced mobs and were confronted by a Canadian gunboat. Even our non-native doctors and nurses, working with dwindling supplies, were harassed by mobs.

We watched the Canadian Army replacing the police with tanks, armored personnel carriers, helicopters, and hundreds of fully armed soldiers. And then they invaded our territory, and most of us stayed because it was our home.

Day 70. 18 September 1990.

A light ground frost shimmers the grass. Bright stars poke in and out of white clouds. I sit in darkness, sipping coffee and thinking of the coming winter. It is time to pick the remaining foods in the garden. As on other mornings in the past few weeks, I try to think of things unrelated to the presence of the Canadian Army surrounding our lands. I am very tired of being a hostage to Canada. I want it to end soon. Why doesn't the government negotiate as they promised?

I am sitting on my porch above the very beach where I learned to swim and to fish as a child, remembering when violence and death were dreamlike happenings in a World War far away—the only visible evidence, back then, in the many uniformed men walking our roads to visit relatives for that final good-bye.

This image of yesteryear ended abruptly with the sudden whacking, roaring sounds of a huge helicopter directly over my house. I was thinking in terms of a rescue mission, or some other such act of humanity, as it crossed the small stretch of water, to hover close to ground and disgorge a fully armed assault team.

Quickly, other choppers appeared and spewed out their loads of troops. At a crouching run, the troops headed for the small bridge which connects the island to the mainland. Other choppers dropped rolls of razor concertina wire, and other equipment to accompany whatever demonic drama was unfolding before my eyes.

The reality of this bizarre scene became evident with the immediate arrival of honking cars from all over town. Mohawks—men, women, and young people—poured onto the bridge, in outrage and anger that our sacred territory was being invaded by an armed force of the military.

The people of Kahnawake, unarmed, crossed the bridge and confronted automatic-weapons-carrying troops. There was no fear on the faces of our Mohawk people, only anger. The Army quickly grouped, weapons at the ready, and ready, too, to say, "We were only following orders."

"Get off our land!" was the main cry of the people, nose to nose with those apprehensive-looking soldiers. As the crowd grew and pushed into the line of soldiers, the first barrage of tear gas and concussion grenades was hurled. Little panic ensued as the people returned the canisters of gas, accompanied by stones and fists.

Another barrage of tear gas, and the people were forced to retreat. The Army moved quickly to cross and take the bridgehead. They didn't make it, the people regrouped, and by sheer force of bodies pushed the soldiers back to the other side. This began a long, drawn-out retreat by the Canadian Army.

I stood at the center of the bridge when the third barrage of tear gas fell. I stood at the center of myself and my people. When I heard the unbelievable chatter of automatic fire I wondered, can it be that they would kill?

Tear gas fell. Screams of outrage echoed across the waters. Rifle butts smashed into bodies to be answered by fists and feet. At least eight helicopters circled and roared overhead, unheard by those creating their own fury of sound. People jumped to water to relieve the burning tear gas. I saw soldiers thrown to ground. There were injured people on the rocks beneath the bridge. I heard fists striking flesh.

The single roll of razor wire the Army managed to unroll was tossed to the side of the bridge. The crowd never let up pressing the Army into retreat, taking their rolls of razor wire with them. The soldiers formed a right-angle wedge, with soldiers behind them. Then, at a command, they stepped back four paces. Then again and again. And again. This went on for a very long time—they were retreating!

We formed our own line thirty feet from the Army. Soldiers in small groups left the wedge and ran to waiting helicopters for evacuation. As it grew dark, we built fires. Spotlights from choppers made the scene glaringly real.

When the last of the soldiers finally left in darkness, a great cheer went up from the crowd. Later, Army Lieutenant Colonel Greg Mitchell, in charge of the invasion of Kahnawake, said, "The strong resistance surprised us. It was amazing the way they reacted, especially since we weren't at the Longhouse or a sacred place."

Dear Mr. Mitchell and Dear Canadians: Will you ever begin to understand the meaning of the soil beneath your very feet? From a grain of sand to a great mountain, all is sacred. Yesterday and tomorrow exist eternally upon this continent. We natives are the guardians of this sacred place.

WTO: The Battle in Seattle

Roni Krouzman

In December 1999 protests disrupted the meeting of the World Trade Organization (WTO) in Seattle. The protests—which came to be known as the Battle in Seattle—in some places broke into riots that shocked local residents, world leaders, and the protesters themselves, most of whom had intended their efforts to be strictly nonviolent. The meeting was supposed to showcase Seattle as a world-class city ready to compete globally as a host of important events. Instead, as an article in the *New York Times* put it, Seattleites were "astonished by the irony of riots and tear gas in a place where pedestrians normally exhibit scrupulous respect for the jay-walking laws." Business owners decried the vandalism of shops, while activists fumed over what they saw as heavy-handed police response and the arrest of more than six hundred protesters.

Observers, meeting delegates, and demonstrators alike were also surprised by the success of the protests. Disruption from human blockades shut down the opening ceremonies of the WTO meeting, preventing President Bill Clinton from delivering his remarks. Negotiations broke down, and the trade talks ended in collapse.

Young journalist and political organizer Roni Krouzman filed the following first-person account of the protests for the Web site TomPaine.com. The account was included in a 2003 anthology, *The Radical Reader: A Documentary History of the American Radical Tradition*. His view from the inside was very different than the mainstream media reports delivered to the world.

AS I LOOKED UPON THE SEA OF PEOPLE occupying Fourth Street in downtown Seattle last Tuesday, I could not help but feel energized and proud. We were occupying the city and dancing in its streets. We were nonviolently stopping the WTO and corporate globalization. We were making history.

But when I left the demonstrations and turned on the local news, I heard talk of rioters and chaos, not singing and dancing. I heard talk of police restraint in the face of "anarchist" violence, not police brutality against nonviolent direct action. I heard talk of a city driven to the brink of collapse by "angry protesters," and not an unjust system of exploitation creatively and beautifully stopped in its tracks.

They say that truth is the first casualty of war. Unfortunately, it is also the first casualty of popular rebellion. Now it's time to set the record straight about what happened and is still happening in Seattle.

I witnessed and took part in an incredible week of action and thought, one that united diverse interests to creatively challenge a global order that places profits over people. On Friday night and all day Saturday, 2,500 of us attended a series of lectures and were motivated and informed by intelligent, inspiring people from across the U.S. and around the world. But the media wasn't there.

Teach-ins and workshops continued on Sunday, when the first sign of protests emerged. Several hundred people, including French farmer and anti-globalization activist Jose Bove, demonstrated in front of a downtown McDonald's, creatively and energetically. Toward the end of the rally, someone broke a window, and that's what the media concentrated on.

That night I stumbled upon the Convergence Center, Seattle's grassroots direct action headquarters, and could not believe what I saw. Hundreds of young people filled this commercial space on Capitol Hill, milling about three massive rooms cluttered with flyers, banners and props. They all seemed so engaged, holding discussions in intimate circles, creating signs and teaching each other about civil disobedience and legal aid, and occasionally studying a giant 200 square foot map of the city that hung from a wall. . . .

I returned to the Convergence Center the next day, and participated in the general spokescouncil meeting, a five hour affair during which delegates, representing one of thirteen clusters of three to four affinity groups each, each themselves composed of five to twenty members, finalized plans for Tuesday's actions. The meeting felt frustrating at times, but it was the essence of grassroots democracy, with each representative speaking his or her mind, and conferring with fellow affinity group representatives that sat beside them to plan a coherent, well-organized strategy.

After that meeting, I understood the giant map. Each cluster would occupy one of thirteen intersections surrounding the Washington Convention and Trade Center, and nonviolently shut it down. Incredible that such a well-organized effort could be planned so creatively and democratically.

That evening, I attended the Peoples' Gala, an anti-corporate festival featuring music, comedy, and inspiring words. And seeing steelworkers sitting beside vegans, old lefties beside new, I was inspired indeed. . . .

Our rain-soaked rally began shortly before 7 a.m., long after dozens of affinity groups had slipped in to the night to occupy the city. We sang and we huddled, and cheered when the head of the longshoreman union announced that there would be no business in West Coast ports that day. And over and over again, we heard the code of nonviolence repeated: no alcohol, no drugs, no physical or verbal assault, no property damage.

As the sun began to filter through the morning clouds, we began our march through a waking city, a contingent of steelworkers leading the way. We hit the first police barricade of many shortly thereafter, thousands of us facing down a few dozen cops, who stood guarding one of the many streets that led to the convention center. And so the march continued around the city, with groups of ten and twenty and fifty at a time leaving the procession to join the activists who had seized those 13 intersections. We cheered, and we chanted, and we felt in control. Everywhere I looked, I saw rivers of demonstrators milling excitedly through the streets.

And then the tear gas and the rubber bullets came. At midmorning, the police went on the offensive, demanding a mass of at least one thousand non-violent demonstrators positioned at the intersection of Sixth and Union disperse to make way for WTO delegates. We did not, and as dozens of demonstrators sat down in front of the police line, a squadron of ten officers carrying what appeared to be automatic or semi-automatic machine guns charged over them from behind, trampling several.

The crowd booed and jeered, refusing to disperse and chanting, "We're nonviolent, how about you?" Riot-gear clad police responded with a barrage of tear gas, overcoming dozens with noxious fumes and causing hundreds of us to flee the intersection. Some protesters quickly donned gas masks, refusing to give up their ground, and were met with a hail of rubber bullets. At least two were struck, one in the leg and one in the mouth. Legal observers reported that neither was seriously injured.

Demonstrators were shocked and confused, but did not panic, as direct action medics and other activists rushed to the aid of the injured. Thousands chanted, "Shame!" and "The World is Watching!" amidst an eerie cloud of white gas and the steady hum of helicopters flying overhead.

By late morning, Seattle's coffee shops were buzzing with talk of the actions, which had now drawn over 5,000 demonstrators and hundreds of police, and diverted car and bus traffic from half the downtown area. As the day progressed and tensions mounted, some protesters adopted more aggressive tactics. Several young activists rolled van-sized garbage dumps into alleyways and intersections, including the intersection of Fourth and University. At noon, police ordered the raucous crowd there to disperse, and fired tear gas canisters when it refused. Hundreds of us fled yet again as some demonstrators threw the canisters back at the officers.

On the northern side of the Convention Center, along Pike Street, several small groups of youths dressed in black and donning ski masks or bandanas damaged property at stores including Nike Town, Old Navy, and Planet Hollywood. To the chagrin of activists who had attempted to enforce a code of nonviolence, they scrawled anti-corporate graffiti on walls and displays, and smashed corporate store windows with hammers, crowbars, and street signs, destroying a Starbucks storefront.

The overwhelming majority of activists did not engage in such activities, successfully blocking access to the Convention Center for 2,500 to 3,000 delegates through well-coordinated, nonviolent civil disobedience. In an effort to break the protesters' grip, police moved to take more intersections, shooting streams of pepper spray at nonviolent protesters who were sitting around the intersection of Sixth and Union, and attempting to break through their lines with an armored personal carrier. The police did not succeed, drawing chants of "Protect and Serve!" from an outraged crowd. Similar clashes erupted throughout downtown, with floods of protesters weaving in and out of key intersections—and securing them with barricades—visible in every direction. Police moved to take the intersections back one by one, and were often surrounded on both sides by thousands of demonstrators. I could not believe what I was seeing.

At 2 p.m., an estimated 25,000 activists, mainly union rank and file, marched into downtown from a rally at Memorial Stadium, joining the ten thousand or so direct action activists who had seized control of the city. The demonstrations displayed a level of diversity rare in American movements, as anarchists, environmentalists, and vegan hippies marched side by side with teamsters, steelworkers, and social justice activists. Though television media is concentrating overwhelmingly on protest violence and the restraint shown by officers, most of the protesters did not engage in violence, despite being assaulted by police. . . .

That night, Seattle's mayor declared a Civil Emergency, and placed downtown under nighttime curfew. The National Guard was mobilized, and police tear-gassed protesters out of downtown and in to Seattle's progressive Capitol Hill neighborhood, where the clashes continued.

After successfully using mass civil disobedience to prevent the WTO from carrying on its business Tuesday, several thousand people returned to the streets on Wednesday in an attempt to do the same. By noon, nearly 300 nonviolent protesters had been arrested and taken to the former Sand Point naval station for booking. Police and national guardsmen maintained a heavy presence throughout much of downtown, especially in a twenty-block area around the Washington Convention and Trade Center, where WTO talks had convened earlier during the day. Dozens of police and guardsmen also surrounded the Westin hotel, where President Clinton was staying, barricading the hotel's front entrance with eight Seattle metro busses.

At 1 p.m., a crowd of protesters assembled around a line of police clad in riot gear stationed in front of Old Navy, whose boarded up windows, like those of many other downtown corporate retailers, displayed anti-corporate graffiti. The small group of demonstrators chanted anti-globalization and anti-police slogans, but violence did not ensue.

Shortly thereafter, close to 1,000 protesters, including steelworkers, environmentalists, students, and social justice activists, gathered in the northern section of downtown for an anti-WTO rally. We joined them, and began a march toward the convention center, where WTO negotiations were well under way. As the lively, nonviolent crowd approached the part of downtown where protests had been banned, police opened fire with tear gas, causing the demonstrators to flee and chant, "Shame!"

Stunned and angry that police had used violence to quell a nonviolent march, we regrouped and continued our procession. Hundreds of police, some riding in armored personnel carriers and carrying pepper spray and rubber bullet launchers, swarmed around the area, intermittently firing tear gas and forcing us from one intersection to the next. For the first time that week, I was frightened. The police seemed bent on hurting people.

Chanting "Peaceful Protest!" and "No Violence!" we grew more and more disoriented, and were eventually cornered. Police, some on horseback, surrounded us, and opened fire with more tear gas and possibly rubber bullets and percussion grenades, causing us to flee down alleyways and disperse.

About half an hour later, hundreds of protesters regrouped and began to march again, occupying an intersection after being stopped by police. Night was falling, and a police helicopter flew overhead, shining a spotlight down on us. Suddenly, people began to shout, "They're surrounding us!" as a squad of twenty police marched in goose-step from behind. Just as I managed to get out of the intersection, a group of officers on horseback quickly rode in, and about one hundred protesters were surrounded on three sides.

The intersection was engulfed by an eerie silence, as trapped demonstrators contemplated their fate and hundreds of us on the outside watched in disbelief. Within minutes, dozens of police cars began arriving on the scene, several riding in an SUV whose back was full of weapons. The officers distributed percussion grenades and donned gas masks, drawing chants of "Fascists!" and "Police State!" from angry onlookers. Suddenly, chaos ensued, as police threw at least a dozen grenades at protesters. Deafening, smoky explosions went off in the middle of the demonstration, forcing protesters to flee up the street. Stunned onlookers yelled angry slogans at police, who marched methodically up the street after the fleeing demonstrators.

One enraged officer returned to the scene, and began pepper spraying a line of onlookers at will, yelling "Yeah!" before being pulled away by a fellow officer. I saw all of this with my own eyes.

Part I: The Roots and Roles of Protest
Chapter 1: Dissent and Liberty

The Magna Carta: Courtesy The British Library.

"J' Accuse": Emile Zola, "Letter to M. Félix Faure, President of the Republic, from The Dreyfus Affair: 'J'Accuse' and Other Writings, edited by Alaine Pages, translated by Eleanor Levieux. Copyright © 1996 by Yale University. Reprinted with the permission of Yale University Press.

Freedom of Speech: Copyright 1943, the Norman Rockwell Family Entities. Reprinted by permission of the Norman Rockwell Family Agency.

"Patriotism is not the *fear* of something; It is the *love* of something": Adlai Stevenson, excerpt from speech, August 1952. From Box 136, Folder 1, Adlai E. Stevenson Papers, Seeley G. Mudd Manuscript Library, Princeton University Library. Published with permission of Princeton University Library.

"Let us proclaim—loudly and all together—so that our cry pierces the sky": Reprinted with the permission of the translator.

"Daddy, you're so quaint to believe in hope": Abbie Hoffman, closing statement at his trial (April 15, 1987). As found in *The Nation* (May 2, 1987).

Speakers' Corner: Copyright © 2000 by Singapore Press Holdings Ltd. Reprinted with the permission of SPH-*The Straits Times.*

Chapter 2: Modes of Protest

"We have no intention whatever of paying your rent to Captain Boycott": Reproduced with permission from the Deputy Keeper of the Records, Public Record Office of Northern Ireland.

"But where is she now?" Aleksandra Chumakova, excerpt from *Samizdat: Voices of the Soviet Opposition,* edited by George Saunders. Copyright © 1974 by Pathfinder Press. Reprinted by permission.

"Strange Fruit": Lewis Allen, "Strange Fruit: Copyright 1939 (Renewed) by Music Sales Corporation (ASCAP). International Copyright Secured. All Rights Reserved. Reprinted by Permission.

Mothers of Plaza de Mayo: Copyright © Associated Press. Reprinted with the permission of AP/Wide World Photos.

Do the Right Thing: Copyright © 1989 by Spike Lee. Reprinted by permission of William Morris Agency, LLC on behalf of the Author.

Mock Parking Tickets: Copyright © Earth on Empty. Reprinted with the permission of Earth on Empty.

Critical Mass Turns 10: A Decade of Defiance: Joe Garofoli, "Critical Mass Turns 10: A Decade of Defiance" from *San Francisco Chronicle* (September 26, 2002). Copyright © 2002 by the San Francisco Chronicle. Reprinted with the permission of the San Francisco Chronicle via the Copyright Clearance Center.

Picasso on the Beach: Copyright © 2004 by Robert Visser/Greenpeace. Reprinted with permission.

Secret Service and White House Charged with Violating Free Speech Rights in ACLU Lawsuit: American Civil Liberties Union, "Secret Service and White House Charged with Violating Free Speech Rights in ACLU Lawsuit" (September 14, 2004). Reprinted with the permission of the American Civil Liberties Union.

"The media landscape shifted": Markos Moulitas Zuniga, "The GOP and 24/7 News" from Daily Kos web site (March 9, 2004). Copyright © 2004 by Markos Moulitas Zuniga.

Camp Casey: Copyright © STF/Associated Press. Reprinted with the permission of AP/Wide World Photos.

Pelosi, Democrats See Only Doom and Gloom: Rush Limbaugh, excerpt from " The Rush Limbaugh Show" (April 7, 2006). Reprinted courtesy of The Rush Limbaugh Show and Premiere Radio Networks, Inc.

Chapter 3: Roots of Dissent

The Bible (the Tanach): Excerpts from *The Tanach, or Hebrew Bible, Second Edition,* edited by Rabbi Nosson Scherman. Reprinted with the permission of Mesorah Publications, Ltd.

Lysistrata: Aristophanes, excerpt from *Lysistrata,* translated by Douglass Parker. Copyright © 1964 by William Arrowsmith. Used by permission of Dutton Signet, a division of Penguin Group (USA) Inc.

A Song of War Chariots: Du Fu, "A Song of War-chariots," translated by Harold Witter Bynner. As found at http://afpc.asso.fr/wengu/wg/wengu.php?l=Tangshi&no=86. Collected in *The Jade Mountain: A Chinese Anthology* (New York: Alfred A. Knopf, 1929). [36 lines]

On the Harmony of Religion and Philosophy: Averroës, excerpt [1302 words] from *On the Harmony of Religion and Philosophy,* by George F. Hourani. Reprinted with the permission of the E J W Gibb Memorial Trust.

The Vision of William concerning Piers Plowman: William Langland, excerpt from *The Vision Concerning Piers Plowman,* translated by H. W. Wells. Copyright 1935 by H. W. Wells. Reprinted with the permission of Sheed & Ward, Ltd.

The Book of the City of Ladies: Christine de Pizan, excerpt from *The Book of the City of Ladies,* translated by Rosalind Brown-Grant. Copyright © 1999 by Rosalind Brown-Grant. Reprinted with the permission of Penguin Group (UK) Ltd.

"To swear it was against my conscience": Sir Thomas More, excerpt [853 words] from a letter to his daughter, Margaret Roger (April 17, 1534) from *St. Thomas More: Selected Letters,* edited by Elizabeth Rogers. Copyright © 1961 by Yale University Press. Reprinted with the permission of Yale University Press.

Part II: Documents of Dissent
Chapter 4: Civil Rights

Protests by the Bonus Expeditionary Army. AP/Wide World Photos

Resignation from the Daughters of the American Revolution: Eleanor Roosevelt, excerpt from letter of resignation to the Daughters of the American Revolution (1939). Reprinted with the permission of Nancy Roosevelt Ireland.

Letter to the Minersville, Pennsylvania, School Directors: Billy Gobitas, letter to Minersville, PA School Board (November 5, 1935). Reprinted with the permission of Lillian Gobitas Klose.

"I have a dream": Martin Luther King, Jr., "I Have a Dream" (August 23, 1963). Copyright © 1963 by Martin Luther King, Jr. renewed 1991 by Coretta Scott King. Reprinted with the permission of the Estate of Martin Luther King, Jr., c/o Writers House, Inc., as agents for the proprietor, New York, NY.

The Autobiography of Malcolm X: Malcolm X, "A Dissenter's View of Dr. King's Speech" from Malcolm X with the assistance of Alex Haley, *The Autobiography of Malcolm X.* Copyright © 1964 by Alex Haley and Malcolm X. Copyright © 1965 by Alex Haley and Betty Shabazz. Reprinted with the permission of Random House, Inc. and John Hawkins & Associates, Inc.

Two-Minute Warning: Bloody Sunday: Copyright © 1965 Spider Martin. All rights reserved. Used with permission.

Statement of Purpose: National Organization for Women, statement of purpose (1966). Reprinted with the permission of the National Organization of Women.

"The unconstitutional provisions of AFM 39-12 relating to the discharge of homosexuals": Leonard Matlovich, letter to The Secretary of the Air Force (March 6, 1975). As found in *Letters of the 20th Century,* edited by Lisa Grunwald and Stephen J. Adler (New York: Dell, 1999). In Number 88–1, Leonard Matlovich Papers, Gay and Lesbian Historical Society of Northern California, San Francisco.

Why We Fight: Vito Russo, excerpt from speech at ACT UP event (1988). Copyright © 1988 by Vito Russo. Reprinted with the permission of the Estate of Vito Russo.

De Colores Means All of Us: Elizabeth Martinez, excerpt from *De Colores Means All of Us: Latina Views for a Multi-Cultural Century.* Copyright © 1998 by Elizabeth Martinez. Reprinted with the permission of the author and South End Press.

The Growing Surveillance Monster: Jay Stanley and Barry Steinhardt, excerpt from the introduction to "Bigger Monster, Weaker Chains: The Growth of American Surveillance Society" (New York: ACLU, January 15, 2003). Reprinted with the permission of the American Civil Liberties Union.

"Si se puede!" AP/Wide World Photos.

Chapter 5: National Self-Determination

Decree of the War to the Death: Simón Bolívar, excerpt from "Decree of War to the Death" from *El Libertador: Writings of Simón Bolívar,* translated from the Spanish by Frederick H. Fornoff. Copyright © 2003 by Oxford University Press. Reprinted with permission of the publisher.

Prague Spring: Liber Hajsky/epa/Corbis

"I couldn't help noticing the crack in the bell": His Holiness the Dalai Lama, excerpt from speech before United States Congress (1991). Reprinted with the permission of the Office of His Holiness the Dalai Lama.

Chapter 6: Economic Justice

"The Negro is still a slave": W.E.B. Du Bois, "The Negro Is Still a Slave" from *The (Cincinnati) Times-Star* (December 5, 1910). Reprinted with the permission of the David Graham Du Bois Trust.

The Torment of Migrant Workers: John Steinbeck, excerpt from "The Torment of Migrant Workers" from *The Nation* (September 12, 1936). Reprinted with the permission of *The Nation.* For subscription information, call 1-800-333-8536. Portions of each week's *The Nation* magazine can be accessed at http://www.thenation.com.

"The Oligarchies": Pablo Neruda, "The Oligarchies," translated by Jack Schmitt, from *Canto General.* Copyright © 1991. Reprinted with the permission of the University of California Press.

Capitalism and Freedom: Milton Friedman, excerpt from *Capitalism and Freedom.* Copyright © 1962 by Milton Friedman. Reprinted with the permission of The University of Chicago Press.

Bark Petitions: Rev. E. A. Wells, excerpt from "Text of a statement prepared by the Rev. E. A. Wells and read at the House of Representatives Select Committee of Enquiry into the Grievances of Yirrkala Aborigines sitting at Yirrkala Mission on 1 October 1963." Published in E. A. Wells, *Reward and Punishment in Arnhem Land.* Copyright © 1982 by the Australian Institute of Aboriginal and Torres Strait Islander Studies. Reprinted with permission. Image courtesy of the National Archives of Australia.

"We are not beasts of burden": Reprinted with the permission of the Cesar E. Chavez Foundation.

The Modern Little Red Hen: Ronald Reagan, "The Modern Little Red Hen" from *Ronald Reagan in His Own Hand*. Copyright © 2001 by The Ronald Reagan Presidential Foundation. Reprinted with the permission of The Ronald Reagan Presidential Foundation.

How can you call it a trade union?: Nic Paget-Clarke, excerpt from "Interview with Ela Bhatt" from *In Motion Magazine* (August 31, 2003). Reprinted with the permission of Nic Paget-Clarke/ *In Motion Magazine*.

Disposable People: Kevin Bales, excerpts from *Disposable People*. Copyright © 1999 by the Regents of the University of California. Reprinted with the permission of the University of California Press.

Resolved to Ruin: Greg Palast, excerpt from "Resolved to Ruin" from *Harper's* (March 2003). Copyright © 2003 by Greg Palast. Reprinted with the permission of Diana Finch Literary Agency.

Wal-Mart: The High Cost of Low Price: Copyright © 2005 Retail Project LLC. Reprinted with permission.

The Great Corporate Jobs-for-Subsidies Con-Job: Jim Hightower, excerpt from *Hightower Lowdown* (July 2005). Reprinted with the permission of the *Hightower Lowdown*. You can read this and other Lowdown issues at www.hightowerlowdown.org.

Youth's Future: Protests Against Changes in French Labor Laws: Copyright © 2006 AP/Wide World Photos. Reprinted with permission.

Chapter 7: Environmental Conservation

Everglades: River of Grass: Marjorie Stoneman Douglas, excerpts from *The Everglades: River of Grass, Fiftieth Anniversary Edition*. Copyright 1947, © 1997 by Marjorie Stoneman Douglas. Reprinted with the permission of Pineapple Press, Inc.

A Sand County Almanac: Aldo Leopold, excerpt from *A Sand County Almanac*. Copyright 1949, 1953, © 1966 by Oxford University Press. Reprinted with the permission of Oxford University Press, Ltd.

"Wilderness Letter": Wallace Stegner, "Wilderness Letter" from *The Sound of Mountain Water*. Copyright © 1946–1980 by Wallace Stegner. Reprinted with the permission of Doubleday, a division of Random House, Inc. and Brandt & Hochman Literary Agents, Inc.

Silent Spring: Rachel Carson, excerpt from "A Fable for Tomorrow" from *Silent Spring*. Copyright © 1962 by Rachel Carson. Reprinted with the permission of Houghton Mifflin Company and Pollinger, Ltd. All rights reserved.

"What is Proposed Here is a Modest Compromise": Sierra Club advertisement from *The New York Times* (June 9, 1966): 35. Reprinted with permission.

"The Energy Crisis: A Radical Solution": Stewart Udall, "The Energy Crisis: A Radical Solution" from *World* (May 8, 1973). Reprinted with the permission of the author.

The Crying Indian: Image courtesy of Keep America Beautiful, Inc., www.kab.org.

The Monkey Wrench Gang: Edward Abbey, excerpt from *The Monkey Wrench Gang*. Copyright © 1975, 1985 by Edward Abbey, renewed 2003 by Clarke Abbey. Reprinted with the permission of HarperCollins Publishers and Harold Matson Co., Inc. and by permission of Don Congdon Associates, Inc.

"Before Love Canal, I knew Nothing About the Environment": Richard Kazis, "Love Canal" from *New Internationalist* 113 (July 1982). Copyright © 1982 by New Internationalist, www.newint.org. Reprinted by kind permission of New Internationalist.

Ecodefense: Dave Foreman, excerpt from "Strategic Monkeywrenching" from Dave Foreman and Bill Haywood, eds., from *Ecodefense: A Field Guide to Monkeywrenching*. Copyright © 1985 by Dave Foreman. Reprinted by permission.

Voices of Chernobyl: Nikolai Fomich Kalugin, father, "Monologue About a Whole Life Written On Doors" From Svetlana Alexievich, from *Voices from Chernobyl: The Oral History of a Nuclear Disaster*, translated by Keith Gessen. Copyright © 1997, 2006 by Svetlana Alexievich. Translation © 2005 by Keith Gessen.

Cry of the Earth, Cry of the Poor: Leonardo Boff, excerpt from *Cry of the Earth, Cry of the Poor*, translated by Philip Berryman. Copyright © 1995 by Leonardo Boff. English translation copyright © 1997 by Orbis Books. Reprinted with the permission of Orbis Books.

The Wisdom That Builds Community: Greg Watson, "The Wisdom That Builds Community" (presented at the 17th Annual E. F. Schumacher Lectures, October 1997). Reprinted with the permission of the author.

Now or Never: What's an Environmentalist to Do?: Bill McKibben, "Now or Never: What's an Environmentalist to Do?" from *In These Times* (April 30, 2001). Reprinted with the permission of *In These Times*, www.inthesetimes.com and Bill McKibben.

Protecting Yellowstone: Earthjustice, "Conservationists Sue to Protect Yellowstone from Snowmobiles" (press release, March 25, 2003). Reprinted with the permission of Earthjustice.

"On the Very First Day We Planted Seven Trees": Amanda Griscom Little, "Maathai on the Prize: An Interview with Nobel Peace Prize Winner Wangari Maathai" from *Grist* (February 15, 2005). Reprinted with permission from Grist.org.

Petition to the Inter American Commission on Human Rights Seeking Relief from Violations Resulting from Global Warming Caused by Acts and Omissions of the United States: Reprinted with the permission of Sheila Watt-Cloutier and the Inuit Circumpolar Conference.

"We should no longer tolerate the low-cost or even free exploitation of public resources": Three Gorges Probe,

"Call for Public Disclosure of Nujiang Hydropower Development's EIA Report in Accordance with the Law" (September 6, 2005). Reprinted with the permission of Three Gorges Probe, www.threegorgesprobe.org.

"Kleercut" Advertisement: Copyright © 2005 by the Natural Resources Defense Council.

Equator Principles; Compliance Complaint: Center for Human Rights and Environment, "Equator Principles: Compliance Complaint, Regarding Proposed Paper Mill Investment in Fray Bentos Uruguay: From the Center for Human Rights (CEDHA) and Environment to ING of the Netherlands" (2005). Reprinted with the permission of the Center for Human Rights and Environment (CEDHA).

Chapter 8: Religious Freedom

Appeal to the President of the United States: Reprinted with the permission of the Karpeles Manuscript Library Museums.

"Christ Climbed Down" from *A Coney Island of the Mind:* Lawrence Ferlinghetti, "Christ Climbed Down" from *A Coney Island of the Mind.* Copyright © 1955, 1958 by Lawrence Ferlinghetti. Reprinted with the permission of New Directions Publishing Corporation.

Letter from Birmingham Jail: Dr. Martin Luther King, Jr., "Letter from Birmingham Jail" (April 16, 1963). Copyright © by The Estate of Martin Luther King, Jr. Reprinted with the permission of Writer's House, LLC. on behalf of the Proprietor.

Responsibility of the Kingdom of God: Archbishop Oscar Romero, "Responsibility of the kingdom of God" (sermon, June 29, 1977). As found at www.romeroes.com

Controversies at Auschwitz: the Convent and the Cross: Elie Wiesel, excerpt from interview (August 29, 1989) in *Memory Offended: The Auschwitz Convent Controversy,* edited by Carol Rittner and John K. Roth. Copyright © 1991 by Carol Rittner and John K. Roth. Reprinted with the permission of Greenwood Publishing Group, Inc. Westport, CT

Presentation of the Ten Commandments Monument at the Alabama Supreme Court: Chief Justice Roy S. Moore, "Presentation of the Ten Commandments Monument at the Alabama Supreme Court" (speech, August 1, 2001). Reprinted with the permission of the author.

Response of the Faithful: A Declaration to the Pope: Voice of the Faithful, "Response of the Faithful: A Declaration to the Pope." Reprinted with the permission of Voice of the Faithful, www.votf.org.

Statement Protesting the Ordination of Bishop V. Gene Robinson: American Anglican Council, statement protesting the ordination of Bishop V. Gene Robinson (November 2, 2003). Reprinted with the permission of The American Anglican Council.

Protest of French Muslim Head Scarf Ban: Copyright © 2004 by Reuters.

"Our Religious Identities Have . . . Become an Increasingly Potent Source of Human Conflict": Sam Harris, excerpt from "Q&A with Sam Harris" from www.samharris.org/index.php/samharris/full-text/qa_with_sam_harris/. Reprinted with the permission of Sam Harris.

Take Back the Faith: Jim Wallis, "Take Back the Faith" from *Sojourners* (September 2004). Copyright © 2004. Reprinted with the permission of *Sojourners* magazine, www.sojo.net, 1-800-714-7474.

"We have to snap out of our denial.": Irshad Manji, "Denial is the Scourge of Islam," letter to Australian Prime Minister John Howard from *The Australian* (August 23, 2005). Reprinted with the permission of the author.

Our Endangered Values: America's Moral Crisis: Jimmy Carter, excerpts from *Our Endangered Values: America's Moral Crisis.* Copyright © 2005 by Jimmy Carter. Reprinted with the permission of Simon & Schuster Adult Publishing Group.

Chapter 9: Peace and War

The Third of May, 1808, or *The Execution on Principe Pio Hill:* Scala / Art Resource, NY

Guernica: Photo: John Bigelow Taylor / Art Resource, NY. Copyright © 2006 Estate of Pablo Picasso/Artists Rights Society (ARS) New York

Catch-22: Joseph Heller, excerpt from *Catch-22.* Copyright © 1961 by Joseph Heller. Reprinted with the permission of Simon & Schuster Adult Publishing and International Creative Management, Inc.

4 Kent State Students Killed by Troops: John Kifner, excerpt from "4 Kent State Students Killed by Troops" from *The New York Times* (May 5, 1970). Copyright © 1970 by The New York Times Company. Reprinted with permission.

"Witness for Peace needs to reflect on the true meaning of peace": Sharon Hostetler, "Old Commitments, New Directions" from *Witness for Peace Newsletter* 10, no. 2 (Summer 1993). Copyright © 1993. Reprinted with the permission of the author.

"Washington Bullets": Michael Geoffrey Jones and John Mellor, "Washington Bullets," as performed by The Clash on *Sandinista*

Statement on the Refusal to Participate in Interventionist Wars: Erik Larsen, excerpt from "Statement of Refusal to Participate in Interventionist War" (August 28, 1990). Reprinted with the permission of the author.

Thoughts in the Presence of Fear: Wendell Berry, "Thoughts in the Presence of Fear" (October 11, 2001). Copyright © 2001 by The Orion Society. Reprinted with the permission of the Orion Society.

"So You Want to be a CO?": "So You Wan to Be a Conscientious Objector?" from www.peace-out.com. Reprinted by permission.

Black Power: AP/World Wide Photos

Criticism and Response to Piss Christ: Reprinted with permission.

"This action was illegal .. but it was legitimate": Reprinted with permission of José Bové.

Protests Against Western Valentine's Day: On Asia Images PTE Ltd.

Chapter 12: Extreme Protest

"An oppressed class which does not strive to . . . use arms . . . deserves to be treated like slaves.": Source: Marxists Internet Archive.

"What happened exceeded our boldest dreams": Copyright © 2004 Yad Vashem The Holocaust Martyrs' and Heroes' Remembrance Authority. Reprinted with permission.

Self-immolations of Vietnamese Buddhist Monks: "His body was slowly withering and shriveling up, his head blackening and charring": Copyright © Bettmann/CORBIS.

"It is an idea for which I am prepared to die": Statement at the Opening of the Rivonia Trial: Nelson Mandela, excerpt from "I Am Prepared to Die: (Statement from the dock at the opening of the defense case in the Rivonia Trial, Pretoria Supreme Court, 20 April 1964)". As found at www.anc.org.za/ancdocs/history/rivonia.html

The Legacy of Luna: Julia Butterfly Hill, excerpt from *The Legacy of Luna: The Story of a Tree, a Woman, and the Struggle to Save the Redwoods*. Copyright © 2000 by Julia Butterfly Hill. Reprinted with the permission of HarperCollins Publishers and the William Morris Agency, LLC.

Letter to America: Osama bin Laden, excerpt [approximately 1145 words] from "Letter to America" from *The Observer* (November 24, 2002). As found at http://observer.guardian.co.uk/international/story/0,,845724,00.html

My Name is Rachel Corrie: Rachel Corrie, excerpt from My Name Is Rachel Corrie, edited by Alan Rickman and Katharine Viner. Copyright © 2005. Reprinted with the permission of Craig Corrie.

Protests Against Cartoons Depicting the Prophet Mohammed: "They featured evil, shameless images": STR/Associated Press. Reprinted with the permission of AP/Wide World Photos. Cartoons reprinted with permission of Jens Julius Hansen and Ramus Sand Hoyer.

Chapter 13: The Experience of Protest

"I Sat Speechless and Prayed to God to Help Me": Mohandas K. Gandhi, excerpt from *An Autobiography: The Story of My Experiments with Truth,* translated by Mahadev Desai. Reprinted with the permission of The Navajivan Trust.

"I did not mince matters, yet there was no arrest": Emma Goldman, excerpt from *Living My Life, Volume II.* Copyright 1931 by Emma Goldman. Reprinted with the permission of Alfred A. Knopf, a division of Random House, Inc.

"Those Who Dare to Stand in a Strong Sun and Cast a Sharp Shadow": Robert Moses, excerpt from a letter written in Magnolia, Mississippi county jail (1961). Reprinted with the permission of Robert Parris Moses, Founder & President, The Algebra Project, Inc.

"Saturday Night, the Pink Panthers are Back in Full Force": Edmund White, excerpt from a letter to Alfred and Ann Corn (1969) from *The Violet Quill Reader: The Emergence of Gay Writing After Stonewall*, edited by David Bergman. Reprinted with the permission of the author.

"Praying Crowd Halts Marcos Tank Column": John Burgess, excerpt from "Praying Crowd Halts Marcos Tank Column" from *The Washington Post* (February 24, 1986). Copyright © 1986 by The Washington Post. Reprinted with permission.

Standoff at Oka: Peter Blue Cloud, excerpt from "Resistance at Oka" From *Native American Testimony, Revised Edition*, edited by Peter Nabokov (New York: Penguin, 1999). Copyright © 1978 by Peter Blue Cloud. Reprinted with the permission of the author.

WTO: The Battle in Seattle: Roni Krouzman, excerpt [approximately 1935 words] from "WTO in Seattle: An Eyewitness Account" (December 6, 1999). Reprinted with the permission of the author.

INDEX OF DOCUMENTS

Advice to a People Called Methodist (Wesley), 324-325
Agreement of the Free People of England, An (Lilburn/Walwyn/Prince/Overton), 420-422
"Am I Not a Man and a Brother?": Anti-slavery Medal from the Shop of Josiah Wedgwood, *423*, 423-424
American Crisis, The (Paine), 172-175
American Forests (Muir), 257-258
"And ain't I a woman?" (Truth), 123-124
Appeal to the President of the United States (Smith), 335-336
Autobiography of Malcolm X, The (Malcolm X), 149-150

Bark Petitions (The Yolngu People), 238-240, *239*
Battle of Algiers, The (Solinas), 193-194
"Before love canal, I knew nothing about the environment" (Gibbs), 283-285
Bible, The (the Tanach), 71-72
Black Power, *481*, 481-482
Book of the City of Ladies (de Pizan), 91-92
"Brief Letter to Donald Walsh (in memoriam)" (Cuadra), 439-440
"But where is she now?" (Chumakova), 49-52

Camp Casey (Sheehan), *67*, 67-68
Capitalism and Freedom (Friedman), 237-238
Capoeira: "The Dance of War," (Rugendas), *47*, 47-48
Catch-22 (Heller), 402-404
"Christ Climbed Down" from *A Coney Island of the Mind* (Ferlinghetti), 343-345
Collection of the Sufferings of the People called Quakers, A (Besse), 381-383
Communist Manifesto, The (Marx/Engels), 212-214
Conservationalists Sue to Protect Yellowstone from Snowmobiles (Earthjustice), 299-301
Controversies at Auschwitz: The Convent and the Cross (Wiesel/Rittner), 352-356
"The Corn Laws" (Davenport), 210-212
Critical Mass Turns 10: a Decade of Defiance (Garofoli), 60-62
Criticism and Response to *Piss Christ* (Helms/Serrano), 484-487
Cry of the Earth, Cry of the Poor (Boff), 290-292
"Crying Indian, The," 279, *279*

"Daddy, you're so quaint to believe in hope" (Hoffman), 40-42
De Colores Means All of Us (Martínez), 156-158
De Profundis (Wilde), 470-472
Declaration from the Poor Oppressed People of England, The (The True Levelers), 202-204
Declaration of Barbados, The, 436-437
Declaration of Independence (Minh), 190-191
Declaration of Independence, The, 169-172
Declaration of Rights of the Stamp Act Congress, 162-163
Declaration of the Immediate Causes Which Induce and Justify the Secession of South Carolina from the
      Federal Union, 176-178
Declaring America's Independence (Rush), 515
Decree of War to the Death (Bolívar), 175-176
Dialogue from the Examination of Mrs. Hutchinson During Her Trial (Hutchinson/Winthrop), 317-321
Dialogue from *United States v. Susan B. Anthony* (Anthony/Hunt), 126-128
Discourse Concerning Unlimited Submission and Non-Resistance to the Higher Powers (Mayhew), 326-328
Discourse on Political Economy, A (Rousseau), 204-206
Disposable People (Bales), 245-248
Dissenting from *Sierra Club v. Morton* (Douglas), 280-281
"Do not let the olive branch fall from my hand" (Arafat), 195-197
Do the Right Thing (Lee), 55-58

Easter proclamation (Provisional Government of the Irish Republic), 188-189
Ecodefense (Foreman/Haywood), 285-288
Encyclopedia (Diderot), 465-466
Energy Crisis: A Radical Solution (Udall), 273-276
Equator Principles: Compliance Complaint (Center for Human Rights and Environment), 312-315
Everglades: River of Grass (Douglas), 261-263

Fascism's Firm Footprint in India (Roy), 454-456
4 Kent State Students Killed by Troops (Kifner), 407-409
Freedom from Fear (Aung San Suu Kyi), 441-444
Freedom of Speech (Rockwell), *36*, 36-37

"Get Up, Stand Up" (Marley/Tosh), 437-439
"Give me liberty or give me death" (Henry), 166-169
"Give us our independence": Speech to the U.S. House of Representatives (Rivera), 186-188
Great Corporate Jobs-for-Subsidies Con-Job (Hightower), 253-255
Growing Surveillance Monster (American Civil Liberties Union), 158-159
Guernica (Picasso), *402*, 402
"Hair" (Rado and Ragni), 479-481
"He Calls That Religion" (The Mississippi Sheiks), 341-343
Hind Swaraj (Gandhi), 184-186
"How can you call it a trade union?" (Bhatt/ *In Motion* Magazine), 244-245
How to Destroy the Boreal, North America's Largest Ancient Forest, in 3 Easy Steps (Greenpeace/Natural
    Resources Defense Council), *311*, 311-312
"I advise, I entreat, I exhort, I admonish" (Ambrose, Bishop of Milan), 83
"I am for peace on almost any terms" (Worth), 389-390
"I am opposed to having the eagle putting its talons on any other land" (Twain), 390-391
"I am opposed to this and all other wars" (Baldwin), 399-400
"I came to Wichita expecting to get in trouble and here I am": A Report of the Carrie Nation (*Topeka
    Daily Capital*), 472-474
"I cannot say it without tears" (Delgados), 105-108
"I confess that I do not entirely approve of this Constitution" (Franklin), 22-24
"I couldn't help noticing the crack in the bell" (Dalai Lama), 197-200
"I did not mince matters, yet there was no arrest" (Goldman), 521-522
"I do not feel that I am a piece of property" (Flood), 153
"I have a dream" (King), 145-148
"I have nothing to lose by standing up for my beliefs" (Ali), 404-405
"I have suffered because I was an Italian" (Vanzetti), 139-140
"I must like them publish a card of denial" (Langston), 493-495
"I neither can nor will retract anything": Speech Before the Diet of Worms (Luther), 93-95
"I never intentionally wronged anyone" (Socrates), 75-78
"I sat speechless and prayed to god to help me" (Gandhi), 519-521
"I saw the soldier ... endeavoring to push me through with his bayonet" (Palmes), 164-165
I Speak of Freedom (Nkrumah), 192
"I will be heard" (Garrison), 113-115
"In the interest of true Americanism": letter to New York governor Alfred Smith (Winter), 138-139
"An inconceivable miscarriage of justice" (Doyle), 425-427
"Is there any point at which all of the legal remedies will not suffice?" (Rudolph), 509-512
"It is an idea for which I am prepared to die": Statement at the Opening of the Rivonia Trial (Mandela),
    499-503
"It is no longer clear what is service and what is disservice' (Clinton), 405-407

"J'accuse" (Zola), 28-31
Jewish State, The (Herzl), 179-181
Journal of the Life, Travels, and Gospel Labours of That Faithful Servant and Minister of Christ, Job Scott (Scott),
    382-384
"Labour is the Producer of All Wealth" (George), 218-220
Land Mines and Measures to Eliminate Them (Williams), 447-449
"The late rising of the people" (Gray), 108-109
Legacy of Luna, The (Hill), 503-504
"Let My People Go" (African-American spiritual), 334-335
"Let us proclaim—loudly and all together—so that our cry pierces the sky" (Aguirre/Tarigo), 38-40
Letter Concerning Toleration, A (Locke), 321-323
Letter from Birmingham Jail (King), 349-350
Letter to America (bin Laden), 504-507
Letter to the Minersville, Pennsylvania, School Directors (Gobitas), 143
Letter to the San Francisco Board of Trustees (Tape), 131-132
Li Peng Meets Fasting Student Protesters (Beijing Television Service), 530-533
Liberty Leading the People (Delacroix), 424-425, *425*
Lysistrata (Aristophanes), 73-75

Magna Carta, 16-19
Man Against Tanks (photograph), 440-441, *441*
Manifesto of Futurism (Marinetti), 474-475

Manifesto of the Equals (Maréchal), 206-208
"The media landscape shifted" (Daily Kos), 65-67
Memorial and Remonstrance Against Religious Assessments (Madison), 328-332
Memorial of the Cherokee Indians (Cherokee Nation), 110-113
Memorial to the Massachusetts Legislature (Dix), 117-118
Mock Parking Tickets (Earth on Empty), 59, *59*
Modern Little Red Hen (Reagan), 242-243
Monkey Wrench Gang, The (Abbey), 281-283
Mothers of Plaza de Mayo, 54-55, *55*
My Name Is Rachel Corrie (play) (Corrie/Rickman/Viner), 507-509
My Official Protest to the Treaty, from *Hawaii's Story by Hawaii's Queen* (Queen Liliuokalani), 181-183

Narrative of the Life of William Brown (Brown), 119-120
"The Negro is still a slave" (Du Bois), 230-231
New York Committee of Vigilance for the Year 1837, Together with Important Facts Relative to Their
    Proceedings (Ruggles), 115-116
Nineteen Eighty-Four (Orwell), 430-433
North Korea: Denial of Right to Food (Amnesty International), 460-461
"The not-raising-hog-business" (Lee), 53-54
Notes for Officers (Tolstoy), 391-395
"The novel is not the crime" (Rushdie), 444-447
Now or Never: What's an Environmentalist to Do? (McKibben), 295-299

Oil War of 1872, The (Tarbell), 225-227
"The Oligarchies" from *Canto general* (Neruda), 235-237
On Child Slavery in Yorkshire (Oastler), 208-210
On Liberty (Mill), 31-34
On the Duty of Civil Disobedience (Thoreau), 385-387
On the Harmony of Religion and Philosophy (Averroës), 85-88
"On the Late Massacre in Piedmont" (Milton), 422-423
"On the very first day we planted seven trees" (Maathai/Little), 301-304
Opinion from *Engel v. Vitale* (Black), 345-348
Opinion on *Abrams v. United States* (Holmes), 34-35
"Opposing arbitrary power" (Zenger), 102-105
"An oppressed class which does not strive to … use arms … deserves to be treated like slaves" (Lenin),
    495-496
Oppression of the Worthy Poor, The (Banks), 221-222
Oral Argument from *Elk Grove Unified School Dist. v. Newdow* (Newdow and the Supreme Court of
    the United States), 365-368
Our Endangered Values: America's Moral Crisis (Carter), 377-379
"Our religious identities have … become an increasingly potent source of human conflict" (Harris), 368-373
"Out of the love that I bear to some of your friends," 491

"Patriotism is not the *fear* of something; it is the *love* of something" (Stevenson), 37-38
Pelosi, Democrats See Only Doom and Gloom (Limbaugh), 68-69
People's Party Platform, 222-225
Petition to the Inter-American Commission on Human Rights Seeking Relief from Violations Resulting from
    Global Warming Caused by Acts and Omissions of the United States (Watt-Cloutier/Inuit Circumpolar
    Conference), 304-308
Picasso on the Beach (Greenpeace), 62-63
Pittsburgh Platform: Declaration of Principles of Reform Judaism 1885 Pittsburgh Conference, The, 336-338
"Please stop using the word 'Negro' " (Terrell), 477-479
Prague Spring, 194-195. *194*
Praying Crowd Halts Marcos Tank Column (Burgess), 527-530
Preamble to the U. S. Constitution, 25
Presentation of the Ten Commandments Monument at the Alabama Supreme Court (Moore), 356-359
Proceedings of Farmington, Connecticut, on the Boston Port Act, 165-166
Profits of Religion, The, 338-341
Protest of French Muslim Head Scarf Ban, *364*, 364
Protests Against Cartoons Depicting the Prophet Mohammad: "They featured evil, shameless images"
    512, *513*
Protests Against Western Valentine's Day (Dukhtaran-e-Millat), 489, *489*
Protests by the Bonus Expeditionary Army, *140*, 140-141

"Rally, Mohawks! Bring out your axes," 491-493
Report of New York City Draft Riot, 387-389
Republic of Fear (Makiya), 449-451

Resignation from the Daughters of the American Revolution (Roosevelt), 141
Resolution of the Citizen's Mass meeting (Montgomery Improvement Association), 143-145
Resolved to Ruin (Palast), 248-251
Response of the Faithful: A Declaration to the Pope (Voice of the Faithful), 359-360
Responsibility of the Kingdom of God (Romero), 350-353

"Same power which protects the white man, should protect the black" (Forten), 109-110
Sand County Almanac, A (Leopold), 263-265
"Saturday night, the pink panthers are back in full force" (White), 525-527
Second Inaugural Address (Lincoln), 26-28
Second Treatise of Government (Locke), 19-20
Secret Service and White House Charged with Violating Free Speech Rights in ACLU Lawsuit (American
    Civil Liberties Union), 63-65
Self-immolations of Vietnamese Buddhist Monks: "His body was slowly withering and shriveling up, his head
    blackening and charring," 498, 498-499
Self-Reliance (Emerson), 466-468
Seneca Falls Declaration of Independence, 1200-123
Sermon on the Mount, The (Jesus Christ), 80-82
"Sexual love is not naturally restricted to pairs" (Noyes), 468-470
"She found herself concerned to go to their Assembly in a very unusual Manner" (Wardell), 46-47
"Sí se puede" (Yes we can), 159-160, 160
Silent Spring (Carson), 268-271
So You Want to Be a CO? (Peace-Out), 417-419
Social Contract, The (Rousseau), 20-22
Song of War Chariots, A (Fu), 84-85
Speaker's Corner (Ng), 42-44
Spirit of the First Earth Day, The (Lewis), 277-278
"The Stalin Epigram" (Mandelstam), 427-428
Standoff at Oka (Blue Cloud), 533-536
Statement Defining the Position of the American Civil Liberties Union on the Issues of the United
    States, A (American Civil Liberties Union founders), 135-138
Statement of Purpose (founders of the National Organization for Women), 151-152
Statement of Refusal to Participate in Interventionist Wars (Larsen), 412-414
Statement Protesting the Ordination of Bishop V. Gene Robinson (American Anglican Council), 362-364
"Strange fruit" (Allen), 52-53
Strike Against War (Keller), 396-399
Summation in the Haywood Trial (Darrow), 227-230

Take Back the Faith (Wallis), 373-375
Ten Years of Madness (Jicai), 433-436
Testimony Before the U.S. Congressional Human Rights Caucus (al-Qahtani), 360-362
"There Is Power in a Union" (Hill), 232-233
The Third of May, 1801, or The Execution on Principe Pio Hill (Goya y Lucientes), 384, 384-385
"This action was illegal, but … it was legitimate" (Bové), 487-489
"This Land Is Your Land" (Guthrie), 142
"This sight froze the blood in my veins" (Moneta), 516-517
"This word as used in the picture is not an oath or a curse" (Selnick), 475-477
"Those who dare to stand in a strong sun and cast a sharp shadow" (Moses), 524-525
"Though I see only gloom before me, I shall follow the Lone Star" (Houston), 178-179
Thoughts in the Presence of Fear (Berry), 414-417
"To swear it was against my conscience" (More), 95-97
To the Workmen (The Committee for the Central Labor Union), 214-215
Torment of Migrant Workers, The (Steinbeck), 233-235
Two-Minute Warning: Bloody Sunday, 150-151, 151

U.S. Bill of Rights, 24-26
"The unconstitutional provisions of AFM 39-12 relating to the discharge of homosexuals" (Matlovich),
    153-154
Underground Rail Road, The (Still), 517-519

Virginia Act for Establishing Freedom, The (Jefferson), 332-333
Vision of William, concerning Piers Plowman (Langland), 88-90
Voices from Chernobyl (Alexievich), 288-290

Wal-Mart: the High Cost of Low Price (Greenwald), 251-252, 252
"The War of Spartacus" from Life of Marcus Licinius Crassus (Plutarch), 78-80
"Washington Bullets" (The Clash), 411-412

"We … demand to be busted by policewomen only" (New York Radical Women), 482-484
"We are against this traffic of men" (German Mennonites), 101-102
"We are not beasts of burden" (Chávez), 240-242
"We don't want other women ever to have to do this over again" (Winslow), 522-524
"We drifted back to our trenches and the fraternization ended" (Niemann), 395-396
"We frankly admit that we are disloyalists" (Debs), 400-402
"We have found you wanting" (Schneiderman), 231-232
"We have no intention whatever of paying your rent to Captain Boycott" (Irish Land League), *48*, 48-49
"We have to snap out of our denial" (Manji), 375-377
"We should no longer tolerate the low-cost or even free exploitation of public resources" (Call for Public Disclosure of Nujiang Hydropower Development's EIA Report), 308-310
        Wealth (Carnegie), 216-218
"What happened exceeded our boldest dreams" (Anielewicz), 497
"What Is Proposed Here Is a Modest Compromise" (Udall), 271-273, *272*
What Shall Be Done with the Negro? (Douglass), 128-131
When Broken Glass Floats (Him), 451-453
"Why can't we have a soldier's pay?" (Gooding), 125-126
"Why should we be kept thus in serfdom?": from a Sermon by John Ball (Froissart), 90-91
Why We Fight (Russo), 154-156
"Wilderness Letter" from *The Sound of Mountain Water* (Stegner), 266-268
"Will We Say 'Never Again' Yet Again?" (Kristof), 458-459
Wisdom That Builds Community, The, 292-295
"Witness for Peace needs to reflect on the true meaning of peace" (Hostetler), 409-411
Woman and the New Race (Sanger), 133-135
"A Woman's Point of View" (Blatch), 132-133, *133*
WTO: The Battle in Seattle (Krouzman), 536-541

A Year in Treblinka Horror Camp (Wiernik), 428-430
Yosemite Against Corporation Greed (Branson), 258-261
"You know the people's choice" (Yushchenko), 456-457
Youth's Future: Protests Against Changes in French Labor Laws, 255

INDEX

Aaron, 71, 72
Abbey, Edward, 281-283
Abernathy, Ralph, 144
Abolition and abolitionist move
    ment, 109, 113-115, 124,
    423-424, 493-495
    medals, *423*, 423-424
Aboriginal peoples, 238-240, 436-
    437
Abrams v. United States, 34, 35
Adams, Abigail, 100
Adams, John, 164, 169, 515
Addams, Jane, 135
Advertising, 279, *279*, *311*, 311-312
African Americans, 55, 100, 109,
    115-116, 119-120, 123-124,
    125-126, 128-131, 143-150,
    230-231,388, 477-479, 517-519
African National Congress, 499
Age of Enlightenment, 465
Agitators, 420
Aguirre, Gonzalo, 38-40
AIDS, 154-156
AIDS Coalition to Unleash Power
    (ACT UP), 155
Alcohol, 472-474
Alexievich, Svetlana, 288-290
Algeria, 193
Algerian National Liberation Front
    (NLF), 193
Ali, Muhammad, 404
Allen, Lewis, 52
al-Qaeda, 504
al-Qahtani, Amal, 360-362
Amazon, 290-292
Ambrose, Bishop of Milan, 83-84
American Anglican Council, 362-
    364
American Anti-Slavery Society, 113
American Civil Liberties Union
    (ACLU), 63-65, 135-138, 158-
    159, 356-357, 399
American Civil War, 26, 387, 387-
    388, 389
American Crisis, The, 172-175
American Missionary Association,
    129
American Revolution, 19, 21, 161,
    166-175, 382-383, 490
Americanism, pure, 138
Amnesty International, 439, 442,
    460-461
Amnista (painting), 62
Anderson, David C., 362
Anderson, Marian, 141
Angier, Natalie, 368
Anglo-Irish Treaty, 188
Anielewicz, Mordecai, 497
Anthony, Susan B., 126-128
Anthropology, 437
Anti-Corn league, 211
Antigone (character), 70-71

Anti-Semitism, 28, 179, 353
Antitrust suits, 225
Apartheid, 499
Apology, 76
Appeals, criminal, 425
Aquino, Benigno, Jr., 527
Aquino, Corazon, 527-528
Arafat, Yasser, 195-197
Argentina, 54, 248-251
Aris, Michael, 441, 442
Aristophanes, 49, 73-75
Aristotle, 86
Armstrong, Jerome, 65
Art, 45-46, 62-63, 232, *238*, 238,
    474-475, 484-487
Athens-Sparta war, 73-75
Augustine, Saint, 80
Aung San Suu Kyi, Daw, 420,
    441-444
Auschwitz, 352
Autonomic Charter of 1897, 186
Averroës, 85-88

Bailey, William S., 517, 518-519
Baldwin, Roger N., 135, 399-400
Bales, Kevin, 245-248
Ball, John, 90
Banks, Louis Albert, 221-222
Barnes, Clive, 479
Barr, E. L., 240
Baseball, 153
Battle in Seattle, 536
Battle of Algiers, The (film), 193-194
Battleship Potemkin, The (film), 55
Bayonet Constitution, 181
Beatitudes, 80, 81
Beijing Television Service, 530-533
Benedict XVI, Pope, 350
Berlin, Irving, 142
Berry, Wendell, 414-417
Besse, Joseph, 46, 381-382
Bible (New Testament), 80-82
Bible (Old Testament), 71-72
Bicycling, 59, 60-62
Bimba, Mestre, 48
bin Laden, Osama, 504-507
Biodiversity, 290-292, 308
Birth control and family planning,
    133-135, 521-522
Birth of a Nation (film), 55
Black, Hugo, 345-348
Black power, *481*, 481-482
Blatch, Harriet Stanton, 132-133,
    133
Blogs, 65, 66-67
Bloody Sunday, 150-151, *152*
Blue Cloud, Peter, 533-536
Boff, Leonardo, 290-292
Boleyn, Anne, 95
Bolívar, Simón, 175-176
Bolsheviks, 495
Bolt, Robert, 95

Bombings, 491, 509
Bonus Expeditionary Army, *140*,
    140-141
Book of Mormon, 335
Boston, Massachusetts, 292-295
Boston Massacre, 164
Boston Port Act, 165
Boston Tea Party, 165, 492
Bourgeoise, 212
Bové, José, 487-489
Boycott, Charles, 45, *48*, 48-49
Boycotts, 45, 48-49, 240, 395
    bus, 144-145
    sexual, 49, 73-75
Bradley, Richard, 102-105
Branson, I. R., 258-261
Brazil, 47-48, 52, 290
Breen, Joseph, 476
*Brief Letter to Donald Walsh (in
    memoriam)* (poem), 439-440
Brower, David, 271
Brown, Clarence, 428
Brown, John, 493
Brown, William Wells, 119-120
Bryan, William Jennings, 10, 223
Buddhists, 498-499
Burgess, John, 527-530
Burma, 441-444
Buses, seating on, 143-145
Bush, George H. W., 412
Bush, George W., 63, 377, 414
Business practices, 221

Cambodia, 451-453
Camp Casey, 67, 67-68
Campaign to Protect America's
    Land, 300
Candeau, Alberto, 39
Canto general (poem), 235-237
Capoeira (martial art), *47*, 47-48
Carlos, John, *481*, 481-482
Carnegie, Andrew, 216-218
Carolina Interfaith Task Force,
    409-411
Carson, Rachel, 268-271
Carter, Bo, 341
Carter, Jimmy, 377-379
Cartoons, 512-513, *513*
Catch-22, 402-404
Catesby, Robert, 491
Catherine of Aragon, 95
Catholics, 491
Center for Human Rights and
    Environment, 312-315
Central Labor Union, 214-215
Charles I, King of England, 326
Charles V, Holy Roman Emperor,
    93
Charles X, King of France, 424
Chávez, Cesar, 240-242
Chernobyl, 288-290
Cherokee Nation, 110-113

Chicano Power, 156
Children, exploitation of, 201, 208-209, 212
China, 308-310, 433-436, 440-441, 530-533
Chinese Exclusion Act, 131
Chirac, Jacques, 255, 487
Christianity, 80, 83, 343-345, 373-375, 377-379
Christmas truce (1914), 395-396
Chumakova, Alesandra, 49-52
Church of England, 95, 324, 328
Church of the Latter Day Saints, 335
Civil disobedience, 326-328, 349-350, 385-387, 391-395, 487
Civil Disobedience, 380, 385-387
Civil liberties, 17-19
    protection of, 24-26, 64, 135-138
Civil rights, 100-161, 499
Civil rights movement, 12, 144, 145-151, 230, 385, 481-482, 524
Clarkson, Thomas, 424
Clash, The (band), 411-412
Clear and present danger test, 34
Clement VII, Pope, 95
Cleveland, Grover, 181
Climate, 292-295
Clinton, Bill, 153, 196, 261, 405-407, 537
Clotel; or, the President's Daughter, 119
Cloward, Richard A., 11
Cody, Iron Eyes, 279
Collection of the Sufferings of the People Called Quakers, 46, 381-383
Colonies
    British, 166-175, 183-186, 188-189, 192
    French, 190, 194
    Spanish, 105-108, 175-176, 186
    United States, 390-391
Common Sense, 172-173
Communism, 212-214
Community redevelopment, 292-295
Comstock, Anthony, 521
Coney Island of the Mind, A, 343-345
Confederate States of America, 178-179
Congress of Angostura, 175
Conscientious objectors, 399-400, 404, 412-414, 417-419
Conscription. *See* Draft.
Conscription Act of 1917, 399
Constantine I, 83
Constitution Hall, Washington, D.C., 141
Constitutions, 17, 24-26
Consumers' League, 221
Convents, 352-356
Copernicus, 464
Copperheads, 389
Corn, 210-212, 487
Corn, Alfred, 525

Corn, Ann, 525
Corn Laws, 210-212
Corn Laws (song), 211-212
Corporations, 223, 253-254
    protests against, 201, 251-252, 311-312, 312-315, 503-504
Corrie, Rachel, 507-509
Cosby, William, 102
Cotton, John, 317
Countries, borders of, 161
Critical Mass, 60-62
Crosses, 352-353
"Crying Indian" advertising campaign, 279
Cuadra, Angel, 420, 439-440
Cuba, 439-440
Cuban Missile Crisis, 37
Cubism, 474
Cukierman, Yitzhak, 497
Cultural Revolution, 433-436
Currency, 108, 223, 382
Currency Act, 162
Cuyahoga River, Ohio, 256
Czechoslovakia, 194-195

D'Avigdor, Sylvie, 180
Dáil Éireann, 188
Daily Kos (blog), 65-66
Dalai Lama, 197-200
Dams, 258-261, 271-273, *272*, 308-310, 311
Dan, Wang, 531
Darfur, Sudan, 458-459
Darrow, Clarence, 227-230
Daughters of the American Revolution (DAR), 141
Davenport, Allen, 210-211
Davis, Jefferson, 178
Davit, Michael, 48
De Lancey, James, 102-105
De Pizan, Christine, 91-92
Debs, Eugene, 400-403
Declaration of Barbados, 436-437
Declaration of Independence, 100, 169-172, 515
Deflation, 223
Delacroix, Eugène, 424-425
Delgado, Fray Carlos José, 105-108
Demonstrations and riots, 54, 60-62, 138-139, 159-160, *160*, 349-350, 440-441, *441*, 456-457, 512, *513*, 525-541
    See also Civil disobedience: Nonviolent resistance.
Dershowitz, Alan, 512
Desaparecidos (disappeared ones), 54
Diderot, Denis, 465-466
Diem, Ngo Dinh, 498, 499
Diet of Worms, 93
Dioxin, 456
Dissent
    principles of, 16-44
    roots of, 70-97
Dix, Dorothea, 117-118
Do the Right Thing (film), 55-58
Douglas, Alfred, 470
Douglas, Marjorie Stoneman, 261-263

Douglas, William O., 280-281
Douglass, Frederick, 11, 119, 128-131
Doyle, Arthur Conan, 425-427
Draft, 387-389, 405-409
    riots, 387-389
Dreyfus, Alfred, 28
Dreyfus, Mathieu, 28
Dreyfus Affair, 28-31, 179
Du Bois, W. E. B., 230-231
Du Paty de Clam, Mercier, 28
Dubcek, Alexander, 194-195
Duchamp, Marcel, 45
Dudley Street, Boston, Massachusetts, 292-295
Dudley Street Neighborhood Initiative (DSNI), 292-295
Dukakis, Michael, 317
Dukhtaran-e-Millat, 489

E. F. Schumacher Society, 292
Earth Day, 256, 277-279
Earth First!, 285
Earth on Empty, 59
Earthjustice, 299-301
East India Company, 165, 492
Easter Uprising of 1916, 188
Ecology, 290-292
Economics, 201-255
    conservative, 237-238, 242-243
    See also Free trade; Globalization.
Ecoterrorism, 285-288
Edalji, George, 425-427
Edict of Milan, 83
Edict of Worms, 93
Education, public, 131-132, 156-158, 212
Eisenhower, Dwight, 37, 141, 266
Eisenstein, Sergei, 55
El Salvador, 350-352
Elk Grove Unified School Dist. v. Newdow, 365-368
Emerson, Ralph Waldo, 11, 464, 466-468
Eminent domain, 292-295
Encampments, *67*, 67-68, 141
Encyclopedia, 465-466
End of Nature, The, 295
Endangered Species Act, 277
Engel v. Vitale, 345-348
Engels, Friedrich, 212-214
England, 420-422
Environment, conservation of, 256-315
Environmental impact assessment, 308-310, 312
Environmental movement, 12, 263-265, 268-271, 295-299
Episcopal (Anglican) Church, 362-364
Equality, 206-208
Equality League of Self-Supporting Women, 132
Equator Principles, 312-315
Erne, Earl of, 48, 49
Ervin, Sam, 345
Esterhazy, Ferdinand, 28-29

Everglades, Florida, 261-263
Everglades National Park, 261

Factories, 208-209, 231-323
Factory Act of 1833, 209
Farmer's Alliance, 223
Farmington, Connecticut, 165-166
Farms and farming, 202, 222,
    230-231, 233-235, 240-242
Fascism, 474
Fatwas, 444-445, 504
Faure, Félix, 28
Fawkes, Guy, 491
Feminism. *See* Women and
    women's rights.
Ferlinghetti, Lawrence, 343-345
Films, 55, 193-194, 234, 521-252,
    252, 475-477
First Amendment. *See* Free speech.
Five Days of Milan, 516
Fleisher, Ari, 65
Flood, Curt, 153
Foraker Act of 1900, 186
Foreman, Dave, 285-288
Forten, James, 109-110
Four Freedoms Speech, 36
France, 255, 255, 364, *364*
Franco, Francisco, 402
Franklin, Benjamin, 22-24, 162,
    169, 424, 490, 492
Frazer, Phillip, 252
Free agents, 153
Free speech, 28, 32, 34-35, *36*,
    36-37, 41, 42-44, 62-63, 63-65,
    102, 308, 512, *513*, 521
Free trade, 210, 212-214, 218-
    220, 248-251, 487
Freedom of Speech (painting), *36*,
    36-37
French Indochina, 190
French Revolution, 21, 206
Freud, Sigmund, 70, 474
Friedan, Betty, 151
Friedman, Milton, 237-238
Friends of the Everglades, 261
Froissart, Jean, 90-91
Fu, Du, 84-85
Fund for Animals, 300
Funders' Network for Smart Growth
    and Livable Communities, 292
Futurism, 474-475

Galbraith, James K., 253
*Game of Capoeira (or the Dance
    of War)* (lithograph), *47*
Gandhi, Mohandas, 80, 183-186,
    385, 490, 514, 519-521
Gang of Four, 433
Garofoli, Joe, 60-62
Garrison, William Lloyd, 113-115
Gay rights, 153-156, 362-364,
    525-527
General Jewish Workers' Union of
    Poland, 429
Genocide, 449, 451, 458-459
Geoghan, John, 358
George V, King of England, 188
George, Henry, 218-220

George-ist movement, 218
Georgia, 110-111, 113
    Get Up, Stand Up (song), 437-439
Ghana, 192
Giap, Vo Nguyen, 190
Gibbs, Lois, 283-285
Gil, Gilberto, 52
Gladiators, 78
Glayd, Charles, 472
Glemp, Cardinal Jozef, 352
Glen Canyon Dam, 281
Global warming, 290-292, 295-
    299, 304-308
Globalization, 45, 212-214, 245-
    246, 248-251, 252, 311, 487,
    536-537
Gobitas, Billy, 143-145
God Bless America (song), 142
Gold Star Families for Peace, 68
Goldman, Emma, 521-522
Gone With the Wind (film), 476
Gooding, James Henry, 125-126
"GOP and 24/7 News" (Daily
    Kos), 66-67
Gospel of Matthew, 80
Government, 16, 19-22, 38-40, 42,
    135, 154, 161, 175, 237-238,
    257, 308, 321, 326, 420, 484,
    495
    corruption, 28
    state, 108-109, 176-176, 345
    totalitarian, 430-436, 439-440,
        449-451, 460-461, 527
Goya y Lucientes, Francisco José
    de, 384-385, 402
Grand Canyon, 271-273, *272*
Grape workers, 240-242
Grapes of Wrath, The (novel/film),
    233, 234
Gray, Dorian, 108-109
Great Depression, 140, 142
Green Belt Movement, 301
Greenpeace, 62-63, 311-312
Greenwald, Robert, 251-252
Griffith, D. W., 55
Guernica (painting), 385, *402*, 402
Guernica, Spain, 402
Guthrie, Woody, 52, 142

Hair (play/song), 479-480
Hairstyles, 479-481
Hajibs, 364, *364*
Halberstam, David, 498-499
Hamilton, Andrew, 102-105
Hancock, John, 515
Harpers Ferry, 493
Harris, Sam, 368-373
Harrison, Benjamin, 181
Hawaii, 181-183
Hawaii's Story by Hawaii's Queen,
    181-183
Haymarket Square, Chicago, 214
Hays, William, 476
Haywood, Big Bill, 227, 232,
    285-288
Haywood trial, 227-230
He Calls That Religion (song),
    341-343

Head scarfs. *See* Hajibs.
Heller, Joseph, 402-404
Helms, Jesse, 464, 484-487
Henry VIII, King of England, 95
Henry, Patrick, 166-169, 328
Henshaw, Jesse G., 389
Heretics, 93, 317, 422
Herzl, Theodor, 179-181
Hetch Hetchy Valley (Yosemite
    National Park), 258-261
Hidalgo, Miguel, 175
Hightower, Jim, 252-254
Hightower Lowdown, 252-254
Hill, Joe, 232-233
Hill, Julia Butterfly, 503-504
Him, Chanrithy, 420, 451-453
Hind Swaraj, 184-186
Hippies, 479
Hochschild, Adam, 423-424
Hoffman, Abbie, 40-42
Hogs, 53-54
Holiday, Billie, 52, 53
Hollywood, 475
Holmes, Eugene J., 405
Holmes, Oliver Wendell, 31, 34-35
Holocaust, 352-356, 428-420, 497
Holzer, Jenny, 45
Homosexuality, 153-154, 470,
    525-527
Hong Lim Park, Singapore, 42
Hoover, Herbert, 141
Hostetler, Sharon, 409-411
Hourani, George F., 86
House arrest, 441
Houston, Cisco, 142
Houston, Sam, 178-179
Hughes, Howard, 476
Hunger strikes, 522-524, 530
Hunt, Ward, 126-128
Hus, Jan, 93
Hussein, Saddam, 449
Hutchinson, Anne, 316, 317-321
Hyde Park, London, 42
Hyndman, H. M., 218

Immigrants, 159-160, 232, 240
    Chinese, 131-132
    Italian, 139-140
    Hispanic and Latino, 156-158,
        159-160
Imprisonment, 524-525
In Motion, 244-245
Independence. *See* Self-determina
    tion, national.
India, 183-186, 454-456, 489
Individuals, 466-468, 470-472
    rights of, 16, 20, 22, 64, 70,
        100, 109-110, 115-116, 117-
        118, 304, 321-323, 484-487
    responsibilities of, 16, 100,
        385-387
    See also Civil rights.
Indulgences, 93
Industrial Revolution, 221
Industrial Workers of the World
    (IWW), 232
ING, 312
Insurrections, 493-495

Inter-American Commission on Human Rights, 304
Intergovernmental Panel on Climate Change, 295
International Campaign to Ban Land Mines, 447-449
International Conference on Freedom of Expression, 445
International Monetary Fund, 248
International Solidarity Movement (ISM), 507
Internet, 65, 66-67
Intolerable Acts, 165, 492
Inuit Circumpolar Conference, 304-308
Inuits, 304
Iran, 444-445
Iraq, 42, 45, 417, 449-451
Iraq War, 67-68, 417
Ireland, 188-189
Irish Free State, 188
Irish Land League, 48
Irish Republican Army, 188
Islam, 86, 360-362, 375-377, 444, 504-507, 512-513
Israel, 179-180, 196
Italy, 516-517

Jackson, Andrew, 111
Jackson, Jimmy Lee, 150
Jacquerie, 88
James, King of England, 491
Janjaweed, 458
Jefferson, Thomas, 10, 169, 316, 321, 328, 332-333
Jehovah's Witnesses, 143
Jenkins, Greg, 64
Jesus Christ, 80-82, 471-472
Jewish State, The, 179-180
Jews, 71-72, 179-181, 196, 336-338, 352-356, 428-430, 497
Jiang, Shao, 532
Jicai, Feng, 433-436
Jim Crow laws, 143
Job, 71, 72
John Brown's Body (song), 493
John, King of England, 16-17
John Paul II, Pope, 359
Johnson, Lyndon, 37, 145, 151, 271
Jones Act, 186-187
Joyce, James, 474
Juarès, Jean, 395
Judaism, Reform, 336-338
July Revolution, 424
Jungle, The, 338
Jyllands Posten, 512

Kaixi, Wu'er, 531, 532
Kalakaua, King of Hawaii, 181
Keep America Beautiful, 279
Keller, Helen, 396-399
Kennedy, John F., 145, 268
Kennedy, X. J., 73
Kent State University, 407-409
Kenya, 301-304
Khmer Rouge, 451-453
Khomeini, Ruhollah, 444
Kifner, John, 407-409

Kimberly-Clark Corporation, 311
King, Martin Luther, Jr., 80, 143-144, 145-148, 349-350, 490
Knighton, Henry, 90
Koran, 86
Kristof, Nicholas D., 458-459
Krouzman, Roni, 536-541
Ku Klux Klan (KKK), 55, 138-139
Kuhn, Bowie, 153
Kurds, 449

Labor and laborers, 212, 218-220, 230-231, 253-255, 255
child, 201, 208-209, 212
working conditions, 201-202, 208-209, 231-232, 240-242
Labor camps, 452-453
Labor movement, 212, 214-215, 227-230, 231-235, 255
Labor unions, 223, 227-230, 231-234
women's, 244-245
Lake Okeechobee, Florida, 261
Land, 202
ethics of, 263-265, 295-299
ownership of, 142, 212, 218, 223, 238-240, 292-295, 533-536
trusts, 294-295
Land mines, 447-449
Langland, William, 88-90
Langston, Charles H., 493-495
Language, 476-478
Larsen, Erik, 412-414
Latin America, 235-236, 436
Law, Cardinal Bernard F., 359
League of the Just, 212
Lee, J. B., Jr., 53-54
Lee, Richard Henry, 169
Lee, Spike, 55-58
Lenin, Vladimir I., 495-496
Leo X, Pope, 93
Leopold, Aldo, 263-265
Let My People Go (song), 52, 334-335
Letters, 53-54
Lewis, Jack, 277-279
Libel, 29, 102
Liberation theology, 290, 350
Liberator, The, 113-115
Liberty Leading the People (painting), 424-425, 425
Licinius, 83
Life of Marcus Licinius Crassus, 78-80
Lilburn, John, 420-422
Liliuokalani, Queen, 181-183
Limbaugh, Rush, 68-69
Lincoln, Abraham, 26-28, 125, 177, 389
Littering, 279
Little Red Song Book, 232
Little, Amanda Griscom, 301-304
Livingston, Robert, 169
Locke, John, 19-20, 161, 321-323, 326
Logging, 311, 503
Louis-Philippe, King of France, 424

Love Canal, Niagara Falls, New York, 283-285
Love Canal Homeowners Association, 283
Luna (tree), 503-504
Luther, Martin, 80, 93-95
Lynchings, 52-53, 55
Lysistrata (play), 49, 73-75

Maathai, Wangari, 301-304
Madison, James, 316, 321, 328-332
Magna Carta, 16-19.
Maimonides, 86
Makiya, Kanan, 449-451
Malcolm X, 149-150
Malls, 63
Man and Nature, 256
Man for All Seasons, A (film), 95
Mandela, Nelson, 499-503
Mandelstam, Nadezhda, 428
Mandelstam, Osip, 427-428
Manji, Irshad, 375-377
Manuscripts, clandestine, 49-50
March on Washington, 145, 149-150
Marches, 145, 149-150, 151, 183 184
silent, 54-55, 55
Marcos, Ferdinand, 527-528
Maréchal, Pierre-Sylvain, 206-208
Marinetti, Filippo T., 474-475
Marley, Bob, 437-439
Marriage, 95, 468-470
Marsh, George Perkins, 256
Martinez, Elizabeth, 156-158
Marx, Karl, 212-214, 474
Massacre of Chios (painting), 424
Materialism, 80
Matlovich, Leonard, 153-154
Mayhew, Jonathan, 326-328
McCarthy, Joseph, 37
McDonald's, 487
McKibben, Bill, 295-299
McKinley, William, 182
Meerpol, Abel. See Allen, Lewis.
Memoirs of a Bolshevik-Leninist, 50
Mendes, Chico, 290-293
Mennonites, 101, 380
Mental illness and the mentally ill, 117-118
Methodists, 324-325
Mexican-American War, 385
Micah, 71, 72
Middle class, 253-254
Migrant workers, 233-235, 240-242
Military service, 153-154, 160, 402-404
Mill, Harriet, 31
Mill, John Stuart, 31-34
Miller, Henry, 474
Milton, John, 422-423
Minh, Ho Chi, 190-191
Miranda v. Arizona, 421
Miss America Pageant, 482-484
Missionaries, 436-437
Mississippi Sheiks (band), 341-343
Mohammad, depictions of, 512-513, 513

Mohawks, 533-534
Moneta, Ernesto Teodoro, 516-517
Monkey Wrench Gang, The, 281-283
Monkeywrenching, 285-288
Monks, Buddhist, 498-499
Monteagle, Lord, 491
Montgomery Improvement Association, 143-145
Moore, Roy S., 316, 356-359
More, Thomas, 95-97
Mormons, 335
Moses, 71, 72
Moses, Robert, 524-525
Mothers of Plaza de Mayo, 54-55, 55
Mott, Lucretia, 120
Moulder, Andrew, 131
Moulitsas Zúniga, Markos, 65
MoveOn.org, 45
Moyer, Charles, 227
Muir, John, 257-258
Music, 411-412, 437
Muslims, 86, 316, 360-362, 364, 489
My Name is Rachel Corrie (play), 507-509
MyDD.com (blog), 65

Nation, Carrie, 472-474
National Association for the Advancement of Colored people (NAACP), 143, 230, 477
National Association of Colored Women (NACW), 477
National Endowment for the Arts, 484
National Organization for Women (NOW), 151-152
National Woman Suffrage Association, 126
National Women's Party, 132
Nationalism, 454-456
Native Americans, 105-108, 110-113, 533-536
Natural Resources Defense Council (NRDC), 311-312
Neruda, Pablo, 235-237
New Hyde Park, New York, 345
New York City, 387-389
New York Committee Vigilance, 115-116
New York Radical Women, 482-484
New York Society for the Suppression of Vice, 521
Newdow, Michael, 316, 365-368
New-York Weekly Journal, 102
Ng, Irene, 42-44
Nicaragua, 409-411
Niemann, Johannes, 395-396
Nietzsche, Friedrich, 474
Nike, 201
Nineteen Eighty-Four, 430-433
Ninety-Five Theses, 93
Nkrumah, Kwame, 192
Nobel Peace Prize, 198, 302, 442, 447, 516
Nonconformity, 10, 464-489

Nonviolent resistance, 80, 149, 183-184, 197-200, 240-242, 244-245, 285-288, 503-504, 507, 519
Norman, Peter, 482
North Korea, 460-461
Notes on Virginia, 332
Noyes, John, 468-470
Nudity, 46-47, 476
Nujian Hydropower Development, 308-310
Nujiang River, China, 308-310

Oastler, Richard, 201, 208-210
Ohio Women's Rights Convention, 124
Oil, 225-227, 273-276, 412
Oil Regions, 225-227
Oka, Canada, 533-536
Olympic Project for Human Rights (OPHR), 481, 482
Olympics, 481-482
Omang, Joanne, 54-55
On the Late Massacre in Piedmont (poem), 422-423
Oneida Community, 468-470
Orange Revolution, 456
Orchard, Harry, 227
Orwell, George, 430-433
Outdoor Recreation Resources Review Commission, 266
Outlaw, The (film), 476
Overton, Richard, 420-422

Pacific Lumber Company, 503
Pacifism, 80, 380, 381-382, 399-403
Paine, Thomas, 172-175
Pakistan, 184
Palast, Greg, 248-251
Palestine, 180, 195-197, 507
Palestine Liberation Organization (PLO), 195
Palmes, Richard, 164-165
Parker, Douglass, 73
Parking tickets (fake), 59, 59
Parks, 256, 299
Parks, Rosa, 143
Parnell, Charles Stewart, 48
Paterson, Jeff, 12
Patriot Act, 158
Patriotism, 37-38, 391
Patti, Archimedes, 190
Peace-Out, 417-419
Peasant Revolt of 1381, 90-91
Peasants, 88-91
Pelosi, Nancy, 68-69
Penance, 83-84
Peng, Li, 530-533
Penn, William, 381
Pennsylvania Abolition Society, 109
People's Party, 223-225
Persian Gulf War, 412-414
Pesticides, 268
Petitions, bark, 238-240, 239
Pettibone, George, 227
Philanthropy, 216
Philippines, 390-391, 527-530

Phillips, U. Utah, 232
Picasso, Pablo, 385, 402
Picasso on the Beach (artwork), 62, 62-63
Pierce, Charlotte Woodward, 120
Piers Plowman tradition, 88-89
Piss Christ (artwork), 484-487
Pittsburgh Conference 1885, 336 338
Pittsburgh Platform, 336-338
Piven, Frances Fox, 11
Place of Peace, 216
Planned Parenthood, 133
Plato, 76
Pledge of Allegiance, 143, 365-368
Plutarch, 78
Poetry, 84-85, 89-90, 439
Police, 12, 55, 138, 150, 214, 425
Political freedoms, international, 420-461
Politics, radical, 139
Pollution, 279, 299, 312
Political prisoners, 441-442
Pompadour, Madame de, 465
Pontecorvo, Gillo, 193
Prague, Czechoslovakia, 194-195, 195
Prague Spring, 194-195
Preston, Thomas, 164
Prince, Thomas, 420-422
Printing press, 45, 70, 93
Privacy, right to, 158-159
Production Code, 475-476
Profanity, 476-477
Programme to Combat Racism, 436-437
Prohibition, 472-474
Proletariat, 212
Prostitution, 246-248
Protest, 11-13, 280
  experience of, 514-541
  extreme, 285-288, 490-513
  modes of, 45-69, 179, 424, 498-499
  roots of, 70-97
  violence against, 138, 150, 164-165
Protestant Reformation, 19, 45, 70, 89, 93
Public health, 154-156
Publishing, secret, 49-50
Puerto Rico, 186-188
Puritans, 317-321

Quakers, 46, 101, 380, 381-384
Quartering Act, 162
Quincy, Josiah, 164

Race relations, 55-58
Radiation, 288-290
Radio, 68-69
Rado, James, 479-481
Ragni, Gerome, 479-481
Railroads, 223
Rain forests, 290-292
Rally, Mohawks! Bring out your axes (song), 492-493
Rank, Jeff, 64

Rank, Nicole, 64
Ratzinger, Cardinal Joseph. *See*
  Benedict XVI, Pope.
Reagan, Ronald, 154, 242-243
Red Guard, 433
Religions
  clerical abuse, 341-343, 359-360
  meetings of, 317-321
  organized, 383-341, 368-373
  persecution for, 335-336
  tolerance for, 321-323, 368-373
  See also Specific religions.
Religious freedom, 46, 76, 93-97,
  143, 317-379, 444-447, 491
Rent, 48-49
Repression, 193
Republican National Convention, 12
Reserves Officers' Training Corps
  (ROTC), 405
Revere, Paul, 164, 492
Revolt of the Ciompi, 88
Revolutions of 1848, 516-517
Richard II, King of England, 90
Richardson, Anna H., 517
Rickman, Alan, 507-509
Right Livelihood Award, 290
Righteousness, 80
Riots. *See* Demonstrations and riots.
Rittner, Carol, 352-356
Rivera, Luis Muñoz, 186-188
Rivonia Trial, 449-503
Road blockades, 533-536
Robinson, V. Gene, 362-364
Rockefeller, John, 225
Rockwell, Norman, 36
Rodney, Caesar, 169
Rodriguez Nieto, Katherine, 439
Roman Catholic Church, 93, 95,
  105-108, 321, 350-356, 422,
  465
  clerical abuse, 359-360
Rome (republic), 78
Romero, Oscar, 350-351
Roosevelt, Eleanor, 141
Roosevelt, Franklin D., 36
Roosevelt, Theodore, 390
Roper, Margaret, 95
Rousseau, Jean-Jacques, 20-22,
  161, 204-206
Roy, Arundhati, 454-456
Royalties, 173
Rudolph, Eric, 509-512
Rugendas, Johann Mortiz, 48
Ruggles, David, 115-116
Rush Limbaugh Show (radio
  show), 68-69
Rush, Benjamin, 515
Rushdie, Salman, 444-447
Russell, Jane, 476
Russo, Vito, 154-156

Sacco, Nicola, 139
Sahkarov, Andrei, 50
Sailormongering, 63
Salt, 183-184
Samizdat, 49-52
San Francisco, California, 258-261
San Martín, José de, 175

Sanger, Margaret, 133-135, 521
Sanger, William, 521
Satanic Verses, The, 444
Saudi Arabia, 360
Schenk v. United States, 34
Schneiderman, Rose, 231-232
School prayer, 345-348
Scott, Job, 382-384
Seattle, Washington, 537
Self-determination, national,
  161-200
Self-Employed Women's
  Association (SEWA), 244
Self-government. *See* Self-determi
  nation, national.
Self-immolations, 498-499
Selznick, David O., 475
Separation of church and state, 316,
  321-323, 328-333, 345-348,
  356-359, 364, 365-368, 377-379
September 11, 2001 attacks, 414,
  504
Sermon on the Mount, The, 80-82
Serrano, Andreas, 484-487
Servile Wars, 78
Sex discrimination, 151
Sharp, Granville, 424
Shaw, Robert Gould, 125
Shays's Rebellion, 108-109
Sheehan, Casey, 68
Sheehan, Cindy, 67, 67-68
Sherman, Roger, 169
Shields, human, 507-509
Sierra Club, 257, 258, 266, 271,
  280-281, 311
Sierra Club v. Morton, 280-281
Sinclair, Upton, 317, 338-341
Sinn Féin, 188
Slavery, 26, 47, 78, 101-102, 109-
  110, 113-116, 119-120, 175,
  177, 334-335, 388, 423-424
  escapes from, 517-519
  modern, 245-248
  rebellions, 78-80
  sexual, 246-248
Smith, Alfred, 138
Smith, Hyrum, 335
Smith, Joseph, Jr., 335-336
Smith, Tommie, *481*, 481-482
Snowcoaches, 300
Snowmobiles, 299-301
Social contracts, 19-22
Social equality, 90
Societal norms, 464-489
Society, 19, 31, 88-89, 212, 420,
  464-489
  democratic, 16, 22, 420-422
  psychosocial viewpoint, 70
Society for the Abolition of the
  Slave Trade, 424
Socrates, 75-78
Socratic method, 75
Sojourners, 373-375
Solinas, Franco, 193-194
Solzhenitsyn, Aleksandr, 50
Songs and singing, 52-53, 142,
  211-212, 232-233, 334-335,
  341-343, 437-439, 492-493

Sound of Mountain Water, The,
  266-268
South Africa, 499, 519-521
South Carolina, 177-178
South Improvement Company, 225
Southern Baptist Convention, 377
Southern Christian Leadership
  Conference, 349
Southern Leadership Christian
  Conference, 150
Soviet Union, 49-50
  occupation of Eastern Europe,
  194-195
Spanish-American War, 390
Spanish Civil War, 402, 430
Spartacus, 78
Speakers' Corner, London, 42
Speakers' corners, 42-44
Speeches, courtroom, 75-78
Spirituals, 334-335
Sporting events, 481-482
Stalin, Joseph, 49, 428
Stalin Epigram, The (poem),
  427-428
Stamp Act, 162
Stamp Act Congress, 162
Standard Oil Company, 225
Stanton, Elizabeth Cady, 120, 126,
  132
Star Chamber, 421
States
  rights, 176-177
  secession of, 176-179
Stegner, Wallace, 266-268, 281
Steinbeck, John, 233-235
Stereotypes, racial, 477-478
Stevens, John, 181
Stevenson, Adlai, 37-38
Stewart, Potter, 345
Still, William, 517-519
Stonewall Inn, 525
Stonewall Riots, 525
Strange fruit (song), 52-53
Street theater, 60
Strikes, labor, 214-215, 240
Student Nonviolent Coordinating
  Committee (SNCC), 150, 524
Stunenberg, Frank, 227
Suburbs, 292-295
Sudan, 458-459
Suffrage, women's, 120, 126-128,
  132-133, 522
Sugar Act, 162
Sunstein, Cass, 10, 31
Surveillance, 158-159
SUVs, 59
Swann, Robert, 292
Sweatshops, 231-232

Tanach. *See* Bible (Old Testament).
Tape, Mamie, 131
Tape, Mary, 131-132
Tarbell, Ida, 225-227
Tarigo, Enrique, 38-40
Tarzan and His Mate (film), 476
Taxes and taxation, 108-109, 162,
  164, 204-206, 212, 216, 218,
  242-243, 328, 382, 385

incentives, 252-254
Tea, 164, 165, 490, 491-493
Tea Act, 492
Technology, 158-159
Temperance movement, 472-474
Ten Commandments Monument, Montgomery, Alabama, 356-359
Ten Hour Movement, 209
Teresa Benedicta of the Cross, Sister, 352
Terrell, Mary Church, 477-479
Territories
  commonwealth, 186-188, 188
  U.S. annexation of, 181-183
Terrorism, 193, 196, 414, 504-507
Texas, 179
Thailand, 246-248
Theodosius I, 83
There Is Power in a Union, 232-233
Thessalonica, 83
Third of May, 1808, The, or, The Execution on Principe Pio Hill (painting), *384*, 384-385, 402
This Land is Your Land (song), 142
Thomas, Mary B., 517-518
Thomas, Norman, 135
Thomas Aquinas, 86
Thomson, Charles, 515
Thoreau, Henry David, 11, 256, 380, 385-387, 493
Three Gorges Dam, 308-310
Tiananmen Square, 440-441, *441*, 530
Tibet, 197-200
Tolstoy, Leo, 80, 385, 391-395
Topeka Daily Capital, 472-474
Torture, 193-194, 491
Tosh, Peter, 437-439
Tourism, 299
Town meetings, 36, 42
Townshend Acts, 164, 491
Toxic waste, 283-285
Transcendentalism, 466
Transportation, 59
Treblinka, 428-430
Trees and forests, 257-258, 301-304, 503-504
Tree-sits, 503-504
Triangle Shirtwaist Factory, 12, 201, 231
Tropicália, 52
True Levelers, 201, 202-204
Truth, Sojourner, 123-124
T-shirts, 63
Twain, Mark, 390-391
Tyler, John, 335

U.S. Central Intelligence Agency, 40, 41-42
U.S. Congressional Human Rights Caucus, 360
U.S Constitution
  amendments, 132
  preamble, 24
  Bill of Rights, 24-26, 135, 332, 345, 365
U.S. National Park Service, 300
U.S. Secret Service, 64-65

Udall, Morris K., 271-273
Udall, Stewart L., 266, 273-276
Ukraine, 456-457
Underground Railroad, 517
Unions. *See* Labor unions.
United Farm Workers (UFM), 240
United Nations, 195-196, 420
United States Constitutional Convention of 1787, 22
United States v. Susan B. Anthony, 126-128
Universal Declaration of Human Rights, 420
University of Massachusetts, 40-41
Uruguay, 38-40

Valentine's Day, 489
Values, Western, 489
Vandalism, 492
Vanzetti, Bartolomeo, 139-140
Veloso, Caetano, 52
Velvet Revolution of 1989, 195
Viet Minh, 190
Vietnam, 190-191, 498-499
Vietnam War, 404-409
Villaraigosa, Antonio, 160
Viner, Katharine, 507-509
Vinson, Walter, 341
Violence, use of, 495-496, 497, 499-503, 509-512, 516-517
Virginia Act for Establishing Religious Freedom, 328, 332-333
Voice of the Faithful, 359-360
Voting, 150-151, 524
  See also Suffrage, women's.
Voting Rights Act of 1965, 151
Vulgarisms, 476-477

Wages, 108, 221, 233-235, 246
  equal, 125-126
  military, 125-126, 140-141
Wahhabism, 360
Walden (Thoreau), 256
Waldensians, 422
Waldo, Peter, 422
Walkouts and blowouts, 156-158
Wallace, George, 150
Wallis, Jim, 373-375
Wal-Mart, 251-252, *252*
Wal-Mart: the High Cost of Low Price (film), 521-252, 252
Walsh, Donald, 439
Walwyn, William, 420-422
War of 1812, 176-177
War of Spartacus, 78-80
Wardell, Lydia, 46-47
Warren, Earl, 421
Warren, Elizabeth, 252
Warren, Joseph, 492
Wars, 84-85, 175-176, 380-418
  protests against, 67-68, 73-75, 389-390, 396-399, 405-411
  See also Specific wars.
Warsaw Ghetto, 497
Washington, George, 22, 169, 173, 382-383
Washington Bullets (song), 411-412
Water, 258, 261

Watson, Greg, 292-295
Watt-Cloutier, Sheila, 304-308
Wealth, distribution of, 142, 201, 202-204, 204, 206, 212-214, 216-218, 242-243
Wedgwood, Josiah, 423-424
Wells, E. A., 238-239
Wesley, Charles, 324
Wesley, John, 316, 324-325
Western Federation of Miners (WFM), 227
White, Edmund, 525-527
White House Advance, 64
Widener, Jeff, 441
Wiernik, Yankel, 428-430
Wiesel, Elie, 352-356
Wilberforce, William, 424
Wilde, Oscar, 470-472
Wilderness, 266-268
Wilderness Act, 257
Williams, Jody, 447-449
Wilson, E. O., 257
Wilson, James, 22
Winslow, Rose, 514, 522-524
Winstanley, Gerrard, 202
Winter, Paul M., 138-139
Winthrop, John, 317-321
Wirt, William, 167
Witness for Peace, 409-411
Witt, Susan, 292
Wobblies. *See* Industrial Workers of the World (IWW).
Women and women's rights, 31, 91-92, 100, 120-124, 126-128, 132-135, 151-152, 244-245, 317, 360-362, 375-377, 482-484, 522
Wood, John, 208
Work day, 209, 214-215
Workers movement. *See* Labor movement.
World Bank, 248
World Council of Churches, 436-437
World Heritage Sites, 308
World Trade Organization (WTO), 536
World War I, 395-403
World Zionist Organization, 180
Worrell, Richard, 101
Worth, Jonathan, 389-390
Wycliffe, John, 93

Yan, Xiong, 531-532
Yanukovich, Viktor, 456
Yellowstone National Park, 299-301
Yolngu People, Yirrkala, Australia, 238-240
Yosemite National Park, 256, 257, 258-261
Young, Brigham, 335
Yushchenko, Viktor, 456-457

Zedong, Mao, 433
Zenger, John Peter, 102-105
Zhixin, Wang, 532
Zionist Congress, 180
Zola, Émile, 28-31